Museums and Archaeology

Museums and Archaeology brings together a wide, but carefully chosen, selection of literature from around the world that connects museums and archaeology. Part of the successful *Leicester Readers in Museum Studies* series, it provides a combination of issue- and practice-based perspectives. As such, it is a volume not only for students and researchers from a range of disciplines interested in museum, gallery and heritage studies, including public archaeology and cultural resource management (CRM), but also the wide range of professionals and volunteers in the museum and heritage sector who work with archaeological collections.

The volume's balance of theory and practice and its thematic and geographical breadth is explored and explained in an extended introduction, which situates the readings in the context of the extensive literature on museum archaeology, highlighting the many tensions that exist between idealistic 'principles' and real-life 'practice' and the debates that surround these. In addition to this, section introductions and the seminal pieces themselves provide a comprehensive and contextualised resource on the interplay of museums and archaeology.

Robin Skeates is Professor in the Department of Archaeology at Durham University in the UK. He was elected a Fellow of the Society of Antiquaries of London in 2005, and has served as General Editor of the *European Journal of Archaeology* since 2010.

Leicester Readers in Museum Studies
Series Editor: Professor Simon J. Knell

Museum Management and Marketing
Richard Sandell and Robert R. Janes

Museums in the Material World
Simon J. Knell

Museums and their Communities
Sheila Watson

Museums in a Digital Age
Ross Parry

Preventive Conservation
Christopher Caple

Museum Objects
Sandra H. Dudley

Museums and Archaeology

Edited by

Robin Skeates

LONDON AND NEW YORK

First published 2017 by Routledge
2 Park Square, Milton Park, Abingdon, Oxon OX14 4RN

and by Routledge
711 Third Avenue, New York, NY 10017

Routledge is an imprint of the Taylor & Francis Group, an informa business

© 2017 Robin Skeates

The right of the editor to be identified as the author of the editorial material, and of the authors for their individual chapters, has been asserted in accordance with sections 77 and 78 of the Copyright, Designs and Patents Act 1988.

All rights reserved. No part of this book may be reprinted or reproduced or utilised in any form or by any electronic, mechanical, or other means, now known or hereafter invented, including photocopying and recording, or in any information storage or retrieval system, without permission in writing from the publishers.

Trademark notice: Product or corporate names may be trademarks or registered trademarks, and are used only for identification and explanation without intent to infringe.

British Library Cataloguing-in-Publication Data
A catalogue record for this book is available from the British Library

Library of Congress Cataloging-in-Publication Data
A catalog record for this book has been requested

ISBN: 978-1-138-02622-3 (hbk)
ISBN. 978-1-138-02623-0 (pbk)

Typeset in Bembo and Bell Gothic
by Saxon Graphics Ltd, Derby

Contents

List of figures	xii
List of tables	xiv
Series preface	xv
Preface	xvii
Acknowledgements	xix

1   Museums and archaeology: principles, practice, and debates   1
    ROBIN SKEATES

PART I

ARCHAEOLOGICAL COLLECTIONS   41

Introduction to Part I   43
ROBIN SKEATES

PART I, SECTION 1

CURATION OF ARCHAEOLOGICAL REMAINS: RESPONSES TO CRISIS   46

2   Managing curated collections: the basics   47
    LYNNE P. SULLIVAN AND S. TERRY CHILDS

3   Archaeological curation in the twenty-first century. Or, making sure the roof doesn't blow off   63
    WENDY BUSTARD

PART I, SECTION 2

ARCHAEOLOGICAL ARCHIVES: SELECTION, RETENTION, USE AND DISPOSAL   71

4   Primal fear: deaccessioning collections   72
ROBERT C. SONDERMAN

5   Archaeological archives: serving the public interest?   77
NICK MERRIMAN AND HEDLEY SWAIN

6   Archaeological archives in Britain and the development of the London Archaeological Archive and Research Centre   93
HEDLEY SWAIN

PART I, SECTION 3

DOCUMENTATION, IDENTIFICATION, AND AUTHENTICATION OF ARCHAEOLOGICAL COLLECTIONS   98

7   Inventory and global management in archaeology: the example of the Neuchâtel Museum   99
MARIE-ODILE VAUDOU

PART I, SECTION 4

MUSEUM CARE, CONSERVATION, AND RESTORATION OF ARCHAEOLOGICAL OBJECTS   108

8   Issues in practice: conservation procedures   109
ELIZABETH PYE

9   Caring for an Egyptian mummy and coffin   142
LAURA S. PHILLIPS AND LINDA ROUNDHILL

PART I, SECTION 5

ARCHAEOLOGY COLLECTIONS RESEARCH 148

10 Gristhorpe Man: an Early Bronze Age log-coffin burial
   scientifically defined 149
   NIGEL MELTON, JANET MONTGOMERY, CHRISTOPHER J. KNÜSEL, CATHY BATT, STUART
   NEEDHAM, MIKE PARKER PEARSON, ALISON SHERIDAN, CARL HERON, TIM HORSLEY,
   ARMIN SCHMIDT, ADRIAN EVANS, ELIZABETH CARTER, HOWELL EDWARDS, MICHAEL
   HARGREAVES, ROB JANAWAY, NIELS LYNNERUP, PETER NORTHOVER, SONIA O'CONNOR,
   ALAN OGDEN, TIMOTHY TAYLOR, VAUGHAN WASTLING, AND ANDREW WILSON

11 History and surface condition of the Lewis Chessmen in the collection
   of the National Museums Scotland (Hebrides, late twelfth to early
   thirteenth centuries) 167
   JIM TATE, INA REICHE, FLAVIA PINZARI, JANE CLARK, AND DAVID CALDWELL

PART II

ARCHAEOLOGY, ETHICS, AND THE LAW 181

Introduction to Part II 183
ROBIN SKEATES

PART II, SECTION 1

LEGAL AND ETHICAL DIMENSIONS OF ARCHAEOLOGICAL MUSEUM COLLECTING AND COLLECTIONS 185

12 From museum to mantelpiece: the antiquities trade in the
   United Kingdom 186
   KATHRYN WALKER TUBB AND NEIL BRODIE

13 The revolution in US museums concerning the ethics of
   acquiring antiquities 201
   JENNIFER ANGLIM KREDER

PART II, SECTION 2

REPATRIATION AND REBURIAL OF ARCHAEOLOGICAL MUSEUM COLLECTIONS — 233

14 Repatriation: Australian perspectives — 234
    MICHAEL GREEN AND PHIL GORDON

15 The Native American Graves Protection and Repatriation Act in its first decade — 242
    JAMES A.R. NAFZIGER AND REBECCA J. DOBKINS

PART II, SECTION 3

MUSEUMS AND THE CARE AND DISPLAY OF ANCIENT HUMAN REMAINS — 268

16 Policy and practice in the treatment of archaeological human remains in North American museums and public agency collections — 269
    FRANCIS P. McMANAMON

17 Covering up the mummies — 285
    TIFFANY JENKINS

PART III

INTERPRETING THE ARCHAEOLOGICAL PAST — 305

Introduction to Part III — 307
ROBIN SKEATES

PART III, SECTION 1

CRITICAL AND POLITICAL PERSPECTIVES ON MUSEUM REPRESENTATIONS OF THE ARCHAEOLOGICAL PAST AND OF ARCHAEOLOGY — 311

18 Presenting the past: towards a redemptive aesthetic for the museum — 312
    MICHAEL SHANKS AND CHRISTOPHER TILLEY

19 Speaking for the past in the present: text, authority, and learning in archaeology museums — 346
    ROBIN SKEATES

20 Towards presenting scientific research in archaeology museums 361
MARK S. COPLEY

21 Prehistory, identity, and archaeological representation in
Nordic museums 379
JANET E. LEVY

22 Is it enough to make the main characters female? An intersectional and social semiotic reading of the exhibition Prehistories 1 at the National Historical Museum in Stockholm, Sweden 399
ANNIKA BÜNZ

PART III, SECTION 2

ARCHAEOLOGICAL SITE MUSEUMS 415

23 The Jorvik Viking Centre: an experiment in archaeological
site interpretation 416
PETER ADDYMAN AND ANTHONY GAYNOR

24 The new Museum of Altamira: finding solutions to tourism pressure 426
JOSÉ ANTONIO LASHERAS CORRUCHAGA AND PILAR FATÁS MONFORTE

25 Archaeological site museums in Latin America 432
HELAINE SILVERMAN

PART III, SECTION 3

NEW ARCHAEOLOGY MUSEUM ARCHITECTURE 448

26 The new Acropolis Museum: where the visual feast trumps education 449
KATIE RASK

27 Development and utilization of underground space for the protection of relics in the Yang Emperor Mausoleum of the Han Dynasty 456
ZHILONG CHEN, PING ZHANG, AND JUXI LI

PART III, SECTION 4

DESIGNING ARCHAEOLOGY DISPLAYS 462

28 The Port Royal Project: a case study in the use of VR technology for the recontextualization of archaeological artifacts and building remains in a museum setting 463
HARRY HELLING, CHARLIE STEINMETZ, ERIC SOLOMON, AND BERNARD FRISCHER

PART III, SECTION 5

TEACHING AND LEARNING THROUGH MUSEUM ARCHAEOLOGY 472

29 Teaching the past in museums 473
JOANNE LEA

30 Interaction or tokenism? The role of 'hands-on activities' in museum archaeology displays 485
JANET OWEN

31 The redisplay of the Alexander Keiller Museum, Avebury, and the National Curriculum in England 500
PETER G. STONE

32 Roman boxes for London's schools: an outreach service by the Museum of London 513
JENNY HALL AND HEDLEY SWAIN

33 Translating archaeology for the public: empowering and engaging museum goers with the past 522
ALEXANDRA A. CHAN

PART III, SECTION 6

PUBLIC ENGAGEMENT IN, AND PERCEPTIONS OF, MUSEUM ARCHAEOLOGY 542

34 Involving the public in museum archaeology 543
NICK MERRIMAN

35	Public archaeology and museums in Japan DEVENA HAGGIS	564
36	Uncovering ancient Egypt: the Petrie Museum and its public SALLY MACDONALD AND CATHERINE SHAW	572
37	Re-imagining Egypt: artefacts, contemporary art, and community engagement in the museum GEMMA TULLY	593
38	Working towards greater equity and understanding: examples of collaborative archaeology and museum initiatives with Indigenous peoples in North America SARAH CARR-LOCKE AND GEORGE NICHOLAS	608
39	Conversations about the production of archaeological knowledge and community museums at Chunchucmil and Kochol, Yucatán, México TRACI ARDREN	617
40	Us and them: who benefits from experimental exhibition making? PETE BROWN	635

Index   *656*

Figures

5.1	Amount of space remaining for archives	84
5.2	The date by which museums predict their archive space will be full	85
9.1	The newly designed stainless steel case built by Snow & Company, Seattle, Washington, was the product of consultations with many experts	146
10.1	The Gristhorpe finds on display (centre, back) in the Rotunda Museum in the late nineteenth century	150
11.1	The 11 chessmen from Lewis in the NMS collection	168
11.2	(a) Base of King (H.NS 19); (b) Base of Queen (H.NS 23); (c) Base of Warder (H.NS 28)	171
11.3	(a) Base of Warder (H.NS 29); (b) Base of Knight (H.NS 27)	172
11.4	(a and b) Showing how King (H.NS 20) has been cut partially through the secondary dentine, while (c) the Warder (H.NS 28) is almost entirely from primary	172
11.5	The ratio of calcium to strontium as measured by XRF from various locations on each chess piece	173
11.6	(a) Surface tool marks where material has been cut away; (b) polishing marks as groups of fine abrasions in different orientations; (c) 'chatter' marks, coarse marks towards the centre, and a finer band down the left of the image.	175
11.7	(a) Post polishing damage channel on the cheek; and (b) carved hair. The channels cross rather than branch (c)	175
18.1	The aesthetic artefact	317
18.2	The past brought back to life	331
19.1	Text panel in the Alexander Keiller Museum, Avebury	351
20.1	Top: the source of respondents' archaeology degree *(n = 39; Q2)*. Bottom: the respondents' highest level of science training (answered by 61/62 respondents; Q3)	367
20.2	Responses (*n = 62*) to the seven statements in Q4 *(a–g)*; the graphs are presented in the order in which the questions were asked. Normalized responses to the fourth statement according to respondent's backgrounds *(h)*	368
21.1	Case in the prehistory exhibition in the National Museum of Finland	388
21.2	*Kota*, reindeer herders' tent, the Sami Museum, Karasjok, Norway	390

22.1	The two top women represent characters in a side story. The women on the bottom row represent characters from the main stories: the woman from Gårdlösa to the left, and the aristocratic woman from Köpingsvik to the right	403
22.2	The woman from Bäckaskog, ca. 7000 BC	404
22.3	A representation of the man from Kvissleby, also mentioned as the man by the coast, buried together with a woman in a burial mound in Kvissleby	405
22.4	The man from further inland, buried in the Krankmården mound	407
23.1	Plan of the Jorvik Viking Centre showing the interrelationships between the principal elements in the design	419
23.2	On the street front of Coppergate are market booths, and recreated Viking buildings and their inhabitants are amongst the most striking features of the Jorvik Viking Centre	423
24.1	The Neocave: ceiling with paintings	429
26.1	The Erechtheion's caryatids on display, now visible from all angles	450
26.2	The Parthenon Gallery interacts with the Athenian Acropolis	450
26.3	The Archaic Gallery on the second floor of the Acropolis Museum	453
26.4	The entrance to the Acropolis Museum includes a view of the recent excavations	454
27.1	The section drawing of the underground museum	459
28.1	Port Royal display case at the Ocean Institute	467
30.1	Muska Mosston's concept of discovery learning	488
30.2	A list of museums sent informal survey questionnaires and a list of museums visited	489
31.1	The symbolic presentation of 'fact' versus 'imagination' through the use of a divided image	507
32.1	One of the Roman School Boxes. The bottom shelf contains the actual Roman artefacts	517
33.1	View south of the Great House and Slave Quarters in close proximity and in complementary architectural style	531
33.2	Graphic representation of the artefact frequency distribution on the site	533
35.1	Public archaeology in Japanese museums	566
35.2	Public preferences in learning about the past	570
39.1	Division of archaeological ruins into five modern community boundaries	621
40.1	Discovering the body: section showing construction with object cases, applied interview quotes, and 'Find out More' shelf with seating	637
40.2	Personal Meaning Map 43	642
40.3	Personal Meaning Map 24	647
40.4	Value to visitors – Generic Learning Outcomes (GLOs)	649
40.5	Personal Meaning Map 73	649

Tables

2.1	Basic standards of repositories	54
5.1	Plans by museums to deal with future archives	86
5.2	Museum archive usage	87
10.1	The measurements and values used to assess humeral bilateral asymmetry	153
10.2	The measurements and values obtained to assess clavicular asymmetry	153
10.3	Lead, strontium, and oxygen isotope data	154
10.4	Carbon and nitrogen isotope data	155
16.1	Examples of quantities of human remains from archaeological contexts in United States public agency or museum collections	270
16.2	United States archaeological laws and human remains	272
16.3	Treatment decisions based upon degree of affinity and age of remains	280
20.1	Responses for Q5: 'For each topic, which best describes how it is incorporated in your museum display?' and Q7 responses: 'Which of the following scientific topics would you like to include more of in your museum?'	370
20.2	Responses for Q6: 'How are the following themes currently included in your museum?'	371
27.1	Optimal environmental condition for preserving relics	459
35.1	Museum categories	565
35.2	Museum activities	565
35.3	Percentages and activities by museum type	567
35.4	Other museum activities	568
36.1	Themes of interest to Petrie Museum user groups	581
36.2	Periods of interest to Petrie Museum user groups	582
37.1	Timeline and artefacts for show/handling	600

Series preface

Leicester Readers in Museum Studies provide students of museums – whether employed in the museum, engaged in a museum studies programme or studying in a cognate area – with a selection of focused readings in core areas of museum thought and practice. Each book has been compiled by a specialist in that field, but all share the Leicester School's belief that the development and effectiveness of museums relies upon informed and creative practice. The series as a whole reflects the core Leicester curriculum which is now visible in programmes around the world and which grew, forty years ago, from a desire to train working professionals, and students prior to entry into the museum, in the technical aspects of museum practice. In some respects the curriculum taught then looks similar to what we teach today. The following, for example, was included in the curriculum in 1968: history and development of the museum movement; the purpose of museum; types of museum and their functions; the law as it relates to museums; staff appointments and duties; sources of funding; preparation of estimates; by-laws and regulations; local, regional, etc. bodies; buildings; heating, ventilation and cleaning; lighting; security systems; control of stores, and so on. Some of the language and focus here, however, indicates a very different world. A single component of the course, for example, focused on collections and dealt with collection management, conservation and exhibitions. Another component covered 'museum activities' from enquiry services to lectures, films, and so on. There was also training in specialist areas, such as local history, and many practical classes which included making plaster casts and models. Many museum workers around the world will recognise these kinds of curriculum topics; they certainly resonate with my early experiences of working in museums.

While the skeleton of that curriculum in some respects remains, there has been a fundamental shift in the flesh we hang upon it. One cannot help but think that the museum world has grown remarkably sophisticated: practices are now regulated by equal opportunities, child protection, cultural property and wildlife conservation laws; collections are now exposed to material culture analysis, contemporary documentation projects, digital capture and so on; communication is now multimedia, inclusive, evaluated and theorised. The museum has over that time become intellectually fashionable, technologically advanced and developed a new social relevance. *Leicester Readers in Museum Studies* address this change. They deal with practice as it is relevant to the museum today, but they are also about expanding horizons beyond one's own experiences. They reflect a more professionalised world and one that has thought very deeply about this wonderfully interesting and significant institution. Museum studies remains a vocational subject but it is now very different. It is, however, sobering to think that the Leicester course was founded in the year Michel Foucault published *The Order of Things* – a book that greatly influenced the way we think about the museum today. The writing was on the wall even then.

Simon J. Knell
Series Editor

Preface

This reader brings together a diverse yet focused selection of literature that connects and questions museums and archaeology. It is intended to complement other volumes in the *Leicester Readers in Museum Studies* series, with their special combination of issue- and practice-based perspectives. As such, it should appeal not simply to students and researchers from a range of disciplines interested in museum, gallery and heritage studies, including public archaeology and cultural resource management (CRM), but also to the wide range of professionals and volunteers in the museum and heritage sector who work with archaeological collections.

With this balance of theory and practice and its thematic and geographical breadth, the reader sits distinctively between – and moves beyond – the two key texts on museum archaeology: Hedley Swain's (2007) *An Introduction to Museum Archaeology* with its museological emphasis on the poetics and politics of contemporary museum archaeology, particularly in the UK; and Lynne Sullivan and Terry Childs' (2003) *Curating Archaeological Collections: From the Field to the Repository*, designed as a toolkit with practical advice for field archaeologists and museum professionals, particularly in the USA. All replace the groundbreaking but now out-of-date *Archaeological Curatorship* written by Susan Pearce (1990).

Selecting what to include (and exclude) has inevitably presented a series of choices and challenges. The goal has been to put together an accessible package of classic and current, long and short, readings that – together – offers readers the opportunity to gain a well-rounded and critical understanding of museum archaeology, with an emphasis on current practices and debates and their development since the 1970s. (A conscious editorial decision was taken to leave out a set of readings on the history of collecting and collections, although an introduction and bibliographic references to this vast field are provided in Chapter 1.) Global coverage is the ideal, but in practice it is difficult to find reflexive academic and professional literature on museum archaeology beyond Europe and North America, although readings on China, Japan, Australia, Mexico, and South America are valuable exceptions included here. Some themes are also better published than others, the best-represented here being museum communication, which has captured the attention of a range of academics as well as museum professionals. Other exclusions of texts and images are simply due to the cost, or denial, of copyright permissions. Nevertheless, the readings included here do provide plenty of food for thought in an important branch of museum work.

References

Pearce, S.M. (1990) *Archaeological Curatorship*. London and New York: Leicester University Press.

Sullivan, L.P. and Childs, S.T. (2003) *Curating Archaeological Collections: From the Field to the Repository*. Walnut Creek, CA: AltaMira Press.

Swain, H. (2007) *An Introduction to Museum Archaeology*. New York: Cambridge University Press.

Acknowledgements

Simon Knell sowed the seed for this book over the course of some pleasant and stimulating conversations, and provided encouragement and advice thereafter. My colleagues Chris Caple and Ben Roberts offered further provocation and helpful suggestions, as did the four readers of the original book proposal, including Alan Saville and Louise Zarmati. Matthew Gibbons and Lola Harre at Taylor & Francis managed everything with quiet competence.

I am very grateful to the authors, publishers, and other copyright holders for kindly granting permission for their works to be reproduced here. I have tried to remain true to their original texts, making only slight changes where necessary, particularly to bibliographic references (adding those missing from book chapters and updating those that were previously 'in press', for example), and also removing abstracts, keywords, and acknowledgements for reasons of space and coherence. Details of the original works and copyright holders are as follows:

Sullivan, L.P. and Childs, S.T. (2003) *Curating Archaeological Collections: From the Field to Repository*. Archaeologist's Toolkit Volume 6. Walnut Creek, CA: AltaMira Press. Chapter 5. Managing curated collections: the basics. pp. 59–77. Reprinted by permission of AltaMira Press.

Bustard, W. (2000) Archaeological curation in the 21st century. Or, making sure the roof doesn't blow off. *CRM Online*, 23(5): 10–15. Reprinted by permission of the author and the U.S. National Parks Service.

Sonderman, R.C. (1996) Primal fear: deaccessioning collections. *Common Ground: Archaeology and Ethnography in the Public Interest*, 1(2): 27–29. Reprinted by permission of the author and the U.S. National Parks Service.

Merriman, N. and Swain, H. (1999) Archaeological archives: serving the public interest? *European Journal of Archaeology*, 2(2): 249–67. Reprinted by permission of the European Association of Archaeologists.

Swain, H. (2006) Archaeological archives in Britain and the development of the London Archaeological Archive and Research Centre. In: N. Agnew and J. Bridgland (eds.), *On the Past, for the Future: Integrating Archaeology and Conservation*.

Proceedings of the Conservation Theme at the 5th World Archaeological Congress, Washington, D.C., 22–26 June 2003. Los Angeles: The Getty Conservation Institute, pp. 211–15. Reprinted by permission of the J. Paul Getty Trust.

Vaudou, M.-O. (2004) Inventory and global management in archaeology: the example of the Neuchâtel Museum. *Museum International*, 56(3): 68–76. Reprinted by permission of John Wiley and Sons.

Pye, E. (2000) Issues in practice: conservation procedures. *Caring for the Past: Issues in Conservation for Archaeology and Museums*. London: James & James. Chapter 7. pp. 121–48. Reprinted by permission of Maney Publishing.

Phillips, L.S. and Roundhill, L. (2007) Caring for an Egyptian mummy and coffin. In: V. Cassman, N. Odegaard and J. Powell (eds.), *Human Remains: Guide for Museums and Academic Institutions*. Lanham, MD: AltaMira Press, pp. 269–73. Reprinted by permission of AltaMira Press.

Melton, N., Montgomery, J., Knüsel, C.J., Batt, C., Needham, S., Parker Pearson, M., Sheridan, A., Heron, C., Horsley, T., Schmidt, A., Evans, A., Carter, E., Edwards, H., Hargreaves, M., Janaway, R., Lynnerup, N., Northover, P., O'Connor, S., Ogden, A., Taylor, T., Wastling, V., and Wilson, A. (2010) Gristhorpe Man: an Early Bronze Age log-coffin burial scientifically defined. *Antiquity*, 84: 796–815. Reprinted by permission of Antiquity Publications.

Tate, J., Reiche, I., Pinzari, F., Clark, J. and Caldwell, D. (2011) History and surface condition of the Lewis Chessmen in the collection of the National Museums Scotland (Hebrides, late 12th-early 13th centuries). *ArchéoSciences: revue d'archéométrie*, 28: 249–58. Reprinted by permission of Presses universitaires de Rennes.

Tubb, K.W. and Brodie, N. (2001) From museum to mantelpiece: the antiquities trade in the United Kingdom. In: R. Layton, P.G. Stone and J. Thomas (eds.), *Destruction and Conservation of Cultural Property*. London: Routledge, pp. 102–16. Reprinted by permission of Taylor & Francis.

Kreder, J.A. (2010) The revolution in U.S. museums concerning the ethics of acquiring antiquities. *University of Miami Law Review*, 64(3): 997–1030. Reprinted by permission of the University of Miami Law Review.

Green, M. and Gordon, P. (2010) Repatriation: Australian perspectives. In: J. Lydon and U.Z. Rizvi (eds.), *Handbook of Postcolonial Archaeology*. Walnut Creek, CA: Left Coast Press Inc., pp. 257–66. Reprinted by permission of Left Coast Press, 2010. All rights reserved.

Nafziger, J.A.R. and Dobkins, R.J. (1999) The Native American Graves Protection and Repatriation Act in its first decade. *International Journal of Cultural Property*, 8(1): 77–107. Reprinted by permission of Cambridge Journals, © The International Cultural Property Society.

McManamon, F.P. (2006) Policy and practice in the treatment of archaeological human remains in North American museums and public agency collections. In: J. Lohman and K. Goodnow (eds.), *Human Remains and Museum Practice*. Paris: UNESCO, pp. 48–59. Reprinted by permission of Berghahn Books.

Jenkins, T. 2011. *Contesting Human Remains in Museum Collections: The Crisis of Cultural Authority*. New York and Abingdon: Routledge. Chapter 6. Covering up the mummies. pp. 121–39. Reprinted by permission of Taylor & Francis.

Shanks, M. and Tilley, C. (1993) *Re-Constructing Archaeology: Theory and Practice*. London: Routledge. 2nd edition. Chapter 4. Presenting the past: towards a redemptive aesthetic for the museum, pp. 68–99. Reprinted by permission of Taylor & Francis.

Skeates, R. (2002) Speaking for the past in the present: text, authority and learning in archaeology museums. *Public Archaeology*, 2(4): 209–18. Reprinted by permission of Taylor & Francis.

Copley, M.S. (2010) Towards presenting scientific research in archaeology museums. *Museum Management and Curatorship*, 25(4): 383–98. Reprinted by permission of Taylor & Francis.

Levy, J.E. (2006) Prehistory, identity, and archaeological representation in Nordic museums. *American Anthropologist*, 108(1): 135–47. Reprinted by permission of the author and the American Anthropological Association.

Bünz, A. (2012) Is it enough to make the main characters female? An intersectional and social semiotic reading of the exhibition *Prehistories 1* at the National Historical Museum in Stockholm, Sweden. In: I.-M. Back Danielsson and S. Thedéen (eds.), *To Tender Gender: The Pasts and Futures of Gender Research in Archaeology*. Stockholm Studies in Archaeology 58. Stockholm: Department of Archaeology and Classical Studies, Stockholm University, pp. 97–115. Reprinted by permission of the author.

Addyman, P. and Gaynor, A. (1984) The Jorvik Viking Centre: an experiment in archaeological site interpretation. *The International Journal of Museum Management and Curatorship*, 3: 7–18. Reprinted by permission of Taylor & Francis.

Lasheras Corruchaga, J.A. and Fatás Monforte, P. (2006) The new Museum of Altamira: finding solutions to tourism pressure. In: N. Agnew and J. Bridgland (eds.) *On the Past, for the Future: Integrating Archaeology and Conservation. Proceedings of the Conservation Theme at the 5th World Archaeological Congress, Washington, D.C., 22–26 June 2003*. Los Angeles: The Getty Conservation Institute, pp. 177–83. Reprinted by permission of the J. Paul Getty Trust.

Silverman, H. (2006) Archaeological site museums in Latin America. In: H. Silverman (ed.), *Archaeological Site Museums in Latin America*. Gainesville, FL: University Press of Florida, pp. 3–17. Reprinted by permission of the University Press of Florida.

Rask, K. (2010) The new Acropolis Museum: where the visual feast trumps education. *Near Eastern Archaeology*, 73(1): 56–59. Reprinted by permission of the American Schools of Oriental Research.

Chen, Z., Zhang, P. and Li, J. (2007) Development and utilization of underground space for the protection of relics in the Yang Emperor Mausoleum of the Han Dynasty. *Frontiers of Architecture and Civil Engineering in China*, 1(2): 229–33. Reprinted by permission of Springer-Verlag.

Helling, H., Steinmetz, C., Solomon, E. and Frischer, B. (2011) The Port Royal Project: a case study in the use of VR technology for the recontextualization of archaeological artifacts and building remains in a museum setting. In: E. Jerem, R. Ferenc and V. Szeverényi (eds.), *On the Road to Reconstructing the Past. Computer Applications and Quantitative Methods in Archaeology (CAA). Proceedings of the 36th International Conference. Budapest, April 2–6, 2008*. Budapest: Archaeolingua, pp. 229–35. Reprinted by permission of Archaeolingua and the authors.

Lea, J. (2000) Teaching the past in museums. In: K. Smardz and S.J. Smith (eds.), *The Archaeology Education Handbook: Sharing the Past with Kids*. Walnut Creek, CA: AltaMira Press, pp. 315–27. Reprinted by permission of AltaMira Press.

Owen, J. (1999) Interaction or tokenism? The role of hands-on activities in museum archaeology displays. In: N. Merriman (ed.), *Making Early Histories in Museums*. London: Leicester University Press, pp. 173–89. Reprinted by permission of Bloomsbury Academic Publishing.

Stone, P.G. (2004) The re-display of the Alexander Keiller Museum, Avebury, and the National Curriculum in England. In: P.G. Stone and B.L. Molyneaux (eds.), *The Presented Past: Heritage, Museums and Education*. London and New York: Routledge, pp. 190–205. Reprinted by permission of Taylor & Francis.

Hall, J. and Swain, H. (2000) Roman boxes for London's schools: an outreach service by the Museum of London. In: P.M. McManus (ed.), *Archaeological Displays and the Public: Museology and Interpretation*. 2nd edition. London: Archetype Publications, pp. 87–95. Reprinted by permission of the Hedley Swain, Arts Council England, and Jenny Hall.

Chan. A.A. (2011) Translating archaeology for the public: empowering and engaging museum goers with the past. *International Journal of Heritage Studies*, 17(2): 169–89. Reprinted by permission of Taylor & Francis.

Merriman, N. (2004) Involving the public in museum archaeology. In: N. Merriman (ed.), *Public Archaeology*. New York: Routledge, pp. 85–108. Reprinted by permission of Taylor & Francis.

Haggis, D. (2008) Public archaeology and museums in Japan. *The International Journal of the Inclusive Museum*, 1(4): 95–102. Reprinted by permission of Common Ground Publishing.

MacDonald, S. and Shaw, C. (2004) Uncovering ancient Egypt: the Petrie Museum and its public. In: N. Merriman (ed.), *Public Archaeology*. London: Routledge, pp. 109–31. Reprinted by permission of Taylor & Francis.

Tully, G. (2015) Re-imagining Egypt: artefacts, contemporary art and community engagement in the museum. Reprinted by permission of the author.

Carr-Locke, S. and Nicholas, G. (2011) Working towards greater equity and understanding: examples of collaborative archaeology and museum initiatives with indigenous peoples in North America. *Society for Applied Anthropology Newsletter*, 22(1): 4–9. Reprinted by permission of the Society for Applied Anthropology and the authors.

Ardren, T. (2002) Conversations about the production of archaeological knowledge and community museums at Chunchucmil and Kochol, Yucatán, México. *World Archaeology*, 34(2): 379–400. Reprinted by permission of Taylor & Francis.

Brown, P. (2011) Us and them: who benefits from experimental exhibition making? *Museum Management and Curation*, 26(2): 129–48. Reprinted by permission of Taylor & Francis.

Chapter 1

Museums and archaeology
Principles, practice, and debates

Robin Skeates

This chapter is intended to provide readers with an overview of the key contemporary principles, practices, and debates relating to museum archaeology. By highlighting a series of questions, it encourages readers to adopt a critical perspective and to use this in their own evaluations of museum theory and work. And, by referring to a significant sample of the professional and academic literature on museum archaeology, it offers not only an introduction to the chapters selected for inclusion in this Reader but also the chance to explore an even wider body of relevant literature.

The focus in this introduction, and throughout the Reader, is on present-day museum archaeology, including its development since the 1970s. Over this period, there has been a clear shift in museums from servicing the needs of archaeologists to serving diverse publics in more dynamic and sustainable ways. There exists, however, an extensive literature on the earlier history of antiquarian and archaeological collecting, dedicated to themes ranging from colonialism and nationalism to classical art and aesthetics (e.g. Leospo 1984; Gilberg 1987; Mitchell 1988; Wilson 1989; Jenkins 1992; Beard 1993; Broschi 1994; Masry 1994; Hebditch 1996; Kristiansen 1996; Wright 1996; Guha-Thakurta 1997; Crawley 1998; Errington 1998: 161–187; St. Clair 1998; Kurtz 2000; Skeates 2000, 2005; Crooke 2001; Jenkins 2001; Browman 2002; Shaw 2003; Tahan 2004, 2005; Moser 2006; Whitehead 2009; Cheape 2010; Garrigan 2012; Quirke 2012; ter Keurs 2011; Savino 2015; and numerous articles in the *Journal of the History of Collections*) – an awareness of which is certainly important when trying to understand the causes of some of the logistical and political challenges facing museum archaeology around the world today. As Hedley Swain (2007) has pointed out, for example, museum displays of cultural remains appropriated by representatives of former colonial powers can still perpetuate politically biased views of ancient civilizations as well as hero-myths about early archaeologists.

In what follows, three main areas – archaeological collections; archaeology, ethics, and the law; and interpreting the archaeological past – and a variety of sub-themes are covered, following the same order and headings as those used to structure the other chapters in this Reader.

Archaeological collections

Curation of archaeological remains: responses to crisis

What are the key principles of archaeological collections management? Is there a crisis in the curation of archaeological collections? How are museum archaeologists responding?

The key principles of good archaeological collections management are now well established (e.g. Museums and Galleries Commission 1992; Sullivan 1992; Sullivan and Childs 2003: 59–77 – **Chapter 2**). The first step is acquisition. This refers to the formal process of adding a set of objects to a collection. Museums and other repositories should agree and follow acquisition policies, and they should aim to obtain legal title to the objects that they acquire. The next step is accessioning, involving assigning an accession number and entering basic information for each object into an accessions register, including an assessment of the object's physical condition. Cataloguing follows on from this. It means gathering together all the primary information known about each object, including details of its provenance. Objects then need to be prepared for storage, and for possible research, exhibition, and loan. This includes being labelled, being assessed for conservation treatment, and being tracked via inventories. Strategic decisions have to be taken where objects and associated records are to be stored, taking account of access requirements and restrictions (notably over the handling and storage of human remains), environmental standards, and security. Deaccessioning and disposal – deciding to, then physically removing, objects from a collection – are also legitimate, if unusual, steps in collections management. In such cases, strenuous efforts should be made to transfer the objects through donation or exchange to responsible new owners (in contrast, for example, to sale on the open market to raise funds). All of these principles are intended to facilitate the controlled use of archaeological collections by a variety of people, whilst maintaining their safety and long-term preservation.

But museum principles and practice do not always neatly overlap. This has become increasingly evident since the mid-1970s, when a series of archaeological curation problems (labelled as 'the curation crisis') surfaced in the USA and elsewhere (e.g. Christenson 1979; Childs 1995, 2006; Kusimba 1996; Bustard 2000 – **Chapter 3**; Thompson 2000; Lyons et al. 2006). Ongoing issues include: large backlogs of uncatalogued collections; extensive archives from recent cultural resources management/developer-funded projects; inadequate museum staffing (and training); increasing curation fees; substandard, overflowing, dispersed, and unsafe storage facilities; limited public access to archaeological collections; and a lack of awareness of these problems amongst the wider archaeological community. Solutions do exist, but funding (which is a constant challenge) underpins almost all of them (Nash and O'Malley 2012). Engaging with the tax-paying public is essential, and digitization and online access to museum documentation is certainly one way forward towards more effective and accountable collections management. However, preserving and sharing digital data bring their own significant set of issues. State-of-the-art archaeological research and curation centres are a curator's dream, but usually remain so. As a consequence, despite a long-lived professional assumption that museum collections should be curated 'in perpetuity', deaccessioning and disposal cannot now be rejected out of hand, although the process has to be managed very carefully.

Given these challenges, Trimble and Marino (2003) go so far as to state that good collections management is an ethical responsibility of museum and field archaeologists. They define ethics in this context as being about making sound professional choices that benefit the long-term care and use of archaeological collections. On one level, before archaeological fieldwork begins, good curation planning is important, including the pursuit of rigorous sampling strategies. On another level, the physical and administrative infrastructure of curation facilities needs to be reviewed – critically and from a long-term perspective. Dynamic fundraising and outreach programmes are regarded as ways forward here. However, when it comes to collections of culturally sensitive materials, other ethical stances are also relevant, as we shall see later on.

Archaeological archives: selection, retention, use, and disposal

Should archaeologists keep everything they find? Can the long-term museum storage and care of (often large) archaeological excavation archives be justified? Who should pay for such storage? How can better use be made of archaeological archives? Should some of this material be disposed of, and if so how?

Archaeological archives comprise finds, environmental samples, paper, photographic, and digital records, and other material arising from archaeological field- and laboratory-work and passed to museums for long-term curation after their primary study and publication. This flow of material has a long and sometimes chequered history, and, in order to promote closer working together of museum and field archaeologists, and to assist museum staff in planning for the care and use of archaeological archives, successive reports, recommendations, and guidelines have been produced (e.g. for the UK, White 1986; Wingfield 1993; Owen 1995; Swain 1998; Perrin 2002). Nevertheless, problems have continued. The traditional archaeological justification for retaining such archives is that they comprise a priceless residue of 'our' archaeological heritage, resulting from public- or developer-funded fieldwork at now largely destroyed archaeological sites, with the potential to be of research or educational value in the future. However, in an economic climate of shrinking budgets and storage space, hard decisions still need to be made about the future of archaeological archives (Sonderman 1996 – **Chapter 4**).

Nick Merriman and Hedley Swain's (1999 – **Chapter 5**) response to the growing problems faced by the curators of often neglected archaeological archives in England in the 1990s (e.g. Swain 1996) was, on the one hand, to remind scholars of their research potential, and, on the other hand, to offer suggestions as to how they might be made more accessible for the benefit of the wider public. Providing online access to digitized museum catalogues and collections was seen as an important first step. The Museum of London's 'London Archaeological Archive and Research Centre' has since been regarded as a model of good practice (Swain 2006 – **Chapter 6**). The

Centre, which cares for the archives of some 5,200 archaeological excavations in London, hosts the Central London Young Archaeologists Club for children and teenagers, provides loans boxes of Roman material for London schools (see later), and offers the public weekend events such as a recreated excavation using real artefacts, themed 'behind-the-scenes' tours, and volunteer opportunities. However, according to a recent survey of museums holding archaeological archives across England, many of the old problems remain at a local level, including lack of storage space, geographical gaps in the collecting areas of museums, understaffing, and limited public awareness and use of the archives (Edwards 2012).

Documentation, identification, and authentication of archaeological collections

How should archaeological collections be documented? What range of terms should be used to describe archaeological remains? How can fakes be identified?

Good documentation is essential to the effective management of museum collections of archaeological material, whether it be newly acquired, on display, in store, under study and conservation, or on loan. Widely shared (even 'universal') documentation standards are ideal – one example being SPECTRUM: The UK Museum Documentation Standard (e.g. Longworth 1998; Longworth and Wood 2000). This approach is particularly relevant to large and widely dispersed collections – notably of Egyptian antiquities, acquired in large quantities, dispersed around the museums of the world, and catalogued in a variety of languages and databases (Saleh 1992). However, local solutions that meet the needs of specific collections and organisations are also necessary. One example is provided by the computerized inventory system devised by staff at Laténium – the Archaeological Museum in Neuchâtel, Switzerland – to cope with the voluminous and varied excavation and field-survey archives from the surrounding canton (Vaudou 2004 – **Chapter 7**; see also Kaeser 2009). To ensure the smooth transfer of archaeological archives from field to repository, the systematic entry of data, and easy access to them, a thesaurus of standard words is shared by excavation and museum staff, a very structured and straightforward form is used for recording objects, and a single index is maintained (as opposed to separate indexes according to archaeological period).

However, despite the knowledge and experience of museum documentation staff, not all archaeological materials are easy to identify correctly, particularly by eye. As a consequence, in the case of ancient marbles, for example, a combination of scientific analyses can help to differentiate between authentic pieces and forgeries (Polikreti 2007). The patina of marble can be investigated using techniques such as optical microscopy, the stone's provenance (quarry) can be identified using a range of physical and geochemical techniques, the freshness of working and breaks can be evaluated under ultraviolet light, and the 'burial age' or length of time an object has been exposed to sunlight can be calculated using thermoluminescence. Not surprisingly, there are advantages and limitations to all of these techniques, and their results are not always conclusive. The same is true of techniques used in the authentication of other archaeological materials, such as ancient bronze artefacts (Robbiola and Portier 2006).

Museum care, conservation, and restoration of archaeological objects

What are the optimum conditions for the care of archaeological collections? What are the consequences of conservation work on archaeological objects? Are minimum intervention and reversibility practicable guiding principles for archaeological conservation work? In what circumstances are conservators justified in seeking to restore to an earlier stage the appearance of an archaeological object?

Despite the existence of clearly defined standards and guidelines for curation and conservation (e.g. Museums and Galleries Commission 1992), not all archaeological collections receive adequate care. For example, China's world-famous terracotta warriors, displayed to large numbers of visitors in the Museum of Qin Terracotta Warriors and Horses near Xi'an, have been discoloured and eroded by air pollution (characterized by high concentrations of acidic aerosols) – the impact of which is particularly high in the summer season when the temperature can reach 30 degrees Centigrade and relative humidity 70 per cent (Cao et al. 2005; Hu et al. 2009). Evidently, the active and long-term involvement of conservators is essential here to establish, monitor, and maintain appropriate environmental controls. More recently, significant negative media attention was generated when it emerged that museum staff at the Egyptian Museum in Cairo had hastily and irreversibly glued back Tutankhamun's beard with epoxy when his gold burial mask was damaged during cleaning (BBC 2015).

The common purpose of conservators is to prolong the lifespan of an object, even though it is not possible to halt the deterioration process completely. But, in practice, conservators are faced with an overlapping array of choices of treatment, ranging from initial investigative work to establish the nature of the object, to preventive treatment and care involving the removal of damaging materials, the consolidation of remaining materials and the establishment of environmental controls to prevent further disintegration, to remedial treatment to repair or support a fragile object, to more interventive cleaning and restoration of the object's shape and appearance (Pye 2000 – **Chapter 8**). Much depends on the actual material (for example, archaeological bronzes are easier to conserve than archaeological iron), the perceived future uses of the object (for study, teaching, or display), and, of course, the funding available. Caution is essential and debate inevitable.

A particularly controversial archaeological example is provided by the restoration of the Bush Barrow lozenge plate (Kinnes et al. 1988). This object comprises one of a group of finely decorated gold objects excavated from a Bronze Age burial mound near Stonehenge, and is owned by the Wiltshire Archaeological and Natural History Society. For the purposes of museum handling and display, it was restored whilst on loan to the British Museum (without the permission of the owners), initially by removing the creases and indentations on the face, but then – more profoundly – by modifying its shape from a flattened state to a deduced 'original' gently domed profile and by polishing its surface. This irreversible restoration has been challenged on both scientific and ethical grounds (Shell and Robinson 1988; Corfield 1988).

A more creative solution to the care and display of a set of valuable archaeological objects is shown by the example of an Egyptian mummy and coffin owned by the Burke Museum of Natural History and Culture in Seattle, Washington (Phillips and Roundhill 2007 – **Chapter 9**). The coffin belongs to the Twenty-First Dynasty (2909–2839 BP) and the unrelated mummy to the Ptolomaic Period (2250–1980 BP). In the late 1990s, museum staff realized that both were in need of conservation and a new protective environment. US$35,000 was successfully raised from the museum's community to design and build an environmentally stable and ethically sensitive storage and display case. A single case was produced with separately sealed compartments: the coffin is situated in the visible upper part in a stable environment, while the mummy and its cartonnage pieces are respectfully placed out of (but potentially in) view in an oxygen-free polyethylene bag in a drawer below.

Archaeology collections research

What is the research potential of old museum collections of archaeological objects? In what ways can new analytical techniques improve understanding of them? What do museum curators get out of archaeological scientists' work on their collections? How might members of the public participate in research on archaeological collections?

New research on old archaeological collections has the potential to transform our understanding of those objects and their wider archaeological contexts, and also to significantly enhance their appeal to the public (e.g. Chapman 1981; Saville 1994; Gaimster 2001). Given that museums generally have less resources to undertake this work themselves, partnerships with academics and the public can prove to be a productive way forward, particularly where research agendas and data are shared.

Take Gristhorpe Man, for example. This well-preserved Early Bronze Age log-coffin burial from North Yorkshire in the UK was excavated in the early nineteenth century and has since been housed in Scarborough Museum. The coffin contained a complete human skeleton accompanied by organic and inorganic grave goods. While the museum was undergoing major renovation, a large international team of archaeological scientists, led by Nigel Melton of Bradford University, used a wide range of modern analytical techniques to shed new light on the dating, diet, and provenance of the man (Melton et al. 2009 – **Chapter 10**). Osteoarchaeological study revealed that the man was relatively tall, physically active, and right-handed, while stable isotope measurements indicated that he spent his childhood in the Scarborough area, and that his nutritious diet was relatively high in meat. Healed fractures are suggestive of injuries sustained during martial exploits. CT scanning showed that, despite his healthy physique, he suffered from a slowly developing intra-cranial tumour, which may have caused physical and behavioural impairment. Gas chromatography-mass spectrometry and stable isotope analysis confirmed that the black material contained in a vial was correctly labelled 'brain'. Metallurgical analysis and the lead isotope ratios of the bronze dagger blade found with the body suggest that it was manufactured in Britain using recycled Irish metal. The dagger's pommel was confirmed to be of rare whalebone. A combination of accelerator mass spectrometry, radiocarbon, and dendrochronological dating of the Gristhorpe assemblage gave a date for the skeleton of 2200–2020 BC, and indicate that the tree for the coffin was felled at around the same time (between 2115 and 2035 BC), but that the branches laid over the coffin were deposited at least 270 years after the death of Gristhorpe Man – perhaps when the barrow was completed. Overall, these results support the hypothesis that the man was of chiefly status, born locally into an elite family, but linked to a wider social network via the sea. The new museum display is now helping to disseminate these research findings to the public.

A comparable example is provided by recent research on the famous Lewis Chessmen in the collection of the National Museums of Scotland (Tate et al. 2011 – **Chapter 11**). The surface condition of the museum's collection of eleven of these pieces was examined using optical microscopy, X-ray fluorescence spectroscopy, and scanning electron microscopy, in order to find out more about the materials from which they were made and about their biographies – from their manufacture in the early medieval period through to their discovery in the nineteenth century. The results suggest that while the majority are of walrus ivory two of the pieces are of sperm whale tooth. Traces of cinnabar-derived mercury identified on the surface of individual pieces also suggest that they were originally decorated by red pigment.

In addition to projects like these where archaeological scientists undertake cutting-edge research on museum collections, the innovative MicroPasts project led by Andrew Bevan of University College London has used web-based, crowd-sourcing methods to allow academics and the public to co-produce large numbers of 3D models of artefacts, enhance existing archaeological databases, add rich new content to images, and micro-fund new collaboratively developed research agendas. Working in partnership with the British Museum, project volunteers have, for example, helped to transcribe more than 30,000 handwritten catalogue cards dating back to the late eighteenth century, and made digital photographs of thousands of ancient bronze artefacts so that they can be stitched together to form 3D images (Kennedy 2014). In return, the catalogue records and the images are freely available, without copyright restrictions, and so a replica of a bronze axe from Jevington housed in the British Museum has been printed out as a 3D plastic model in a public library in Washington DC during the course of an archaeology open day.

Archaeology, ethics, and the law

Legal and ethical dimensions of archaeological museum collecting and collections

What is the relationship between museum collecting and the licit and illicit trade in antiquities? How can museums practice due diligence when acquiring archaeological collections? What are the limitations to existing cultural property legislation?

Caution has been growing in museum archaeology towards the collecting of cultural material, especially since the late 1980s (e.g. Shestack 1989; Cook 1991;

Gaimster 1993; Tubb 1995; O'Keefe 1997; Brodie et al. 2000; McIntosh et al. 2000). Although not all would agree that archaeologists should think of themselves as the absolute guardians of heritage (e.g. Boardman 2006), concern has centred on the legality and ethics of collecting cultural material that might have been destructively looted from archaeological sites and then illicitly traded (e.g. Tubb and Brodie 2001 – **Chapter 12**). In particular, concerns have been voiced by archaeologists and national heritage agencies over acquisitions of antiquities made by prestigious museums in Europe and the USA. For example, David Gill and Christopher Chippindale (Gill and Chippindale 1993; Chippindale and Gill 2000; cf. Broodbank 1992) have documented the calamitous consequences of connoisseurs' esteem for classical art objects and prehistoric Cycladic marble figurines, which has driven their competitive private and public collecting, their illicit trading, the looting of archaeological sites and museums, the production of fakes, and a distortion of these objects' contextual significance in past societies. Another particularly scandalous example is the J. Paul Getty Museum in Los Angeles, allegedly known in the Swiss antiquities trade as the 'museum of the *tombaroli*' ('tomb-robbers') (Watson and Todeschini 2006). Its former curator of antiquities, Marion True, was indicted by the Italian government in 2005, along with the American antiquities dealer, Robert E. Hecht, for conspiracy to traffic in illicit antiquities, based on evidence from a police raid of the Geneva warehouse of an Italian art dealer, Giacomo Medici, who had acted as the middleman for items purchased by the Getty, including Etruscan bronzes and Greek vases illegally excavated and exported from Italy. True resigned from the museum the following year, complaining that she had been made the scapegoat for practices that were known and condoned by the Getty's Board of Directors.

Following a series of high-profile exposés of the sometimes close connection between museums and the illicit trade in antiquities, museum archaeologists are now much more aware of their legal obligations and ethical responsibilities when collecting archaeological materials. In particular, they pay closer attention to the claimed provenance and recent histories of potential archaeological acquisitions, to ensure that they have not been illegally looted, exported, and sold. They are also making new efforts to educate their publics as to the destructive effects of the illicit trade in antiquities (e.g. Argyropoulos et al. 2014). In the UK, this new attitude has been codified in guidelines produced by the government's Cultural Property Unit (DCMS 2005a). These state that museums should reject an item offered to them for acquisition or loan if there is any suspicion about it, or about the circumstances surrounding it, after checking that it was not illegally excavated or exported since 1970 (the date UNESCO adopted the Convention on the Means of Prohibiting and Preventing the Illicit Import, Export and Transfer of Cultural Property). More specifically, it describes the process of 'due diligence'. This involves examining the object, considering its type and likely place of origin, taking expert advice, determining whether the item was lawfully exported to the UK, and evaluating the account given by the vendor or donor. These worthy principles were described as 'daunting and difficult' in practice by Paul Roberts, Curator of Roman Art and Archaeology at the British Museum, although he remained upbeat about the likelihood of the Museum continuing to add to its archaeological collections for the purposes of display and research (Roberts 2006: 60). In the USA, a law and ethics revolution pertaining to museums' acquisitions of antiquities can also be claimed to have taken place, with both the Association of Art Museum Directors and the American Association of Museums adopting new ethics guidelines for acquisitions of ancient art and archaeological material (Kreder 2010 – **Chapter 13**). However, still fearing the loss of important unprovenanced archaeological objects to private collections, their guidelines intentionally leave loopholes for museums to use 'informed judgement' when the complete documented ownership history of a work is unavailable. A comparable tension exists in Norway, where museum staff have been criticized for legitimating unlawful metal detecting by praising metal detector users who hand in objects to them (Munch Rasmussen 2014).

Despite this tightening up of the legal and ethical dimensions of museum acquisitions in Europe and the USA, the looting of national museums during recent and ongoing wars in the Arab world highlights the continued value and vulnerability of cultural property in 'source' countries. For example, in 2003, following the U.S. invasion of Iraq and the chaotic fall of Baghdad, the inadequately protected National Museum in Baghdad was looted by Iraqi civilians, resulting in the loss of thousands of artworks and artefacts. One of the most valuable pieces was a headless stone statue of the Sumerian King Entemena; it was eventually recovered in the USA and restituted to Iraq. Upon reflection, it became clear that UNESCO's widely ratified 1954 Hague Convention on the Protection of Cultural Property in the Event of Armed Conflict did not explicitly contemplate civilian looting (as opposed to state-sponsored looting and destruction) and therefore does not address responsibility for preventing civilian looting (Paroff 2004; cf. Stone and Farchakh Bajjaly 2011). However, this has been partly addressed in the Second Protocol to the 1954 Hague Convention, which entered into force in 2004. Nevertheless, museums and their collections will never be entirely safe in times of war. Indeed, in Syria, at the time of writing, museums and archaeological sites are being actively targeted, looted, and destroyed.

Repatriation and reburial of archaeological museum collections

How is 'ownership' understood by different interest groups? What is repatriation? How should museums respond to repatriation requests? What impact have repatriation requests had on museums and their collections around the world? What should be done with unprovenanced ancestral remains held in museums?

Repatriation is traditionally defined as returning a person to their place of origin. However, in the museum context, it has come to refer to the return of an item of cultural patrimony from a museum collection to a party found to be its true owner or traditional guardian, or their heir and descendants. As such, the act of repatriation can also be understood as an act of reparation – making amends for a wrong done, often by members of former colonial powers (Greenfield 2007).

In Australia, systematic repatriation of Australian Aboriginal and Torres Strait Islander artefacts and human remains began in the 1970s, in response to growing Aboriginal political activism, and, despite resistance from anthropologists and archaeologists, is now actively pursued by Australian governments and cultural institutions as a matter of policy (e.g. Turnbull 2002; Green and Gordon 2010 – **Chapter 14**). Perhaps the best known, and most archaeologically contentious, example was the repatriation and reburial of human remains excavated at the Kow Swamp late Pleistocene burial site in central Victoria, dating back to at least 15,000 years ago, and arguably unrelated to modern Aboriginal populations. These were returned by the Government of Victoria in 1990 at the request of the Yorta Yorta Aboriginal community. However, casts of some of the Kow Swamp skulls and mandibles have been retained by museums. Today, negotiation between museums and Aboriginal communities, and repatriation on request of ancestral remains and secret-sacred objects, are enshrined in the policy of Museums Australia – Australia's national museums association. But the large number of effectively unprovenanced ancestral remains still held in Australian museums represents an unresolved problem.

In the USA, repatriation is now closely associated with the Native American Graves Protection and Repatriation Act (NAGPRA). This was enacted in 1990, following two decades of campaigning by the Native American human rights (and associated burial rights) movement. The legislation confirmed Indigenous ownership or control over native cultural items discovered on federal and tribal lands, criminalized trafficking in Native American human remains, and established a process of repatriation of material from museums and federal agencies to Native groups. Museums have consequently been obliged to compile detailed inventories of Native American remains and cultural items in their possession, and to return any material to a claimant that has established the requisite link of linear descendancy, cultural affiliation, or ownership or control. It has also required museums to consult and collaborate with Native groups: to classify objects correctly and – where possible – determine their cultural affiliation. In practice, tensions have arisen over definitions of 'cultural affiliation', what to do with nearly 119,000 sets of 'culturally unidentifiable human remains', the level of scientific documentation to be undertaken, and the amount of time and work involved (e.g. Nafziger and Dobkins 1999 – **Chapter 15**; Killion 2008; Daehnke and Lonetree 2010). The experience of Harvard University's Peabody Museum of Archaeology and Ethnology offers a good example of some of these issues (Isaac 2002). But positive relations between museums and Native American communities have often been established through the restitution process. It is also worth noting that not all Native American items have been restituted, nor all restituted items reburied – some being left in the care of the original museums for the educational benefit of tribal members and non-tribal researchers, many receiving more culturally sensitive care through the incorporation of indigenous curation methods, and some gaining greater visibility as part of new tribal museum collections.

In the UK, official guidelines for good practice in responding to requests for restitution and repatriation of cultural property were published by the former Museums and Galleries Commission (Legget 2000) – the Government's advisory body for museums – and have since been widely adopted as part of museums' collections management policies. When considering a request, thirteen keys steps to consider are usefully defined:

- acknowledging the request
- delegating the preparation of the response to one person
- informing the museum's governing body of the request
- clarifying the status of those making the request
- contacting other museums to establish if they have received similar requests
- understanding the reasons behind the request
- gauging the cultural and religious importance of the material
- checking the status and condition of the material
- checking the acquisition history of the material
- referring to current museum policies
- considering professional ethical concerns
- checking international legislation and conventions, and
- considering the proposed future of the material if returned.

However, it is worth noting that such requests are relatively rare in the UK, and generally relate to material in ethnographic or fine art collections – one classic archaeological exception being the Parthenon Marbles, held by the British Museum since the early nineteenth century (St. Clair 1998), against Greek politicians' wishes, who have optimistically reserved space for them in the New Acropolis Museum (to which we will return below).

Another way forward in the repatriation debate can be found in a change of attitude towards collections mobility, encapsulated in a report published by the UK Museums Association entitled *Collections for the Future* (Museums Association 2005). Essentially, the report recommended that museums (including national museums) develop more partnerships with each other, and that they share – to a much greater extent – collections, expertise, and skills. This new dynamic attitude has played a significant part in responding to, and mitigating demands for, the repatriation of Scottish cultural artefacts from English and Scottish national museums. A good example is provided by the Lewis Chessmen (already mentioned earlier). Of the 93 pieces known to us today, 82 are held by the British Museum (BM) and 11 by the National Museum of Scotland (NMS). They are an iconic set of objects within the British Museum's collection, and an extensive range of Lewis Chessmen merchandise features prominently in the Museum's shop. The Celtic League, an independent pressure group championing the cultural rights of the indigenous people of Scotland and other Celtic regions has been calling for the restitution of the Lewis Chessmen and other Celtic artefacts for a number of years. Their cause was boosted in 2007 when Alex Salmond, the then leader of the Scottish National Party and First Minister, began arguing for their return to an independent Scotland. Local politicians and campaigners on the Isle of Lewis responded by stating that they would certainly like some of the pieces back, particularly to help boost their tourist industry. In the context of the Museums Association's recommendations and this political debate, in 2010 and 2011 the British Museum worked in partnership with National Museums Scotland, and with funding from the Scottish Government, to lay on the largest travelling exhibition to date (involving 30 of the chessmen – 24 from the BM and 6 from the NMS). The exhibition opened at the National Museum in Edinburgh, then toured to Aberdeen Art Gallery, Shetland Museum and Archives, and the Western Isles Museum in Stornoway. In this way, a diplomatic solution was sought in which these special objects could be kept 'alive' and relevant to the modern world by being kept circulating in the public domain, while sidestepping the entrenched issue of all-out transfer of ownership. The British Museum was, anyway, not inexperienced in politically sensitive negotiations, having, for example, previously hosted a blockbuster exhibition of the terracotta warriors – which remain highly visible symbols of Chinese cultural diplomacy (Feuchtwang 2011).

Museums and the care and display of ancient human remains

What archaeological human remains might be retained by museums? How should these remains be treated? Should they be displayed? And who should decide?

The care and display of ancient human remains in museums has been the subject of enduring and heated debate between researchers, museum curators, and descendant communities, all of whom have asserted claims for access or control based upon their different perspectives (e.g. Lohman 2012; Giesen 2013). This debate has been particularly intense in the USA, where it led to the enactment of NAGPRA. This has had significant consequences for federally funded museums holding collections of Native American and Native Hawaiian human remains and other cultural items (McManamon 2006 – **Chapter 16**). Leaving aside repatriation (discussed earlier), NAGPRA and its associated regulations require federal officials to ensure that retained collections of human remains are preserved and made available for scientific, educational, and religious uses, although recognized tribes with demonstrable cultural affiliation to the remains are generally allowed to control access to them. Public agencies and museums have also established their own policies concerning research on, and display of, human remains from archaeological contexts in their collections. In general, they allow study of human remains by qualified researchers, including destructive analysis, subject to review of a detailed research proposal and to consultation with traditionally associated peoples. By contrast, they do not allow the public display of Native American human remains and photographs of them, in order to avoid causing offense and distress to Native American people. Human remains of individuals from other ethnic groups are occasionally displayed, but only after careful consideration.

Debate over the appropriate treatment of human remains in museums has also been growing in the rather different political context of the UK (e.g. Swain 2002; Curtis 2003; Giesen 2013). In response to the Australian government's request for the UK to increase efforts to repatriate human remains to Australian Indigenous communities, the UK Government's Department of Culture, Media, and Sport (DCMS) published guidance for the care of human remains in museums, including procedural guidance on the return of human remains (DCMS 2005b). The report acknowledges that, 'The vast majority of work on human remains held by museums in the United Kingdom is uncontroversial and has wide popular and academic support' (p. 8). In other words, most visitors 'trust' museums to be professional in how they treat human remains (Kilmister 2003). But the DCMS also recommends that museums should always have a clear understanding as to why they are holding human remains, should store those remains in a designated area, treat them with dignity and respect, display them only when their presence makes a material contribution to a particular interpretation, and in such a way as to avoid visitors coming across them unawares.

Some UK museum archaeologists have since encouraged debate over the question of whether or not human remains should be displayed in museums, and have experimented with the redisplay of previously uncontested human remains (Alberti et al. 2009; Jenkins 2011 – **Chapter 17**). This has been stimulated by the international debate, by the controversial 'Bodyworlds' travelling exhibition of plastinated human bodies stripped down to reveal their inner anatomical structures, and by national outrage over Alder Hey hospital's removal of organs from the bodies of deceased children without their families' consent. Set in the context of this debate, a temporary exhibition held between 2008 and 2009 at Manchester Museum focused on Lindow Man, a well-preserved Iron Age bog-body found near Manchester, and invited a range of stakeholders (including curators, archaeologists, Pagans, and local people) to contribute to an inclusive and respectful exhibition that presented multiple views of Lindow Man in the light of present-day concerns. (The design of, and audience responses to, this exhibition are returned to later.) This contrasted with previous exhibitions of Lindow Man in the British Museum, which drew primarily upon archaeological research to interpret the man's life and death in the past (e.g. Stead et al. 1986). At the same time, Manchester Museum took the decision to cover up three unwrapped Egyptian mummies with white sheets, in order to raise questions through public consultation about the most respectful and appropriate way for the museum to display human remains. However, this strategy provoked a strongly negative public and professional reaction, to which the museum responded by uncovering some of the mummies.

Interpreting the archaeological past

Critical and political perspectives on museum representations of the archaeological past and of archaeology

Museum displays have been critically evaluated by visitors for longer than we might imagine. D.H. Lawrence, for example, in his book about Etruscan places, wrote: 'Museum, museums, museums, object-lessons rigged out to illustrate the unsound theories of archaeologists, crazy attempts to co-ordinate and get into a fixed order that which has no fixed order and will not be co-ordinated! It is sickening!' (Lawrence 1932: 185). However, it was in the late 1980s and early 1990s, as part of a broader intellectual revolution informed by critical theory, that an alliance of scholars and other commentators began to question many aspects of the museum institution, with the goal of establishing a 'new museology' (Vergo 1989). Particular attention was paid to the conventions used to represent the past in museum displays, whose orders were found to be far from politically neutral. This led to a fundamental question: how objective can and should museum displays about the past be?

In archaeology, Michael Shanks and Christopher Tilley (1987a; 1987b) led the charge, challenging the archaeological orthodoxy with a new brand of social theory which promoted a self-reflexive, critical, and political archaeology that linked the past to the present. This radical manifesto extended to museum representations of archaeological collections and of archaeological work (Shanks and Tilley 1993: 68–99 – **Chapter 18**). Their key argument was that museums can misrepresent the past: distorting it through processes of selection and classification, objectification and aestheticization, revelation and signification – processes through which archaeological artefacts are ultimately turned into ahistorical commodities and visitors into voyeuristic consumers. They also deconstructed the presentation at the Jorvik Viking Centre in York of 'the archaeologist as hero', in which archaeologists are portrayed as industrious scientific experts discovering truths about the past. Reacting against established modes of museum representation, Shanks and Tilley proposed a new interpretative agenda to redeem museum archaeology – one that would embrace heterogeneity, difference, contradiction, discontinuity, and conflict. More specifically, they argued that: (1) to reflexively acknowledge how the past may be manipulated and misrepresented for present-day purposes, political content should be introduced into conventional displays; (2) to acknowledge that artefacts' meanings change according to their specific engagements with the present, artefacts should be reordered and juxtaposed together with contemporary objects; (3) to emphasize that historical authorship is a dynamic, incomplete work-in-progress, impermanent displays should be produced; and (4) to democratize historical authorship, communities should be allowed to construct their own pasts in the museum and to use artefacts outside the institutional space of the museum.

This critical agenda had a significant impact on museum archaeology, particularly within the UK (e.g. Owen 1996; Merriman 1999, 2000). This was evident, for example, in texts accompanying exhibitions of prehistoric material in England and Scotland developed in the 1990s (Skeates 2002 – **Chapter 19**). Analysis of information panels and artefact labels revealed a curatorial shift away from using museum text as an authoritative aid to education and communication towards the expression of more critically aware and easy-to-read curatorial messages. For example, the redisplay of the Alexander Keiller Museum (Stone 2004), discussed later, and the new display of the Kilmartin House Museum of Ancient Culture (which, incidentally, won the Scottish Museum of the Year and the Gulbenkian Prize for Museums and Galleries) (Heywood 2000) were testimony to a theoretically informed desire shared by members of a new generation of museum professionals to deconstruct and reconstruct archaeology.

But the most contentious example was the 'People before London' prehistory gallery in the Museum of London, opened in 1994 and closed prematurely in 2000 (Cotton and Wood 1996; Merriman 1996; Wood 1996; Cotton 1997; cf. Merriman 1997 on the Museum of London's comparable 'Peopling of London' project). Front-end visitor studies revealed the restricted prior knowledge of audiences, who often equated 'prehistoric' with 'dinosaurs', and their preference for large images over text. At the same time, Shanks and Tilley's radical proposals were explicitly taken into account by the curators, who introduced a degree of political content into the displays, juxtaposed archaeological artefacts with contemporary objects, emphasized authorship and the historical contingency of archaeological interpretations, and encouraged visitors to construct their own pasts in the museum. For example, the first text panel in the gallery, signed by the curators, asked visitors, 'Can you believe what we say?' and also acknowledged that green and gender issues had been given prominence in the display, while the final panel asked, 'Now what does prehistory mean to you?' Although there were some dissenters amongst more conservative visitors and commentators, who accused the curators of political correctness, academic relativism, distasteful over-personalisation, and the dumbing-down of culture, summative evaluation indicated that most visitors appreciated this new approach. Nevertheless, this example also exposes a fundamental flaw in Shanks and Tilley's agenda: unequal relations of power were still inherent in the display, whose curators still spoke for the past and manipulated the visitor, ultimately establishing a new form of curatorial authority – one that was more subtly masked by written admissions of bias and offers of democratic learning.

It is worth adding that not all museum archaeologists in the UK adopted Shanks and Tilley's approach in the 1990s or have done so since then. This is especially the case with curatorial staff based in the national museums, where scholarly allegiance to their vast archaeological collections has traditionally been an important priority. For example, the 'Early Peoples' gallery in the National Museum of Scotland is dominated by artefacts from the museum's rich archaeological collections, complemented by specially commissioned contemporary artworks, and accompanied by texts that reassert an anonymous curatorial authority to communicate and educate – albeit in engaging, poetic language (Clarke 1996, 1998, 2000; Ascherson 2000). Furthermore, according to Mark Copley's (2010 – **Chapter 20**) survey of 62 curatorial staff responsible for archaeology exhibits in the UK, most staff, even if not generally trained as scientists, are largely supportive of the UK Government's strategy to enhance the public understanding of science and of current scientific research (ranging in archaeology from dating techniques to palaeopathology). The same is probably true in the USA, where, for example, a temporary exhibition in 2001 at the Science Museum of Minnesota focused on science as a social process exemplified by the ongoing archaeological research at the Neolithic site of Çatalhöyük in Turkey, as part of a broader strategy to advance the public understanding of science funded by the National Science Foundation (Pohlman 2004).

Nevertheless, since the late 1990s, the critiquing of museum representations of the archaeological past has become more mainstream in academic archaeology, both within and beyond the UK. Shanks and Tilley's groundbreaking ideas may be less explicitly acknowledged in the large body of literature in this area, but their impact continues to be felt in archaeological museology (i.e. the study of the history, theory, and practice of museums), if less so in museum practice.

Museum displays of human origins, for example, have been critically appraised by Stephanie Moser (2003), along similar lines to those proposed by Shanks and Tilley (cf. Scott 2007). Moser argues that, in the twentieth century, such visual displays created a highly formulaic and restrictive account of human evolution. Life-size dioramas in particular represented our early ancestors as 'primitive', with slouched and hairy bodies, recurrently associated with clubs, animal skins, and caves. As an alternative to this display canon, Moser calls for new displays of human origins that: (1) challenge the associations that are still made between our hominid ancestors and modern black African peoples; (2) challenge the traditional 'caveman' iconography of human evolution; (3) replace the traditional narrative of unilinear and sequential evolutionary progress with combined chronological and thematic exhibits; (4) tell new stories – for example, about socializing or the preoccupations of juvenile hominids; and (5) harness the emotional power of empathy and humour to communicate with visitors.

The variable representation of Saami (Lapp) prehistory and identity in museums in Sweden, Finland, and Norway has been thoughtfully evaluated by Janet Levy (2006 – **Chapter 21**). In particular, she has identified ideology-based contrasts between messages expressed by Scandinavian national and regional museums and by indigenous Saami community museums, particularly in the context of political tensions over claims to land and resources in Lapland. In the national and regional museums, an authoritative view of Scandinavian antiquity is presented, from which the Saami are largely marginalized. By contrast, in the Saami community museums, Saami history and culture are closely tied to the natural setting and climate of Lapland, and the time depth of Saami occupation is emphasized. Levy acknowledges the interpretative problems presented by both kinds of museum display, but, rather than calling for the depoliticization of archaeology, she acknowledges that representations of the past are inevitably political.

Persuasive critiques of gender and age bias in traditional archaeological museum exhibitions have also been published. For example, back in the 1990s Vivienne Holgate (1996: 85) noted that in museum displays about Roman Britain women were 'shown performing stereotypical tasks in domestic situations such as food production, food preparation, and looking after children.' And in Greek museums Dimitra Kokkinidou and Marianna Nikolaidou (2000) have argued that women have tended to be represented as passive or ambiguous participants in history, while female archaeologists have been rendered invisible, by displays that reflect the deep-rooted scholarly male chauvinism in Greek archaeology. As a consequence of such critiques some progress has been made in recent years over the museum representation of women in archaeology displays. However, Annika Bünz (2012 – **Chapter 22**) argues that further changes need to be made in order to achieve complete equity. Focusing on the 'Prehistories 1' permanent exhibition, which opened in 2005 at the National Historical Museum in Stockholm, Sweden, her detailed analysis reveals that women have been included in the exhibition narratives to a greater extent than in previous exhibitions but that male characters are still represented as older, more authoritative, and powerful, and women as closer to nature. Children and childhood are, likewise, often under-represented in museum archaeology, despite the high proportion of children among museum visitors (Sofaer Derevenski 1999; Brookshaw 2010).

Archaeological site museums

Museums at archaeological sites and parks focus on the excavated remains and historic landscapes of particular places, but they do not exist in isolation, either museologically or socially (Mgomezulu 2004). As a consequence, they raise many questions. How should such archaeological museums be managed? How should their archaeological remains be preserved? To what extent should reconstruction be used in their public presentation? And how might they work with local urban and rural communities? Certainly archaeological site museums have multiple responsibilities: to undertake on-site preservation, documentation, research, exhibition, and interpretation, as well as to raise public awareness of the archaeological heritage and to provide a source of economic income for local people (e.g. Ertürk 2006; Hachlili 1998).

In contrast to regional and national archaeological museums with extensive collections, site museums have the significant interpretative and ethical advantage of being able to present the histories of archaeological remains in context – or at least close to their places of discovery. But they do not always capture the imagination of visitors, due to the removal of star finds to more prominent museums, or a lack of funding to revive old displays of often large archaeological collections, or because of the presence of complicated and decayed archaeological remains. A curatorial emphasis on preservation, education, and tourism (particularly at designated World Heritage Sites) can also make them feel rather heavy going (e.g. Ennabli 1998; Matos Moctezuma 1998; Sarma 1998). In some cases, full-scale and partial reconstruction can lead to new archaeological understandings and memorable visitor experiences, while archaeological tours, experiments, and workshops can prompt dialogues between visitors and experts (e.g. Edgren 1998; Paardckooper 2012). However, as with archaeological artefacts, reconstruction must be used with caution. For example, York Archaeological Trust's painstaking excavation, multi-sensory reconstruction, and prominent marketing of the exceptionally well preserved Anglo-Scandinavian alley on the Coppergate site at the Jorvik Viking Centre has proved a great commercial success, at the same time as challenging public preconceptions of the Vikings (Addyman and Gaynor 1984 – **Chapter 23**; Jones 1999). The centrepiece for visitors is a 'timecar' ride through a reconstructed street scene, complete with evocative sounds and smells (Aggleton and Waskett 1999). Yet, this project has been harshly criticized by archaeological theorists, who question the museum's emphasis on empirical accuracy and the passivity of visitor experiences (Shanks and Tilley 1992). Conceptual concerns could also be raised about the authenticity of the visitor experience at the replica of the famous Palaeolithic painted cave in the new Museum of Altamira, opened in 2001 in response to growing anxiety over the preservation of the original (Lasheras Corruchaga and Fatás Monforte 2006 – **Chapter 24**). Digital technologies now offer virtual alternatives to more permanent reconstructions (e.g. Callebaut and Sunderland 1998), but tend to provide primarily visual experiences.

The Viking Ship Museum at Roskilde in Denmark offers visitors a more active experience, whilst also operating as an economically important tourist attraction (Bærenholdt and Haldrup 2006). Until the early 1980s, the central asset of the museum was its well-researched exhibition of five well-preserved Viking wrecks excavated from Roskilde Fjord. But since then, as the museum has gained growing media attention for its experimental work in constructing and sailing replica ships, the museum has increased activities which involve visitors more directly. In particular, it has constructed, with the financial backing of the local municipality, a 'Museum Island' for a variety of experiences relating to the Viking Age and its ships, ranging from painting shields and stamping coins, to dressing up as Vikings, to discussions with professional shipbuilders, to sailing trips in replica Viking boats. This, in turn, has contributed to the wider redevelopment of the harbour area in Roskilde, and has boosted local pride and identity.

Beyond Europe, managers of archaeological site museums have also sometimes tried to acknowledge local communities and cultural minorities and their socio-economic needs. For example, one of the key challenges for managers of the Luxor Museum of Ancient Egyptian Art since the mid-1970s has been to involve the local community in the programme of this site museum, which was (until recently) one of the world's foremost international tourist destinations (El Mallah 1998). Here, the museum's strategy has been to educate the inhabitants of modern Luxor – informing them about new archaeological discoveries and about the significance of on-going conservation work. But 'education' can be criticized as a one-way communication process. In Latin America, by contrast, tensions arising from growing international tourism, on the one hand, and the political articulation of the socio-economic aspirations of relatively disadvantaged local and/or descendant communities, on the other hand, have sometimes led ethically minded site managers to develop more creative strategies. Local stewardship, consultation, public education and outreach, accessibility, and training of local people have all been tried and tested here within the context of a global economy, with mixed benefits for protecting ancient archaeological sites and for developing living local communities (Silverman 2006 – **Chapter 25**). Examples range from the troubled story of the San Lorenzo Tenochtitlán Community Museum in Mexico, centred on a contested colossal sculpted Olmec head (Cyphers and Morales-Cano 2006), to the more positive scenario of the community site museum at Agua Blanca in Ecuador, where the local community has been enabled by a long-term archaeological project to incorporate ideas about stewardship, education and archaeological heritage into their value system and economic needs (McEwan et al. 2006). Analogies can be drawn here with ecomuseums, dedicated to encapsulating the special nature of places, building sustainable and empowered local communities, and caring for and exhibiting their tangible and intangible heritage (Davis 1999). But precisely why community museums have become part of indigenous groups' identities – given the place of archaeology and the museum in colonial and Western history – raises more questions than answers (Hastorf 2006).

New archaeology museum architecture

What kinds of modern museum architecture work best at archaeological sites and with archaeological collections?

In contrast to old-fashioned, dark, and crowded museums, some new archaeology museum buildings have used glass walls, floors, and ceilings to great effect. A pioneering example is Kevin Roche, John Dinkeloo and Associates' glass pavilion, constructed in 1976 to showcase the Egyptian Temple of Dendur in the Metropolitan Museum of Art in New York, complete with a lake representing the River Nile and a view of Central Park (Gissen 2009; Rosenblatt 2001). (However, the Roche building has now fallen out of favour with the Museum's Trustees, who in 2015 selected David Chipperfield to replace it with a new design.) Other outstanding examples include Norman Foster's Great Court in the British Museum in London (Anderson 2000), and Bernard Tschumi's new Acropolis Museum in Athens (Rask 2010 – **Chapter 26**). More local European examples are Patroklos Karantinos's Archaeological Museum of Thessaloniki (Grammenos 2011), Henri Ciriani's Arles Museum of Antiquity (Ryan 2012), Philippe Chaix and Jean-Paul Morel's archaeological museum at Saint-Romain-en-Gal, Tschumi's archaeological visitor centre at Alésia (Barreneche 1997), and Holzer Kobler Architekturen's *paläon* museum and research centre dedicated to the 300,000 year old Schöningen spears and their golden-clad Nebra Ark visitor centre at Wangen. Glass makes their galleries seem bright, spacious, clean, and cool. It illuminates objects with natural light, it enables visitors to walk over and look down on excavated remains, and it sets up visual dialogues with adjacent archaeological sites and landscapes. Such glittering architectural designs can be stunning, but we should not suspend our critical faculties regarding their underpinning Modernist aesthetics (sometimes combined with Classical gestures), for this often comes with a museological tendency to transform ancient, broken, and decayed objects into sterilized artworks to be appreciated visually, without the clutter of contextualization.

An alternative trend has been towards the burial of new archaeological museum buildings, to minimize their visual impact above-ground and to enhance the protection of archaeological collections housed within them. For example, the Museum of the Yang Emperor Mausoleum of the Han Dynasty at Xi'an is an entirely underground structure, designed to be quake-proof, insulated from outside temperature fluctuations, illuminated by natural light, and masked by a roof lawn (Chen et al. 2007 – **Chapter 27**). Henning Larsen Architects' new Moesgaard Museum of prehistory and ethnography near Aarhus in Denmark is also partly submerged on the side of a hill, and features a sloping roof covered in grass, moss, and flowers. But the desire for iconic architecture (albeit now with eco-friendly credentials) will continue to outweigh more humble curatorial concerns, if current architectural proposals are anything to judge by. For example, Coop Himmelb(l)au's project for a new Archaeological Museum in Egypt, to be situated near the excavation site of Tell el-Daba, envisages a landmark pyramid-shaped building, accessed via a large spiral ramp and powered by the sun. And in Turkey, where a policy of museum renovation is currently underway, numerous new archaeology museums are being constructed in a variety of bold architectural styles (Republic of Turkey Ministry of Culture and Tourism 2014). Restoration of old museum buildings is less fashionable, but can be effective, particularly in the case of David Chipperfield's restoration of the Neues Museum in Berlin, which intentionally retains the spirit of the war-damaged ruin (Moore 2009).

Designing archaeology displays

What are the most effective ways to display archaeological collections in museums? What key concepts underlie the designs of museum archaeology exhibitions? How can such displays offer more enjoyable and engaging experiences for visitors?

When it actually comes to mounting archaeology exhibitions, a series of competing constraints and considerations have to be negotiated. These include: the nature of the archaeological objects themselves; available space; proposed curatorial narratives; designers' visions; conservation, security, and safety concerns; exhibition budgets; and the attitudes of visitors. In response, it is now well-established that having an aim, a plan of action, close collaboration, compromise, clarity, knowledge of one's audience, and evaluations are all essential (Schadla-Hall and Davidson 1982). Building an archaeology exhibition around an attractive theme or storyline also helps. Traditional themes tend to be rather 'archaeological' in focus, including: typology/chronology, finds from major sites, production techniques/technology, food and cooking, imports/trade, ethnic groups, social relations (including gender and power) in the past, archaeological site formation processes, and the work of archaeologists. By contrast, more popular focal themes used by the British Museum in recent years have included: a personality (such as an emperor or a leader), beauty, beliefs (held by past people), discovery (of the past), warfare and violence, exotic journeys (that visitors can be taken on), sex, and death (B. Roberts pers. comm. 2015). But archaeology exhibitions also present some persistent challenges, not least of which is how to represent the duration and passage of time, particularly to visitors whose sense of time-depth may not extend much beyond their grandparents.

One published example of a thoughtfully designed archaeology display is the Port Royal Project, which created a combined artefact-based and interactive virtual reality exhibition about the archaeology of Port Royal in Jamaica – the major English colony in the Caribbean during the seventeenth century (Helling et al. 2011 – **Chapter 28**). Its main aim, informed by constructivist theories of learning, was to arouse the curiosity of school children and other visitors to the Ocean Institute in Dana Point, California. It involved collaboration between the UCLA Cultural Virtual Reality Laboratory, MIT's Deep Water Archaeology Laboratory, Texas A&M University's Institute of Nautical Archaeology, and the Ocean Institute. Due to time and budgetary constraints, a student in Art History at UCLA took on the key roles of chief modeller and researcher for the project, with expert information provided by a variety of sources. The resultant computer model offered visitors the opportunity to 'walk' through and explore the town of Port Royal, and middle school children the opportunity to 'swim' within the underwater archaeological site in search of the real artefacts exhibited alongside the computer equipment, together with text panels – all housed in a replica shipping crate. Evaluations showed that the interactivity of the computer model helped make the Port Royal story relevant to visitors, and helped them understand how archaeologists employ technology to record sites. It was especially appealing to teenage students. However, it is hoped that a new, user-friendly, public interface will be added to the exhibit, because visitors can only navigate the model with the assistance of the Institute's staff or volunteers.

There is always room for improvement, and recent research is offering new insights into what makes effective object-based displays in museums. Conspicuous objects tend to be attractive to visitors. Egyptian mummies, for example, whose material qualities (such as size, colour, shape, symmetry, and texture) and non-material attributes (age, iconicity, and familiarity), easily attract and hold the visitor's attention. However, research by Francesca Monti suggests that inconspicuous 'silent' objects, such as Egyptian figurines (or 'shabtis'), can also be displayed effectively, particularly when exhibition designers take account of the key factors that encourage visitor interaction with the displays (Monti and Keene 2013: 221–40). These include: uninterrupted sight lines, strategic positioning of objects, moving images, striking colours, sound, graphic (as opposed to text-based) display of information, opportunities for personal discovery, selection of communicative objects, and the use of varied, multi-sensory media.

Visitor-focused factors have informed, for example, the recent redisplay of the Tomb-chapel of Nebamun gallery in the British Museum (Monti and Keene 2013). The design of this room generates a fresh and relaxed atmosphere, being relatively light and spacious, with sky-blue walls and case interiors and a limestone-coloured floor and ceiling. Its careful layout echoes that of an ancient tomb-chapel. Large fragments of eleven beautiful paintings from the ancient structure are displayed, with graphic panels below drawing attention to and explaining details. The scenes in these paintings (which represent the lives of elite and 'ordinary' Egyptians) are complemented by an even distribution of spectacular and inconspicuous contemporary objects. Eye-catching large photographs of Egypt, drawings, and a 3D video (without an intrusive soundtrack) also help to contextualize and reconstruct the tomb-chapel. Evaluations have confirmed that this gallery has a relatively high 'holding power', with many visitors slowing down to concentrate on the exhibition, and consequently learn from its messages about ancient Egyptian life and death.

Teaching and learning through museum archaeology

What and how should museum visitors learn through archaeology?

Although the public can encounter archaeology across a wide variety of contexts and media, museums with archaeological collections remain an important place for teaching and learning about archaeology. Here, museum education programmes seek to cater for a variety of audiences, although young visitors – and school groups in particular – are a key target. The museum educators' aim has become not simply to teach people about the importance, techniques, and ideas of archaeology, but (in line with constructivist theory) to empower them to develop to their own experience and knowledge of the past through engaging with its objects – both 'real' and replica.

In practice, a wide variety of formats are used to deliver such educational programmes (Lea 2000 – **Chapter 29**). The standard approach of museums, and the least-costly in terms of staff time, is to invite the public to access their collections through self-guided tours of permanent or temporary exhibitions, which inevitably contain explanatory text panels and labels, sometimes supplemented by traditional worksheets for children. But deeper engagement is usually achieved in less restricted situations involving more direct interaction with museum collections and staff. Guided tours or lectures can be interesting and informative, particularly for adults. But children learn best by doing rather than looking and listening, and for museum educators this usually means 'hands-on', demanding as it is in terms of staffing. The scope of 'hands-on' possibilities is broad, ranging from handling and recording ancient artefacts to making and trying out replicas and models, and having the potential to stimulate not only touch but all the senses for the benefit of visitors with differing degrees of sensory and learning ability (Coles 1984).

Museum archaeologists have been particularly successful in using hands-on experiences to capture the attention and imagination of younger visitors, especially by involving them in active and enjoyable problem-solving. Tasks can include sorting mixed assemblages by material and reconstructing complete objects from fragments. A classic example is provided by the award-winning Archaeological Resource Centre (ARC) in York (today rebranded as 'Jorvik DIG') (e.g. Jones 1995, 1999; Moussouri 1998). The prime objective of the archaeological activity area and its friendly staff is to allow visitors of all ages and abilities to learn more about how people lived in the past through handling and sorting archaeological finds and experimenting with different crafts and technologies, such as stitching together copies of one-piece Roman leather shoes. Active visitor participation is the key concept here. However, Janet Owen (1999 – **Chapter 30**), commenting on hands-on activities connected to museum archaeology displays in the UK in the 1990s, has argued that such learning experiences can actually remain passive and intellectually closed: their outcomes being predetermined and stage-managed, with little encouragement to think further (and critically) about the archaeological objects and alternative interpretations of them.

Constraints and opportunities to explore the past in new ways are presented by the necessity to make museum education programmes relevant to school curriculums (ultimately, to ensure their attractiveness to visiting school groups) (e.g. Henson 2002). A good example is provided by the redisplay of the Alexander Keiller Museum in Avebury, UK in the 1990s (Stone 2004 – **Chapter 31**). The World Heritage Site of Avebury, with its cluster of important prehistoric monuments, is a popular venue for school visits, especially those with children in the 7 to 11 age range. When the time came to redisplay its archaeology collection, the English Heritage team recognized the importance of connecting the new exhibition to the National Curriculum. This was not easy, since none of the core units of the history curriculum (then) covered any prehistoric period. Nevertheless, connections were made to the curriculum's target to introduce students to the use of historical sources, including the fragmentary nature of historical (archaeological) evidence and the subjectivity of interpretation based on such evidence. At the same time, the team tried to respond to the results of a survey of the interests of local school children regarding the monuments' builders. They wanted to know about things central to their own world such as: where did they go to the toilet and what did they wash with, what clothes did they wear, what were their houses and weapons like, what animals did they have, how did they die, did children go to school, and what games did they have? Despite the difficulty of answering many of these questions, the team came up with some innovative solutions, which sought to be interesting, educational, and fun. For example, they included a life-size Neolithic human figure in the display, but one that was presented in two 'schizophrenic' halves – one side showing a ragged person, the other side showing a more sophisticated individual (painted, tattooed, with well-made clothes and jewellery) – and with a caption below acknowledging that archaeologists are unsure about what people really looked like in the Neolithic, although they are sure that they did not look like stereotypical cartoon cavemen.

Museum educators' determination to demonstrate the relevance of their collections to schools can also be seen in the development of outreach activities, aimed both at enhancing access to museum collections and at extending the reach of the museum into the classroom. The Museum of London, for example, developed a series of 200 'mini-museum' boxes of Roman archaeological material, suitably packed and presented, to be lent to a large number of schools in the Greater London area (Hall and Swain 2000 – **Chapter 32**). They used modified metal tool boxes with drawers, which combined durability with display potential. Real objects (including fragments of pottery and building tile), from old collections of limited archaeological value, were packed in polystyrene boxes. Replica objects (including a samian cup, a clay lamp, a bronze manicure set, a glass perfume bottle, a writing tablet and stylus, coins, and a figurine head) were set into foam recesses. Each box also contained a graphic panel about the Romans, the Museum of London, and archaeology, and teachers' resource packs. But museum outreach does not need to end in the classroom. Penrith Museum in North West England, for example, successfully established a two-way process connecting the museum to local schools through outreach projects designed to complement their special exhibitions in 2002 and 2006 on prehistoric rock art in Cumbria (Clarke and MacDougall 2010; cf. Owen 2003). Importantly, a museum visit by each school was a condition of participation in the project, which then involved one-day school-based workshops led by a professional artist to create new artworks inspired by the rock art, and culminated in the incorporation of the new works in the museum exhibitions, which proved to be two of the most popular ever held there.

Another recent example, which builds upon many of the principles and practices outlined above, is provided by the archaeology programme offered to visitors at the Isaac Royall House museum in Massachusetts (Chan 2011 – **Chapter 33**). This was home to one of the largest slaveholders and traders in New England during the eighteenth century. The elegant mid-Georgian architecture and its period rooms were originally foregrounded in presentations to the public, together with a narrative of Isaac Royall as a 'benevolent patriarch and self-made man'. However, archaeological excavations at this site encountered the hidden history of slavery, and consequently investigated the social relations between master and slave, the cultural process of creating distinct race and class categories, and the part played by material things in these dynamic relations and processes. Following on from this, heritage professionals now present a more critical history of the site. They also strive to empower the public to understand, appreciate, and question what archaeology has to offer, through a new archaeology exhibition, signage, interactive guided tours (oriented around the movements and responsibilities of enslaved people), workshops, teacher seminars, after-school programmes, and family events. And this formula has evidently been successful, since school groups from all over Massachusetts now come to Royall House as a regular part of their history curriculum.

Public engagement in, and perceptions of, museum archaeology

Who is 'the public' that visits (or does not visit) museums with archaeology collections? What do these people want from museums with archaeological collections, what preconceptions do they bring to such museums, and what do they take away from their encounters with archaeology? How can museum archaeologists make such encounters more effective? And how might traditionally alienated groups be persuaded to contribute to the work of museum archaeology?

Archaeological curators traditionally served the needs of the archaeological community: allowing their museums to be used in particular as repositories for excavated artefacts and in general for archaeological collection, preservation, interpretation, education, and research (e.g. Peers 1999). Museum archaeologists now recognize that they should also serve the needs of a wider, culturally diverse, and (often) tax-paying public. This 'turn towards the public' (Merriman 2004: 88 – **Chapter 34**) has taken many forms in the work of museum archaeologists, some of which have been discussed above, including hands-on exhibits, more culturally inclusive exhibitions, behind the scenes tours, and loan boxes. Another example is that of digital access to museum archaeology, including the digitization of museum collections and related information and the creation of new opportunities to explore and interact with them both within museums and via the Internet. Despite an initial reluctance by some museums, particularly towards virtual-reality technologies, this field has expanded enormously during the early years of the twenty-first century and will continue to do so in ever more creative ways (e.g. Hall et al. 2002; Sanders 2002; Bruno et al. 2010). The British Museum's extensive website (www.britishmuseum.org/), for example, provides information on visiting, the work of the museum and how to support it, the museum's research projects and exhibitions, access to the museum's collections online, educational resources for different kinds of learners, curatorial blogs with space to post comments, and a shop. It also offers short videos of curators introducing potential visitors to the objects, thinking, and work underpinning current exhibitions. Another example is the Burke Museum's 'The Archaeology of Seattle's West Point' interactive online exhibition, which won a *Communication Arts* Interactive Design Award in 2006 (www.burkemuseum.org/westpoint/). This exhibit tells the story of the archaeological investigation of a prehistoric site in Seattle's Discovery Park and of the people who lived there 4000 years ago, using text, images, and audio-visual videos. A third example is the website of the Shandong University Museum in China (Xiang et al. 2003). This makes use of several multimedia technologies to present its archaeological collections, including a searchable database, interactive texts, audio commentaries, photographs, video, virtual reconstructions of artefacts, animations, and a virtual tour of the museum. But we still need to understand more about the people who (physically and virtually) visit museums with archaeological collections.

We have some idea of what works best for visitors. According to a survey of visitors to museums in Japan with archaeological collections (Haggis 2008 – **Chapter 35**), intended to ascertain which museum activities people find interesting or most useful in learning about archaeology and the past, members of the public prefer a more participatory, practical, and 'hands-on' experience at a museum. Examples include working together with archaeologists on excavations, and joining in with experimental activities, such as pottery making, fire starting, and making stone tools.

We also know that visitors bring not only prior knowledge to archaeological exhibitions, but sometimes also misconceptions and prejudices. Research undertaken for the Petrie Museum of Egyptian Archaeology in London, designed to explore the nature and limits of the public's fascination with Ancient Egypt, found that focus groups (of varying ages and knowledge of Egypt) generally understood Ancient Egypt through a self-contained and self-satisfying set of popular myths and stereotypes, which included pharaohs, slaves, pyramids, tombs, buried treasure, and the mummy's curse (MacDonald 2003; MacDonald and Shaw 2004 – **Chapter 36**). They were positive in their view of archaeology, seeing it as a virtuous search for artefacts. By contrast, they had very limited understanding of, or interest in, how ordinary people lived in Ancient Egypt, or in its African context, its chronology and transformation over time, and its relation to modern Egypt. Black participants, however, were more critical, feeling, for instance, that Ancient Egypt had been appropriated as part of white history. Similar findings emerged from a more recent study undertaken by Gemma Tully (2011), who asked members of an Egyptian community about their opinions on the British Museum's plans to redisplay the tomb-chapel paintings of Nebamun (discussed earlier). They wished to see new, peopled, daily life narratives that would challenge stereotypes and enable audiences to make connections with their own lives. As Sally MacDonald (2003: 99) points out to the curators of Western museums with collections of Ancient Egypt, 'The challenge is to exploit the subject's popularity while questioning some of the assumptions on which that popularity is based.' In Egypt itself, the appropriation of Ancient Egypt by foreign archaeologists and tourists has also led to the alienation of local communities. For example, Madline El Mallah, Director of the Luxor Museum of Ancient Egyptian Art, acknowledged some years ago: 'the museum constitutes nothing of value to the townspeople' (El Mallah 1998: 18). However, a recent study suggests that a postcolonial museum tradition has now been established in Egypt, which has redefined and reclaimed Egypt's indigenous heritage for an increasingly local audience (Doyon 2008). This perspective has also informed a recent museum exhibition in the UK dedicated to 'Re-imaging Egypt', which involved close collaboration with an Egyptian contemporary artist whose work actively commented on the archaeological collections and on past and present-day societies (Tully, this volume – **Chapter 37**).

If museum archaeology is to challenge its own colonialist and racist history, it must, then, collaborate with members of those communities whose own cultural histories are entangled in archaeological collections. In North America in particular, following the watershed moment of the 1990 enactment of NAGPRA (discussed above) — which describes the rights of Native American and Native Hawaiian groups with respect to cultural items held in museums and calls for field archaeologists to consult with those groups — new forms of good practice are beginning to be established (Carr-Locke and Nicholas 2011 – **Chapter 38**). These characteristically view heritage as living and dynamic rather than static and artefact-based, acknowledge different ways of interpreting the past, respect Indigenous cultural values, encourage collaboration, and disrupt the academic boundaries separating archaeology from anthropology, history, ethnology, and museum studies. In Canada, for example, constructive collaboration between the Assembly of First Nations, the Canadian Museums Association Task Force on Museums and First Nations, and the Canadian Archaeological Association Aboriginal Heritage Committee led to the development of new collections policies and exhibitions (Holm and Pokotylo 1997). And in Mexico, members of local descendant communities and archaeologists have co-developed a 'living museum' around the ancient Maya archaeological site of Chunchucmil (Ardren 2002 – **Chapter 39**). Going one step further, at the Makah Cultural and Research Center in Washington State, which was established as a museum by the Makah Indian Nation following a collaborative archaeological excavation by Washington State University of the pre-contact village of Ozette, the collections are not sorted, stored, and labelled according to established archaeological or museological categories, but by ownership according to household. Similarly, a collaborative project between the A:shiwi A:wan Museum and Heritage Center of Zuni, the University of California Los Angeles (UCLA) and the Museum of Anthropology and Archaeology at Cambridge University in the UK has sought to re-document knowledge about the Cambridge museum collections of Zuni objects, incorporating descriptions of digitized collections by Indigenous source communities (Srinivasan et al. 2010). As a consequence, the Cambridge catalogue has been enhanced, with meaningful stories and narratives about the objects, as well as information about their historical and modern uses in the context of rituals, activities, and lived experiences.

A more controversial example is provided by Manchester Museum's 2008 temporary exhibition of the 2000-year-old 'bog-body' of Lindow Man, found not far from Manchester in the UK (James 2008; Sitch 2009; Brown 2011 – **Chapter 40**; Hutton 2011). In order to increase the relevance of the display to contemporary society and to attract new audiences, this exhibition questioned traditional museum expertise, shared authority through a public consultation exercise, and experimented with exhibition making conventions (using rough, everyday materials and finishes). In so doing, it encouraged debate about the appropriateness of the museum display and interpretation of human remains (as discussed above). It used as its core structure interviews of seven people with personal experience of Lindow Man: one of the peat diggers who discovered the body, a local woman who campaigned for the 'repatriation' of the body from the British Museum to Manchester, a forensic scientist who examined the body, a neo-Druid priest, a landscape archaeologist, a curator from the Manchester Museum, and a curator from the British Museum. Despite some commentators criticising this approach as postmodern self-indulgence, and the exhibition as bewildering and alienating, wider audience evaluation indicated that the majority of visitors did learn something from the exhibition, were moved by the experience, and felt able to contribute to debate about the bog-body.

Final questions

Given the questioning approach advocated here, it seems appropriate to end with yet more questions. Is the future of museum archaeology safe? Will museum archaeology retain its distinct professional identity? Will professional standards in museum archaeology become more universal? Who will pay for museum archaeology and conservation? How much political and popular support can museum archaeology count on? How successfully will archaeological site museums compete with other tourist attractions? Will traditionally disenfranchised groups be persuaded that museum archaeology matters? Will the illicit trade in antiquities ever be defeated? Will repatriation requests decline? Will museums cease to collect and display human remains? Will archaeological collections continue to inform and inspire future generations? What new stories about past people will result from collections research? Will museum designers create more effective, engaging, and enjoyable archaeological exhibitions? What new messages will museum displays present and visitors learn about the past and its relation to the present? What will publics around the world expect of museum archaeology?

References

Addyman, P. and Gaynor, A. (1984) The Jorvik Viking Centre: an experiment in archaeological site interpretation. *The International Journal of Museum Management and Curatorship*, 3: 7–18.

Aggleton, J.P. and Waskett, L. (1999) The ability of odours to serve as state-dependent cues for real-world memories: can Viking smells aid the recall of Viking experiences? *British Journal of Psychology*, 90: 1–7.

Alberti, S.J.M.M., Bienkowski, P., Chapman, M.J., and Drew, R. (2009). Should we display the dead? *Museum and Society*, 7(3): 133–49.

Anderson, R. (2000) *The Great Court and the British Museum*. London: The British Museum Press.

Ardren, T. (2002) Conversations about the production of archaeological knowledge and community museums at Chunchucmil and Kochol, Yucatán, México. *World Archaeology*, 34(2): 379–400.

Argyropoulos, V., Aloupi-Siotis, E., Polikreti, K., Apostolides, R., El Saddik, W., Gottschalk, R., Abd el Nazeer, M., Vryonidou Yiangou, M., Ashdjian, P., Yannoulatou, M.-C., Simon, S., Davis, W., and Kassianidou, V. (2014) Museum education and archaeological ethics: an approach to the illicit trade of antiquities. *Journal of Conservation and Museum Studies*, 12(1). Available at: www.jcms-journal.com/articles/10.5334/jcms.1021210/. Accessed 10/07/2015.

Ascherson, N. (2000) The Museum of Scotland: review. *Public Archaeology*, 1: 82–84.

Bærenholdt, J.O. and Haldrup, M. (2006) Mobile networks and place making in cultural tourism: staging Viking ships and rock music in Roskilde. *European Urban and Regional Studies*, 13(3): 209–24.

Barker, A. (2010) Exhibiting archaeology: archaeology and museums. *Annual Review of Anthropology*, 39: 293–308.

Barreneche, R.A. (1997) Digging history: a streamlined antiquities museum in southern France by Parisian architects Chaix Morel and Associates reveals the scientific process of archaeology. *Architecture: The AIA Journal*, 86(10): 102–05.

BBC (2015) Egypt inquiry after Tutankhamun's beard glued back on. BBC News, 22 January 2015. Available at: www.bbc.co.uk/news/world-middle-east-30931369. Accessed 16/10/2015.

Beard, M. (1993) Casts and cast-offs: the origins of the museum of classical archaeology. *Proceedings of the Cambridge Philological Society*, 39: 1–29.

Boardman, J. (2006) Archaeologists, collectors, and museums. In: E. Robson, L. Treadwell and C. Gosden (eds.), *Who Owns Objects? The Ethics and Politics of Collecting Cultural Artefacts*. Oxford: Oxbow Books, pp. 33–46.

Brodie, N., Doole, J., and Watson, P. (2000) *Stealing History: The Illicit Trade in Cultural Material*. Cambridge: The McDonald Institute for Archaeological Research.

Broodbank, C. (1992) The spirit is willing. *Antiquity*, 66: 542–6.

Brookshaw, S. (2010) The archaeology of childhood: a museum perspective. *Complutum*, 21(2): 215–32.

Broschi, M. 1994. Archaeological museums in Israel: reflecting on problems of national identity. In: F.S. Kaplan (ed.), *Museums and the Making of 'Ourselves': The Role of Objects in National Identity*. London and New York: Leicester University Press, pp. 314–29.

Browman, D.L. (2002) The Peabody Museum, Frederic W. Putnam, and the rise of U.S. anthropology, 1866–1903. *American Anthropologist*, 104(2): 508–19.

Brown, P. (2011) Us and them: who benefits from experimental exhibition making? *Museum Management and Curation*, 26(2): 129–48.

Bruno, F., Bruno, S., De Sensi, G., Luchi, M.-L., Mancuso, S., and Muzzupappa, M. (2010) From 3D reconstruction to virtual reality: a complete methodology for digital archaeological exhibition. *Journal of Cultural Heritage*, 11: 42–9.

Bünz, A. (2012) Is it enough to make the main characters female? An intersectional and social semiotic reading of the exhibition *Prehistories 1* at the National Historical Museum in Stockholm, Sweden. In: I.-M. Back Danielsson and S. Thedéen (eds.), *To Tender Gender: The Pasts and Futures of Gender Research in Archaeology*. Stockholm Studies in Archaeology 58. Stockholm: Department of Archaeology and Classical Studies, Stockholm University, pp. 97–115.

Bustard, W. (2000) Archaeological curation in the 21st century. Or, making sure the roof doesn't blow off. *CRM Online*, 23(5): 10–15.

Callebaut, D. and Sunderland, J. (1998) Ename: new technologies perpetuate the past. *Museum International*, 50(2): 50–54.

Cao, J., Rong, B., Lee, S., Chow, J.C., Jo, K., Liu, S., and Zhu, C. (2005) Composition of indoor aerosols at Emperor Qin's Terra-cotta Museum, Xi'an, China, during summer, 2004. *China Particuology*, 3(3): 170–75.

Carr-Locke, S. and Nicholas, G. (2011) Working towards greater equity and understanding: examples of collaborative archaeology and museum initiatives with indigenous peoples in North America. *Society for Applied Anthropology Newsletter*, 22(1): 4–9.

Chan. A.A. (2011) Translating archaeology for the public: empowering and engaging museum goers with the past. *International Journal of Heritage Studies*, 17(2): 169–89.

Chapman, J.C. (1981) The value of Dalmatian museum collections to settlement patterns. In: A.-M.E. Cantwell, J.B. Griffin, and N.A. Rothschild (eds.), *The Research Potential of Anthropological Museum Collections*. New York: The New York Academy of Sciences, pp. 529–55.

Cheape, H. (2010) The Society of Antiquaries of Scotland and their museum: Scotland's national collection and a national discourse. *International Journal of Historical Archaeology*, 14: 357–73.

Chen, Z., Zhang, P., and Li, J. (2007) Development and utilization of underground space for the protection of relics in the Yang Emperor Mausoleum of the Han Dynasty. *Frontiers of Architecture and Civil Engineering in China*, 1(2): 229–33.

Childs, S.T. (1995) The curation crisis. What's being done? *Federal Archaeology*, 7(4): 11–15.

——(2006) Archaeological collections: valuing and managing an emerging frontier. In: N. Agnew and J. Bridgland (eds.), *Of the Past, for the Future: Integrating Archaeology and Conservation. Proceedings of the Conservation Theme at the 5th World Archaeological Congress, Washington, D.C., 22–26 June 2003*. Los Angeles: The Getty Conservation Institute, pp. 204–08.

Chippindale, C. and Gill, D. (2000) Material consequences of contemporary classical collecting. *American Journal of Archaeology*, 104(3): 463–511.

Christenson, A.L. (1979) The role of museums in cultural resource management. *American Antiquity*, 44: 161–3.

Clarke, D.V. (1996) Presenting a national perspective of prehistory and early history in the Museum of Scotland. In: J.A. Atkinson, I. Banks, and J. O'Sullivan (eds.), *Nationalism and Archaeology. Scottish Archaeological Forum*. Glasgow: Cruithne Press, pp. 67–76.

——(1998) New things set in many landscapes: aspects of the Museum of Scotland. *Proceedings of the Society of Antiquaries of Scotland*, 128: 1–12.

——(2000) Creating the Museum of Scotland: a reply to Neal Ascherson. *Public Archaeology*, 1: 220–21.

Clarke, J. and MacDougall, K. (2010) Rock art in Cumbria: inspiring future generations. Education projects at Penrith Museum. In: T. Barnett and K. Sharpe (eds.), *Carving a Future for British Rock Art. New Directions for Research, Management, and Presentation*. Oxford: Oxbow Books, pp. 151–8.

Coles, P. (1984) *Please Touch. An Evaluation of the 'Please Touch' Exhibition at the British Museum, 31 March to 8 May 1983*. Committee of Inquiry into the Arts and Disabled People.

Cook, B.F. (1991) The archaeologist and the art market: policies and practice. *Antiquity*, 65: 533–7.

Copley, M.S. (2010) Towards presenting scientific research in archaeology museums. *Museum Management and Curatorship*, 25(4): 383–98.

Corfield, M. (1988) The reshaping of archaeological objects: some ethical considerations. *Antiquity*, 62: 261–5.

Cotton, J. (1997) Illuminating the twilight zone? The new prehistoric gallery at the Museum of London. In: G.T. Denford (ed.), *Representing Archaeology in Museums*.

The Museum Archaeologist Volume 22. Winchester: Society of Museum Archaeologists, pp. 6–12.

Cotton, J. and Wood, B. (1996) Retrieving prehistories at the Museum of London: a gallery case study. In: P.M. McManus (ed.), *Archaeological Displays and the Public: Museology and Interpretation*. London: Institute of Archaeology, University College London, pp. 53–71.

Crawley, P. (1998) Making use of prehistory: narratives of human evolution and the Natural History Museum. In: J. Arnold, K. Davies, and S. Ditchfield (eds.), *History and Heritage: Consuming the Past in Contemporary Culture*. Shaftesbury: Donhead, pp. 3–15.

Crooke, E. (2001) *Politics, Archaeology and the Creation of a National Museum of Ireland: An Expression of National Life*. Dublin and Portland, OR: Irish Academic Press.

Curtis, N.G.W. (2003) Human remains: the sacred, museums and archaeology. *Public Archaeology*, 3: 21–32.

Cyphers, A. and Morales-Cano, L. (2006) Community museums in the San Lorenzo Tenochtitlán region, Mexico. In: H. Silverman (ed.), *Archaeological Site Museums in Latin America*. Gainesville, FL: University Press of Florida, pp. 30–46.

Daehnke, J. and Lonetree, A. (2010) Repatriation in the United States: the current state of NAGPRA. In: J. Lydon and U.Z. Rizvi (eds.), *Handbook of Postcolonial Archaeology*. Walnut Creek, CA: Left Coast Press, pp. 245–55.

Davis, P. (1999) *Ecomuseums: A Sense of Place*. London and New York: Leicester University Press.

Department for Culture, Media and Sport (DCMS) (2005a) *Combating Illicit Trade: Due Diligence Guidelines for Museums, Libraries and Archives on Collecting and Borrowing Cultural Material*. London: Department for Culture, Media and Sport.

——(2005b) *Guidance for the Care of Human Remains in Museums*. London: Department for Culture, Media and Sport.

Doyon, W. (2008) The poetics of Egyptian museum practice. *British Museum Studies in Ancient Egypt and Sudan*, 10: 1–37.

Edgren, B. (1998) Eketorp Rediviva: 'an ongoing scientific discussion'. *Museum International*, 50(2): 10–15.

Edwards, R. (2012) *Archaeological Archives and Museums 2012*. Society of Museum Archaeologists.

El Mallah, M.Y. (1998) The Luxor Museum of Ancient Egyptian Art: the challenge of abundance. *Museum International*, 50(2): 16–22.

Ennabli, A. (1998) The Museum of Carthage: a living history lesson. *Museum International*, 50(2): 23–32.

Errington, S. (1998) *The Death of Authentic Primitive Art and Other Tales of Progress*. Berkley, Los Angeles, London: University of California Press.

Ertürk, N. (2006) A management model for archaeological site museums in Turkey. *Museum Management and Curatorship*, 21(4): 336–48.

Feuchtwang, S. (2011) Exhibition and awe: regimes of visibility in the presentation of an emperor. *Journal of Material Culture*, 16: 64–79.

Gaimster, D. (1993) Sitting comfortably? Museums and the antiquities market. In: E. Southworth (ed.), *'Picking up the Pieces' – Adapting to Change in Museums and Archaeology*. The Museum Archaeologist Volume 18. Liverpool: Society of Museum Archaeologists, pp. 30–32.

——(2001) Archaeological curatorship in the national sector: reviewing the British Museum's research function. In: P.J. Wise (ed.), *Indulgence or Necessity? Research in Museum Archaeology*. The Museum Archaeologist Volume 26. Colchester: Society of Museum Archaeologists, pp. 3–9.

Garrigan, S.E. (2012) *Collecting Mexico. Museums, Monuments, and the Creation of National Identity*. Minneapolis and London: University of Minnesota Press.

Giesen, M. ed. (2013) *Curating Human Remains: Caring for the Dead in the United Kingdom*. Woodbridge: The Boydell Press.

Gilberg, M. (1987) Friedrich Rathgen: the father of modern archaeological conservation. *Journal of the American Institute for Conservation*, 26(2): 105–20.

Gill, D.W.J. and Chippindale, C. (1993) Material and intellectual consequences of esteem for Cycladic figures. *American Journal of Archaeology*, 97(4): 601–59.

Gissen, D. (2009) The architectural production of nature, Dendur/New York. *Grey Room*, 34: 58–79.

Grammenos, D.V. (2011) The reconstruction and redisplay of the Archaeological Museum of Thessaloniki. *Museology*, 6: 21–9.

Green, M. and Gordon, P. (2010) Repatriation: Australian perspectives. In: J. Lydon and U.Z. Rizvi (eds.), *Handbook of Postcolonial Archaeology*. Walnut Creek, CA: Left Coast Press, pp. 257–66.

Greenfield, J. (2007) *The Return of Cultural Treasures*. Third edition. Cambridge and New York: Cambridge University Press.

Guha-Thakurta, T. (1997) The museumised relic: archaeology and the first museum of colonial India. *The Indian Economic and Social History Review*, 34(1): 21–51.

Hachlili, R. (1998) A question of interpretation. *Museum International*, 50(2): 4–5.

Haggis, D. (2008) Public archaeology and museums in Japan. *The International Journal of the Inclusive Museum*, 1(4): 95–102.

Hall, J. and Swain, H. (2000) Roman boxes for London's schools: an outreach service by the Museum of London. In: P. McManus, P.M. (ed.), *Archaeological Displays and the Public: Museology and Interpretation*. Second edition. London: Archetype Publications, pp. 87–95.

Hall, T., Ciolfi, L., Bannon, L., Fraser, M., Benford, S., Bowers, J., Greenhalgh, C., Hellström, S.-O., Izadi, S., Schnädelbach, H., and Flintham, M. (2002) The visitor as virtual archaeologist: explorations in mixed reality technology to enhance educational and social interaction in the museum. In: *VAST'01. Virtual Reality, Archaeology, and Cultural Heritage. Athens, Greece – November 28–30, 2001*. New York: Association for Computing Machinery, pp. 91–6, 365.

Hastorf, C.A. (2006) Building the community museum at Chiripa, Bolivia. In: H. Silverman (ed.), *Archaeological Site Museums in Latin America*. Gainesville, FL: University Press of Florida, pp. 85–98.

Hebditch, M. (1996) The display of Roman London. In: J. Bird, M. Hassall, and H. Sheldon (eds.), *Interpreting Roman London: Papers in Memory of Hugh Chapman*. Oxford: Oxbow Books, pp. 253–61.

Helling, H., Steinmetz, C., Solomon, E., and Frischer, B. (2011) The Port Royal Project: a case study in the use of VR technology for the recontextualization of archaeological artifacts and building remains in a museum setting. In: E. Jerem, R. Ferenc, and V. Szeverényi (eds.), *On the Road to Reconstructing the Past. Computer Applications and Quantitative Methods in Archaeology (CAA). Proceedings of the 36th*

International Conference. Budapest, 2–6 April 2008. Budapest: Archaeolingua, pp. 229–35.
Henson, D. (2002) Opportunities for museums in archaeological education. In: P.J. Wise (ed.), *Public Archaeology: Remains to be Seen.* The Museum Archaeologist Volume 27. Colchester: Society of Museum Archaeologists, pp. 46–51.
Heywood, F. (2000) Against the grain. *Museums Journal*, 100(10): 18–19.
Holgate, V. (1996) Portraying working women: the approach taken at Verulamium Museum. In: A. Devonshire and B. Wood (eds.), *Women in Industry and Technology from Prehistory to the Present Day. Current Research and the Museum Experience. Proceedings from the 1994 WHAM Conference.* London: Museum of London, pp. 85–91.
Holm, M. and Pokotylo, D. (1997) From policy to practice: a case study in collaborative exhibits with First Nations. *Journal Canadien d'Archéologie*, 21: 33–43.
Hu, T., Lee, S., Cao, J., Chow, J.C., Watson, J.G., Ho, K., Ho, W., Rong, B., and An, Z. 2009. Characterization of winter airborne particles at Emperor Qin's Terracotta Museum, China. *Science of the Total Environment*, 407: 5319–27.
Hutton, R. (2011) Why does Lindow Man matter? *Time and Mind*, 4(2): 135–48.
Isaac, B. (2002) Implementation of NAGPRA: the Peabody Museum of Archaeology and Ethnology, Harvard. In: C. Fforde, J. Hubert, and P. Turnbull (eds.), *The Dead and their Possessions: Repatriation in Principle, Policy, and Practice.* London and New York: Routledge, pp. 160–70.
James, S. (2008) Repatriation, display and interpretation. *Antiquity*, 82: 770–77.
Jenkins, I. (1992) *Archaeologists and Aesthetes in the Sculpture Galleries of the British Museum, 1800–1939.* London: British Museum Press.
—— (2001) *Cleaning and Controversy: The Parthenon Sculptures, 1811–1939.* London: British Museum.
Jenkins, T. (2011) *Contesting Human Remains in Museum Collections: The Crisis of Cultural Authority.* New York and Abingdon: Routledge.
Jones, A. (1995) Integrating school visits, tourists and the community at the Archaeological Resource Centre, York, UK. In: E. Hooper-Greenhill (ed.), *Museum, Media, Message.* London and New York: Routledge, pp. 159–67.
—— (1999) Archaeological reconstruction and education at the Jorvik Viking Centre, York, UK. In: P.G. Stone and P.G. Planel (eds.), *The Constructed Past: Experimental Archaeology, Education and the Public.* London and New York: Routledge, pp. 258–68.
Kaeser, M.-A. (2009) Manifeste architectural d'une archéologie intégrée : le Laténium (Neuchâtel, Suisse). *Les nouvelles de l'archéologie*, 117: 27–34.
Kennedy, M. (2014) Volunteers help British Museum in crowdsourcing archaeology project. *The Guardian*, 18 August 2014.
Killion, T.W. (2008) A view from the trenches. Memories of repatriation at the National Museum of Natural History, Smithsonian Institution. In: T.W. Killion (ed.), *Opening Archaeology: Repatriation's Impact of Contemporary Research and Practice.* Santa Fe: School for Advanced Research Press, pp. 133–50.
Kilmister, H. (2003) Visitor perceptions of ancient Egyptian human remains in three United Kingdom museums. *Papers from the Institute of Archaeology*, 14: 57–69.
Kinnes, I.A., Longworth, I.H., McIntyre, I.M., Needham, S.P., and Oddy, W.A. (1988) Bush Barrow gold. *Antiquity*, 62: 24–39.

Kokkinidou, D. and Nikolaidou, M. (2000) A sexist present, a human-less past: museum archaeology in Greece. In: M. Donald and L. Hurcombe (eds.), *Gender and Material Culture in Archaeological Perspective*. St. Martin's, New York: Palgrave Macmillan, pp. 33–55.

Kreder, J.A. (2010) The revolution in U.S. museums concerning the ethics of acquiring antiquities. *University of Miami Law Review*, 64(3): 997–1030.

Kristiansen, K. (1996) Destruction of the archaeological heritage and the formation of museum collections: the case of Denmark. In: W.D. Kingery (ed.), *Learning from Things: Method and Theory of Material Culture Studies*. Washington, D.C.: Smithsonian Institution Press, pp. 89–101.

Kurtz, D.C. (2000) *The Reception of Classical Art in Britain: An Oxford Story of Plaster Casts from the Antique*. British Archaeological Reports 308. Oxford: Archaeopress.

Kusimba, C.M. (1996) Archaeology in African museums. *African Archaeological Review*, 13(3): 165–70.

Lasheras Corruchaga, J.A. and Fatás Monforte, P. (2006) The new Museum of Altamira: finding solutions to tourism pressure. In: N. Agnew and J. Bridgland (eds.), *On the Past, for the Future: Integrating Archaeology and Conservation. Proceedings of the Conservation Theme at the 5th World Archaeological Congress, Washington, D.C., 22–26 June 2003*. Los Angeles: The Getty Conservation Institute, pp. 177–83.

Lawrence, D.H. (1932) *Etruscan Places*. New York: The Viking Press.

Lea, J. (2000) Teaching the past in museums. In: K. Smardz and S.J. Smith (eds.), *The Archaeology Education Handbook: Sharing the Past with Kids*. Walnut Creek, CA: AltaMira Press, pp. 315–27.

Legget, J. (2000) *Restitution and Repatriation: Guidelines for Good Practice*. London: Museums and Galleries Commission.

Leospo, E. (1984) The archaeological discoveries in Egypt and the formation of the main collections of Egyptian antiquities. In: S. Curto and A. Roccati (eds.), *Treasures of the Pharaohs: Cairo Egyptian Museum*. Milano: Arnoldo Mondadori Editore.

Levy, J.E. (2006) Prehistory, identity, and archaeological representation in Nordic museums. *American Anthropologist*, 108(1): 135–47.

Lohman, J. (2012) Contested human remains. In: G. Were and J.C.H. Kings (eds.), *Extreme Collecting: Challenging Practices for 21st Century Museums*. New York and Oxford: Berghahn Books, pp. 49–57.

Longworth, C. (1998) SPECTRUM: a ray of light for archaeologists. In: G.T. Denford (ed.), *Museums in the Landscape: Bridging the Gap*. The Museum Archaeologist 23. Winchester: Society of Museum Archaeologists, pp. 60–62.

Longworth, C. and Wood, B. (2000) *Standards in Action. Working with Archaeology. Book 3. Guidelines for Use in the Channel Islands, England, Isle of Man, Northern Ireland, Scotland, and Wales*. Cambridge: mda.

Lyons, P.D., Adams, E.C., Altschul, J.H., Barton, C.M., and Roll, C.M. 2006. *The Archaeological Curation Crisis in Arizona: Analysis and Possible Solutions. A Report Prepared by the Governor's Archaeology Advisory Commission Curation Subcommittee*. Available at: http://azstateparks.com/committees/downloads/GAAC_Curation_Crisis_Full.pdf. Accessed 09/07/2015.

MacDonald, S. (2003) Lost in time and space: ancient Egypt in museums. In: S. MacDonald and M. Rice (eds.), *Consuming Ancient Egypt*. London: UCL Press, pp. 87–99.

MacDonald, S. and Shaw, C. (2004) Uncovering Ancient Egypt: the Petrie Museum and its public. In: N. Merriman (ed.), *Public Archaeology*. London and New York: Routledge, pp. 109–31.

Masry, A.H. (1994) Archaeology and the establishment of museums in Saudia Arabia. In: F.S. Kaplan (ed.), *Museums and the Making of 'Ourselves': The Role of Objects in National Identity*. London and New York: Leicester University Press, pp. 125–68.

Matos Moctezuma, E. (1998) Reaching beyond the site: the Great Temple Museum in Mexico City. *Museum International*, 50(2): 40–43.

McEwan, C., Silva, M.-I., and Hudson, C. (2006) Using the past to forge the future: the genesis of the community site museum at Agua Blanca, Ecuador. In: H. Silverman (ed.), *Archaeological Site Museums in Latin America*. Gainesville, FL: University Press of Florida, pp. 187–216.

McIntosh, S.K., Renfrew, C., and Vincent, S. (2000) 'The good collector': fabulous beast or endangered species? *Public Archaeology*, 1: 73–81.

McManamon, F.P. (2006) Policy and practice in the treatment of archaeological human remains in North American museums and public agency collections. In: J. Lohman and K. Goodnow (eds.), *Human Remains and Museum Practice*. Paris: UNESCO, pp. 48–59.

Melton, N., Montgomery, J., Knüsel, C.J., Batt, C., Needham, S., Parker Pearson, M., Sheridan, A., Heron, C., Horsley, T., Schmidt, A., Evans, A., Carter, E., Edwards, H., Hargreaves, M., Janaway, R., Lynnerup, N., Northover, P., O'Connor, S., Ogden, A., Taylor, T., Wastling, V., and Wilson, A. (2010) Gristhorpe Man: an Early Bronze Age log-coffin burial scientifically defined. *Antiquity*, 84: 796–815.

Merriman, N. (1996) Displaying archaeology in the Museum of London. In: G.T. Denford (ed.), *Museum Archaeology – What's New?* Winchester: Society of Museum Archaeologists, pp. 60–65.

——(1997) The Peopling of London project. In: E. Hooper-Greenhill (ed.), *Cultural Diversity: Developing Museum Audiences in Britain*. London and Washington: Leicester University Press, pp. 119–48.

——ed. (1999) *Making Early Histories in Museums*. London and New York: Leicester University Press.

——(2000) The crisis of representation in archaeological museums. In: F.P. McManamon and A. Hatton (eds.), *Cultural Resource Management in Contemporary Society. Perspectives on Managing and Presenting the Past*. London and New York: Routledge, pp. 300–09.

——(2004) Involving the public in museum archaeology. In: N. Merriman (ed.), *Public Archaeology*. New York: Routledge, pp. 85–108.

Merriman, N. and Swain, H. (1999) Archaeological archives: serving the public interest? *European Journal of Archaeology*, 2(2): 249–67.

Mgomezulu, G.G.Y. (2004) Editorial. *Museum International*, 56(3): 4–6.

Mitchell, T. (1988) *Colonising Egypt*. Cambridge: Cambridge University Press.

Monti, F. and Keene, S. (2013) *Museums and Silent Objects: Designing Effective Exhibitions*. Farnham and Burlington (VT): Ashgate.

Moore, R. (2009) Neues Museum by David Chipperfield Architects, Berlin, Germany. *The Architectural Review*. Available at: www.architectural-review.com/today/neues-museum-by-david-chipperfield-architects-berlin-germany/8601182.fullarticle (accessed 27 May 2016).

Moser, S. (2003) Representing archaeological knowledge in museums: exhibiting human origins and strategies for change. *Public Archaeology*, 3: 3–20.

——(2006) *Wondrous Curiosities: Ancient Egypt at the British Museum*. Chicago: University of Chicago Press.

Moussouri, T. (1998) Family agendas and the museum experience. In: G.T. Denford (ed.), *Museums for the 21st Century*. The Museum Archaeologist Volume 24. Winchester: Society of Museum Archaeologists, pp. 20–30.

Munch Rasmussen, J. (2014) Securing cultural heritage objects and fencing stolen goods? A case study on museums and metal detecting in Norway. *Norwegian Archaeological Review*, 47(1): 83–107.

Museums and Galleries Commission (1992) *Standards in the Museum Care of Archaeological Collections*. London: Museums and Galleries Commission.

Museums Association (2005) *Collections for the Future. Report of a Museums Association Inquiry*. London: Museums Association.

Nafziger, J.A.R. and Dobkins, R.J. (1999) The Native American Graves Protection and Repatriation Act in its first decade. *International Journal of Cultural Property*, 8(1): 77–107.

Nash, S.E. and O'Malley, N. (2012) The changing mission of museums. In: M. Rockman and J. Flatman (eds.), *Archaeology in Society: Its Relevance to the Modern World*. New York: Springer, pp. 97–109.

O'Keefe, P.J. (1997) *Trade in Antiquities. Reducing Destruction and Theft*. London and Paris: Archetype and UNESCO.

Owen, J. ed. (1995) *Towards an Accessible Archaeological Archive. The Transfer of Archaeological Archives to Museums: Guidelines for Use in England, Northern Ireland, Scotland, and Wales*. Society of Museum Archaeologists.

——(1996) Making histories from archaeology. In: G. Kavanagh (ed.), *Making Histories from Museums*. London and New York: Leicester University Press, pp. 200–15.

——(1999) Interaction or tokenism? The role of hands-on activities in museum archaeology displays. In: N. Merriman (ed.), *Making Early Histories in Museums*. London: Leicester University Press, pp. 173–89.

——(2003) The art of archaeology initiative – a summary report. In: P.J. Wise (ed.), *The Art of Archaeology*. The Museum Archaeologist Volume 28. Colchester: Society of Museum Archaeologists, pp. 1–21.

Paardekooper, R.P. (2012) *The Value of an Archaeological Open-Air Museum is in its Use. Understanding Archaeological Open-Air Museums and their Visitors*. Leiden: Sidestone Press.

Paroff, S.P. (2004) Another victim of the war in Iraq: the looting of the National Museum in Baghdad and the inadequacies of international protection of cultural property. *Emory Law Journal*, 53(4): 2021–54.

Peers, R. (1999) Museums and archaeology. In: J. Beavis and A. Hunt (eds.), *Communicating Archaeology*. Oxford: Oxbow Books, pp. 113–18.

Perrin, K. (2002) *Archaeological Archives: Documentation, Access and Deposition. A Way Forward*. London: English Heritage.

Phillips, L.S. and Roundhill, L. (2007) Caring for an Egyptian mummy and coffin. In: V. Cassman, N. Odegaard, and J. Powell (eds.), *Human Remains: Guide for Museums and Academic Institutions*. Lanham, MD: AltaMira Press, pp. 269–73.

Pohlman, D. (2004) Catching science in the act: *Mysteries of Çatalhöyük*. In: D. Chittenden, G. Farmelo, and B.V. Lewenstein (eds.), *Creating Connections: Museums and the Public Understanding of Current Research*. Walnut Creek, CA: AltaMira Press, pp. 267–75.

Polikreti, K. (2007) Detection of ancient marble forgery: techniques and limitations. *Archaeometry*, 49(4): 603–19.

Pye, E. (2000) *Caring for the Past: Issues in Conservation for Archaeology and Museums*. London: James & James.

Quirke, S. (2012) Lyricism and offence in Egyptian archaeology collections. In: G. Were and J.C.H. King (eds.), *Extreme Collecting: Challenging Practices for 21st Century Museums*. New York and Oxford: Berghahn Books, pp. 37–48.

Rask, K. (2010) The New Acropolis Museum: where the visual feast trumps education. *Near Eastern Archaeology*, 73(1): 56–9.

Republic of Turkey Ministry of Culture and Tourism (2014) *Progressive Museums in Turkey*. Ankara: General Directorate for Cultural Heritage and Museums, Republic of Turkey Ministry of Culture and Tourism.

Robbiola, L. and Portier, R. (2006) A global approach to the authentication of ancient bronzes based on the characterization of the alloy-patina-environment system. *Journal of Cultural Heritage*, 7: 1–12.

Roberts, P. (2006) Barriers or bridges? Museums and acquisitions in the light of new legal and voluntary codes. In: E. Robson, L. Treadwell, and C. Gosden (eds.), *Who Owns Objects? The Ethics and Politics of Collecting Cultural Artefacts*. Oxford: Oxbow Books, pp. 47–60.

Rosenblatt, A. (2001) *Building Type Basics for Museums*. New York and Toronto: John Wiley & Sons.

Ryan, R. (2012) Blue heaven. *The Architectural Review*, 1382: 35–40.

Saleh, F. (1992) Documentation issues in Egyptian museums. In: *What Museums for Africa? Heritage in the Future. Proceedings of the Encounters. Benin, Ghana, Togo. 18–23 November 1991*. Paris: ICOM, pp. 205–10.

Sanders, D.H. (2002) Virtual archaeology and museums: where are the exhibits? In: F. Niccolucci (ed.), *Virtual Archaeology: Proceedings of the VAST Euroconference, Arezzo 24–25 November 2000*. BAR International Series 1075. Oxford: Archaeopress, pp. 187–94.

Sarma, I.K. (1998) Archaeological site museums in India: the backbone of cultural education. *Museum International*, 50(2): 44–9.

Saville, A. (1994) Artefact research in the National Museums of Scotland. In: D. Gaimster (ed.), *Museum Archaeology in Europe*. The Museum Archaeologist 19. Oxford: Oxbow Books, pp. 155–66.

Savino, M. (2015) Aziz Ogan and the development of archaeological museums in the Turkish Republic. *Museum History Journal*, 8: 88–101.

Schadla-Hall, T. and Davidson, J. (1982) It's very grand but who's it for? Designing archaeology galleries. *Museums Journal*, March: 171–5.

Scott, M.R. (2007) *Rethinking Evolution in the Museum: Envisioning African Origins*. Abingdon: Routledge.

Shanks, M. and Tilley, C. (1987a) *Reconstructing Archaeology. Theory and Practice*. Cambridge: Cambridge University Press.

——(1987b) *Social Theory and Archaeology*. Oxford: Polity Press.

——(1993) *Re-Constructing Archaeology: Theory and Practice*. Second edition. London: Routledge.

Shaw, W.M.K. (2003) *Possessors and Possessed: Museums, Archaeology, and the Visualization of History in the Late Ottoman Empire.* Berkeley and Los Angeles, CA and London: University of California Press.

Shell, C.A. and Robinson, P. (1988) The recent reconstruction of the Bush Barrow lozenge plate. *Antiquity,* 62: 248–60.

Shestack, A. (1989) The museum and cultural property: the transformation of institutional ethics. In: P. Mauch Messenger (ed.), *The Ethics of Collecting Cultural Property: Whose Culture? Whose Property?* Albuquerque: University of New Mexico Press, pp. 93–101.

Silverman, H. (2006) Archaeological site museums in Latin America. In: H. Silverman (ed.), *Archaeological Site Museums in Latin America.* Gainesville, FL: University Press of Florida, pp. 3–17.

Sitch, B. (2009) Courting controversy: the Lindow Man exhibition at the Manchester Museum. *University Museums and Collections Journal,* 2: 51–4.

Skeates, R. (2000) *The Collecting of Origins. Collectors and Collections of Italian Prehistory and the Cultural Transformation of Value (1550–1999).* BAR International Series 868. Oxford: British Archaeological Reports.

——(2002) Speaking for the past in the present: text, authority and learning in archaeology museums. *Public Archaeology,* 2(4): 209–18.

——(2005) Museum archaeology and the Mediterranean cultural heritage. In: E. Blake and A.B. Knapp (eds.), *The Archaeology of Mediterranean Prehistory.* Malden, MA, Oxford and Victoria: Blackwell Publishing, pp. 303–20.

Sofaer Derevenski, J. (1999) Children in archaeological narrative. *Museum Archaeologists News,* 28: 6–9.

Sonderman, R.C. (1996) Primal fear: deaccessioning collections. *Common Ground: Archaeology and Ethnography in the Public Interest,* 1(2): 27–9.

Srinivasan, R., Becvar, K.M., Boast, R., and Enote, J. (2010) Diverse knowledges and contact zones within the digital museum. *Science, Technology & Human Values,* 35(5): 735–68.

St. Clair, W. (1998) *Lord Elgin and the Marbles. The Controversial History of the Parthenon Sculptures.* Oxford and New York: Oxford University Press.

Stead, I.M., Bourk, J. and Brothwell, D. (1986) *Lindow Man: The Body in the Bog.* London: The British Museum Press.

Stone, P.G. (2004) The redisplay of the Alexander Keiller Museum, Avebury, and the National Curriculum in England. In: P.G. Stone and B.L. Molyneaux (eds.), *The Presented Past: Heritage, Museums, and Education.* London and New York: Routledge, pp. 190–205.

Stone, P.G. and Farchakh Bajjaly, J. (2011) *The Destruction of Cultural Heritage in Iraq.* Woodbridge: Boydell Press.

Sullivan, L.P. (1992) *Managing Archaeological Resources from the Museum Perspective.* Technical Brief No. 13. Washington, D.C.: U.S. Department of the Interior, National Park Service.

Sullivan, L.P. and Childs, S.T. (2003) *Curating Archaeological Collections: From the Field to Repository.* Archaeologist's Toolkit Volume 6. Walnut Creek, CA: AltaMira Press.

Swain, H. (1996) Here comes a national museums crisis. *British Archaeology,* 12: 11.

——(1998) *A Survey of Archaeological Archives in England.* London: Museums and Galleries Commission and English Heritage.

——(2002) The ethics of displaying human remains from British archaeological sites. *Public Archaeology*, 2: 95–100.

——(2006) Archaeological archives in Britain and the development of the London Archaeological Archive and Research Centre. In: N. Agnew and J. Bridgland (eds.), *On the Past, for the Future: Integrating Archaeology and Conservation. Proceedings of the Conservation Theme at the 5th World Archaeological Congress, Washington, D.C., 22–26 June 2003*. Los Angeles: The Getty Conservation Institute, pp. 211–15.

——(2007) *An Introduction to Museum Archaeology*. New York: Cambridge University Press.

Tahan, L.G. (2004) The archaeology of ethnicity in Lebanon: the case of the National Museum of Beirut. *Archaeological Review from Cambridge*, 19(2): 102–17.

——(2005) Investigating colonialism and post-colonialism in the archaeological museum space: the case of the Lebanon and France. In: C. Briault, J. Green, A. Kaldelis, and A. Stellatou (eds.), *SOMA 2003. Symposium on Mediterranean Archaeology*. BAR International Series 1391. Oxford: Archaeopress, pp. 151–5.

Tate, J., Reiche, I., Pinzari, F., Clark, J., and Caldwell, D. 2011. History and surface condition of the Lewis Chessmen in the Collection of the National Museums Scotland (Hebrides, late 12th–early13th centuries). *ArchéoSciences: revue d'archéométrie*, 28: 249–58.

ter Keurs, P. (2011) Agency, prestige and politics: Dutch collecting abroad and local responses. In: S. Byrne, A. Clarke, R. Harrison, and R. Torrence (eds.), *Unpacking the Collection: Networks of Material and Social Agency in the Museum*. New York: Springer, pp. 165–82.

Thompson, R.H. (2000) The crisis in archaeological collection management. *CRM*, 5: 4–6.

Trimble, M.K. and Marino, E.A. (2003) Archaeological curation: an ethical imperative for the twenty-first century. In: L.J. Zimmerman, K.D. Vitelli, and J. Hollowell-Zimmer (eds.), *Ethical Issues in Archaeology*. Walnut Creek, CA: AltaMira Press, pp. 99–114.

Tubb, K.W. ed. (1995) *Antiquities Trade or Betrayed. Legal, Ethical and Conservation Issues*. London: Archetype.

Tubb, K.W. and Brodie, N. (2001) From museum to mantelpiece: the antiquities trade in the United Kingdom. In: R. Layton, P.G. Stone, and J. Thomas (eds.), *Destruction and Conservation of Cultural Property*. London: Routledge, pp. 102–16.

Tully, G. (2011) Re-presenting ancient Egypt: reengaging communities through collaborative archaeological methodologies for museum displays. *Archaeological Review from Cambridge*, 26(2): 137–52.

Turnbull, P. (2002) Indigenous Australian people, their defence of the dead and native title. In: C. Fforde, J. Hubert and P. Turnbull (eds.), *The Dead and their Possessions: Repatriation in Principle, Policy, and Practice*. London and New York: Routledge, pp. 63–86.

Vaudou, M.-O. (2004) Inventory and global management in archaeology: the example of the Neuchâtel Museum. *Museum International*, 56(3): 68–76.

Vergo, P. ed. (1989) *The New Museology*. London: Reaktion Books.

Watson, P. and Todeschini, C. (2006) *The Medici Conspiracy: The Illicit Journey of Looted Antiquities, From Italy's Tomb Raiders to the World's Greatest Museums*. New York: Public Affairs.

White, A.J. ed. (1986) *Dust to Dust? Field Archaeology and Museums. Conference Proceedings Vol. II.* Society of Museum Archaeologists.

Whitehead, C. (2009) *Museums and the Construction of Disciplines: Art and Archaeology in Nineteenth-Century Britain.* London: Duckworth.

Wilson, D.M. (1989) *The British Museum: Purpose and Politics.* London: British Museum Publications.

Wingfield, C. ed. (1993) *Selection, Retention and Dispersal of Archaeological Collections. Guidelines for Use in England, Wales, and Northern Ireland.* Society of Museum Archaeologists.

Wood, B. (1996) Wot! No dinosaurs? Interpretation of prehistory and a new gallery at the Museum of London. In: A. Devonshire and B. Wood (eds.), *Women in Industry and Technology from Prehistory to the Present Day. Current Research and the Museum Experience. Proceedings from the 1994 WHAM Conference.* London: Museum of London, pp. 53–63.

Wright, G. ed. (1996) *The Formation of National Collections of Art and Archaeology.* Washington, D.C.: National Gallery of Art.

Xiang, H., Meng, X., and Yang, C. (2003) Design and implementation of digital archaeology museum of Shandong University. *Journal of System Simulation*, 15(3): 319–21.

PART I

Archaeological collections

Introduction to Part I

Robin Skeates

This section explores the principles and practices of working with archaeological collections. In addition to introducing the basics of archaeological collections management, it outlines the long-lasting crisis in archaeological curation and explores the range of strategies being pursued by museum and heritage professionals to overcome these problems. Archaeological archives represent a particularly relevant example, with heated debates surrounding the deaccessioning of stored archaeological material and the uses to which the retained archival material might be put. Digitized documentation is fundamental. However, sound authentication and identification of less well-provenanced collections is not always possible. Conservation of archaeological objects is equally important. Clear standards in the museum care of archaeological collections exist, but in practice debates arise over particular procedures, especially when objects are prepared for and presented in public displays. Unfortunately, collections research is increasingly marginalized in cash-strapped museums, but it should remain central to the curatorial process, and can be better managed and communicated to various audiences.

We begin this section with a pair of readings on the management of archaeological collections – an area that has often been described as being in crisis. **Chapter 2** presents archaeologists with the basics of collections management. It covers: acquisition policies and practices, accessioning, cataloguing, object labelling and conservation, storage, inventory control and data management, deaccessioning, and public access to and use of collections. It comes from a helpful handbook intended to teach professionals and students the key practices relating to curating archaeological collections. The authors, who draw upon their experiences both in museum archaeology and field archaeology, write primarily from an American perspective. Nevertheless, they usefully outline some widely applicable principles. **Chapter 3** then reveals how these principles are not always followed in practice. It outlines five top concerns of curators in North America with archaeological collections: the failure of agencies and institutions to manage collections to professional standards and especially to deal with backlogs of uncatalogued objects and archives; the lack of museum staff and space to enable researchers, managers, and the general public to access archaeological collections; the housing of many bulk archaeological collections in substandard conditions; the need to incorporate deaccession policies into collection management plans; and the need for additional storage space of a suitable standard. A key example is the museum collection of the Chaco Culture National Historical Park, located on the campus of the University of New Mexico, Albuquerque. The author ends by urging archaeologists to work on solutions to this archaeological curation crisis, particularly by becoming more involved in curation policies and implementation.

Our next set of readings looks at issues surrounding archaeological archives, including debates over the selection, retention, use, and disposal of archaeological remains. The engagingly written **Chapter 4** acknowledges archaeologists' 'primal fear' when the issue of deaccessioning archaeological material is raised, but also that the climate of opinion may be changing, and that archaeologists will have to be more selective in what field projects retain for future analysis. Examples are drawn in particular from the author's experience of working for the National Park Service in the Capital Area of Washington, DC. On a more positive note, the following two readings champion the proactive use of archaeological collections. Referring to a major survey of archaeological archives in England undertaken in 1997, the seminal **Chapter 5** highlights the neglected role of archaeological archives in archaeology, and explores how they might be better used and integrated into a more public-oriented discipline. The authors mobilize examples based on their professional experiences in the Museum of London and the UK's Society of Museum Archaeologists. Among other proposals, they recognize the use of information technology as a key way forward. **Chapter 6** follows on neatly. It describes how the Museum of London, through the creation of the London Archaeological Archive and Research Centre, is attempting to redefine the value of archives, not just by emphasizing the importance of proper curation but also by linking it to access and research.

The next reading offers insights into the documentation of archaeological collections. Informed by the theory and practice of contextual archaeology, **Chapter 7** describes a new method of computerized inventory that was developed between 1996 and 2003 at Latenium, the Museum of Archaeology in Neuchâtel, Switzerland. This method was designed to deal with the entire yield of material from the archaeological excavation at the Iron Age site of Marin/La Tène, including both cultural and environmental remains, and its movement from excavation site to storage in repositories or presentation in display cases. In this example, the museum staff could be sure that the objects were indeed archaeological, but occasionally curators and scholars have to contend with forgeries.

We then turn to the museum care and conservation of archaeological objects. **Chapter 8** comes from a key textbook on issues in conservation for archaeology and museums. It explores, in general terms, the range of possible options available to the conservator when considering how to deal with the conservation of an object. These range from doing nothing to changing the way in which an object is used, undertaking preventive conservation or remedial conservation, or even restoration. This chapter is followed by a case study. **Chapter 9** describes the careful decisions and work undertaken by staff at the Burke Museum of Natural History and Culture in Seattle to conserve, display, and store an Egyptian mummy and coffin in an innovative, environmentally and ethically sensitive manner.

The final set of readings in this section deals with archaeology collections research. **Chapter 10** provides an excellent example of how modern analytical techniques can transform our understanding of old museum collections. Here, the full armoury of modern scientific investigation was applied to a well-preserved Bronze Age log-coffin and its contents from Gristhorpe in North Yorkshire, housed since the early nineteenth century in Scarborough Museum in the UK. **Chapter 11** offers another example of recent scientific research on archaeological artefacts. In this case, microscopy and spectroscopy were used to obtain new biographical information about the famous Lewis Chessmen, held by the National Museums Scotland.

Part I, Section 1

Curation of archaeological remains

Responses to crisis

Chapter 2

Managing curated collections
The basics

Lynne P. Sullivan and S. Terry Childs

Few archaeologists have formal training in managing collections. Courses in collections management more typically are taught in museum studies programs than in university anthropology departments. Even when anthropology departments offer courses in museum work, these classes tend to focus on developing exhibits rather than on managing collections. Although archaeologists do not need to become experts in collections management, a working knowledge of basic principles, issues, and terminology is useful for enjoying effective communication with repository staffs and for being sensitive to their concerns, policies, and procedures.

This chapter offers an introduction to the mechanics of collections management. It begins with the entry of items into the repository and ends with use of curated collections by repository patrons. We discuss the policies and procedures repositories use to acquire collections, conduct initial processing and storage, preserve the physical integrity of the objects, maintain accessibility and inventory control, deaccession objects, and enable public use. In the museum world, these policies and procedures generally fall under the rubric of *registration methods* and may be handled by a staff member called a *registrar* (Buck and Gilmore 1998). Repositories differ in the specifics of managing collections, but all face similar challenges and thus have collections management programs that generally are similar.

Acquisition policies and practices

Repositories use the term *acquisition* to refer to the process of obtaining legal title to an object or collection of objects and formally adding it (or them) to the collections. Legal title is obtained through a *transfer of title,* which is the formal process of a change of ownership of an object from one person or organization to another (Malaro 1994). To transfer title, a *deed of gift* often is the contractual statement that must be signed by the appropriate parties, typically the owner of the object(s) and a repository representative. Examples of typical deed of gift forms can be found on several websites. Repositories do not like to acquire objects if there is any doubt

Source: *Archaeologist's Toolkit* Volume 6. Walnut Creek, CA: AltaMira Press, 2003. pp. 59–77.

about the vendor's or donor's rights of ownership because investment in the care of an object is not prudent if the object's owner can take it from the repository at any time. Questionable acquisition also may violate laws, such as the Archaeological Resources Protection Act (ARPA), that deal with the illicit trade of antiquities, as well as professional museum and archaeological ethics. When public money is used to care for privately owned items, these issues especially are problematic. Archaeologists need to make every effort to ascertain the ownership of collections and to transfer legal title to the repository or appropriate public agency.

A written transfer of title from a private landowner is preferred because a verbal agreement is difficult to document. Repositories often can assist with obtaining title from a recalcitrant private landowner because the public generally views repositories (especially museums) as desirable institutions. On the other hand, the contract archaeologist may be unsuccessful in obtaining title to collections because she or he may be associated with a project that the landowner did not want to occur. ARPA permits should specify repositories for federally owned collections. The contract archaeologist will need to consult with repository staff about policies relevant to curating federal collections because the repository will not actually acquire such materials. Federal and other government collections remain the property of the public entity.

Repositories have policies covering the acquisition of objects. An *acquisition policy* typically includes the following:

- a collecting policy governing what is acquired, aligning the composition of the collections with the institutional mission;
- an authorization policy for agreeing to acquisitions, specifying who has the authority to accept materials on behalf of the repository;
- a statement of the terms and conditions under which objects will normally be acquired.
- guidelines for determining costs for additional processing, storage, transport; conservation (what these may cost the repository if the collection is acquired), as well as to what extent the repository will provide or arrange for such services.

The governing board of a repository most often approves acquisitions, because this board is legally responsible for the repository's activities (Malaro 1998). Staff members are usually responsible for recommending acquisitions to the board. Beyond the "fit" of a particular collection with a repository's collecting policy, factors that can influence a repository's decision to acquire collections can include the amount of time and money that will be required to process, conserve, and store the objects. An ethic of the museum profession is that collections should not be acquired unless the institution can properly care for them.

Accessioning

Once a repository acquires an object or collection, its formal inclusion into the institution's collections is called *accessioning* (Carnell and Buck 1998). This process follows the transfer of title and includes assigning an accession number and entry of information about the acquired object or collection into the accessions register. An accession file that contains records about the acquisition also typically is developed as part of the accessioning procedure.

A repository that agrees to care for a federal or state collection in perpetuity does not gain title of ownership to that collection unless a transfer of title is completed. Nevertheless, a repository will usually go through the accessioning procedure for those collections to optimize their long-term care.

The typical steps for accessioning a collection or object are these:

1. Evaluate and authorize an acquisition according to agreed museum policy and retain written documentation of this process.
2. Ensure that the receipt of the object is properly planned for and that appropriate long-term storage or display space is available for the object(s) to be acquired.
3. Complete a *condition report* for the object(s) to be acquired (a condition report is a brief description of the physical condition of the objects in order to highlight any hidden costs of conservation that can be planned for or avoided).
4. Obtain unambiguous evidence of title to the object.
5. Describe the method of acquisition (e.g., bequest, field collection, gift).
6. Assign a unique number to the object or collection.
7. Record the information about the acquisition in the accessions register.

Each repository keeps an *accessions register* as a permanent record of all objects that are or have been part of the institution's collections. Entries in the accessions register include the accession number, a brief description of the object or collection, and the date of accession. An accessions register may be handwritten, generated from computer records, or a computer database. Repositories ideally should keep a copy of their accessions register in a secure place, such as microfiche or digital copies held at an outside location.

All of the documents compiled for acquisition of objects and associated records during the accessioning process are called *accession records*. These records provide written evidence of the original title to an object and the transfer of the title to the acquiring institution, and they contain a unique number (accession number) that is physically associated with all objects in an acquisition. Because they describe all acquisitions and list them by number, accession records ensure that an accessions register is maintained and information about the acquisition process is retained. Accession records also are the central place where all subsequent information about a collection's history may be maintained or cross-referenced, such as loans and conservation treatments.

Repositories generally use one of two systems for *accession numbers*. The first assigns a separate number to each item, while the second assigns the same number to all items in one accession group or individual collection and then a suffix to create a unique identity number. The second system works best for archaeological collections, which typically include many small objects. Accession numbers may take the form of a simple running sequence (e.g., 14603; 14604; 14605) or the year of accession followed by a running number (e.g., 1991.3; 1991.4; 1991.5). Identity numbers follow the accession number and may be assigned during the cataloging process. Actual placement of numbers on objects is discussed later in the section on collections preparation.

Cataloging

Cataloging is the assembly of all primary information about each item in the collection. Archaeologists sometimes confuse cataloging with analysis, although if an object is analyzed as a single item, it usually should be catalogued as a single item. For an archaeological collection, the most important aspect of cataloging is permanently associating a specimen with its archaeological context or provenience. This correlation usually is done as part of typical archaeological laboratory procedures and involves keying a number that is associated with the specimen to a written record of its provenience. Cataloging should be done by, or under the supervision of, someone with subject knowledge as well as familiarity with the cataloging system used by the repository that will curate the collection.

The main purpose of cataloging is to identify and document an object or group of like objects, especially to collect information that is likely to be valuable as an index heading or computerized search term. Such information may include an object's identification number or code and its provenience. While the purpose of cataloging is not to record attributes or collect data for research purposes, catalogue information is essential and useful for the research process. Cataloging allows the researcher to know what objects are in a collection, and the identifications made for cataloging purposes often can be used for very general analyses (e.g., sherd counts). Until it is catalogued, an item cannot be indexed properly and will not be easily accessible to museum staff or the public. A repository may also catalogue the records associated with an archaeological collection, although repositories handle these records in different ways. A common way is to link the accession number to both the specimens and the records that comprise an individual archaeological collection.

There are no standards for cataloging archaeological collections used by repositories across the United States. Some federal and state repositories have clear policies and guidelines for cataloging (e.g., Department of the Interior 1997). Most repositories commonly collect the following types of information: accession number, catalogue number, object name or description, material type, form, quantity, measurements, weight, cataloguer name, cataloging date, location in repository, site number, state site number, provenience or collection unit, state, county, Universal Transverse Mercator (UTM) coordinates or township/range/section, field collector, date collected, and conservation and treatment comments (Griset and Kodack 1999).

Catalogue or *identity numbers* provide a code for uniquely identifying objects and for linking archaeological objects to their provenience. The form they take varies among repositories, depending on individual needs and past practice. The accession number may serve as the identity number if different accession numbers are given to each item. Otherwise, an item suffix must be added to create a unique identity number. For example, a group of four projectile points brought into the museum together might be accessioned as 1991.24. Each individual point would then be numbered 1991.24.1, 1991.24.2, 1991.24.3, and 1991.24.4. Another common archaeological numbering practice is to use the tripartite Smithsonian site number (i.e. state number/county abbreviation/site number) in lieu of an accession number, but in combination with identity numbers—for example:

$$\frac{11Ms38}{15} \text{ or } \frac{40Mg31}{123}$$

A problem with this system arises when multiple investigations are conducted at the same site because there is no unique designation for the year of investigation. Collections made in different years and by different investigators thus could have objects with identical numbers. This situation should be avoided because it can cause confusion between discrete collections and lead to loss of provenience data. Therefore, a unique set of catalog numbers should be used for each phase of an investigation at a particular site.

Sometimes repositories have to work with numbering systems that they have not created. For example, a collection generated by an amateur archaeologist may already have its own numbering system. These numbers must be preserved as a link to the original records, but they can play havoc with computerized data management systems if they use a different format from the numbering system used by the repository.

Collections preparation: labeling and conservation

After objects are cataloged, they must be prepared for storage and for possible research, exhibit, and loans. The primary objectives of collections preparation are to preserve objects and associated records in a stable condition for the long term and to maintain their research, heritage, and educational values (Jacobson 1998). The latter requires that any action applied to a collection:

- be reversible;
- be well documented;
- be respectful of the object's integrity and of the culture from which it originated and is affiliated;
- utilize non-reactive materials; and
- always maintain the connection between the object and its documentation.

A critical step during collections preparation is to *label* or mark each accessioned item or, where appropriate, group of items with its permanent identity number (Segal 1998). Labeling should use methods and materials that do not damage the object and its surface yet ensure that the labels cannot be removed accidentally. Label placement should not negatively affect the appearance of an object or its detail yet must be sufficiently visible to minimize the need to handle the object. It should not be placed in areas that might receive wear or friction, including the bottom of objects. The materials used for labeling should be reversible so they can be removed intentionally with minimal trace, even after fifty to one hundred years. They should have good aging properties and be as chemically stable as possible yet be safe for staff use without posing health risks.

Many factors influence the choice of the most appropriate labeling technique for a specific object. Most factors are closely related to the object's constituent materials and to the physical stability and roughness of the object's surface, the object's porosity, physical strength, and flexibility (Segal 1998; Sease 1994).

Taking into account the basic principles and limitations of labeling, most repositories choose to use semi-permanent methods and materials to label their collections. Procedures generally involve thorough examination of the object, cleaning the surface where it is to be marked, applying a base coat of clear, reversible varnish, writing the number on the base coat with a permanent pigment-based ink or acrylic paint, and placing a thin coat of clear varnish over the number. Sufficient drying time must be allowed for each coat. For paper and photographs, writing the number in the same location in pencil is optimal. Repositories may use temporary labeling methods and materials (e.g., attachable tags, outside labels on storage boxes, loose labels) for archaeological objects or records. These are used only for highly unstable items, temporary deposits, loans, tiny objects, and objects stored outdoors.

For archaeological objects whose research value depends on their link to provenience, some repositories choose to use more permanent marking methods and materials. These procedures may help ensure that the label is not damaged or lost over time, although the semi-permanent techniques are often adequate. It is important to consult with a conservator if there is any doubt about appropriate methods and materials. It also is critical to know what materials are *not* good to use for labels, primarily due to their effects over time as summarized in the list below (Segal 1998; Sease 1994):

- Typewriter correction fluids can flake and may resist solvents.
- Nail polish made of cellulose nitrate can yellow, shrink, peel, and become brittle.
- Nail polish remover often contains contaminants other than the solvent.
- Rubber cement adhesive can deteriorate, and it can stain organics.
- Pressure-sensitive tape or label adhesive can deteriorate.
- Paper labels moistened by water are often hard to remove and can stain.
- Ballpoint ink may fade, smear, and resist solvents.
- Metal fasteners and metal-edged tags can corrode, stain, abrade, and cause cracking of some materials.

The other task that is critical to collections preparation involves *condition assessment* and *conservation*. The condition of objects and conservation must be considered during project design, in the field, and in the laboratory. Once in the repository, an assessment is necessary to document the current condition of an object or record and to recommend necessary conservation treatment. The goal of conservation, then, is to maintain the preservation and survival of an object or record in its original state, to the extent possible, often through the use of interventions such as physical strengthening or chemical stabilization.

Conservation may be costly, particularly for submerged or underwater archaeology, and should be carefully budgeted. Conservation also should be a collaborative process that involves archaeologists, collections managers or registrars, curators, and conservators (Cronyn 1990). However, treatment requires the expertise and experience of a conservator who is familiar with the best interventions or treatment available for the particular constituent materials of an object. All decisions and interventions must be well documented.

Storage

Integral to the long-term care and preservation of collections is how they are stored (Ford 1980). *Storage* refers to both the overall conditions of the spaces where collections are kept and the safekeeping of individual objects and associated records (Swain 1998; Department of the Interior 1997).

Collections storage within a repository requires attention to spatial layout, environmental controls for different types of collections, security, fire protection, and disaster planning (Table 2.1). Many repositories have areas for long-term storage that are separate from other key activities, such as exhibits, exhibit preparation, research, temporary storage, object preparation, and administration. Such physical separation enhances security as well as protection from fire and other disasters. Some repositories have off-site storage, but this alternative can hinder access, security, and monitoring.

Maintaining environmental standards minimizes the rate of deterioration, extends the lives of objects and records, and reduces the need for conservation treatment. Extreme levels and significant fluctuations in temperature and humidity may damage archaeological objects, especially those made of unstable materials such as metal or wood, bone, and other organics. They also can severely affect documents, photographs, electronic media, and audio-visual recordings. Therefore, temperature and humidity should be monitored and recorded and kept within acceptable ranges. Establishing an appropriate range of relative humidity (RH) involves consideration of local climate, the collection materials and their condition, mould growth prevention, repository structure and layout, and the RH levels to which the collection had been adapted.

Other environmental conditions that require consideration are visible light, ultraviolet radiation (i.e., sunlight), pollutants, and pests. In general, no visible light should be present in a storage area except for short periods of time. Ultraviolet light (UV) should be monitored periodically and controlled with filters if found to be excessive. UV can be particularly harmful to photographs. Gaseous and particulate pollution (e.g., dust, chemical off-gassing from unsealed wooden shelving, solvents, and acidic paper) should be monitored and controlled when appropriate. A rigorous pest management program should be developed because rodents and insects can severely damage organic objects and archival materials. Many repositories have an integrated pest management program to monitor and treat pest infiltration (Jessup 1995).

Table 2.1 Basic standards of repositories

Environmental controls

- Temperature and humidity
- Level and duration of visible light
- Ultraviolet radiation
- Pests
- Air pollution

Security

- Mechanical and/or electrical system for detecting and deterring intruders
- Policy on access to collections and associated documents, including systems for visitor and researcher registration, opening and closing storage and exhibition areas, and control of keys to particular areas of the repository

Fire protection

- Fire detection and suppression equipment appropriate for the collections housed in storage and exhibition areas
- Storage of repository and collection records in appropriate fire-resistant container that is also locked when not in use
- Fire plan for the needs of the collections to prevent, detect, and suppress fire

Housekeeping

- Regular cleaning of storage and exhibit spaces based on established procedures and policy
- Maintenance and calibration of monitoring equipment

Physical examination and inventory

- Regular examination to detect deterioration of collections' contents
- Inventory policy to regularly confirm locations of collections and prevent loss or theft

Conservation

- Maintenance of objects in stable condition using professional conservation standards and practices

Disaster planning

- Procedures to protect collections in the event of a natural or human-inflicted disaster

Exhibition

- Consideration of how to best preserve, protect, and minimize risk to objects when planning an exhibit
- Design and use exhibit cases and areas to promote security, housekeeping, and preservation of objects

Individual objects and associated records are packed and housed in an *artifact container* (e.g., bag or box) and then a *storage container* (e.g., box, larger bag, cabinet, or drawer). Two critical principles must be followed in all storage decision-making. First, *provenience information must be maintained at all times*. Provenience labels must be placed on all containers so that their contents can be reunited if they become separated. Second, *all storage materials must be archival quality for long-term use*.

Several factors must be considered when deciding how to store objects and records. One is the frequency of use of the items. If an object is a type specimen that may be regularly studied or used, it is more appropriate to place it in a drawer rather than a box on a high shelf. Another factor is the diversity of materials in the collection. In general, objects and associated records are stored in artifact containers by material class: all the shells from one provenience should be in one bag, all the ceramics in another, and all the photographs in acid-free or inert plastic photographic sleeves. Objects and associated records, particularly those that are fragile or made of unstable materials that require special environmental conditions, should be separated by both artifact container and storage container. Another consideration is the size and weight of the objects. Obviously, a large mortar and pestle should not be placed in the same bag as obsidian flakes, nor should a bag containing a large mortar and pestle be placed in the same storage container as a bag of thin-walled pottery sherds. Some oddly shaped or fragile items may need special support mechanisms to prevent them from further deterioration or to enhance their visibility so as to decrease handling.

Storage of human remains and objects held sacred by various groups require additional considerations. Human remains must be handled with respect and stored in a separate area. The Native American Graves Protection and Repatriation Act of 1990 (NAGPRA) also requires that culturally affiliated, federally recognized American Indian tribes be consulted about the disposition of any remains, as well as sacred objects and objects of cultural patrimony. Therefore, these items should be accessible for consultation. Tribal members also may want to conduct ceremonies in the storage area for various purposes (McKeown et al. 1998).

The most common and suitable artifact container for most objects is the polyethylene zip-top plastic bag. It is easy to handle, lightweight, and economical and can be directly labeled. Bag thickness, no less than two millimeters, is important for long-term curation of the objects inside. Most bags should be perforated with small holes to promote air circulation and prevent the creation of micro-environments that promote mold. Bags containing objects that are sensitive to the environment, such as iron, should not be perforated (Vogt-O'Connor 1996).

Care of records even from a single archaeological project is not a simple task due to the wide variety of formats and media used. The Chickamauga Basin case study provides an example. Records from this project include handwritten field notes on notebook paper, standardized mimeographed field and laboratory forms that are filled out with typing and handwriting in ink and pencil, artifact catalog cards on 3 × 5-inch card stock, analytical notes and tallies that are either typed or handwritten on ledger paper, photographs and negatives (the latter of which are typical of the time period with self-destructing silver nitrate), artifact illustrations on vellum, large excavation plats on graph paper, progress reports and preliminary site reports, and correspondence (both typed and handwritten) between the various investigators and with the WPA. To maintain the rich research potential of the collections, these critical and often fragile documents must be carefully preserved.

Appropriate document containers vary by document format and size. Paper records may be contained in acid-free or buffered folders or files or in polypropylene, polyethylene, or polyester sleeves. Each map should be stored in an acid-free folder, although a divider sheet of acid-free tissue between multiple maps is minimally acceptable when expense is a significant issue. Photographs (print, negative, and transparency) should be placed in individual envelopes or sleeves made of acid-free paper or an inert plastic of polypropylene, polyethylene, or polyester. Older nitrate-based negatives can be considered hazardous materials as they deteriorate. Freezing can deter total degradation. The long-term solution is to make copies of all of these negatives. Audio and videotapes should be stored in acid-free boxes of suitable sizes, while electronic records can be placed in appropriate plastic containers. Tapes and disks should be stored in areas free from harmful electromagnetic fields.

Unacceptable containers for objects include lightweight sandwich and food storage bags, brown paper bags, cigar boxes, plastic (not polyethylene) film vials, and glass containers that are not well insulated and may break. It is also unacceptable to use rubber bands, twist ties, adhesive tape, string, staples, or heat sealing to close artifact containers.

Storage containers, the larger boxes or polyethylene bags that contain one or more smaller artifact containers, should be made of archivally stable materials. They should also be of standard sizes for optimal stacking on shelves. Repositories vary in their box size requirements, although boxes of approximately 0.03 cubic meter (one cubic foot) are most common for objects.

Inventory control and data management

An *inventory* document is a permanent record of the physical location of all accessioned and cataloged objects and associated records. It is periodically updated during the process of *inventorying* when the physical locations of items are checked against the list of objects. The inventory process also enables an inspection of the condition of each object and document, and it identifies items that may be lost, missing, or stolen.

An inventory thus is an important means of accounting for and managing data on collections (Malaro 1998; Cowan 1998). At its most basic level, it documents what a repository has and where to find it. It can also relate to other important information critical to the mission of a repository. For federal and state agencies that depend on non-federal and non-state repositories to care for their collections, inventories provide a critical check on their property, helping fulfill ethical and legal obligations. It is for these reasons that 36 CFR Part 79.11 specifies periodic inventories and inspections of federal collections. For bureaus with the Department of the Interior, for example, a 100 per cent inventory and inspection of all museum property above a certain value and a random sample inventory of all other cataloged items must be done on an annual basis (Department of Interior 1997). A well-documented inventory also is essential for complying with requirements of NAGPRA (McKeown et al. 1998).

A repository benefits from inventory control and good data management. Good location and description information not only enhances security, it also facilitates tracing lost, stolen, or missing objects. When such information is cross-referenced to title, it may further enhance retrieval and help resolve disputes about legal ownership. Accounting for collections increases the repository's credibility in the eyes of funding agencies, potential donors, and the general public. Also, inventories facilitate access to specific items by repository staff, researchers, and educators; access to information about the contents of collections; and data needed for planning and budgeting exhibits and educational programs.

Deaccessioning

Despite the claims that all archaeological collections should be preserved in perpetuity for their present and future research value and potential, there are times when a collection or specific objects may legitimately be deaccessioned (Childs 1999). *Deaccessioning* is "the process used to remove permanently an object from a museum's collection" (Malaro 1998: 217). The decision-making process is usually lengthy and well documented because deaccessions often have been controversial. Critics include local communities who felt their cultural heritage was being discarded, donors offended that their gifts were no longer worthwhile, and various support groups who disapproved of how the repository spent auction proceeds (e.g., *not* for new acquisitions). Once a decision is made to deaccession one or more objects, the subsequent action of removal from the repository is *disposal* (Morris 1998).

The primary reasons to deaccession and dispose of archaeological objects are when they are:

- outside the repository's scope of collections;
- subject to repatriation under NAGPRA;
- physically deteriorated beyond viable research or educational value;
- hazardous;
- incapable of being adequately cared for by the repository; or
- determined to have been acquired illegally or unethically.

The decision to deaccession involves a number of steps (Morris 1998):

- initiation of action with a written justification that lays out the reason to deaccession in relation to the repository's mission, collecting plan, scope of collections, and any relevant federal or state laws;
- confirmation that the object(s) was accessioned, cataloged, and well documented—a good deaccessioning policy is intimately related to a good accessions policy (Malaro 1998);
- physical inspection by a conservator to help identify the best method of disposal;
- confirmation of title and a check of the records for any donor restrictions;
- when applicable, an outside appraisal of the monetary and research value;
- internal review to ensure full knowledge of the deaccessioning plan;
- approval by the repository director and governing board, and review committee, if established;
- assignment of a deaccession number to each item to be disposed of;
- public relations, particularly with local community groups whose cultural heritage may be the subject of deaccessioning and disposal.

The final act of the deaccessioning process is disposal. There are several options for archaeological objects, although every effort should be made to transfer, through donation or exchange, the objects to another repository in the vicinity for research and educational use. The primary means of disposition are as follows:

- donation and transfer of title to another repository to maintain educational use;
- repatriation (the restoration of control over) of human remains, funerary objects, sacred objects, and objects of cultural patrimony to affiliated Native American tribes, other appropriate culture groups, or countries of origin. Packing and delivery of repatriated objects should be done in consultation with the recipient group in order to respect traditional practices and beliefs (McKeown et al. 1998);
- exchange with other repositories, usually of items of equal value and significance. This involves transfer of title;
- physical destruction. This disposal technique may be applied to hazardous items, severely deteriorated items, and counterfeits. The exact method chosen should be permanent, irreversible, and well documented. Destructive analysis for research purposes, when total, is often placed in this category;
- return to rightful owner if it is determined that the donor was not the legal owner;
- public auction, usually to raise funds for future acquisitions. This option usually is not appropriate for archaeological items recovered in a research or CRM context for ethical reasons.

Public access and use

Use of collections is both a bane and a blessing for repositories. The purpose of having collections is to use them. However, their use puts them at risk because individual items may accidentally become damaged, proveniences can get lost if objects are not labeled, and a range of other problems can occur. Policies and procedures for use of collections are designed to allow use in ways that minimize the risks to collections. Here, we discuss what a repository does to enable access and use of collections including issues of accessibility and consultation, on-site use and loans, and publications.

To make collections accessible and useable, a repository must have good systems of inventory control and data management. These systems should allow repository staff to provide access to those materials that are needed by the user. Repository staff members have to try to anticipate the kinds of questions users will ask about the collections. They must then structure their data and information management systems in ways that are likely to provide answers to the most common kinds of questions or, at a minimum, to furnish leads to information sources that can be used to answer the questions. For example, it should be easy for a repository to answer the question "Do you have archaeological artifacts from Illinois?" On the other hand, answering the question "Do you have a Madison point from Feature 315 at the Goody Site that was excavated in 1902 by Hiram D. Igers?" could entail a records search for a number of similar objects unless the repository has a very sophisticated computer database or a very small collection. The inquirer may be invited to conduct the records search, depending on the number of objects and volume of records. In any case, a repository has to decide just how accessible information about its collections will be based on its individual circumstances, including the size and nature of its collections, funding, and staff.

Repositories also must decide the circumstances under which physical access to collections will be allowed. Not just anyone can walk into a repository and ask to use the collections; "curiosity seekers" almost never are granted physical access to collections. Because of the potential risks, repositories almost always limit physical access to collections to those persons who have needs linked to legitimate scholarly research or public education purposes such as exhibits. Even then, access usually is limited to those items pertinent to the user's needs. Users typically are not let loose in storage areas. Secure exhibitions, not storage areas, are the appropriate venue for the browser.

NAGPRA affects collections access and use at repositories that hold Native American human remains, funerary objects, sacred objects, and objects of cultural patrimony (McKeown et al. 1998). The process of inventory for NAGPRA compliance entails determining cultural affiliation through consultation with tribes. Consultation may involve tours through collections, careful consideration of appropriate handling of objects, and the need to accommodate traditional rites such as purification rituals.

Loans of collections to other institutions may be made for exhibitions or for research and teaching when in-house use is not feasible. Even small repositories often process a large volume of outgoing loans for exhibition and research. Some repositories do not have the facilities for scholars to use collections or do not have exhibits, so loaning collections is a way to provide access to both scholars and the general public. Procedures for loans made for both purposes are often identical and are intended to meet the needs of both the repository and the borrower.

Repositories have *loan policies* governing outgoing and incoming loans and the conditions under which they are made. *Loan agreements* are contracts that spell out the conditions of a specific loan, which must be signed by representatives of the borrowing and loaning institutions. Loan conditions may differ depending on the nature and intended use of the items. Borrowers almost always are responsible for the items they borrow, so repositories should make loans to institutions, not individuals. At large repositories, loan requests may be considered by a loan review committee and may need approval by the director or other administrator.

Other typical stipulations of loan policies include the following:

- Only properly accessioned and cataloged material are loaned unless there is a specific agreement that the borrower will do some of this work for the repository.
- Loans generally are made for the period of one year or less, subject to annual recall. The term *permanent loan,* although in common use, is a misnomer. *Permanent* implies that the borrower will always have the loaned item and thus may as well have title to it. The term *continuing loan* is preferable if an object

will be loaned for an indefinite or lengthy period of time. Some repositories will not renew loans for more than five years.
- Unless alternate arrangements are agreed on in writing, all loaned items must be returned to the repository in the condition in which they leave.
- For research loans, collections returned must be accompanied by a report of findings, whether or not formal publication results. If formally published, the repository receives a complimentary copy of the report.
- Borrowers may be subject to fees or costs involved in arranging the loan.

Procedures for setting up a loan usually include the following steps:

- Requests must be submitted in writing and addressed to the appropriate curator, collections manager, registrar, or director. Information on the intended use of collections, the requested duration of the loan period, and any other details pertinent to the request are necessary. Requests must stipulate the nature of collections use or type of research to be conducted, the accession and catalogue numbers of the objects requested, and a time framework. Research requests should also discuss expected results.
- A completed *facility report* must accompany exhibition loan requests. Facility reports describe the borrowing institution's security system, climate control, and so forth, as pertains to exhibitions. The American Association of Museums has standard forms that many institutions use.
- Each object or group of objects lent is documented on a loan agreement and may be photographed for record-keeping purposes.
- Specification of loan return is made at the time of the initial loan negotiation. Notification of loan return must be made in advance.

Repositories often receive requests for photographs of objects to be used in publications. Publicly owned repositories usually do not hold copyright to the images of the objects they curate, but private institutions may. Policies on use of photographs differ widely among repositories, but almost all institutions ask to receive a credit line on the published photograph, and users usually must pay the costs of photography. Many larger repositories prefer to have their own in-house photographer make photographs for publication purposes so they can ensure the quality of images of their objects and safety in handling.

Some repositories also publish their own series of research reports, catalogs, or other collections-related materials. Digital publications and catalogs, especially on the World Wide Web, provide new frontiers of public access to curated collections. In general, publications make collections more accessible because they provide detailed information in a format that can be widely circulated. Publication policies and procedures differ considerably among institutions, depending on the kinds of series and available support.

Conclusion

Repositories have standard sets of policies and procedures for managing collections. Acquisition, accession, and cataloging procedures document the ownership status of objects and ensure that an object stays linked to its documentation. Inventory control and data management procedures establish an institution's accountability for its holdings and facilitate finding objects in the repository. Conservation, collections preparation, and storage procedures help maintain the physical integrity of curated objects. The intent of all of these procedures is to enable controlled use of collections in order to maintain the safety and long-term preservation of the objects and associated records.

References

Buck, R.A. and Gilmore, J.A. eds. (1998) *The New Museum Registration Methods*. Third edition. Washington, D.C.: American Association of Museums.

Carnell, C. and Buck, R. (1998) Acquisitions and accessioning. In: R.A. Buck and J.A. Gilmore (eds.), *The New Museum Registration Methods*. Third edition. Washington, D.C.: American Association of Museums, pp. 157–65.

Childs, S.T. (1999) Contemplating the future: deaccessioning federal archaeological collections. *Museum Anthropology*, 23(2): 38–45.

Cowan, S. (1998) Inventory. In: R.A. Buck and J.A. Gilmore (eds.), *The New Museum Registration Methods*. Third edition. Washington, D.C.: American Association of Museums, pp. 117–19.

Cronyn, J.M. (1990) *The Elements of Archaeological Conservation*. London: Routledge.

Department of the Interior (1997) *Policies and Standards for Managing Museum Collections*. Departmental manual Part 411. Washington, D.C.: U.S. Department of the Interior.

Ford, R.I. (1980) A three-part system for storage of archaeological collections. *Curator*, 23(1): 55–62.

Griset, S. and Kodack, M. (1999) *Guidelines for the Field Collection of Archaeological Materials and Standard Operating Procedures for Curation of Department of Defense Archaeological Collections*. Legacy project No. 98-1714. St. Louis, MO: Mandatory Center of Expertise for the Curation and Management of Archaeological Collections, U.S. Army Corps of Engineers, St. Louis District.

Jacobson, C. (1998) Preparation. In: R.A. Buck and J.A. Gilmore (eds.), *The New Museum Registration Methods*. Third edition. Washington, D.C.: American Association of Museums, pp. 121–5.

Jessup, W.C. (1995) Pest management. In: C. Rose, C. Hawks, and H. Genoways (eds.), *Storage of Natural History Collections: A Preventive Conservation Approach*. Iowa City, IA: Society for the Preservation of Natural History Collections, pp. 211–20.

Malaro, M.C. (1994) *Museum Governance: Mission, Ethics, Policy*. Washington, D.C.: Smithsonian Institution Press.

——(1998) *A Legal Primer on Managing Museum Collections*. Second edition. Washington, D.C.: Smithsonian Institution Press.

McKeown, C.T., Murphy, A., and Schansberg, J. (1998) Complying with NAGPRA. In: R.A. Buck and J.A. Gilmore (eds.), *The New Museum Registration Methods*. Third edition. Washington, D.C.: American Association of Museums, pp. 311–19.

Morris, M. (1998) Deaccessioning. In: R.A. Buck and J.A. Gilmore (eds.), *The New Museum Registration Methods*. Third edition. Washington, D.C.: American Association of Museums, pp. 167–76.

Sease, C. (1994) *A Conservation Manual for the Field Archaeologist*. Third edition. Archaeological Research Tools, Volume 4. Los Angeles, CA: Institute of Archaeology, University of California Los Angeles.

Segal, T. (1998) Marking. In: R.A. Buck and J.A. Gilmore (eds.), *The New Museum Registration Methods*. Third edition. Washington, D.C.: American Association of Museums, pp. 65–78.

Swain, L. (1998) Storage. In: R.A. Buck and J.A. Gilmore (eds.), *The New Museum Registration Methods*. Third edition. Washington, D.C.: American Association of Museums, pp. 109–19.

Vogt-O'Connor, D. (1996) *Care of Archival Digital and Magnetic Data*. Conserve O Gram, 19/20. Washington, D.C.: National Park Service, Department of the Interior.

Chapter 3

Archaeological curation in the twenty-first century
Or, making sure the roof doesn't blow off

Wendy Bustard

Over the past few years it has become apparent that a crisis in American archaeology exists (Novick 1980). Those words were written in 1980 in response to a symposium, "The Curation of Archaeological Collections", at the 44th Annual Meeting of the Society for American Archaeology (SAA) in Vancouver, British Columbia, April 1979. Exactly 20 years later, Verna L. Cowin organized a symposium entitled "The Crisis in Curation: Problems and Solutions" at the 64th Annual Meeting of the SAA in Philadelphia, April 2000. The speakers in this symposium touched on a series of curation problems: large backlogs of uncataloged collections; extensive collections from recent cultural resources management (CRM) projects; inadequate staff; increasing curation fees; substandard and overflowing storage facilities; and the lack of awareness in the archaeological community of just how bad things are. The fall 1999 thematic volume of *Museum Anthropology* on the management of federal archaeological collections included articles on curation accountability, funding, accessibility, partnerships, and deaccession policies. It seems that once again a number of people are thinking about the state of archaeological curation and, unfortunately, finding many of the same problems cited in 1980. I recently did an informal poll of curators with archaeological collections to learn what their top concerns were. Generally, recurring themes regarding archaeological collections fall into five categories: accountability, accessibility, conservation/preservation, deaccession policies, and storage.

Accountability

In 1990, regulations entitled *Curation of Federally Owned and Administered Archaeological Collections* (36 CFR pt. 79) were published (CFR 1990), partly as a result of a 1980s General Accounting Office audit of the status of federal archaeological collections. The 1987 GAO report found that agency accountability was poor, largely due to the lack of records and guidelines. Three years later, 36

Source: *CRM Online*. National Park Service, 2000. 23(5): 10–15.

CFR pt. 79 was finalized. Unfortunately, a decade after its publication, federal agency accountability shows only sporadic improvement (Ferguson and Giesen 1999). Today, some agencies still do not have formal policies on curation, making accountability difficult to achieve. Other agencies, including the Departments of Defense and Interior, have made significant progress in terms of accountability.

Accountability asks two questions: what do you have and where is it? Problems with answering the first question generally center on the backlog: the number of uncataloged objects and archives. Until material is cataloged, we don't really have a handle on what we have, and the numbers can be overwhelming. Ten years ago, Chaco Culture National Historical Park calculated its archaeological and archival backlog to be around 1.5 million items. Today, about 54 per cent of the backlog has been cataloged. Unfortunately, the backlog continues to grow as new collections are accessioned each year.

Trouble answering the second question usually arises when we deal with older collections or federal agency collections. Often, older collections were divided, traded, or even sold off. For instance, archaeological collections from Chaco Canyon, excavated in the late-nineteenth and early-twentieth centuries, are now located in museums around the world. Old collections, dispersed among different institutions, sometimes with poor or no documentation, nonetheless can be useful for exhibits and type or comparative collections. As Joan Schneider of the University of California's Center for Archaeology and Paleontology observes, even with just general provenience information, these old collections can also be useful for research, if we know what and where they are (Joan Schneider, personal communication, March 2000). Sometimes, unfortunately, collections have simply been lost. Old field school collections are a good example—occasionally languishing, forgotten, in an attic or basement. Other collections, moved from storage room to storage room get lost along the way. Today, computerized accession and catalog records provide us with tools to track storage location moves and, with cooperation among institutions, to intellectually re-unite dispersed collections to facilitate research (McVicker 2000).

At the federal level, responsibility to protect and preserve archaeological resources on federal land dates back to the 1906 Antiquities Act. Agencies and bureaus whose primary mission does not include managing cultural resources (such as the U.S. Army Corps of Engineers or U.S. Fish and Wildlife Service) typically place most of their cultural collections in local or regional repositories. Since 1906, some of these agencies and bureaus have lost track of their collections. Federal compliance with the deadlines imposed by the 1990 Native American Graves Protection and Repatriation Act (NAGPRA) has had the beneficial effect of forcing agencies to locate and inventory their collections, and to make formal arrangements with non-federal repositories. The publication of 36 CFR pt. 79 in the same year as NAGPRA reinforced federal accountability for archaeological collections. The Department of Defense, through its U.S. Army Corps of Engineers Mandatory Center of Expertise for the Curation and Management of Archaeological Collections, has been particularly aggressive and effective in locating its collections, assessing conditions at repositories, and making recommendations for long-term curation.

The problem of locating collections is not limited to past practices. The rise of CRM projects over the last three decades has resulted in large, well-documented collections. However, we don't always know where these collections are. Although a repository agreement is required before a State Historic Preservation Officer will grant a permit, there is no way to monitor if the collection, after excavation and sometimes years of analysis, actually ends up in the specified repository (Otto 2000). According to Verna Cowin of the Carnegie Museum, CRM firms often cite a lack of staff to pack collections to repository standards and the high cost of curation fees as reasons for their failure to comply with state and federal regulations concerning archaeological collections (Cowin 2000).

Accountability is the responsibility of the agency or institution. Archaeologists and curators must ensure that agencies and institutions acknowledge their responsibility to manage collections to professional and regulatory standards. We must also encourage the public to hold us accountable for our cultural heritage.

Accessibility

Accessibility generally refers to whether or not researchers, managers, and the general public can use archaeological collections. This in turn relates to the question of accountability—if we don't know what we have and/or where it is, we cannot make collections available for use. This is not a trivial problem. According to 36 CFR pt. 79, federal collections must be made available for "scientific, educational, and religious uses." The general public pays for federal collections through taxes and, therefore, is entitled to use them appropriately. The Smithsonian Institution's creation of a Museum Support Center was in response to the need to appropriately care for collections and make them accessible. From 1983 to 1996, the National Museum of Natural History moved its archaeological and ethnographic collections to the new facility. During the move, inventories were completed, a new database system was installed, artifact storage locations were barcoded by catalog number, and storage was upgraded (Krakker et al. 1999). Researchers can now query electronic databases and easily locate artifacts for study. The Smithsonian Institution's curation center is an excellent model, but most of us do not have the good fortune to work in such well-designed facilities.

From a curator's perspective, the lack of accessibility relates directly to space and staff. Staff is necessary to catalog the artifacts. Even when you know what you have and where it is, without staff to retrieve requested items, collections are still not fully accessible for research. Overcrowded, unsafe storage conditions also physically hamper a curator's ability to pull items for researchers. Researchers face other accessibility challenges. For instance, collections dispersed in multiple repositories across the country (or world) make research physically difficult and often expensive. Sometimes just finding out what collections exist is a problem. The result is a lack of research use of important but little-known collections. Joan Schneider cites the example of the Elizabeth and William Campbell collection at Joshua Tree National Park, an important historical collection about which few outside the local academic community know. The University of New Mexico's

Chaco Field School collections from the 1930s and 1940s are uncataloged and information about these important small site assemblages is unavailable to researchers. Other field school collections no doubt suffer the same fate—forgotten on shelves in university storage rooms. As Schneider asks, "What is the purpose of curating collections if no use is made of them?" The American public, who pays for much of this work, would like an answer to that question as well. One way to increase accessibility would be to create a single, indexed, searchable website with links to all archaeological collections in the United States.

Conservation/preservation

Conservation is another concern. As Karin Roberts of the National Park Service Midwest Archeological Center points out, storage facilities for archaeological collections must be appropriate for a wide variety of materials, from stone to metal to textiles to celluloid (Karin Roberts, personal communication, April 2000). Often, storage conditions are geared toward generic, stable materials and fragile specimens may suffer over the long term. Roberts also observes that while archaeological collections should be accorded the same protection as other museum collections, this is not always the case. In my experience, bulk archaeological collections in particular are often housed in substandard conditions.

Increasingly, attention is focusing on archival collections. Without documentation, archaeological collections are generally not useful for research. When documentation exists, it can be considerable. The Chaco Museum Collection has seen an exponential growth in the amount of field notes, personal papers, photographs, and maps donated as researchers finish projects and/or retire. Preserving these records that are on non-archival paper is expensive and time-consuming. Another archival issue concerns electronic media. Managing data on computer tape, diskette, CD-ROM, and zip disk is a challenge. The media change so quickly that long-term preservation studies are non-existent and would be largely irrelevant. For now, we must keep old hardware so that we can read data on old media. The temptation is to get rid of obsolete technology as quickly as possible, but we must be careful not to throw out equipment before salvaging associated data files. The Chaco Museum Collection is currently engaged in an electronic database rescue project: we are converting 1970s–1980s data on old mainframe data tapes to CD-ROM format before the tapes disintegrate and the data are lost. This will not be a long-term solution, however, as technology changes faster than we can keep up with it. Migrating data files to new media every five years or so is a worthy goal, but one that may not be realistic, given other curatorial concerns and crises. National curatorial standards for electronic data migration, verification, and preservation would be useful.

Deaccession policies

Archaeological collecting in the United States dates back to the beginning of the republic. Americans of European ancestry shared the continental interest in curiosities from other cultures. The founding of the Smithsonian Institution in

1846 provided both the impetus, via funding, and a national home for the collection of antiquities on a large scale. By the late 1800s, institutions vied with each other to acquire antiquities for display in museums. The Antiquities Act of 1906 required that collections recovered under the Act be deposited in a public museum or national repository (CFR 1990). Over the last 150 years, a staggering number of artifacts has been collected and housed in the Smithsonian Institution, private museums, universities, federal agency repositories, state and local historical museums, and in some cases, garages and basements. Today, we face the problem of managing these collections and, sometimes, deciding what we will curate "in perpetuity" and what we will not.

Culling collections for cost, management, and research considerations is a touchy subject. However, several curators who responded to my informal poll brought up this problem, and S. Terry Childs of the National Park Service Archeology and Ethnography Program has argued for the need to incorporate deaccession policies into collection management plans (Childs 1999). In times of decreasing funds for museum support, increasing curation costs, and lack of space, curators are looking more closely at what is piled in the storage rooms. What we could (or should) discard, who should make those decisions, and how we justify our decisions are difficult questions, and should not be made in haste to solve short-term storage problems.

For private museums, deaccessioning is usually a policy issue, and these institutions can work with their boards of directors to develop such policies. However, at the state and federal level, legislative authority is required to dispose of publicly owned property. Within the federal government, some federal agencies and bureaus have the authority to deaccession inappropriate collections, and some do not. For example, the Department of Defense, the Department of State, and the Smithsonian Institution have deaccessioning authority, but in the Department of the Interior only the National Park Service and the Department of the Interior Museum have this legislative authority. The NPS deaccessioning authority was granted in 1955 and broadened in 1996, and the NPS museum program has had formal guidelines in place for deaccessioning since 1967. However, other bureaus in the Department of the Interior do not have general legislative authority to deaccession, with the exception of NAGPRA. This authority is needed. As Nancy Coulam of the Bureau of Reclamation notes, deaccessioning objects with limited or no value would be fiscally responsible and in the public interest (Nancy Coulam, personal communication, March 2000). The American Association of Museums (AAM), the American Anthropological Association (AAA), and the SAA could and should work with state and federal agencies to obtain the legislative authority needed to deaccession inappropriate archaeological collections through such mechanisms as transfer, exchange, or donation.

Storage

"The roof blew off the car wash last week." Not words that normally strike fear in a curator's heart, unless of course you have archaeological collections stored in the car wash. This actually happened to a university anthropology museum in March

2016. This museum had outgrown its storage space long ago and was desperate for additional storage space. Several years ago, the university's board of regents came up with a temporary solution—use an abandoned two-bay car wash for overflow storage. Since it was to be temporary, the university did not renovate the building. To stop the roof from leaking, it constructed a metal roof above the original roof. This is what blew off in a wind and rainstorm. Luckily, this story has a happy ending: a generous private donor has given the university money to construct an archaeological research and curation center.

While most of us do not have to worry about roofs blowing off, there are few state-of-the art facilities such as the Smithsonian Institution's Museum Support Center in Suitland, Maryland, and the National Park Service's new Museum Resource Center in Landover, Maryland. I suspect most of us labor in small, overcrowded, ill-lit storage facilities never designed to hold museum collections. The Chaco Museum Collection is currently housed in six locations: three in the park and three on the campus of the University of New Mexico in partnership with the Maxwell Museum of Anthropology. One of our shared facilities is the Maxwell Museum Warehouse, a 16-foot-high warehouse stacked floor to ceiling with archaeological collections from the Southwest. The Chaco Archive is housed in the 1930s book stacks section of the University of New Mexico's main library. I imagine a great many repositories across the country are similar: retrofitted spaces with limited or no environmental controls, security, or fire protection. Most of all, repositories are full—packed to the rafters and beyond, every inch of floor space taken up by piles of boxes. Even the Smithsonian Institution's Museum Support Center is now facing a scarcity of storage space (Hansen and Zwiesler Sawdey 1999). Archaeological collections and their accompanying archival collections grow steadily—sometimes slowly, sometimes at an alarming rate. Real estate is expensive, especially real estate that must be built to strict federal standards for curation and have room to expand. Not surprisingly, universities, private museums, and federal agencies are not overly anxious to undertake expensive construction projects to build the kinds of facilities required.

Not only do many (most?) repositories fail to meet the standards of 36 CFR pt. 79 for the curation of federal archaeological collections, many present severe safety and health concerns. Before the Museum Support Center was built, the National Museum of Natural History's anthropological collections were physically and figuratively stored in the "nation's attic," as the Smithsonian Institution is affectionately nicknamed. In this case, the conceptual charm of an overflowing attic was counterbalanced by the reality of asbestos contamination. Two of the Chaco Museum Collection storage areas in the park are infested with hantavirus-carrying mice. The 16-foot-high storage shelves in the Maxwell Museum Warehouse are a potential Occupational Safety and Health Administration (OSHA) nightmare. The list could go on.

Where do we go from here?

It seems to me that the pressing issues concerning archaeological collections can be characterized from two different standpoints: policy and implementation. The policy aspects of accountability and accessibility can and should be dealt with by the museum profession. The implementation aspects of accountability, accessibility, conservation/preservation, and storage require funding. Securing legislative authority for state and federal agencies and bureaus to deaccession inappropriate collections may require the political assistance of non-governmental entities such as the American Association of Museums (AAM), American Anthropological Association (AAA), and Society for American Archaeology (SAA).

Discussing the papers presented at the "Crisis in Curation" symposium, Francis P. McManamon, Departmental Consulting Archeologist for the Department of the Interior, observed that the infrastructure of curation is crucial: facilities and staff. It is this infrastructure that implements curation. Without an adequate and solid infrastructure, there will be no meaningful solutions to the problems facing us. Unfortunately, the curation infrastructure is expensive. Facilities that meet the standards of 36 CFR pt. 79 are costly to build and operate. Professional staff with the necessary expertise does not come cheap. Asking Congress, boards of directors, boards of regents, state legislatures, and city governments for more money for curation is not easy. We must compete with social programs that directly impact the public welfare. How? We need to do a better job educating the public about the importance of caring for the objects of our past and preserving them for future generations. Professional initiatives and public education are the tools to which we have immediate access. We must use them wisely to find solutions.

Archaeologists also must become more involved in curation. The SAA has a newly formed Committee on Curation; a good, if curiously late, start. However, in a cursory examination of the Society for American Archaeology's recently published *Teaching Archaeology,* I found only one reference to the need for professional, effective curation and collections management (Bender 2000). There is a strong emphasis on the preservation ethic in this volume, but it focuses on site preservation. Curation does not seem to be part of either undergraduate or graduate archaeological curricula. It is as though archaeologists collect things and then the objects disappear into another realm of responsibility. In 1980, Alexander Lindsay and Glenna Williams-Dean wrote:

> It is our opinion that many of the curatorial problems are created and can be solved or ameliorated by archaeologists themselves. The apparent lack of a positive ethic for the preservation, care, and use of collections in the training of archaeologists is one cause of the problem.
> (Lindsay and Williams-Dean 1980)

I can personally attest to the fact that some graduate schools today still do not train archaeologists in the care and use of collections. Ironically, as Ann Hitchcock of the National Park Service has noted, many museum studies programs developed within anthropology programs, such as those at the University of Arizona, the University of Colorado, the University of Denver, and the University of Washington (Ann Hitchcock, personal communication, May 2000).

If archaeologists do not become involved in curation policies and implementation, decisions will be made by boards of directors, federal and state managers, and administrators in the private sector. I suspect that most archaeologists will not be comfortable with the decisions these individuals make. It is up to us. If we want to make sure the roof doesn't blow off, we must all work on solutions to the archaeological curation crisis.

References

Bender, S.J. (2000) A proposal to guide curricular reform for the twenty-first century. In: S.J. Bender and G.S. Smith (eds.) *Teaching Archaeology*. Washington, D.C.: Society for American Archaeology, pp. 31–48.

CFR (1990) *Code of Federal Regulations. Title 36: Parks, Forests, and Public Property. Part 79: Curation of Federally Owned and Administered Archaeological Collections.* Washington, D.C.: US Government Publishing Office.

Childs, S.T. (1999) Contemplating the future: deaccessioning federal archaeological collections. *Museum Anthropology*, 23(2): 38–45.

Cowin, V.L. (2000) Caring for collections: a case study of Carnegie Museum of Natural History. Unpublished paper presented at the 65th Annual Meeting of the Society for American Archaeology, April 2000, Philadelphia, Pennsylvania.

Ferguson, B. and Giesen, M. (1999) Accountability in the management of federally associated archeological collections. *Museum Anthropology*, 23(2): 19–33.

Hansen, G. and Zwiesler Sawdey, C. (1999) A moving experience: thirteen years and two million objects later. *Curator*, 42(1): 13–35.

Krakker, J.J., Rosenthal, D.J., and Hull-Walski, D. (1999) Managing a scholarly resource: archaeological collections at the National Museum of Natural History. *Museum Anthropology*, 23(1): 9–18.

Lindsay, A.J. and Williams-Dean, G. (1980) Artifacts, documents, and data: a new frontier for American archaeology. *Curator*, 23(1): 19–29.

McVicker, D. (2000) All the king's horses and all the king's men: putting old collections together again. Unpublished paper presented at the 65th Annual Meeting of the Society for American Archaeology, April 2000, Philadelphia, Pennsylvania.

Novick, A.L. (1980) Symposium on the curation of archaeological collections. *Curator*, 23(1): 5–6.

Otto, M.P. (2000) CRM Curation in Ohio. Unpublished paper presented at the 65th Annual Meeting of the Society for American Archaeology, April 2000, Philadelphia, Pennsylvania.

Shingleton, K.L., Kozuch, L., and Trimble, M.K. (2000) The Department of Defense National Archaeological Curation Assessment Project. Unpublished paper presented at the 65th Annual Meeting of the Society for American Archaeology, April 2000, Philadelphia, Pennsylvania.

Part I, Section 2

Archaeological archives

Selection, retention, use and disposal

Chapter 4

Primal fear
Deaccessioning collections

Robert C. Sonderman

A few months after beginning a new job as an archaeologist with the National Park Service, my boss informed me that the regional director was coming to visit our storage facility. After several days of cleaning and preparing for his visit, I had my assistant and a small group of volunteers huddled around tables, sorting, counting, labeling, and cataloging a typical historic period archaeological assemblage of nails, broken glass, ceramics, and bone. Everyone looked very studious and scientific, the way many folks view archaeological lab work. In walks the director, who introduces himself, proceeds to look over someone's shoulder, and looks up at me and says, "Well, Bob, why do we keep all those chicken bones?"

The question that faces all of us responsible for the long-term care of archaeological collections is how do we address this far-reaching and fundamental issue. Before launching into the subject, let's establish a definition. Taken from an article by Marie Malaro, an expert in the field, deaccessioning "is the permanent removal of an object that was once accessioned into a museum collection" (Malaro 1991). This may seem rather restrictive for some archaeologists. It has been my experience that most of them don't even know what an accession is, let alone how to remove something from it. But we do know how to collect archaeological objects—millions and millions of them.

Most archaeologists practicing in the United States have been trained in a tradition of keeping everything that we find. Everything gets washed, labeled, inventoried, and cataloged; nothing is discarded, and with few exceptions, it is all deemed precious.

Armed with that paradigm, it is no wonder that the archaeological community has generated tens of millions of objects during the past 50 years. Both public and private collections have been kept in abysmal storage conditions with little regard to their long-term care or any acknowledgment of the ethical responsibility we as collection managers have towards them. The point has been well articulated by prominent voices such as Edward B. Jelks (1989), Alexander Lindsay (et al. 1980),

Source: *Common Ground: Archaeology and Ethnography in the Public Interest.* National Park Service, 1996. 1(2): 27–29.

and Michael Trimble (1990) and underscored by a 1986 Government Accounting Office report (GAO 1987). As a result, another question arises: "If these collections are so precious, why don't we take better care of them?" The next level of logic is, of course, "If we don't take care of them, why should we keep them?" This brings us back to the original question, "Why keep all those chicken bones?"

There are three standard responses. The first, which I refer to as the "flag-waving response," is that these objects represent the tangible remains of our national heritage and we are obligated to preserve and protect them. The second is the "It's the law response." We all know there are numerous federal, state, and local statutes that obligate archaeological collections managers to provide for long-term care. The third is the idea that new technologies and methods will allow archaeologists in the future to look at these collections differently and may provide valuable insights into human behaviour and, as a consequence, we must keep them.

Indeed many new discoveries have altered the way archaeologists look at collections. In the Chesapeake region, archaeologists working on prehistoric and historic sites may recover thousands of oyster shells, which until recently were viewed as another redundant artifact class. Recent research, however, has demonstrated that the shells can help determine the health of the oyster population, establish seasonal hunting patterns, and even help date archaeological sites. These collections can also hold research value to other disciplines. Citing the oyster shell example again, marine biologists can gain valuable insights into climate, water quality, and bottom conditions of the Chesapeake Bay in the past and diagnose methods to improve the oyster population in the present.

A sherd is not a chair

Now let's examine some distinctions between 'museum collections' and archaeological collections. Despite protestations to the contrary, museum collections – commonly perceived as paintings, sculpture, historic furnishings, and the like – are not intrinsically the same as archaeological collections. Both kinds of objects are certainly museum property but the manner in which they become part of the collection and how they are perceived once in it are quite different.

In the United States, most museums and federal repositories have clear collection acquisition policies and scope of collections statements. With these policies in hand, the collections manager, curator, or board of directors can restrict the type and flow of objects that enter the museum or repository. Conversely, archaeological projects, the vast majority of which are federally funded, generate millions of objects annually with little or no restrictions on the type or volume to be recovered and ultimately accessioned.

Given the nature of how archaeology is conducted in the States, it would be unethical for an archaeologist armed with a clear research design and scope of work – for example, to study Native American settlement patterns in upstate New York – to encounter a French colonial site and not collect the French material because it doesn't specifically relate to the research design or the repository's scope of collections statement. The traditional approach in federally funded archaeology is essentially a carte blanche: to recover all archaeological material – prehistoric, historic, extraterrestrial – that might be affected as a result of a federal undertaking. The archaeologist does not simply collect the material that is of research interest but rather, as a matter of ethics, recovers or samples everything. Federally generated archaeological collections are exempted from standard narrowly defined scope of collections statements.

Archaeological objects are not viewed as individual objects, such as tables and chairs might be, but rather, each flake or sherd is seen as part of the context from which it is recovered. It is not the individual object but the entire assemblage that is used to interpret the past. It is that paradigm that releases such an overwhelming sense of primal fear when the thought of deaccessioning archaeological material is raised.

Making the hard decisions

In 1990, when the federal government issued its curation standards and guidelines in 'Curation of Federally Owned and Administered Archaeological Collections' 36 CFR part 79, a proposed rule for deaccessioning archaeological collections was floated for comment. It was met with some opposition and withdrawn for further study. No scholarly archaeological organizations in the United States have expressed a willingness to tackle the issue. Passions pro and con on the subject run deep, but the climate may be changing.

Whether archaeologists are cognizant of it or not, federal agencies for the past several years have embarked on a massive deaccessioning programme. Driven by the Native American Graves Protection and Repatriation Act (NAGPRA), tens of thousands of archaeological objects recovered from Native American sites on public lands have been repatriated to their rightful owners. Repatriation is de facto deaccessioning – the permanent removal of an object that was once accessioned into a museum collection. In most cases, this repatriation/deaccessioning process has no strings attached. The receiving group can do with the objects as they choose.

The IRS has its own form of deaccessioning archaeological collections. Recently, the IRS seized the collections of a museum for failure to pay taxes. Assuming that once in IRS hands it became federal property, the Archeology Program of the National Park Service suggested that the IRS treat the collection as federal property and as a consequence, the collection was subject to 36 CFR Part 79. The IRS ruled otherwise and sold portions of the collection at auction. The issue of whether forced sale constitutes adequate federal control to apply 36 CFR Part 79 and NAGPRA is currently under review by the IRS office of general counsel. It is against this backdrop that archaeologists and collections managers must face the new climate of budget limitations, a downsized work force, restructuring, space limitations, and storage costs. Recognizing this reality, archaeological collections managers must begin to make the hard decisions. And it must be the archaeologists who take the lead in this decision process, for only archaeologists can fully comprehend the nature, public education value, and research potential of these remnants of our nation's patrimony.

In the late 1920s, the director of the Smithsonian's Museum of Natural History, an ornithologist facing a severe storage crisis, ordered the culling of collections. At the same time, in the Southwest, archaeologists had just made the famous Folsom complex discoveries, which included a distinctive type of fluted projectile point dating to the end of the last Ice Age, nearly 10,000 years ago. Unbeknownst to the technicians at the Smithsonian who were culling the archaeological collections, several of these same projectile points had been found around Washington, DC, and were held by the museum.

Later, scientists began to link the development of this culture complex with similar artifacts found in the East. Unfortunately, researchers at the Smithsonian discovered that some of the rare fluted points had been culled and destroyed. My point here is clear, archaeologists must take the lead. It must be a thoughtful, intellectual decision-making process with clear justifications and must also include a clear understanding of what is the most appropriate method of disposal or dispersion of those objects, if we take that step.

Why keep it?

Though deaccessioning may be a painful inevitability, a far better approach is to be more selective in what field projects retain and begin training archaeologists while at the university in sound museum policies, collection management principles, and procedures.

Particularly in the early stages of preparing scopes of work or research designs, archaeologists must start to think about sampling redundant artifact types, such as fire-cracked rock or brick fragments. Thinking about how many "chicken bones" need to be kept to conduct solid research may prevent the culling of accessioned collections while providing solid data for future analysis.

In the National Capital area of the Park Service, we have been experimenting with what we euphemistically refer to as "pre-accession deaccessioning." All material recovered in the field is returned to the lab, where it is processed and inventoried. It is at this time that the project archaeologist makes the determination to keep or reject artifacts or groups of artifacts for permanent accessioning. Although we do not have a written policy at this moment, we know we should have one. At present it is admittedly subjective, but it is based on a sampling strategy of per cents of redundant object classes, and the perceived research or public educational potential of the object.

We recognize, however, that there are clear dangers in this approach. No one can know what questions will be asked in the future and no one can know what objects will be needed for scientific analysis.

In the National Capital area, the decision is made by the same individual or group of individuals. There is no discussion of discarding diagnostic or museum quality objects during this "gleaning" process. Contract archaeological firms must consult with the area archaeologist in concert with the archaeological curator before any objects are considered for disposal prior to accessioning.

The state of Maryland is preparing to initiate a fee for collections storage as many states already have. One of the principal concerns of the local professional community is whether this fee will foster a trend of not recovering artifacts in an effort to avoid large storage fees. A clearly articulated recovery policy that allows for sampling certain redundant artifact categories may help avoid this sticky issue.

An alternative solution to permanent removal is placing objects selected for deaccession or of low research interest into inactive storage (in underground military bunkers, for example). The accessioned assemblage could undergo a triage system to identify the redundant artifact classes and those objects of little research potential. The selected objects could then be placed in lower cost, lower maintenance inactive storage, though in principle still accessible. The remaining portions of the assemblage would stay in active storage. This may be a viable solution for collections that require very little maintenance. The downside, however, is that portions of the collection will have limited accessibility which could invite the rejoinder—why keep it?

In a climate where space is equated with money, archaeologists must face the hard reality that we simply can't keep everything. The professional community must take the lead on this issue or we face the possibility of having the decisions made for us. Our new paradigm should be that the best deaccession policy is a good accession policy.

References

GAO (1987) *Cultural Resources: Problems Protecting and Preserving Federal Archeology Resources*. GAO/RCED-88-3. Washington, D.C.: U.S. General Accounting Office.

Jelks, E.B. (1989) Curation of archaeological collections of the Southwestern Division, U.S. Army Corps of Engineers. Manuscript report on file. Normal, IL: Southwestern Division, U.S. Army Corps of Engineers.

Lindsay, A.J., Williams-Dean, G., and Haas, J. (1980) *The Curation and Management of Archaeological Collections: A Pilot Study*. Cultural Resource Management Series, 59. Washington, D.C.: U.S. Department of the Interior, Heritage Conservation, and Recreation Service.

Malaro, M.C. (1991) Deaccessioning: the American perspective. *Museum Management and Curatorship*, 10: 273–79.

Trimble, M. (1990) *Saving the Past for the Future: Archaeological Curation in the St. Louis District*. St. Louis, MO: St. Louis District, U.S. Army Corps of Engineers.

Chapter 5

Archaeological archives
Serving the public interest?

Nick Merriman and Hedley Swain

Introduction

Under the model of Cultural Resource Management described as 'public archaeology' by writers such as McGimsey (1972) onwards, archaeology is seen to serve the public interest by preserving cultural remains *in situ*, or excavating them and preserving the records for future generations. Within such a framework, 'the public interest' is vaguely defined and oriented towards a similarly vague 'posterity'. An examination of the historical growth of archaeological archives from the 1960s onwards shows that a concentration on the specialist needs of the discipline of archaeology and a neglect of the wider public has led to the crisis in the curation of archives – a crisis revealed by a recent major survey. In this paper, we argue that such a limited view of the public interest is inadequate as it leads to a lack of appreciation for, and interest in, archaeological archives amongst today's public, which in turn leads to their low use, neglect, and underfunding. As a result, the role of archaeological archives needs to be re-thought as part of a reconstitution of archaeology towards being a more truly public-oriented discipline.

Archaeology and the accumulation of data

Archaeology has always been a fieldwork-based discipline that has generated records and finds as a result of its investigations. The importance of the long-term preservation of these records and finds as often the only vestiges of a destroyed site has long been recognized. Archaeological excavation, the adage runs, is 'the unrepeatable experiment' or 'destruction' (Wheeler 1954:15). The retention of the finds and records from fieldwork have been deemed to preserve the site 'by record' on the assumption that, if a site is sufficiently well recorded, it should be possible to reconstruct it totally from the records once it is destroyed. The body of finds, environmental samples, paper, photographic and digital records, and other material arising from an excavation, together with any analytical reports, comprise what has

Source: *European Journal of Archaeology*. European Association of Archaeologists, 1999. 2(2): 249–267. Reprinted with permission of the author and the EAA.

become known as 'the archaeological archive'. These archives have usually been passed to museums for long-term curation after completion of the principal phase of analysis and publication.

For at least a century, however, archaeologists have been concerned that museums or similar repositories should be adequately funded to be able to preserve and make available ever-increasing amounts of material generated from excavations. In 1904, for example, Flinders Petrie was already concerned about the inadequate space in English museums for the preservation of archaeological material, and suggested the building of a National Repository:

> A square mile of land, within an hour's journey from London, should be secured; and built over with uniform plain brickwork and cement galleries, at the rate of 20,000 square feet a year, so providing 8 miles of galleries 50 feet wide in a century, with room yet for several centuries of expansion at the same rate.
>
> (Petrie 1904:133–4)

The principal concern of archaeologists from Petrie onwards has been that adequate provision be made for museums to play their role in what is seen as the proper functioning of the discipline, by housing and preserving archaeological material for the use of current and future scholars, and by providing public dissemination of the results of archaeological work through displays, publications, public lectures, and the like (Pearce 1993: 232–6).

The growth in rescue archaeology in the late 1960s/early 1970s (Rahtz 1974; Jones 1984) brought about something of a crisis in the structure and funding of archaeology in England (Fowler 1970a, 1970b). Intense lobbying led to the announcement in 1973 of substantial increases in funds for rescue excavations in England and Wales and the establishment of various regional archaeological excavation units. Whilst some of these units were established in museums, the majority were established in local government departments, universities, or were independently constituted, often as charitable trusts. The wider implications of the boom in rescue archaeology, i.e. the recovery of a vastly increased volume of archaeological data which needed to be stored in perpetuity, took a little longer to filter through. This was partly because the concerns of museums were handled in a different government department from that concerned with archaeology and partly because much of the fieldwork was undertaken outside the museum framework. These factors led to a split between field archaeology and museum archaeology, which despite efforts of mitigation (some of which are outlined in this paper), continues to this day.

Responses to the growth in archives

By 1974, it was recognized that 'the present state of museums in this country is inadequate to cope with the present demands made on them, let alone the extra archaeological material that will become their responsibility' (Rescue/CBA 1974:15), and it was argued that a nucleus of regional museums be equipped to provide back-up facilities for rescue archaeology and offer long-term care of finds. Subsequent to this, a series of reports recognized the importance of properly curated archaeological archives as an integral element of the archaeological process. The 'Frere Report' (DoE 1975) on publication of archaeological fieldwork noted that the four different levels of dissemination identified all depended on the condition 'that all the original records of the excavation, properly organized and curated, are housed in readily accessible form in a permanent archive' (DoE 1975:3). The report crucially recognized both the need for standardization in recording and that a much greater commitment had to be made in funding terms towards post-excavation work and archive preparation.

The Dimbleby Report (DoE 1978) took these principles further by arguing that 'the creation, housing, and use of an archive is a single continuous process', that all archives should be stored in a museum building 'capable of meeting agreed standards of security, storage, conservation, and curatorial care', and that 'ideally no excavation should take place until arrangements for the adequate future storage, conservation, and maintenance of the archive have been made'. This meant 'total museum involvement', to ensure that 'the archive is organized in advance of deposition to agreed standards', and that time and money would be saved 'if the recording methods used in the field and the recording system used in the recipient museum were integrated' (DoE 1978:24).

A scheme was announced in 1981, which provided funding for approved museums for the storage of finds from excavations funded by the government's agency (DoE 1981). A system was established whereby museums could apply to the Museums and Galleries Commission (MGC) for 'approval' as an archaeological store meeting certain criteria regarding, for example, in-house expertise, availability of space, and adequate environment. Once approved, these museums could then apply for grants to store the archives from English Heritage-funded excavations (MGC 1986). For museums, this was an extremely significant step, as it represented for the first time an explicit recognition of the special nature of museum archaeology. In all other discipline, it is the museum itself that actively controls the rate at which it collects material, so that it can keep its collecting in balance with the availability of resources to curate the material. However, decisions to undertake archaeological fieldwork resulting in the generation of archives destined for museums are made as a part of the planning process, which does not involve input from museum. Museum archaeologists, therefore, have no real control over the rate at which archaeological archives are generated and therefore cannot ensure that the rate of collection is kept in balance with the resources available to curate them in the long term. Thus, although museums play a vital role in the archaeological process by housing archives from excavations 'in perpetuity', they are not involved in the rest of the process, and, before 1981, received no funding for this role. The expectation that museums would continue to accept, at their own expense, archaeological material that was being accumulated at an unpredictable rate was one with which few museum directors would ultimately be comfortable. The MGC/English Heritage storage grant scheme was thus an explicit acknowledgement of the special role that museum archaeology plays in the wider system of archaeological resource management, and a recognition that additional funds needed to be provided.

By the early 1980s, there was an apparent awareness of the problems created for museums by the growth in rescue archaeology, a realization of the importance of the archives held by museums and a system in place to assist with costs of curation. However, the reality of the situation for museum archaeology curators was rather different. Whilst the MGC/English Heritage storage grant scheme provided much-needed funding for some museums to upgrade their facilities, rarely was there liaison between field archaeologists and museum curators in advance of fieldwork; museum archaeologists rarely provided standards to field units detailing how they wished archives to be prepared, and museums continued to act as dumping grounds for the results of fieldwork.

By the mid-1980s, responsibility for funding archaeological excavation work was gradually shifting from the state through its system of grant aid, to property developers who wished to undertake new developments, which would destroy archaeological remains. This meant that, as fewer excavations were being funded by English Heritage, fewer sites were eligible for storage grants. After being persuaded to fund excavation and sometimes post-excavation processing, developers themselves were understandably reluctant also to fund the long-term curation of archives, which, after all, they were usually donating to the museum as the owners of the land. The split between field archaeology and museum, which had been healed temporarily and only partially successfully by the storage grant scheme, began to open up again. Museums were once more largely left on their own to find additional resources to curate in perpetuity archaeological material, which was accumulated at a rate beyond their control.

The split between museums and the rest of archaeology was further emphasized in the early 1990s by the publication of two important documents – *Planning Policy Guidance Note 16: Archaeology and Planning* (PPG16, DoE 1990) and *Management of Archaeological Projects* (MAP 2, English Heritage 1991a). In common with previous documents, they emphasized the importance of the mutually supporting dyad of archive and publication as the ultimate result – even the aim – of archaeological work, but provided no mechanism for funding the long-term preservation of the archive itself. PPG16 in particular was a major development through its establishment of archaeology for the first time as a material consideration in the planning process, which ensured that development proposals are assessed for their likely impact on the archaeological resource. It lays out two principal mitigation strategies: preservation *in situ*, and preservation 'by record'. Whilst it therefore makes arrangements for the adequate recording of archaeological remains threatened by development, it makes no provision for the preservation of the record itself. Museums, archives, and long-term preservation of the record are entirely absent from the document. MAP 2 integrates archives into the management process, but is silent about the mechanisms to facilitate this and about the means to fund it.

In the early 1990s, the virtual monopoly held by regional units to undertake archaeological work in 'their' areas began to be broken down by 'competitive tendering' or contract archaeology, whereby different units were invited to tender for a particular project (Swain 1991). Many archaeological units now operate without any form of public subsidy and compete for archaeological work over a wide area of the country or abroad, and produce archives for a large number of different museums. Here, the issue of standards has become extremely important, to ensure some degree of consistency in terminology and preparation to permit searching across different sites (Owen 1995).

In the meantime, a variety of evidence from museums, some anecdotal and some gathered via surveys, suggested that archaeological archives in museums were underfunded, and relatively little consulted (Swain 1996, 1997). Responses by museums to the problem of the underfunding of archaeological archives ranged from refusing to accept any more material to levying a charge for their acceptance. The latter response was a worrying development without legislative backing or even a consistent policy to support its use.

Concerned by the accumulation of archaeological material as 'unpublished backlog' or underfunded archive, the Society of Antiquaries of London held a major seminar in 1991 to address the issue. The seminar produced a number of potential initiatives, some of which were returned to in later studies. A survey of museum archaeological collections conducted in the same year (Merriman 1993) showed that the great majority had less than 10 per cent of their material on display, and the majority received less than 10 requests to view the stored material per year. Part of the problem, it was argued at the time, was that 'even the best project archives are frequently seen as repositories of records of finds too boring to keep, of retained artefacts too tedious to record, and of research results too dull to publish' (Hinton 1993:8)

Developments in museums

A further factor in the crisis in archaeological archive curation has been the increasingly divergent agendas of the archaeological resource management system and of museums. Until recently, the accepted definition of a museum in the UK was 'an institution that collects, documents, preserves, exhibits, and interprets material evidence and associated information for the public benefit' (Museums Association 1997:19). Here, the emphasis is first and foremost on the material evidence and its curation. This reflected a long-standing conception of the role and purpose of museums.

In 1998, a new definition was approved in response to a shift in emphasis in museum work over the previous decade:

> Museums enable people to explore collections for inspiration, learning and enjoyment. They are institutions that collect, safeguard and make accessible artefacts and specimens, which they hold in trust for society.
> (Museums Association 1998:40)

The shift in emphasis here is significant, stressing as it does people as well as objects and the provision of services in the present as being at least as important as the role of long-term custodianship. In response to calls for greater accountability for public funds, to the priorities of local authority and government funding bodies, and to the wishes of visitors and non-visitors as revealed in surveys over the last decade, museums have made huge efforts to render themselves more attractive and accessible to a wider range of visitors than ever before. Whereas 25 years ago writings about museums tended to concern themselves with technical matters such as storage, conservation, and security, a large literature has now grown up concerned with understanding museum visitors and the popularization of museum services (e.g. Merriman 1991; Falk and Dierking 1992; Hooper-Greenhill 1994a, 1994b). In a climate of shrinking public resources, museums have had to become more commercially oriented in order to survive. They have had to learn to compete with other leisure attractions by marketing themselves effectively, raising funds through sponsorship, donations, lettings, and other commercial activities, and by generally making their institutions more welcoming and attractive. Current policies of the government, local authorities, and the Heritage Lottery Fund emphasize 'access' to museums, 'for the many, not for the few', as one of their highest priorities, and encourage museums to develop their roles in lifelong learning (Anderson 1997) and in tackling issues such as social exclusion (DCMS 1998). Many museums have undertaken imaginative and successful projects opening them up to wider audiences, including ones that have used archaeological collections (Batey 1995; Merriman 1997).

The reinvigoration of museums towards providing services for the majority of people potentially meets well their role in the public dissemination of archaeological results. However, it sits rather uneasily with their other role of providing conservation, storage, and access services for archaeological archives, which by their very nature tend to be of more specialist interest. Archives tend to be consulted by relatively few people in comparison to their size and the annual costs of looking after them. A publication on the long-term costs of collecting (Lord et al. 1989) focused the attention of curators and museum managers on the expense of long-term storage and created increased concern about the accountability of public funds used to store large collections, which are rarely consulted.

A Society of Museum Archaeologists (SMA) discussion document developed in response to these growing concerns (SMA 1995) confirmed unanimous agreement amongst museums and museum bodies that the long-term storage of archaeological archives was a problem needing urgent attention, but no immediate solutions were offered. In 1996, following cuts in its grant from the government, the Museum of London, which holds the largest volume of archaeological archives in the country, closed its doors to further archaeological archives. One of the reasons it did this is that it felt it could no longer justify the proportion of its resources that it spent annually on curating its huge archaeological archive without additional funding in recognition of this special role it played in the archaeological process (CBA 1996; Merriman 1998).

The problems many museums were clearly having in the accommodation and management of the growing number of archaeological archives presented to them, and the refusal of the major archive holder to accept further material without additional resourcing, brought to the surface structural problems within English archaeology that arose from the lack of proper recognition of the museum's role in the overall archaeological resource management system, and prompted deeper questions about the purpose of archaeology: what are these archives for? Why is so much money being spent on archaeological fieldwork if adequate provision is not being made for the long-term preservation of the results? If they are not so important, is it necessary to retain them? Who will ultimately use them? These in turn raise questions about the balance to be struck between the slightly contradictory aims of preservation for posterity and access in the present.

The national survey of archaeological archives

In an attempt to gather reliable data on the scale of the problem across England, the Museum and Galleries Commission (MGC) and English Heritage (EH), the UK government agencies responsible for, respectively, museums in Britain and archaeology in England, commissioned a survey early in 1997. The survey was undertaken that summer and its results published the following year (Swain 1998).

The survey included a detailed questionnaire sent to 168 museums in England which were identified as being actively involved in accepting and curating archaeological archives, and to 79 archaeological contracting organizations. Responses were very good, with 115 from museums (a 70 per cent return) and 48 from contractors (a 60 per cent return). Detailed analysis of the questionnaire returns was supported by visits to museums and contractors.

The generation of archives

The vast majority of archaeological fieldwork in England is now undertaken on a commercial basis through the planning system (see for example Swain 1991 and Hunter and Ralston 1993). This means there is, in most cases, no organizational link between the contractor and local museum. Many contractors work widely throughout the country; four from the survey worked in over 20 museum-collecting areas. In these circumstances, it is essential that museums have the necessary expertise to monitor archaeological activity in their area and ensure both the preparation of archives to standards, which are suitable for curation in their museum, and the planning for the appropriate quantity and rate of archive deposition.

The survey found, however, that only about 50 per cent of museums had issued standards or guidelines on how archives should be prepared and that these were being included in well under 50 per cent of archaeological project briefs. The feeling in the museum profession appeared to be confirmed that archaeological archives have been prepared to a widely differing set of standards, and are therefore difficult to use collectively.

Most worryingly, museums in England do not provide a unified collecting coverage for the whole country. An already patchy coverage has been made more complex by local government reorganization, which in some cases has divided a larger county into several small 'unitary authorities'. Many areas are not covered by a museum that meets nationally accepted standards for archaeological curation, and there are a number of regions where there are no museums to accept archives at all. This leaves a series of 'vacuums' where no organization has responsibility for ensuring archives are properly prepared and cared for.

Quantity of material and its curation

The quantity of material in archaeological archives held by museums for the survey sample is about 40,000 cu. m.; 35 per cent of this is held by five museums, with the Museum of London holding about 18 per cent of the entire volume of archaeological archives in the country. The vast majority of the archive, 86 per cent, is composed of artefacts; 8 per cent is environmental material; 6 per cent is paper and other records; less than 1 per cent is digital material. This information is of limited use in its own right other than to confirm that finds material make up the bulk of archives. Of greater relevance is the rate at which archives are being generated and the ability of museums to store the material in a sustainable fashion.

About 70 per cent of the archives surveyed have been in museums for over ten years, and 30 per cent have arrived during the last ten years. Material is predicted to continue arriving at the same rate. It is difficult to link these figures with those on archaeological field activity. However, recent surveys commissioned by English Heritage suggest that archaeological fieldwork is increasing, and has done so particularly since the introduction of PPG16 (English Heritage 1995).

The survey showed that museums had very little space to continue collecting archaeological material. Figures 5.1 and 5.2 show respectively the amount of space available in museums to store archives and the rate at which it is likely to become full.

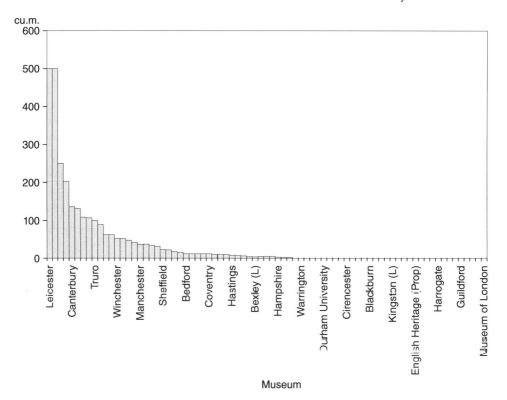

Figure 5.1 Amount of space remaining for archives (not all museums are named). Source: Swain 1998: 32.

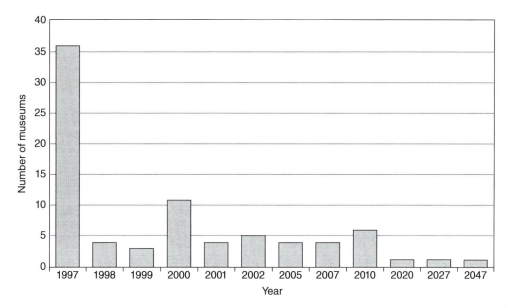

Figure 5.2 The date by which museums predict their archive space will be full. Source: Swain 1998: 33.

In summary, 38 archaeological units (48 per cent of all) report they have about 13,000 cu.m. of material to transfer to museums in the near future, while 77 museums (45 per cent of all) report having about 2000 cu. m. of free capacity.

This suggests a very acute shortage of space in museums to store archives. However, these global figures are slightly misleading. Detailed analysis shows that there is a relatively small number of large museum services with a major storage problem and a relatively small number of archaeological contractors with large bodies of material that should be transferred to a relatively small number of museums. Nevertheless, storage of archaeological material remains an acute problem in most English museums.

The survey revealed overall that much archaeological material is being stored in poor, inaccessible, and cramped conditions both by museums and by contracting organizations that have held on to material.

The cost of archiving

Only a few museums and contractors were able to produce detailed costs for archive care, and attempts to produce an average cost are fraught with difficulty. Bearing this in mind, from the limited figures provided, it is possible to calculate a provisional average cost for archive care at £34.30 per cu. m. per annum for museums and £22.50 per cu. m. per year for contractors.

Thirty museums in the sample (18 per cent) are already charging for accepting archives or are considering whether to do so. Almost all those museums that charge use the rate from the English Heritage box grant scheme of nearly £13 per box. Such charges are made as one-off payments when the archive is transferred to the museum.

Table 5.1 Plans by museums to deal with future archives

Archiving plan	(%)
Project under way to review problem:	19.1
New store planned:	17.0
Stop or suspend collecting:	10.6
Selective disposal of material:	9.6
Reorganize to maximize existing space:	8.5
Look for storage elsewhere:	6.4
'Panic':	6.4
Lottery bid planned:	5.3
Everything okay:	4.3
No comment:	12.8
Total	100 (N = 94)

Source: Swain 1998: 38.

These figures would seem to suggest that charging these rates would cover the cost of archive storage. If invested, the box grant figure should give a return of at least £34.30 per annum. However, many feel that it is unreasonable to charge developers for long-term storage, and that such a scheme is unenforceable and fraught with risks. This is because the developers tend to own the land they are developing and therefore also own the material recovered from it by archaeologists. A simple solution to the demand for storage payment for their own property might therefore be for the developers to retain it, or to dispose of it.

To a certain extent, attempts to quantify the archive problem on the basis of cost miss the point. Very few museums in England have budgets that are flexible enough to increase as extra funds are needed. A clearer picture was given when the survey asked museums how they planned to deal with future archives (Table 5.1). This shows that only 17 per cent of museums felt the situation to be 'fine', or made no comment. The other 83 per cent were either doing something actively about coping with future storage demand, or considering drastic action ranging from ceasing collecting, to disposing of material.

How archives are being used once in museums

The survey shows that archaeological archives are not being exploited to their full potential by museums, either to serve the archaeological profession or the general public. Table 5.2 shows instances mentioned in the survey of the ways in which archaeological archives are used. The commonest uses are the traditional ones of museum collections – the provision of material for displays, data for researchers, and resources for school parties. It is however not clear what proportion of the archives are used for these activities, and actual instances of use are still numerically

Table 5.2 Museum archive usage

How archives are used	Instances mentioned in survey
For display/exhibitions	73
Use by researchers	44
Education work	43
Staff research projects	20
General enquiries	14
Community projects	10
No use/no response	10
For type series/reference collections	4
By commercial archaeologists	4
For development control or sites and monuments record	3

Source: Swain 1998: 43.

low. The responses also show that archives are not being widely used by museum staff doing their own research, or by the general non-specialist public. Very few community projects are taking place and there are few general enquiries. Even within the archaeological profession, archives remain largely unused as reference collections, as support to sites and monuments records or as resources for contractors, even though they represent the prime evidence for the archaeology of an area.

The survey found that 29 per cent of museums replying to the survey received no visits or enquiries to their archives in the previous year. Most types of visit average less than 20 per year, and annual total visits of all types to archives average at 46. It tends to be the larger museum, which often have important collections and an academic reputation, that are most used, but even here the majority of enquiries are by specialists. Archives in general are underused as a commercial resource.

It is a fact that archives tend to be intractable and inaccessible as prime resources for study. However, it is the responsibility of the archaeological community to ensure they are prepared in such a way as to overcome this. One major potential to open them up to greater use is provided by digital technology. However, the survey shows there is still much further work to do in this area.

Digital archives

As already shown, if nothing else, digital archives do not cause a storage problem. However, the survey revealed a growing concern about computerized records and the ability of museums to deal with these. The survey asked: are you having problems dealing with computer records from archaeological archives?

48 museums said no
31 museums said yes
14 failed to answer

Many of those museums who claimed not to have encountered a problem had either not yet received any digital archives; or had had no problem because they had made no attempt to read or use digital material that had been deposited with them.

A number of regional and national initiatives are currently under way, which have the potential to revolutionize the way archaeological information is managed. It is recognized that more and more archaeological information is being recorded, manipulated, and stored in digital form. This includes sites' and monuments' records, other strategic management resources, and prime data from archaeological excavations and fieldwork. It is only a matter of time before archaeological plans and record sheets are a thing of the past, replaced by AutoCAD drawings and computerized databases. Museums need to ensure they are properly integrated with the wider archaeological community, where awareness of the value of digital information in dealing with archives is more advanced.

Conclusions of the survey

The survey showed that archives are large in number and bulk, but that the main collections are concentrated in a small number of museums and units. The number of archives are predicted to grow at a steady rate and museum predictions of future available space is clearly inadequate to cope with future growth. Archives are largely unstandardized, which makes them difficult to use, and there are gaps in museum provision so that archives from some areas have no long-term destination. Storage conditions are often cramped and inadequate, and little funding is available for long-term curation costs. Perhaps most worrying, archives remain greatly underused both by archaeologists and the wider community.

It has become clear that there will be no single solution to the problems faced and that, in some areas, much has to be achieved within the archaeological/museum infrastructure before the more straightforward question of archive quantity and access can be addressed. The survey report lists nine principal recommendations (Swain 1998:10–11):

- promoting expertise amongst the curators of archives;
- the redefinition of museum archaeological collecting areas;
- the preparation of a set of core standards for the transfer of archaeological archives;
- a redefinition of guidelines for the disposal or dispersal of archaeological archives;
- a review of the physical condition of the major archives held by archaeological contractors;
- an analysis of the feasibility of a network of regional Archaeological Resource Centres;
- a review of the storage grant scheme;
- a study of how to increase the use of archaeological archives;
- a review of the nature and long-term curation of digital data being included in archives.

English Heritage and the Museums and Galleries Commission have established working parties that are actively pursuing the achievement of all of these recommendations.

Discussion: promoting access and use

The national survey has confirmed for the first time, and in a rigorous manner, some of the developments consequent on the growth of rescue archaeology and the historic split between museums and the rest of the archaeological profession. While the recommendations will go some way towards alleviating some of the problems, deeper structural problems remain to be addressed. The archaeological resource management system is based on a model of objective knowledge, facilitated by an ever-increasing accumulation of data. The public interest is felt to be served by the 'rescuing' of sites on behalf of the public by professional archaeological teams and by their archiving for the public of the future. Archaeology continues, both in the mind of the public and that of the discipline itself, to place greater value on romantic-heroic notions of discovery of new data through fieldwork than on the analysis of material that has already been excavated. However, for museums, increasingly orienting themselves towards accountability for public funding and delivery of services to wide audiences, the idea that archives can be accumulated in ever-increasing numbers and barely used in the present is difficult to sustain.

The answer must be to give archaeological archives a higher value in the eyes of both the profession and the wider public. A truly 'public' archaeology should place much greater emphasis on the use of archaeology in the present by a wider audience, as well as on the preservation of data for a future community of scholars. As far as archaeological archives are concerned, this must involve the proper integration of museums and their role of archive curation into the overall archaeological resource management process, and the development of coherent strategies for public involvement in archaeology as a whole. As a discipline, archaeology needs to be able to answer some of the questions raised earlier in this paper: what are these archives for? Who will Ultimately use them? How much needs to be retained in perpetuity? How can funding be secured for this?

The first step must be to make the contents of archives better known. At present, one of the major barriers to their further use is that even specialist researchers are often unaware of the existence and location of many archaeological archives. Here, digital resources must be able to play a major role. The potential revolution in digital technology in archaeological resource management already alluded to is significant in that it opens up a whole new vista of possibilities in the use of data. Thanks to the Internet, there is the potential for a researcher to gain electronic access to the records and reports for a site direct to their personal computer, perhaps using the Archaeology Data Service (a service established to provide a home for digital resources created through archaeological research) or an online Sites and Monuments Record as their point of entry. There is also the potential to make generic enquiries that cut across site archives.

However, there is a real risk that museums will once again be left out of the system. Most archaeological contractors use computers very heavily, while many museums do not have the funds for the computer hardware or software to support archives they may accept, or have not given thought to setting standards for the transfer and storage of material in such a way that it can be used. Care must therefore be taken to ensure that, if the digital indexes and primary digital data that will be the key to unlocking archives are held and managed by central facilities outside the museum system, museums are able to have the facilities to access the online electronic archive.

If digital information can provide the mechanism by which archive information is made more accessible to a wider audience it must still be underpinned by research strategies to ensure its coherent and productive use (e.g. English Heritage 1991b, 1997). At present, however, the deposition of an archive in a museum is seen as the (dead) end of a linear archaeological resource management process, once the analysis and research of a site has been completed for the foreseeable future. It may be useful to begin to conceive of the process as a unified and circular one, in which the holdings of an archive feed back into research strategies for future work. One element of this has to be the development of strategies for what may be termed the *'ex-situ* resource', alongside the more familiar ones for the *in situ* resource. Ideally, archive holders should produce statements on the research potential of their archives in order to promote further research, and develop proactive relationships with universities regarding collaborative projects. Initiatives might include undergraduate and postgraduate dissertations and theses in archaeology, history, photography, computing, geography, or environmental sciences, possibly written as elements of a wider programme of research on a particular issue. With amateur archaeological societies finding it increasingly difficult to undertake fieldwork, there is a strong argument for encouraging their involvement with the further development of archaeological archives. For example, the Museum of London's proposals for a new London Archaeological Archive Resource Centre have been discussed with local societies and opportunities identified for their involvement.

Although research agendas do have the potential to address matters of wider public interest, at present they are mainly serving the archaeological profession and specialist needs. A few initiatives, perhaps most notably the Archaeological Resource Centres in Toronto and York, have shown some of the potential for 'mundane' archaeological material being used in stimulating ways. Can archives be linked in with the widespread popular interest in family and local history, for example? Information technology has a role to play here. It has the ability to make archaeological data, at various levels, accessible to essentially non-archaeological audiences. It is probable that many members of the general public have little interest in site codes, matrices, and dating tables but would be fascinated to know that Roman remains had been found in their street or parish. Schools' use of archaeological archives might be encouraged by targeted projects on particular aspects of archives, which link in with the National Curriculum and allow some measure of original work. The availability of some (interpreted) archive data on the World Wide Web, which is specifically aimed at schools, might be linked in to practical projects on the material itself. Perhaps unusual uses of archives should be explored. The Society of Museum Archaeologists is at present discussing a programme to bring in artists into archives, for example, to create artworks inspired by the material, to use the material itself in their work, and/ or to work with local people and schools in creative uses and responses to archives.

In conclusion, for many years, archaeological archives have been viewed very narrowly as a resource for scholars and a storage problem for museums. There is now a recognition that their true value must depend upon their far greater importance as a resource to the widest possible archaeological community from scholars to the general public. The national survey will, it is hoped, pave the way for solutions to the storage problem and better working relationships amongst archaeologists with differing responsibilities. However, if the full potential of archives is to be realized, we must maximize the use of information technology and be far more imaginative in how we use the *ex-situ* resource to interpret the past.

References

Anderson, D. (1997) *A Common Wealth. Museums and Learning in the United Kingdom.* London: Department of National Heritage.

Batey, C. (1995) In touch with the past at Glasgow museums. In: G. Denford (ed.), *Museum Archaeology – What's New? The Museum Archaeologist 21. Conference Proceedings Edinburgh 1994.* Winchester: Society of Museum Archaeologists, pp. 19–23.

CBA (1996) Threat to urban research as archive faces closure. *British Archaeology*, 12: 4.

DCMS (1998) *A New Cultural Framework.* London: Department for Culture, Media, and Sport.

DoE (1975) *Principles of Publication in Field Archaeology (The Frere Report).* London: Department of the Environment.

——(1978) *The Scientific Treatment of Material from Rescue Excavations.* London: Department of the Environment.

——(1981) *Storage of Finds from Grant-Aided Rescue Excavations.* Advisory Note 31. London: Department of the Environment.

——(1990) *Planning Policy Guidance 16: Archaeology and Planning.* (PPG16). London: Department of the Environment.

English Heritage (1991a) *Management of Archaeological Projects.* Second Edition. London: English Heritage.

——(1991b) *Exploring Our Past. Strategies for the Archaeology of England.* London: English Heritage.

——(1995) *Planning for the Past. Volume 1. A Review of Archaeological Assessment Procedures in England 1982–1991.* London: English Heritage.

——(1997) *English Heritage Archaeology Division Research Agenda.* London: English Heritage.

Falk, J.H. and Dierking, L.D. (1992) *The Museum Experience.* Washington D.C.: Whalesback Books.

Fowler, P.J. (1970a) The crisis in field archaeology. *Current Archaeology*, 23: 343–5.

——(1970b) Archaeology and museum, 1970–2000 AD. *Museums Journal*, 70(3): 120–21.

Hinton, P. (1993) Archives and publication in the real world. In: E. Southworth (ed.), *'Picking Up The Pieces' – Adapting to Change in Museums and Archaeology. The Museum*

Archaeologist 18. Conference Proceedings Sheffield 1991. Liverpool: Society of Museum Archaeologists, pp. 6–9.

Hooper-Greenhill, E. ed. (1994a) *The Educational Role of the Museum.* London: Routledge.

——(1994b) *Museums and their Visitors.* London: Routledge.

Hunter, J. and Ralston, I. eds. (1993) *Archaeological Resource Management in the UK.* Stroud: Institute of Field Archaeologists/Alan Sutton.

Jones, B. (1984) *Past Imperfect. The Story of Rescue Archaeology.* London: Heinemann.

Lord, B., Lord, G.D., and Nicks, J. (1989) *The Cost of Collecting. Collection Management in UK Museums.* London: HMSO.

McGimsey, C.R. (1972) *Public Archaeology.* New York: Seminar Press.

Merriman, N. (1991) *Beyond The Glass Case. The Past, the Heritage, and the Public in Britain.* Leicester: Leicester University Press.

——(1993) The use of collections: the need for a positive approach. In: E. Southworth (ed.), *'Picking Up The Pieces' – Adapting to Change in Museums and Archaeology. The Museum Archaeologist 18. Conference Proceedings Sheffield 1991.* Liverpool: Society of Museum Archaeologists, pp. 10–17.

——(1997) The Peopling of London project. In: E. Hooper-Greenhill (ed.), *Cultural Diversity. Developing Museum Audiences in Britain.* Leicester: Leicester University Press, pp. 119–48.

——(1998) Records of metropolitan archaeology: unwanted residues or primary sources? In: M.V. Roberts (ed.), *Archives and the Metropolis.* London: Corporation of London, pp. 57–64.

MGC (1986) *Eligibility Criteria for the Grant-Aided Storage of Excavation Archives.* London: Museums and Galleries Commission.

Museums Association (1997) *Codes of Ethics.* Second edn. London: Museums Association.

——(1998) Definition of a museum. *Museums Journal,* 98(11): 40.

Owen, J. ed. (1995) *Towards an Accessible Archaeological Archive. The Transfer of Archaeological Archives to Museums; Guidelines for use in England, Northern Ireland, Scotland, and Wales.* London: Society of Museum Archaeologists.

Pearce, S. (1993) Museum archaeology. In: J. Hunter and I. Ralston (eds.), *Archaeological Resource Management in the UK.* Stroud: Institute of Field Archaeologists/Alan Sutton, pp. 232–42.

Petrie, W.M.F. (1904) *Methods and Aims in Archaeology.* New York: Blom.

Rahtz, P.A. ed. (1974) *Rescue Archaeology.* Harmondsworth: Penguin.

Rescue/CBA (1974) *Archaeology and Government. A Plan for Archaeology in Britain.* London: Rescue/CBA.

SMA (1995) Long-term storage and curation of archaeological archives. Unpublished discussion document. Society of Museum Archaeologists.

Swain, H. ed. (1991) *Competitive Tendering in Archaeology.* Hertford: Rescue/SCAUM.

——(1996) Here comes a national museums crisis. *British Archaeology,* 12: 11.

Swain, H. (1997) Archaeological archive transfer: theory and practice. In: G.T. Denford (ed.), *Representing Archaeology in Museum, The Museum Archaeologist 22. Conference Proceedings, London 1995.* Winchester. Society of Museum Archaeologists, pp. 122–44.

——(1998) *A Survey of Archaeological Archives in England.* London: Museums and Galleries Commission/English Heritage.

Wheeler, R.E.M. (1954) *Archaeology from the Earth.* Harmondsworth: Penguin.

Chapter 6

Archaeological archives in Britain and the development of the London Archaeological Archive and Research Centre

Hedley Swain

As long ago as 1904 archaeologists in Britain were expressing concern about the ability of museums to store and curate the material from archaeological excavations. In that year Flinders Petrie (1904:134) suggested the provision of a national repository: "A square mile of land, within an hour's journey from London, should be secured; and built over with uniform plain brickwork and cement galleries at a rate of 20,000 square feet a year, so providing 8 miles of galleries 50 feet wide in a century, with room yet for several centuries of expansion space."

Three elements of this description are worth noting: "within an hour's journey from London" suggests the need for rapid access; "20,000 square feet a year" suggests a large mass of material; and "several centuries of expansion space" suggests that the rate of deposition will be continuous. These observations remain true for British and indeed European archaeology today. There is a lot of it, it keeps coming, and we believe that we should provide ready access to it.

Archaeological archives (the term normally used in England for the collective records and finds and associated reports and data from an excavation) should represent a prime research and heritage asset; yet they have been under-resourced and underused. For many years British museums have struggled to find the resources to properly store archives, never mind maximize their research and educational value. This situation has been made worse by the organization of archaeology in Britain today whereby the practitioners are primarily commercial organizations whose peripatetic activities are quite separate from the museums that are expected to curate archives (see, e.g., Merriman and Swain 1999).

In London in the past thirty years this situation has become acute. The unprecedented level of excavation in the historic urban core has resulted in the largest body of archaeological records and finds of its kind. This is an immense

Source: *On the Past, for the Future: Integrating Archaeology and Conservation. Proceedings of the Conservation Theme at the 5th World Archaeological Congress*, Washington, D.C., 22–26 June 2003. N. Agnew and J. Bridgland (eds.). Los Angeles: The Getty Conservation Institute, 2006. pp. 211–215. Reprinted with permission of the J. Paul Getty Trust.

research resource, making London one of the best-understood historical cities in Europe (Museum of London Archaeology Service 2000). However, it has brought with it huge logistical problems for the Museum of London, which takes and cares for the archives from excavations.

The London Archive and Research Centre

In the last few years, the Museum of London has attempted to embrace the need for an easily accessible and sustainable home for the material from previous London excavations. Since its foundation in 1976 the Museum of London has acted as the home for archaeology in the capital (Ross and Swain 2001; Sheppard 1991). The museum's field units, in their different incarnations, have carried out the vast majority of excavations in Greater London. The museum's main galleries tell London's story from prehistory to the twentieth century and draw heavily on archaeology, as have some of its recent temporary exhibitions such as *London Bodies* (Werner 1998), which used human skeletons to demonstrate how the appearance of Londoners has changed through the ages, and *High Street Londinium* (Hall and Swain 2000a), which focused on how excavations had helped to reconstruct the appearance of Roman Londinium. Behind the scenes the museum also cares for the archives from excavations in Greater London. It has long been realized that this material offers both great challenges in terms of its sheer quantity and an incredible untapped resource for research. In creating the London Archaeological Archive and Research Centre (LAARC) the museum has tried to meet these challenges.

The LAARC was opened in February 2002; it is housed in the museum's Mortimer Wheeler House resource center, about two miles from the main museum building and its galleries. It shares the building with the offices of the museum's archaeology service and much of the museum's social and working history collections. A grant from the Heritage Lottery Fund (the U.K.'s national lottery) provided about 50 per cent of the funding. Other funds came from central government, the Getty Grant Program, and many other organizations, archaeological societies, and individuals. Two new large storage areas have been created, as well as a visitor center and two study rooms. State-of-the-art roller storage has been installed, and computerized index and access systems (the latter available on the Internet) have been developed. The LAARC project, which included building and equipping the new spaces, designing the computer systems, and undertaking a minimum standards program on the archive, cost about £2.5 million. Funds for the six-person team that manages the LAARC are found from the museum's recurrent costs.

The core staff for the LAARC is adequate for day to day management and curation. Extra project funds are sought to undertake specific enhancement and research projects. These currently include a major project funded by the Wellcome Trust to produce an online database of the human skeletons held in the archive.

The London archive is by far the largest in Britain. It currently contains about 150,000 individual boxes of finds stored on 10,000 meters of shelving and includes finds and records from about 5,200 individual excavations from Greater London. And, of course, these figures are growing every year. Therefore, about twenty years' expansion space has been built into the plans. This will be achieved partly through current spare space but also by the rationalization of existing material. For example, a current program entails recording and then discarding some assemblages of mundane and repetitive ceramic building materials from past excavations that would not have been retained under modern excavation methodologies.

The museum has set rigorous standards for the preparation of new archives resulting from excavations and expects the archives from all excavations in Greater London to be deposited in the LAARC. It has taken a while for the twenty or so archaeological contractors who regularly operate in London to become accustomed to this new, disciplined approach, but the will seems to be there, and material is now being deposited at an increased rate.

Meanwhile, the LAARC has also turned its attention to material that is already in its care. This material was generated over about one hundred years by many different archaeologists working for many different organizations. Currently, this material is not compatible and often not easily accessible. A huge effort is being made to bring all this material up to an acceptable level of care and accessibility, not only for its long-term well-being but also to encourage research.

Research has been spearheaded by the publication of a London archaeological research framework (McAdam et al. 2002) and a series of partnerships with London's archaeologists and universities. The international research potential of material held at the LAARC is also being recognized. The museum already has formal partnerships in place with La Trobe University in Melbourne to study eighteenth and nineteenth-century assemblages and with Pennsylvania State University to study DNA from some of the skeletons held in the archive.

Another key part of the London archaeological community is its local societies; the museum is working with these groups to encourage research and use of the LAARC. Several societies were actively involved in the planning of the LAARC and donated funds for its creation. It is hoped that society projects either researching London's past or helping with collections management in the LAARC will allow local members to feel actively involved in London's archaeology—something that has been very difficult in the past ten years as more and more archaeology has been funded commercially by developers. Under another initiative, the LAARC is hosting the Central London Young Archaeologists Club for children and teenagers.

The LAARC is not an alternative to the museum's galleries, and it is fully appreciated that archives may not be the best way to introduce the general public to archaeology. There are public weekend events at the LAARC, but its main value is as a foundation for other activities. The *London Bodies* exhibition would have been impossible without the museum's archive of human remains; other such projects will follow. The sorting and rationalization of material in the archive has also made possible the museum's Roman Boxes for Schools scheme, whereby unstratified material has been turned into teaching collections (Hall and Swain 2000b). Such material was also used in *The Dig*, a recreated excavation using real artifacts, which was the museum's summer family event in 2001 (Martin 2002).

The LAARC's philosophy is simple, but it calls on the archaeological community to refocus its priorities. Over thirty years we have become expert at excavating and recording archaeological material in the face of threats from development. But we have been not sufficiently used the results of excavation to further public knowledge and appreciation of the past. A vast unrealized resource has slowly accumulated. By its proper curation, we are now ready to put it to a variety of uses, led by research. It is hoped that the LAARC will develop as a strong foundation for archaeological activity in London and a model for similar endeavors elsewhere.

The wider challenge

The challenges posed by the curation of archaeological archives are not restricted to London. A number of reports and surveys have highlighted the plight of archaeological archives throughout Britain (Swain 1998). Archaeological digging units have been slow to transfer archives to museums, and museums in their turn have struggled to find the space and resources to care for them to acceptable standards. There has also been a poor record of dialogue between museums and archaeologists.

The initial success of the LAARC hides underlying contradictions in British archaeology that undermine much of the philosophical basis for archaeology. As archaeologists, we have long learned that excavation is destruction and that it is imperative therefore that we properly preserve and "archive" our records and finds, and publish the results. Developing from the idea of archiving is the concept that the archive should be a valuable research tool, allowing archaeologists to "test" the conclusions made—in the same way that a scientific experiment is valid only if it can be repeated—but also allowing new research by comparing the results from more than one dig or studying a different aspect of the archive.

Experience has shown that professional archaeologists, and the archaeological community in general, have been reluctant to archive material and to use archives as a valid research resource—obviously, by so doing undermining the original premise for preservation in the first place. There is a tendency in the profession to fall back on the argument that material must be preserved because it is part of our heritage and is unique. This will not do. It is not justifiable to spend large amounts of money and resources preserving something just because it was dug up and is old. It must have a demonstrable value to society now and be valued as a resource for future research, display, and education.

In Britain, much progress has been made in the past five years to recognize the poor state in which archives are being curated and the threats so posed to them. However, the profession still has some way to go in realizing that the material is of real value and to demonstrate this by using the archives, thus demonstrating the need for care. We hope that the LAARC can play an important part in this task by demonstrating how archives can be used once they are valued.

It is not enough simply to keep archives because they are a record of excavations. They must be put to use. Archives must be properly curated. If they are properly curated they can be used for research and as a foundation for other archaeological endeavors: display, education, management. It is only worth curating them if they are used in these ways.

References

Hall, J. and Swain, H. (2000a) *High Street Londinium*. London: Museum of London.

——(2000b) Roman boxes for London's schools: an outreach service by the Museum of London. In: P.M. McManus (ed.), *Archaeological Displays and the Public*. London: Archetype Publications, pp. 87–95.

Martin, D. (2002) Great excavations. *Museum Practice*, 7(1): 21–3.

McAdam, E., Nixon, T., Swain, H., and Tomber, R. eds. (2002) *A Research Framework for London Archaeology 2002*. London: Museum of London.

Merriman, N. and Swain, H. (1999) Archaeological archives: serving the public interest? *European Journal of Archaeology*, 2(2): 249–67.

Museum of London Archaeology Service (2000) *The Archaeology of Greater London*. London: MoLAS.

Petrie, W.M.F. (1904) *Methods and Aims in Archaeology*. New York: Bloom.

Ross, C. and Swain, H. (2001) *Museum of London: 25 Years*. London: Museum of London.

Sheppard, F. (1991) *The Treasury of London's Past*. London: HMSO.

Swain, H. (1998) *A Survey of Archaeological Archives in England*. London: Museums & Galleries Commission.

Werner, A. (1998) *London Bodies*. London: Museum of London.

Part I, Section 3

Documentation, identification, and authentication of archaeological collections

# Chapter 7

Inventory and global management in archaeology
The example of the Neuchâtel Museum

Marie-Odile Vaudou

Stemming from a global reflection, the new method of inventory in archaeology that was developed from 1996 to 2003 at the Museum of Archaeology (SMA) in Neuchâtel, Switzerland, is part of a multidisciplinary approach that aims at managing the entire yield of an excavation. This approach includes all the productions of humankind and its environment. It accompanies, in a single process, the archaeological object from the excavation site to its storage in repositories or its presentation in display cases. This management is part of the cycle of the conservation, study, and showcasing of local heritage. The computerized inventory constitutes a crucial stage within this chain of operations, because it facilitates classifying objects, no longer only for themselves, but in relation to the context of discovery. It is therefore possible to treat from the same perspective, objects, plant, and animal samples, lithic matter as well as archival documentation and related studies. This approach is influenced by the evolution of archaeology, which from the mid-1960s integrated new research tools by having recourse to earth sciences and fundamental sciences such as chemistry or computer science.

The growth of archaeological and archival documentation produced by systematic excavations, as well as the diversity of jointly conducted studies, has required the management of an increasingly voluminous and varied mass of information. The definitive disappearance of sites, following rescue excavations that precede public works, has led us to pay particular attention to records and methods for recording data. As a corollary to these changes, reflection on the management of material on a much larger scale than previously has become necessary.

Controlling the quantity and diversity of the material

The creation of a new system inventory at Laténium, the archaeological park museum in the commune of Hauterive,[1] facilitated the systematic and uniform

Source: *Museum International*. International Council of Museums (ICOM), 2004. 56(3): 68-76. Reprinted with permission of John Wiley & Sons, Inc.

management of the quantity and diversity of archaeological material preserved in the museum. Rescue excavations and surveys conducted since 1964 along the highway on the northern shore of the lake and in the rest of the canton, brought extensive material up to date, completing the national and international collections that were created as from the end of the nineteenth and beginning of the twentieth century (Société Suisse de Préhistoire et d'Archéologie 2002). They are spread over a period of 50,000 years, from the Middle Palaeolithic (the oldest vestige is a Neanderthal jaw dating from approximately 45,000 BC) up to the modern era. The wealth of movable property, amounting to several tonnes of material, is largely explained by the geography, the history of the spot, and the satisfactory conservation of objects in lacustrine sediment.

Whatever their state of conservation, their origin or their dimensions, the objects are classified without any discriminatory criteria. For the inventory, equal importance is given to an amber bead, a menhir, a bone, a pin, or a nail! The only possible distinctions, which can arise during the recording, have to do with the complexity of the object, such as the specificity of a form or a decor, or a particular exploitation of property for a study or exhibition.

The inventory must ensure the cataloguing, identification, and documentation of this immense collective memory. Its goal is to quantify and qualify the material according to scientific criteria, and to localize and manage the movements of objects. The standardized system facilitates counting and reveals series that are not visible without it; it should facilitate the selection of items according to precise characteristics in order to create corpora for studies or exhibitions. It is a tool for interpretation and synthesis that affords a direct, individual or global vision of objects and avoids long manual sortings. Through the inventory of the mass and the control of the inflation of material as a result of contemporary excavations, rationalized storage is ensured in the repositories as well. Managing the quantity means preserving it in order to enhance its utilization. In the urgency of discoveries linked to rescue excavations, the inventory provides a stable framework. It ensures fundamental management of the material, which can be completed later. The computerized input of movable property takes place on-site, simultaneously with the excavation.

Legal framework and Swiss specificity

In view of the absence of centralized power in Switzerland (the federal state grants a certain autonomy to cantons), disparities result between the various cantonal archaeological services, according to the region of the country, the type of find, and the importance of deposits. In order to guarantee a certain consistency in the management of Swiss heritage, a federal decree, as from 1961, stipulated that the financing of archaeological excavations undertaken on the path of future motorways is the responsibility of the government.[2] On the other hand, responsibility for the conservation and publication of findings lies with the cantons where the excavations are located. The cantons become the owners of the objects (Tissot 1991). In agreement with the statutes of ICOM and the conditions for joining the Association of Swiss museums, Helvetian institutions must take into account the following criteria for the management of their collections: 'Collections have a recognized heritage value and are managed according to delineated criteria. An inventory exists (completed or in progress) of collections established according to scientific bases available to researchers. The quality and integrity of collections cannot be reduced by the sale of objects from these collections' (Bruelisauer 1998). The mission of the Museum of Archaeology is therefore to exhibit, identify, inventory, document, restore, place in reserve collections, and protect the archaeological as well as the archival material.

An attempt at shared management of cultural heritage in its entirety was developed in 1996 through the Database of Swiss Cultural Property. It was not, however, applied to the whole country. This system of cataloguing included property from a diversity of disciplines, such as archaeology, fine arts, history, ethnography, etc. This System for Museographic and Archaeological Inventory and Management (SIGMA), which uses Texto software, was developed at the Museum of Archaeology and History in Lausanne, in 1989.

Inventory and global management

In addition to the legal obligation to conduct inventories for museums, the prospect of the opening of Latenium[3] (Architecture Suisse 2002) and moving objects into new premises was one of the decisive factors in completing a new inventory system. In fact, it was urgent to prioritize registering all objects and lots intended for exhibition in the future museum. Finally, as from September 2001, the grouping together of the Museum, the Excavations Service and the University Institute of Prehistory, at Latenium, influenced the design and structure of the inventory. At Latenium, the desire to manage collectively the global yield of excavations, the collections of the museum and archives (reports, studies, etc.) triggered an in-depth reflection, led by Béat Arnold, a local archaeologist. The result is an approach jointly characterized by problems arising in the field and in collections. The structure of the inventory used thesauri shared by the department of excavations and the museum to take into account data from the field as well as typological and museographical information specific to objects. This synergy constitutes one of the specificities of Latenium's inventory. Using descriptive language which is sufficiently precise to describe the degree of finesse of an object and intelligible in a way that is applicable to all the material, the developed system establishes a bridge between the general level and that of the specialist. In order to guarantee maximum efficiency during recordings, which can be concise or detailed, the hierarchical structure does not exceed four degrees of precision within the headings.[4]

Since the 1970s, different systems of recording data, aimed at developing a concise, shared descriptive language, have been experimented with on the D-Base system for lacustrine excavations. The information was very difficult to use because it was distributed in a fixed manner throughout hundreds of notebooks. Ten years later the desire to structure archaeological data in order to make it available to other researchers prevailed. Experience derived from different databases for excavation sites during this period made it essential to create uniform and standardized systems of management. Thanks to the development of correlation tables, the present inventory was able to recover some of this earlier data. This new general database is therefore designed to control the different bases, from prospection to storage in repositories, including excavation, conservation-restoration, inventory, and study activities. Its objective is to optimize conditions of analysis, thanks to an operating system and maximum accessibility of data. It is an evolving documentary tool, developed with Access software. Meant to be used over the long term, it should benefit from current as well as future experiments. Its efficiency increases in relation to the quantity of information to be managed. This system of centralized management facilitates the consultation of data and enables the researcher to work on his/her own bases or from those of colleagues. Thanks to the development of a computerized network, each database is accessible, in reader format, for the collaborators of the Service and Museum of Archaeology (SMA) in Neuchâtel.

A common platform

The desire to manage vestiges comprehensively required the development of a thesaurus, shared by different departments, concerning the origins, material, eras, typologies, and types of sites. This shared platform facilitated a uniform grouping of information and a pathway for the identification of an artefact during the various stages of the operating chain. It is therefore possible to use the inventory number of the object to consult the different specific bases and find information related to the property. Was it the subject of a specialized study or a specific excavation? We then consult the base for specialists or the base for excavations. Some headings are specific to the inventory of the property and do not appear in the database for excavations such as the usual precautions to be taken during the handling of items or the names of collectors. On the other hand, data that is specific to excavations, such as stratigraphic relationships, do not feature in the object database.

A complete version of the thesauri exists, intended for the inventory of the museum, and an abridged version, intended for excavation sites. The latter contains terms and headings frequently used in the field. In fact, certain terms, like armour or a crossbow window are not very useful in current excavations! However, the complete version can always be activated, even in the field, if a specialist provides specific information concerning a subject or a typology, or during unusual discoveries.

A single general index

The mass and diversity of material facilitated the creation of a single computerized index. Access to information, through requests, is obtained through a single operation, because all the data are unified and centralized. Separate indexes according to period can create a dispersion of data and confusion for pieces existing during several eras or that are difficult to date accurately. Requests facilitate sortings, locating individual pieces or ensembles. The interest, and the advantage, of a single index enables diverse data concerning property to be integrated into one file. In the framework of a computerized network that links different departments, the single file facilitates the consultation and circulation of information. It also makes it easier to detect errors more directly in the recording of items and to complete or correct data in a uniform manner.

Maintaining specificities and a shared perspective for exploitation

In the case of the inventory, vocabulary specific to an individual researcher disappears in favour of a common syntax that everyone understands. Some thesauri – such as the origin, era, typology, material, technique, surface treatment, and type of clay for ceramics – are used by both museum departments and those of excavations. This standard core, which the user can draw on, facilitates consulting the general inventory base of the museum, and benefiting, for the same object, from precise field data by consulting the excavation base. The standard thesauri therefore can be read on two levels, maintaining uniformity in the syntax of fundamental headings. The specificities of departments are maintained (because the inventory of the museum contains specific headings, such as the names of collectors, as does the excavation database with stratigraphic data). The 'restrictive' aspect of standard thesauri is compensated by the accessibility of the system and the constitution of corpora for the purpose of analysis. These two levels of management create a shared perspective for the ensemble of archaeological documentation and, consequently, better scientific exploitation. It is an opportunity to bring several skills into contact with each other. By making data accessible, we stimulate and decompartmentalize different units. However, it is imperative that an object be named in the same way in the different databases, in order to benefit from comprehensive corpora.

Stages of development

Several stages were required for the development of the inventory system. First of all, it was necessary to evaluate the needs of collaborators, before anticipating possible scenarios dictated by the material (the structure, once established, authorizes developments, but not fundamental changes). Headings were created and grouped according to theme, with their respective levels of precision. The final phase consisted of recording, experimentally, a fixed ensemble of property, made up of different decor, shapes, dimensions, and descriptions, in order to verify that the system functioned correctly. This stage is essential for ensuring the pertinence and viability of the method. The detailed management of the first recordings of objects subsequently facilitated mastering larger ensembles, such as lots. The system increased in efficiency and introduced exchanges with other institutions and researchers. Computerized connections are intentionally rare at this stage, because conversion into a more efficient software, such as Oracle, can be envisaged later. Protective measures were developed to avoid duplications, notably for the heading of the inventory number, which is primordial, as it is the link with other bases.

The input form

In order to facilitate input and increase efficiency, the form for recording objects is intentionally very structured and straightforward. It contains headings in hierarchical order, from the general to the specific, in order to establish different degrees of precision. Some fundamental headings, like the inventory number, the description, origin, material, and general era, are mandatory. On the other hand, more specific headings, such as typology, decor, eras, and specific materials (from the 'third or fourth level') are only filled in if the information provided by the object, or the degree of knowledge by the person in charge of input, are sufficient. Different types of headings exist:

Scrolling list: Some thesauri, those with descriptions, materials, eras or techniques, scroll automatically in alphabetical order when they are activated. This system dictates the term to the user, guaranteeing the uniformity of syntax and anticipating input errors or the arbitrary addition of terms. The thesauri can be completed by the person in charge of their management.

Filter: Filters exist between some thesauri, notably those with descriptions, typologies, eras or material, which facilitate automatic sorting at a level of additional precision. For example, the selection of a term from the list of general periods, that is to say 'first level' (such as the Bronze Age) determines the related sub-periods (the 'second level') such as Ancient Bronze or Final Bronze, etc.

Combination list: This kind of list allows adding or specifying a term already present in the thesaurus. This is notably the case for descriptions of decors.

Automatic heading: Some headings have recurring contents that are listed 'by default', automatically. This is notably the case for the heading Copy/Fake (the 'original' term is listed with each new index). Whether a facsimile or a replica, the user scrolls the list and selects the appropriate term.

Field text: The 'field texts', like the commentary heading, are exclusively reserved for remarks that cannot be included under the normal headings.

Window: Windows open on to headings, notably concerning decors, dimensions, preserved items, acquisitions, and loans. The titles, on the buttons, are automatically underlined when the window contains information.

Requests: The ensemble 'Request and Print' is a research module for the consultation and printing of indexes. Requests are multiple and can contain an indefinite number of criteria. All the tags can be selected, for example, for a site or typology that is not from the Iron Age, or, as another example, all clear ceramics with a surface dating from the Roman era.

Single responsibility for management

The optimal ulterior exploitation of data is the result of careful and efficient recording. Each index acquires its real meaning only after it is inscribed quantitatively and in the long term. Such an approach also helps overcome the occasionally tedious nature of data input! The results of a request are only pertinent within the exhaustiveness of the recording, as similarities or differences between artefacts become distinguishable. In case of ambiguity between several terms, during the input, the person in charge makes a choice and decides to record all the items in the same way. However, objects often take on different denominations according to specialists or eras (occasionally there are as many authors as appellations!). When in doubt, it is preferable to choose a neutral term without interpretive nuance that will always be registered in the same way. If one alternatively registers, for example, the term 'torque' or 'necklace' to designate the same object, during requests, an erroneous count results, along with incomplete corpora. We should be aware of such ambiguities and make clear choices. In the case of an artefact whose description is later specified, it is possible globally to replace one term by another. This operation is only possible if a type of object has been recorded in a systematic way.

By using descriptive language that is sufficiently precise to account for the degree of finesse of an object and intelligible in a way that can be applied to all items, a bridge is established between requests and responses. Standardized syntax anticipates the pitfalls of individual language. This is why a system of standard data is much more complex to develop than an individual base. Supervising the management of inventory must be the job of a qualified and competent reference person who is responsible for additions, substitutions, even suppressions of terms in the thesauri while respecting the initial structure. He/she centralizes the data, manages those responsible for the data input, corrects and prints the files; all modifications are thus made by the same person thereby standardizing data and facilitating research (in particular when it is a question of recordings made by several people). If the file presents an anomaly or an ambiguity, returning to the object is necessary.

Cataloguing policy

The efficiency of recording items is intimately linked to the policy of cataloguing, which must be clearly defined in the long term. As one of the important aspects for the preservation of ensembles of vestiges, it is ultimately anticipated to record all items. This does not mean that it will be studied globally! In order to conduct consistent recordings, it is necessary to define in advance what is going to be inventoried, grouping the material by site, content, and era. The level of precision of the data input depends on the subsequent exploitation of the material. Precision can increase if the object is going to be published or exhibited (as was the case for the display case material), or reduced if it is to be stored in crates or repositories. In certain cases, treatment by lot allows the unity of ensembles that have not (yet) been analysed to be preserved. It will therefore be possible to recover original items that will ultimately be restored, inventoried in detail, and sketched.

In general and without differentiation, the person responsible for data input always fills in the headings with as much precision as possible. The recording is always done starting from the object that is the 'primary archive'. Information that results from records, excavation reports or labels accompanying the objects should also be mentioned. This does not, however, constitute the basic data because it is considered to be from 'secondary archives'. Standardized input can also ensure avoiding significant loss of time during the correction of indexes.

Evaluation and perspectives

As it is also called upon to become an archival document dependent on the evolution of archaeology, the computerized inventory is intended to have its own cycle of conservation, just as any other document. This link between the object and its documentation guarantees controlled evolution of the stages of the operating chain. The grid for analysis, according to the explicit parameters of the inventory, results from a rigorous approach whose structure meets the rigour of models and objectivity specific to physical sciences advocated by the New Archaeology in the English-speaking countries. This grid does preserve a degree of flexibility in the sense that it does not isolate the material in a restrictive yoke, but provides it with an opportunity for continual interpretation and new history. From this point of view, our approach is similar to the 'contextual archaeology' of Ian Hodder (1987), who gives meaning to vestiges, through establishing strict typologies and facilitating, among other things, a precise description of relationships of similarity or dissimilarity between artefacts.

Notes

1 The former Cantonal Museum of archaeology in Neuchâtel has become the Latenium and was inaugurated on 7 September 2001. It is the result of a synergy between museum, park, cantonal archaeology service, Institute of Pre-history attached to the University, laboratory of conservation-restoration and dendrochronology. The Latenium gets its name from the nearby site of Marin/La Tène, which is known for having given its name to the Second Iron Age. Constructed across from the lake, on the site of two villages built on piles, dating back respectively from 3800 and 1050 to 870 BC, the museum is surrounded by the archaeological park. The visitor therefore benefits from a continuity between exhibition halls, which mainly display objects of local heritage, and, outdoors, completely reconstituted structures (houses on piles, tumulus, Roman garden, etc.). Henceforth, the Latenium belongs to the history of the site; it received the Museum Prize from the Council of Europe in 2003. The repository open to visitors preserves more than 800,000 objects and concentrates on the presentation of typological ensembles of material, grouped according to era or culture. The permanent exhibition comprises 3,000 objects from this ensemble.
2 This ruling is equally applied to the financing of archaeological excavations carried out along railway routes.
3 The people of Neuchâtel, aware of the value of their heritage, voted to allocate funds for the construction of the museum and its museography.
4 As a comparison, The Museum of National Antiquities in Saint-Germain-en-Laye (France) uses a system that provides a level of extreme precision: the hierarchy within

the headings can range to seven degrees and there are multiple fields. On the other hand, the Department of Greek and Roman Antiquities at the Louvre uses a much more concise system. The precision of the tool thus varies considerably from one museum to another.

References

Architecture Suisse (2002) Laténium – Parc et musée d'archéologie, Hauterive/NE. *Architecture suisse*, 145(1): 1–4.

Bruelisauer, J. (1998) Der Verband der Museen der Schweiz. *Archäologie Suisse*, 21(2): 48–9.

Hodder, I. (1987) *The Archaeology of Contextual Meanings*. Cambridge: Cambridge University Press.

Société Suisse de Préhistoire et d'Archéologie (2002) *L'archéologie neuchâteloise revisitée*. Archéologie Suisse 25(2). Basle: Société Suisse de Préhistoire et d'Archéologie.

Tissot, N. (1991) *Protection juridique des vestiges archéologiques – Problèmes liés au droit des expropriations et de l'aménagement du territoire*. Neuchâtel: Éditions Ides et Calendes.

Part I, Section 4

Museum care, conservation, and restoration of archaeological objects

Chapter 8

Issues in practice
Conservation procedures

Elizabeth Pye

Introduction

In reaching a decision about the procedures to be used the conservator will have considered a range of possible options and drawn up a conservation proposal. Conservation choices depend on a range of factors, not just the condition of the object, thus there are no 'standard' approaches. Different options have different effects on the significance of the objects, and there are no clear dividing lines between various conservation procedures since some will have more than one effect. The effect will vary too, depending on the level of conservation applied. This chapter explores, in general terms, the range of possible options.

Conservation in practice

Conservation and change

Conservation processes are intended to change the object, or its environment, and to lead to the object's long-term survival by managing the rate of change. Conservation procedures are undertaken in order to maintain an acceptable state or to improve on an unacceptable state. Unfortunately some conservation actions may bring about further unintended reactions. Conservation, therefore, is not static but dynamic, and a single procedure cannot be assumed to have solved the problem of continuing change within the object; monitoring and further action will be needed in the future (e.g. Ward 1986; Plowden and Halahan 1987; Oddy 1992; Thompson 1992).

Some conservation procedures, such as 'cleaning', repairing and re-leading a decorated glass window are complex and lead to changes in the longevity, strength, and appearance of the object and in its material and conceptual significance. Some conservation procedures are minimal, such as providing better packaging, but nevertheless may slow deterioration. Most preventive and remedial procedures will prolong the lifespan of the object to a greater or lesser extent. Some will clarify the

Source: *Caring for the Past: Issues in Conservation for Archaeology and Museums*. London: James & James, 2007. pp. 121–148. © Taylor & Francis.

appearance and readability of the object (e.g. through reconstruction), some will strengthen and make objects safe to handle, and some, through revealing technological information or aesthetic detail, will help to establish a clearer understanding of the object and its significance. However, changes that may superficially improve the appearance of the object (it may look 'cleaner'), may have been brought about at the cost of removal of surface accretions (which may be protective or contain evidence) or at the cost of change to the internal structure (e.g. stress and microscopic damage to individual fibres when washing a textile).

Some superficial changes may be seen as improvements by some, but not by others. A consolidant or surface coating may not only strengthen or protect the underlying structure but intensify colour and so be seen by some as refreshing the look of an object, but by others as masking the appearance which is the result of change and deterioration. Attitudes vary. For example, the lacquer on scientific instruments may be renewed because it reinstates, the presumed original appearance (Brenni 1999) but a consolidant on a matt and powdery ethnographic paint could be considered unacceptable because it changes the appearance from matt and opaque to glossy and translucent, quite unlike its appearance 'as found' (Hansen et al. 1993).

Different approaches to conservation

Different adjectives have been used to qualify types of conservation and they can be divided into those that describe intent and those that describe the degree of interaction with the object. Thus investigative, preventive, and remedial conservation (as well as restoration) all express the aim of the process, whereas active, passive, and interventive conservation are normally taken to describe the way in which the conservator interacts with the object. Here, passive conservation is considered to involve changing the environment surrounding the object rather than doing anything directly to the object itself, but active and interventive conservation imply working directly on the object and probably changing it.

Preventive conservation has taken on more than one meaning. The term is used to describe the intention of preventing deterioration, but it is also often considered to be synonymous with what has been called passive conservation, involving modification and control of the environment alone. This ignores the fact that many treatments, such as neutralization of acids in paper, are applied directly to an object with the aim of preventing further change. One of the characteristics which has moved conservation from craft-restoration to a scientific discipline is the anticipation and management of future change. Thus, even if the initial intent of a treatment is to remedy past damage this should be done in such a way as to minimize the likelihood of future change, or it should be coupled with preventive measures. In an earlier chapter it was proposed that the activities involved in preventive conservation need clearer definition, and the terms 'preventive care' and 'preventive treatment' were suggested.

There has been an assumption that preventive measures are 'better' because they interfere less (or not at all) with the material significance (integrity) than interventive ones, but this is to assume firstly that preventive measures are limited to modifying the environment, and secondly that preventive measures make no change to significance. With a growing understanding of the meanings encompassed by or implied by significance, it becomes clear that it is not possible to state that preventive care has no effect on significance, nor that all interventive treatments automatically affect significance. It cannot be assumed that a procedure limited to changing the object's environment will not affect significance, nor that any work undertaken directly on an object will automatically change its significance. For example, if the changed environment involves a change of context (e.g. enclosing a state bed in a protective glass case in the setting of a historic house where all other furniture remains in the open room, or taking outdoor statuary from its garden setting into a sheltered display area), it can have a marked effect on conceptual significance. Some measures that undoubtedly prevent further deterioration (preventive treatments) at the same time can involve change to the object's significance (e.g. the removal of salts or soils which may be highly relevant to the burial history of the object, or to its use). By contrast, some other forms of preventive treatment, such as removal of superficial museum dust, or of recent mould spores, or even of some forms of current repair, may have minimal effect on significance.

When making choices of treatment, consideration of the degree to which different forms of conservation are likely to affect significance and use, i.e. consideration of the outcome of the procedure in terms of significance, is more helpful than the present, rather blurred, distinctions made between intent and degree of intervention. The examples given are, of course, debatable but the injunctions that conservators should preserve the integrity of objects and adopt minimum intervention as a guiding principle are intended to limit the possibilities of changing significance.

The continuum of conservation

The processes of conservation are not always distinct from one another in aim or effect (Brooks et al. 1994; Berducou 1996). Although conservators talk about apparently separate activities such as 'preventive conservation' or 'reconstruction', the processes can be seen as features of a continuum from initial investigation through to restoration, and many serve more than one purpose. The initial investigative phase, which may involve removing accretions from an excavated object, not only reveals material information (establishing the nature of the object) but may remove damaging materials (preventive treatment), and, if taken further, may restore the shape and something of the appearance (restoration). Repairing a broken ceramic or stitching a fragile textile to a support (remedial treatment) can also be seen to contribute to restoration. Removal of damaging salts from within porous ceramics and stone will prevent future damage, and it will also aid successful remedial treatment of the crumbling surface: unless the salts are removed it is unlikely that attempts to strengthen the object will be effective. Building a sympathetic internal support for a costume, normally considered an aspect of preventive care because the support will distribute the weight of the costume while it is on display, will also restore the shape of the costume so that the viewer can understand better what it would have looked like when worn.

The treatment of waterlogged wood is a good example. Keeping it wet in the field prevents collapse and distortion (preventive care); treatment with a polymer which bonds to the damaged cellulose prevents disintegration (preventive treatment) and at the same time remedies the effect of deterioration. After treatment, individual pieces of wood may be joined to reconstruct the shape of the object (remedial and restoration) and the object will be given continual preventive care (Pearson 1987).

Not only is there this continuum, or overlapping, of conservation processes but there is also the paradox that conservation can destroy. Thus removal of 'dirt', for example in washing a textile, can 'improve' the appearance (restoration) and minimize some forms of future damage, for example by removing acids or mould spores (preventive treatment). But looked at under a high-powered microscope there may be signs that the swelling of the fibres, which occurred during washing, has caused a permanent change (damage) (Cooke 1990). Consolidating a porous surface weakened by salts without either removing the salts or ensuring adequate penetration of the consolidant may cause damage to the surface and all the information it carries (Giusti 1999). Cleaning away accretions on a coin is undertaken to clarify the image and make the coin identifiable, but it also has the power (even inadvertently) to distort details, such as the mint mark, and so change the significance and archaeological value of the coin (Casey and Cronyn 1980).

Thus not only do deteriorating objects present multifaceted problems, but conservation actions will inevitably be variable in their intention and effects. Taken together, these factors require that conservators consider very carefully both the object itself and all the possible consequences of the proposed conservation actions (as far as it is possible to predict them).

Selection and levels of conservation

Early versions of some codes of practice enjoined conservators not to discriminate between objects, to give the same care to every object (Sease 1998), but it is not possible to conserve everything to the same level, and this is now recognized. Conservation can never be absolute and conservators apply different levels of conservation to different objects.

There are several reasons for different objects being given different levels of attention. The amount of assessment and conservation any one object is given is, of course, influenced by how significant (or how 'useful') it is perceived to be at the time. Major national monuments cannot be allowed to crumble because there would be a public outcry, so normally they are well maintained: in contrast, minor monuments may get inadequate attention. Changes in fashion and thus in significance may mean that hitherto disregarded classes of object or building may become the subject of conservation projects (and major objects or monuments may suffer from too many attempts to conserve them).

Archaeological material often needs elucidation in order to establish how informative (how useful) it is, so anything that looks potentially informative may be investigated further. Some materials are easier to conserve than others – for example, conservators have more effective means for conserving archaeological bronzes than archaeological iron, and bronzes are often more obviously interesting (perhaps decorated) than highly corroded and misshapen iron, so iron may get little attention. Some materials are very difficult to deal with, for instance deteriorating early plastic objects – other than permanent storage in a deep freezer, there is as yet no apparent way to retain their original characteristics (Reilly 1991; Fenn 1995).

There are examples of scales of treatment devised to match either condition or value of objects. This concept lies behind the UKIC Archaeology Section's proposal of five levels of conservation to deal with the enormous range of material coming from excavations (UKIC Archaeology Section 1982). A similar designation of specific levels of care for different categories or values of object was made during the Delta Plan (Ashley-Smith 1999; Talley 1999). Using this general approach, all museum objects, or monuments, should be given the basic care of assessment and preventive care or maintenance. Both objects and structures may be given some minimal cleaning in order to clarify their nature and condition. In some cases the condition, the context, the significance, or the proposed use of the object may dictate a more detailed approach involving more extensive investigation, remedial conservation, and possibly some restoration in order to prepare the object or structure for display. In other words, at one end of the spectrum there is preventive care and minimum remedial work, and at the other end there are 'the full works', including restoration.

Current limitations

At its best, conservation enhances the use and understanding of objects and structures, but it also has its limitations. Change is difficult to prevent and conservation cannot achieve stability for all objects and structures. Some materials are inherently unstable and deteriorate more readily than others (e.g. organics, including early plastics). For some materials there are apparently successful treatments (e.g. the use of corrosion inhibitors on excavated bronzes), while for others none has yet been developed. Many early treatments have proved to be less effective than was hoped (or have even proved to be damaging) and some treatments in current use are not yet proven.

Putting the conservation proposal into action

Doing nothing

In some cases the decision will be made to do nothing. One situation in which this decision may be taken arises when it is simply not practicable to conserve, other than possibly in the short term. This was the case with many of the medieval and Roman waterfront structures revealed along the bank of the river Thames in London. Building work would have destroyed the structures but constraints of space (both for treatment and, later, for storage and display) and of other resources including money and staff, meant that it was impossible to conserve in the long term. So emphasis was put on conserving *in situ* (by keeping wet while exposed) for long enough to gain as much information as possible from the structures. In other cases wooden structures may not be under threat from building work but in such poor condition that it would not be viable to do more than record and monitor (e.g. many timbers appearing in the intertidal zone along the edge of the Thames).

More frequently, the decision to do nothing may be taken because, other than maintaining adequate preventive care, nothing more is needed, or because other options might be seen to carry little benefit and too much risk. A particular situation in which no conservation treatment may be undertaken is when the conceptual significance of the material is such that it is considered inappropriate to do more than provide preventive care. The growing understanding of conceptual significance has changed the conservation approach to human remains, and to secret or sacred objects. An interesting example arose at the Canadian Conservation Institute over the proposed conservation of a rare and very deteriorated Mi'kmaq prayer book. Initially, a representative of the Mi'kmaq, who was helping the conservator, felt that it would be inappropriate to apply any remedial treatments because of the spiritual nature of the book. Eventually, the conservator flew to Newfoundland to explain possible conservation processes and consult the Mi'kmaq community, and it was decided to treat the book, which has now been returned to the community (Hanington 2000).

It is not only ethnographic material that may be left unconserved. Conceptual artists may prefer their works to be left alone, indeed many artists of different periods may have anticipated deterioration as part of the 'life' of their works 'with certain works, preservation is interference – interference with a process which has been dictated (or tacitly accepted) by the artist' (Fry R 1997: 56).

Change of use

There may be obvious reasons for changing the way in which an object is used, for example to minimize wear and tear caused by handling or over-visiting. Thus, one possible objective of changing use may be to safeguard the material integrity of an object or structure. Another objective may be to reinstate conceptual significance as when an object is cared for in traditional ways in a museum or is lent for use in ceremony (Clavir et al. 1986; Welsh et al. 1992; Clavir 1994; Simpson 1996; Paterson and Greenfield 1998; Peers 1999). Change of use also occurs when artefacts are returned to an indigenous community or when human remains are repatriated so that they can be reburied (Hubert 1989; Greenfield 1995; Coote 1998; Leggett 1999). Some changes of use are contentious. When 'Seahenge' (a Bronze Age timber circle in the intertidal zone at Holme next the Sea, in Norfolk, UK) was excavated and removed in order to preserve it, it ceased to be a feature of the local landscape, which appeared and disappeared with the tides and became a subject for scientific study. Its removal for analysis and conservation, and possibly for eventual display, transformed it into a 'museum' object and for some people, at least, this change of use robbed it of its conceptual significance (Miles 2000).

An example of an object with dual uses, as both museum object and ceremonial object, is the Lord Mayor's coach, which now spends most of its life on display in the Museum of London but leaves the museum to be used in procession on ceremonial occasions. Its use in ceremony requires that it is maintained in working order so that it can carry passengers, and be pulled by horses, while in the museum preventive care ensures that the whole remains in good condition.

Preventive conservation

Preventive care

Preventive care is now seen to be vital to the management of change and the long-term conservation of individual objects and collections. In any well-managed organization all objects will be given basic standards of preventive care, which means ensuring that they are handled safely, that stored material is kept in well-regulated and clean areas with appropriate environmental control, and that objects on display are as far as possible protected from exposure to touching, excessive light levels, and so on. Any object that is given some form of preventive or remedial treatment will also be given long-term preventive care. Thus, preventive care should be applied to *all* objects that are held in a museum (and to historic monuments).

This form of care involves appropriate control of all the external factors that affect type and rate of change: light, temperature, relative humidity, and pollutants (MGC 1992 onwards; Dollery 1994; Erhardt and Mecklenburg 1994; *Museum Practice* 1996 onwards). It also involves minimizing stress, which might otherwise be caused by inadequate support or vibration, or by poor handling (Bradley 1990; Rose and de Torres 1992; Robinson and Pardoe 2000). Application of preventive care, without remedial treatment, involves accepting the current state of an object, and presupposes that the conservator is confident that changes to packaging, handling or environment alone will ensure reasonable future stability. The benefits of preventive and remedial treatments will be maintained through follow-up preventive care (La Rocca and Nardi 1994).

LOCAL ENVIRONMENT

Preventive care in a museum or historic house should take place within a framework of environmental management for the building as a whole, but preventive care of individual objects (or groups of objects) may involve 'local' management, e.g. through controlling the environment in specific parts of a building, or in individual storage boxes. Achieving better conditions involves assessing the state of the objects or collections, identifying causes of deterioration, then deciding on an appropriate environment and preventive care regime. Adjustment may mean modifying the environment or changing policies on handling or other aspects of use. It may mean moving an object from one environment to another, e.g. from outdoor to indoor, or from open display to display in a showcase. For example, some medieval stone sculptures at Lincoln Cathedral were removed from the exterior of the building and replaced by replicas, in order to protect what remains of the original carvings

(Price 2000). Excavated wooden structures, such as the Rose Theatre (the remains of Shakespeare's theatre in London) or waterlogged boats, have been reburied in order to recreate an environment that will prevent further deterioration (Wainwright 1989; Fry M F 1996).

Preventive treatment

Preventive treatment was defined earlier as treatment intended to prevent future change while not necessarily remedying past damage, so less intrusive than applying the full range of remedial treatment. The clearest examples of preventive treatment involve removal of materials that are causing ongoing deterioration (or may cause future deterioration), including processes, such as elimination of insect pests through heating or freezing, or elimination of soluble salts which, if left, may cause disintegration of the object. Some 'cleaning' processes can be seen as preventive in that removal of dust and dirt may not only 'improve' the appearance of an object but at the same time remove sources of future deterioration such as mould spores. Preventive treatments might also include removal of (recent) metal dowels if they are corroding and disrupting the structure of the object (whereas original metal dowels, as found in classical statuary, would normally be retained because of their significance, and some other means would be found for controlling corrosion).

A minimal repair may play an important part in preventing further deterioration, such as securing loose tesserae at the edge of a mosaic before greater loss occurs, or securing paint flakes before they become detached. Applying a support to a weak and fragile object, such as a painting or textile, is part remedial and part preventive (Durham 1995; Morgan and Cruikshank 1995). Another form of preventive treatment involves removing stresses. For example, a textile or mat with very hard creases or folds resulting from poor storage may be humidified to allow the fibres to relax and the creases to be removed, so preventing breakage of fibres along the line of stress. Regular maintenance of working machinery could be considered to be preventive treatment. 'It is recognized that preventive maintenance of equipment, such as cleaning and lubrication, can prolong utility and avoid costly repairs' (Williams 1997: 198).

There is one situation where changing the *structure* of an object could be described both as a preventive measure and a way of enhancing use. This is the case of firing unfired clay cuneiform writing tablets, which are badly affected by damaging salts. The salts cannot be soaked out of the tablets in the normal way because the water would soften the clay and cause the tablets to disintegrate. Firing permanently changes the clay structure but makes the tablets resistant to water and thus allows removal of the salts. This is an example of a treatment that would not normally be considered but which makes it possible to handle the tablets and read the texts. It is worth noting that it was Rathgen who first devised this treatment more than a century ago, and that it is still in use today (Organ 1961).

EXCAVATION AND PREVENTIVE TREATMENT

During excavation, objects are exposed to an abrupt change in environment (e.g. an object in damp soil is exposed to sunlight and drying winds; or an object in an oxygen-free deposit is exposed to air) and, at the same time, the soil and adjacent objects, which have provided physical support in the ground, are removed, leaving weak objects very vulnerable. Thus, the first conservation process that an archaeological object may undergo is excavation using conservation procedures intended to prevent unnecessary collapse or disintegration.

Many objects are, of course, in reasonably robust state and once partially revealed can be exposed further, rapidly assessed and removed safely from the surrounding soil. However, exposure of an object may reveal that it is already very fragile, or likely to deteriorate rapidly (e.g. waterlogged wood). Before anything more can be done it may need emergency treatment. This is a form of 'first aid' conservation and may involve the use of temporary adhesives (to hold a crumbling ceramic together), or special protective or storage conditions (e.g. keeping waterlogged organic materials properly wet) (Watkinson and Neal 1998).

Some objects are so complex, fragmentary or fragile that they cannot be removed without providing additional protection during the process of excavation. In this case they may be given exterior support (e.g. bandaging or polyurethane foam) in order to hold the whole together while it is released from the ground. Lifting in a block maintains the three-dimensional relationship between different objects in an assemblage and enables conservators to excavate the block and record relationships in the conservation laboratory An alternative approach with structures, such as kilns or mosaics, is to partially dismantle and remove them in well-documented and manageable pieces (Scase 1987; Payton 1992; Watkinson and Neal 1998). Some of these processes are feats of engineering such as the release of the mass of lime-plaster figures from the site of 'Ain Ghazal in Jordan (Tubb and Grissom 1995) or the dramatic lifting of the *Mary Rose* from the seabed in the UK (Rule 1982).

The general principle is that the shock of uncovering and moving the object should be minimized as far as possible by using appropriate materials and techniques, and that conservation treatments should follow. The exposure of the object may set up a succession of deterioration processes leading to loss of information, and possibly loss of the object, unless assessment and conservation go ahead as soon as possible. An important issue is that, as excavation is potentially damaging, it is unethical to remove objects from an unthreatened site unless provision for conservation (and use) is assured (though it may, of course, be necessary to 'save' an object or structure during a rescue or salvage excavation).

Where it is inevitable that building development will damage or destroy important remains, means are sought to minimize the impact, e.g. through modification of the building design to leave most of the remains accessible, or through excavation and removal for study and display. The responsibility for mitigation of the impact of development on the site and its contents is increasingly placed on the developer. In the UK, this is now built into the development planning process (UK Department of the Environment Planning Policy Guidance 16: Archaeology and Planning, 'PPG16').

Is preventive conservation better than remedial conservation?

Codes of practice (e.g. AIC 1996) stress the importance of preventive conservation.

> The conservation professional should recognize the critical importance of preventive conservation as the most effective means of promoting the long-term preservation of cultural property.
> (AIC 1996: 29)

> Preventive conservation is more than a physical activity. It is consistent with philosophies and practices that are basic to ethical standards endorsed by the museum community.
> (Williams 1997: 199)

The implication in both these quotes is that preventive conservation is better than any other approach to conservation. While not disagreeing with the view that preventive conservation is crucial to the preservation of museum collections, it is important to examine whether preventive conservation is always 'better'.

If preventive conservation is taken to mean procedures that do not involve direct interaction with objects (what has been called earlier 'preventive care'), there are some clear advantages because the procedures used should not change the material significance of the object, thus it can be said to satisfy the criterion of minimum intervention. In terms of efficiency of managing change, preventive care is efficient *only* if objects have been properly assessed and given an appropriate environment, and it remains efficient only if the environment is monitored, and modified if necessary. Assessment should have revealed whether an object requires some direct treatment before it can be stabilized in an appropriate environment. Only if this form of preventive conservation is efficient will it safeguard the significance of the object.

Preventive care can be said to be better because it is assumed to be cost-effective, in that it should obviate the need to remedy the effects of deterioration on individual objects (Staniforth 1990; Keene 1996). Using this approach to conservation it is possible to minimize change in whole collections rather than deal with objects individually. It should remain cost-effective provided it is effectively monitored, but if it is not monitored and the environment fails (allowing a major problem to arise such as an insect infestation or an outbreak of corrosion on metal artefacts), large-scale and expensive remedial measures may be needed. Monitoring the environmental conditions, e.g. light levels and relative humidity levels, does not require specialist conservation expertise, but monitoring the effects of the environment, and proposing modifications, does.

It can be said that limiting conservation to both preventive care and preventive treatments is 'better' than undertaking remedial treatments, since even applying preventive treatments is less intrusive and less expensive than also applying remedial measures (so, for example, treatment of excavated ceramic can be limited to removing potentially harmful salts rather than also rejoining the sherds in order to remedy the damage caused by breakage or crushing). Preventive care does not make objects readily accessible as it is at its most effective in well-monitored storage areas where it is possible to exclude light and dust, and buffer against vibration and humidity changes with suitable packaging, but in that environment material is neither visible nor easily accessible.

Prevention alone may not render an object useful either to the public or to specialists, indeed it may be thought to 'sterilize' it. If the intention of conservation is to enable objects to be interpreted and used (thus aiding access to them), then it is almost certain that some remedial treatments will be needed. The point of elucidating the significance of an object is to make it available for study, or teaching, or for demonstration or display, but preventive conservation cannot necessarily do this since it normally results in maintenance of current use-value. This is in contrast to remedial conservation, which should result in enhancement of use-value. In many cases remedial and restoration skills are vital tools for understanding objects and aiding interpretation, as in the example of excavating a mass of objects lifted in a soil block to reveal the fragile remains of a trinket box and its contents. Thus, although preventive measures are undoubtedly important from both the ethical and the practical points of view, the possibilities of gaining information and of using objects would be limited without remedial and restoration measures.

Assessment of excavated archaeological objects (particularly recently excavated ones) in terms of condition and potential for providing information is often impossible to do without investigative work on the object itself. This may be limited to discovering what kind of object is beneath an encrustation, and the object may be stored thereafter in a controlled environment, but investigative skills will be required to reveal significance. When dealing with existing collections, removal of old repairs or restorations, which may be damaging the material or object, or distorting its conceptual significance, will also require remedial conservation.

Preventive care has the advantages that it should minimize material change and can be used as a tool for maintaining condition in whole groups of objects. In these senses it presents significant advantages over labour-intensive remedial treatments applied to individual objects. However, there is a distinct danger that many museum managers will assume that environmental management is all that is needed to keep collections in good condition, and that monitoring by conservators is not needed. In fact, many problems cannot simply be solved by modifying the environment, and the skills of the experienced practical conservator are still essential, especially when the condition of collections may be taken to be an indicator of performance in preservation of collections (DCMS 2000). Experienced conservators are needed to modify and monitor the environment, and to monitor the condition of the displayed and stored objects, since if control mechanisms fail and the failure goes undetected, lasting damage may be done to collections.

In fact management of the environment, far from being the passive business implied by the term 'passive conservation', is a dynamic activity since the systems of control require to be checked regularly to ensure appropriate conditions are achieved and maintained (Sandwith and Stainton 1991; MGC 1992 onwards; *Museum Practice* 1996 onwards; Pinniger and Winsor 1998). However, the increasing demands for access, new displays, and greater communication with the public mean that it is difficult for conservators also to keep up an effective programme of monitoring and care of material in permanent storage.

Remedial conservation

Some problems of poor condition or illegibility can be alleviated by applying remedial treatment. Broadly, remedial treatments can be divided into those that involve removing materials from the object (because they may be obscuring shape or surface detail), those that involve adding materials such as adhesives (to strengthen a weakened structure, or to reconstruct a broken object, or to replace [compensate for] losses) and others which may involve either modifying the shape, e.g. where an object has been crushed, or changing the chemistry to produce a more stable material. In each case the object will be changed, so there should be a valid reason for undertaking the treatment; remedial conservation should not be undertaken simply because it is possible. It is also important to remember that any treatment, which makes a visible change to an object, is interpretative and affected by the views of the conservator:

> despite the trend of minimalism, interventions of some sort are often inevitable and usually, by implication, involve a statement, realised on the object through the actual treatment.
>
> (van de Wetering 1996: 197)

Removing materials

Many objects and structures have accumulations of materials on part or all of the surface such as dust and oily deposits. These accretions or changes alter the colour and texture of the surface and may obscure surface features and details of decoration or design. Some of these changes are seen as the inevitable and desirable indications of age and use (patina). However, they may make it difficult to interpret the object (in the case of highly encrusted excavated objects) or to assess and understand the condition of an object or structure, and, worse, some accretions may consist of materials that are also involved in active deterioration processes.

Some of the accretions will be foreign to the object (soil on the surface of excavated objects, dust on the surface of museum objects) but some will have been formed as a result of the reaction between the object and the environment (corrosion on metal, changes to the surface of glass). Still others will be a mixture of intrinsic and extrinsic accretions (corrosion on metals incorporating soil and plant material) and many accretions will be indicative of the history or use of an object (bloodstains on a military uniform, carbon on a cooking pot, textiles trapped in corrosion products on a brooch). Thus, not only should some accretions not be removed, but removal should be approached with caution because it makes a permanent change and can affect all aspects of significance and use. Just like excavation, removal of accretions can reveal one form of evidence while destroying another, and it can change the overall appearance of an object very considerably. It is difficult to ensure that only damaging materials are removed; for example washing textiles may remove adhering dirt, mould spores and acid deterioration products, but it may also remove dyes and stains or other deposits that provide evidence of manufacture and use (Brooks et al. 1996; Eastop and Brooks 1996). Because of the evidence contained in accretions some conservators prefer to undertake partial removal only, for example to reveal part of the underlying surface on a metal object, but this may not always be the best way to ensure long-term stability. The skill of the conservator lies in detailed examination of the object and accretions, careful choice, and execution of removal technique and knowing where to stop in order to safeguard the integrity of the object.

'CLEANING'

Removal of materials from an object is often described as cleaning. This is an unfortunate term since it makes the many different actions, which can be referred to as 'cleaning', sound like one simple and innocuous procedure. It is also unfortunate because it has connotations of purity and of achieving an object unsullied by 'dirt', when in reality conservators and other stakeholders aim to retain informative accretions. Use of this term may also encourage non-specialists to see it as a procedure anyone can undertake. The procedures that involve removal of obscuring or damaging materials are some of the most difficult to control and the results can be highly controversial. In fact, 'cleaning' covers a range of activities from the scientific investigation of archaeological objects to the aesthetic exercise of elucidating a painting. Because the state of the object beneath the stains, concretions, or earlier restoration is difficult to establish, even with sophisticated examination techniques, and because objects react in different ways to conservation treatments, removal of materials is always a 'new' experience and may produce unexpected results. Conservators have to make choices during these processes, thus the activity is subjective and relies on their interpretation of the object.

REMOVAL OF MATERIALS FROM MUSEUM OBJECTS

Removal of materials from museum artefacts is not necessarily undertaken in order to make them look 'clean' but to clarify significance. It can have a number of different effects so the reasons for the procedure may be varied. Many procedures are undertaken to remove deposits or stains, which prevent appreciation of the colour, gloss, or texture of the underlying surface. Some may be undertaken to locate the surface, and clarify its topography, or to clarify condition by revealing cracks, breaks, or earlier repairs. Some, particularly washing techniques, remove contaminants so may prevent further deterioration, and they may also remove stresses by enabling creases or folds to be eased out.

Since the significance of many museum objects depends (partly) on their being old, 'cleaning' involves achieving a balance between clarification of surface features and retention of the signs of age.

> An ideal restoration should not at first glance be evident. The work should appear in good order, legible in all its parts, but showing also its age. A

> balanced and careful cleaning has the fundamental purpose of achieving this.
>
> (Schleicher 1997: 152)

Achieving this balance is difficult, and removal procedures are problematic because they make irreversible changes to the object. Although the intention is to regain something of an earlier appearance so as to clarify the meaning of the object, procedures can remove not just the signs of age but evidence that may aid present or future interpretation. For example, at the root of some of the controversies over the 'cleaning' of paintings is the knowledge that subtle shading or gradation of colour consisting of thin paint layers or transparent coloured glazes can be removed during the process (Hedley 1990). It may also result in the removal of materials that have not been detected, either because they have not been looked for, or because there is no means yet of revealing their presence. This problem is particularly likely to occur when dealing with archaeological material where evidence, such as lice on a comb or blood on stone tools, are difficult to detect and could easily disappear while removing other materials (Fell 1996; Wilson et al. 1996).

Although 'cleaning' may result in clarification of colour because overlying veils of dirt or salts have been removed, it is important to distinguish between this situation and colour change, which is inherent to the object. Fading of pigments in paintings or natural history specimens, darkening of some woods in furniture, or yellowing of paper cannot normally be improved. Taking removal of stains or accretions too far can result in too bright an object and loss of the 'magic' of age; this can be particularly problematic on a composite object since the result may be that some components appear brighter than others and so affect the whole balance, or accentuate differences in condition.

Inadequate knowledge of the materials and technique of the object, or of the effects of deterioration, can lead to poor choice of removal method. This was the case with the thirteenth-century Norwegian Haug crucifix, which was mistakenly assumed to be painted in egg tempera when in fact the medium was oil. Removal of later overpainting, rather than leaving the original paint unaffected, caused devastating damage (Kollandsrud 1997). This can be compared with the loss of information caused by indiscriminate electrolytic or electrochemical treatment of archaeological metalwork (commonly practised in the first half of the twentieth century), which stripped off all corrosion and much surface detail. In this case the damage was caused by the failure to appreciate that much of the surface information lay within the corrosion layers. Much recent research into 'cleaning' procedures concerns the development of processes (such as laser cleaning, or the use of gels), which enable the conservator to work cautiously by removing one layer of 'dirt' at a time, and limiting the effects of the treatment on the underlying object (Mills and Smith 1990; Cooper 1998). Finally, it is important for curator and conservator to realize the extent to which fashion dictates appreciation of objects and thus their conservation and restoration. Larson's discussion of the early twentieth-century removal of what was presumably original polychromy on Renaissance terracotta busts (to leave a bare terracotta surface) is particularly instructive (Larson 1997; Larson 1990).

All these disadvantages strengthen the argument for a cautious approach to removal of dirt or accretions, and for partial treatment where this is appropriate. However, provided the conservator has good understanding of the object, and provided the process is skilfully and carefully undertaken, it can have undoubted advantages. Removal of yellowing and dirty varnish reveals colour and detail in paintings, removal of corrosion on excavated metal objects reveals ornament and toolmarks, all of which would otherwise remain invisible and unappreciated. Hunter and Foley discussed the complexities of dealing with the corroded enamelwork of the Anglo-Saxon Lincoln hanging bowl. Their objective was to reveal the original colour of the red enamel, as well as other technological details; they left small areas of corrosion in order to preserve surface evidence for future re-examination but decided that 'when considering a display object of this stature it was important to make accessible to the public and specialists alike the brilliancy and fine detail of the original enamel work' (Hunter and Foley 1984: 18).

Although 'cleaning' has the potential to damage it is one way of understanding objects, just as excavation is one way of understanding a site. If obscuring or damaging materials were never removed many objects would have little apparent significance or use. It is becoming more possible to interpret some objects using non-interventive examination techniques such as X-radiography (just as it is becoming possible to interpret archaeological sites using different types of non-interventive survey), but to detect details and phases of construction, effects of use and modification, as well as to expose the extraordinary range of technological and aesthetic achievements of past peoples, some intervention remains necessary. Thus, 'cleaning' is one possible way of making some aspects of the past visible.

REMOVING MATERIALS FROM ARCHAEOLOGICAL OBJECTS: CONCEPTUAL ISSUES

Conservators know that many of their treatments change the appearance of objects. Should consideration of the maker's or user's intent affect what archaeological conservators do? This has not been considered often enough although a recent conference in France opened up discussion (ARAAFU 1996).

> When nineteenth- and twentieth-century works are conserved, our views are focused not so much on the passage of time but on the ideas and techniques which the artist used to create the work originally. The artist's original intent is rarely mentioned when conserving ancient works.
> (Heuman 1997: 121)

In fact, the consideration of artist's intent is always problematic because it is impossible to know the intent of a long-dead artist, and changes in the object have almost always changed the appearance. This point was made by Hedley: 'in paintings which have undergone significant changes, we cannot any longer have the artist's original intention' (Hedley 1990: 9). However, the fact that it is impossible to envisage the intent of the makers and users of archaeological objects does not mean that their possible expectations should not be considered.

This question of maker's intent arises, for example, over the role of colour in ancient artefacts. Some deep red glass becomes green because of the effects of burial on the copper salts, which impart colour to the glass. The question then arises whether to retain the green appearance or to reveal the intended red colour, even though this means removal of some of the original glass surface, albeit now altered (Smith 1999). Ancient bronze objects (e.g. brooches, small figures, tools) may have been intended when in use to be either bright (polished) or dark with a 'tarnish' corrosion layer. The makers would have been familiar with the eventual formation of green corrosion in a neglected or weathered object, but they would probably not have expected the objects to look liver-red or part red and part green (sometimes spotted), which is the effect that can result when conservators remove overlying corrosion to reveal surface features such as engraved decoration. Many archaeological conservators will say that colour is not as important as surface detail: 'we look for an epidermis that is on occasion admirably conserved under a crust of mineral products. Colour itself means nothing' (France-Lanord 1996: 247). But should considerations of colour be sacrificed to reveal surface characteristics (which could in many cases be detected with X-radiography)?

Different standards of 'cleaning' clearly produce different visual and conceptual effects. To consideration of maker's intent must be added the conceptual, or aesthetic value for today's audience, of corrosion ('patina') resulting from burial. It would not be surprising if museum visitors assumed that most excavated copper-alloy (bronze) utensils were green when in use, since they are commonly displayed with a green corrosion layer, so is this misleading? For some people, however, the patina not only indicates the history of the object but may embody additional aesthetic significance. Thus, conservators should consider the effects of removal or retention of accretions on the possible interpretations of the historic evidence, as well as on the appreciation of the object for its aesthetic qualities and its age-value.

In fact, there are inconsistencies in visual presentation of corroded ancient metals. Where the condition allows, silver is frequently polished to provide a brilliant shine, but bronze, even when it is in a condition that would allow it, is not. Highly polished silver may lose any signs of history and age, as was apparent at the 1989 British Museum exhibition entitled 'The Work of Angels', in which a range of Celtic metalwork from several different museums, each with its own approach to 'cleaning' (or not 'cleaning') its objects, was exhibited together. Some of the highly polished silver looked as if it could have been made yesterday, and this is apparent in the photographs in the catalogue (Young 1989). Polishing silver may be imposing today's values, as little is known about the appearance of silver during its original use, though it has been proposed that, during classical times, not only was silver allowed to acquire a smooth black stable tarnished surface but that red and black figure ware are representations (skeuomorphs) of gold and silver vessels (Vickers 1995). There are no clear answers here for the curator and archaeological conservator, but these issues should be considered and discussed.

Adding materials

Another approach to prolonging the use of an object is to add materials to strengthen a weakened structure, or to join dissociated fragments or to replace missing features. The issue here is that, although repair and replacement are intended to enhance conceptual significance, adding materials may make just as permanent a change to the material significance as removing materials. A number of different materials may be added, such as corrosion inhibitors, protective coatings, adhesives, or consolidants.

CONSOLIDANTS

Some materials may be seriously weakened by the effects of loss of a component material, e.g. loss of cementing material in stones. To maintain or regain structural coherence it may be necessary to introduce a material (a consolidant) that will penetrate into the weakened structure and strengthen it. This procedure is used only if absolutely necessary as it is never possible to remove more than a very small proportion of the consolidant, in other words consolidation makes a permanent change to the structure of the material.

Introducing a consolidant can be seen to be partly preventive in that it is intended to safeguard the object against future disintegration, but it can also be seen to be remedial in that it is countering the damage which has already taken place. A good example is the treatment of waterlogged wood, which has lost much of the cellulose that strengthens the cell walls. Introducing a material that bonds to the remaining cellulose and fills the voids in the degraded cell-structure, while at the same time allowing water to evaporate from the wood, results in an artefact which can be handled and displayed (Pearson 1987). The extraordinary 9000-year-old lime-plaster statues from 'Ain Ghazal in Jordan provide another example of severely weakened objects, which could not be studied or appreciated without remedial treatment. They were lifted as a cemented and friable mass and required consolidation in order to separate and reconstruct them. Without this treatment it would have been impossible to study them in any detail, or to discover how they were made (Tubb and Grissom 1995).

REPAIR AND RECONSTRUCTION

Reconstruction contributes to revealing both historical and archaeological evidence and reinstating conceptual significance since the reconstructed whole provides information on size, shape, and possibly on original use. Repair or reconstruction may also play an important role in stabilizing an object or structure. A ceramic or glass vessel in fragments may be illegible, and the individual sherds vulnerable to damage if they are not well packaged. Reconstruction can make vessels comprehensible for display (but specialists may prefer to examine sherds in order to see the inside as well as the outside).

The normal method used is to join fragments with an adhesive. Where necessary, for strength, joins are sometimes supported by the insertion of dowels (which involves drilling into the original material, thus involving loss of substrate and possible damage to the object). Repair can also involve filling or bridging gaps in order to strengthen reconstructed areas, for example when parts of an object, such as a ceramic vessel, are missing. Even though the intention here is to strengthen, filling any gap has the effect of partially completing the shape and so compensating for losses.

In some cases original structural material is so weakened that it is removed and replaced rather than strengthened. This is the approach often used in buildings where individual components, such as beams, must continue to bear loads (and in such cases an insect-eaten wooden beam might be replaced rather than consolidated). Similarly, in order to maintain a weatherproof outer surface, deteriorating exterior stonework may be replaced at intervals as part of a normal maintenance programme on an ancient building.

MODERN ADHESIVES

The use of natural adhesives, such as bone glue, has a long history, but at about the same time that conservation was evolving as a recognizable discipline (in the 1930s), modem synthetic polymers (plastics) were being developed. When these came onto the market in the form of adhesives they appeared to offer significant advantages because they were more versatile and less visible, when applied to objects, than traditional materials. However, the subsequent discovery that many of these adhesives had poor long-term properties and that many are difficult to remove has led to a much more cautious approach to their use (e.g. Sease 1981; Hanna 1990).

A significant problem for conservators is the fact that modem adhesives are formulated for industrial applications, which seldom match conservation requirements. On the other hand, it is an advantage that there are many available adhesives and conservators can test and select from a wide range (although there are limitations to the reliability of short-term testing). Conservators look for an adhesive that is weaker than the substrate (the object) so that the adhesive fails rather than causing damage to the object. They also look for compatibility with other factors such as the flexibility of an object (e.g. plant fibre in basketry) or the climate in which the adhesive is used (some adhesives fail in high temperatures). The acknowledged instability of many modern adhesives remains a disadvantage and research into adhesives for conservation is now going in two directions. One is to re-evaluate natural adhesives, such as starch pastes, since their long-term behaviour is at least well known (Cruickshank and Tinker 1995). The other is to continue the search for modern adhesives with better long-term stability.

The issue of reversibility is particularly relevant to added materials such as adhesives. Although it is not possible to reverse the process of adding an adhesive, most conservators wish to apply only those materials that they expect to be at least partially removable at a future date, so that permanent material changes can be minimized. This was broadly the intention of the principle of reversibility when it was first proposed. However, adhesives often prove difficult to remove because they have become firmly bonded to the object, or have changed with age and can no longer be dissolved, and even when it is possible to remove enough of an adhesive to separate old joins, traces will almost certainly remain. Conservators may choose to use two different adhesives at different positions on a join not only to improve bonding but to aid future separation.

Reversibility is also sometimes mentioned in relation to consolidants, for example, polyethylene glycol, the polymer used to consolidate and strengthen waterlogged wood, appears to remain water-soluble in laboratory conditions, and thus theoretically it could be removed from treated wood. However, attempting to remove a consolidant from any weakened object would put the object at great risk, thus treatments of this kind are considered to be permanent. In some cases it is possible to keep the added consolidant to a minimum in order to satisfy the principle of minimum intervention. This was the approach used by Daintith (1995) when consolidating powdering pigments on the surface of ethnographic pottery from Papua New Guinea, because it was known that the pottery would be handled only rarely.

ADDING MATERIALS: COMPENSATING FOR LOSSES

Loss of parts of objects affects conceptual significance, particularly when the loss is great enough to distort the appearance or image. Losses can also be important evidence of history as, for example, the jagged holes in the stonework of buildings such as the Victoria and Albert Museum in London, which are left as a record of war damage (Ashley-Smith 1999). The intention of completing missing areas and reconstructing missing features (sometimes known as loss-compensation) is to regain an approximation of the original appearance (or function, in the case of replacing moving parts in a working object). This completion may have no effect on the long-term conservation of the object in that it is not necessarily intended to manage change.

Issues arise over the choice of materials used to complete missing features. Some conservators argue that as far as possible the same materials should be used (stone with stone, leather with leather) because only in this way can it be ensured that both original and added materials react in the same way to environmental changes (e.g. organic materials expanding and contracting at the same rate) thus safeguarding material integrity. They may also argue that this is the only way to achieve a sympathetic appearance. Other conservators argue that missing parts should be completed in different materials because only in this way will it be possible to distinguish the added from the original, and only in this way will it be possible to avoid compromising material significance. Most archaeological conservators use different materials to complete missing areas, but these materials are chosen to be compatible with the behaviour of the original. Gap-filling materials, such as micro-balloons mixed with a polymer, or paper-pulp, have been designed to put minimal stress on a fragile original (Barclay and Mathias 1989; Podany et al. 1995). Japanese papers are frequently used for their strength and compatibility to repair and support other organic materials such as barkcloth, basketwork and even some textiles (Wills 1995).

In situations where the object is intended to continue its original function (e.g. a working object such as a clock with moving parts, or a building which must be structurally safe, or a boat which continues to be used in the water) the same or closely similar materials are normally used in replacing lost or damaged features. In this situation the question arises as to whether original or modern working methods should be used since each will provide a different surface finish and appearance. For example, should a replacement wooden beam be hand sawn or machine sawn?

Completion of missing areas or features and colouring and texturing the added materials to 'match' the original, is intended to regain conceptual significance and is one of the activities that contributes to restoration. It will not return an object to its original state because use, deterioration, and earlier conservation will have changed it, but it is possible to regain some of the superficial visual characteristics.

Changing composition

Some conservation treatments make a change to the composition and structure of materials present in artefacts, either to produce a more stable structure, less susceptible to change, or to regain something of the original appearance. Examples include retanning disintegrating vegetable tanned leather with a modern tanning agent (Calnan 1992; Wills et al. 1992), or treating deteriorating building stone or wall paintings to convert soluble calcium sulphate into insoluble barium sulphate (Giusti 1999). In each case the change in chemistry is intended to induce stability (the latter method is analogous to treating human teeth with fluoride). Chemical treatment to convert blackened white lead pigments to a different but more stable white form, or refiring blackened lead-glazed ceramics, are examples of regaining legibility (Tennent et al. 1996; Daniels 1999).

Understandably, conservators are reluctant to use such treatments because of the loss of material evidence. However, the objective is to regain conceptual significance, thus to retain the use of the object. Some objects, which are deteriorating very rapidly, may simply not survive without this kind of intervention, while others may lose much of their meaning unless they are treated. Detailed documentation is intended to ensure that the changes made to the object are recorded and material significance is not misinterpreted in the future. Even though apparently effective, the long-term effects of some of these treatments (e.g. retanning) have still to be fully evaluated.

Changing shape

Many objects have been crushed or distorted during burial, or use, or through poor storage. In some cases (e.g. a crushed ceramic) it is possible to reconstruct the three-dimensional shape from the fragments, but a misshapen metal object or a squashed basket may need to be reshaped if its original form is to be understood. There are three reasons for caution: firstly, some objects may have been crushed as part of original use (e.g. ritual breakage of weapons, or deliberate folds in a garment); secondly, the reshaping procedures may affect internal structure; thirdly, reshaping is interpretative because the aim of the treatment is to induce a temporary malleable or flexible state in the object, which allows the conservator to manipulate it into a semblance of the supposed original shape. To these reservations may be added the fact that even the later crushing caused by burial may be considered to be part of the history of the object.

Most controversial is reshaping metals because in many cases some heating is needed, which changes metallographic structure. Less contentious is reshaping organic materials (paper, textiles, baskets), but exposing them to moisture to render them flexible almost certainly induces some swelling in the cell structure, which may leave permanent change.

Provided the crushing or distortion is not thought to be a feature of original use and does not contribute important information on the history of the object, reshaping can do much to regain conceptual significance. In some cases the results are extraordinary and transform the understanding of the object, as in the reshaping of Roman crocodile skin armour (Sully 1992), or the restoration of an Egyptian dress (Landi and Hall 1979). Here, too, documentation provides a record of what has been done so that any changes detected in the future should be interpreted knowing that a reshaping process has been used.

Restoration

Any conservation process that contributes to enhancing the visual or functional understanding of an object may be described as restoration; thus, 'cleaning', reshaping, and filling losses may each have a role in restoration. The objective of restoration is to aid the interpretation of an object, so paintings are restored in order to complete the image and industrial machinery may be restored to demonstrate its function (Keene 1994). Unlike much nineteenth-century and earlier craft restoration, today's restoration follows investigation and conservation of the object. The validity of a restoration depends on the conservator's investigation, and the approach to restoration is influenced by the conservation requirements of the object. The continuum of conservation means that some treatments provide both conservation and restoration; thus, supporting a damaged textile on a backing may be intended primarily to strengthen the original, but if the backing is of similar colour and texture it helps to minimize visible gaps and holes and so restore something of the original appearance.

The processes that are most frequently associated with restoration are removal of accretions and completion of losses, though treatments such as coating degraded glass with a polymer to restore transparency (Smith 1999) could also be included. Accretions are removed to reveal surface colour and detail, and missing parts are modelled, coloured, and finished to give the appearance of a whole and undamaged object. Of these processes, compensation for losses is more controllable than cleaning, and in many cases can be largely undone at some later stage. Restoration does not necessarily contribute to long-term preservation in the material sense, but it may mean that an object is treated with greater physical respect because it appears undamaged or is more immediately understandable; in all cases restoration is intended to preserve conceptual significance.

Restoration is controversial because it depends on the conservator or restorer's *interpretation* of the object. Even though restoration should never be based on conjecture, different conservators will interpret differently the available evidence on which restoration might be based. Another reason for controversy is that skilfully matched restoration may be considered to be close to faking, indeed, if the continuum of conservation is taken beyond restoration it could be said to reach faking (which employs many of the same techniques and skills as restoration).

The dilemma of restoration

In a frequently used quote the nineteenth-century French architect, Viollet-le-Duc, said of restoration:

> Both the word and the thing are modern. To restore an edifice means neither to maintain it nor to rebuild it: it means to reestablish it in a finished state, which may in fact never have actually existed at any given time.
>
> (Viollet-le-Duc 1996: 314)

In fact, here he was pointing out the essential problems that arise with all restoration, and perhaps particularly with the restoration of buildings, that the original state has inevitably been changed through age and alterations to the fabric. Thus, it follows that a completed restoration represents not a former state but *another* state. If the dirty or damaged state is considered not to demonstrate the significance of an object, then the curator and conservator choose to 'improve' that state in order to make the object more understandable. Conservation cannot reverse changes, it can only move the object to a different condition or appearance. Thus, curators, conservators, and restorers must realize that:

> simple removal of patina on a bronze or a painting will not recover the object's original appearance, but only uncover the present state of the original material.
>
> (Philippot 1976: 374)

Furthermore, objects continue to change and conservators should manage this change rather than 'freeze' the object into a state of suspended animation.

> Should our function as conservators, then, be to impose our own perspective concerning durability onto the creative process of the artist? The odd result would be the ideals of the conservator taking precedence over those of the artist, as an attempt is made to permanently lock a work of art into a single moment in time.
>
> (Albano 1996: 183)

Sometimes treatment involves a conscious decision to choose a particular stage in the life of the building or object as a basis for restoration, for example in the treatment of polychrome sculpture (Larson 1992). With complex objects this can be the subject of much debate. It is agreed, however, that restorations should respect the appearance of age so it is inappropriate as well as impossible to attempt to restore to a 'pristine' state.

Restoring to an earlier stage

It may be decided that one particular stage in the life of an object is more significant than the present state, but stripping away all later additions or changes can not only destroy age-value but remove character without clarifying meaning. A good example is the proposal, in the 1970s, to strip out the eighteenth-century houses built into the ruins of the medieval abbey at Bury St Edmunds, Suffolk, UK. If this had been done it would have robbed the ruins both of later history and considerable charm, and would have left only a rubble shell to represent the medieval work (see Baker 1999).

In some cases the decision to return an object to an approximation of an earlier state is made in order to provide visual information not otherwise readily available. This is sometimes done with costume, which, altered to suit a later fashion, retains the stitch- and cut-lines of the original shape (Doré 1978; Brooks et al. 1994). Industrial machinery and wheeled vehicles, which are to be used in demonstration, are often returned to a functioning state (Mann 1994); however a less intrusive conservation approach is now being developed (Newey and Meehan 1999).

Different approaches to, and standards of, restoration

An important issue is whether it is appropriate to restore so that additions are not detectable to the viewer. Effects of damage and loss can be masked more successfully on some types of object than others. While losses in paintings can be filled and coloured with paint, and losses in furniture can be repaired and concealed with careful choice of replacement veneer, even the most skilful repair of glass or fine textiles is detectable on close viewing. The approach to restoration depends, obviously, on the significance of the object. A statue from an archaeological context will normally be left uncompleted (e.g. with missing limbs); however, Molina and Pincevin (1994) discussed some examples of religious statuary where the views of parishioners and priest (the users) influenced a more extensive restoration than might otherwise have been undertaken, including the replacement of a hand and a missing cross.

Where it is possible to match shape, colour, and texture (as in paintings) is it appropriate to do so? An exact match makes it impossible for the viewer to detect which is original and which restoration. However, where an object has been completed and the new material has not been toned to match the original (e.g. a ceramic with white plaster of Paris fills), the distraction of the obtrusive new fill may make it difficult to appreciate the original. Archaeological conservators attempt to steer a path between these two extremes, in accordance with Philippot's statement that the aim of painting a restored area is to reintegrate the visual whole (Philippot 1976). Adopting this approach means that restored areas are detectable on close viewing but are coloured and textured so as not to detract from appreciation of the whole. An 'archaeological' approach to restoration of paintings (frequently applied to wall paintings) is to use an impressionistic technique, which involves building up colour and shading through the application of fine streaks of separate colours (tratteggio). Viewed from a distance this should complete the image, viewed close-to the restored areas should be apparent (Philippot 1976; Mora et al. 1984).

The case of the Lansdowne *Herakles* provides a particularly interesting example of the contrast between an eighteenth-century artist's restoration and a 1970s 'evidential' re-restoration. Eventually, the starkly honest (in that it made no attempt to conceal filled areas) twentieth-century restoration was removed and the eighteenth-century one reinstated on the grounds that the 'honest' approach detracted from, rather than enhanced, appreciation of the original (Podany 1994).

Detachable restorations

The principle of minimum intervention has affected the extent of restorations and the techniques used, and has now given rise to the concept of detachable restorations. Although there are many examples of attached material being removed at a later stage in order to attempt different and 'better' restorations (e.g. Williams 1992; Podany 1994), the concept of easily detachable restored features is relatively new. The objective is to position the restored feature in such a way that it can be removed with minimal application of solvents or other direct intervention on the object. The sixth-century BC Greek marble kouros at the J Paul Getty Museum was reconstructed and the missing areas filled in such a way that it is 'possible to disassemble the object with ease and without adverse effect on the individual segments' (Podany 1987: 376). Detachable gap-fills in ceramics have been demonstrated by Koob (1987) and non-intrusive detachable upholstery by Balfour et al. (1999): here, one of the aims was to allow access to the frame of the furniture for future examination of technological details.

Another approach that can restore the appearance of a fragmentary object is to locate the fragments in their assumed relationship on some form of support without attaching the fragments one to another (Fig 20). This was the method chosen to reconstruct degraded fragments of a workman's waistcoat (possibly as early as fifteenth century in date) found in a coal mine (Brooks et al. 1994).

Retreatment; re-restoration

Objects frequently need reconservation and are sometimes considered to need re-restoration. Retreatment may become necessary if an earlier treatment has failed, or has proved unsuitable for present circumstances. The new treatment may 'reinforce' what has been done before (e.g. reconsolidate a still-friable object), or may counteract an unsuitable method (e.g. removal of metal dowels which are now corroding). The concept behind the principle of reversibility was that of facilitating retreatment (after removing the earlier applied material) and some have proposed a principle of 'retreatability' (i.e. designing treatments to allow for further treatment) to take the place of the problematic principle of reversibility (Appelbaum 1987). Conservation processes are not permanent, the object continues to change and added materials change too. In any case 'maintenance' conservation (i.e. small interventions at regular intervals) is more likely to manage change and achieve minimum intervention overall, than major and intrusive remedial treatments at irregular intervals.

Re-restoration may be undertaken because the earlier restoration has deteriorated (e.g. painted reintegration has changed colour and become obtrusive) or because the object itself is at risk. This was the reason for the re-restoration of the Portland Vase (the famous Roman cameo glass vase) at the British Museum. The vase had been restored more than once and the latest adhesive appeared to have failed. A new restoration would also allow for the incorporation of small fragments, which had been left out of earlier restorations (Smith 1992). More complex is the situation where an earlier restoration represents an unfashionable, or possibly inaccurate, interpretation of an object. Re-restoration, in the sense of a new interpretation, will introduce another view of the object, which, in its turn, may fall out of favour in the future (as in the case of the Lansdowne *Herakles,* see Podany 1994). Re-restoration may also remove significant evidence of how the object was seen at an earlier stage in its history so is normally undertaken only if further evidence indicates a different interpretation. The *Laocoon* (a renowned Hellenistic marble sculpture) had been restored more than once during the Renaissance, then in 1905 part of a missing arm was rediscovered. Eventually this original arm was replaced (which changed the image considerably) but the influential Renaissance restoration, by Montosorli, was recorded in a plaster cast (Philippot 1996; Pinelli 1996). Much re-restoration falls somewhere between these examples (e.g. Elston 1998), but remedial retreatment, or re-restoration, should never be undertaken simply because it is possible, only if there is a valid objective. The Anglo-Saxon Sutton Hoo helmet was re-restored in order to achieve a more accurate interpretation (Bruce-Mitford 1978; Williams 1992).

Virtual restoration

With the advent of digital imaging it is becoming possible to test potential approaches to reconstruction, restoration (or re-restoration) by manipulating the image of the object rather than interacting with the object itself. Digital imaging also has the ability to 'restore' lost colour, so faded colour can be intensified on the image in order to regain the impression of a more or less unchanged state. This approach, too, is interpretative, but it has the advantages of allowing curator and conservator to produce more than one interpretation and to compare them, and it satisfies the principle of minimum intervention because it leaves the object in its present state.

Replicas

Replicas can be used not only to make objects more readily understandable but as an alternative to restoring the original. Thus they, too, can support the principle of minimum intervention. However, a replica has the problem that it is an even clearer statement than a restoration of what may be only one possible interpretation, and some replicas are so powerful that reinterpretation could well be hindered (even though the original may remain unrestored). Nevertheless, replicas can have a useful role. Sometimes an object is so changed that both colour and detail have disappeared. This is the case with the Sutton Hoo helmet, which is now a drab brown because, during burial, the iron of the helm was converted to rusty corrosion products, which also affected other metals present. The replica, made in collaboration with the Royal Armouries, and now displayed with the original at the British Museum, shows what the helmet may have looked like when first made. The brilliant tinned, gilded, and ornamented surface would have made the helmet an impressive sight. The replica had a further role in that it confirmed that the new reconstruction provided a viable shape which would have fitted the head, and provided adequate protection for ears and neck (which the earlier restoration would not have done) (Bruce-Mitford 1978, Williams 1992).

Replicas can be used to construct a whole where only part of an object has survived. The lines of ships and boats can be extrapolated from the incomplete remains of vessels, and replicas (or scale models) can be made and tested to see how the original might have handled on the water (Greenhill 1976). Replicas can also have a role when the decision is made to do little or no remedial conservation on an object. This was the case with a doublet that was not prepared for display, but a replica was made in order to show the probable original appearance of the garment (Brooks et al. 1996).

Effective conservation

Management of change is complex and multifaceted. Effective conservation is dependent on thorough assessment of the object, which requires communication and collaboration between conservators and colleagues, or other stakeholders, and it must facilitate the use of the object, not prevent it. Conservation itself embraces a range of activities from investigation to restoration, with preventive conservation being viewed, rightly, as increasingly important. However, while preventive conservation makes a crucial contribution to preservation, remedial conservation and restoration arc needed to aid interpretation of objects, so may play an important role in facilitating use.

References

AIC (American Institute for Conservation of Historic and Artistic Works) (1996) Code of ethics and guidelines for practice. In: *AIC Directory*. Washington, D.C.: AIC, pp. 24–31.

Albano, A. (1996) Art in transition. In: N. Stanley-Price, M.K. Talley, and A.M. Vaccaro (eds.), *Historical and Philosophical Issues in the Conservation of Cultural Heritage*. Los Angeles, CA: The Getty Conservation Institute, pp. 176–84.

Appelbaum, B. (1987) Criteria for treatment: reversibility. *Journal of the American Institute for Conservation*, 26: 65–73.

ARAAFU (Association des Restaurateurs d'Art et d'Archéologie de Formation Universitaire) (1996) *Les aspects esthétiques de la restauration des objets archéologiques*. Paris: ARAAFU.

Ashley-Smith, J. (1999) *Risk Assessment for Object Conservation.* Oxford: Butterworth-Heinemann.

Baker, D. (1999) Introduction: contexts for collaboration and conflict. In: G. Chitty and D. Baker (eds.), *Managing Historic Sites and Buildings: Reconciling Presentation and Preservation.* London: Routledge, pp. 1–22.

Balfour, D., Metcalf, S. and Collard, F. (1999) The first non-intrusive upholstery treatment at the Victoria & Albert Museum. *The Conservator*, 23: 22–9.

Barclay, R. and Mathias, C. (1989) An epoxy/microballoon mixture for gap filling in wooden objects. *Journal of the American Institute for Conservation*, 28: 31–42.

Berducou, M. (1996) Introduction to archaeological conservation. In: N. Stanley-Price, M.K. Talley, and A.M. Vaccaro (eds.), *Historical and Philosophical Issues in the Conservation of Cultural Heritage.* Los Angeles, CA: The Getty Conservation Institute, pp. 248–259.

Bradley, S. (1990) *A Guide to the Storage, Exhibition, and Handling of Antiquities, Ethnographia, and Pictorial Art.* British Museum Occasional Paper 66. London: British Museum Publications.

Brenni, P. (1999) Restoration or repair? The dilemma of ancient scientific instruments. In: A. Oddy and S. Carroll (eds.), *Reversibility – Does it Exist?* British Museum Occasional Paper 135. London: British Museum, pp. 19–25.

Brooks, M., Clark, C., Eastop, D., and Petcheck, C. (1994) Restoration or conservation – issues for textile conservators, a textile conservation perspective. In: A. Oddy (ed.), *Restoration. Is it Acceptable?* British Museum Occasional Paper 99. London: British Museum, pp. 103–22.

Brooks, M. Lister, A., Eastop, D., and Bennett, T. (1996) Artifact or information? Articulating the conflicts in conserving archaeological textiles. In: A. Roy and P. Smith (eds.), *Archaeological Conservation and its Consequences. Preprints of the Contributions to the Copenhagen Congress.* London: IIC, pp. 16–21.

Bruce-Mitford, R. (1978) *The Sutton Hoo Ship Burial, Vol 2 Arms, Armour and Regalia.* London: British Museum Publications.

Calnan, C. (1992) The conservation of Spanish gilt leather. In: H.W.M. Hodges, J.S. Mills, and P. Smith (eds.), *Conservation of the Iberian and Latin American Cultural Heritage. Preprints of the Contributions to the Madrid Congress, 9–12 September 1992.* London: IIC, pp. 23–6.

Casey, P.J. and Cronyn, J.M. eds. (1980) *Numismatics and Conservation.* Occasional Paper 1. Durham: Department of Archaeology, University of Durham,

Clavir, M. (1994) Preserving conceptual integrity: ethics and theory in preventive conservation. In: A. Roy and P. Smith (eds.), *Preventive Conservation, Practice Theory and Research. Preprints of the Contributions to the Ottawa Congress. September 1994.* London: IIC, pp. 149–53.

Clavir, M., Johnson, E., and Shane, A. (1986) A discussion on the use of museum artifacts by their original owners. In: R. Barclay, M. Gilberg, J. McCawley, and T. Stone (eds.), *Symposium 86, The Care and Preservation of Ethnological Materials.* Ottawa: CCI, pp. 80–89.

Cooke, B. (1990) Fibre damage in archaeological textiles. In: S. O'Connor and M. Brooks (eds.), *Archaeological Textiles.* UKIC Occasional Papers 10. London: UKIC, pp. 5–14.

Cooper, M. (1998) *Laser Cleaning in Conservation. An Introduction.* Oxford: Butterworth-Heinemann.

Coote, K. ed. (1998) *Care of Collections*. Committee for Aboriginal and Torres Straits Islander Keeping Places and Cultural Centres. Sydney: Australian Museum.

Cruickshank, P. and Tinker, Z. eds. (1995) *Starch and Other Carbohydrate Adhesives for Use in Textile Conservation*. London: UKIC.

Daintith, C. (1995) A consolidation treatment for ethnographic pottery from New Guinea. In: L. Hill and S. Giles (eds.) *Where to Start, Where to Stop. Papers from the British Museum / MEG Ethnographic Conservation Colloquium*. Museum Ethnographers Group Occasional Papers 4. Hull: Museum Ethnographers Group, pp. 121–30.

Daniels, V. (1999) Imperfect reversibility in paper conservation. In: A. Oddy (ed.), *Restoration. Is it Acceptable?* British Museum Occasional Paper 99. London: British Museum, pp. 47–52.

DCMS (Department for Culture, Media and Sport) (2000) *Portable Antiquities Annual Report 1997–1998*. London: DCMS.

Dollery, D. (1994) A methodology of preventive conservation for a large expanding and mixed archaeological collection. In: A. Roy and P. Smith (eds.), *Preventive Conservation, Practice Theory, and Research. Preprints of the Contributions to the Ottawa Congress. September 1994*. London: IIC, pp. 69–72.

Doré, J. (1978) The conservation of two eighteenth-century court mantuas. *Studies in Conservation*, 23: 1–14.

Durham, A. ed. (1995) *Lining and Backing. The Support of Paintings, Paper and Textiles*. London: UKIC.

Eastop, D. and Brooks, M. (1996) To clean or not to clean: the value of soils and creases. In: *ICOM Committee for Conservation. Preprints of the 11th Triennial Meeting. Edinburgh. September 1996*. London: James & James, pp. 687–91.

Elston, M. (1998) A corrective treatment on the 5th century BC Attic Krater. In: A. Paterakis (ed.), *Glass, Ceramics and Related Materials*. Interim Meeting of the ICOM-CC Working Group. Vantaa: EVTEK Institute of Arts and Design, pp. 106–14.

Erhardt, D. and Mecklenburg, M. (1994) Relative humidity re-examined. In: A. Roy and P. Smith (eds.), *Preventive Conservation, Practice Theory and Research. Preprints of the Contributions to the Ottawa Congress. September 1994*. London: IIC, pp. 32–8.

Fell, V. (1996) Washing away the evidence. In: A. Roy and P. Smith (eds.), *Archaeological Conservation and its Consequences. Preprints of the Contributions to the Copenhagen Congress*. London: IIC, pp. 48–51.

Fenn, J. (1995) The cellulose nitrate time bomb: using sulfonephthalein indicators to evaluate storage strategies. In: J. Heuman (ed.), *From Marble to Chocolate: The Conservation of Modern Sculpture. Tate Gallery Conference, September 1995*. London: Archetype, pp. 87–92.

France-Lanord, A. (1996) Knowing how to 'question' the object before restoring it. In: N. Stanley-Price, M.K. Talley, and A.M. Vaccaro (eds.), *Historical and Philosophical Issues in the Conservation of Cultural Heritage*. Los Angeles, CA: The Getty Conservation Institute, pp. 244–7.

Fry, M.F. (1996) Buried but not forgotten: sensitivity in disposing of major archaeological timbers. In: A. Roy and P. Smith (eds.), *Archaeological Conservation and its Consequences. Preprints of the Contributions to the Copenhagen Congress*. London: IIC, pp. 52–4.

Fry, R. (1997) Preservation or desecration? The legal position of the restorer. In: P. Lindley (ed.), *Sculpture Conservation: Preservation or Interference?* Aldershot: Scolar Press, pp. 55–62.

Giusti. A. (1999) Reversibility in the restoration of stone artifacts: real possibilities and objective limits. In: A. Oddy and S. Carroll (eds.), *Reversibility – Does it Exist?* British Museum Occasional Paper 135. London: British Museum, pp. 91–8.

Greenfield, J. (1995) *The Return of Cultural Treasures.* Cambridge: Cambridge University Press.

Greenhill, B. (1976) *Archaeology of the Boat: A New Introductory Study.* London: Adam and Charles Black.

Hanington, D. (2000) To treat or not to treat – that is the question. *CCI Newsletter,* 25: 1–3.

Hanna, S. (1990) The cleaning and removal of surface coatings from a seventh-century BC sandstone shrine from Nubia. In: J.S. Mills and P. Smith (eds.), *Cleaning, Retouching and Coatings: Technology and Practice for Easel Paintings and Polychrome Sculpture. Preprints of the Contributions to the Brussels Congress.* London: IIC, pp. 23–7.

Hansen, E.F., Walston, S., and Bishop, M.H. eds. (1993) *Matte Paint. Its History and Technology, Analysis, Properties and Conservation Treatment with Special Emphasis on Ethnographic Objects.* Marina del Rey, CA: Getty Conservation Institute and IIC.

Hedley, G. (1990) Long-lost relations and new found relatives: issues in the cleaning of paintings. In: V. Todd (ed.), *Appearance, Opinion, Change: Evaluating the Look of Paintings.* London: UKIC, pp. 8–13.

Hubert, J. (1989) A proper place for the dead: a critical review of the reburial issue. In: R. Layton (ed.), *Conflict in the Archaeology of Living Traditions.* London: Routledge, pp. 131–66.

Hunter, K. and Foley, K. (1984) The Lincoln hanging bowl. In: L. Bacon and B. Knight (eds.), *From Pinheads to Hanging Bowls.* UKIC Occasional Papers 7. London: UKIC, pp. 16–18.

Keene, S. (1994) Objects as systems: a new challenge for conservation. In: A. Oddy and S. Carroll (eds.), *Reversibility – Does it Exist?* British Museum Occasional Paper 135. London: British Museum, pp. 19–26.

——(1996) *Managing Conservation in Museums.* Oxford: Butterworth-Heinemann.

Kollandsrud, K. (1997) Vasari's theory on the origins of oil painting and its influence on cleaning methods: the ruined polychromy of the early thirteenth-century crucifix from Haug, Norway. In: P. Lindley (ed.), *Sculpture Conservation: Preservation or Interference?* Aldershot: Scolar Press, pp. 139–50.

Koob, S. (1987) Detachable plaster restorations for archaeological ceramics. In: J. Black (ed.), *Recent Advances in the Conservation and Analysis of Artifacts.* London: Summer Schools Press, pp. 63–5.

Landi, S. and Hall, R. (1979) The discovery and conservation of an ancient Egyptian linen tunic. *Studies in Conservation,* 24: 141.

La Rocca, E. and Nardi, R. (1994) Preventive conservation and restoration: a matter of costs. In: A. Roy and P. Smith (eds.), *Preventive Conservation, Practice Theory and Research. Preprints of the Contributions to the Ottawa Congress. September 1994.* London: IIC, pp. 24–7.

Larson, J. (1990) The treatment and examination of painted surfaces on eighteenth-century terracotta sculptures. In: J.S. Mills and P. Smith (eds.), *Cleaning, Retouching* and Coatings: Technology and Practice for Easel Paintings and Polychrome Sculpture. Preprints of the Contributions to the Brussels Congress. London: IIC, pp. 28–32.

——(1992) Statue of the Bodhisattva Guanyin. In: A. Oddy (ed.), *The Art of the Conservator*. London: British Museum Press, pp. 177–89.

——(1997) Sculpture conservation treatment or reinterpretation? In: P. Lindley (ed.), *Sculpture Conservation: Preservation or Interference?* Aldershot: Scolar Press, pp. 69–82.

Leggett, J. (1999) National consciousness. *Museums Journal*, October: 17.

Mann, P.R. (1994) The restoration of vehicles for use in research, exhibition and demonstration. In: A. Oddy (ed.), *Restoration. Is it Acceptable?* British Museum Occasional Paper 99. London: British Museum, pp. 131–8.

MGC (Museums and Galleries Commission) (1992) *Standards in the Museum Care of Collections*. London: Museums and Galleries Commission.

Miles, D. (2000) Hole timber circle: excavation, removal and scientific analysis. *Conservation Bulletin*, 37: 6–7.

Mills, J.S. and Smith, P. eds. (1990) *Cleaning, Retouching and Coatings: Technology and Practice for Easel Paintings and Polychrome Sculpture. Preprints of the Contributions to the Brussels Congress*. London: IIC.

Molina, T. and Pincevin, M. (1994) Restoration: acceptable to whom? A. Oddy (ed.), *Restoration. Is it Acceptable?* British Museum Occasional Paper 99. London: British Museum, pp. 77–84.

Mora, P., Mora, L., and Philippot, P. (1984) *Conservation of Wall Paintings*. London: Butterworth.

Morgan, H. and Cruikshank, P. (1995) The conservation of the shroud of Resti – an 18th Dynasty linen *Book of the Dead*. In: C. Brown, F. Macalister, and M. Wright (eds.), *Conservation in Ancient Egyptian Collections*. London: Archetype, pp. 1–12.

Newey, H. and Meehan, P. (1999) The conservation of the 1895 Panhard et Levassor and the 1922 prototype Austin Seven motorcars: new approaches in the preservation of vehicles. *The Conservator*, 2: 11–21.

Oddy, A. (1992) Introduction. In: A. Oddy (ed.), *The Art of the Conservator*. London: British Museum Press, pp. 7–27.

Organ, R. (1961) The conservation of cuneiform tablets. *British Museum Quarterly*, 23: 52–7.

Paterson, C. and Greenfield, J. (1998) Storage considerations for native arts: a joint project between Denver Art Museum and the Native American Community. In: M. Wright and Y.M.T. Player-Dahnsjö (eds.), *Site Effects: The Impact of Location on Conservation Treatments*. Edinburgh: The Scottish Society for Conservation and Restoration, pp. 40–45.

Payton, R. ed. (1992) *Retrieval of Objects from Archaeological Sites*. London: Archetype.

Pearson, C. ed. (1987) *Conservation of Marine Archaeological Objects*. London: Butterworth.

Peers, L. (1999) Curating Native American art. *British Museum Magazine. The Journal of the British Museum Society*, 34: 24–7.

Philippot, P. (1976) Historic Preservation: philosophy, criteria, guidelines. In: International Centre for Conservation, Rome, and International Centre Committee of the Advisory Council on Historic Preservation, *Preservation and Conservation: Principles and Practices. Proceedings of the North American International Regional Conference, 1972*. Washington, D.C.: Preservation Press, pp. 367–82.

——(1996) Restoration from the perspective of the humanities. In: N. Stanley-Price, M.K. Talley, and A.M. Vaccaro (eds.), *Historical and Philosophical Issues in the*

Conservation of Cultural Heritage. Los Angeles, CA: The Getty Conservation Institute, pp. 216–29.

Pinelli, O.R. (1996) The surgery of memory: ancient sculpture and historical restorations. In: N. Stanley-Price, M.K. Talley, and A.M. Vaccaro (eds.), *Historical and Philosophical Issues in the Conservation of Cultural Heritage*. Los Angeles, CA: The Getty Conservation Institute, pp. 288–305.

Pinniger, D. and Winsor, P. (1998) *Integrated Pest Management*. London: Museums and Galleries Commission.

Plowden, A. and Halahan, F. (1987) *Looking after Antiques*. London and Sydney: Pan Books.

Podany, J.C. (1987) Advances in the reassembly of large stone sculpture at the J Paul Getty Museum. In: J. Black (ed.), *Recent Advances in the Conservation and Analysis of Artifacts*. London: Summer Schools Press, pp. 375–82.

——(1994) Restoring what wasn't there: reconstruction of the eighteenth-century restorations to the Lansdowne Herakles in the collection of the J Paul Getty Museum. In: A. Oddy (ed.), *Restoration. Is it Acceptable?* British Museum Occasional Paper 99. London: British Museum, pp. 9–18.

Podany, J.C., Elston, M., Thoresen, L., and Maish, S.L. (1995) The use of paper-pulp-based fill material for compensation of losses to sculpture. In: J. Heuman (ed.), *From Marble to Chocolate: The Conservation of Modern Sculpture*. Tate Gallery Conference, September 1995. London: Archetype, pp. 59–64.

Price, C.A. (2000) Following fashion: the ethics of archaeological conservation. In: F.P. McManamon and A. Hatton (eds.), *Cultural Resource Management in Contemporary Society: Perspectives on Managing and Presenting the Past*. London and New York: Routledge, pp. 213–30.

Reilly, J.A. (1991) Celluloid objects: their chemistry and preservation. *Journal of the American Institute for Conservation*, 30: 145–62.

Robinson, J. and Pardoe, T. (2000) *An Illustrated Guide to the Care of Costume and Textile Collections*. London: Museums and Galleries Commission.

Rose, C.I. and de Torres, A.R. eds. (1992) *Storage of Natural History Collections: Ideas and Practical Solutions*. Pittsburgh: Society for the Preservation of Natural History Collections.

Rule, M. (1982) *The Mary Rose*. London: Conway Maritime Press.

Sandwith, H. and Stainton, S. (1991) *The National Trust Manual of Housekeeping*. London: Penguin Books and National Trust.

Schleicher, B. (1997) Problems in the cleaning of polychromed wood sculpture. In: P. Lindley (ed.), *Sculpture Conservation: Preservation or Interference?* Aldershot: Scolar Press, pp. 151–4.

Sease, C. (1981) The case against using soluble nylon in conservation work. *Studies in Conservation*, 26: 102–10.

——(1987) *A Conservation Manual for the Field Archaeologist*. Third Edition. Los Angeles, CA: Institute of Archaeology, UCLA.

——(1998) Codes of ethics for conservation. *International Journal of Cultural Property*, 7: 98–114.

Simpson, M.G. (1996) No deceit, no conspiracy, just a Reubens through and through. *London Evening Standard*, 2nd June.

Smith, S. (1992) The Portland Vase. In: A. Oddy (ed.), *The Art of the Conservator*. London: British Museum Press, pp. 42–58.

——(1999) Opacity contrariwise: the reversibility of deteriorated surfaces on vessel glass. In: A. Oddy and S. Carroll (eds.), *Reversibility – Does it Exist?* British Museum Occasional Paper 135. London: British Museum, pp. 135–40.

Staniforth, S. (1990) Benefits versus costs in environmental control. In: S. Keene (ed.), *Managing Conservation. Papers Given at a Conference Held Jointly by UKIC and the Museum of London.* London: UKIC, pp. 28–30.

Sully, D. (1992) Humidification: the reshaping of leather, skin, and gut objects for display. In: P. Hallebeek, M. Kite, and C. Calnan (eds.), *Conservation of Leathercraft and Related Objects. Interim Symposium.* London: Victoria and Albert Museum, pp. 50–54.

Talley, M.K. (1999) The Delta Plan: a nationwide rescue operation. *Museum International,* 51: 11–15.

Tennent, N.H., Baird, T., and Gibson, L. (1996) The technical examination and conservation of blackened Delftware from anaerobic sites. In: A. Roy and P. Smith (eds.), *Archaeological Conservation and its Consequences. Preprints of the Contributions to the Copenhagen Congress.* London: IIC, pp. 182–7.

Thompson, J.M.A. ed. (1992) *The Manual of Curatorship.* Oxford: Butterworth-Heinemann.

Tubb, K.W. and Grissom, C.A. (1995) Ayn Ghazal, a comparative study of the 1983 and 1985 statuary caches. *Studies in the History and Archaeology of Jordan,* 5: 437–47.

UKIC Archaeology Section (1982) *Excavated Artifacts for Publication, UK Sites.* Guidelines 1. London: UKIC.

van de Wetering, E. (1996) The autonomy of restoration: ethical considerations in relation to artistic concepts. In: N. Stanley-Price, M.K. Talley, and A.M. Vaccaro (eds.), *Historical and Philosophical Issues in the Conservation of Cultural Heritage.* Los Angeles, CA: The Getty Conservation Institute, pp. 193–9.

Vickers, M. (1995) Surface colour transfer from metal, ivory and stone to ceramic and glass. In: *Materials Issues in Art and Archaeology IV.* Pittsburgh: Materials Research Society, pp. 189–99.

Viollet-le-Duc, E.-E. (1996) Restoration. In: N. Stanley-Price, M.K. Talley, and A.M. Vaccaro (eds.), *Historical and Philosophical Issues in the Conservation of Cultural Heritage.* Los Angeles, CA: The Getty Conservation Institute, pp. 314–18.

Wainwright, G. (1989) Saving the Rose. *Antiquity,* 63: 430–35.

Ward, P. (1986) *The Nature of Conservation. A Race against Time.* Marina del Rey, CA: The Getty Conservation Institute.

Watkinson, D. and Neal, V. (1998) *First Aid for Finds.* Third edition. London: Rescue – The British Archaeological Trust, and Archaeology Section of the UK Institute for Conservation, with the Museum of London.

Welsh, E., Sease, C., Rhodes, B., Brow, S., and Clavir, M. (1992) Multicultural participation in conservation decision-making. *AAAC (Western Association for Art Conservation) Newsletter,* 14(1): 13–22.

Williams, N. (1992) The Sutton Hoo helmet. In: A. Oddy (ed.), *The Art of the Conservator.* London: British Museum Press, pp. 73–88.

Williams, S.L. (1997) Preventive conservation: the evolution of a museum ethic. In: G. Edson (ed.), *Museum Ethics.* London and New York: Routledge, pp. 198–206.

Wills, B. (1995) Some methods of basketry repair, using Japanese tissue paper and starch paste. In: L. Hill and S. Giles (eds.) *Where to Start, Where to Stop. Papers from the British Museum / MEG Ethnographic Conservation Colloquium.* Museum

Ethnographers Group Occasional Papers 4. Hull: Museum Ethnographers Group, pp. 109–14.

Wills, B., Shashoua, Y., and Sully, D. (1992) Approach to the conservation of a Mexican saddle and *anquera*. In: H.W.M. Hodges, J.S. Mills, and P. Smith (eds.), *Conservation of the Iberian and Latin American Cultural Heritage. Preprints of the Contributions to the Madrid Congress, 9–12 September 1992*. London: IIC, pp. 179–83.

Wilson, A., Tuross, N., and Wachowiak, M. (1996) Blood residues on archaeological objects – a conservation perspective. In: A. Roy and P. Smith (eds.), *Archaeological Conservation and its Consequences. Preprints of the Contributions to the Copenhagen Congress*. London: IIC, pp. 213–18.

Young, S. (1989) *'The Work of Angels': Masterpieces of Celtic Art, Sixth to Ninth Centuries AD*. London: British Museum Publications.

Chapter 9

Caring for an Egyptian mummy and coffin

Laura S. Phillips and Linda Roundhill

During pharaonic times in Egypt, mummification, as well as funerary scenes decorated on coffins, served to protect the deceased during the perilous journey through the underworld on the way toward obtaining eternal life. This journey was frequently interrupted when tombs were robbed for valuables by local thieves and even government officials (Taylor 2001). Much later, in the late nineteenth and early twentieth centuries, European and American museums encouraged yet more raiding in response to the Western fascination with Egyptian civilization. The Washington State Museum, now the Burke Museum of Natural History and Culture in Seattle, Washington, got caught up in this fad when, in 1902, a University of Washington regent purchased for the museum a Ptolemaic Period (2250–1980 BP) mummy and a Twenty-first Dynasty (2909–2839 BP) coffin from the National Museum of Egyptian Antiquities. Nearly a century later, this mummy and coffin have become an important part of Seattle's history.

Finding a home

More than one hundred years of research and exhibition have taken their toll, and the Burke Museum's mummy and coffin were identified in the late 1990s as badly in need of conservation and a stable, protective environment. By this time, the museum had redefined its mission to focus on the Pacific Rim, and it recognized that the Egyptian collection fell outside its scope. The expense required for proper care might be better spent finding them a more appropriate home. Other institutions with more extensive Egyptian holdings had contacted the museum in the past, and one museum in 1998 wanted to offer Pacific Rim collections in exchange.

Intensive internal museum discussions ensued. Not only were the mummy and coffin outside the museum's mission, but the display of human remains is now a significant concern for the community. Native American remains are not displayed; other human remains are rarely displayed, and then only after consultation with the affected community. It seemed obvious, therefore, that the best solution was to

Source: *Human Remains: Guide for Museums and Academic Institutions.* V. Cassman, N. Odegaard and J. Powell (eds.). Lanham, MD: AltaMira Press, 2007. pp. 269–273.

transfer the collection. However, the mummy and coffin had become closely linked to the history and identity of the Burke Museum. For decades, schoolchildren eagerly flocked to the museum to see Seattle's only Egyptian mummy and coffin. Today, nostalgic requests to view the mummy and coffin occur frequently.

Constructing storage: multiple considerations

The museum's ultimate decision to keep and properly care for the mummy and coffin derived from the outpouring of community care, support, and continued interest. More than $35,000 was contributed to conserve the collection, as well as to design and build an environmentally stable case. While the museum anticipated the conservation work to take more than a year, the exhibit case, based on a hermetically sealed case design by the Getty Conservation Institute (GCI), was expected to take little or no design time, and to be built quickly, easily, and locally (Maekawa 1998). Although the conservation work was completed within the estimated time frame by Linda Roundhill, Art and Antiquities Conservation, the case could not be built as planned.

The new case needed to be designed for both display and storage, and would need to address specific environmental conditions and contextual factors. For almost ninety years, the mummy and coffin were continually displayed one inside the other as if they belonged together. The possible continuation of this practice created many problems for a variety of reasons: interpretive, spiritual, curatorial, and matters pertaining to public accessibility.

Interpretive

Displaying the mummy and coffin as one object, while visually dramatic, creates the impression that they belong to the same artistic and ritual traditions. While both are recognizably Egyptian examples of funerary sacraments, their provenances were separated in time by nearly one thousand years. Both artistic styles and burial customs had changed considerably in that time, and even though the label may be explicit, the visual impact would be misleading.

Spiritual

Although the deceased has been dead for more than two thousand years and has already suffered the indignity of being removed from her burial context, displayed, studied, and handled, would it be proper to continue this trend? Should this mummy be forced to rest in the coffin of another individual whose name is clearly painted in the inside? Are the prayers and incantations depicted all over the coffin the correct ones for this deceased? From the perspective of the deceased, whose spirit may well be still conscious of the present (most religious traditions imply this), are we honouring the dead by continuing to display the body in this way?

Curatorial

Both the coffin and the mummy are fragile, have suffered from overexposure, and require an environment free of ultraviolet light radiation. Yet, they require different stable, controlled environments to ensure survival. The coffin's gessoed and painted wood must be kept at constant temperature and normalized relative humidity to minimize movement of the wood relative to the brittle paint layers. The mummy, though it would benefit as well from such conditions, should furthermore have an oxygen-free atmosphere to control biological degradation of the remains and prevent further deterioration of the extremely degraded linen.

Public accessibility

The coffin is a funerary device but also a work of art. The entire coffin (minus the foot end and the undersides) is painted with ceremonial art and depictions of the underworld journey. The art on the inside is by far the most interesting visually and from a scholarly viewpoint. The mummy, on the other hand, is not primarily an art object, but human remains, despite traditional treatments of mummies in museums that often imply otherwise. The mummy, however, has a beautiful gilded mask and painted cartonnage (plaster-soaked linen) panels that are artistically significant. The museum is not interested in parading the coffin and mummy for the benefit of those with morbid fascinations but as a fine example of Egyptian funerary art and as representative of the beliefs of a past civilization.

Addressing multiple considerations

The coffin and mummy continue to instruct and inspire awe. It was therefore essential for the museum to develop a method of display and storage that would speak to all four of the aspects mentioned. The mummy and coffin would need to be in proximity because they share the same acquisition source and broad cultural context, but they must be in separate spaces to prevent misinterpretation and to provide the best possible environments. Furthermore, the coffin needs to be viewed from all angles with adequate safe lighting within, while the mummy should be provided with a private space that can be accessed on occasion for viewing or study, but is respectful of the spirit of the deceased.

It was with all these requirements in mind that the museum staff consulted with several professionals in the fields of storage, display, manufacturing, and conservation and ultimately developed the display case assembly described here.

Initial planning

Based on the storage criteria just described, the museum's initial plan included separate cases that could be stacked for more efficient storage. Each case would have unique environmental conditions based on the GCI's design specifications. GCI specifications were sent to two local museum case fabricators, and both said it was too technical for them. In addition, the extruded metal frame parts essential to the hermetically sealed system could not be fabricated locally and would be cost-prohibitive because new die had to be made. As an alternative, one case fabricator provided an estimate for a fir-framed case; the other quoted the cost to design (not build) a medite MDF-framed case for $4,500. Out of frustration, GCI was contacted. Staff there were quite helpful and generously offered one of their extra cases, gratis. Unfortunately, the size of the case did not meet the museum's needs.

A revised plan

Based on further discussions with the conservator, the museum decided that neither the mummy nor the coffin required a hermetically sealed case as long as the environment could be controlled. The museum then hired Snow & Company, a small contracting firm with experience in metal fabrication, as well as home and boat construction. This company suggested a single case with separately sealed compartments. The frame would be constructed of stainless steel with interior anodized aluminum extrusions. Air exchange would be minimal due to gaskets, but the case would not be hermetically sealed.

Our concern about storing the coffin and mummy together was minimized by the new design (Figure 9.1). The coffin is placed in an upper partition with one-quarter-inch UV-filtered laminated glass on four sides and on top to ensure adequate views from all angles for research and display purposes. The mummy is respectfully placed in a discrete, nearly flush drawer below. The drawer can be pulled out and locked in place for display. Visitors and researchers can view the mummy through a glass covering on the top of the drawer. When not on display, the drawer is kept closed and locked.

The coffin, housed in the top portion of the case, is composed of a lid and base. The lid is mounted at an angle on Ethafoam-covered solid-anodized-aluminium frames with stainless steel sockets, and formed to the lid interior to ensure adequate weight distribution and minimal movement during earthquakes. The base rests on one-quarter-inch-thick Ethafoam to prevent direct contact with the steel base.

The stabilization of environmental conditions is particularly important for the coffin, given its sycamore wood construction and gesso and paint overlay. The frame of the case top was sealed with silicone gaskets, then four holes were drilled in the bottom of the top portion of the case. In one hole is a removable, gasketed screw fitted with an ACR SmartReader Plus 2 datalogger to measure temperature and relative humidity. One hole houses a fiber-optic cable (discussed later). The other two holes are fitted with tubes, part of a passive system designed to regulate the relative humidity and air quality. CICU Air-Safe System (developed by NoUVIR Research in Seaford, Delaware) conditions and recirculates the air in the top portion of the case. Air in the top portion of the case is expelled through one polypropylene tube into two cartridges fitted with microparticulate filters, a NIOSH/MSHA-certified acid gas/organic vapour filter, and a NIOSH/MSHA-certified formaldehyde/ammonia filter, and forty cubic inches of conditioned silica gel. The filtered air is then circulated back into the case through the second hose. The replaceable cartridges, enclosed in a 0.0005-inch-thick polyethylene bag, are accessible via a locked, separate side compartment in the lower portion of the case.

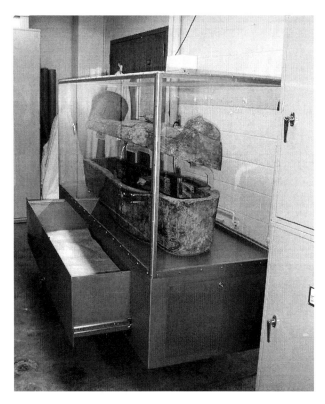

Figure 9.1 The newly designed stainless steel case built by Snow & Company, Seattle, Washington, was the product of consultations with many experts. Photo courtesy of Burke Museum.

In order to adequately view the funerary texts and ritual scenes painted on the coffin, interior case lighting was essential. To prevent light and heat damage, a five-foot-long aluminum tube housing a three-hundred-strand capacity fiber optic cable was attached to the lid mount. Fiber-optic light is emitted in a sixty-degree cone from fifty-eight holes arrayed linearly along the one-inch-square tube. The fiber optics provide an even light that illuminates the painted interior of the coffin. The light source, a 120-volt, 60-hertz illuminator with a 100-watt MR16 quartz halogen lamp and fan, is stored in a separate, vented compartment in the lower portion of the case, on the opposite end of the case from the compartment that houses the passive air quality system and provides access to the datalogger. A dimmer was added to the illuminator to provide variations in light as needed.

The mummy comprises the human remains as well as her accompanying cartonnage mask and body panels. An oxygen-free environment would help prevent further linen deterioration and insect damage. The cartonnage pieces are important for the mummy's journey to the afterlife and need to rest on top of her. The solution is a custom made anoxic keepsake bag. This nearly clear polyethylene bag houses the mummy as well as an oxygen scavenger and is heat sealed to provide a permanent oxygen-free environment. It can be opened and resealed as many as twelve times. A padded muslin cover fits over the entire case for storage. The case rests on lockable casters, which are removable for display and storage.

The journey continues

Sadly, disassociated Egyptian mummies and coffins abound in museums around the world. In the future, respect for these burial objects and human remains may require returning them to proper entombment. However, many are in poor condition and cannot be returned to their original provenience due to the lack of adequate field collecting data. Museums can serve a positive role as respectful caretakers and educators. Successful attempts to rehouse these mummies and coffins require careful, considered thought along with expert and community involvement to preserve the dignity of the deceased and ensure their continued journey.

References

Maekawa, S. (1998) Design and construction of the GCI's hermetically sealed display and storage case. In: S. Maekawa (ed.), *Oxygen Free Museum Cases*. Los Angeles, CA: Getty Conservation Institute, pp. 31–51.

Taylor, J.H. (2001) *Death and the Afterlife in Ancient Egypt*. Chicago: University of Chicago Press.

Part I, Section 5

Archaeology collections research

Chapter 10

Gristhorpe Man
An Early Bronze Age log-coffin burial scientifically defined

Nigel Melton, Janet Montgomery, Christopher J. Knüsel, Cathy Batt, Stuart Needham, Mike Parker Pearson, Alison Sheridan, Carl Heron, Tim Horsley, Armin Schmidt, Adrian Evans, Elizabeth Carter, Howell Edwards, Michael Hargreaves, Rob Janaway, Niels Lynnerup, Peter Northover, Sonia O'Connor, Alan Ogden, Timothy Taylor, Vaughan Wastling, and Andrew Wilson

The Gristhorpe discovery and Early Bronze Age log-coffin burials in Britain

In July 1834 William Beswick, the local landowner, and a group of friends opened a barrow at Gristhorpe, just north of Filey, North Yorkshire (Williamson 1896: 44). The barrow was the central and most prominent in a group of three on the clifftop. They recovered an intact log-coffin containing a flexed skeleton laid on its right side, with the head to the south and facing east. Organic and inorganic grave goods were recovered, too, and the complete skeleton, which was stained black in the manner of a bog body, was conserved by simmering it in a solution of glue. The skeleton was subsequently articulated and wired together for display by local doctors William Harland and Thomas Weddell (Scarborough Philosophical Society Minute Book for 1834; Harland 1932; K. Snowden pers. comm.). The finds were donated to the Scarborough Museum where, except for a brief period in storage during the Second World War, they have remained on display ever since (Figure 10.1).

William Crawford Williamson, the 17-year-old son of Scarborough Museum curator John Williamson, swiftly published a report: Gristhorpe Man was powerfully built, over 6ft tall and of advanced age, and a Brigantian chief (Williamson 1834). The technique of phrenology, then in vogue, was used to identify his personal

Figure 10.1 The Gristhorpe finds on display (centre, back) in the Rotunda Museum in the late nineteenth century. Courtesy of Scarborough Museums Trust.

qualities: combativeness, destructiveness, firmness, perseverance, and self-esteem, traits necessary to fit him for 'high and important office' and to 'overawe a wild and uncivilized people' (Williamson 1834: 16). The skull subsequently featured in *Crania Britannica* (Davis and Thurman 1865).

Parallels between the Gristhorpe coffin and Danish log-coffins were noted at the time of its discovery, and in 1836 the Gristhorpe coffin was compared to the log-coffin found at Toppehoj, Bjolderup (Rowley-Conwy 2007: 118), and illustrated alongside the Danish example in *Antiqvarisk Tidsskrift* (reproduced in Jensen 1998: 40). The perceived close connection with the Danish finds meant that when Thoms published his English translation of Worsaae's *The Primeval Antiquities of Denmark* in 1849, he did so in Worsaae's stated belief that the 'close connection which in old time existed between Denmark and the British islands, renders it natural that British antiquaries should turn to the antiquities of Denmark, and compare them with those of their own countries' (Worsaae trans. 1849: iv). Thoms' translation of Worsaae's 1843 work, which helped to make Thomsen's 'Three Age System' readily available in Britain, used as the prime example of such comparisons the Gristhorpe coffin and its contents, quoting Williamson's 1834 report in detail (Thoms, Preface to Worsaae trans. 1849: xi–xix). The Three Age System itself was developed in 1819, published in Danish in 1836 and translated into English in 1848. This fundamental advance in understanding enabled Williamson to revise his report 38 years later, assigning the coffin and its contents to the Early Bronze Age and distinguishing them from similar finds made in Denmark, which he correctly identified as being of later Bronze Age date (Williamson 1872).

The Gristhorpe log-coffin burial is one of 75 recorded in Britain that range in date from the twenty-third to seventeenth centuries cal BC (Parker Pearson et al. 2013). Although no certain example is known from Ireland, they are found throughout Britain from Scotland to the south coast and from East Anglia to Wales. Log-coffin burial was also practised during the Early Bronze Age in The Netherlands, Germany, and Central Europe (Harding 2000: 105–07; Drenth and Lohof 2005: 439–40). Within Britain, three particular concentrations occur, in Wessex, Yorkshire and eastern England (the East Midlands and East Anglia). Intriguingly, large expanses within two if not all three of these regions were substantially lacking in mature woodland by the Early Bronze Age (French 2003; French et al. 2007), so the distribution of log-coffin burials does not necessarily reflect availability of supplies of suitable timber.

Gristhorpe is one of three Bronze Age log-coffins in Britain to have survived intact to the present day, the two others being from Disgwylfa Fawr, near Ponterwyd, Ceredigion (Savory 1980: 22). Many log-coffins were found intact upon discovery but have subsequently perished or survive just as fragments. These include the coffins from Hove, Sussex (Phillips 1856); Stoborough, Dorset (Hutchins 1767); Cairngall, Dalrigh, and Dumglow, Scotland (Mowat 1996: 83, 85, 102–3; D. Bertie pers. comm.); Loose Howe (Elgee and Elgee 1949) and Rylstone (Greenwell 1877: 375–7), North Yorkshire; and two from Winterbourne Stoke, Wiltshire (Colt Hoare 1812: 122–4). One of the latter two was reported to be of elm, but the others appear to have been of oak.

Most log-coffins have been recorded as soil stains recognizable only through careful excavation. It can be difficult to differentiate between plank-built coffins and log-coffins in such circumstances (Petersen 1969). The former are known from the fourth millennium BC onwards, whereas the earliest log-coffins for single graves appear as an innovation in the climax Beaker period (Period 2, Needham 2005), although the predominant ceramic associations are Food Vessels. Log-coffins were clearly in their heyday after 2000 cal BC.

A good case can be made that even those log-coffins without observable grave goods were probably the graves of individuals of some distinction. Symbolic associations with woodland and occasionally with boats can be identified on the basis of material, shape, and in cases such as Gristhorpe, the grave's location overlooking the sea. Some individuals may have had specialist ties to woodland with status roles connected to forestry and hunting, while others may have had associations with the maritime interaction networks that were becoming such a major social force during the Early Bronze Age (Frank 1993; Kristiansen and Larsson 2005; Needham 2009).

Our re-examination of Gristhorpe Man reported here included the analysis of the skeleton and grave goods, using modern techniques for dating, diet, and provenance. The original barrow and its nineteenth-century excavation were also located using geophysical methods and confirmed by test excavation. The results suggest a new context for the burial and the use of log-coffins on the British side of the North Sea.

'Gristhorpe Man': an osteobiography

Gristhorpe Man was a physically active male who had attained the prime of life, being at least 36 to 45 years and probably much older at the time of his death (following the methods of Brothwell 1981; Meindl and Lovejoy 1985; Iscan and Loth 1986). This is an assessment strengthened by the extent of age-related infracranial enthesial modification and the presence of ossified tracheal cartilage rings that Williamson had misidentified (as a broken horn ring possibly used for 'fastening a light scarf' [Williamson 1834: 9]). Standing between 178.27cm (5' 10") and 181.2cm (6') (using the equations of Trotter [1970] and Fully [1956], respectively), he was of above average height for the Early Bronze Age compared with the statures of other individuals from Early Bronze Age barrows (mean height =174.5 ± 5.0cm 1sd). Taking the more accurate Fully (cf. Raxter et al. 2006) result of 178.27cm, Gristhorpe Man is at the top end of the stature range (161.6–185.3cm) and nearly a standard deviation from the mean for the group (Wastling 2006). A body mass estimate, ranging between 69.8kg and 74.6kg (using the methods of Ruff et al. 1991; McHenry 1992; Grine et al. 1995), suggests a body mass index of roughly 22, which is in the heart of the normal range of 19 to 25 of modern standards (Frisancho 1993: 428). The maximum bi-iliac breadth method (Ruff 2000) suggests a body mass index of between about 24 and 25, which falls towards the upper end of the normal range of 19 to 25 of modern standards (Frisancho 1993: 428). The estimates of body mass are based on articular surface measurements that are set at physiological maturity (Ruff et al. 1991), when growth ceases. This means that in his prime, Gristhorpe Man possessed a lithe, muscular build that would be considered healthy by modern standards. Some form of strenuous physical activity involving extension, abduction, and lateral rotation of the hip resulted in bilateral third trochanters and marked hypotrochanteric fossae on the posterior surfaces of the femora, a combination of physical changes indicative of strenuous activity of the hips and lower limbs. Comparing favourably with the previously analysed and very robust Towton medieval combatants (Knüsel 2000), Gristhorpe Man appears to have been right-handed and strongly lateralized, indicating that he engaged in activities requiring strenuous use of his dominant right upper limb (Tables 10.1 and 10.2). This could have been from weapon use, although other activities requiring the use of a single hand, technological or subsistence-linked, could also have contributed to this asymmetry.

Gristhorpe Man's origins and diet were investigated using a combination of stable isotope measurements. Strontium, lead, and phosphate oxygen isotope ratios from the mandibular second molar tooth enamel, which mineralizes between the ages of two-and-a-half and eight (Gustafson and Koch 1974), are all consistent with origins on the Jurassic silicate rocks of the Scarborough region but not Jurassic limestones or the Cretaceous chalk of the Wolds (Montgomery 2002; Darling et al. 2003; Montgomery et al. 2005; Evans et al. 2010) (Table 10.3). The results cannot rule out origins in other regions of Europe where a similar combination of values might be found, but the most parsimonious explanation for such results is that he spent his childhood in north-east Yorkshire. Childhood (second molar root dentine)

Table 10.1 The measurements and values used to assess humeral bilateral asymmetry

Humeral measurement	Right (mm)	Left (mm)	Asymmetry (%)
Maximum transverse head diameter	49	48	2.62 %
Maximum breadth of the greater tubercle	34	34	0 %
Minimum circumference of the humeral shaft	65	60	8 %
Epicondylar breadth	67	63	6.2 %
Articular breadth	49	47	4.1 %
Maximum length	336	330	1.8 %

Table 10.2 The measurements and values obtained to assess clavicular asymmetry

Clavicle	Right (mm)	Left (mm)	Asymmetry (%)
Maximum length	155	159	− 2.55 %
Sagittal diameter at midshaft	14	13	7.41 %
Vertical diameter at midshaft	10	9.5	6.67%

and later life (cortical femur) diet were investigated using carbon and nitrogen isotope analysis of collagen (Table 10.4). Both provide a similar result: $\delta^{15}N$ = 11.3‰ (dentine) and 10.7‰ (femur); $\delta^{13}C$ = −21.0‰ (dentine) and −21.1‰ (femur). This indicates that his diet contained a substantial amount of protein of terrestrial origin from an early age, placing him at the upper end of the range for other East Yorkshire and British Late Neolithic and Bronze Age individuals (Jay and Richards 2007; Jay et al. 2012). Relatively reduced dental wear and lack of enamel hypoplastic lines (the presence of which would indicate a stressed growth period) and robust skeletal development testify to an individual who benefited from good nutrition and a diet that contained cariogenic foodstuffs from birth (as suggested by the presence of dental caries).

Three small, spherical objects, *ca.* 5mm in diameter, originally thought to have been 'mistletoe berries', were found in the coffin (Williamson 1834, 1872). The chemical composition of one of these was investigated by Raman Spectroscopy. The Raman spectra from the outer surface and inner core revealed the presence of peaks typically associated with phosphate and degraded protein (Edwards et al. 2010). Their composition is similar to modern kidney or gallstone calculus, a result that is consistent with his age-at-death and also high nitrogen values associated with a meat-based diet that would have predisposed him to suffer these abdominal stones during his advanced years (cf. Blackman et al. 1991).

Brachycrany (cranial index of 82.7), typical for the Bronze Age, as well as his height and strong build, with isotope evidence for a high-protein diet, support the hypothesis that Gristhorpe Man was probably a member of an elite from birth. The

Table 10.3 Lead, strontium, and oxygen isotope data

Sample	Material	Pb ppm	$^{206}Pb/^{204}Pb$[1]	$^{207}Pb/^{204}Pb$	$^{208}Pb/^{204}Pb$	$^{207}Pb/^{206}Pb$	$^{208}Pb/^{206}Pb$	Sr ppm	$^{87}Sr/^{86}Sr$[2]	$^{18}O_{bp}$ ‰[3]	$^{18}O_{dw}$ ‰[4]
Dagger	Bronze	0.003	18.2428	15.6308	38.2600	0.85684	2.09736				
Second molar	enamel		18.45	15.63	38.44	0.847	2.083	66.3	0.710689	17.2+0.18	-7.8 ±0.4
	dentine							173.9	0.710619		

[1] External reproducibility for the dagger measured by MC-ICP-MS at NIGL, Keyworth: ±0.0124% for $^{208}Pb/^{204}Pb$; ±0.0108% for $^{207}Pb/^{204}Pb$; ±0.0078% for $^{206}Pb/^{204}Pb$; ±0.0043% for $^{207}Pb/^{206}Pb$; ±0.0068% for $^{208}Pb/^{206}Pb$ 2σ and data are normalized and errors propagated to within run measurements of NBS 981. For the tooth measured by TIMS: ±0.15% for $^{208}Pb/^{204}Pb$; ±0.11% for $^{207}Pb/^{204}Pb$; ±0.07% for $^{206}Pb/^{204}Pb$; ±0.04% for $^{207}Pb/^{206}Pb$ and ±0.08% for $^{208}Pb/^{206}Pb$ (2σ, η=19).

[2] External reproducibility was estimated at ±0.004% (2σ).

[3] External and sample reproducibility for phosphate oxygen measurements was estimated at ±0.18 (1σ).

[4] Calculated using Levinson's equation (Levinson et al. 1987) after correction for the difference between the average published values for NBS120C and NBS120B used by Levinson (Chenery et al. 2010).

Table 10.4 Carbon and nitrogen isotope data

Sample	d¹³C	d¹⁵N	%C	%N	C/N	n
Femur – surface removed	−21.2	10.7	44.7	16.4	3.2	2
Femur – surface removed repeat	−21.2	10.8	43.6	16.1	3.2	2
Femur – surface removed small fraction	−21.3	10.6	42.3	15.2	3.2	2
Femur – surface removed small fraction repeat	−21.4	10.7	42.3	15.1	3.2	2
Femur surface – small fraction	−21.4	10.5	40.3	13.5	3.4	2
Femur surface – small fraction repeat	−21.7	10.5	40.0	13.1	3.6	1
Bone 'dust'	−21.6	10.5	45.0	15.6	3.4	1
Bone 'dust' – small fraction	−21.1	10.7	40.6	14.3	3.3	2
Bone 'dust' – small fraction repeat	−21.2	10.7	41.4	14.4	3.2	1
Mean of bone	−21.3	10.6	42.2	14.8	3.3	
1 sd	0.2	0.1	1.9	1.1	0.1	
Tooth dentine from second molar	−21.0	11.3	45.0	16.9	3.1	2
'Brain'	−23.6	11.7	54.9	8.1	7.9	2
Beeswax from inside the cranium	−26.8	n/a	81.8	0.1	n/a	2

Carbon and nitrogen stable isotope measurements were undertaken by continuous-flow isotope ratio mass spectrometry at the Stable Light Isotope Facility, University of Bradford. 'Small fraction' refers to the collagenous proteins that go through the ultrafilter and hence have a molecular weight less than 30 000. Analytical error determined from repeat measurements of internal and international standards was 0.2 per mil or better.

presence of traumatic injuries – two healed fractures of left ribs six and nine, and damage to cervical vertebrae two and three that resulted in left apophyseal joint fusion – in addition to vertebral degenerative osteophytes of vertebral bodies and a large syndesmophyte extending from the right side of the first sacral vertebra, attests to the effects of physical rigours and advanced age. In addition to dental disease (caries), he had suffered further episodes of trauma to the lower central incisors resulting in dead tooth roots and cyst formation. Furthermore, a large cyst had formed above the left maxillary molars and into the maxillary antrum.

Since the nineteenth-century wiring could not be interfered with, the skeleton was submitted for CT scanning to obtain 3D visualization and virtual dissection. This enabled articular surfaces to be examined and revealed that, despite his healthy physique and physical evidence for social advantage for much of his life, Gristhorpe Man suffered from a slowly developing intra-osseous, benign intracranial tumour in the left anterior parieto-temporal region, the increased intra-cranial pressure from which probably had an impact on cerebral function. A lesion in this location may have had behavioural consequences prior to death, ranging from intermittent headaches, vomiting, aphasia (i.e. impaired speech and speech comprehension) and hemiparesis (i.e. muscle weakness) to impaired consciousness and seizure (Aufderheide and Rodríguez-Martín 1998: 250–51; De Angelis et al. 2002: 68).

Gas chromatography-mass spectrometry (GC-MS) was undertaken on a small (1–2mg) sample of black material contained in a vial labelled 'brain'. Although lipid analysis of degraded brain tissue from archaeological contexts is uncommon (Gülacara et al. 1990), analysis revealed the presence of stanols and stanones in high abundance including coprostanol (5β–cholestanol), epicoprostanol and coprostanone (5β–cholestan–3–one). These are microbial alteration products of cholesterol. The brain is the most cholesterol-rich organ in the human body. Cholesterol is the only sterol present in the adult human brain and accounts for 25 per cent of total lipid of the tissue (Norton 1981). Although no cholesterol was present in the Gristhorpe sample, the abundance of cholesterol alteration products suggests that the sample could indeed be remnant brain tissue. Stable isotope analysis supports this interpretation: the nitrogen isotope ratio obtained from the black material ($\delta^{15}N$ = 11.7‰) is very similar to that obtained from the tooth dentine ($\delta^{15}N$ = 11.3‰), whilst the carbon isotope ratio ($\delta^{13}C$ = −23.6‰) is 2.6‰ more negative than that for the dentine ($\delta^{13}C$ = −21.0‰). This situation would be consistent with the expected carbon isotope ratio offset between collagen and a fatty, lipid-rich tissue such as the brain (Jim et al. 2004).

The coffin and grave goods

On discovery, the 2.29 × 0.99m coffin was aligned north-south and in an excellent state of preservation. It was roughly square cut at the foot (i.e. northern) end, but the base and lid had been rounded off at the head (i.e. southern) end to give it a 'canoe' shape. More explicitly canoe-shaped examples have been found at Loose Howe (Elgee and Elgee 1949) (for example, see Grinsell 1941). Only the coffin lid, which now measures 2.26 × 0.79m, survives.

In 1834 the excavators identified 'a rude figure of a human face' carved into the foot end of the lid, i.e. at the opposite end to the head of the body inside (Williamson 1834: 5–6). This carving, now much degraded, is surrounded by a cut that flares, possibly to indicate shoulders (Maron 2007), and which distinguishes it from the surrounding wood. There is no bark present on the carved 'face' and an area of flattened sapwood and a slightly curving gash may be the results of damage during the lifting of the coffin in 1834 (Williamson 1834: 5–6, 1872: 6).

The artefacts accompanying the burial are characteristic of other Early Bronze Age adult males in Yorkshire and elsewhere in Britain, except that they include organic materials that do not normally survive. According to Williamson's account (1834: 10, 1872: 15), the body lay on 'vegetable substance' described as rushes, and was wrapped in animal hide fixed at the chest with a polished bone pin, 72mm long, which has been fashioned from a pig fibula (T. O'Connor pers. comm.)

On the lower chest was 'a double rose of a ribband, with two loose ends' decorated with raised lines made of a brittle material that disintegrated on exposure to air (Williamson 1834: 10, 1872: 15). No other garments or human hair, nails, and skin were reported. The animal skin may have survived because it had been treated, perhaps tanned, before burial.

Several other objects accompanied the corpse; unfortunately, their original positions were mostly not recorded. These comprise: 1) a dagger blade and pommel; 2) a knife and two flint flakes; 3) a bark container, found beside the body; 4) a small wooden object, probably a fastener; and 5) fox metatarsal and pine marten phalanges, originally identified by William Buckland as from a weasel. The 'horn ring', and 'mistletoe berries' (Williamson 1834) or 'seeds of a leguminous plant' (Williamson 1872) have, as already discussed, now been identified as ossified tracheal cartilage rings and kidney stones (see earlier).

The dagger has a short, slender flat bronze blade, classified by Gerloff within her *Type Merthyr Mawr, Variant Parwich* (Gerloff 1975: 51). A revised classification (Woodward et al. 2015) confirms that it can be grouped with early flat bronze daggers (series 2) despite being one of the shortest examples; this may in part be due to sharpening. It is placed in type F3 (*Merthyr Mawr*), which seems to be specifically late within the overall currency of series 2 weapons, dating close to the turn of the millennium. The cutting edge was cold-worked and annealed through several cycles at a temperature high enough to ensure a homogeneous bronze. The organic hilt, of which no trace survives, was riveted to the blade with two metal peg rivets. The original 1834 illustration of the blade appears to depict a scabbard, which would have been made from wooden plates lined and/or covered with hide (Henshall 1968; Cameron 2003; Gabra-Sanders et al. 2003). This no longer survives except perhaps in the form of traces of animal collagen on the blade, which were visible on scanning electron micrographs.

Metallurgical analysis of the blade shows it to have been of an unleaded medium tin-bronze with 12.00 per cent tin, which is within the 9–12 per cent range characteristic of Early Bronze Age alloys (Northover 2007). The principal impurities are 0.38 per cent arsenic, 0.09 per cent antimony, 0.14 per cent silver, and 0.07 per cent lead, with traces of nickel, zinc, and bismuth (Northover 2007). The arsenic/antimony/silver impurity pattern and the negligible nickel are consistent with Northover's Group A3, long attributed to Ireland (Rohl and Needham 1998; O'Brien et al. 2004). Detailed typological studies suggest that the Gristhorpe dagger, like most contemporary British objects, would have been manufactured in Britain using recycled Irish metal (Needham 2004). The lead isotope ratios (Table 10.3) are also consistent with the presence of Irish copper ore, as they overlap with those of Chalcolithic 'A' metal from Ireland and Wales.

Perhaps the most extraordinary item in the assemblage is the perfectly preserved pommel, the sides of which splay out to a flat oval top *ca.* 52mm wide dwarfing the blade, whose maximum width is about 38mm. The top and sides are polished to a high sheen, but it is unclear whether or not this is partly due to use-wear. Originally identified as whalebone, reappraisal confirms it as a cetacean jawbone. Its form is intermediate between two clearly defined classes of socketed pommels; broadly speaking, pre-2000 BC examples (class 2) are oval in plan and rectangular/gently trapezoidal in face view, whereas post-2000 BC (class 3) pommels are elliptical or lenticular in plan and more strongly expanded, usually with a 'lip' at the top (Woodward et al. 2015). The Gristhorpe pommel is unusual in combining characteristics of both classes.

Three lithic artefacts recovered from the log-coffin comprise a finely retouched blade described in the original report as the head of a small javelin (Williamson 1834: 8) but identifiable as a knife, and two unmodified flakes, described originally as 'rude heads of arrows' (Williamson 1834: 9). In the 1872 report the retouched blade is described as an 'implement of flint ... [these were] ... probably used as knives, or occasionally as scrapers for cleaning skins' (Williamson 1872: 14). The other two pieces were correctly described as flint flakes. These artefacts are readily paralleled in Early Bronze Age graves from Yorkshire and elsewhere in Britain, with numerous examples from the East Riding of Yorkshire as illustrated by Mortimer (1905).

The bark container, now a quantity of warped and degraded pieces of wood and bark, had a flat wooden base to which bark sides had been attached. It was first described as 'a kind of dish, or shallow basket of wicker work' (Williamson 1834: 9) and later as 'a kind of dish composed of pieces of bark stitched together with strips of skin or of animal sinews' (Williamson 1872: 15). Williamson (1834: 9) described a deposit of organic material found inside the container as 'a quantity of decomposed matter, which has not yet been analysed'. At some stage it was labelled as 'food residue' and a handwritten note in the museum archive records that it was investigated by Stuart Piggott in the 1950s, but the analysis proved indeterminate.

GC-MS analysis of solvent extracts of this deposit suggests a plant origin. However, there appears to be contamination of the sample from lignin-derived molecules that may have leached from the oak coffin. Analysis of a tiny fragment of the coffin supported such a view. Although further work is required, it may be that the deposit is not a food residue but a plant-based product used to make the interior waterproof. Whether the fibrous material, hair, and sinew traces found embedded in it represent accidental inclusions or the last traces of some foodstuff is unclear.

A small wooden object, 44 × 6.4mm, rounded at one end and slightly waisted, tapers to a spatulate shape at the other end. It is manufactured from a small piece of roundwood not identifiable to species. A slight notch across the waist on one side, created through use, makes it likely that this was a fastener, shaped so that the tapered surface would lie flat when fastened. A possible use is as a pouch fastener (analogous to the V-perforated buttons probably used in this way at Rudston, barrow 68a and at Acklam Wold barrow 124, Yorkshire [Greenwell 1877: 265; Mortimer 1905: 91; Shepherd 1973, 2009]) or else as a fastener for the bark container.

The black-stained fox metatarsal and pine marten phalanges found among the vegetable matter in the coffin may be the remnants of fox and pine marten furs, as paws are often retained with the pelt when an animal is skinned. Alternatively, the bones may simply attest to the presence of animal remains, perhaps as amulets.

The date of the burial

A combination of AMS radiocarbon and dendrochronological dating of the Gristhorpe assemblage provides insight into the sequence of events related to burial and permits comparison with similar finds. All radiocarbon dates are quoted at

95 per cent confidence and full details are given in Melton et al. (2013). Dagger blade and pommel typologies suggest a date of around 2000 BC, and a conventional radiocarbon date obtained in the 1980s on the branches overlying the coffin provided a date of 2300–1650 cal BC (HAR-4424).

The longest possible dendrochronological sequence was obtained from two sections from the oak coffin lid. A section from the 'foot' end, near the carving, including the bark and outer rings, produced 126 rings, and one from the 'head' end, 108 rings. Together these provide a 173-year composite ring sequence. The relatively small number of rings for the size of section suggests fast growth in a favourable environment (Tyers pers. comm.). Unfortunately, it was not possible to match this floating ring sequence with others from the region to obtain a calendar date because the sequence was relatively short and there are few dated dendrochronological records for this Early Bronze Age period (Tyers pers. comm.).

AMS radiocarbon dating was carried out on tooth root dentine, on femoral samples and on the branches overlying the coffin. In addition, a sequence of six evenly spaced tree-ring samples was obtained from the dendrochronology section from the coffin lid to allow a more precise wiggle-matched radiocarbon date for felling. Two factors had to be borne in mind when dating the skeleton: first, whether the attempt in 1834 to consolidate the 'very rotten' bones by simmering them for eight hours in a 'thin solution of glue' (Williamson 1872: 7) had introduced animal collagen; and, second, whether the skeleton is a nineteenth-century composite or replacement, with Indian ink (J. Ambers pers. comm.) used to 'touch up' substitute bones. The survival of so much bone mineral from an oak coffin burial is highly unusual, as conditions are not normally conducive to bone mineral preservation (Glob trans. 1983; Randsborg and Christensen 2006: 35–6).

The tooth root dentine provided a date of 2140–1940 cal BC (OxA-16844), while the femur gave a date of 2280–2030 cal BC (OxA-19219). These combine to give a date for the skeleton of 2200–2020 cal BC at 95 per cent confidence. In addition, the level of lead in the tooth enamel (three ppb) is extremely low even compared to other Bronze Age or pre-metallurgical Neolithic populations (Montgomery et al. 2000, 2005; Montgomery 2002). Such a low level of lead indicates Gristhorpe Man inhabited a remarkably unpolluted environment, which was not the case for people living in nineteenth-century England (Montgomery et al. 2010). This finding thus supports the dating evidence that shows the skeleton is of Early Bronze Age date and not that of a nineteenth-century individual.

The stable carbon and nitrogen isotope ratios of the dated collagen are inconsistent with terrestrial herbivores, marine fish, or marine mammal collagen, so the skeleton seems to have been unaffected by nineteenth-century attempts at conservation with glue. The same is true for the surface and sub-surface femur samples, and for the separated, ultra-filtered and small fraction samples where degraded animal collagen might be detected if present. All of these samples provided very similar carbon and nitrogen stable isotope results (Table 10.4), which leaves open the question of why the skeleton survived so well and, furthermore, how the unusual nineteenth-century conservation method worked. There is no apparent evidence for any protein that does not come from an Early Bronze Age human. The section of femur used for dating, although stained, was greasy and dense, with a high collagen yield. This strongly suggests that original collagen preservation was very good. Moreover, any mineral loss was not so extensive as to render the bones soft; there is no evidence for bone warping and deformation. Unfortunately, although a chemical analysis of the coffin water was made in 1834, the pH is unknown, but it is likely that any acid in the burial environment was buffered by the presence in the water of 'much sulphate of lime' (Williamson 1872: 8) and this, coupled with anaerobic conditions, led to the preservation of both mineral and organic materials.

The branches over the coffin dated to 1750–1530 cal BC (OxA-16812). Wiggle-matching of the radiocarbon dates for the coffin lid (Bronk Ramsey et al. 2001) confirmed a date of 2115–2035 cal BC for the date of felling.

The combined dating evidence indicates that the tree for the coffin was felled between 2115 cal BC and 2035 cal BC and that Gristhorpe Man died between 2200 cal BC and 2020 cal BC, indicating that these could have been contemporary events. The branches over the coffin were cut between 1750 cal BC and 1530 cal BC, meaning that this cannot have occurred at the same time, and that the branches were laid over the coffin at least 270 years after the death of Gristhorpe Man. The tree-ring sequence from the coffin can now be incorporated into the dated master records for the region.

Discussion

The unusual preservation circumstances of Gristhorpe Man provide a rare insight into Early Bronze Age funerary practices and the social networks that supported them. Parallels can be found for most, if not all, of the burial goods. In particular, the hide wrapping and the dagger with its pommel of rare cetacean bone represent items of conspicuous display that, along with the coffin and the structure and location of the funerary monument, emphasize a pre-eminent social status that is perhaps closely paralleled by the log-coffin grave unearthed at Stoborough, Dorset (Hutchins 1767).

Among these distinctive interments, where individual social identities appear to be emphasized (cf. Treherne 1995; Stig Sørensen 1997; Whitley 2002), is a group of males accompanied by metal weapons. These weapons, along with the conspicuous consumption usually involved in the construction of the funerary monuments, would have served to justify and legitimate a pre-eminent social position in life and in death.

Well-excavated burial sites frequently show complex histories of construction and successive burial deposits. The oak branches were described as 'carelessly thrown over the coffin; they are from five to eight inches in diameter, and, like the coffin, are still covered with their rough bark' (Williamson 1872: 16). If these are the axe-trimmed logs curated in the museum today, there is at least a 270-year difference between them and the oak coffin. It may be that Gristhorpe is an example of an interment that remained accessible for a time before the barrow was completed over it, or – more likely, given the coffin's state of preservation – the subject of a later intrusion or interment unrecognized by the nineteenth-century excavators.

The choice of grave goods may well have had special symbolic significance. The cetacean bone pommel indicates a connection with the sea that might also be echoed in the boat-like shape of the coffin. It is also curious that this senior dagger-accompanied male, a class of individual almost invariably laid on the left side at this time, is here laid on his right side looking out to sea. It is clear that travel, and the long-distance movement of materials and objects, was important to the operation of Early Bronze Age society (e.g. Needham 2009). Gristhorpe Man appears to be a paramount chief born locally, as indicated by his local isotope ratios, but linked into a wide network by the sea, with his burial accoutrements being part of a regional tradition of interment. The bark container with its probable internal coating of sealant appears to be a vessel or container paralleled by the characteristic Beaker or Food Vessel found with other near-contemporary single burials (see Ashbee 1960; Needham 2005; Woodward et al. 2005).

The ostentation of the Gristhorpe grave appears to have been matched by the physical attributes of the man himself. His prominent stature and body mass suggest that he benefited from good nutrition and living conditions from birth. The high nitrogen isotope ratio for the period indicates a substantial meat component to his diet that predisposed him to develop renal stones or gallstones, a condition associated with older, well-fed males of higher socio-economic status today. The skeletal and isotope evidence for good nutrition from early childhood would be consistent with inherited rather than acquired status. It is likely that this pre-eminent social standing was built upon an active lifestyle that included strong lateralized use of his right upper limb, perhaps in martial exploits that exposed him to several traumatic injuries in the form of healed fractures. In later life, he developed an intra-cranial tumour that may have caused physical and behavioural impairment, particularly of his dominant limb and those qualities that aided his rise to social prominence such as the use and comprehension of speech, physical strength, and co-ordinated movement.

Conclusion

The early discovery and publication of the Gristhorpe burial in 1834 and its reworking by the same author nearly half a century later in 1872 afford a rare opportunity to appraise changes in nineteenth-century archaeological thought. The interpretation of the find in 1834 is very much in the antiquarian manner, with heavy emphasis on classical sources, mainly that of Julius Caesar, which we now know describes societies at a 2000-year remove from the Gristhorpe burial. By 1872, Williamson was able to employ Thomsen's/Worsaae's 'Three Age System', both Thomsen and Worsaae having previously compared the Gristhorpe remains with similar Danish log-coffins in the formulation of this bedrock of archaeological interpretation (Rowley-Conwy 2007: 118; Worsaae trans. 1849: fn. 96). Our new programme of dating on the Gristhorpe skeleton and coffin, along with recent dendrochronological dating of the Danish examples (Randsborg and Christensen 2006), shows conclusively that Gristhorpe Man is the earlier by some 700 years.

This type of chronological resolution epitomizes the advances made in the discipline over the years since 1872. Other noteworthy developments include residue analyses of proteins and chemical constituents of both artefacts and human remains that clarify the identification, preservation, manufacture, and use of material and biological remains found in funerary contexts. Major advances have been made in analyses of human remains. This subject has been entirely reinvented from its origin as part of medicine and reliant upon now-defunct methods, such as phrenology, the latter being present in the 1834 analysis of Gristhorpe Man but reproduced with due scepticism in 1872. New methods include standards for determining age at death, sex, body proportions, and health status, enhanced most recently by the application of medical imaging techniques. Isotopic analyses now provide means to examine the diet, provenance and movement of people to explore the origin and social relationships implicit in funerary contexts. The use of these studies, in conjunction with continued scholarly synthesis of archaeological discoveries, highlights the value of the retention and curation of finds. The Gristhorpe remains have resided in the Rotunda Museum since 1834, and their new display ensures public dissemination of research findings, as well as their availability for future study in light of even newer techniques and ideas.

References

Ashbee, P. (1960) *The Bronze Age Round Barrow in Britain*. London: Phoenix House.

Aufderheide, A.C. and C. Rodríguez-Martín (1998) *The Cambridge Encyclopedia of Human Paleopathology*. Cambridge: Cambridge University Press.

Blackman, J., Allison, M.J., Aufderheide, A.C., Oldroyd, N., and Steinbock, R.T. (1991) Secondary hyperparathyroidism in an Andean mummy. In: D.J. Ortner and A.C. Aufderheide (eds.), *Human Paleopathology: Current Syntheses and Future Options*. Washington, D.C. and London: Smithsonian Institution Press, pp. 291–6.

Bronk Ramsey, C., Van Der Plicht, J., and Weninger, B. (2001) Wiggle matching radiocarbon dates. *Radiocarbon*, 43: 381–9.

Brothwell, D.R. (1981) *Digging up Bones: The Excavation, Treatment and Study of Human Skeletal Remains*. Third edition. London: British Museum (Natural History); Oxford: Oxford University Press.

Cameron, E. (2003) The dagger: hilt and scabbard. In: L. Baker, J.A. Sheridan, and T.G. Cowie, An Early Bronze Age 'dagger grave' from Rameldry Farm, near Kingskettle, Fife. *Proceedings of the Society of Antiquaries of Scotland*, 133: 85–123.

Chenery, C.A., Müldner, G., Evans, J., Eckhardt, H., Leach, S., and Lewis, M. (2010) Strontium and stable isotope evidence for diet and mobility in Roman Gloucester, UK. *Journal of Archaeological Science*, 37: 150–63.

Colt Hoare, R. (1812) *The History of Ancient Wiltshire: Volume 1*. London: W. Miller.

Darling, W.G., Bath, A.H., and Talbot. J.C. (2003) The O and H stable isotopic composition of fresh waters in the British Isles 2: surface waters and groundwater. *Hydrology and Earth System Sciences*, 7(2): 183–95.

Davis, J.B. and Thurnam, J. (1865) *Crania Britannica: Delineations and Descriptions of the Skulls of the Early Inhabitants of the British islands, together with Notices of their Other Remains: Volume 2*. London: Printed for the subscribers.

De Angelis, L.M., Gutin, P.H., Leibel, S.A., and Posner, J.B. (2002) *Intracranial Tumours: Diagnosis and Treatment*. London: Martin Dunitz.

Drenth, E. and Lohof, E. (2005) Mounds for the dead: funerary and burial ritual in Beaker period, Early and Middle Bronze Age. In: L.P. Louwe Kooijmans, P.W. van den Broeke, H. Fokkens, and A.L. van Gijn (eds.) *The Prehistory of the Netherlands: Volume 1*. Amsterdam: Amsterdam University Press, pp. 433–54.

Edwards, H.G.M., Montgomery, J. Melton, N.D., Hargreaves, M.D., Wilson, A.S., and Carter, E.A. (2010) Gristhorpe Man: Raman spectroscopic study of a Bronze Age log-coffin burial. *Journal of Raman Spectroscopy*. 41(11): 1533–6.

Elgee, H.W. and Elgee, F. (1949) An Early Bronze Age burial in a boat-shaped wooden coffin from north-east Yorkshire. *Proceedings of the Prehistoric Society*, 15: 87–106.

Evans, J.A., Montgomery, J., Wildman, G., and Boulton, N. (2010) Spatial variations in biosphere $^{87}Sr/^{86}Sr$ in Britain. *Journal of the Geological Society, London*, 167: 1–4.

Frank, A.G. (1993) Bronze Age world system cycles. *Current Anthropology*, 34(4): 383–429.

French, C.A.I. (2003) *Geoarchaeology in Action: Studies in Soil Micromorphology and Landscape Evolution*. London: Routledge.

French, C.A.I., Allen, M.J., and Lewis, H. eds. (2007) *Prehistoric Landscape Development and Human Impact in the Upper Allen Valley, Cranborne Chase, Dorset*. Cambridge: McDonald Institute for Archaeological Research.

Frisancho, A.R. (1993) *Human Adaptation and Accommodation*. Ann Arbor, MI: University of Michigan Press.

Fully, G. (1956) Une nouvelle méthode de détermination de la taille. *Annuaire de Médecine Légale*, 35: 266–73.

Gabra-Sanders, T., Cressey, M., and Clarke, C. (2003) The scabbard. In: M. Cressey and J.A. Sheridan, The excavation of a Bronze Age cemetery at Seafield West, near Inverness, Highland. *Proceedings of the Society of Antiquaries of Scotland* 133: 47–84.

Gerloff, S. (1975) *The Early Bronze Age Daggers in Great Britain and a Reconsideration of the Wessex Culture*. Prähistorische Bronzefunde 6: 2. Munich: Beck.

Glob, P.V. (1973) (trans. 1983). *The Mound People: Danish Bronze-Age Man Preserved*. Translated by J. Bulman. London: Paladin.

Greenwell, W. (1877) *British Barrows*. Oxford: Clarendon.

Grine, F.E., Jungers, W.L., Tobias, P.V., and Pearson, O.M. (1995) Fossil *Homo* femur from Berg Aukas, Northern Namibia. *American Journal of Physical Anthropology*, 97: 151–85.

Grinsell, L.V. (1941) The boat of the dead in the Bronze Age. *Antiquity*, 15: 360–70.

Gülacara, F.O., Susini, A., and Klohn, M. (1990) Preservation and post-mortem transformations of lipids in samples from a 4000-year-old Nubian mummy. *Journal of Archaeological Science*, 17: 691–705.

Gustafson, G. and Koch, G. (1974) Age estimation up to 16 years of age based on dental development. *Odontologisk Revy*, 25: 297–306.

Harding, A.F. (2000) *European Societies in the Bronze Age*. Cambridge: Cambridge University Press.

Harland, N. (1932) Letter to F. Elgee dated 28 February 1932. Frank Elgee Archive, Yorkshire Archaeological Society, 23 Clarendon Road, Leeds LS2 9NZ, UK.

Henshall, A.S. (1968) Scottish dagger graves. In: J.M. Coles and D.D.A. Simpson (eds.), *Studies in Ancient Europe*. Leicester: Leicester University Press, pp. 273–95.

Hutchins, J. (1767). Archaeology: part I. *Gentleman's Magazine*: 94–5.

Iscan, M.Y. and Loth, S.R. (1986) Estimation of age and determination of sex from the sternal rib. In: K.J. Reichs (ed.), *Forensic Osteology*. Springfield, IL: Charles C. Thomas, pp. 68–89.

Jay, M. and Richards, M. (2007) The Beaker People Project: progress and prospects for the carbon, nitrogen and sulphur isotopic analysis of collagen. In: M. Larsson and M. Parker Pearson (eds.), *From Stonehenge to the Baltic: Living with Cultural Diversity in the Third Millennium* BC. British Archaeological Reports International series 1692. Oxford: Archaeopress, pp. 77–82.

Jay, M., Parker Pearson, M., Richards, M., Nehlich, O., Montgomery, J., Chamberlain, A., and Sheridan, A. (2012) The Beaker People Project: an interim report on the progress of the isotopic analysis of the organic skeletal material. In: M.J. Allen, J. Gardiner, and A. Sheridan (eds.), *Is there a British Chalcolithic? People, Place and Polity in the Later 3rd Millennium*. Prehistoric Society Research Paper 4. Oxford: Oxbow Books, pp. 226–36.

Jensen, J. (1998) *Manden i kisten, hvad bronzealdererens gravhøje gemte*. Copenhagen: Gyldendal.

Jim, S., Ambrose, S.H., and Evershed, R.P. (2004) Stable carbon isotopic evidence for differences in the biosynthetic origin of bone cholesterol, collagen and apatite: implications for their use in palaeodietary reconstruction. *Geochimica et Cosmochimica Acta*, 68: 61–72.

Knüsel, C.J. (2000) Activity-related skeletal change. In: V. Fiorato, A. Boylston, and C.J. Knüsel (eds.) *Blood Red Roses: The Archaeology of a Mass Grave from the Battle of Towton AD 1461*. Oxford: Oxbow, pp. 103–18.

Kristiansen, K. and Larsson, T.B. (2005) *The Rise of Bronze Age Society: Travels, Transmissions and Transformations*. Cambridge: Cambridge University Press.

Levinson, A.A., Luz, B., and Kolodny, Y. (1987) Variations in oxygen isotope compositions of human teeth and urinary stones. *Applied Geochemistry*, 2: 367–71.

Mchenry, H.M. (1992) Body size and proportions in early hominids. *American Journal of Physical Anthropology*, 87: 407–31.

Maron, D.R. (2007) The Bronze Age tree trunk coffin from Gristhorpe, East Yorkshire: curation, scholarship, and new research agenda. Unpublished MSc dissertation, Bradford University.

Meindl, R.S. and Lovejoy, C.O. (1985) Ectocranial suture closure: a revised method for the determination of skeletal age based on the lateral-anterior sutures. *American Journal of Physical Anthropology*, 68: 57–66.

Melton, N.D., Montgomery, J., and Knüsel, C.J. eds. (2013) *Gristhorpe Man: A life and Death in the Bronze Age*. Yorkshire Archaeological Society Occasional Monograph Series. Oxford: Oxbow Books.

Montgomery, J. (2002) Lead and strontium isotope compositions of human dental tissues as an indicator of ancient exposure and population dynamics. Unpublished PhD dissertation, Bradford University.

Montgomery, J., Budd P., and Evans, J. (2000) Reconstructing the lifetime movements of ancient people: a Neolithic case study from southern England. *European Journal of Archaeology*, 3(3): 407–22.

Montgomery, J., Evans, J.A., Powlesland, D., and Roberts, C.A. (2005) Continuity or colonization in Anglo-Saxon England? Isotope evidence for mobility, subsistence practice, and status at West Heslerton. *American Journal of Physical Anthropology*, 126(2): 12–38.

Montgomery, J., Evans, J.A., Chenery, S.R., Pashley, V., and Killgrove, K. (2010) 'Gleaming, white and deadly': the use of lead to track human exposure and geographic origins in the Roman period in Britain. In H. Eckardt (ed.), *Roman Diasporas: Archeological Approaches to Mobility and Diversity in the Roman Empire*. Portsmouth (RI): Journal of Roman Archaeology, pp. 204–26.

Mortimer, J.R. (1905) *Forty Years Researches in British and Saxon Burial Mounds of East Yorkshire*. London: A. Brown and Sons.

Mowat, R.J.C. (1996) *The Log-Boats of Scotland*. Oxford: Oxbow.

Needham, S. (2004). Migdale-Marnoch: sunburst of Scottish metallurgy. In: I.A.G. Shepherd and G. Barclay (eds.), *Scotland in Ancient Europe: the Neolithic and Early Bronze Age of Scotland in their European Context*. Edinburgh: Society of Antiquaries of Scotland, pp. 278–87.

——(2005) Transforming Beaker culture in north-west Europe: processes of fusion and fission. *Proceedings of the Prehistoric Society*, 71: 171–217.

——(2009) Encompassing the sea: 'maritories' and Bronze Age maritime interactions. In: P. Clark (ed.), *Bronze Age Connections: Cultural Contact in prehistoric Europe*. Oxford: Oxbow, pp. 12–37.

Northover, P. (2007) Analysis and metallography of the Gristhorpe Dagger. Report No. R3005 prepared for Oxford Materials Characterisation Service.

Norton, W.T. (1981) Formation, structure and biochemistry of myelin. In: G.J. Siegel, A.R. Wayne, B.W. Agranoff, and R. Katzman (eds.), *Basic neurochemistry*. Boston: Little Brown, pp. 63–92.

O'Brien, W., Northover, J.P., and Stos, S. (2004) Lead isotopes and circulation. In: W. O'Brien (ed.), *Ross Island: Mining, Metal and Society in Early Ireland*. Bronze Age Studies 6. Galway: Dept. of Archaeology, National University of Ireland, Galway, pp. 538–51.

Parker Pearson, M., Needham, S., and Sheridan, J.A. (2013) Bronze Age tree-trunk coffin burials in Britain. In: N. Melton, J. Montgomery, and C. Knüsel (eds.) *Gristhorpe Man: A Life and Death in the Bronze Age*. Yorkshire Archaeological Society Occasional Monograph Series. Oxford: Oxbow Books, pp. 29–66.

Petersen, F. (1969) Early Bronze Age timber graves and coffin burials on the Yorkshire Wolds. *Yorkshire Archaeological Journal*, 42: 262–7.

Phillips, B. (1856) Untitled communication. *Archaeological Journal*, 13: 183–4.

Randsborg, K. and Christensen, K. (2006) *Bronze Age Oak-Coffin Graves: Archaeology and Dendro-Dating*. Acta Archaeologica 77. Copenhagen: Blackwell Munksgaard.

Raxter, M.H., Auerbach, B.M., and Ruff, C.B. (2006) Revision of the Fully technique for estimating statures. *American Journal of Physical Anthropology*, 130: 374–84.

Rohl, B. (1996) Lead isotope data from the Isotrace Laboratory, Oxford: archaeometry data base 2, galena from Britain and Ireland. *Archaeometry*, 38: 165–80.

Rohl, B.M. and Needham, S.P. (1998) *The Circulation of Metal in the British Bronze Age: The Application of Lead Isotope Analysis*. British Museum Occasional Paper 102. London: British Museum.

Rowley-Conwy, P. (2007) *From Genesis to Prehistory: The Archaeological Three Age System and its Contested Reception in Denmark, Britain and Ireland*. Oxford: Oxford University Press.

Ruff, C.B. (2000) Body mass prediction from skeletal frame size in elite athletes. *American Journal of Physical Anthropology*, 113: 507–17.

Ruff, C.B., W.W. Scott, and A.Y.-C. Liu. (1991) Articular and diaphyseal remodeling of the proximal femur with changes in body mass in adults. *American Journal of Physical Anthropology*, 86: 397–413.

Savory, H.N. (1980) *Guide Catalogue of the Bronze Age Collections*. Cardiff: National Museum of Wales.

Shepherd, I.A.G. (1973) The V-bored buttons of Great Britain. Unpublished MA dissertation, Edinburgh University.

——(2009) The V-bored buttons of Great Britain and Ireland. *Proceedings of the Prehistoric Society*, 75: 335–69.

Stig Sørensen, M.L. (1997) Reading dress: the construction of social categories in Bronze Age Europe. *Journal of European Archaeology*, 5(1): 93–114.

Treherne, P. (1995) The warrior's beauty: the masculine body and self-identity in Bronze-Age Europe. *Journal of European Archaeology*, 3(1): 105–44.

Trotter, M. (1970) Estimation of stature from intact limb bones. In: T.D. Stewart (ed.), *Personal Identification in Mass Disasters*. Washington, D.C.: Smithsonian Institution, pp. 71–83.

Wastling, V.J. (2006) Gristhorpe Man: a modern assessment of an Early Bronze Age Tree Trunk Burial. Unpublished MSc dissertation, Bradford University.

Whitley, J. (2002) Objects with attitude: biographical facts and fallacies in the study of Late Bronze Age and Early Iron Age warrior graves. *Cambridge Archaeological Journal*, 12(2): 217–32.

Williamson, W.C. (1834) *Description of the Tumulus, lately Opened at Gristhorpe, near Scarborough*. Scarborough: C.R. Todd.

——(1872) *Description of the Tumulus Opened at Gristhorpe, near Scarborough*. Scarborough: S.W. Theakston.

——(1896) *Reminiscences of a Yorkshire Naturalist*. London: George Redway.

Woodward, A., Hunter, J., Ixer, R., Maltby, M., Potts, P.J., Webb, P.C., Watson, J.S., and Jones, M.C. (2005) Ritual in some early Bronze Age grave goods. *Archaeological Journal*, 162: 31–64.

Woodward, A., Hunter, J.. Needham, S., Bray, P., and O'Connor, S. (2015) Items of equipment I: daggers, pommels and belt fittings. In: A. Woodward and J. Hunter, *Ritual in Early Bronze Age Grave Goods*. Oxford: Oxbow Books, pp. 23–68.

Worsaae, J.J.A. (1843) (trans. 1849). *The Primeval Antiquities of Denmark*. Translated and applied to the illustration of similar remains in England by W.J. Thoms. London: John Henry Parker.

History and surface condition of the Lewis Chessmen in the collection of the National Museums Scotland (Hebrides, late twelfth to early thirteenth centuries)

Jim Tate, Ina Reiche, Flavia Pinzari, Jane Clark, and David Caldwell

Introduction

The Lewis Chessmen (Figure 11.1) are widely recognized to be amongst the most appealing pieces of early medieval sculpture that survive. The miniature figures, each carved in ivory and most less than 100mm tall, have charm and individual personalities. Some were clearly for playing chess, the game as we know it being comparatively new in northern Europe when they were carved, but other non-figurative pieces in the hoard may well have been for playing the Scandinavian board game *hnefatafl* (Caldwell et al. 2009). Where and how they were found is uncertain, with various more or less plausible proposals having been enriched by good story telling since the early nineteenth century. Nor do we know for sure where they were made, or for whom, leading to attributions – and claims – from several different countries. Although there are many other carved playing pieces the questions raised by the Lewis hoard continues to intrigue scholars and the public alike, while the figures themselves retain their enigmatic expressions – resigned, worried, fierce, bored, or just generally preoccupied.

It has been generally accepted that the hoard was found in 1831 in Uig, on the west coast of the island of Lewis. Surprisingly, there is little direct contemporary evidence, and recent research (Caldwell et al. 2009) has proposed that Mèalasta, still on the coast but several miles south of Uig Strand, is possibly a more likely location. It was not long before various different legends about their finding became established. Madden (1832) says that they were found by a 'peasant ... while digging a sand bank'. Wilson (1851) says that the peasant found the pieces in a 'small subterranean stone building like an oven, some depth beneath the surface'. By 1861

Figure 11.1 The 11 chessmen from Lewis in the NMS collection.

Thomas (1863) reported an earlier and far more elaborate story told by Donald Morrison who died in 1834, which starts in the early seventeenth century with a seaman escaping from a shipwreck with a bag containing 'the wealth the ship was supposed to contain'. The sailor was observed and killed, but when the contents of the bag were examined his murderer decided that they were too incriminating and went some ten miles to bury them in a sand bank in Uig – where they remained until found in 1831 by Malcolm Macleod. Robinson (2009) notes how a cow joins into the story in other versions, while both he and Caldwell et al. (2009) point out that the tales say more about the significance of story telling in the Hebrides than about the history of the pieces.

Even after they were discovered the history of the pieces has some gaps. They were acquired from the finder by Roderick Ririe, who permitted their display in Edinburgh in April 1831 and then bought by T A Forrest who, after failing in Edinburgh, successfully sold the majority of them to the British Museum. Thus, 82 pieces (including 6 Kings, 5 Queens, 13 Bishops, 14 Knights, 10 Warders, 19 Pawns or games pieces, and a small belt buckle also in ivory) were acquired by the BM in 1831/2 and were comprehensively published by the Keeper Sir Frederick Madden (Madden 1832).

However, Ririe had a further 11 pieces (10 from the hoard and a further piece which he obtained from Lewis) which he sold to Charles Kirkpatrick Sharpe, an Edinburgh dealer. These pieces remained with Sharpe until 1851 when they were sold to Lord Londesborough, in whose collection they remained until eventually, in 1888, they were acquired by the National Museum of Antiquities of Scotland, now the National Museums Scotland (NMS): two Kings, three Queens, three Bishops, one Knight, and two Warders.

The collecting history of the chess pieces has been outlined to illustrate that there are several possible scenarios in the life of the pieces since they were carved in the late twelfth or early thirteenth century and deposited (however this came about) in the hoard not long afterwards (Caldwell et al. 2009, 2010). Were they buried in a sand dune, or in a vaulted chamber? Does the buckle mean that some or all were together in a bag? Were they recovered earlier than 1831 and kept in different conditions? And when they moved into private and public collections what was done to clean and preserve them?

The purpose of this study on the 11 pieces now in the NMS collection was to see whether the surface condition of the pieces might help to understanding their history. The pieces have often been illustrated and described (Glenn 2003; Stratford 1997; Robinson 2009; Caldwell et al. 2009, 2010) as well as being on permanent display. However, for the reasons outlined above they were not included in the first and fullest account by Madden (1832) who noted particularly how a number of the pieces newly acquired by the BM had traces of red colour. Nor were the NMS pieces included in the technical examination undertaken at the BM department of scientific research reported by Stratford (1997). A more comprehensive study is now planned of the full collection from the hoard in both museums to allow more detailed comparison of the surface appearance and condition and particularly to relate this to different cleaning and conservation treatments since they were collected.

The work so far has considered four questions:

- Are the pieces all from Walrus ivory, and can we say anything about the tusks they came from?
- Are there tool marks that might distinguish working methods?
- What is the nature of the surface damage and can that tell us anything about the environment to which they have been subjected?
- Is there any remaining evidence of colouring?

All 11 pieces from the NMS collection were examined, i.e.:

Kings H.NS 19 and H.NS 20
Queens H.NS 21, H.NS 22, and H.NS 23
Bishops H.NS 24, H.NS 25, and H.NS 26
Knight H.NS 27
Warders H.NS 28 and H.NS 29

Methods

Investigations of Lewis chess pieces

The pieces were examined with an Olympus SZX12 stereo microscope with magnification between x7 and x50 with direct observation, digital image capture, and linear measurement using AnalySIS software.

Selected areas of the pieces were examined using X-ray Fluorescence (XRF) with a modified Oxford Instruments ED 2000 with Oxford Instruments software ED 2000SW version 1.31 with open sample geometry and a short airpath between sample and X-ray source and Si(Li) detector. Standard conditions use a Rhodium X-ray tube at 48kV and up to 1mA, the primary beam exciting an analytical area approximately 2 x 3 mm on the sample, the position of the analysis shown by the intersection of two laser pointers. The system detects atomic number elements greater than 19, the detection limits and analytical depth depending on the sample matrix. Data are recorded as energy spectra between 3 and 40keV with a detector energy resolution of 140eV at 6keV. In order to compare results from different analyses net peak area values were extracted and presented either as ratios, or by comparison normalized to the main K-alpha peak from calcium.

Artificial fungal aging experiments on modern ivory

A boar (*Sus scrofa*, L.) tusk about 30 years old was used for the investigation of the effect of fungi damage on ivory. Cut into 1–2cm diameter pieces the tusk was cleaned with ethanol 70 per cetn (water:alcohol V:V), sterilized under 254nm UV light for 45 minutes at approximately 40mWs^{-1}cm^{-2}. They were separated into two experiments. Two pieces were inoculated with an *Aspergillus niger* van Tieghem strain (from the ICRCPAL culture collection) and placed in sterilized Petri dishes at 100 per cent RH at 25°C for ten days along with two controls with no inoculation. Further pieces were treated in the same way but immersed in nutritive agar. Full details are given in Pinzari et al. (2013).

The ivory samples were examined by optical microscopy before and after fungal growth using a Leica MZ16 stereoscopic microscope fitted with low temperature fibre-optic illumination. The system was equipped with a digital camera connected with a computer and software (L.A.S. Leica) that allow the multifocal composition of images.

The samples were also analysed before and after fungal growth using a Carl-Zeiss EVO50 variable pressure scanning electron microscope (VP SEM) with a backscattered electron detector (BSE) and Oxford Instruments INCA 250 energy dispersion spectroscopy (EDS).

Results and discussion

The species of ivory and possible location within the tusk

The chess pieces are generally referred to as being made from Walrus ivory, with a few possibly of whale tooth. A characteristic of walrus ivory is that the main bulk of the tusk consists of dentine that is clearly divided into two forms: the outermost primary dentine, which is smooth and uniform, and an inner secondary dentine that has a granular 'oatmeal-'like structure (Webster 1958; Locke 2008). In section the tusks are oval and the distinction between the different dentine layers can be clearly seen. In contrast sperm whale teeth are more uniform, with a more circular cross section with concentric growth rings (e.g. Espinoza and Mann 1991). Elephant and hippopotamus ivory have characteristic forms, although their identification is not always straightforward, but it is known that these materials were very scarce in northern Europe in the eleventh and twelfth centuries (Robinson 2009). Walrus ivory and whale teeth are hollow at the base pulp cavity, becoming solid in moving towards the distal end. Narwhale tusks are smaller in diameter with a hollow core along the bulk of their length.

We do not have polished cross sections of the Lewis chess pieces, but the bases do provide evidence of characteristic differences. The base of the King (H.NS 19, Figure 11.2a) shows the roughly oval shape of the darker patterned secondary dentine at the centre, surrounded by paler primary dentine. For the Queen (H.NS 23, Figure 11.2b) the same structure is clear, the void showing that the piece was carved from the proximal end of the tusk where the formation the globular secondary dentine starts. However the Warder (H.NS 28, Figure 11.2c) has a quite different base; the conical void is surrounded by a more circular structure as well as being a paler chalk-like colour. The second Warder (H.NS 29, Figure 11.3a) was at one point classified as whale tooth: however the base shows quite clearly the secondary dentine structure of walrus.

The material of the only Knight in the NMS collections (H.NS 27, Figure 11.3b) is less clear. While the overall shape suggests the likely use of a wide walrus tusk, the appearance of the surface is more chalk-like than the other walrus pieces, and the pattern on the base less diagnostic of the species. It is in generally poor condition, with material loss and serious longitudinal cracking.

To carve the pieces the craftsman had to remove significant depths of ivory from the surface: for example in the King (H.NS 19) each side of the face is about 15mm deeper in that the sides of the throne, and there is a similar depth between the front of his chest and his knees. The carver did not avoid cutting through the primary dentine to expose the marbled secondary dentine layer. On what we might see as the 'better' pieces this has been minimized so that, for example, the King's face is smooth and the secondary dentine is only apparent as a band up the sides and across the top of the head. This is similar for one of the Queens and the three Bishops. For the other King (H.NS 20) and two Queens there is considerably more secondary dentine exposed (Figure 11.4a and 11.4b); this might have been because the carver appreciated the contrasting effect, was simply less skilled, or because the ivory available had a thinner primary dentine layer.

Figure 11.2 (a) Base of King (H.NS 19); (b) Base of Queen (H.NS 23); (c) Base of Warder (H.NS 28).

172 JIM TATE, ET AL.

Figure 11.3 (a) Base of Warder (H.NS 29); (b) Base of Knight (H.NS 27).

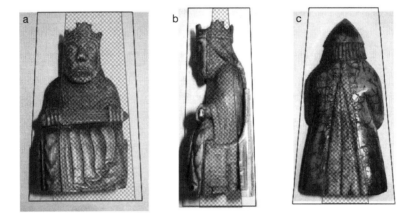

Figure 11.4 (a and b) Showing how King (H.NS 20) has been cut partially through the secondary dentine, while (c) the Warder (H.NS 28) is almost entirely from primary.

In contrast, the smaller NMS Warder (H.NS 29) only shows the secondary dentine at the base, very little is revealed near the head (Figure 11.4c). We conclude that this piece was carved from the distal end of the tusk, passing the upper reach of the secondary dentine. An X-ray radiograph taken of natural walrus tusk specimens does not clearly reveal the extent of the secondary dentine, the small difference in density being masked by longitudinal surface cracks and marks. Interestingly, the radiograph does reveal cracks across the inner part of the tusk, suggesting that the secondary dentine is separating and therefore may well be fragile. Some indication of such cracks was also found on a small sample of sectioned tusk in the NMS collection.

Clearly, the form of the pieces depended on the nature and quality of the tusk that the carver had available. Robinson (2009) illustrates how several pieces might have fitted in to one tusk, and Poplin (2006) has pointed out how two of the Bishops in the BM collection appear to have been carved back-to-back from the same piece of tusk. Since the cross-section of the primary/secondary interface has quite varied shape and dimensions, there does seem to be scope for investigating this more closely with a view to matching pieces. High-resolution Computerized X-ray Tomography (CT) scanning offers a possible way of obtaining virtual cross sections to allow comparison and potential matching of any pieces from the same tusk (Reiche et al. 2011).

As part of the overall examination of the pieces using X-Ray Fluorescence (XRF) we compared the relative amounts of calcium (Ca) and strontium (Sr) in the different chess pieces. The average relative values for each chess piece are shown in Figure 11.5. These measurements were made on various parts of the chessmen rather than concentrating on the directly comparable areas of each (such as the cut base) and have a certain amount of scatter. Nevertheless they show that two of the pieces have a lower Ca/Sr ratio than the first eight. We made the same measurements on three specimens of walrus tusk and three whale teeth from the collections, and found that, from this small sample, the whale teeth had a lower Ca/Sr ratio. We cannot obtain quantified data for Ca and Sr from the XRF data obtained in these experiments, nor can we separate surface and bulk compositional differences, and we report the data simply as a qualitative observation. The existence of strontium within bone and enamel has been extensively studied in relation to the determination of diet from $^{87}Sr/^{86}Sr$ isotopic ratios, with attention particularly to the relative stability within the matrix of Sr arising from diet or from post-mortem burial environment (e.g. Sillen and Kavanagh 1982; Burton and Wright 1995; Burton et al. 1999; Budd et al. 2000; Price et al. 2002; Lee-Thorpe 2008). Godfrey et al. (2002) record low values (200ppm) of Sr for modern elephant ivory and higher (720 to 1440ppm) for elephant ivory recovered from a seventeenth-century shipwreck, presumably showing the effect of prolonged immersion in seawater. As both walrus and sperm whale are marine animals, fairly high levels of Sr are not unexpected and although we do not know the impact of their habitats, different

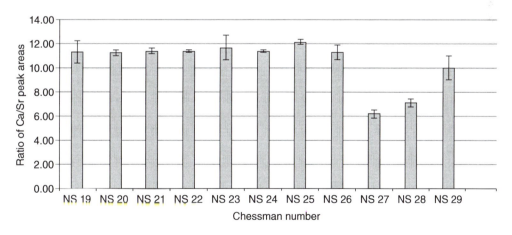

Figure 11.5 The ratio of calcium to strontium as measured by XRF from various locations on each chess piece. The lower values for H.NS 27 and H.NS 28 correspond to lower ratios found for whale teeth compared to walrus tusks.

feeding regimes or diagenesis, Müller and Reiche (2011) have also noted different Sr/Ca ratios from sperm whale compared to other marine ivory in a study using PIXE/PIGE of a wider range of samples. It seems reasonable therefore for us to hypothesize that both the Warder (H.NS 28) and the Knight (H.NS 27) are whale tooth, while the Warder (H.NS 29) is walrus ivory like the other pieces.

Surface evidence of tool marks

As outlined above we know nothing about the chessmen between the time they were lost or buried and their finding in 1831. We do not know if they were continuously buried until they were found, or if they might have spent some of the time between being abandoned (presumably in the thirteenth century) and found (in the nineteenth century) in different burial conditions and environments. Anything that we can deduce from the condition of the chess pieces, which will tell us about the environments to which they have been exposed, will increase our understanding of the history of the pieces.

Visual and microscopic examination of the surface shows evidence firstly of toolmarks as quite coarse grooves, presumed to be from fine chisels with slightly damaged cutting edges (Figure 11.6a). These marks suggest tools of less than 0.5mm, the main decorative grooves are typically 0.2 to 0.3mm wide at their base. There are also groups of parallel scratches oriented in different directions from polishing or fine scraping to achieve the smooth surfaces, individual scratches being around 0.1mm (Figure 11.6b). These marks, and the way in which the ivory has been cut to highlight features, for example the sharpness of the cutting lines around the eyelids, could be used to compare tools between pieces, something which was not possible in the limited time available for this study.

Groups of parallel 'chatter marks' were also observed on otherwise smoothed surfaces (Figure 11.6c). The marks look at first like the impressions that might come from vice marks, the short parallel lines forming tracks like the scale of a ruler. The separation of the lines varies between 50 and 300μm, consistent within each track but apparently with no basic size 'unit' between tracks. We conclude that they are caused by a blade vibrating as it is dragged across the ivory surface, the frequency of vibration depending on the pressure, the characteristics of the blade, and the structure of the ivory. We have observed that similar marks occur on other pieces of cleaned or worked ivory.

Other surface damage

The chess pieces all exhibit even more prominent and very characteristic damage: the surfaces are covered with a network of fine channels (Figures 11.6 and 11.7). These channels:

- are typically 0.5mm across and of a similar depth, none are bore holes; wander irregularly across the surface;
- vary in length – some are just spots, while others can be followed for several millimetres;

- cross and join together, or sometimes run side by side, but do not have any systematic branching form, nor is there any tapering of the widths along the length of the tracks;
- have rough edges and grainy bottoms with dark mineral inclusions;
- cover pretty much all surfaces evenly; there are very few sides of any of the chess pieces that do not have this damage, including the bases.

The damage must have occurred after the pieces were carved. It is evident from simple visual examination that the channels cause disfigurement to the carved and polished surfaces. For example, the face of the King (H.NM 19, Figure 11.7a) has a groove on one cheek: it is hard to imagine that the carver would have left such a scar. The damage is on surfaces that have only been revealed because the overlying ivory material has been removed during carving, and there are no boreholes into the ivory on the areas that were closer to the outer original surface. We can also see examples where some of the channels cross over carved details: for example across the sharply carved hair of Bishop (H.NS 25, Figure 11.7b–c).

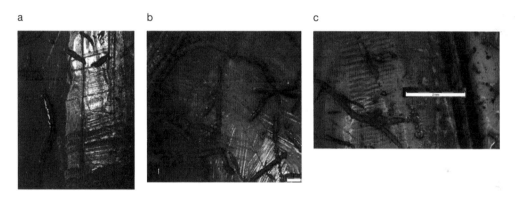

Figure 11.6 (a) Surface tool marks where material has been cut away; (b) polishing marks as groups of fine abrasions in different orientations; (c) 'chatter' marks, coarse marks towards the centre, and a finer band down the left of the image.

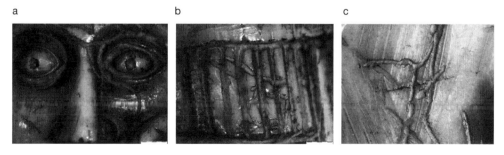

Figure 11.7 (a) Post polishing damage channel on the cheek; and (b) carved hair. The channels cross rather than branch (c).

The tracks have been attributed to 'the burrowing of tiny termites such as are common in sand' (Stratford 1997) 'etching by acids secreted by plant rootlets or alternatively by grazing organisms' and 'the burrowing action of insects that live in the sand' (Robinson 2009).

Although the damage tracks look very like those found on organic material, especially beneath the bark layer of wood, there are no insects that eat ivory in a similar way. Marine polychaetes digest minerals, for example limestone, producing both surface channels and holes and tunnels. These may be of similar dimensions to the chessmen tracks, but the fact that they burrow into the stone is quite different from the surface channels on the chess pieces, and the condition of the chessmen is not like that of ivory which has been submerged in salt water for any length of time (Godfrey et al. 2002) and without traces or marks, such as biogenic calcareous material, which would be expected from a marine environment. Cliona (marine sponges) also cause damage but more as spots rather than tracks. Uncarved walrus tusks in the natural history collections of NMS did not reveal any with similar channelling on the visible surfaces, suggesting that this type of damage does not occur during the life of the animal when marine exposure is of course the norm.

We have, however, found examples of very similar damage on a fragment of boar tusk excavated from Cnip on Lewis (O. Lelong pers. comm. 2010), a site only a few miles along the coast from Uig bay. This fragment shows a higher level of damage, in terms of channel density, than the chessmen. Unfortunately, it does not have a secure date from the stratigraphy of the excavation and may come from an earlier period.

As noted, the sides of the channels are often stained or 'dirty' looking and there are small dark particles, which appear to be enclosed in the mineral material, suggesting that an intimate relationship with the soil has occurred. This, together with the dimensions and the overlapping is consistent with damage caused by chemical action of a tightly overlapping root system. The chemotrophic activity of roots is documented, especially in poor, sandy soils (Crowther 2002) where dissolution of calcitic material by the combination of the root and associated fungi (mycorrhizas) can take place. There is a considerable literature concerning the damage to buried bone from roots, fungi, and microbacteria, but little that considers damage to ivory. The action of fungi alone is possible, but in itself seems unlikely to lead to channels of the size observed, while microbacterial attack leads to pits and staining rather than channels.

In bone, the damage caused by roots is reported as leading to tunnelling as well as surface damage, presumably because of the more porous nature of the bone surface compared to ivory (Grupe and Dreses-Werringlöer 1993). Acid soils are generally considered to favour bone pitting by roots and fungi, and there are of course differences according to the plant species (Binford 1981; Swift et al. 1979). It has been suggested that in some nutrient-poor soils mycorrhizal fungi may have direct involvement in bone decomposition caused by the excretion of acid metabolites (Marchiafava et al. 1974 Grupe and Dreses-Werringlöer 1993).

Results from preliminary experiments on modern ivory

The control samples, inoculated only with broth, showed no alteration of the surface. Samples of ivory inoculated with *Aspergillus niger* showed tunnelling on the dentine layer and a change in microscopic surface appearance. Fungal mycelia formed a dense layer around the whole sample and a subtle white crust appeared raised from the ivory surface in some points of the sample. Variable pressure SEM examination revealed that the white crusts are made of biogenic crystals produced in the fungal matter and presumably leached from the ivory surface. The appearance of the crystals precipitated between hyphal matter resemble calcium oxalate, while the crystals that cover the surface of the sample and that crystallize on fungal hyphae have the appearance of calcite. The surface of the samples was covered by a dense pattern of crystals and crossed by channels, tracks, and calcified hyphae.

Energy dispersive microanalysis confirmed the elemental composition of the different crystalline areas, and also showed that the action of the fungi is to selectively leach calcium (Ca) from the body of the tusk to form calcite crystals on the surface: Phosphorus (P), which is clearly present in the unattacked tusk, does not occur in the new surface layer.

The metabolic activity of fungi has been found to be implicated in the biodeterioration of cultural monuments causing pitting, encrustations, and discolouration (Sterflinger 2000). Among pitting causing fungi, *Aspergillus niger* has been widely studied for enzymatic formation of oxalate from oxaloacetate (Gadd 2007) and its ability in biochemical transformation of rocks. Our results demonstrate that *Aspergillus niger* causes similar leaching of apatite from ivory and the biogenic formation of new minerals such as calcium oxalates: if these minerals can be detected in future analysis of the chessmen their existence could be taken as reasonable proof of fungal activity on the surface.

These experiments are reported on in a separate paper (Pinzari et al. 2013). As noted, we do not anticipate that fungi alone can produce large tunnelling and plan therefore to extend the experiment using soil and the marram grass (*Ammophila* spp.) typical to the west coast of Lewis. With these experiments we aim to reproduce the track formation and establish parameters for the rate of damage, information that may allow some estimation of the length of time the chessmen would have been exposed to this type of burial condition. We will also be able to examine the track damage in more detail, particularly using VP-SEM-EDS and possibly both FTIR and Raman spectroscopy to characterize changes of the organic and inorganic composition induced.

Physical damage

For playthings the chess pieces are in remarkably good physical condition. Generally, the damage is more from the environment to which they must have been exposed (detailed above) than to abrupt physical stress or knocks, which might be expected from extensive handling. However, on some pieces, such as the knight H.NS 27, which is in quite poor condition compared to the other pieces, discolourations and cracks might be due to fire damage. This hypothesis needs however to be confirmed by more detailed investigations of heat-induced damage of different types of ivory.

It may be that only those in good condition were gathered in the hoard, but it seems that they must have been well cared for. There has been erosion of some of the surface details, some pieces have splits and lifting surfaces, and there is surface discolouration or staining. Where there is physical damage, such as the chipped crown of King H.NS 19, some of this may well have occurred after the pieces were found in 1831.

The pieces might have had some protection if they were wrapped or enclosed in a bag. The ivory buckle found with the hoard may have come from a textile or leather bag, which subsequently decayed providing an organic layer attractive to plant roots and fungi. As noted, the channel damage covers all surfaces of the chess pieces, meaning that they would have to have been tightly surrounded with roots. They could have been repositioned in moving sand, although we might expect any significant changes – for example if they were in a sand dune that was eroded by the wind so that they were occasionally exposed – to have led to more surface abrasion. If all were wrapped tightly together in one bag it might be expected that some areas would be protected from exposure to roots. Perhaps then they were initially fairly loosely together, possibly individually wrapped, in a bag or bags. To be damaged by roots they must all have been at about the same depth in the sand: and because each channel is presumably the action of an individual root tip over a growing season they might not have been within an active root system for the whole period of burial.

Colour

A particularly interesting outcome of this study has been finding traces of mercury on various parts of the surface of individual pieces by XRF analysis. This is reported in detail elsewhere (Tate et al. in press) and we note here simply the finding and the exciting conclusion that the mercury comes from traces of cinnabar, a mineral well known to have been used as a red pigment in the medieval period (Eastaugh et al. 2004). In his 1832 report on the chess pieces acquired by the British Museum, Madden says, 'For the sake of distinction, part of them were originally stained of a dark red or beet-root colour; but from having been so long subject to the action of the salt water, the colouring matter, in most cases, has been discharged' (Madden 1832: 212). No traces of this colour can now be convincingly seen, (although we would not expect it still to look red [McCormack 2000]) nor could any be found when the British Museum undertook a comprehensive study of the pieces (C. Higgitt pers. comm. 2010). However this is the first time that the NMS pieces have been analytically examined and it may be that the traces we have found reflect the rather different treatment that the two groups of chess pieces have received since they were found. There was insufficient time in the scope of our study to map the distribution of Hg across the pieces and to draw any conclusions about the extent of decoration, or any correlation with the density of the damage tracks. Both of these are planned for a further in-depth study.

Conclusions

In this preliminary study we have clarified that while nine of the eleven chess pieces in the NMS collection are made from walrus ivory, two are different and most probably are sperm whale teeth, basing this conclusion on a combination of visual examination and non-destructive elemental analysis. We confirm the presence of working tool marks in the ivory and the possibility of their being used to compare the tools used on different pieces, including the existence of mechanical looking striations, which we believe to be 'chatter marks' from surface scrapers. We have recorded the characteristics of the surface 'channels', which we believe most likely to be the action of ectomycorrhizal fungi associated with plant rootlets. We have completed a preliminary experiment to demonstrate the action of fungi on boar tusk ivory and are investigating this further with walrus ivory and the flora on Lewis to learn about the environmental exposure of the pieces. And finally, we note the detection of traces of what we believe to be cinnabar, evidence found for the first time that the pieces were at least partly decorated with red pigment.

References

Binford, L.R. (1981) *Bones: Ancient Men and Modern Myths*. New York, NY: Academic Press.

Budd, P., Montgomery, J., Barreiro, B., and Thomas, R.G. (2000) Differential diagenesis of strontium in archaeological human dental tissue. *Applied Geology*, 15: 687–94.

Burton, J.H. and Wright, L.E. (1995) Nonlinearity in the relationship between bone Sr/Ca and diet: paleodietary implications. *American Journal of Physical Anthropology*, 96: 372–82.

Burton, J.H. Price, T.D., and Middleton, W.D. (1999) Correlation of bone Ba/Ca and Sr/Ca due to biological purification of calcium. *Journal of Archaeological Science*, 26: 609–16.

Caldwell, D.H.C., Hall, M.A., and Wilkinson, C.M. (2009) The Lewis hoard of gaming pieces: a re-examination of their context, meanings, discovery and manufacture. *Medieval Archaeology*, 53: 155–203.

——(2010) *The Lewis Chessmen Unmasked*. Edinburgh: NMS Enterprises.

Crowther, J. (2002) The experimental earthwork at Wareham, Dorset after 33 years: retention and leaching of phosphate released in the decomposition of buried bone. *Journal of Archaeological Science*, 29: 405–11.

Eastaugh, N., Walsh, V., Chaplin, T., and Siddall, R. (2004) *The Pigment Compendium: A Dictionary of Historical Pigments*. Oxford: Elsevier Butterworth-Heinemann.

Espinoza, E.O. and Man, M.J. (1991) *Identification Guide for Ivory and Ivory Substitutes*. Baltimore: World Wildlife Fund and Conservation Foundation.

Gadd, G.M. (2007) Geomycology: biogeochemical transformations of rocks, minerals, metals and radionuclides by fungi, bioweathering and bioremediation. *Mycological Research*, 111: 3–49.

Glenn, V. (2003) *Romanesque and Gothic*. Edinburgh: NMSE Publishing.

Godfrey, I.M., Ghisalberti, E.L., Beng, E.W., Byrne, L.T., and Richardson, G.W. (2002) The analysis of ivory from a marine environment. *Studies in Conservation*, 47: 29–45.

Grupe, G. and Dreses-Werringlöer, U. (1993) Decomposition phenomena in thin sections of excavated human bones. In: G. Grupe and A.N. Garland (eds.), *Histology of Ancient Human Bone: Methods and Diagnosis*. Berlin: Springer-Verlag, pp. 27–36.

Lee-Thorpe, J.A. (2008) On isotopes and old bones. *Archaeometry*, 50(6): 925–50.

Locke, M. (2008) The structure of ivory. *Journal of Morphology*, 269: 423–50.

Marchiafava, V., Bonucci, L., and Acenzi, A. (1974) Fungal Osteoclasia: a model of dead bone resorption. *Calcified Tissue Research*, 14: 195–210.

Madden, F. (1832) Historical remarks on the introduction of the game of chess into Europe, and the ancient chess-men discovered in the Isle of Lewis. *Archaeologica*, 24: 203–91.

McCormack, J.K. (2000) The darkening of cinnabar in sunlight. *Mineralium Deposita*, 35: 796–8.

Müller, K. and Reiche, I. (2011) Differentiation of archaeological ivory and bone materials by micro-PIXE/PIGE with emphasis on two Upper Paleolithic key sites at Abri Pataud and Isturitz, France. *Journal of Archaeological Science*, 38: 3234–43.

Pinzari, F., Tate, J., Bicchieri, M., Rhee, Y.J., and Gadd, G.M. (2013) Biodegradation of ivory (natural apatite): possible involvement of fungal activity in biodeterioration of the Lewis Chessmen. *Environmental Microbiology*, 15(4): 1050–62.

Poplin, F. (2006) L'ivoire de rhinocéros et les ivoires du Proche-Orient ancien. *Comptes Rendus de l'Académie des Inscriptions*, 1116: 1130.

Price, T.D., Burton, J.H., and Bentley, R.A. (2002) The characterisation of biologically available strontium isotope ratios for the study of prehistoric migration. *Archaeometry*, 44(1): 117–35.

Reiche, I., Müller, K., Staude, A., Goebbels, J., and Riesemeier, H. (2011) Synchrotron radiation and laboratory micro X-ray computed tomography – useful tools for the material identification of prehistoric objects made of ivory, bone or antler. *Journal of Analytical Atomic Spectroscopy*, 26: 1802–12.

Robinson, J., 2009. *The Lewis Chessmen*. London: BM Press.

Sillen, A. and Kavanagh, M. (1982) Strontium and palaeodietary research: a review. *Yearbook of Anthropology*, 25: 67–90.

Sterflinger, K. and Claeys, P. (2005) Fungi as geological agents. *Geomicrobiological Journal*, 17: 97–124.

Stratford, N. (1997) *The Lewis Chessmen and the Enigma of the Hoard*. London: BM Press.

Swift, M.J., Heal, O.W., and Anderson, J.M. (1979) *Decomposition in Terrestrial Ecosystems*. Oxford: Blackwell Scientific Publications.

Tate, J., Reiche, I., and Pinzari, F. (in press). The Lewis Chessmen: what can examination of the surfaces tell us? In: D.H. Caldwell and M.A. Hall (eds.), *The Lewis Gaming Hoard in Context – New Analyses of their Art, Purpose and Place in History*. Edinburgh, Birlinn.

Thomas, F.W.L. (1863) Notes on the Lewis Chessmen. *Proceedings of the Society of Antiquaries of Scotland*, 4: 411–13.

Webster, R. (1958) Ivory, bone and horn. *The Gemmologist*, 27: 91–8.

Wilson, D. (1851) *The Archaeology and Prehistoric Annuals of Scotland*. Edinburgh: Sutherland and Knox.

PART II

ARCHAEOLOGY, ETHICS, AND THE LAW

Introduction to Part II

Robin Skeates

This section covers a selection of the legal and ethical issues affecting museum archaeology. Legal specialists are obviously well-placed to introduce and also discuss the limitations of current legislation, such as the hugely influential US Native American Graves Protection and Repatriation Act (NAGPRA), and its implications for future museum practice and ethics. But it is also important to consider the perspectives of other stakeholders, including museum professionals, journalists, and government agencies with responsibilities for culture, particularly when it comes to the professional dilemmas over the acquisition, exhibition, and publication of cultural material that may have been illegally excavated and traded. Museum collections of ancient human remains present equally challenging issues in terms of their treatment in laws, policies, guidelines, and practice, particularly when repatriation is the required course of action.

The first two readings offer various insights into the legal and ethical dimensions of archaeological museum collecting and collections. **Chapter 12**, written by a conservator and an expert on the illicit trade in cultural material, provides a critical insight into the growing antiquities trade in the UK during the 1990s. In addition to questioning the attitude of the British government (which belatedly ratified the 1970 UNESCO Convention on the Means of Prohibiting and Preventing the Illicit Import, Export and Transfer of Ownership of Cultural Property), the authors call upon archaeologists, conservators, museum curators, and other heritage professionals to develop a more unified and ethical approach to this area of activity, which is often connected to the looting of archaeological sites and to the loss of important provenance information for artefacts. **Chapter 13** then analyses the recent law and ethics revolution pertaining to US museums' acquisitions of antiquities, and the impact of this revolution on the antiquities market.

The following pair of readings focuses on the repatriation and reburial of archaeological museum collections. **Chapter 14** provides an Australian perspective on issues relating to repatriation of Indigenous cultural property and human remains. It presents a brief history of how relevant collections came to be created and how Indigenous Australian communities reacted to them. It then discusses the contemporary legal, policy, and political repatriation landscape in Australia. **Chapter 15** then offers a useful contrast. Written by both a professor of law and a curator of Native American art, it considers some of the legal questions and controversies that have arisen during the first decade of NAGPRA. In particular, it highlights the limitations of formal dispute resolution as a means of developing and implementing the law.

The third set of readings in this section concentrates on a related theme: museums and the collecting and display of human remains. **Chapter 16** considers the challenging questions of how to treat the human remains from archaeological contexts in the collections of a large number of public museums and agencies in the US and of who should be responsible for determining this, with reference to national laws and regulations, written policies and guidance, and patterns of practice. **Chapter 17**, by contrast, explores the controversy that broke out when the Manchester Museum in the UK took the decision to cover up three displayed unwrapped Egyptian mummies with white sheets, with the aim of raising questions through public consultation about the respectful treatment of human remains in museums.

Part II, Section 1

Legal and ethical dimensions of archaeological museum collecting and collections

From museum to mantelpiece
The antiquities trade in the United Kingdom

Kathryn Walker Tubb and Neil Brodie

Introduction

The 'museum' and 'mantelpiece' of the title are not intended to be precise and self-explanatory terms but rather to be alliterative and catchy, alluding to the destinies of collectable antiquities, available for purchase and which, rightly or wrongly, have already undergone the process of commodification. It may be helpful to give the reader an insight into the authors' rather nebulous weighting of meaning behind the two terms. First, such concepts as a public, systematic, classified collection situated in a centre dedicated to guardianship, conservation, scholarship, and accessibility are comprised in 'museum'. 'Mantelpiece', on the other hand, has been used to denote the individual and the casual, the quirky and impulsive, the isolated artefact gathering dust in uncategorized splendour. Clearly, such distinctions have been somewhat arbitrarily made and are artificial to a degree. Perhaps the following selection of quotes may illuminate this prefatory apologia however.

Marketing strategies

In March 1990, the arts correspondent, Geraldine Norman wrote: 'Jerome Eisenberg has brought the supermarket approach to selling antiquities to London', and went on 'The price range of Eisenberg antiquities is from £50 to £1m. He claims to have over 2000 objects priced under £500. They include ancient terracottas, scarabs, glass, and south Italian pottery'. This article appeared in the Weekend Collecting section of the *Independent* and was entitled 'Antiquities off the shelf' (Norman 1990a).

In September 1993, again under Collecting, but this time in the *Daily Telegraph*, Madeleine Marsh 'gives a guide to antiquities on the cheap'. In her article entitled 'How to hunt out treasure' she states that: 'One of the more remarkable things about collecting ancient objects is how cheap they can be at the lower end of the market – within the reach of the pocket-money collector'. Richard Lobel, the proprietor of Coincraft, is quoted as saying of small antiquities that: 'You can put them on display, they make fascinating conversation pieces, and burglars wouldn't know what they were, so the chances of their being stolen are minimal'. The article goes on to say that 'Goods on sale range in value from £5 to £3000 and include pots, amulets, daggers, axe-heads, glass, and ancient coins – what Mr Lobel describes as "everyday antiquities"'. Pains are taken to point out that 'At the British Museum shop, a reproduction necklace based on an Egyptian design will cost you £49.95' whereas 'At Coincraft ... you can buy a string of beads that are 5000 years old for £17.95'.

In July 1995 in the Weekend Shopping section of the *Independent,* John Windsor, under the banner headline 'From the dawn of time, a bargain' reports that 'Antiquities are plentiful and cheap' (Windsor 1995). This article is based in large part on the wares on offer from Chris Martin, 'Britain's biggest mail-order antiquities dealer'. Mr Martin is said to provide other dealers with Roman terracotta oil lamps by the thousand. Such lamps in turn are sold via newspaper advertisements and TV shopping channels. The article continues 'Mr Martin retails Palestinian and Phoenician cloak pins from 1500 BC to 1000 BC for £15 and Persian dress brooches (eighth to fifth century BC) for £11. Roman glass? He charges £50 for a simple bottle. For £32.50: a perspex stand with a Greek or Roman egg-shaped lead slingshot, a Greek bronze arrowhead (eighth to third century BC) and a Roman iron arrowhead (third to second century BC). Dagger and spear blades? He retails by the dozen Phoenician and Hittite specimens (2400–800 BC) for £30 £40 each to multinational companies who present them to distinguished guests as paper knives'.

In November 1996, in the Homes and Gardens section of the *Guardian Weekend,* Chris Martin is again featured under the headline 'Sale of the centuries'. Fiona Murphy sums up the gist of her article as follows: 'Roman glass vases for £45, Mesopotamian jugs for £35. Who needs a fake when the original is yours for the same price?' The talk is of a 'vast number of domestic items to be had at no great cost', which appeals to 'the contemporary taste for the rough-hewn and the simple'. A former marketing executive is said to have persuaded Chris Martin 'to put an element of glamour into his business'. Nowhere is this more evident than in his Winter 1996/97 catalogue. Attractive colour photographs of his wares are interspersed with black-and-white shots of a female nude, artfully cropped so as not to be too revealing, depicting here a scattering of silver pennies over an abdomen or there a pair of crossed bronze blades pressed flat against breasts and chest. The occasional literary quote appears as a caption. This is just one of a series of alluringly illustrated and attractive catalogues. Chris Martin has also advertised his company, Ancient Art, in such publications as the Heritage Shop Catalogue, which is 'the buyer's guide for museums, galleries, historic houses, and visitor attractions' (1996, inside back cover).

Television has delivered the same message overtly as items on such programmes as *This Morning* (Finnigan and Madeley 1996) and *The Antiques Show* (Stock 1997). In a feature in the latter on collecting antiquities entitled 'Museum Piece', Francine Stock, the presenter, begins 'Antiques three or four hundred years old are rare enough; ones from ancient civilizations you'd expect to find only in a museum. But *if you really think your home wouldn't be complete without a one-thousand-five-*

hundred-year-old Roman oil lamp or an Egyptian statue on your mantelpiece then it could be yours thanks to a thriving if controversial trade in antiquities' (authors' italics). She adds: 'With just a phone call and a credit card, a chunk of the ancient world could be yours for as little as a tenner'.

Chris Martin of Ancient Art explains: 'We've been in the business for about twenty-five years in coins and antiquities and seeing how the reproduction catalogues were selling reproductions of ancient objects for basically the same price as we could provide the originals and *we would like to promote the idea that people can own a piece of ancient history'* (authors' italics). In observing preparation for the new issue of the catalogue she remarks: 'And just like any Next directory or Habitat catalogue, presentation is laid on thick', naming two well-known mail-order catalogues for clothes and home furnishings. Ms Stock sets the scene for the next dealership to be visited with: 'If buying through mail order isn't quite your style then there are alternatives, but you have to know where to look. Behind discreet brass plaques in Mayfair *you can spend thousands bringing ancient history to your living room, something for the mantelpiece to impress the neighbours perhaps'* (authors' italics).

Television also displays artefacts in general as part of the stage settings in dramas, light entertainment, interviews, and commercials. The example of a diver casually swimming past an amphora and breaking it with a pickaxe for no apparent reason was used in 1996 by Cheltenham and Gloucester Building Society in an advertisement for mortgages.

In June 1997 Desiderata, a division of the Corsellis-Montford Group plc, was advertising for antiquities dealers to join its 'premier antiquities and collectables information service' on the Internet (*Minerva*, May/June 1997). Websites exhibiting artefacts for sale in infinite variety are easily accessed. Even such sensitive material as human remains is not exempt. In October 1995, what was claimed to be a mummified Egyptian princess's hand, together with its certificate of authenticity, was being hawked around touting for bids for this treasure. The lucky buyer would then 'walk away with a piece of history' (Rudd 1995).

What does the above reflect of current market trends as they have been developing over the past ten years? Clearly, the impulse would seem to be striving to generate new consumers in a particular, reasonably specialized and relatively small segment of the art market: the trade in antiquities. Perhaps a sufficiently high proportion of today's consumer-oriented population can now not only satisfy its needs but also its desires. What was once the exotic, the rare, and the appealing in the emporia and department stores in the earlier twentieth century has become mundane; too available to be satisfying for the individual and too commonplace to provoke envy and reflect the erudition, taste, and uniqueness of the possessor. Perhaps mass production coupled with the boom years of the 1980s has led to satiety with such products and is leading to the desire for something scarcer. Perhaps deriving an almost spiritual sense of satisfaction from mass-produced articles is being deemed inadequate. And yet the belief that fulfilment can still be derived from the marketplace persists. What better solution than to identify another category of goods endowed with a numinous aura by virtue of its age and rarity? This sanctification of the past has been previously discussed by such authors as David

Lowenthal (1996) and Russell Belk (1995). Noted and famous collectors have been
feted, lauded, and esteemed as saviours, benefactors, and donors of precious objects,
their collections often entering the public domain. And Belk observes that: We
generally regard museum collections as normal and accept that they legitimize
objects that are acceptable for individuals to collect: if it's good enough for the Met,
no further questions need be asked' (ibid.: 147). Emulation of these hallowed
individuals is presented as being achievable and at bargain rates. The humdrum and
mediocre are both, at one and the same time, elevated to a higher plane and
diminished by the price and apparent abundance. The desire for a sense of
connectedness with the past is easily recognizable and exploitable, although a
propensity for fetishizing artefactual remains, particularly those from a basic low-
level craft tradition, mystifies many both inter- and intra-culturally. Marketing
ploys are merely taking advantage of a pre-disposition toward seizing bargains
imbued with the added fillip of rarity value and an almost mystical character. There
is no need to engage in collecting even in a modest way; simple acquisition will
suffice. The siting of this information in the hobby pages and its shift to the shopping
pages of the newspapers attests to this. A single piece to decorate the mantelpiece
is sufficiently gratifying.

The discussion thus far is missing crucially important facts that should be
obvious to all but which remain obscure even to some within the heritage
professions. The exclusive reference to antiquities as *commodities* is jarring. To those
accustomed to valuing such material for the assistance it gives in the interpretation
of the past such a narrow focus is desperately skewed with disastrous consequences
for the archaeological heritage. Context is the *sine qua non* for the archaeologist, the
essence of archaeology; information retrieval the goal consequent upon context.
Artefacts divested of contextual information are pitifully dispossessed, impoverished
of meaning and, as such, are an anathema. At the first Courtauld Debate on the
subject of the antiquities trade and its contribution to the study of the art of the past
(20 November 1997), Lord Renfrew of Kaimsthorn gave an impassioned address
in which he illustrated the importance of context using Philip II of Macedon's
tomb as an example. Similarly, the examples of an Anglo-Saxon bed-burial
excavated in Cambridgeshire and an Assyrian tassel from Nimrud in Iraq have been
used (Tubb 1995: 258–59). This message remains unheard and is easily dismissed
– a vital lie for antiquities dealers and collectors acting as a group whose 'capacity
to keep information out of frame can fall prey to a collusion that buys social coziness
at the expense of important truths … warping social reality to suppress unpleasant
information' (Goleman 1997: 224). James Ede, an eminent dealer in ancient art, in
the heat of the debate referred to above, denounced context, misrepresenting it as
simply position in the soil, '2cm or 4cm' under the ground. Given preservation of
context, archaeologists are less concerned about the eventual disposition of a given
object (Renfrew 1995: xviii).

Implicit in these marketing strategies is the question of supply. No distinction
has been made between reproducible goods and goods derived from a finite
resource. Although dealers and collectors argue strongly for a free market in art and
antiques generally, including antiquities, the movement of such material is the

subject of substantial legal controls. The difficulty of supply exposes the inherent danger of this tactic of broadening the market. The consequence of increased demand has been increased looting of archaeological sites. Archaeologists are witnessing massive destruction of the archaeological record. Areas formerly relatively free from such depredation because of their peripheral position to the accepted major civilizations and whose artefactual remains were by and large not identified as high art are now sustaining severe and irreparable loss. One case, which serves well to illustrate this point, is that of the biblical settlement of Zoar, whose despoliation has, unusually, been documented and reported (Politis 1994). Another example from Jordan concerns the large multi-period site of Tell es-Sa'idiyeh, ancient Zarethan. Seasonal excavation of this site has been proceeding under licence for the past fifteen years, either annually or every other year, by the British Museum under the direction of Jonathan Tubb. During one of the fallow years, an unexpected visit revealed that the site guard, employed to protect the site year round, was potholing part of a 3000-year-old cemetery. Only part of this area had been being excavated and clearly, the guard thought his marauding would go undetected since he was taking pains to backfill the holes and, by the time the excavators were to return the following year, vegetation would have obscured his activities. The damage sustained by the site would only have been detected if formal excavation of the cemetery were to have been extended. Fortunately, the adventitious visit by the excavators put a stop to the destruction (J. Tubb, personal communication).

But not everybody agrees that the majority of antiquities new to the market are looted. It has sometimes been claimed that they are in fact chance finds, the result of construction projects or agricultural operations (Ortiz 1997: 22). While it is no doubt true that many antiquities do come to light during the course of such activities it must be emphasized that they are not chance finds, but that they are more probably recovered from archaeological sites damaged or destroyed during the course of development. Archaeological fieldwork has shown that true chance finds are difficult to come by. During the past twenty years or so large tracts of land in the Mediterranean area in particular have been field-walked by archaeological teams intent on mapping out presently surviving surface indications of ancient sites. Many of these surveys have been published and the results are available for all to see (for instance Runnels et al. 1995; Cavanagh et al. 1996). Very few, if any, intact antiquities have been found. The published material consists largely of pieces of broken pottery and small architectural fragments. The idea that there are large quantities of antiquities lying about waiting to be found is a myth.

There can be little doubt that the majority of antiquities without demonstrable provenance, which are now flooding the market have been looted from archaeological sites of one form or another. They are illicit and it is foolish to pretend otherwise. In 1990, Norman observed that '80 per cent of all antiquities coming on to the market have been illegally excavated and smuggled from their country of origin' (Norman 1990b). Peter Watson reports on results of research in this area by David Gill and Christopher Chippindale. Their research has found that 'up to 90 per cent of the antiquities that appear on the London auction market are unprovenanced – many of which may have been illegally excavated and smuggled out of their countries of origin' (Watson 1997). The sale and collection of these unprovenanced artefacts are the ultimate causes of the looting, and it follows that anything that deters unethical collecting must certainly help to diminish the destruction, and conserve the information-rich contexts.

What do the dealers think?

O'Keefe (1997: 103) has suggested that a short-term increase in the supply of licit antiquities of known provenance might go some way towards discouraging the trade in those that are illicit. He also discusses some of the associated problems. But what do the dealers themselves think? A common suggestion is that museum storerooms contain large collections of duplicate or surplus artefacts, and that if these were properly documented and released on to the legitimate market then the volume of the trade in illicit material would decrease accordingly (Eisenberg 1995: 220; Ede 1996: 56). From an archaeological perspective, however, there are several objections to this suggestion.

In the first place, it is not at all clear that there is any necessary inverse correlation between the respective volumes of the trades in licit and illicit antiquities. This is certainly not the case in other sectors of the economy where the black market is more rather than less active for stolen or copied items of leading brand names – as the total volume of the market increases so too does the volume of the black market. This has been shown to be true of the antiquities markets in Peru and the United States (O'Keefe 1997: 66–7) and the onus really is on members of the trade to demonstrate otherwise.

Second, without prior investigation it is premature to assume that the number of objects in museums is great. One of the authors (Brodie) has worked in the storerooms of several regional museums in the Mediterranean area and has seen large quantities of fragmentary sherd material and broken pieces of carved masonry but very few complete antiquities, which would be considered collectable. The collectable objects are usually on display. Perhaps the situation is different in the large national museums – perhaps the material available in the storerooms of American and British museums is more marketable. It is difficult to say. The argument that much of this material is without value to the archaeologist as it has no recorded context is specious (Ede 1996: 56). While it is true that without a properly recorded excavation context much information is lost, location alone is sometimes of great interest. The distribution map is a fundamental tool of archaeological analysis.

It has in the past been argued by archaeologists that the duplicate objects presently stored behind the scenes in museums would not be of interest to collectors or dealers who want one-offs, the unique pieces. The small utilitarian objects that were produced in large quantities in antiquity would be of less interest to the trade as they do not command a high price. But the force of this argument has been diminished over the past few years by the attempts of some dealers to market these antiquities, to place them on the mantelpiece, as described earlier. Yet these artefacts, which might never find a place in a museum display case, are often of great interest to the archaeologist precisely because they were produced (and survive) in large numbers – they are ideal for typological analysis and provide the backbone of relative chronologies. Thus, although the monetary value of a single object is probably very small, its scholarly value might be quite high when its context is known.

Finally, the idea that archaeological material may be subject to a single process of examination and documentation is archaic. In archaeology, as in any academic discipline, the context of enquiry is kaleidoscopic. It changes constantly as different or novel attributes of the material under study come into view. Sometimes this is because of the development of new scientific techniques; more often it is simply because new questions are asked. The constant search for novel interpretations is a fundamental feature of scholarly endeavour. As O'Keefe (1997: 73) has pointed out, the material collected during the course of an excavation constitutes an archive that can be returned to again and again. If it is broken up and sold off without record then the possibility of any further advance in understanding disappears along with it.

Dealers also maintain that a system of due compensation should be put in place to reward farmers who turn in antiquities they have found on their land, and that these antiquities might then be offered up for resale on the legitimate market (Ede 1995: 213; 1996: 56). Doubts have already been expressed about the true status of 'chance' finds, but nevertheless they will continue to turn up as small sites are accidentally or deliberately disturbed. But any system of compensation will only work to protect archaeological sites if the rewards offered can match the prices fetched in the open market – not a viable proposition when the market is inflating and expanding. If a state-sponsored scheme of compensation offered prices to match those of dealers or collectors, then it would encourage farmers to seek out antiquities actively and destroy archaeological sites in the process. It might also bankrupt the state. If the state did not match prices available privately then objects would still be sold on the black market. A sensible compensation scheme will only work in the presence of a well-regulated and modest market.

An ethical trade?

Up to now the focus of this discussion has been on the trade in illicit antiquities, those that have in the first instance been illegally acquired. Yet it remains the case that there is a sizeable trade in licit antiquities, antiquities which have been legally removed from their country of origin at some time in the past and which will not now be returned. It would not be practical, nor in many cases desirable, for this to happen. These objects will remain in circulation. It is also possible to foresee a time when the spiralling cost of long-term storage and conservation will cause artefacts from properly controlled archaeological excavations to come on to the market. Thus, there is, and will continue to be, a legitimate trade. Whether archaeologists like it or not, they must come to terms with this fact and try to establish a constructive dialogue with dealers.

Increasingly, archaeologists are choosing not to collaborate with dealers or collectors so as not to add a gloss of legitimacy to their activities. Some have gone further and taken great pains to document the damage inflicted by unethical collecting. But if a legitimate trade in antiquities is inevitable then the challenge is to encourage not only a legitimate trade but also an ethical one. There has been a move recently in archaeological circles towards developing the concept of the 'Good Collector' (McIntosh et al. 1995; O'Keefe 1997: 95). The Good Collector recognizes that the aesthetic qualities of an artefact are not such as to merit the destruction of the cultural and historical information embodied in its context. He or she actively opposes the trade in illicit antiquities, does not 'turn a blind eye' to questionable provenances, and encourages scholarly study of the collection and its use for educational purposes. Archaeologists might be persuaded to co-operate with Good Collectors and, by extension one would assume, 'Good Dealers'. But what would a Good Dealer look like?

Reputable antiquities dealers do have a professional body with its own code of ethics. The International Association of Dealers in Ancient Art (IADAA) was formed in 1993 and membership is dependent upon observation of a code of ethics, which, among other things, forbids members to deal in stolen or looted antiquities (Ede 1995: 214). Is a member of IADAA to be considered a Good Dealer then? There is a certain convergence of interests with those of archaeologists, but the critical Article 12.2 of the code is weaker than might appear on first reading. The text reads as follows:

> The members of IADAA undertake not to purchase or sell objects until they have established to the best of their ability that such objects were not stolen from excavations, architectural monuments, public institutions or private property.

It should be noticed at once that the sale of chance finds is not vetoed, although doubts have already been expressed about the true status of such finds. The IADAA code entertains no such doubts. But ultimately the article stands or falls by the interpretation given to the term 'best of their ability'. How good is their best and to what extent are they able?

There is a certain willingness expressed to investigate the provenance of an artefact, but by and large, dealers seem more inclined to accept that an antiquity is not looted unless there is positive evidence to the contrary. James Ede, for instance, has insisted that the principle of guilty until proven innocent is not acceptable (Ede 1995: 211; 1996: 55). Yet when it is the authenticity of a piece that is in question rather than its provenance it becomes a principle dealers are much happier with. The archaeologist Ricardo Elia, for instance, has been taken to task for daring to suggest that 'art dealers ... assume that everything is genuine'. 'How brazen a statement,' replied Eisenberg (1997: 20), shocked by the suggestion that dealers should assume that everything is innocently genuine rather than guiltily fake. Dealers are strenuous in their efforts to establish authenticity (Eisenberg 1995: 216): there is big money at stake. It is not a question of principle, it is a judgement of value. Quite simply, the authenticity of a piece is of more interest to a collector than its provenance – a piece with no provenance might command a lower price than one with, but an inauthentic piece is valueless. Thus, a dealer might understandably be exercised to establish the authenticity of a piece, but not its good provenance. The 'best' of their ability seems, then, as far as provenance is concerned at any rate, to be less than it could be.

But in any case, the ability of dealers to investigate provenance is hopelessly compromised by the code of anonymity, which is adhered to and defended by dealers and collectors alike, keeping secret the identities of buyers and sellers. This frustrates at the outset any attempt to reconstruct a chain of ownership aimed at establishing the original provenance of a piece. Several reasons have been proposed to justify this policy of non-disclosure. The most convincing is that it keeps collections away from the attention of potential thieves. Some are less convincing, such as Ede's (1996: 55) example of the owner who was unwilling to have his name published because he wanted to hide from his wife the fact that he was selling off the family heirlooms! More cynically, it has been suggested that non-disclosure of a vendor's identity protects a dubious source and guarantees full employment for forgers, grave robbers, smugglers, and other crooks (Elsen 1992: 129).

The recent example of the Salisbury Hoard is a case in point (Stead 1998). This is an Iron Age hoard of bronze objects, part of which was purchased in 1989 by the British Museum from the antiquities dealer Lord McAlpine for the sum of £55,000. The hoard was subsequently shown by museum staff to have been illegally excavated by two people using metal detectors. The British Museum returned the hoard voluntarily to the landowner (an ethical but not legally necessary action) and the finders were tried, pleaded guilty to theft, and sentenced. The British Museum was £55,000 out of pocket. McAlpine would not reimburse the Museum as he himself had bought the hoard in good faith from another dealer, and indeed he maintained that the hoard had passed through the hands of several anonymous dealers and as a result its initial provenance could not be ascertained. Thus, the end result was that the original excavators were convicted of a crime from which a series of anonymous dealers did quite nicely, and in doing the right thing the British Museum lost £55,000 out of an ever-decreasing acquisitions budget. While such a code of *omertá* continues to obscure the identities of those who buy and sell, dealers are simply not able to investigate provenance in a manner that is effective. Article 12.2 of the IADAA code is rendered meaningless. An ethical trade needs to be a transparent trade with the identities of transacting parties made public.

The situation in the United Kingdom is deplorable

The trade in illicit antiquities is an international problem with pragmatic and ethical dimensions. Some countries profess to an ethical stance that is beyond reproach while in practice their implementation of policy is hampered or obstructed by limited resources. The ethics of other countries are less clearly defined when they adopt a pragmatic approach governed by the ideology of the market. The poor record of many 'source' nations in protecting their archaeology has often been used by proponents of the trade to justify their own activities. They argue that they are conserving artefacts that would otherwise deteriorate or be lost if not removed from their country of origin (Chesterman 1991: 538; Ede 1995: 214; Eisenberg 1995: 220). It simply will not do, however, to point the finger at deficiencies in the museums, governments, or civil services of source countries while at the same time glossing over the inequitable role played by the governments and citizens of the wealthier 'market' nations. Such a diversionary tactic comes perilously close to an accusation of contributory negligence. In this chapter, the focus is on the situation in the United Kingdom which is, sad to say, deplorable. The UK is one of the major centres of the present-day trade in antiquities, and in particular of the trade in illicit antiquities. It is not against the law to deal openly in antiquities that may in the first instance have been obtained illegally, often through looting. The British government has also consistently refused to sign or ratify major international conventions designed to obstruct or curtail the free flow of stolen and looted cultural material.

An antiquity without provenance holds within it the threat of recovery. At any time it might be identified as stolen and claimed back by its original owner. Its monetary value is in consequence less than that of its legitimate cousin with an impeccable provenance. The majority of unprovenanced antiquities of course have not been stolen from established collections, they have been looted, and will not be immediately identifiable. But without a provenance it is impossible to distinguish between the potentially identifiable and the unidentifiable, and the threat of recovery discourages their purchase. In the United Kingdom at the present time, however, collectors can enjoy possession of their unprovenanced antiquities confident in the knowledge that any attempt at recovery will most likely fail as, due to a combination of historical circumstance and government intransigence, the available legislation is relatively ineffectual. There is therefore no real deterrence.

The British government has failed to ratify the 1970 UNESCO Convention on the Means of Prohibiting and Preventing the Illicit Import, Export, and Transfer of Ownership of Cultural Property, which would allow other states party to the convention to sue for the return of stolen or illegally exported antiquities. It has given many reasons for this failure, among which the cost of establishing a national register and a belief in self-regulation figure prominently (Palmer 1995: 15); as a result, any action for recovery must proceed through a British court. However, in Britain the police are not able to act when theft is merely assumed, as is the case with most unprovenanced antiquities when there is no proof of illegal excavation or cross-border transit. The police can only act to recover material known to be stolen, that is to say when its prior ownership or location is recorded and open to demonstration (Ellis 1995: 223). But the effectiveness of the police is limited further by poor communication. They can act only if they are in receipt of good information, and although the information seems sometimes to be available, it does not always end up in their hands. Channels of communication between the police and concerned authorities of source states are not well established.

The efforts of the British police are further obstructed by the presence of a loophole in international law. This allows good title to a stolen or looted antiquity to be acquired by means of a 'good faith' purchase in a third country, such as Switzerland, where that country's law has the effect of giving good title to a buyer, thus making its subsequent sale in Britain legal and taking it outside the limits of police competence (Ellis 1995: 223). The loophole has been closed by the 1995 UNIDROIT Convention on Stolen or Illegally Exported Cultural Objects. The convention is specifically designed to circumvent issues of ownership. It allows a state party to the Convention or a citizen thereof to request the return of archaeological objects that have in the first instance been illegally excavated or exported, and which are by definition of the Convention stolen, despite their role in any subsequent transactions. Sadly, the Department of National Heritage announced in 1995 that the British government would not sign the UNIDROIT Convention, although the reasons for this decision were not forthcoming. As a result, there is no simple recourse under British law for the recovery of objects illegally removed from their country of origin when good title has been obtained through purchase in a third country. The 'international loophole' remains open.

The UNIDROIT Convention also makes provision for a good faith purchaser to receive compensation when required to return looted antiquities, so long as it can be shown convincingly that due diligence was exercised at the time of purchase. It has been pointed out that convincing demonstration of due diligence would require clear proof that any relevant publication such as that of Gill and Chippindale (1993) had been consulted (Prott 1995: 64). Further studies in a similar vein will become invaluable if and when the British government accedes to UNIDROIT.

The United Kingdom is currently required to adhere to European Union legislation. The Council Directive 93/7 on the Return of Cultural Objects Unlawfully Removed from the Territory of a Member State was implemented in 1994 as the Return of Cultural Objects Regulations. The Directive provides a means for states to recover cultural objects of designated importance ('national treasures'), which have been exported unlawfully from their territory to that of another member state. Like the UNESCO Convention, however, the Directive fails to close the international loophole in property laws and makes no provision for private individuals to reclaim objects. Palmer (1995: 16) has expressed doubts about the likely effectiveness of the Directive on account of its elaborate machinery and discouraging bureaucracy, and to date it has not been invoked.

Dealers and collectors have to be exceedingly foolish or excessively greedy to fall foul of British law. Tokeley-Parry for instance was convicted of two charges of handling stolen goods because although he claimed to have passed stolen Egyptian antiquities through the 'international loophole', by buying them in Switzerland and Germany, the investigating authorities were able to establish that he had in fact smuggled them directly to Britain.

The reluctance of successive British governments to accede to the UNESCO and UNIDROIT conventions, or at least adhere to their principles, is a serious enough matter in itself, but there is evidence to suggest that it is actively undermining the efforts of other states. The United States, for instance, has now enacted a series of bilateral agreements with other states party to the UNESCO Convention in an attempt to curtail the destruction of certain specified classes of cultural material. Several of these agreements are with Latin American countries. While they have acted to lessen the flow northwards of antiquities, there is evidence to suggest that it has been rerouted through the salesrooms of Britain (Yemma 1997: A28), so much so that the London market is said to be glutted with smuggled pre-Columbian antiquities, with 60 per cent of sales revenue coming from Americans (Windsor 1997).

The role of the United Kingdom as a conduit in this unfortunate trade is facilitated further by the diaphanous nature of British export controls. British customs will not enforce foreign export restrictions and will not stop the import into Britain of artefacts exported illegally from their country of origin as this would in effect burden the British taxpayer with the cost of enforcing the export laws of other countries. It is not an offence to import illegally exported artefacts (Ellis 1995: 222). Before the police can act, artefacts must be shown to be stolen (ibid.), as already discussed. There are export controls, however, even for material that has been in the country for only a short period of time, although their scope is so limited that the use of the word 'control' is hardly warranted.

A European licence is required for the export of antiquities to destinations outside the European Union as the EU Council Regulation 3911/92 on the Export of Cultural Goods is currently directly applicable to the United Kingdom. The British government has diluted the effect of this regulation, however, by excluding from licensing requirements any objects that possess no special features of form, size, material, decoration, inscription, or iconography and which are not in especially fine condition – most archaeological material in fact. The government took this decision to ward off large numbers of licence applications that it could not provide the resources to support (Morrison 1995: 208). This seems to imply that the underlying rationale of the Regulation to restrict or register the flow of antiquities through or out of Europe was not recognized or, more likely, was unpalatable.

The guiding principles of British export licensing seem to be avoidance of cost to the taxpayer and of loss to the economy. There is little recognition of the problems engendered by the trade or there might be good ethical reasons to regulate it more closely. The legislation and the method of its administration combine to provide what is in effect an 'open door' regime for the trade in illicit antiquities. From an archaeological point of view it is a disaster, as there is no system in place which could provide a means even to monitor and record the movement of antiquities through Britain and in so doing constitute an information archive.

This discussion has returned again and again to the theme of lost information. Whether low-cost objects emerge from a looted site, or treasures to bid high for, the information loss is the same, and the British legal system contains no credible deterrent. An opportunity to recover some of the lost information at points of transit fails to materialize because of the frailty of the export licensing system. Another chance to trace the movement of antiquities is at most only dimly perceived through the almost impenetrable opacity in which the trade operates. The situation in the United Kingdom, as was stated at the outset, is deplorable.

Conclusion

The appeal of artefacts is strong for many and varied reasons, but a hyped-up demand for personal ownership must be balanced by effective communication of the resultant destruction. Prospective purchasers need incontrovertible, graphic exposition of the damage caused to sites by looting. Delivery of this message must be sufficiently clear to persuade the buyer and collector to reject illicit material. Disclosure of provenance should become the norm and, even then, such provenance should be viewed with healthy scepticism. The concept of guardianship of the archaeological heritage for future generations needs to be inculcated and fostered. There is a clear need for education as well.

Archaeologists, conservators, museum curators, and other heritage professionals should develop a unified approach in these areas and it is encouraging to note that there have been recent moves to adopt a recognized ethical stance when confronted with unprovenanced archaeological material. In May 1995 the Standing Conference on Portable Antiquities was established on the initiative of the Council for British Archaeology to provide a forum for British archaeologists and museum and other heritage professionals. This conference has been quoted frequently by government ministers who are pleased to recognize it as speaking for all those responsible for the historic and archaeological heritage (Renfrew 1997). In 1997 this conference unanimously passed a resolution calling upon the government of the United Kingdom to adopt and ratify the UNESCO and UNIDROIT conventions. In 1998, the British Academy, a professional association of academics, also passed a resolution urging the British government to adhere to the spirit of these conventions, whether as a signatory or not. The British Academy has advised that written certificates of authenticity or valuation should not be provided by academics for antiquities of doubtful provenance. These are small steps perhaps, but steps nevertheless, and in the right direction.

We must remember that utilization of artefacts as research tools need not, perhaps even should not, preclude their veneration. Scientific objectivity essential in the academic realm need not eclipse or invalidate an appreciation of consummate craftsmanship, exquisite beauty, or the imprint of an ancestral thumb in the interior of that most humble of objects, the ceramic lamp. It is also obvious that the arguments put forward here must be reiterated time and time again in the hope that voracious consumption of this non-renewable resource – our own unique history – can be controlled so as to avoid its expunction. The need to put an end to the widespread looting of archaeological sites is now of great urgency. The destruction has reached unprecedented levels – another two decades in Latin America and there will not be much left to destroy (Melikian 1997: 9).

Note

After this chapter was submitted for publication (in 1999) the UK Government's Culture, Media and Sport Committee conducted an extensive investigation into issues of the illicit trade and restitution, which was published in three volumes entitled *Cultural Property: Return and Illicit Trade* (July 2000) HC 371–1, II, III. London: The Stationery Office. Additionally, in May 2000, a Ministerial Advisory Panel on Illicit Trade was appointed which published its report in December 2000. Among other things, the report recommended that the UK trade should accede to the 1970 UNESCO Convention on the Means of Prohibiting and Preventing the Illicit Import, Export and Transfer of Ownership of Cultural Property, and that its system of export control should be reviewed. In March 2001, the UK Government announced its intention to sign the UNESCO Convention. The chapter also makes no account of the explosion in internet trading that has occurred over the past few years, as predicted by the authors, which is pushing the marketing of antiquities to its very limit.

References

Belk, R.W. (1995) *Collecting in a Consumer Society*. London and New York: Routledge.

Cavanagh, W., Crouwel, J., Catling, R.W.V., and Shipley, G. (1996) *The Laconia Survey* Volume II. Supplementary Volume 27. London: British School at Athens.

Chesterman, J. (1991) A collector/dealer's view of antiquities. *Antiquity*, 65: 538–9.

Desiderata (1997) *Minerva*, 8(3): 44.

Ede, J. (1995) The antiquities trade: towards a more balanced view. In: K.W. Tubb (ed.), *Antiquities Trade or Betrayed*. London: Archetype in association with UKIC Archaeology Section, pp. 211–14.

——(1996) Art theft and control. *Minerva*, 7(1): 55–6.

Eisenberg, J. (1995) Ethics and the antiquity trade. In: K.W. Tubb (ed.), *Antiquities Trade or Betrayed*. London: Archetype in association with UKIC Archaeology Section, pp. 215–21.

——(1997) Enough is enough, Lord Renfrew. *Minerva*, 8(5): 20.

Ellis, R. (1995) The antiquities trade: a police perspective. In: K.W. Tubb (ed.), *Antiquities Trade or Betrayed*. London: Archetype in association with UKIC Archaeology section, pp. 222–5.

Elsen, A. (1992) An outrageous anomaly. *International Journal of Cultural Property*, 1: 129–31.

Finnigan, J. and Madeley, R. (1996) *This Morning*. Granada Television, 7 November 1996.

Gill, D. and Chippindale, C. (1993) Material and intellectual consequences of esteem for Cycladic figurines. *American Journal of Archaeology*, 97: 601–59.

Goleman, D. (1997) *Vital Lies and Simple Truths: Psychology of Self-Deception*. London: Bloomsbury.

Heritage Shop Catalogue Autumn 1996–Spring 1997. Leighton Buzzard: IMS.

Lowenthal, D. (1996) *The Heritage Crusade and the Spoils of History*. London: Viking.

McIntosh, R.J., Togola, T., and McIntosh, S.K. (1995) The good collector and the premise of mutual respect among nations. *African Arts* (autumn): 60.

Marsh, M. (1993) How to hunt out treasure. *Daily Telegraph* (London), 16 September 1993.

Melikian, S. (1997) Salesroom enigmas, pre-Columbian art market booms. *International Herald Tribune*, 7 June 1997, 9.

Morrison, C.R. (1995) United Kingdom export policies in relation to antiquities. In: K.W. Tubb (ed.), *Antiquities Trade or Betrayed*. London: Archetype in association with UKIC Archaeology Section, pp. 205–10.

Murphy, F. (1996) Sale of the centuries. *Guardian* (London), 2 November 1996.

Norman, G. (1990a) Antiquities off the shelf. *Independent* (London), 24 March 1990.

——(1990b) Great sale of the centuries. *Independent* (London), 24 November 1990.
O'Keefe, P.J. (1997) *Trade in Antiquities: Reducing Destruction and Theft*. London and Paris: Archetype Publications and UNESCO.
Ortiz, G. (1997) Unidroit is a potential disaster – enough of disinformation and ideology. *The Art Newspaper,* February 1997: 21–2.
Palmer, N. (1995) Recovering stolen art. In: K.W. Tubb (ed.) *Antiquities Trade or Betrayed*. London: Archetype in association with UKIC Archaeology Section, pp. 1–37.
Politis, K.D. (1994) Biblical Zoar: the looting of an archaeological site. *Minerva*, 5(6): 12–15.
Prott, L.V. (1995) National and international laws on the protection of cultural heritage. In: KW. Tubb (ed.), *Antiquities Trade or Betrayed*. London: Archetype in association with UKIC Archaeology section, pp. 57–72.
Renfrew, C. (1995) Introduction. In: KW. Tubb (ed.) *Antiquities Trade or Betrayed*. London: Archetype in association with UKIC Archaeology section, pp. xvii–xxi.
——(1997) Stemming the flood of looted antiquities. *British Archaeology*, December: 11.
Rudd, S. (1995) mummy@webcreations.com
Runnels, C.N., Pullen, D.J., and Langdon, S. (1995) *Artefact and Assemblage. The Finds from a Regional Survey of the Southern Argolid, Greece*. California: Stanford University Press.
Stead, I.M. (1998) *The Salisbury Hoard*. Gloucestershire: Tempus.
Stock, F. (1997) Museum piece. *The Antiques Show*. BBC2 television, 14 April 1997.
Tubb, K.W. (1995) The antiquities trade: an archaeological conservator's perspective. In: K.W. Tubb (ed.), *Antiquities Trade or Betrayed*. London: Archetype in association with UKIC Archaeology Section, pp. 256–62.
Watson, P. (1997) Ancient art without a history. *Times* (London), 14 August 1997.
Windsor, J. (1995) From the dawn of time a bargain. *Independent* (London), 1 July 1997.
——(1997) Potted history up for sale. *Independent* (London) 31 May 1997.
Yemma, J. (1997) In the underworld of the looters, a growing violence. *Boston Globe,* 4 December: A24.

Chapter 13

The revolution in US museums concerning the ethics of acquiring antiquities

Jennifer Anglim Kreder

"When I saw the vase ... I knew I had found what I had been searching for all my life."[1]

"I thought I knew where it must have come from. An intact red-figured Greek vase of the early sixth century B.C. could only have been found in Etruscan territory in Italy, by illegal excavators."[2]

"We would consciously avoid knowledge of the history of the vase."[3]

"I was already thinking how to get the money to get this treasure. At the split second I first looked at it, I had vowed to myself to get it. ... This was the single most perfect work of art I had ever encountered."[4]

Former Metropolitan Museum of Art Director Tom Hoving speaking about the now-infamous *Euphronios krater* since restituted to Italy after the below described scandals that rocked the art and antiquities world.

In 2008, we witnessed the dramatic culmination of various scandals in the museum and cultural heritage community. To name just a few of the high-profile events: (1) restitutions of spectacular Etruscan and Greek objects from some of the United States' most prestigious museums and elite collectors to Italy;[5] (2) FBI raids on four California museums whose employees allegedly engaged in antiquities trafficking and the exchange of inflated appraisals for donations to perpetuate tax fraud;[6] and (3) the death of renowned archaeologist and Director of the Southeast Asian Ceramics Museum in Bangkok, Roxanna Brown, while she was in FBI custody.[7] These scandals did not arise in a vacuum. The law and ethics of the cultural property market is changing—dramatically. This article will analyze the law and ethics revolution pertaining to museums' acquisitions of antiquities along with the revolution's impact on the market and knowledge of our collective history.

Those interested in the law and ethics pertaining to the acquisition of antiquities will appreciate the value of some history to understand the current environment and thus, Part I lays out some basic history of the modern era of acquisition law and ethics. Part II highlights the most high-profile scandal to shake the museum and

Source: *University of Miami Law Review*. University of Miami School of Law, 2010. 64(3): 997–1030.

cultural property community—restitutions of exquisite Etruscan[8] and Greek objects from some of the United States' most prestigious museums and collectors. Part III analyzes ethics guidelines adopted by the Association of Art Museum Directors (AAMD) and American Association of Museums (AAM). Part IV concludes that we are in a new era in terms of both law and ethics pertaining to the acquisition of antiquities, which may have a profound impact on the education of the American museum-going public concerning ancient cultures.

The dawn and debate of the modern era of acquisition ethics

In 1969, archaeologist Clemency Coggins laid bare the unauthorized destruction of pre-Colombian archaeological sites causing the irreversible loss of historical and archaeological data in order to obtain objects to sell on the international market.[9] Coggins's famous article begins:

> In the last ten years there has been an incalculable increase in the number of monuments systematically stolen, mutilated and illicitly exported from Guatemala and Mexico in order to feed the international art market. Not since the sixteenth century has Latin America been so ruthlessly plundered.[10]

Well-known archaeologist and cultural property law expert Patty Gerstenblith succinctly explained the damage to sites resulting from looting when she stated, "Only carefully preserved, original contexts can furnish the data upon which the reconstruction of our past depends. Once this context is lost, the inherent value, that is the historic, cultural, and scientific information that informs U.S. about the object, is irreparably injured."[11]

The damage is particularly acute when integrated architectural sculptures and reliefs are hacked away from monuments to be sold as moveable chattels.[12] To smuggle artifacts out of source nations,[13] smugglers often "cut [artifacts] into pieces or deliberately deface" them to conceal their value from customs officers.[14] Collectors have purchased an astronomical number of antiquities over the years for billions of dollars,[15] often without knowing an object's provenance—history tracing its path from find-spot to present.[16] Their motivations are varied, often including a desire to act as a steward of history.[17] Perhaps more often, however, collectors are mesmerized by the object's beauty and mystique, as exemplified by the quotations of former Director of the Met, Tom Hoving, which opened this article.[18] Profit potential also is a common motivator within the antiquities market.[19] Finally, as Coggins put it in 2001: "Without an historical context, owning such objects simply becomes part of an expensive hobby."[20]

Museums in the United States acquire objects through purchase or donation and accept objects on short or long-term loan.[21] Coggins "traced a substantial portion of this stolen and mutilated art from the jungles of Central America into some of America's most respectable museums."[22] Coggins's work led to demands by source nations for the return of some of the most treasured items in museum collections along with the adoption of the Importation of Pre-Columbian

Monumental or Architectural Sculpture or Murals Act.[23] According to Professor of Archaeology, Ricardo J. Elia: "People think that there is an illicit market and a legitimate market ... [i]n fact, it is the same."[24] Ever since Professor Elia's comment, there has been a raw, polarizing philosophical and ethical debate raging between the archaeologists' "camp,"[25] and the collector/dealer/museum "camp,"[26] as to the extent of the antiquity market's trickle down impact upon archaeological sites worldwide.[27] Despite the relatively small number of purchase acquisitions made directly by museums, they still receive many financial and in-kind donations from collectors who do acquire items on the market and, therefore, should act as leaders to exemplify best practices to combat the illicit trade in cultural property.[28] Museums have responded by adopting increasingly stringent acquisitions guidelines, the most stringent of which were adopted in late 2008.[29] As demonstrated below, acquisitions practices and philosophy have changed dramatically since the year 1970.[30]

Coggins's work was also an impetus for the drafting of the UNESCO Convention on the Means of Prohibiting and Preventing the Illicit Import, Export and Transfer of Ownership of Cultural Property of 1970 (UNESCO Convention).[31] The purpose of the UNESCO Convention is to curb widespread pillaging of archaeological sites.[32] Initially, the UNESCO Convention did little to directly change the legal landscape in the United States with the exception of a few categories of objects to which the United States agreed to prohibit importation pursuant to various statutes and bilateral agreements.[33] The Convention adopted what has been referred to critically as the "blank check" approach, which requires art importing signatories to block importation of any object exported in violation of any source nation's export regulations.[34] As explained by Professor John H. Merryman of Stanford Law School, a renowned scholar in the cultural property field:

> Article 3 [of UNESCO] defines as "illicit" any trade in cultural property that "is effected contrary to the provisions adopted under this Convention by the States Parties thereto." Thus, if Guatemala were to adopt legislation and administrative practices that, in effect, prohibited the export of all pre-Columbian artifacts, as it has done, then the export of any pre-Columbian object from Guatemala would be "illicit" under UNESCO 1970. Several source nations that are parties to UNESCO 1970 have such laws. This feature of UNESCO 1970 has been called a "blank check" by interests in market nations; the nation of origin is given the power to define "illicit" as it pleases. Dealers, collectors, and museums in market nations have no opportunity to participate in that decision. That is why legislation implementing United States adherence to UNESCO 1970 took 10 years to enact. Dealer, collector and museum interests sought, with some success, to limit the effect on the trade in cultural property that would follow if the United States automatically acquiesced in the retentive policies of some source nations.[35]

In another essay lamenting the wide divide between archaeologists, specialists,[36] and source nations, versus collectors and art dealers, Clemency Coggins responded to another of Professor Merryman's essays in a way that encapsulates the breadth of the current divide:

> In outlining the archaeological point of view Professor John Merryman suggests, disbelievingly, in his essay that archaeologists would eliminate all commercial demand for such objects, if possible, that archaeology is at war with the market, and that some archaeologists are delighted when fakes appear on the market. But this is all absolutely true. Furthermore, archaeologists do, indeed, assume that an ancient object was illicitly acquired unless there is convincing proof to the contrary. Guilty until proven innocent.[37]

Litigation has also shaped the debate. The *Hollinshead*,[38] *McClain*,[39] and *Schultz*[40] cases have established that one may be prosecuted under the National Stolen Property Act for removing an object from a source nation in violation of a clear national ownership law.[41] This has become known as the "*McClain* doctrine."[42] The widespread adoption of the Convention[43] and the entrenchment of the *McClain* doctrine have strengthened the position of archaeologists in the ongoing debate about the antiquities market and museum acquisition practices, but the debate continues on many fronts as looted antiquities continue to flow throughout the world.[44] The most common framework for the debate has been that of "cultural nationalism" versus "cultural internationalism," as was first articulated by Professor Merryman.[45]

Of course, all actors in the antiquities trade are bound to follow applicable law. However, the debate continues as to whether one in the United States should acquire an object without detailed documentation showing it was exported from a source nation in compliance with that nation's export laws when no U.S. law has been broken.[46] In other words, should objects be "guilty until proven innocent," as stated by Professor Coggins.[47] Regardless of the philosophical debate, if the source nation lacks a clear national ownership law applying to objects excavated after its enactment, then the risk of criminal prosecution and civil liability in the United States is minimal under the *McClain* doctrine.[48] Basically, the ability to win a civil or criminal law suit concerning an allegedly looted antiquity with possible find-spots in multiple nations (some with in-the-ground statutes and others without), turns primarily on which party bears the burden of proof.[49]

Assuming compliance with both U.S. customs regulations and the source nation's clear ownership law, the next step in the inquiry, under the *McClain* doctrine, is to evaluate civil litigation risk in the United States as an evidentiary matter concerning whether the claimant can show (1) that the object was removed from a find-spot within the modern source nation[50] (2) after enactment of the ownership law.[51] A criminal prosecution would also require a showing (3) that the acquirer possessed the requisite level of intent to deprive the owner of the benefit of ownership[52]—and (4) a prosecutor willing to bring the case.[53] A case might be brought by the U.S. government in the form of a civil forfeiture action,[54] which would shift the burden of establishing right of possession onto the purchaser claiming title.[55]

A number of prominent U.S. museums have been caught in the center of it all, often without clear documentation demonstrating proper title.[56] Perhaps the most important impetus for the dramatic change in law and ethics pertaining to the antiquities market is the recent revelation as to the extent of criminal activity providing a steady stream of illicit objects to the high-end antiquities market.[57] Although some still cling to the due process notion of "innocent until proven guilty," the recent scandals, in addition to the work of Professor Coggins and others dating back to 1969, seem to demonstrate that most antiquities being offered on the market for the first time were recently looted.[58] In particular, developments originating in Italy have shown that the market in Etruscan artifacts has been infected with illicit excavation and organized international crime for quite some time.[59] Illicit objects were laundered for years by sophisticated dealers into the international market eventually making their way into respected collections and esteemed museums in the United States.[60] Due to this activity we have seen the prosecution of previously esteemed collectors, a museum curator, and *tombaroli*, which is an Italian word meaning "tomb robber[s]."[61]

Italian criminal investigations and prosecutions

Popular press has attributed Italy's recent success reclaiming its cultural patrimony to the book *The Medici Conspiracy* by Peter Watson and Cecilia Todeschini.[62] Although the book is interesting, Italy's recent successes are better attributed to events dating back to 1902 when the first "in-the-ground" statute passed, thereby vesting ownership of unearthed ancient artifacts in the state.[63] Italy ratified the UNESCO Convention in 1979[64] and later signed a Memorandum of Understanding (MOU) with the United States in 2001.[65] Pursuant to the MOU, which was renewed in 2006, the United States agreed to protect pre-Classical, Classical, and Imperial Roman architectural material,[66] thus committing US customs and enforcement agents to the goal of recovering artifacts.[67] Just this year that MOU has led to over 1,000 artifacts being returned to Italy.[68] However, Italy has been proactive in its recovery efforts, declining to wait for the United States to do the "heavy lifting."

In the mid-1990s, Italy began to press US museums to return objects Italy believed had been illegally exported.[69] It has long been known that artifacts illegally excavated in Italy are often transported through Switzerland before reaching the international market.[70] Accordingly, Italian police sought assistance from Swiss police in 1995 to conduct raids on the Geneva warehouses of Italian art dealer Giacomo Medici.[71] As relayed in The Medici Conspiracy, the raid uncovered a vast treasure trove of smuggled antiquities—many fresh from the ground and others in various stages of preparation for market.[72] A parallel investigation in Italy uncovered a paper referred to as "the organigram," which hints at a vast smuggling ring implicating key players in the international antiquities market.[73] The Italian government viewed the organigram in conjunction with other evidence, particularly photographs found at the Medici warehouses,[74] and brought criminal charges against key and lesser players including prominent art dealer Robert Hecht and former Getty Museum curator Marion True. A raid of Hecht's residence uncovered his personal journal seeming to detail his activities (although he claims it is a draft novel), which has been pivotal in his prosecution.[75]

Hecht was (in)famous for having sold the *Euphronios krater* to the Met for a controversial $1 million in 1972, the first million-dollar sale of an antiquity.[76] Additionally, as articulated in Hoving's book, *Making the Mummies Dance*,[77] and numerous other sources including *The Medici Conspiracy*,[78] there was much speculation at the time of the sale that the krater was overpriced. The sale was a landmark in rendering art theft more profitable than ever.[79]

True, who had tightened the Getty's questionable acquisition policies during her tenure as curator there,[80] was the first U.S. museum employee ever to be indicted for allegedly trading in illegal antiquities.[81] Under True's stewardship, the Getty implemented a policy requiring objects to be acquired from "established, well-documented collections" and to have been published before 1995.[82] In 2006, after True's indictment and in the midst of the below-described negotiations, the Getty again tightened its acquisitions policy.[83]

Negotiations between the Italians and the Getty were difficult—it took several years before they could agree on which antiquities the Getty would return to Italy.[84] On October 25, 2007, the Getty formally agreed to return forty of the fifty-one artifacts demanded,[85] including the prized *Cult Goddess* limestone and marble statue *(a/k/a Aphrodite)*.[86] In the agreement, the Italian Culture Ministry agreed the *Cult Goddess* could remain on display at the Getty until 2010, but the other artifacts were to be returned immediately.[87] Pursuant to the agreement, Italy has loaned other artifacts and will continue to engage in "cultural cooperation," including research projects and joint exhibitions.[88]

In the midst of the negotiations in August 2007, Italy dropped the civil charges against True and reduced the criminal charges, but the criminal trial of True and Hecht continues.[89] It is likely that the Italian statute of limitations, which continues to run until the conclusion of a prosecution and appeal,[90] will expire before the end of True's trial, and possibly also Hecht's, which would preclude their conviction.[91]

Meanwhile, on February 21, 2006, the Italian government finalized negotiations with the Met for the return of the prized *Euphronios krater*, other vases, and Hellenistic silver.[92] The museum continues to dispute Italy's claim that the silver's find-spot is located in Morgantina.[93] Elsewhere, in September 2006, the Museum of Fine Arts, Boston agreed to return thirteen objects, including a statue of Sabina (wife of the Roman emperor, Hadrian).[94] On October 30, 2007, the Princeton University Art Museum agreed to return four objects immediately and four more in four years.[95] In January 2008, the University of Virginia agreed to return two ancient Greek sculptures,[96] and, on November 19, 2008, Italy and the Cleveland Museum of Art issued a joint press release announcing the return of fourteen items.[97]

The Italians also turned their sights to dealers and collectors implicated in the photo chain linking *tombaroli* looting to the market.[98] New York art dealer Jerome Eisenberg of Royal Athena Galleries agreed to return eight Etruscan and Roman artifacts on November 6, 2007.[99] Collector Shelby White returned nine objects in

January 2008 and returned another on loan with the Museum of Modern Art in New York in 2010.[100]

Finally, in January 2008 the Italian government broke up an international ring of antiquities smugglers,[101] which led to the largest criminal case against antiquities smugglers to date.[102] On January 17, 2008, General Giovanni Nistri, head of the art squad within the Italian *Carabinieri*, reported statistics that in his opinion show that international trafficking is "surely declining."[103] If General Nistri is correct, Italy's active pursuit of restitutions from high-profile entities and individuals and its criminal prosecutions are significant factors in the decline. Another likely factor is the 2006 bilateral agreement signed by Italy and Switzerland requiring Swiss customs agents to verify proof of origin and legal export of antiquities arriving in Switzerland from Italy.[104] This is a dramatic legal change to the Geneva Freeport procedures described in The Medici Conspiracy.[105] The Rome trial of True and Hecht continues in its fourth year[106]—and police raids have uncovered additional dealer's archives containing "some 10,000[sic] further Polaroids … waiting to be processed."[107] Also, "there [were] the Polaroids seized in Greece which have yet to be exploited to the same degree as Italy."[108] These restitution efforts are far from over.

The US museum community's reactions

Naturally, the American museum community reacted to these scandals. Some historical background is necessary to understand the significance of these recent events.

2001 AAMD Position Paper

In October 2001, the AAMD issued a Position Paper that underscored that "acquiring works … is a vital part of a museum's mission."[109] That report stated:

> [W]hile it is highly desirable to know the archaeological context in which an artifact was discovered because this can reveal information about the origin of the work and the culture that produced it, this is not always possible. Nevertheless, much information may be gleaned from works of art even when the circumstances of their discovery are unknown. Indeed, most of what we know about early civilizations has been learned from artifacts whose archeological context has been lost.[110]

Since the Position Paper came out in 2001, the museum community has been steadfast in supporting the cultural internationalist position,[111] which maintains that liberal exchange of cultural objects is preferable.[112] The Position Paper described the nature of museums' due diligence concerning title and legal importation of an object noting "[c]onclusive proof is not always possible, because documentation and physical evidence may be inaccessible or lost."[113] Finally, the Position Paper noted that in an effort "[t]o deter illicit trade and to ensure that the importation of art and artifacts from other countries is conducted in a lawful and responsible manner,"[114] museum directors should consider elements such as the jeopardy to the country's cultural patrimony from pillaging, international community interests, compliance with domestic and international laws, and the provenance of the piece.[115]

The Position Paper did not give any firm direction to art museum directors as to how the individual questions should be weighed or balanced in the evaluation process. Particularly significant is the last question regarding legal exportation. During the debates concerning the drafting and U.S. implementation of the UNESCO Convention, U.S. collectors and the U.S. museum community adamantly opposed the "blank check" approach, which would have required the United States to give effect to all foreign nations' export restrictions. Thus, it is quite significant that in 2001 the AAMD decided to include the legality of the exportation of an object among the factors directors should consider.[116]

2004–2007 AAMD Reports

In 2004, the AAMD revisited the issue of acquisition of archaeological materials and ancient art in its June 4, 2004, Task Force Report.[117] It reaffirmed within the Report's Statement of Principles that "in the absence of any breach of law or of the Principles"[118] incomplete documentation of ownership history should be excused, at least in some cases because of an object's "rarity, importance, and aesthetic merit."[119] Such objects may be "acquired and made accessible not only to the public and to scholars but to potential claimants as well."[120] Thus, the Report takes the position that in some cases acquisition of an incompletely documented object might benefit a true owner whose chances of finding the object may be increased.

The 2004 Report also noted that it is important that the museum "rigorously research the provenance of a work."[121] The 2004 Report, like the 2001 Position Paper, provided a list of factors for a museum to consider before acquiring a work.[122] These factors, which are relevant to affirmative defenses to defeat a civil legal claim, include the ownership, exhibition, and publication history, the countries in which the work of art has been located and when, whether a claim of ownership of the work of art has been made, "whether the [art] work appears in ... databases of stolen works[,] and the circumstances under which the ... art is being offered."[123]

These 2004 factors are directly relevant to affirmative defenses that may be raised to defeat a civil legal claim to the work of art, such as statute of limitations, laches, and waiver.[124] Legal claims and litigation are costly for museums to evaluate and defend against.[125]

Additionally, Guideline A(2) instructs that museums should "make a concerted effort to obtain accurate written documentation with respect to the history of the work of art, including import and export documents."[126] And Guideline A(3) states that museums "should require sellers, donors, and their representatives to provide all available information and documentation, as well as appropriate warranties regarding the origins and provenance of a work of art offered for acquisition."[127]

Additionally, Guideline C is entitled "Legal Considerations."[128] It requires that museums "comply with all applicable local, state, and federal U.S. laws, most notably those governing ownership and title, import, and other issues critical to acquisition decisions."[129] It continues to note the problematic complexity of the law applicable to antiquities cases:

> The law relevant to the acquisition of archaeological materials and ancient art has become increasingly complex and continues to evolve. Since the status of a work of art under foreign law may bear on its legal status under U.S. law [pursuant to the *McClain* doctrine], member museums must be familiar with relevant U.S. and foreign laws before making an acquisition.[130]

Moreover, Guideline D deals exclusively with the UNESCO Convention.[131] It provides that member museums should not acquire objects falling into any of the below three categories:

[(1)] any archaeological material or work of ancient art known to have been 'stolen from a museum, or a religious, or secular public monument or similar institution'...
[(2)] objects known to have been part of an official archaeological excavation and removed in contravention of the laws of the country of origin [; or]
[(3)] any such works of art that were removed after November 1970 regardless of any applicable statutes of limitation and notwithstanding the fact that the U.S. did not accede to the Convention until 1983.[132]

In comparison to the 2001 factors, the 2004 factors focus with precision on key legal standards. Although the 2001 factors mention "applicable law,"[133] which presumably meant criminal law and U.S. import regulations, and one factor implicates foreign export law, the 2001 factors' core theme reflects concern about the impact of museum acquisitions upon unauthorized excavation in foreign lands and destruction of the archaeological record.[134] In contrast, the 2004 factors take on a more legalistic—and defensive—approach that primarily reflects fear of costly lawsuits.[135] They inherently implicate legal evaluation of the ability to defeat claims that may be brought.

This is not to say that the Guidelines foreclosed acquiring an object with knowledge that there was a distinct chance it might later be restituted, but as a general rule museum deaccessioning is strongly disfavored.[136] Guideline F in the 2004 Report states that if a member receives a claim to an object, it should seek an "equitable resolution"[137] "even though this claim may not be enforceable under U.S. law."[138] "Possible options that should be considered include: transfer or sale of the work of art to the claimant; payment to the claimant; loan or exchange of the work of art; or retention of the work of art."[139]

Additionally, archaeological ethics remained a concern for the AAMD Guideline E of the 2004 Report entitled "Incomplete Provenance" provides that in cases where rigorous research could not provide "sufficient information on the recent history of a proposed acquisition," that "museums must use their professional judgment ... in accordance with the Statement of Principles," to determine whether to nonetheless acquire an object.[140] The exercise of judgment should "recogniz[e] that the work of art, the culture it represents, scholarship, and the public may be served best through the acquisition of the work of art by a public institution dedicated to the conservation, exhibition, study, and interpretation of works of art."[141] Examples are provided:

> [(1) if] the work of art is in danger of destruction or deterioration; or [(2)] the acquisition would make the work of art publicly accessible, providing a singular and material contribution to knowledge, as well as facilitating the reconstruction of its provenance thereby allowing possible claimants to come forward.[142]

Another notable factor museums were instructed to take into account was:

> [W]hether the work of art has been outside its probable country or countries of origin for a sufficiently long time that its acquisition would not provide a direct, material incentive to looting or illegal excavation; while each member museum should determine its own policy as to length of time and appropriate documentation, a period of 10 years is recommended.[143]

In this very important respect, the 2004 Guidelines injected a factual assessment of the acquisition's likely impact upon looting. In 2004, the AAMD's view was that a ten-year separation between the likely date an object was improperly excavated and its acquisition date meant that the acquisition likely had no "direct, material incentive to looting or illegal excavation."[144] Most archaeologists would dispute this assessment.[145]

Regardless of who was right factually, by 2004, the AAMD approach to weighing the pros and cons of a possible acquisition became primarily, but not exclusively, a legalistic one. Although the AAMD recognized that acquisitions—even those that would not violate any applicable law—should not encourage destruction of the archaeological record, risk to the museum's budget became the primary guiding light.

On February 27, 2006, the AAMD Subcommittee on Incoming Loans of Archaeological Material and Ancient Art issued a report largely extending the 2004 Principles and Guidelines to loans,[146] particularly to "long-term loans" like those arranged between various U.S. museums and Italy.[147] However, there are a few important distinctions in the 2006 Report. For example, in regard to determining ownership history, in addition to asking lenders for information and appropriate warranties, the Guidelines provide that "[i]n some cases, the museum may decide that it is responsible and prudent to make further inquiries from other possible sources of information and/or databases."[148] As to loans for visiting exhibitions, the Guidelines state the principal responsibility for researching ownership history falls upon the AAMD member museum primarily responsible for organizing it.[149] The Guidelines also caution that while the borrowing institution will generally accept the lending institution's assessment of the ownership history, legal issues may arise for the borrowing institution.[150]

The AAMD's January 2007 Position Paper, *Art Museums, Private Collectors, and the Public Benefit*, contains a "laundry list" of factors to evaluate a potential loan or donation.[151] Additionally, because the Position Paper applies to all art acquisitions and loans, the de-emphasis of issues related to archaeological ethics does not signify a departure from the Principles and Guidelines previously expressed. It is also significant that whereas the prior Reports, Guidelines, and Position Papers did not address how to weigh or balance the factors, the 2007 Position Paper states that "[e]ach of the 176 institutions … answers these questions according to the unique mandate of its mission and the interests of its community."[152] Thus, AAMD member museums have now been given the directive to individually determine how the factors should be weighed or balanced.

AAMD 2008 New Report

On 4 June 2008, the AAMD issued its *New Report on Acquisition of Archaeological Materials and Ancient Art*, which signifies a shift in AAMD philosophy.[153] It announced the creation of a new AAMD website "where museums will publish images and information" about new acquisitions.[154] Instead of leaving it to individual museums to assess the potential legal risks and the object's possible link to clandestine excavation within the last ten years on a case-by-case basis, it, in part, adopts the "blank check" approach, previously rejected in the United States, in relation to UNESCO.[155] It "[r]ecognize[s] the 1970 UNESCO Convention as providing the most pertinent threshold date for the application of more rigorous standards to the acquisition of archaeological material and ancient art" as well as for the development of "a unified set of expectations for museums, sellers, and donors."[156] Guideline E states, in relevant part, that AAMD member museums "should not acquire a work unless its provenance research [(1)] substantiates that the work was outside its country of probable modern discovery before 1970 or [(2)] was legally exported from its probable country of modern discovery after 1970."[157]

Nonetheless, Principle F still retains flexibility to exercise judgment when complete ownership history is unavailable.[158] Guideline F expands upon this flexibility, which fairly can be described as an intentional loophole in providing that museums use an informed judgment when assessing the provenance of a piece:

> The AAMD recognizes that even after the most extensive research, many works will lack a complete documented ownership history. In some instances, an informed judgment can indicate that the work was outside its probable country of modern discovery before 1970 or legally exported from its probable country of modern discovery after 1970, and therefore can be acquired. In other instances, the cumulative facts and circumstances resulting from provenance research, including, but not limited to, the independent exhibition and publication of the work, the length of time it has been on public display and its recent ownership history, allow a museum to make an informed judgment to acquire the work, consistent with the Statement of Principles above.[159]

The overarching "guiding light" to operating within the loophole and deciding whether to acquire an object with incomplete ownership history back to 1970 is stated in Guideline F (second paragraph): "In both instances, the museum must carefully balance the possible *financial and reputational harm* of taking such a step against the benefit of collecting, presenting, and preserving the work in trust for the educational benefit of present and future generations."[160] In sum, this emphasis is less legalistic than that of the 2004 Report. And, the guiding light is not that of preserving archaeological context, but that of the bottom line of the museum.[161]

AAM Standards and Guidelines

The American Association of Museums also weighed in on the debate in 2008 in its Standards Regarding Archaeological Material and Ancient Art. According to the new standards, even if an acquisition would be legal, museums "should not acquire any object that, to the knowledge of the museum, has been illegally exported from its country of modern discovery or the country where it was last legally owned."[162] The standards "recommend[ ]"[163] that "museums require documentation that the object was"[164] (1) "out of its probable country of modern discovery" by 1970; or (2) "legally exported [out of] its country of modern discovery."[165] The AAM policy also contains a loophole "when there is substantial but not full documentation" of provenance,[166] and states that if a museum utilizes the loophole, "it should be transparent about why this is an appropriate decision in alignment with the institution's collections policy and applicable ethics codes."[167]

Dr. Kwame Opoku, a frequent contributor to the debate concerning repatriation of African objects from Western museums, who wrote an essay in 2008 that attracted a rejoinder on Afrikanet.info from de Montebello, critiqued the AAM loophole:

> The solution of the AAM is what one often finds where there is division of opinion and both sides are almost equally strong: a bold general principle with an exception which almost negates totally the general principle. Both sides win. One step forward and one back.[168]

But surely the expression of the U.S. museum community's new attitude toward the "blank check" approach represents a significant development. Also significant is the fact that the Getty and the Indianapolis Museum of Art had already adopted the 1970 "blank check" approach for new acquisitions—without a loophole—in 2006 and 2007, respectively.[169]

These AAM standards apply to new acquisitions, but the standards take a revolutionary position in regard to existing collections. They state in relevant part:

> In order to advance further research, public trust, and accountability museums should make available the known ownership history of archaeological material and ancient art in their collections, and make serious efforts to allocate time and funding to conduct research on objects where

provenance is incomplete or uncertain. Museums may continue to respect requests for anonymity by donors.[170]

This standard is revolutionary because there is no limit to the number of objects within a museum's collection to which the standard applies, and some of the most prestigious institutions' collections' contain hundreds of thousands of objects.[171] The task of full provenance research as to all archaeological and ancient art objects obtained after 1970 would be enormous.[172] As stated by Lee Rosenbaum, who pens the influential CultureGrrl blog: "Did they realize what they were saying?"[173] It should be noted, however, that the new standards are aspirational in nature, not requirements.[174]

The language of the new AAM Standard 4 seems to reveal a more reconciliatory approach toward handling claims by suggesting museums "respectfully and diligently address ownership claims to antiquities and archaeological material."[175] It also suggests that "[w]hen appropriate and reasonably practical, museums should seek to resolve claims through voluntary discussions directly with a claimant or facilitated by a third party."[176] This new standard heavily reflects the cooperative approach to claims to Nazi-looted art previously advanced by the AAMD and the AAM, as well as the "Washington Principles."[177]

Nazi-confiscated art precedents

On June 4, 1998, the AAMD issued guidelines that called on member museums to resolve legitimate Nazi-era claims to art in their collections "in an equitable, appropriate, and mutually agreeable manner."[178] The Washington Principles drew heavily from the AAMD guidelines and called for nations to reach "just and fair solution[s]" to Nazi-looted art claims.[179] The AAM November 1999 Guidelines, amended April 2001, echo the AAMD standard.[180] Although conciliatory in nature, the guidelines and principles are vague and lack instruction as to what is "equitable"[181] or "appropriate"[182] in difficult cases. Moreover, things have changed since this conciliatory tone was struck in 1998.

A little over a decade since publication of the pivotal AAMD Report and The Washington Principles in 1998, we have moved into an era in which museums have begun to file declaratory judgment actions against claimants.[183] Museums are throwing down the litigation gauntlet against fragile, arguably weak, claims.[184] It is telling that in May 2007, the AAMD issued a Position Paper stating that despite the large amount of Nazi-era provenance research that had been conducted in museums between 1998 and July 2006 (which one should note had not been uniformly progressive in all institutions), only "twenty-two works in American museum collections have been identified as having been stolen by the Nazis and not properly restituted after the war."[185] The filing of declaratory judgment actions certainly seems a dramatic turn away from the spirit of 1998. Is the same in store for antiquities? Will we transition out of this new phase of purported openness to a period of pre-emptive litigation strike to defeat claims?

Conclusion

The questions presented boil down to these: Should one presume, without more empirical research, that objects lacking impeccable documentation are looted—and, assuming so, should they nonetheless be purchased under any circumstances? If we ban such objects from museums and scholarly study, what consequences will the market experience? What information will we lose in the overarching fight to preserve archaeological context?[186]

Many archaeologists, consistent with policies of the Archaeological Institute of America (AIA) and American Schools of Oriental Research (ASOR), believe undocumented antiquities should be shunned.[187] As recently stated by archaeologist Elizabeth Stone:

> The place we ought to be is where we are when it comes to buying Brazilian parrots, buying fur coats and things like that. It's no longer a thing you do. It's no longer fashionable. And what you need to do is make clear to the wealthy—that it's no longer fashionable to collect antiquities because of the ethical problems. When you've done that, it's going to stop. It's really going to stop.[188]

To try to stop archaeologists from inadvertently enhancing the value of looted artifacts, the AIA and ASOR prohibit initial publication in their journals of unprovenanced objects (with the exception of an article highlighting the looting problem).[189] Scholars "who lend their expertise to the trade are now considered unethical, and are seen as collaborators in the mutilation and corruption of the past."[190]

These policies reflect concern about the destruction of the archaeological record discussed above, as well as other weaknesses that a market filled with unprovenanced objects poses for science.[191] For example, the market demand for undocumented Coptic sculptures allowed fakes to infiltrate museum and private collections for more than forty years, thus distorting our understanding of ancient Egypt and the importance of Christian iconography there.[192] At the Brooklyn Museum alone, approximately one third of its formerly prized collection of Coptic sculptures are believed to be fakes.[193] At this point, it will be hard even for experts to tease out all of the fakes from collections throughout the United States and the world.[194]

The Coptic market is not unique in being infiltrated with fakes. Another market includes a Himalayan Buddhist art form known as thangkas.[195] Thangkas are composite objects, meaning the various pieces of the thangka are repaired and replaced over time thus making their authenticity harder to verify.[196] In some cases the thangkas have been made as "intentional fakes" with the intent to defraud, while in other cases these unconventional thangkas are used in the traditional manner by the people who create them.[197] This dynamic, obviously, creates a "complex challenge in the spectrum of fakes, forgeries, and fabrications" in the thangka marketplace.[198]

The Buddhist religion is not the only religion with fakes on the market. Pieces of art associated with Christian iconography have created a firestorm of newsworthy fodder over the past couple of years.[199] The scope of forged works is wide including burial remains alleged to be that of Jesus's brother James,[200] a burial box with references to Jesus,[201] and a stone tablet with biblical passages.[202] The case involving the alleged remains of Jesus's brother has even raised suspicion that several world-renowned top scholars have ties to the forgery group primarily responsible for many of these religious fakes.[203] However, their ties and ultimate guilt are questionable. This was, perhaps, stated best by the judge in the case when he wondered aloud how he could accurately "determine the authenticity of the items [when] the professors could not [even] agree among[st] themselves."[204]

Other markets and places being affected by the recent forgery surge include auctions and sales both online on sites like Ebay,[205] and offline in places like auction houses, museums, and art galleries.[206] In Canada, a new art-fraud task force recently charged a man with seventy-five counts of fraud, forgery, and possession of goods after officers found upwards of eighty reproductions of works by Riopelle, Paul Émile Borduas, and Marcelle Ferron in his home.[207] In France, renowned artist S. H. Raza "unwittingly inaugurated a show of ... fakes" of his own works put together by his own nephew; Raza later sued his nephew for his actions regarding the auction.[208] Meanwhile, in America there are plenty of instances of forgery as well ranging from a "prominent New York and Miami art dealer ... arrested on charges of selling forged paintings"[209] to an FBI investigation at the Weisman Museum at the University of Minnesota.[210]

Despite the thriving market in forgeries, collectors and many within the museum community believe we should rescue unprovenanced antiquities and not "pretend they didn't exist," as recently stated by Michael Conforti, President of the AAMD.[211] The custom of the collecting market has never previously required such a high level of proof of ownership—even if it should have.[212] Additionally, chance finds are possible—floods and earthquakes happen, people find objects on private property to which national ownership laws may not apply, and old collections do exist.[213]

Some scholars of antiquity are caught in the middle. In August 2007, the Biblical Archaeology Society issued a Statement of Concern in relation to the "movement that has received much publicity lately that condemns the use of unprovenanced antiquities from consideration in the reconstruction of ancient history."[214] Although they noted their uniform condemnation of looting,[215] as has the AAMD[216] and the AAM,[217] they stated that a history of the ancient Near East and the Mediterranean basin "cannot be written without the evidence from unprovenanced antiquities."[218] The Statement identifies many important unprovenanced and looted antiquities including "the Dead Sea Scrolls, the Nag Hammadi Codices, the recently reported Gospel of Judas, the Wadi Daliyeh papyri," coins, stone seals, and hundreds of thousands of cuneiform tables that are the basis of our understanding of Mesopotamian history.[219] The Statement in particular criticizes the AIA and ASOR publication policies, claiming that it is "almost universally recognized" that the policies have "had little or no effect on looting."[220] In the words of the Biblical Archaeology Society's Statement itself, "Scholars cannot close their eyes to important information."[221] It continued:

> 7. We do not encourage private collection of antiquities. But important artifacts and inscriptions must be rescued and made available to scholars even though unprovenanced. When such objects have been looted, the antiquities market is often the means by which they are rescued, either by a private party or a museum. To vilify such activity results only in the loss of important scholarly information.
> 8. We would encourage private collectors of important artifacts and inscriptions to make them available to scholars for study and publication. Too often collectors who do make their objects available to scholars are subject to public obloquy. As a result, collectors are disinclined to allow scholars to study their collections, and the public is the poorer.[222]

In summary, as a result of the various antiquities markets' infection with fraudulent and looted goods and various policies adopted in response thereto, there has been a dramatic shift in significant segments of *both* the archaeologist and museum/collector/dealer camps concerning the best approach for all those with an interest in antiquities—including the museum-going public. The initial cultural nationalism versus cultural internationalism framework was useful to start discussion, but eventually seemed too polarized to lead to useful solutions. Regardless of one's view of cultural nationalism, the existence of an antiquities market, or politics,[223] present acquisitions invite a whole host of more complex issues to consider. Although hard empirical data would be useful to understand the full ramifications of acquisition and publication policies, such data necessarily will be very difficult or impossible to obtain because of the clandestine, and often criminal, nature of activities at an object's source and path to the seemingly licit market.[224] Logic and hard evidence about the extent of looting of antiquities throughout the world have demonstrated that "guilty until proven innocent" is the right presumption going forward, but it can be overcome! Thus, we cannot allow the lack of firm data concerning the extent of the illicit market to become an excuse to close down open communication.

Museums are on the defensive, as is plainly seen in the evolution of AAMD and AAM policies discussed above and the Universal Museum Statement issued in response to the restitution movement wherein some of the world's largest museums in possession of antiquities are essentially justifying their existence.[225] The fear seems to be that, by the end of the "war,"[226] the museums will be left with "bare walls."[227] The Statement does not instruct museums to refuse all repatriation requests by any means; it calls for a case-by-case determination in light of the benefit to humanity of "universal museums,"[228] much as the new AAMD and AAM Reports and Guidelines call for a balancing of the benefits and harms of deaccessioning an item.

Thus, despite the call by many in the anti-collecting camp for eliminating the market, it would be naïve to believe that many museums will support elimination of the market at any time in the near future. They will continue to acquire objects and confront the archaeological "camp," and collectors and donors will continue to buy spectacular objects even if the price for documented ones rises.[229] Conforti and others in the pro-collecting "camp" call for the promotion of licit markets, much like Professor Merryman did starting in the 1980s.[230] They maintain that so long as a market exists outside of institutional buying, which, in their opinion, should remain the norm, source nations should provide legal avenues for dealers and collectors to acquire antiquities.[231] If source nations do not support a licit market and the price for spectacular documented antiquities rises even further, we will see even more incentive for looting and more sophisticated forgery of objects.

On the one hand, there is hope that we have entered a new era that will lead to a détente between the pro-collecting and anti-collecting camps, which both share the common mission of education about ancient cultures. There is value in acquiring and preserving objects and there is value in acquiring and preserving archaeological data. Museums can—and are—taking the lead and slowing down acquisitions. They are looking for documentation. Perhaps they could slow down even further and display some of the less visually spectacular objects from storage and create exhibits that emphasize their historical significance more than their physical aspects.[232] These practices would have significant market impacts and would even increase knowledge about objects in museum collections.

We will likely see fewer outright purchases by museums; in the past, outright purchases were limited—the Getty was the exception not the rule. Donations will continue, although the IRS may monitor them more closely as a result of the criminal indictments following the overvaluing of antiquities donated to California museums so that donors could take overly generous tax deductions.[233] Additionally, we will also likely see many more loans, like those from Italy to the museums that have recently restituted objects. Also likely are more touring exhibitions.[234] Hopefully, those in the anti-collecting camp can find some comfort in the new AAMD and AAM guidelines and the increased transparency as a result of the AAMD database.[235] It would also be ideal if some museums followed the examples of museums like the Indianapolis Museum of Art and published information discovered via their own thorough provenance research on their own websites.[236]

On the other hand, we may be on a collision course. Many in the anti-collecting "camp" will not be satisfied until the market is eliminated. Museums will conclude that their concessions are not enhancing their reputations, but have added fuel to the repatriation movement if increased transparency translates into the receipt of more claims that they do not view as being meritorious.[237] The risk to the anti-collecting camp is that the museums could withdraw from the dialogue and slowdown or halt publication—and in some cases even exhibition—of objects lacking full documentation.[238] The risk to the museum/collector/dealer camp is reputational as well as legal. If the burden of proof in civil litigation remains on the claimant in the future, then perhaps we will see an increase in prosecutions by U.S. Attorneys and States' Attorneys General in the United States. Perhaps we will see more curators and dealers prosecuted abroad. Or, perhaps U.S. Attorneys will utilize the civil forfeiture procedure to seize objects and shift the burden onto the museum (and other claimants).

In conclusion, members of the cultural heritage community must continue to let informed logic and ethics guide their policies and practices as they act as stewards of objects for the public trust. The biblical scholars have demonstrated that we cannot "turn a blind eye" to all undocumented antiquities. Nor, however, can we continue to accept the lack of documentation with no questions asked as the norm. In light of the overwhelming evidence of the extent of the infection of the market with illicit and fraudulent objects, a presumption of "guilty until proven innocent" is appropriate for most objects. The idea that we must "save" all undocumented antiquities from destruction or disappearance into the oblivion of private collections is naïve. It is remotely possible that some may be destroyed if they cannot find a buyer, but proper ethics dictates that museums and their esteemed patrons, the collectors of the finest (and hence most profitable) objects, not play that role. Failure to change would result in looters continuing to dig *en masse* for spectacular objects, destroying archaeological context and countless other objects in the process—and hence our historical record. Finally, acquisition of the object, even with the best of intentions, risks prosecution under anti-trafficking laws, including the National Stolen Property Act, and subsequent deaccessioning at great cost to the public.

Notes and references

1. Reported in JOHN L. HESS, THE GRAND ACQUISITORS 143 (1974).
2. THOMAS HOVING, MAKING THE MUMMIES DANCE 309 (1993).
3. *Id.* at 310.
4. *Id.* at 312.
5. *See* discussion *infra* Part II.
6. *See* Edward Wyatt, *Four Museums are Raided in Looted Antiquities Case*, N.Y. TIMES, Jan. 25, 2008, at A14. *See also* Jason Felch and Doug Smith, *You Say that Art is Worth how Much?*, L.A. TIMES, Mar. 2, 2008, at A1; Jeff McDonald and Jeanette Steele, *Balancing Art, Ethics*, SAN DIEGO UNION-TRIB., Feb. 17, 2008, at B1; Matthew L. Wald, *Tax Scheme Is Blamed for Damage to Artifacts*, N.Y. TIMES, Feb. 4, 2008, at E1; Laura Bleiberg, *More Questions About Bowers*, ORANGE COUNTY REG., Jan. 31, 2008, at B1; Jason Felch and Mike Boehm, *Federal Probe of Stolen Art Goes National*, L.A. TIMES, Jan. 29, 2008, at B1; Edward Wyatt, *Museum Workers Are Called Complicit*, N.Y. TIMES, Jan. 26, 2008, at B7; Associated Press, *Raids by Federal Agents Newest Black Eye to American Museums*, KomoNews, Jan. 25, 2008.
7. *See* Jason Felch, *A Life in Shards: A Passion for Art, a Perilous Pursuit*, L.A. TIMES, Sept. 11, 2008, at A1. (providing details about the antiquities smuggling scandal that led to the indictment and arrest after five-year investigation); Lawrence Van Gelder, *Museum Director Is Found Dead*, N.Y. TIMES, May 16, 2008, at E4 (discussing death in custody). *See also* Robert Faturechi, *Lawsuit Filed in Death of Roxana Brown, Held at Detention Center*, SEATTLE TIMES, July 15, 2008, at B2; John Berthelsen, *A Museum Director's Death in an American Jail*, ASIA SENTINEL, June 8, 2008, http://www.asiasentinel.com/index.php?option=com_content&task=view&id=1244&Itemid=367; Mike Boehm, *Museum Didn't Need This Publicity*, L.A. TIMES, Jan. 26, 2008, at A1. *See generally* Randy Dotinga, *Art Museums Struggle with Provenance Issues*, CHRISTIAN SCI. MONITOR, Apr. 2, 2008, at 13.

8 Etruscan objects derive from Etruria, an "ancient country of west-central Italy in present-day Tuscany and parts of Umbria." AM. HERITAGE DICTIONARY, 612–13 (4th ed. 2000).
9 Clemency Coggins, *Illicit Traffic of Pre-Columbian Antiquities*, 29 ART J. 94 (1969).
10 *Id.* at 94. *See also, e.g.*, Jamison K. Shedwill, Comment, *Is the "Lost Civilization" of the Maya Lost Forever?: The US and Illicit Trade in Pre-Columbian Artifacts*, 23 CAL. W. INT'L L.J. 227, 229 (1992) (discussing legal framework applicable to pre-Columbian artifacts found throughout Central and South America).
11 Patty Gerstenblith, *The Public Interest in the Restitution of Cultural Objects*, 16 CONN. J. INT'L L. 197, 198–9 (2001). *See also* Lisa J. Borodkin, Note, *The Economics of Antiquities Looting and a Proposed Legal Alternative*, 95 COLUM. L. REV. 377 (1995)

> Once a site has been worked over by looters in order to remove a few salable objects, the fragile fabric of its history is largely destroyed. Changes in soil color, the traces of ancient floors and fires, the imprint of vanished textiles and foodstuffs, the relation between one object and another, and the position of a skeleton—all of these sources of fugitive information are ignored and obliterated by archaeological looters.
>
> Moreover, antiquities traffickers often deliberately deface artifacts to render them less recognizable and easier to smuggle. Treasure hunters have been known to destroy human remains, break up artifacts, behead statues, melt down ancient coins, and chisel reliefs from tombs.
>
> The historical damage extends beyond the defacement of physical evidence to the corruption of the archaeological record. The finders of artifacts often conceal the sites, either to protect a needed source of income or to shield their illegal activities from law enforcement agents. Fear of inviting looters has even intimidated some legitimate archaeologists from publishing their findings. More disturbingly, professional smugglers routinely forge export papers and falsify the provenance, or origin, of the artifacts they sell. As one commentator noted, such falsifications amount to a "quite horrifying distortion of history."

Id. at 382–3 (internal footnotes and citations omitted). *Accord* Lyndel V. Prott, *National and International Laws on the Protection of the Cultural Heritage*, in ANTIQUITIES TRADE OR BETRAYED: LEGAL, ETHICAL & CONSERVATION ISSUES 57 (Kathryn W. Tubb, ed. 1995):

> [Illicit excavation] destroys the scientific value of the site by damaging the site's stratigraphy, and of the object, by wrenching it out of its context. Information for comparative dating, style assessment or relation to other objects in the site is thus lost. The site is destroyed by inexpert excavation ... Part of the cultural record is also lost to expert reassessment by the disappearance of these objects into private collections which are not accessible to the public or to researchers and by the find itself being not professionally recorded, curated and published.

See generally ARCHAEOLOGY, CULTURAL HERITAGE, AND THE ANTIQUITIES TRADE (Neil Brodie et al. eds., 2006).
12 *See* Coggins, *Illicit Traffic*, *supra* note 9, at 96.
13 *See generally* John Henry Merryman, *Two Ways of Thinking About Cultural Property*, 80 AM. J. INT'L L. 831, 832 (1986) (coining phrases "source nation" and "market nation" in the antiquities context).

14 *See* Jane Warring, Comment, *Underground Debates: The Fundamental Differences of Opinion That Thwart UNESCO's Progress in Fighting the Illicit Trade in Cultural Property*, 19 Emory Int'l L. Rev. 227, 242 (2005).

15 *E.g.*, Clemency Coggins, *Cultural Property and Ownership: Antiquities*, 16 Conn. J. Int'l L. 183, 186 (2001) (discussing wealth spent to collect antiquities); *see also, e.g.*, Alia Szopa, Comment, *Hoarding History: A Survey of Antiquity Looting and Black Market Trade*, 13 U. Miami Bus. L. Rev. 55, 75–6 (2004); Borodkin, *supra* note 11, at 377–8. (discussing multibillion dollar illicit art market).

16 *See* Patty Gerstenblith, *Controlling the International Market in Antiquities: Reducing the Harm, Preserving the Past*, 8 Chi. J. Int'l L. 169, 178 n.38 (2007) (defining provenience).

17 *E.g.*, Warring, *supra* note 14, at 237.

18 Hoving, *supra* note 2, at 309. *See also* Sarah Harding, *Value, Obligation and Cultural Heritage*, 31 Ariz. St. L.J. 291, 316–21 (1999) (discussing the "intrinsic value" of antiquities); James Cuno, *Museums and the Acquisition of Antiquities*, 19 Cardozo Arts & Ent. L.J. 83, 88 (2001) (discussing acquisition of collection of Greek vase fragments: "On seeing them, my first thought was how beautiful they were and how important they could be for teaching.").

Oscar White Muscarella is a Near East expert who was fired (three times) from the Metropolitan Museum of Art after publicly opposing the purchase of the *Euphronios krater* discussed below, of which then-Director Tom Hoving approved. Muscarella's saga and multiple reinstatements at the Met are reported in many sources, including Peter Watson & Cecilia Todeschini, The Medici Conspiracy: The Illicit Journey of Looted Antiquities, from Italy's Tomb Raiders to the World's Greatest Museum (2006). In a December 2005 interview with Suzan Mazur (SM), an independent journalist who published scathing reports about the Euphronios affair discussed in Section II below, Muscarella (OWM) described collectors' motives in collecting antiquities as follows:

> OWM: With all the euphemisms of [those involved in the trade], it's rape. All these people are justifying their destruction, their power to have these objects in their apartment. Bring their guests in and say "Golly gee look what I have!" [sic] Power and perversion of the wealthy. These are the people who are encouraging it. Who are authorizing it. Who are the recipients of it. Plunder does not exist without the existence of these people... .
>
> SM: And is it intentional? Do they want to erase the history?
>
> OWM: They don't care. I've talked to the dealers and collectors. One dealer stated he "wanted it [a plundered object] madly."

Suzan Mazur, *Antiquities Whistleblower Oscar White Muscarella: The Whistleblower & the Politics of the Met's Euphronios Purchase: A Talk with Oscar White Muscarella*, Scoop Independent News, Dec. 25, 2005, www.scoop.co.nz/stories/print.html?path=HL0512/S00252.htm (accessed 14 October 2016). For more information about Hoving and the *Euphronios krater*, see Hess, *supra* note 1.

19 *E.g.*, Borodkin, *supra* note 11, at 377–8. Independent journalist Suzan Mazur offered this anecdote about the profit motive in regard to a kylix, a prize amphora that was awarded at the Panathenaic Games in Athens, which she viewed and discussed with a Sotheby's antiquities expert: "The piece went at auction to New York dealer Ed Merrin for $190,000. Merrin once told me for an Economist magazine story that he does it all 'for love.' Corporate raider Asher Edelman (inspiration for Michael Douglas'

character Gordon Gekko in the film *Wall Street*) had $10 million invested in Merrin Gallery ... ." Suzan Mazur, *Mazur: Sotheby's Pre-Auction Euphronios Transcript*, SCOOP INDEPENDENT NEWS, Jan. 11, 2006.
20 Coggins, *Cultural Property*, supra note 15, at 186.
21 *See generally* Cuno, *Museums and the Acquisition*, supra note 18, at 83. *See also* James Cuno, *US Art Museums and Cultural Property*, 16 CONN. J. INT'L L. 189, 189 (2001); Linda F. Pinkerton, *Museums Can Do Better: Acquisitions Policies Concerning Stolen and Illegally Exported Art*, 5 VILL. SPORTS & ENT. L.J. 59, 62 (1998); John W. O'Hagan, *Art Museums: Collections, Deaccessioning and Donations*, 22 J. CULTURAL ECON. 197, 198 (1998).
22 Paul M. Bator, *An Essay on the International Trade in Art*, 34 STAN. L. REV. 275, 279, 306 (1982) (seminal article in cultural property law field describing "art as a good ambassador").
23 19 USC. §§ 2091–5 (1982); *see also* Leo J. Harris, *From the Collector's Perspective: The Legality of Importing Pre-Columbian Art and Artifacts*, in THE ETHICS OF COLLECTING CULTURAL PROPERTY: WHOSE CULTURE? WHOSE PROPERTY? 155, 155–68 (Phyllis Mauch Messenger, ed., 1989) (discussing all laws implicated by export and import of pre-Columbian art and artifacts).
24 Barry Meier & Martin Gottlieb, *An Illicit Journey Out of Egypt, Only a Few Questions Asked*, N.Y. TIMES, Feb. 23, 2004, at A1 (quoting Associate Professor of Archaeology at Boston University).
25 Oscar White Muscarella (OWM) is one of the most vocal and critical of museum acquisition practices, as exemplified in the below exchange during his December 2005 interview with Suzan Mazur (SM):

> SM: You contend that what percentage of the artifacts in the museum are looted?
>
> OWM: In my department [Ancient Near East] it's mixed and there's been a pullback on buying antiquities. If you go to the Greek and Roman room—I call it "The Temple of Plunder"—the great majority are plundered over the years. There's even one object stolen from another museum. They [the museum administrators] know it's stolen from a museum. They refuse to return it. It's a griffin head.
>
> In the Department of Arts of Africa, etc., every pre-Columbian object—every one—is plundered and the tomb sites totally destroyed... .
>
> But other departments that play a major role in plunder are the Asian Art department:
>
> Hundreds and hundreds from temples and tombs all over Cambodia, Thailand, China, just to decorate vitrines in the Metropolitan Museum of Art.

Mazur, *Antiquities Whistleblower*, supra note 18, at 10.
26 Perhaps the two most vocal advocates of the cultural internationalism position are Professor John H. Merryman of Stanford Law School and James Cuno of the Art Institute of Chicago. Their scholarship is discussed extensively herein.
27 *E.g.*, John H. Merryman, *Legal Issues in Museum Administration*, SL077 ALI-ABA, at ★3, ★10–★11 (2006) (Am. Law. Inst.) (stating that there has been a "revolution in acquisition ethics" initiated by "the extremely effective archaeologists' Crusade against the international trade in antiquities"); *accord*, Paul M. Bator, *The International Trade in Art*, 254 PLI/PAT 659, 664 (1988) (available in Westlaw):

> [I]t is my impression that over the past 20 years there has been an important change in consciousness. Art-importing societies such as the United States have become increasingly aware that the preservation and conservation of humanity's artistic and

archaeological heritage constitutes a general human obligation, to be shared by all the world's societies and not arbitrarily restricted to those countries that happen to be rich in archaeological materials.

See also Colin Renfrew, *A Scandal That Rocked the Art World*, EVENING STANDARD (LONDON, UK), June 26, 2006, at 34, *available at* 2006 WLNR 11071727 (Lord Renfrew is an esteemed archaeologist who on January 9, 2009, was presented with an award from the SAFE (Saving Antiquities for Everyone) archaeological preservation organization); Phyllis Halterman, *SAFE Beacon Award Lecture & Reception Honoring Professor Colin Renfrew*, SAFE, (Jan. 10, 2009).

28 *E.g.*, Pinkerton, *Museums Can Do Better*, *supra* note 21, at 59; *see also* Colin Renfrew, *Museum Acquisitions: Responsibilities for the Illicit Traffic in Antiquities*, in ARCHAEOLOGY, CULTURAL HERITAGE, AND THE ANTIQUITIES TRADE 245 (Neil Brodie et al. eds., 2006):

> The disaster that befell the Iraqi National Museum immediately after the coalition occupation of Baghdad in 2003 reminds the U.S. again of the widespread practice of looting, both adventitious and organized, both of existing museum collections and of still unexcavated areas of archaeological sites. The looters are financed, whether before or more often after the event, by collectors. But I argue that the climate of opinion is to a large extent set by museum curators. For it is the content of public exhibitions that establishes the conventions in this matter, and it is the acquisitions of museums, as often by gift or bequest as by purchase, that sets the tone. I argue, moreover, that what is shown in a major museum on temporary loan is as relevant as the permanent acquisition. Very few museums exercise the same degree of due diligence in this area as they do for permanent acquisitions. And some museums consider it one of the criteria for acquisition that an unprovenanced piece has already been publicly exhibited and published in a major museum exhibition. I argue that "reputation laundering by public exhibition" is the up-market version of money laundering in the traffic of drugs. *Id.* at 245.

29 *See* discussion *infra* Part III.C.
30 *See* Prott, *supra* note 11, at 59–61; Patrick J. Boylan, *Illicit Trafficking in Antiquities and Museum Ethics*, in ANTIQUITIES TRADE OR BETRAYED, *supra* note 11, at 94–104; James Ede, *The Antiquities Trade: Towards a More Balanced View*, in ANTIQUITIES TRADE OR BETRAYED, *supra* note 11, at 211–14; Jerome M. Eisenberg, *Ethics and the Antiquity Trade*, in ANTIQUITIES TRADE OR BETRAYED, *supra* note 11, at 216–21.
31 *See generally* UNESCO Convention on the Means of Prohibiting and Preventing the Illicit Import, Export and Transfer of Ownership of Cultural Property, *opened for signature* Nov. 14, 1970, 823 U.N.T.S. 231.
32 *Id.* at introduction; Merryman, *Two Ways*, *supra* note 13, at 843.
33 Edward M. Cottrell, Comment, *Keeping the Barbarians Outside the Gate: Toward a Comprehensive International Agreement Protecting Cultural Property*, 9 CHI. J. INT'L. L. 627, 643 (2009).
34 Merryman, *Two Ways*, *supra* note 13, at 844; *see* Janene Marie Podesta, *Saving Culture, but Passing the Buck: How the 1970 UNESCO Convention Undermines its Goals by Unduly Targeting Market Nations*, 16 CARDOZO J. INT'L & COMP. L. 457, 461–5 (2008).
35 Merryman, *Two Ways*, *supra* note 13, at 844–5 (internal footnotes with citations omitted). The United States ratified UNESCO in 1983 although the US Congress via the Cultural Property Implementation Act has implemented only Paragraphs 7(b) and 9. *See generally* Leonard D. Duboff et al., *Proceedings of the Panel on the US Enabling Legislation of the UNESCO Convention on the Means of Prohibiting and Preventing the Illicit*

Import, Export and Transfer of Ownership of Cultural Property, 4 SYRACUSE J. INT'L L. & COM. 97, 114 (1976) (stating that the United States was "not prepared to give the rest of the world a blank check in that [the United States] would not automatically enforce, through import controls, whatever export controls were established by the other country" except as narrowly limited by Article 9, which calls for controls during a time of crisis). *See generally* Ann Guthrie Hingston, *US Implementation of the UNESCO Cultural Property Convention*, in THE ETHICS OF COLLECTING CULTURAL PROPERTY, *supra* note 23, at 129, 129–46 (providing a general discussion of the Cultural Property Implementation Act); Maria Papageorge Kouroupas, *United States Efforts to Protect Cultural Property: Implementation of the 1970 UNESCO Convention*, in ANTIQUITIES TRADE OR BETRAYED, *supra* note 11, at 83–9. For an opinion that the Cultural Property Implementation Act, adopted by Congress in 1983 to implement UNESCO, did not comport with promises made to the museum and dealer community in exchange for their support, see Douglas C. Ewing, *What Is "Stolen"? The McClain Case Revisited*, in THE ETHICS OF COLLECTING CULTURAL PROPERTY, *supra* note 23, at 177, 177–83.

36 Specialists are defined in this context as including "archaeologists, art historians, curators, conservators—all those professionally dedicated to the preservation of ancient art." Clemency Chase Coggins, *A Licit International Traffic in Ancient Art: Let There Be Light!*, 4 INT'L J. CULT. PROP. 61, 76 n.2 (1995).

37 *Id.* at 62. (internal footnotes omitted). Professor Coggins was responding to John H. Merryman, *A Licit International Trade in Cultural Objects*, in WHO OWNS THE PAST: CULTURAL POLICY, CULTURAL PROPERTY, AND THE LAW 269, 269–289 (Kate Fitz Gibbon, ed. 2005).

38 United States v. Hollinshead, 495 F.2d 1154, 1155 (9th Cir. 1974)

39 United States v. McClain, 545 F.2d 988, 992 (5th Cir. 1977), *conviction on retrial upheld by* 593 F.2d 658 (1979).

40 United States v. Schultz, 333 F.3d 393, 398 (2d Cir. 2003).

41 *See Hollinshead*, 495 F.2d at 1155; *McClain*, 545 F.2d at 992; *Schultz*, 333 F.3d at 410.

42 *E.g.*, Jennifer Anglim Kreder, *The Choice Between Civil and Criminal Remedies in Stolen Art Litigation*, 38 VAND. J. TRANSNAT'L. L. 1199, 1246 n.335, n.339 (2005).

43 Podesta, *supra* note 34, at 475 (noting that 110 nations have adopted the Convention).

44 *E.g.*, David Sassoon, *Considering the Perspective of the Victim: The Antiquities of Nepal*, in THE ETHICS OF COLLECTING CULTURAL PROPERTY, *supra* note 23, at 61, 62 ("We saw the passage of the Cultural Property Act of 1983 which has done close to nothing to stem the tide of illicit trade."). *See* note 35, *supra*, and accompanying text.

45 John Henry Merryman, *Thinking About the Elgin Marbles*, 83 MICH. L. REV. 1881, 1911–21 (1985).

46 *See, e.g.*, Ewing, *supra* note 35, at 181.

47 Coggins, *A Licit International Traffic*, *supra* note 36, at 62.

48 Kreder, *The Choice*, *supra* note 42, at 1211.

49 *Cf.* Jennifer Anglim Kreder, *The New Battleground of Museum Ethics and Holocaust-Era Claims: Technicalities Trumping Justice or Responsible Stewardship for the Public Trust?*, 88 OR. L. REV 37, 69 (2009).

50 *McClain*, 545 F.2d at 1003.

51 *Id.* at 1001.

52 *Id.* at 995, 1002.

53 *E.g.*, Kreder, *The Choice*, *supra* note 42, at 1220–22.

54 *Id.* at 1222–45.

55 *Id.* at 1223.

56 *E.g.*, JAMES CUNO, WHO OWNS ANTIQUITY? 1–20 (2008).

57 Chauncey D. Steele IV, Note, *The Morgantina Treasure: Italy's Quest for Repatriation of Looted Artifacts*, 23 SUFFOLK TRANSNAT'L L. REV. 667, 667–8 (2000). *See also U.S. to Return 1,000 Smuggled Iraqi Artifacts*, AGENCE FRANCE PRESSE, Sept. 22, 2008, available at 9/22/08 AGFRP 10:21:00; Jennifer Modenessi, *Given Up as Lost, Afghan Treasures Make a Triumphant Return in New Exhibit*, ALAMEDA TIMES-STAR, Oct. 26, 2008, available at 2008 WLNR 20306086 (stating that many illicit objects find their way onto the market as a result of armed conflict, such as in Iraq and Afghanistan); Patrick Radden Keefe, *The Idol Thief: Inside One of the Biggest Antiquities-Smuggling Rings in History*, THE NEW YORKER, May 7, 2007, at 58, 60 (explaining that in 2003, police arrested Vaman Ghiya who ran an antiquities smuggling ring under the noses of Indian law enforcement for thirty years); Jori Frinkel, *Thai Antiquities, Resting Uneasily*, N.Y. TIMES, Feb. 17, 2008, at 29; Edward Wyatt, *An Investigation Focuses on Antiquities Dealer*, N.Y. Times, Jan 31, 2008, at A20 (explaining that four California museums were raided as part of a federal investigation into the smuggling of antiquities from Thailand. The investigation revealed a tax fraud scheme in which antiquities dealers donated Thai antiques to museums at inflated values); Tania Branigan, *Chinese Fury at Sale of Plundered Treasures*, THE GUARDIAN, Nov. 3, 2008, http://www.guardian.co.uk/world/2008/nov/03/china-fashion-yves-saint-laurent (stating that the auction of the art collection of fashion designer Yves Saint Laurent included two bronze sculptures originally from an imperial summer palace destroyed by the British in 1860. China alleges that the objects are war plunder, while the auction house "Christie's says there is ... clear legal title for each" sculpture); Marjorie Olster, *Egypt Faces Obstacles in Recovering Antiquities*, ASSOCIATED PRESS, Nov. 23, 2008, available at 11/23/08 AP DataStream 16:44:16 (reporting that the Egyptian Government and the St. Louis Art Museum dispute the ownership of an ancient mummy mask discovered in Egypt in 1952 that resurfaced in 1998 and was purchased by the St. Louis Art Museum); Simon Bahceli, *Nine Arrested Over 2,000 Year-Old Syrian Bible*, CYPRUS MAIL, Feb. 4, 2009, available at 2009 WLNR 2119747; *More Antiquities Arrests in the North*, CYPRUS MAIL, Feb. 8, 2009, available at 2009 WLNR 2466721 (both explaining that a raid on an antiquities dealer's apartment revealed smuggled church relics believed to be of Cypriot origin).

58 Coggins, *Illicit Traffic*, *supra* note 9, at 94.

59 *See* discussion *infra* Part II.

60 *Id*. This is not to imply by any means that this was the first scandal involving museum antiquities purchases. Many other scandals, such as that involving the Lydian Hoard, predated this one, but, as discussed below, this one has triggered restitution of more objects than any other. For a discussion of the Lydian Hoard case by those who litigated it, see Lawrence M. Kaye and Carla T. Main, *The Saga of the Lydian Hoard: From Uşak to New York and Back Again*, in ANTIQUITIES TRADE OR BETRAYED, *supra* note 11, at 150–60.

61 Steele, *supra* note 57, at 667.

62 WATSON and TODESCHINI, *supra* note 18.

63 Michael Kimmelman, *Stolen Objects? Shady Dealers? Time for a Change*, NEWS & OBSERVER, Mar. 27, 2006.

64 WATSON and TODESCHINI, *supra* note 18, at 29; UNESCO, *supra* note 31.

65 Agreement Between the Government of the United States of America and the Government of the Republic of Italy Concerning the Imposition of Import Restrictions on Categories of Archaeological Material Representing the Pre-Classical, Classical, and Imperial Roman Periods of Italy, US-Italy, Jan. 19, 2001.

66 Extension and Amendment to the Agreement Between the Government of the United States of America and The Government of The Republic of Italy Concerning the

Imposition of Import Restrictions on Categories of Archaeological Material Representing the Pre-Classical, Classical and Imperial Roman Periods of Italy, US-Italy, Jan. 13–19, 2006. [hereinafter Extension of US-Italy Agreement]. *See also* Hugh Eakin, *Italy Goes on the Offensive with Antiquities*, N.Y. TIMES, Dec. 26, 2005, at E5.

67 *Cf.* Charles S. Koczka, *The Need for Enforcing Regulations on the International Art Trade*, in THE ETHICS OF COLLECTING CULTURAL PROPERTY *supra* note 23, at 185, 195 (discussing March 5, 1986, letter to the editor of the *New York Times* from Douglas Ewing, President of the American Association of Dealers in Ancient, Oriental, and Primitive Art, entitled "Customs Service Is Overzealous on Art Seizures"). Koczka's perspective was that "[w]hen law enforcers are criticized for being overzealous in their work, they must be doing something right to receive such a backhanded compliment."). *Id.* Vernon Silver, *Met's Antiquities Case Shows Donor, Trustee Ties to Looted Art*, BLOOMBERG.COM, Feb. 23 2006,; Eakin, *supra* note 66.

68 *See* Daniel Flynn, *FBI Help Return over 1,000 Artifacts to Italy*, REUTERS INDIA, Sept. 24, 2009, http://in.reuters.com/article/lifestyleMolt/idINTRE58N2DD20090924. *See also* David Perlmutt, *ICE Finds Stolen Italian Bust in Charlotte*, THE CHARLOTTE OBSERVER, Mar. 19, 2009.

69 Steve Scherer and Adam L. Freeman, *Italy Cracks Down on Stolen Art, Doubling Recoveries*, BLOOMBERG.COM, Jan. 13, 2009.

70 *E.g.*, Michele Kunitz, Comment, *Switzerland & the International Trade in Art & Antiquities*, 21 Nw. J. INT'L L. & BUS. 519, 520 (2001) ("After theft from their source countries, stolen artifacts are cleaned and laundered through various countries, most notably Switzerland.").

71 WATSON and TODESCHINI, *supra* note 18, at 20. *See also* PETER WATSON, SOTHEBY'S: THE INSIDE STORY (Random House 1997) (providing additional background for the culmination of the raids on Medici's warehouses).

72 WATSON and TODESCHINI, *supra* note 18, at 21; *Stolen Italian Artifact Smuggled into the United States Found at Auction House*, US IMMIGRATION AND CUSTOMS ENFORCEMENT, June 1, 2009.

73 WATSON and TODESCHINI, *supra* note 18, at 16–18. Unfortunately for Italian investigators, the author of the organigram was dead by the time it was found, and the organigram alone does not indicate if the key players knew they were trading in looted antiquities. *Id.*

74 *Id.* at 13. *See also* Elisabetta Povoledo, *US Antiquities Dealer at Center of Inquiry Italy Contends it Lost Art to Looting*, INT'L HERALD TRIB., June 21, 2006, at 2, *available at* 2006 WLNR 10688988.

75 WATSON and TODESCHINI, *supra* note 18, at 16–18. For more information on the pending trials see Dan Bischoff, *Deal Life: This Old Art*, DAILY DEAL, Sept. 25, 2006, *available at* 2006 WLNR 16510029 (explaining that research has revealed no reported change in status of Medici's appeal); Peter Watson and Cecilia Todeschini, *Raiders of the Lost Art*, L.A. TIMES, May 8, 2006. A raid of Hecht's residence uncovered his personal journal seeming to detail his activities (although he claims it is a draft novel), which has been pivotal in his prosecution. *See* Jason Felch and Ralph Frammolino, *The Nation; Several Museums May Possess Looted Art*, L.A. TIMES, Nov. 8, 2005, at A16; Steve Scherer, *Rome Court Upholds Conviction of Antiquities Dealer*, BLOOMBERG.COM, July 15, 2009.

76 WATSON and TODESCHINI, *supra* at note 18, at ix. *See also* Randy Kennedy and Hugh Eakin, *The Met, Ending 30-year Stance, Is Set to Yield Prized Vase to Italy*, N.Y. TIMES, Feb. 3, 2006, at A1.

77 HOVING, *supra* note 2, at 307–40.

78 WATSON and TODESCHINI, *supra* note 18, at ix–x.
79 *See, e.g.*, Thomas K. Grose, *Stealing History: Cultural Treasures Are Being Looted—and Museums and Collectors Are Turning a Blind Eye*, US NEWS & WORLD REP., June 19, 2006, at 40, *available at* 2006 WLNR 23825148.
80 Monica M. Jackson, *Archaeology, Looting and the Luxury Arts in the XXI Century*, 13 ART & ANTIQUITY LAW 59, 70 (2008). *See generally* Linda F. Pinkerton, *Due Diligence in Fine Art Transactions*, 22 CASE W. RES. J. INT'L L. 1, 25 n.140 (1990).
81 Felch and Frammolino, *The Nation*, *supra* note 75, at A16.
82 This policy has since been tightened further, as discussed in Part III below.
83 Posting of Mike Boehm to Culture Monster, (Jan. 1, 2009, 6:00 PST) (discussing then upcoming Renfrew presentation entitled "Combating the Illicit Antiquities Trade: The 1970 Rule As a Turning Point (or How the Metropolitan Museum Lags Behind the Getty)"). The last revision to the Met's Collection Management Policy was November 2008. Press Release, Metropolitan Museum of Art, Metropolitan Museum's Collection Management Policy (Revised November 2008) (Jan. 6, 2009).
84 Jason Felch and Livia Borghese, *Italy, Getty End Rift*, L.A. TIMES, Sept. 26, 2007, at E1. Negotiations concerning *Victorious Youth* are ongoing, with the Getty claiming it had been found in international waters and thus is not subject to restitution. CultureGrrl (Nov. 23, 2006,11:40 EST); Nicole Winfield, *Italy Court Orders Getty's Bronze Confiscated*, ASSOCIATED PRESS, Feb. 11, 2010, *available at* 2/11/10 APWIRES 19:55:34 (The Getty maintains that it will "appeal the [Pesaro court's decision to confiscate] to Italy's highest court and … 'vigorously defend' its right to keep the bronze 'Victorious Youth.'").
85 *Looted Antiquities Return to Italy from Getty, Other U.S. Collections*, AGENCE FRANCE PRESS, Dec. 17, 2007.
86 Diane Rozas, *Past is Present*, ART & ANTIQUES, Oct. 1, 2007.
87 Elisabetta Povoledo, *Italy Lends the Getty a Bounty of Berninis*, N.Y. TIMES, Feb. 2, 2008, at B7; Felch and Borghese, *supra* note 84. *See also* Elisabetta Povoledo, *Italy Makes Its Choice of Antiquities to Lend Met*, N.Y. TIMES, Mar. 15, 2006, at E2.
88 *See* Povoledo, *Italy Makes Its Choice*, *supra* note 87, at E2 (On February 1, 2008, Italy lent the Getty "a bounty of Berninis"); CultureGrrl, www.artsjournal.com/culturegrrl/2008/11/more_on_cleveland_museums_retu.html (Nov. 20, 2008 11:26 EST) (Pursuant to the agreement, such loans will be of a four-year duration, which many criticize as too short to accommodate serious academic study); *Getty Launches Antiquities Partnership With Sicily*, ARTINFO.COM, Feb. 18, 2010, http://www.artinfo.com/news/story/33938/getty-launches-antiquities-partnership-with-sicily/ (describing the Getty's new "proposal" by which "the museum would team with Sicilian archaeologists and museum officials to conserve objects, consult on earthquake protection, and jointly develop exhibitions").
89 Felch and Borghese, *supra* note 84. It was reported in the press that the Getty tried to condition the return upon the dropping of charges against Truc and that the Italians refused this request. Jason Felch and Ralph Frammolino, *The Return of Antiquities a Blow to Getty*, L.A. TIMES, Aug. 2, 2007, at A1. One report seems to contradict this characterization of events. The *L.A. Times* quoted Getty spokesman Ron Hartwig as having stated, "Marion's situation is tragic … [w]e have, however, tried throughout this process to keep the two issues separate and focus on resolving the claims for the objects with Italy with the great hope that it would have a positive impact on Marion's situation." Ralph Frammolino and Jason Felch, *Getty Agrees to Return Antiquities to Italy*, L.A. TIMES, Aug. 1, 2007.

90 Heinz Duthel, Guilty as Charged! A Case for the International Criminal Court 333 (2008).
91 Kate Fitz Gibbon, *Museums Into the Fray: The Marion True Trial*, The Magazine Antiques, Mar. 26, 2009, http://www.themagazineantiques.com/news-opinion/current-and-coming/2009-03-26/museums-into-the-fray-the-marion-true-saga/ (describing how True's trial has been ongoing for the past four years).
92 Suzan Mazur, Opinion, *The Italy-Met Euphronios Accord?*, Scoop Independent News, Feb. 22, 2006, http://www.scoop.co.nz/stories/HL0602/S00265.htm. For a discussion of the silver, see Steele, *supra* note 57, at 670; *Getty Launches Antiquities Partnership With Sicily*, *supra* note 88.
93 Steele, *supra* note 57, at 670.
94 Press Release, Museum of Fine Arts, Boston, Museum of Fine Arts, Boston and Italian Ministry of Culture Sign Agreement Marking New Era of Cultural Exchange (Sept. 28, 2006), http://www.mfa.org/press/sub.asp?key=82&subkey=3444.
95 Rudy Larini, *Princeton Agrees to Return Art to Italy*, Star-Ledger (Newark), Nov. 19, 2007, at 13. *See* David Gill and Christopher Chippindale, *From Malibu to Rome: Further Developments on the Return of Antiquities*, 14 Int'l J. Cultural Prop. 205, 224–5 (2007).
96 News Release, UVA Today, University of Virginia Returns Rare Archaic Sculptures to Italy (Jan. 3, 2008).
97 Press Release, Cleveland Museum of Art & Ministero per I Beni e Attivita´ Culturali, The Cleveland Museum of Art and Italy Agree to Exchange of Antiquities and Scholarship (Nov. 19, 2008). Initially, there were conflicting reports in the media concerning whether an agreement had been reached with the Cleveland Museum of Art, but Sandro Bondi, the current Italian Minister of Culture, issued a statement September 10, 2008, that, contrary to earlier statements by prior Italian Minister of Culture Francesco Rutelli, no agreement had been reached. Steven Litt, *The Cleveland Museum of Art Still Has No Deal with Italy on Returning Allegedly Looted Antiquities*, Plain Dealer, Sept. 10, 2008.
98 Posting of Philip Willan to Museum Security Network, www.museum-security.org/?p=1563 (Feb. 28, 2009, 13:27 EST).
99 *Dealer Repatriates Art*, N.Y. Times, Nov. 7, 2007, at E2.
100 Elisabetta Povoledo, *Collector Returns Art Italy Says Was Looted*, N.Y. Times, Jan. 18, 2008, at B1.
101 Posting to Museum Security Network, www.museum-security.org/?p=160 (Jan. 29, 2008, 10:44 EST).
102 *Id.*
103 Marta Falconi, *Italy's Art Squad Says Archaeological Looting Declining*, Associated Press Worldstream, Jan. 17, 2008.
104 Frank Jordans, *Swiss to Return Stolen Antiquities to Italy*, USA Today, Nov. 6. 2008.
105 Watson and Todeschini, *supra* note 18, at 53–65.
106 Posting of Elisabetta Povoledo to Arts Beat, http://artsbeat.blogs.nytimes.com/2009/01/23/ex-getty-curators-four-year-trial-resumes-in-rome/ (Jan. 23, 2009, 13:34 EST).
107 Posting of David Gill to Looting Matters, http://lootingmatters.blogspot.com/2008/11/cleveland-museum-of-art-why-history-of.html (Nov. 24, 2008, 06:50 EST).
108 *Id.*
109 Ass'n of Art Museum Dirs., Art Museums and the International Exchange of Cultural Artifacts 1 (Oct. 2001), [hereinafter AAMD Position Paper].

110 *Id.* at 1–2.
111 Ass'n of Art Museum Dirs., New Report on Acquisition of Archaeological Materials and Ancient Art, (Jun. 4, 2008), [hereinafter 2008 New Report].
112 *See, e.g.*, Merryman, *International Trade, supra* note 37, at 269–89; CUNO, *supra* note 56, at 26–43, 160–62.
113 AAMD Position Paper, *supra* note 109, at 2.
114 *Id.*
115 *Id.*
116 *Id.*
117 Ass'n of Art Museum Dirs., Report of the AAMD Task Force on the Acquisition of Archaeological Materials and Ancient Art (June 4, 2004), [hereinafter 2004 Report on Acquisition].
118 *Id.* at Part I(D).
119 *Id.*
120 *Id.* Other AAMD Reports, Position Papers and Guidelines are the subject of evaluating claims and de-accessioning objects.
121 *Id.* at Part II(A)(1).
122 *Id.*
123 *Id.*
124 *See* Marilyn E. Phelan, *Scope of Due Diligence Investigation in Obtaining Title to Valuable Artwork*, 23 SEATTLE U. L. REV. 631, 638–9 (2000).
125 *See* Daniel Range, Comment, *Deaccessioning and Its Costs in the Holocaust Art Context: The United States and Great Britain*, 39 TEX. INT'L L.J. 655, 666–7 (2004).
126 2004 Report on Acquisition, *supra* note 117, at Part II(A)(2).
127 *Id.* at Part II(A)(3).
128 *Id.* at Part II(C).
129 *Id.* at Part II(C)(1).
130 *Id.*
131 *Id.* at Part II(D).
132 *Id.*
133 AAMD Position Paper, *supra* note 109, at 2.
134 *Id.*
135 2004 Report on Acquisition, *supra* note 117, at Part II(C)(1).
136 *Id.* at Part II(E).
137 *Id.* at Part II(F).
138 *Id.*
139 *Id.* It should be noted here that the AAMD in a November 2007 Position Paper stated that one consideration when determining whether to deaccession an object is whether "evidence [has] come to light that the work was stolen from another institution or that it was illegally exported or imported in violation of the laws of the jurisdiction in which the museum is located." Ass'n of Art Museum Dirs., Art Museums and the Practice of Deaccessioning (Nov. 2007). Note that the concept of the violation of a foreign nation's export regulation is not to be considered.
140 2004 Report on Acquisition, *supra* note 117, at Part II(E).
141 *Id.*
142 *Id.*
143 *Id.*
144 *Id.*
145 *See, e.g.*, Neil Brodie and Colin Renfrew, *Looting and the World's Archaeological Heritage: The Inadequate Response*, 34 ANN. REV. ANTHROPOLOGY 343, 352–3 (2005).

146 Ass'n of Art Museum Dirs., Report of the AAMD Subcommittee on Incoming Loans of Archaeological Material and Ancient Art (Feb. 27, 2006).
147 *Id.*
148 *Id.* at Part II(C).
149 *Id.*
150 *Id.*
151 Ass'n of Art Museum Dirs., Art Museums, Private Collectors, and the Public Benefit (Jan. 2007).
152 *Id.*
153 2008 New Report, *supra* note 111.
154 Press Release, Association of Art Museum Directors, New Report on Acquisition of Archaeological Materials and Ancient Art Issued by Ass'n of Art Museum Dir., (Jun. 4, 2008) [hereinafter 2008 Press Release]. 2008 New Report, *supra* note 111. Nothing is yet posted on the site.
155 *See* 2008 New Report, *supra* note 111, at Part I(F) (explaining "blank check" approach).
156 2008 Press Release, *supra* note 154.
157 2008 New Report, *supra* note 111, at Part II(E).
158 *Id.* at Part I(F).

> Recognizing that a complete recent ownership history may not be obtainable for all archaeological material and every work of ancient art, the AAMD believes that its member museums should have the right to exercise their institutional responsibility to make informed and defensible judgments about the appropriateness of acquiring such an object if, in their opinion, doing so would satisfy the requirements set forth in the Guidelines below and meet the highest standards of due diligence and transparency as articulated in this Statement of Principles.

Id.
159 2008 New Report, *supra* note 111, at Part II(F).
160 *Id.* (emphasis added).
161 The 2008 Report largely repeats the due diligence standards of the 2004 Report, but a few differences should be noted. Guideline A seems to strengthen the due diligence standard by suggesting that "museums should *thoroughly* research the ownership history ... prior to their acquisition, including making a *rigorous* effort to obtain accurate written documentation with respect to their history... ." *Id.* at Part II(A) (emphasis added). Moreover, Guideline C states that "[m]ember museums should require sellers, donors, and their representatives to provide all information of which they have knowledge, and documentation that they possess, related to the work being offered ...." *Id.* at Part II(C). Thus, the AAMD is recognizing that the old days—when almost unquestioned faith in representations by esteemed donors about an object's ownership history was the norm—are over.
162 Am. Ass'n of Museums, Standards Regarding Archaeological Material and Ancient Art sec. 2, para. 3 (July 2008), [hereinafter AAM Standards].
163 *Id.* at sec. 2, para. 4.
164 *Id.*
165 *Id.* at sec. 2, para. 5.
166 *Id.* at sec. 2, para. 6.
167 *Id.*
168 Kwame Opoku, *New AAM Standards for the Acquisition of Archaeological Material and Ancient Art: A Minor "American Revolution"?*, MODERN GHANA, Sept. 6, 2008,

www.modernghana.com/news/181668/50/new-aam-standards-for-the-acquisition-of-archaeolo.html.
169 Policy Statement on Acquisitions by the J. Paul Getty Museum (Oct. 23, 2006), www.getty.edu/about/governance/pdfs/acquisitions_policy.pdf; Illicit Cultural Property, http://illicit-cultural-property.blogspot.com/2007/05/yesterday-artnewspaper-published.html (May 1, 2007, 06:12 EST). The Indianapolis Museum of Art policy was a stop-gap pending the adoption of new standards by the AAMD. According to a statement issued by its Director, Maxwell Anderson, and published in *The Art Newspaper* on April 30, 2007, the IMA acknowledged 1970 as a bright line in March 2004. *See id.*
170 AAM Standards, *supra* note 162, at sec. 3.
171 CultureGrrl, www.artsjournal.com/culturegrrl/2008/08/aams_new_antiquities_acquisiti.html (Aug. 12, 2008, 11:20 EST).
172 *Id.*
173 *Id.*
174 Am. Ass'n of Museums, AAM Standards and Best Practices for US Museums.
175 AAM Standards, *supra* note 162, at sec. 4, para. 1.
176 *Id.*
177 On December 3, 1998, forty-four governments acceded to principles at a conference held in Washington, D.C. Nations met again in 2000 to build upon the Washington Principles in Vilnius, Lithuania, under the auspices of the Parliamentary Assembly of the Council of Europe. COMMISSION FOR LOOTED ART IN EUROPE, WASHINGTON CONFERENCE PRINCIPLES ON NAZI-CONFISCATED ART (Dec. 3, 1998), www.lootedartcommission.com/Washington-principles. The Vilnius Forum generated a declaration expressing continued support of the Washington Principles without significantly refining them or expanding upon them. COMMISSION FOR LOOTED ART IN EUROPE, VILNIUS FORUM DECLARATION (Oct. 5, 2000).
178 Ass'n of Art Museum Dirs., Report of the AAMD Task Force on the Spoliation of Art During the Nazi/World War II Era (1933–1945) (June 4, 1998) [hereinafter Task Force].
179 US State Dep't Bureau of European and Eurasian Affairs, Washington Conference Principles on Nazi-Confiscated Art (Dec. 3, 1998), www.state.gov/p/eur/rt/hlcst/122038.htm.
180 Am. Ass'n of Museums, Guidelines Concerning the Unlawful Appropriation of Objects During the Nazi Era (Nov. 1999) (Amended Apr. 2001).
181 *Id.*
182 *Id.*
183 *See* Kreder, *The New Battleground*, *supra* note 49, at 60–61 (citing Toledo Museum of Art v. Ullin, 477 F. Supp. 2d 802, 803 (N.D. Ohio 2006); Detroit Inst. of Arts v. Ullin, No. 06-10333, 2007 WL 1016996, at *1 (E.D. Mich. March 31, 2007)).
184 *See id.*
185 Ass'n of Art Museum Dirs., Art Museums and the Identification and Restitution of Works Stolen by the Nazis 1 (May 2007), www.aamd.org/papers/documents/Nazi-lootedart_clean_06_2007.pdf.
186 *See generally* Manlio Frigo, *Ethical Rules and Codes of Honor Related to Museum Activities: A Complementary Support to the Private International Law Approach Concerning the Circulation of Cultural Property*, 16 INT'L J. CULTURAL PROP. 49 (2009) (answering questions on the ever-changing ethical rules and codes of conduct in the field of art law while focusing on the main codes of conduct drafted by international, national, public, and private institutions, federations, and associations and those code's influence on art market regulation).

187 *See* John Henry Merryman, *Museum Ethics*, 2006 A.L.I.-A.B.A. COURSE OF STUDY: LEGAL ISSUES IN MUSEUM ADMIN. 3, 9 (2006).
188 Suzan Mazur, *New York Times & Met Museum Sing to Collectors*, SCOOP INDEPENDENT NEWS, Mar. 17, 2006, http://www.scoop.co.nz/stories/HL0603/S00246.htm.
189 Archaeological Inst. of Am., Annual Meeting: Ethical Standards Requirement (2009), www.archaeological.org/webinfo.php?page=10288; Am. Sch. of Oriental Research Bd. of Trs., Statement of ASOR Policy on Preservation and Protection of Archaeological Resources 2 (Nov. 18, 1995) (modified Nov. 22, 2003).
190 Coggins, *A Licit International Traffic*, *supra* note 36, at 62.
191 *See* Archaeological Inst. of Am., *supra* note 189; Am. Sch. of Oriental Research, *supra* note 189, at 1, 3.
192 *See* Martin Bailey, *Revealed: One third of Brooklyn Museum's Coptic Collection is Fake*, THE ART NEWSPAPER, July 1, 2008. The fakes themselves seem to date back to the 20th century.
193 *See id.*
194 *See id.*
195 Ann Shaftel, *Spiritual but Fake?*, 1 J. ART CRIME 16, 17 (2009).
196 *See id.* at 17.
197 *Id.* at 17–18.
198 *Id.* at 21.
199 *See, e.g.*, Stuart Laidlaw, *Forgery of Antiquities is Big Business*, TORONTO STAR, Nov. 4, 2008, at L1 (discussing a case involving the alleged burial remains of Jesus's brother); Etgar Lefkovits, *Justice Ministry Weighs how to Proceed in "Jesus Ossuary" Fraud Trial*, JERUSALEM POST, Nov. 3, 2008, at 4; Jonathan Lopez, *Books: "Unholy Business" Spins a Good Yarn About Faith, Fraud, and Forgery*, ASSOCIATED PRESS, Nov. 17, 2008; Nina Burleigh, *Faith and Fraud*, L.A. TIMES, Nov. 29, 2008, at A21; Matthew Kalman, *Antiquities Authority Chief: Top Scholars Were Suspected of Ties to Forgery Group*, JERUSALEM POST, Sept. 9, 2009, at 4.
200 *See* Laidlaw, *supra* note 199, at L1.
201 *See* Lefkovits, *supra* note 199, at 4.
202 *See id.*
203 *See* Kalman, *supra* note 199, at 4.
204 *Id.*
205 Mike Boehm, *Relic sellers are Faking it on eBay*, L.A. TIMES, May 29, 2009, at D1. *But see Online Sales of Illicit Cultural Goods Halted*, SWISSINFO.CH, Nov. 4, 2008.
206 *See* ARTinvestment.RU, *Outline Makovsky Led Antiques in the Colony*, ARTINVESTMENT. RU, July 8 2008, http://artinvestment.ru/en/news/artnews/20080807_spouses_preobrazhenskie_convicted.html; *see also* Dareh Gregorian, *Forgery a Work of Art*, NEW YORK POST, Nov. 15, 2008, at 007.
207 CBC News, *Canadian Police Unveil New Art-Fraud Task Force*, CBC.CA, Jan. 27, 2009.
208 *See* Neha S. Bajpai, *Forgers' Canvas*, THE WEEK, Feb. 7, 2009.
209 Larry Neumeister, *NY, Fla. Art Dealer Accused of Selling Forgeries*, ASSOCIATED PRESS, Nov. 21, 2008.
210 *See* Bea Chang, *FBI Painting Forgery Probe Leads Investigators to Twin Cities*, KARE11.COM.
211 *See* Helen Stoilas, *New Guidelines for US Museums Acquiring Antiquities*, THE ART NEWSPAPER, Jul. 24, 2008.
212 *See id.*
213 JAMES CUNO, WHOSE CULTURE?: THE PROMISE OF MUSEUMS AND THE DEBATE OVER ANTIQUITIES 65 (Princeton University Press 2009).

214 Biblical Archaeology Society, Publication of Unprovenanced Antiquities: Statement of Concern (Aug. 2007).
215 *See id.* at para. 1.
216 *See* Task Force, *supra* note 178.
217 *See* Press Release, American Association of Museums, AAM Establishes New Standards on Collecting of Archaeological Material and Ancient Art (Aug. 13, 2008), www.aam-us.org/pressreleases.cfm?mode=list&id=147.
218 Biblical Archaeology Society, *supra* note 214.
219 *Id.* at para. 4. *See also* Lefkovits, *supra* note 199, at 4.
220 Biblical Archaeology Society, *supra* note 214, at para. 6. At an October 2008 conference in Chicago at DePaul University College of Law attended by the author, some in the museum community were saying the same is true of museum acquisitions.
221 *Id.* at para. 5.
222 *Id.* at para. 7–8.
223 *See generally* CUNO, WHO OWNS ANTIQUITY?, *supra* note 56, at 119–25 (railing against "nationalist retentionist cultural property laws").
224 *See* Ricardo J. Elia, *Looting, Collecting, and the Destruction of Archaeological Resources*, 6 NONRENEWABLE RESOURCES 85, 88 (1997).
225 *See* Bizot Group of Museum Directions, Declaration on the Importance and Value of Universal Museums (Dec. 2002).
226 *See* Coggins, *A Licit International Traffic*, *supra* note 36, at 62.
227 *See* Jennifer Anglim Kreder, *The Holocaust, Museum Ethics and Legalism*, 18 S. CAL. REV. L. & SOC. JUST. 1, 30 (2008) (describing the concerns that the Holocaust restitution movement would lead to "bare walls"); *see also* George Abungu, *The Declaration: A Contested Issue*, ICOM NEWS (Int'l Council of Museums, France), 2004.
228 *See* Bizot Group, *supra* note 225, at para. 4.
229 *See supra* note 25 and accompanying text.
230 *See* Stoilas, *supra* note 211; Merryman, *supra* note 37, at 269.
231 *See* Stoilas, *supra* note 211; Merryman, *supra* note 37, at 270.
232 *See* Brooklyn Museum, Provenance Research Project, www.brooklynmuseum.org/collections/provenance_research_project.php (last visited Mar. 12, 2010.)
233 *See* Wyatt, *Four Museums*, *supra* note 6, at A14.
234 *See* CultureGrrl, www.artsjournal.com/culturegrrl/2009/01/mario_rescas_whirlwind_tour_of.html (Jan. 14, 2009, 14:00 EST).
235 Additionally, dealers associations have adopted ethics codes—some as early as 1984. *See* Coggins, *A Licit International Traffic*, *supra* note 36, at 66.
236 *See* Indianapolis Museum of Art, Provenance Research, www.imamuseum.org/art/research/provenance (last visited Mar. 12, 2009); *see also* Robin Pogrebin, *At Public Board Meeting, Smithsonian Practices New Openness*, N.Y. TIMES, Nov. 18, 2008, at A13 (describing the Smithsonian's "new commitment to openness" in regard to such issues as diminishment of endowment fund as a result of lavish expense-account spending and the market).
237 *See* Kreder, *The New Battleground*, *supra* note 49, at 60–61.
238 *See* Clemency Chase Coggins, *United States Cultural Property Legislation: Observations of a Combatant*, 7 INT'L J. CULTURAL PROP. 52, 53 (1998) (explaining that in the next few years after UNESCO some museums "went underground and stopped publishing, or even exhibiting, their questionable new acquisitions from the New World and the Old").

Part II, Section 2

Repatriation and reburial of archaeological museum collections

Chapter 14

Repatriation
Australian perspectives

Michael Green and Phil Gordon

In its broadest sense, "repatriation" is the act of returning or restoring something, usually a person, to the country of origin. It is an action that occurs worldwide, probably on a daily basis, as the bodies of recently deceased tourists, soldiers on overseas tours of duty, and travelling businessmen and women (among others) are recovered by local authorities and returned to their homelands, to waiting families and friends. From a cultural heritage perspective, however, the word has recently been imbued with a more specific meaning—namely, the return, back to their communities of origin, of Indigenous cultural patrimony (ancestral property) whose historical removal was facilitated by a colonial regime. An inference often attached to such acts of repatriation is that the initial removal was undertaken in a way that would not be sanctioned by today's ethical or legal standards (this is not to say that these same actions were condoned at the time). The act of repatriation then becomes an act of reparation (Skrydstrup 2005), an action of making amends for a wrong done. At this point, all sorts of values can be, and often are, applied to the act itself and should be supported, indeed endorsed, by us all.

This chapter provides an Australian perspective on issues relating to the repatriation of Indigenous cultural property and human remains. We present a brief historical commentary on how relevant collections came to be created and how Indigenous Australian communities reacted to them. This is followed with a discussion of the contemporary legal, policy, and political repatriation landscape in Australia. The chapter concludes with some personal observations on the future of repatriation in Australia, and touches on the issues that we believe are most likely to occupy Australians over the next decade.

Historical overview

Australia is one of the places in the world where European colonists encountered hunter-gatherers (Pardoe 2004). Knowledge of Australian Aboriginal society

Source: *Handbook of Postcolonial Archaeology*. J. Lydon and U.Z. Rizvi (eds.). Walnut Creek, CA: Left Coast Press Inc., 2006. pp. 257–266 © Taylor & Francis.

became vital to eighteenth- and nineteenth-century European thinkers who were pondering the place of the human in nature. While some romantically viewed Aboriginal peoples as being the closest to a pure state of nature, others saw them as occupying the bottom of various biological and cultural evolutionary trees.

Consequently, there was a great demand for Australian Aboriginal and other Indigenous cultural material and biological specimens (e.g., bodies, skulls) to be made available to the scholars of the day, most of whom directed their intellectual campaigns remotely from the armchairs of Europe. Large amounts of ethnographic material culture and Indigenous skeletal remains (hereafter referred to as ancestral remains) were shipped to Europe and used to inform the further development of these varied and often contradictory ideas (MacDonald 2005: 96–135; Turnbull 1999, 2001, 2007). The newly acquired materials required storage with easy accessibility, and in a short time they found their way into recently created museums of natural history and ethnography. Hundreds of Aboriginal and Torres Strait Islander crania and other skeletal elements were sent to museums and universities across Europe, and a few made their way to North America. Many more were collected and held in newly established Australian museums in Sydney, Hobart, Melbourne, and Adelaide. These activities commenced very shortly after the establishment of the first European settlement at Botany Bay in 1788, and, at least in Victoria, continued well into 1950s (Sunderland and Ray 1959). The collections of ancestral remains held in Australia, Europe, and North America have been used to investigate general theories of human evolution and the origins of anatomically modern humans; human variation and such evolutionary mechanisms as selection, migration, and drift; palaeopathology; and osteometric and nonmetric anatomical variation (see Donlon 1994; Pardoe 1991, 2004).

The systematic repatriation of Australian Aboriginal and Torres Strait Islander artifacts and ancestral remains to their Indigenous communities of origin is a relatively recent phenomenon. In New South Wales, the Australian Museum Trust has been actively implementing a policy of sympathetic consideration of repatriation requests since 1974. Their first formal repatriation was of an artifact to the Solomon Islands National Museum and Cultural Centre, in honor of that county's impending independence; and their first repatriation of ancestral remains occurred in 1980 to a south coast New South Wales Aboriginal community. In each case, the repatriations occurred in response to specific claims of cultural and spiritual significance made by the respective traditional Indigenous owners. In the case of Victoria's state museum (Museum Victoria), the first formal record of repatriated ancestral remains relates to the public reburial in 1985 of the remains of eight Aboriginal people in the King's Domain, adjacent to Melbourne's Royal Botanic Gardens, during a memorial ceremony conducted by Aboriginal communities from across Victoria.

Repatriation is now vigorously and routinely pursued by Australian territory, state, and federal governments and cultural institutions as a matter of public policy. It did not always receive such a high level of support, however, and many in the museum profession and related disciplines of anthropology and archaeology considered the disposal of material culture and ancestral remains in this way as something akin to scientific or intellectual vandalism (Mulvaney 1989, 1991).

Although Indigenous concerns about holding ancestral remains in museum collections goes back many years, the genesis of the repatriation movement in Australia lies in the worldwide Indigenous political activism of the 1970s. The political and cultural environment at that time was quite foreign to many Australian museums. During this period, the quest for independence by many colonized nations reached its zenith across the globe. This growing independence movement and associated political world view manifested itself in many ways that affected a host of cultural institutions, including museums. The very existence of some museums, especially those holding extensive ethnographic collections, was viewed by many as an explicitly tangible expression of colonial power. It is no surprise that museums became targets for the many frustrations felt by Indigenous people worldwide, and these led to demands for the return of cultural patrimony, especially that held outside of their home countries.

The Pacific region was not isolated from these worldwide trends. In fact, Australia was, and still is, viewed by many Aboriginal and Torres Strait Islanders as a colonial power, and many of the demands being made of European cultural institutions at that time were also being made of Australian museums, which soon became the target of vocal protests regarding the treatment of Indigenous cultural property. Many Aboriginal people began to lobby for a say in the management and display of ethnographic collections. Such calls become increasingly prevalent as Australia moved from a conservative to a more liberal federal government approach to Indigenous land rights and the development of a legitimate Aboriginal political voice.

The late 1970s also saw a generational change in museum employment at all levels, from directors through to curators and collection managers. Many of the people employed at this time came from outside the "classic" museum environment, which had previously encouraged promotion from within. They came from universities and Indigenous communities and brought with them few preconceptions about how collections could or should be accessed or used. New intellectual frameworks were applied to the development of museum policy. This, in turn, facilitated great change in the ways that museums and Indigenous communities communicated with each other and how they each perceived the other's point of view with regard to the significant issues confronting them. In the 1980s and 1990s, these changes translated into new institutional policies relating to a whole range of cultural issues that Indigenous people saw as critically important, such as community access to collections, the appropriate display of cultural objects, and training and employment within the museum sector.

From a historical perspective, a number of events in the early to mid 1980s crystallized issues surrounding increasing calls for the repatriation of Indigenous cultural patrimony in Australia. Two in particular had a major influence on the Australian repatriation scene. The first was the delivery of a paper by Ros Langford of the Tasmanian Aboriginal Centre to the annual conference of the Australian Archaeological Association in 1982 (Langford 1983), titled "Our heritage—your playground," in which she argued that archaeologists had appropriated Aboriginal cultural heritage under a colonial paradigm for personal, professional, and intellectual gain. Langford demanded that full control of that culture should be in the hands of Aboriginal people, saying "it is our past, our culture and our heritage, and forms part of our present life. As such it is ours to control and it is ours to share on our terms" (1983: 2). Much of Langford's argument challenges concepts of ownership and control, issues central to the rationales underpinning repatriation today.

The second event was the 1984 action brought against the University of Melbourne by the Victorian Aboriginal Legal Service for holding a collection of Aboriginal skeletal remains without a permit, contrary to the provisions of the Archaeological and Aboriginal Relics Preservation Act 1972 (Victoria). The Legal Service managed to obtain an injunction against the university, and the remains in question (the Murray Black Collection, named after the Victorian collector who assembled it during the 1940s and 1950s) were temporarily transferred to the National Museum of Victoria (now Museum Victoria) for safekeeping while the Victorian state government determined how it should act with respect to demands by Aboriginal communities for the return of the remains for reburial. The state government passed legislative amendments that, although not requiring the repatriation of ancestral remains, did allow it to return these and other ancestral remains held in the National Museum of Victoria's collections to Indigenous communities across Australia. This was the first repatriation of an entire Australian collection of ancestral remains, representing over 800 individuals. This policy position was again invoked in 1990 when the Victorian state government responded positively to requests from the Yorta Yorta Aboriginal community for the repatriation and reburial of 9,000- to 14,500-year-old ancestral remains from Kow Swamp in central Victoria.

Contemporary repatriation landscape in Australia

There is no nationally uniform federal or state legislation in Australia that compels museums to repatriate cultural patrimony to Indigenous communities, unlike in the United States where the Native American Graves Protection and Repatriation Act (1990) requires that all federal agencies and museums and all state and private museums in receipt of federal funding make holdings of Native American ancestral remains and other significant cultural patrimony available for repatriation. The most relevant Australian Commonwealth legislation is the Aboriginal and Torres Strait Islander Heritage Protection Act of 1984 (Commonwealth), which contains provisions for issuing protective declarations over significant Aboriginal cultural property that is under threat of injury or desecration (Section 12), and directs the relevant minister to consult with Aboriginal communities regarding the possible repatriation of remains that are delivered to the minister (Section 21).

Each Australian state and territory has passed legislation that protects Aboriginal cultural heritage, and in some instances these contain specific repatriation provisions. The most comprehensive and specifically relevant piece of legislation to date is probably Victoria's Aboriginal Heritage Act of 2006 (Victoria), which recognizes Aboriginal people with a traditional or familial link to Aboriginal ancestral remains as the owners of those remains (Section 13). The act further identifies Museum Victoria as the official repository for ancestral remains in the care of the State (Section 14); requires the museum to repatriate ancestral remains to identified Aboriginal owners on request (Section 15); and requires that all other Aboriginal ancestral remains found in Victoria be passed to the custody of the relevant departmental secretary for repatriation to identified Aboriginal owners (Sections 19–20). The same provisions effectively apply to Aboriginal secret-sacred objects found in Victoria, although non-state holders of secret-sacred objects are not compelled to surrender them to the state.

Generally speaking, the successful repatriation outcomes achieved by Australian state and territory governments are the result of negotiated policy rather than legislatively imposed obligation. The level of consultation with Aboriginal communities on these polices has varied from state to state, but as a rule there has been significant Indigenous involvement in the drafting of these documents. All major Australian national, state, and territory museums now have policies that require them to negotiate with relevant Indigenous interests regarding the management and display of Aboriginal cultural heritage. Many of these institutions also maintain Aboriginal cultural heritage advisory committees, which actively engage in the development of relevant policy and also provide day-to-day advice on its operational implementation. These policies generally require that significant Aboriginal cultural patrimony, especially ancestral remains and secret-sacred objects, be made available to relevant Indigenous interests for repatriation. Australia's national museums association, Museums Australia, also maintains a policy titled *Continuous Cultures, Ongoing Responsibilities*, which requires collaborative relationships between museums and Indigenous Australian communities and the repatriation of ancestral remains and secret-sacred objects on request (Museums Australia Inc. 2005).

Currently, there is a national Australian scheme, the Return of Indigenous Cultural Property (RICP) Program, that deals specifically with the repatriation of human remains and secret-sacred objects in Australia. The program is an initiative of the Cultural Ministers Council, which is comprised of Australian state and territory ministers, in association with ministers from New Zealand who generally oversee the arts. The RICP Program represents a collaborative effort between the Australian and state/territory governments and the museum sector to resolve issues surrounding collections of ancestral remains and sacred objects. The major aim is the return of cultural material and/or the implementation of negotiations with appropriate Indigenous people about objects and remains held by the main state and territory museums across Australia. Since 2000, over $7.7 million has been provided by the Cultural Minister's Council for the RICP Program. This includes a recent Australian government grant of $4.7 million to be spent over the next four years (2008–2012). The aim of the RICP Program is to repatriate all ancestral remains and secret-sacred objects from eligible participating museums to their communities of origin. The four specific objectives of the program are to:

1. identify (where possible) the origins of all ancestral remains and secret-sacred objects held in participating museums;
2. notify all communities who have ancestral remains and secret-sacred objects held in these museums;

3 appropriately store ancestral remains and secret-sacred objects held in these museums at the request of the relevant community; and
4 arrange for repatriation where and when it is requested.

The RICP Program has two major funding categories: the Museum Support Program provides funds for museums to prepare collections for return to Indigenous communities, while the Community Support Program funds Indigenous communities' participation in the repatriation process.

Present and future issues in Australian repatriation

According to unpublished statistics compiled by the Australian Department of Communications, Information Technology and the Arts, the government department that administers the RICP Program, over 1,200 lots of ancestral remains and 380 secret-sacred objects were returned to Indigenous communities across Australia during the last six years. Ownership of a further 340 lots of ancestral remains and 230 secret-sacred objects was transferred during that time from museums to Indigenous communities. However, conservative estimates put the number of lots of ancestral remains and secret-sacred objects still remaining in Australian museums at 8,200 and 11,200, respectively. The job has only just begun, and it is clear that repatriation will continue to be a focus of museum and Indigenous community activities for many years to come.

Here, we identify eight issues that we believe must be dealt with if Australia is going to be able to claim a satisfactory result in its repatriation engagement with its Indigenous communities:

1 Indigenous communities require assistance and resources to establish and maintain infrastructure, such as for the upkeep of organizations that support repatriation outcomes. These are critical to the appropriate management of cultural heritage material, such as secret-sacred objects, which require ongoing curation within the community.
2 A very large proportion of the ancestral remains still held in Australian museums are effectively unprovenanced. A real challenge for Australia's Indigenous communities will be to develop a sustainable and effective solution to this issue, with support from all levels of government.
3 Australia's Indigenous communities are engaged in an ongoing struggle to have ancestral remains returned from overseas institutions. Advocacy by the Australian government has been crucial in advancing this issue in the United Kingdom over the last few years, and more recently in France, Germany, and the United States, on a government-to-government basis. A downside to this, however, is that Indigenous communities, and sometimes the overseas collecting institutions themselves, feel sidelined and sometimes excluded from the process. A secondary aspect to this is the strong likelihood that Australian Indigenous communities will demand the repatriation of secret-sacred objects. These, as well as ancestral remains, are automatically available for repatriation from

Australian museums under the RICP Program, and it is likely that Indigenous communities will demand that both classes of cultural patrimony should also be repatriated from overseas.

4   There is currently a confusing array of state, territory, and federal bureaucratic structures that all have a stake in repatriation. Sometimes they get in one another's way in the effective delivery of successful repatriation outcomes. The challenge for governments and the museum sector is to collaborate in the development of effective whole-of-government processes that minimize unnecessary impacts on Indigenous communities.

5   Australian museums hold Indigenous ancestral remains derived from other countries, a legacy of the historical body trade. The Australian government has indicated that in the next round of the RICP Program, commencing in 2008, it will develop a repatriation policy in relation to these remains.

6   There is an urgent need for biological anthropologists to reopen a dialogue with Australian Indigenous communities regarding the potential for access to biological data that may be recorded from ancestral remains prior to their reburial. Over the last 20 years, there has been almost no research conducted into prehistoric Australian Indigenous skeletal biology. As Pardoe points out, the complete repatriation of all Australian human remains without the chance to record useful, meaningful biological data would be a great loss to science and to the representation of Indigenous Australians in the story of human evolution (2004: 144).

7   The RICP Program has made many Indigenous communities aware of their rights under various existing museum policies. Many of these policies make reference not only to ancestral remains and secret-sacred objects but to all Indigenous cultural property. Museums are already grappling with requests for the repatriation of "open" or non-restricted cultural material, and the likelihood is that such requests will only increase in number.

8   We need to refine and clarify the language of repatriation. For many Australians, "repatriation" has come to mean the return of something to its place of origin in an effort to right a perceived or acknowledged wrong, and museums and governments are happy to oblige, given their policy positions and reactions to the often unsavory historical circumstances under which many ancestral remains and secret-sacred objects were collected. Should this perspective extend to all traditional Indigenous material culture? Although open material may be requested for return, should the rationale for the request be differently couched? Rather than phrasing the action in terms of righting a wrong (i.e., questioning the legitimacy of the collecting action), should it not be considered in terms of acknowledging a legitimate and legal ownership of the material in the first place as a basic right of Indigenous peoples?

Conclusion

Repatriation, along with other activities that Australian museums are pursuing to support Indigenous cultural objectives, is a positive response to reconciliation, even if not always voluntary. Museums have reacted to Indigenous political and cultural concerns in a variety of supportive ways, and in conjunction with flexible and supportive management structures, they will continue to build on the foundational relationships established over the last 25 years. In having to deal with such a highly emotional subject as repatriation, these relationships have been tested and strengthened over time. We hope that they will deliver opportunities, such as the use of new and emergent digital technologies, to facilitate the repatriation of material to communities. Repatriation has led to increasing collaboration with Australia's Indigenous communities in the development, management, and public understanding of Australia's rich Indigenous history.

References

Donlon, D. (1994) Aboriginal skeletal collections and research in physical anthropology: an historical perspective. *Australian Archaeology*, 39: 73–82.
Langford, R. (1983) Our heritage – your playground. *Australian Archaeology*, 16: 1–6.
MacDonald, H. (2005) *Human Remains: Episodes in Human Dissection*. Carlton: Melbourne University Press.
Mulvaney, D.J. (1989) Reflections on the Murray Black Collection. *Australian Natural History*, 23: 66–72.
——(1991) Past regained, future lost: the Kow Swamp Pleistocene burials. *Antiquity*, 15: 100–02.
Museums Australia Inc. (2005) *Continuous Cultures, Ongoing Responsibilities: Principles and Guidelines for Australian Museums Working with Aboriginal and Torres Strait Islander Cultural Heritage*. Canberra: Museums Australia Inc.
Pardoe, C. (1991) Competing paradigms and ancient human remains: the state of the discipline. *Archaeology in Oceania*, 26: 79–85.
——(2004) Australian biological anthropology for archaeologists. In: T. Murray (ed.), *Archaeology from Australia*. Melbourne: Australian Scholarly Publishing, pp. 131–50.
Skrydstrup, M. (2005) Claiming cultural property across international borders. Paper presented at the conference, The Meanings and Values of Repatriation: A Multidisciplinary Conference, The Australian National University, Canberra, Australia, 8–10 July 2005.
Sunderland, S. and Ray, L.J. (1959) A note on the Murray Black Collection of Australian Aboriginal skeletons. *Royal Society of Victoria Proceedings*, 71: 45–8.
Turnbull, P. (1999) Enlightenment anthropology and the bodily remains of Indigenous Australian peoples. In: A. Calder, J. Lamb, and B. Orr (eds.), *Voyages and Beaches: Pacific Encounters, 1769–1840*. Honolulu: University of Hawai'i Press, pp. 202–25.
——(2001) "Rare work amongst the professors": the capture of indigenous skulls within phrenological knowledge in early colonial Australia. In: B. Creed and J. Hoorn (eds.), *Body Trade: Captivity, Cannibalism and Colonialism in the Pacific*. New York: Routledge, pp. 3–23.
——(2007) British anatomists, phrenologists and the construction of the Aboriginal race, c. 1790–1830. *History Compass*, 5: 26–50.

Chapter 15

The Native American Graves Protection and Repatriation Act in its first decade

James A.R. Nafziger and Rebecca J. Dobkins

The Native American Graves Protection and Repatriation Act (NAGPRA)[1] is the keystone in the legal framework for protecting and repatriating indigenous heritage within the United States, despite its recent enactment in 1990 and the limiting word "graves" in its title. NAGPRA substantially elaborates and broadens the framework of federal and state law to protect the indigenous heritage.[2] Until NAGPRA, this framework was quite limited.[3] Federal and state laws largely sought to protect historic and archaeological resources found on federal, tribal, or state land. Only a few state laws specifically regulated commercial or donative transactions in indigenous heritage or provided for the return of material to indigenous sources. Export controls were, and still are, generally limited to cultural material that has been taken illegally from federal or tribal lands.

This article will examine issues of implementation and dispute resolution that have emerged during NAGPRA's first decade. We will begin with a summary of the law's provisions, origins, legal foundations, and benefits.

Summary of provisions

NAGPRA first confirms indigenous ownership or control over native cultural items found on federal and tribal lands. The governing body of a pertinent Indian tribe or Native Hawaiian organization may, however, relinquish title or control to such items.[4] Ancillary provisions restrict the availability of permits for excavation and removal of Native American human remains or cultural items[5] and require notification of inadvertent discoveries of such material.[6] To enforce these provisions, NAGPRA amends the federal code by criminalizing illegal trafficking in Native American human remains and cultural items obtained in violation of the law's provisions.[7] Arguably, criminal sanctions against what would otherwise be normal dealing in cultural items might drive the market further underground and thereby imperil the public values and opportunities that inhere in open trading.[8] Although NAGPRA does not seem to have produced this result, the risk of a black market bespeaks the need for vigilance, education of dealers and prospective collectors, strong professional and institutional codes of ethics, and improved recording or registration of cultural items.

The most innovative part of NAGPRA—some might say its heart—is a scheme for repatriation of Native American human remains and other cultural items from museums and federal agencies.[9] They are required to compile inventories or provide summaries[10] of Native American remains and cultural items[11] in their possession. A lineal descendant of a deceased Native American, a culturally affiliated[12] Indian tribe, a culturally affiliated Native Hawaiian organization, or a tribe or organization that can show ownership or control of an item may then request material listed in an inventory or summary.[13] Under pain of civil penalty,[14] museums and federal agencies must expeditiously return any such material to a claimant that has established the requisite link of lineal descendancy, cultural affiliation, or ownership or control as the case may be.[15]

Determination of whether an object is properly classified, particularly as a "sacred object"[16] or an "object of cultural patrimony,"[17] may pose particular difficulties. Such issues of classification have often been resolved by consultation and collaboration between native groups and museums or federal agencies. Aside from understandable delays that may result from having to resolve these kinds of issues, there are four statutory qualifications on the requirement of expeditious return of material. First, if an inventory or summary does not itself establish cultural affiliation of the item with a requesting tribe or organization, a federal agency or museum may retain an item until the requesting party can demonstrate cultural affiliation by a preponderance of evidence based on several factors. These factors include "geographical, kinship, biological archaeological, anthropological, linguistic, folkloric, oral traditional historical, or other relevant information or expert opinion."[18] Second, if a cultural item is "indispensable for completion of a specific scientific study, the outcome of which would be of major benefit to the United States," repatriation may be delayed until no later than ninety days after completion of the study.[19] Third, the claimant of an unassociated funerary object, sacred object, or object of cultural patrimony must present evidence "which, if standing alone before the introduction of evidence to the contrary, would support a finding that the federal agency or museum did not have the right of possession."[20] In response, the particular museum or federal agency is given an opportunity to prove its right of possession to the item.[21] Finally, a museum or federal agency may retain an item disputed by multiple (competing) claimants until they agree upon its disposition or until, the dispute is otherwise resolved under either internal NAGPRA procedures or a court of competent jurisdiction.[22]

NAGPRA establishes a review committee within the United States Department of the Interior to monitor and review implementation of the inventory and identification process and repatriation activities.[23] Concluding sections of the legislation provide for grants of assistance by the federal government to Indian tribes, Native Hawaiian organizations, and museums;[24] require the Secretary of the Interior to promulgate regulations to carry out the law;[25] and establish the jurisdiction of federal district courts over alleged violations of NAGPRA.[26]

Origins, legal foundations, and benefits

Origins

The proper disposition of *non*-Indian remains in the American West has often been significant. For example, when William F ("Buffalo Bill") Cody, the legendary impresario of the American West, died in 1917, the location of his gravesite became a major controversy. At his widow's request, he was buried on Lookout Mountain near Denver rather than, as expected, in the town he founded, Cody, Wyoming. The circumstances remain unclear under which Buffalo Bill, on his deathbed, is said to have changed his preference of a gravesite from Cody to Lookout Mountain. What is clear is that resentment simmered in Cody for over thirty years. In 1948, fearing removal of his bones under a bounty offered by the Cody American Legion Post, Denver city officials dug a new tomb twenty-five feet deep, lined it with thick casing, installed steel support rails, and poured more than thirty tons of concrete over the grave to prevent its plunder.[27]

By contrast, Native American remains, even those of the greatest tribal chiefs, have enjoyed very little protection until recently. State laws criminalizing any disturbance or desecration of marked graves seldom barred excavation of Native American sites, either because they were usually unmarked[28] or because they did not otherwise satisfy definitions of protected graves or cemeteries.[29] It is no exaggeration to conclude that American law historically has "protect[ed] the sanctity of the non-Indian at all costs, while tolerating the promiscuous snatching of the Indian dead on a massive scale."[30] Science and human curiosity have normally trumped the sanctity and human dignity of Native American remains.

During the 1970s and 1980s, however, an Indian burial-rights movement, which was opposed to the use of ancestral remains as scientific resources, began fighting for the return of remains to the tribes for reburial.[31] It would no longer be acceptable to ignore Native American rights simply in the interests of physical anthropology. Native Americans also became more assertive about their entitlement to important cultural items, especially sacred objects. The Zunis, in particular, began to request the return of their *Ahayu:da* (wooden figures that represent twin gods).[32] More generally, the tribes demanded to be put on a more equal footing with science in the control of indigenous cultural material.

The normative origins of the burial-rights movement are international.[33] They lie in the regime of human rights and self-determination that emerged after the Second World War. This regime, by confirming the dignity of individual human beings (and by natural extension, their remains), inspired national claims for the protection of cultural heritage. A growing awareness of extensive looting and destruction of cultural material led to the establishment of a new regime, with rights vested in national patrimonies, to deter illegal trafficking and to return stolen and illegally exported objects to countries of origin.[34] Repatriation, restitution, or return of such objects and the concept of cultural patrimony, on a basis of general rights, became enshrined in international law. Moreover, the acknowledgment by this international law regime of a *collective*, so-called third-generation right of repatriation on behalf of nations and groups is noteworthy because it eased the way for the assertion within the United States of tribal and organizational claims under NAGPRA.[35]

Four factors contributed to the extension of the international regime to the domestic indigenous heritage: United States leadership in establishing and implementing the international regime, a concentration by the United States on protecting the heritage of the Americas (including eventually the country's own indigenous heritage), diplomatic gains and public satisfaction derived from implementing the regime, and explicit acknowledgement by the United States of the applicability to Native Americans of human rights provisions such as those crystallized in the Helsinki Accords of 1976.[36] Consequently, by the late 1980s, the museum community, galleries, and individual collectors had become accustomed to constraints on questionable acquisitions and to the requirements of international return, restitution, or repatriation of cultural material.

Against this backdrop of international law and practice, the stage was set for translating into domestic law the aspirations of the native burial movement and claimants of significant cultural material. Native American activism played a major role in this process. In 1989, the World Archaeological Congress, led by tribal leaders and responding in part to a position paper prepared by the International Indian Treaty Council, adopted the Vermillion Accord as a basis for protection and repatriation of human remains and sacred items.[37] During the same year, the Smithsonian Institution, given the opportunity to acquire a major collection of Native American material, agreed to repatriate human remains and sacred objects in its possession to the tribes.[38] This agreement was incorporated into the National Museum of the American Indian Act.[39] The next year the Report of the Panel for a National Dialogue on Museum/Native American Relations[40] proposed similar legislation to be binding on all federal agencies and federally funded institutions (museums). The result was NAGPRA.

Legal foundations

NAGPRA is essentially human rights law.[41] Its legislative history confirms this foundation: "Such human rights include religious, cultural, and group survival rights, as understood within the context of U.S. and international standards of human rights and rights of self-determination."[42] In this regard, the United States is bound by the Universal Declaration of Human Rights,[43] as evidence of international custom, and by the International Covenant on Civil and Political Rights,[44] as a party. Although neither of these instruments articulates a specific right of repatriation, reburial, or cultural patrimony, their provisions for "security of person,"[45] "right to recognition everywhere as a person before the law"[46] and "self-determination"[47] can be interpreted, at least in concert, to embrace a right to repose, that is, a right to non-interference with personal remains as well as associated cultural items. The collective right of self-determination established under international law has been repeatedly invoked to justify claims for repatriation of sacred objects and other significant cultural items. Whether or not there exists a right of cultural patrimony, human rights law clearly ensures equal footing or protection to Native Americans and Native Hawaiians in the use and disposition of their cultural material.

Within the United States constitutional order, NAGPRA manifests the historic relationship of entrustment between the federal government, on the one hand, and indigenous groups, on the other.[48] In practice, the underlying trust doctrine requires a liberal construction of public enactments to the benefit of native peoples.[49]

Benefits

The most obvious benefit of NAGPRA is its systematic promotion of human rights, self-determination, and distributive justice on behalf of Indian tribes and Native Hawaiian organizations. Although private agreements and state legislation may serve the same purposes, they are inadequate to the complex task of providing for comprehensive protection and repatriation of indigenous heritage. Selective repatriation of sacred and other objects serves vital community needs, and repatriation of cultural items for such purposes as tribal museum development enhances the avowed national policy of tribal economic development and education. Also, as an expression of civil rights and ethnic reconciliation, NAGPRA, as implemented, helps redress historic grievances against the dominant culture and, in the long run, serves as a catalyst for cross-cultural understanding.

Required processes of inventorying, consultation, and reporting have had the beneficial effect of highlighting the history of what many regard as a form of colonialism in the United States.[50] NAGPRA reveals this legacy and at the same time fundamentally alters the power dynamics between tribes and collecting institutions. Drawing from the international law of human rights and the international regime for protecting cultural property, NAGPRA recognizes "tribal property interests in various cultural resources, including property now held by museums and institutions," and "group entitlement to cultural property that stems from tribal law and tradition."[51] The statute specifies that a right of possession must mean "possession obtained with the voluntary consent of an individual *or group that had authority of alienation*"[52] and reiterates this aspect by defining cultural patrimony as an object that should be considered "inalienable" by *any* individual, even a tribal member, because of its significance to the entire group.[53] Concomitantly, NAGPRA employs tribal law or custom to address the legal questions of "voluntary consent" and "authority of alienation" when establishing rights of possession.[54] It is important to note, however, that by giving this right only to federally recognized tribes, NAGPRA leaves unfinished the business of redressing power imbalances over the control of cultural property. In this way, NAGPRA reinforces the federal government's power to define, in legal terms, what is and is not an Indian tribe.

For museums, NAGPRA has had the benefit of encouraging closer communication with knowledgeable tribal historians and other members. It has also stimulated museums to undertake comprehensive re-examination and improved documentation of their collections.[55] NAGPRA's requirements of consultation and cooperation between Indian tribes and Native Hawaiian organizations, on the one hand, and museums, on the other, foster broader respect and interchange.[56] Although the communication has sometimes been difficult or even acrimonious, it nevertheless has been essential. It has been observed, for example, that NAGPRA's definitions of such terms as cultural affiliation and cultural patrimony virtually require consideration of indigenous views.[57] In this and other ways the legislation provides a basis for enduring association and partnership.

Although discussions in the NAGPRA Review Committee have been heated, and although some litigation has erupted, our review of the minutes and transcripts of Committee meetings indicates far more consensus than acrimony. Only one spokesperson appearing before the Review Committee, Pemina Yellow Bird of the North Dakota Intertribal Reinterment Committee, seems to have disavowed NAGPRA's emphasis on consultation.[58] In sum, NAGPRA proved a promising framework for both indigenous and national community-building.[59]

NAGPRA implementation issues: reflections from a case study

In this section we will comment on three of the most significant aspects of implementing NAGPRA: the summary and inventory process undertaken by museums and institutions, the continuing problems surrounding the determination of cultural affiliation of human remains and objects in collections, and the various forms of "consultation" and their promise for revitalizing relationships between Native Americans and museums and other collecting institutions. We will examine these aspects through the lens of experience at our institution, Willamette University, in Salem, Oregon. Although Willamette's Native American collection is relatively modest in scale, the university's experience under NAGPRA generally conforms with that of other institutions grappling with NAGPRA. The description of Willamette's experience is therefore of broad relevance.

By way of background, we should note that Willamette is the oldest university in the western part of the United States. It was founded in 1842 by Methodist missionaries who had come to the Oregon Territory in order to convert Native Americans. Over the years, American Indian baskets, ethnographic materials, and surface lithic materials were given to Willamette by amateur hobbyists. In addition, some students and faculty participated in archaeological excavations in the Willamette Valley, particularly between the 1930s and 1960s. They brought materials back from their digs for storage at the university. None of the participating faculty were professionally trained archaeologists, and most of these materials, if documented at all, were identified only by descriptive terms and the general locations from which they were removed.

Thus, by the 1900s, Willamette had amassed a collection numbering over 2,000 objects of Native American origin stored in various locations on campus. Although the university had never received federal funds for excavations or care of the collection, several members of the faculty and staff on campus realized that, as a private institution that receives federal funds for other dimensions of university operations, Willamette was subject to NAGPRA. In December 1995, a specific request by a Native American graduate of Willamette, seeking information about the university's collection, prompted initial steps under NAGPRA. Partly due to lack of trained personnel and partly due to the delayed publication of federal regulations to guide the process, however, the university, like most institutions, did not prepare the required summary or inventory of its collection before the required deadlines.[60] Instead, the formal process of inventorying items was begun in 1997, when, in addition to the clear need to comply with NAGPRA, the imminent opening of a new art museum on campus required a thorough assessment of the university's Native American collection.

As with many institutions, the full extent of Willamette's collection was not clear until a detailed survey was underway. It was therefore decided, partly because the collection had been inaccessible to the public for so long, to conduct a complete inventory of all holdings, not just the required inventory (of human remains and associated funerary objects) and summary (of unassociated funerary objects, sacred objects, and objects of cultural patrimony). It was also decided to approach the summary and inventory process by being open with the tribes about gaps in knowledge as well as collaborating with them to establish cultural affiliation. This process took until July 1998, as new materials continually came to light.[61] Full reports on the university's entire holdings were immediately made to the United States Department of the Interior and to 350 tribal entities with potential interest in the collections.

Summary and inventory process

Many museums and institutions have struggled with the summary and inventory process in order to come into compliance with NAGPRA. The process has exposed, first, how incomplete the collections records are of many museums. In Willamette's case, since there had been no systematic curation of the collection, there were limited records about the materials. A large part of the summary and inventory process therefore revolved around detective work: first, determining what the university had in scattered locations, then determining the origins of material by piecing together the history of collections development at the university. We were fortunate that detailed reports about some of the twelve sets of human remains in the university's possession had been published in *American Antiquity*.[62] In regard to a historic collection of Native American basketry, identifications had been assigned to most of the nearly 300 items in the 1960s. We hired a basketry consultant to re-examine the university's collection and make new assessments of tribal affiliation. We used both sets of identifications, which frequently overlapped, when reporting on the collection to Indian tribes. In addition, as part of the consultation process, the university sought and continues to seek advice from the tribes for further identification of materials.

The experience of Willamette University broadly demonstrates the complex consequences of amateur archaeological and ethnographic collecting in the United States. This legacy has left many institutions—not to mention private individuals, who are not covered under the inventory and repatriation provisions of NAGPRA—with Native American cultural property and human remains whose provenance is uncertain. Several observers have commented on the links between collecting Native American cultural property and American identity building, particularly in the nineteenth and early twentieth centuries, as non-Indians sought to create a sense of cultural heritage in North America somehow distinct from, yet equivalent to, their own European origins.[63] Amateur collectors pursued this objective by literally digging up their newly settled lands and appropriating and displaying archaeological objects and even human remains as evidence of local and national heritage. Ethnographic objects, such as baskets, took a somewhat different route into collectors' hands. Driven by the belief that Indian people were disappearing, collectors bought great quantities of baskets, in particular, around the turn of the century. They were then seen as essential to Victorian, and later, Arts and Crafts décor. Fortunately, basket collectors sometimes left evidence of interaction with weavers, such as photographs or other documentation, in contrast to the disembodied knowledge assembled by artifact hunters.

Collecting institutions and interested tribes alike are at a loss when trying to determine cultural affiliation in cases where documentation is minimal or non-existent, and this difficulty has undoubtedly slowed the repatriation process. In determining the requisite affiliation, NAGPRA's preponderance-of-evidence test encourages a mutual (and mutually educational) consideration of "geographical, kinship, biological, archaeological, anthropological, linguistic, folkloric, oral traditional, historical, or other relevant information or expert opinion,"[64] Although this test is complex, it is also productive in encouraging collaborative investigation.

Amateur collecting continues throughout the United States, as does more malevolent pot hunting and site desecration.[65] The new Hallie Brown Ford Museum of Art at Willamette University gets frequent calls from individuals offering to donate surface finds. After consulting with local tribes, the museum now instructs individual donors to contact the tribes directly and offer such objects directly to them. Assuming the donors do this, the tribes then are empowered to choose whether to take in such material.

The documentation process required by NAGPRA has meant that most collecting institutions and museums have had to clean house, both literally and figuratively. Knowledge once mainly stored in institutional memory has had to be made part of the public record, and gaps in documentation of collections have been laid bare. These gaps, unfortunately, sometimes become evident only after repatriation has taken place. Recently, for example, it has come to light that 11 wampum belts returned by the Museum of the American Indian Heye Foundation to the Iroquois of the Six Nations Reserve in Canada in 1998 (prior to the National Museum of the American Indian Act) may not be the belts they were presumed to be.[66] It had been thought that they belonged to an Onondaga chief who was keeper of the wampum belts of the Iroquois League in the late 1800s, but instead, six are likely those of a Cayuga chief living at the Six Nations Reserve at the turn of the century, and five are of unknown origin, Photographic and archival evidence unintentionally overlooked by both museum staff and the requesting group demonstrates the complex and often confusing journey objects take once they leave the hands of their makers and enter the context of collecting. Whether the museum's decision to repatriate would have been different is unclear, but this example demonstrates the problem of basing repatriation decisions on incomplete or inaccurate documentation of collections.

Problems of cultural affiliation

NAGPRA's requirement of establishing "cultural affiliation" rests on an anthropological understanding of the concept of culture. Yet, in the discipline of anthropology, the understanding of culture itself is in the process of reformation.[67] For much of the discipline's history, culture has been seen as bounded, definable, and homogenous. Following this assumption, material culture has been seen as having similar boundaries and being ultimately classifiable as to group of origin. In recent decades, however, this concept of culture has been discarded in favour of a more contingent notion in which "culture" (and, by extension, cultural identity) is understood to be a process involving intergroup exchange and continual recreation of the self. It is ironic that just when anthropological theory and native peoples themselves are seeing cultural identity as fluid and contextually constructed NAGPRA potentially insists that it be determined and fixed in time and space.[68] Issues of cultural affiliation therefore represent a paradoxical dimension of NAGPRA.

In part growing out of this paradox, the issue of how to deal with "culturally unidentifiable" human remains has been one of the most difficult for the NAGPRA Review Committee, which is still in the process of drafting recommendations for disposition of such remains.[69] The most intractable case under NAGPRA, that of the Kennewick Man,[70] in large part centers on the question of establishing cultural affiliation for ancient remains.

Beyond strict concern with human remains, however, establishing cultural affiliation may be problematic for several reasons. When relocation, displacement, or widespread decimation of a population has been part of a patrimonial history, establishing cultural affiliation with objects made by past groups becomes even more complex. If materials in museum collections are largely or entirely undocumented, cultural affiliation may be impossible to determine or, at best, must be determined through a preponderance-of-evidence test that necessarily relies on often highly subjective processes of interpretation. Finally, a serious, unresolved issue relates to claims by federally unrecognized tribes, which are not covered by NAGPRA but which frequently have strong interests in repatriation. Some of these claims compete or conflict with claims by federally recognized tribes, while some of them do not.

The history of the Willamette Valley offers an example of how complex the question of "cultural affiliation" can be. Widespread decimation of population through epidemics occurred in the early 1800s, and during the period of reservation establishment in the Northwest (1850s–1870s), the surviving Willamette Valley Indians, along with dozens of highly localized Indian groups from up and down the Oregon and even Washington coasts, northwest California, and southwest Oregon, were removed to reservations in the Oregon coastal range. These reservations were themselves terminated in the 1950s and then restored in the 1970s and 1980s. It is fortuitous that these tribes were restored to federal recognition and thus able to make claims under NAGPRA. Cultural identity at these reservations must be understood as having been shaped by the historical experiences of depopulation, relocation, and now, in the late twentieth century, renewal.

At Willamette University, the problem of cultural affiliation has emerged primarily in the process of identifying human remains. In the last stages of the inventory process, twelve partial sets of human remains were discovered on campus. Identifying information, including published reports, associated with some of these sets strongly suggested that they were excavated from Willamette Valley burial sites, but an absolute identification was impossible.

As a general matter, we proceeded to develop summaries and inventories by first consulting with specialists in the National Park Service, who suggested that, based on the preponderance of evidence, the university could tentatively identify these materials with the Willamette Valley. The next step was to consult with the State of Oregon Indian Commission, which is responsible for identifying tribal affiliation under NAGPRA. The commission confirmed the tribal confederacies to be consulted. We then contacted the confederacies, explaining what we had found, the limitations of our documentation, and our deductions about the affiliations of the material. When we also asked them whether they wanted scientific analysis to ascertain further identification of the materials, they declined. Upon further consultation with Willamette and with each other, one of the tribal confederacies submitted a request for repatriation, which has been approved by the university's own NAGPRA Review Committee.[71]

In reflecting upon questions of establishing cultural affiliation, several archaeologists have made the point that scientific and oral traditional knowledge can intersect.[72] NAGPRA, at its best, has required that archaeologists and anthropologists collaborate with tribes and Native Hawaiian organizations during the identification process. Yet, under the statute, it is often Indian tribes who alone can effectively establish or explain cultural affiliation data, with or without input from other sources such as museums or federal agencies.[73] As noted earlier, this presents a deeply paradoxical dimension to NAGPRA insofar as it asks tribes to fix identity in scientific terms but also allows for a process of establishing cultural identity based on tribal oral tradition and non-Western notions of evidence. This dimension of NAGPRA highlights the tension within the law between a socially constructed and historically situated concept of cultural identity and the reification of a fixed definition of identity.

The thorny issue of establishing cultural affiliation captures the significance of the entire NAGPRA process, for it is very much a process of identity establishment.[74] As a process designed to restore access to cultural resources of the past, NAGPRA itself becomes a vehicle for the contemporary reassertion and re-establishment of identity. It is to be hoped that NAGPRA will not result in a retrenchment of identity as a fixed entity. A less rigid definition of cultural identity will avoid trapping Native Americans and the fields of archaeology and anthropology in a time warp with set standards of traditionality and authenticity.

Unrecognized tribes and the complexity of Native American removals

The issue of cultural affiliation is compounded by the existence of many federally unrecognized tribes. Their status under NAGPRA has not yet been a problem at Willamette but has caused a good deal of frustration elsewhere. Technically, unrecognized tribes are not eligible to make claims under NAGPRA. In many instances, however, they have engaged in repatriation processes. Perhaps nowhere is this issue more salient than in California, where a history of ungratified treaties has left many of the state's Indian people without federal recognition. Though excluded from eligibility under NAGPRA, unacknowledged tribes may pursue repatriation from the collections in the University of California system, under whose rules California groups may seek repatriation if they are recognized by the state for any purpose.[75] Since many federally unrecognized tribes are recognized by the state for such purposes as cultural resources management and preservation, these groups have been eligible to make repatriation claims under state practice[76]

Federally unrecognized tribes have pursued repatriation by enlisting the support of culturally related recognized groups, which may then make requests for repatriation on their behalf.[77] This has led, in some instances, to partnerships between recognized and unrecognized groups.[78] Unfortunately, however, the process creates a dynamic of dependency with which some unrecognized groups may be uncomfortable or which they may resist.[79]

The complexity of Native American removals from their original territories during the nineteenth century has also inhibited implementation of NAGPRA in some parts of the country.[80] In Texas, for example, nearly all Indians resident at the time of European contact have been either destroyed by disease or violence or removed outside of the state. Conversely, none of the three federally recognized tribes currently residing in Texas is indigenous to the state. Some of the tribes removed from Texas, notably the Apache, Caddo, Comanche, and Tonkawa, have successfully submitted repatriation claims to federal military entities in Texas.[81] Although NAGPRA requires museums to notify tribes affiliated with their collections regardless of then current location, the concern among some advocates of repatriation in Texas is that tribes have not been properly identified and notified. Intertribal activism, manifested in the American Indian Resource and Education Coalition, has played an advocacy role for the state's original indigenous inhabitants.

Forms of consultation

The NAGPRA process has strengthened Willamette's working relationships with regional tribes. In gathering and recording required data about the university's collection, we erred on the side of widespread notification. Even though many of Willamette's 2,000 objects are unlikely to be eligible for repatriation under NAGPRA, the university notified nearly 350 separate tribal entities about materials in our collection that might be associated with their contemporary communities, based on a very expansive understanding of "cultural affiliation." The consultation and post-reporting inquiry processes have led to identification of previously unidentified objects in the university's collection. Further, the repatriation process has opened the doors to the potential return of objects to tribes outside the parameters of NAGPRA, when doing so conforms to the Hallie Brown Ford Art Museum's deaccession policy. In one significant instance, many of the objects potentially under consideration for return may become part of a new tribal museum. Thus, objects out of sight for years could gain greater visibility as they enter a new institutional context.

"Consultation" has many meanings, of course. The term may be defined very differently by the government, native groups, institutions, and collecting agencies, respectively.[82] Some institutions and agencies seem to view the requirement of "consultation" as entailing little more than the initiation of contacts with indigenous groups.[83] In considering the definitional issue, it is well to keep in mind that "[i]nherent in the tribal consultation process are the elements of sovereignty, the governments' trust relationship, government-to-government communication, respect for cultural and linguistic diversity, and sensitivity to traditional cultural and religious practices."[84] Those elements can be seen in some consultative practices. For example, in the celebrated case of the Zuni tribe's quest for the return of *Ahayu:da*, or war gods, tribal consultation with museums was a multi-year, complex process which began well before the passage of NAGPRA and was successful in communicating Zuni religious values to non-Zumis.[85]

On perhaps the broadest scale in the country, the National Museum of the American Indian (NMAI) has, since its inception in 1989, been involved in a process of consultation on issues of both repatriation and museum development in order to "integrate Name world views into standard museum practices."[86] Tribal delegations visiting the museum for purposes of preparing repatriation requests have been the most significant source of information about preferred traditional care procedures for museum collections. In this process, it has become clear at NMAI that there can be no uniform "pan-Indian" traditional care policies because different tribes have very different beliefs and practices. NMAI therefore seeks out specific care instructions, in the absence of which it leaves "care of the collection to the discretion of Native staff members to treat the objects in the most respectful way possible according to their own cultural knowledge and customs."[87] The NMAI has emphasized that consultation is an ongoing process, perhaps initiated under NAGPRA but not confined to its requirements.

Consultation introduces many new phenomena with lasting importance for museums and tribal communities. One is the incorporation of indigenous curation methods into museum practice, as described above for NMAI. Another is the employment of Native Americans as staff members in museums and as tribal NAGPRA liaisons and consultants. NAGPRA has unquestionably revitalized the field of museum anthropology and archaeology, perhaps even bringing "disciplinary renewal out of national disgrace."[88]

The future of the repatriation process

Some conclusions about the repatriation process drawn from the experience at Zuni Pueblo are instructive.[89] One is that, resonant with NMAI policy and the practice of the NAGPRA Review Committee, museums must adopt a case-by-case resolution of repatriation issues, being sensitive to the specific perspectives of each tribal group and even different constituencies within a group. Another conclusion is that, for museums and native groups alike, the amount of work required by NAGPRA to complete the process of repatriation is staggering. Additional Congressional funding is necessary to support the work needed to implement the law fairly. Since 1994, the first year funding was awarded for NAGPRA consultation projects, approximately $6.5 million has been granted to tribes and $4.25 million to museums.[90] The future of such funding is, however, uncertain. Without funding, NAGPRA-related projects undertaken by smaller institutions and tribes with limited resources may be impossible. Since there is no statute of limitations on the operation of NAGPRA, what happens if tribes many years hence wish to seek repatriation, long after current sources of funding have dried up?

The full impact of NAGPRA is far from being completely felt or assessed. The process will unfold for years, posing both logistical and psychological burdens on museums and native groups. The inventories and summaries of tribal collections arriving on the desks of NAGPRA tribal liaisons indicate the truly astonishing number of cultural items and human remains that were transferred from native communities to the dominant society.[91] Continuous consultation and collaboration on the disposition of this material will be essential.

Dispute resolution

NAGPRA provides two avenues for resolving disputes arising out of its implementation: its own Review Committee and federal court jurisdiction.

The Review Committee

NAGPRA's seven-person Review Committee, which was chartered in 1991, is an advisory group appointed by the United States Secretary of the Interior. It is composed of three members nominated by the indigenous community, three members nominated by national museum and scientific organizations, and a seventh member chosen by the other six members. In making recommendations to the Secretary of the Interior, the Committee is charged with nine responsibilities:[92]

1 to appoint one of its members as chair;
2 to monitor the inventory and identification process;
3 on request of "any affected party," to review and make findings related to the identity or cultural affiliation of cultural items or the return of such items;
4 to facilitate the resolution of disputes relating to return of cultural items, "including convening the parties to a dispute if deemed desirable";
5 to compile an inventory of culturally unidentifiable human remains in the possession of federal agencies and museums and develop a process for disposing of them;
6 to consult with Indian tribes, Native Hawaiian organizations, and museums on pertinent matters;

7   to consult with the Secretary of the Interior in developing regulations to implement the law;
8   to perform other functions assigned by the Secretary of the interior; and
9   to make recommendations regarding future care of repatriated items.

The Review Committee met fifteen times between April 1992 and June 1998, each time in a different location. According to the official minutes of these meeting,[93] the Review Committee's agenda has spanned all nine of its responsibilities. Not surprisingly, its initial meetings were devoted to organizational tasks and review of proposed regulation, whereas substantive issues have dominated its later meetings. The most frequent discussions have focused on developing definitions and a process for the disposition of unidentifiable remains (at nine of the meetings), monitoring implementation of the law (in nine meetings), and reviewing regulations (in six meetings).

The problem of culturally unidentifiable human remains

Perhaps the most difficult problem for the Committee has been to develop a process for the disposition of culturally unidentifiable human remains. The risk of misattribution is serious. Repatriation of the wrong remains to a tribe may involve repatriation of a non-Indian or non–culturally affiliated Indian for reburial.[94] The Committee has struggled with a range of related issues, including the linkage of particular funerary objects with human remains; the status of ancient remains for which there is no specific burial location or information (and hence uncertain cultural affiliation at best); and a workable definition of "shared group identity" within the definition of "cultural affiliation." The Review Committee has acknowledged that "shared group identity" might include geographical, temporal, and cultural links as well as the historical links upon which the definition of cultural affiliation is essentially based.[95]

The minutes of the Review Committee reveal several examples of collaborative solutions to the problem of what to do when human remains, in particular, are unidentifiable under NAGPRA's regulation. On the state level, tribes and agencies have dealt with the problem in a number of ways. In Arkansas, for example, tribes repatriate such remains on the basis of geographical affiliation when cultural affiliation is unknown.[96] In Minnesota, a systematic reburial program has been developed. The Minnesota Native American Reburial Project, which is overseen by the Minnesota Indian Affairs Council, is made up of representatives of all eleven federally recognized tribes in the state. In consultation with the state of Minnesota and the Minnesota archaeological community, the reburial project arrived at a set of guidelines for the reburial of culturally unidentifiable human remains, which allow for the repatriation of such "remains and associated burial objects for reburial to tribal communities presently residing in the regions where the human remains originated."[97] Since NAGPRA does not provide for the repatriation of culturally unidentifiable remains or associated funerary objects, however, representatives from the state Minnesota requested that the Review Committee allow them to proceed according to their guidelines. The Committee is empowered to make such recommendations.[98] After some discussion, the Review Committee endorsed Minnesota's approach, but with some qualifications: that the reburial project secure written approval of the reburial process from pertinent federally recognized tribes, that information recorded about the human remains be accessible to the public, and that the process of reburial adhere to all the procedural requirements of NAGPRA.[99]

Facilitation of dispute resolution

In facilitating the resolution of disputes, the Committee may make recommendations and findings related to four general topics: the applicability of a definition of human remains and cultural items to a particular object, its cultural affiliation, its ownership, and its appropriate disposition. The Committee chair and the departmental consulting archaeologist in the National Park Service screen and coordinate all requests for review of a dispute.[100]

The Committee has attempted to facilitate the resolution of five disputes that have been brought to it for formal review. The first of these[101] involved a request by a Native Hawaiian organization to the Phoebe Hearst Museum for the return of two sets of remains of uncertain ethnicity. In an interesting application of the precautionary principle of environmental law, the museum emphasized the need to retain the remains until such time as research tools might permit their identification. The claimant organization minimized the importance of close cultural affiliation, noting that reburial would benefit everyone by restoring a spiritual force. The Committee indicated that it would review three types of evidence: osteological (or physical anthropological), contextual (where and under what circumstances the bones were found), and spiritual. In regard to the latter procedure, one member of the Committee normally reserved judgment until he could "go to the spirits for guidance." In applying NAGPRA's preponderance-of-evidence test, the Committee recommended that one set of remains be returned to the Native Hawaiian organization and the other transferred to a museum in Hawaii (the Bishop Museum in Honolulu) for safekeeping and further analysis. Both parties to the dispute accepted these recommendations, and both sets of remains were eventually reburied.[102]

The second dispute[103] also involved Native Hawaiian claims for human remains, this time for 1,500 sets from a U.S. naval air station on the island of Oahu. Although the Marine Corps, which was in command of the station, was willing to repatriate the remains to someone, the question was, to which of fifteen claimants? The Committee recommended that the Marine Corps hold the remains until the claimants had mutually decided on an appropriate disposition. The Committee's consideration of the dispute is puzzling insofar as a federal court already had jurisdiction over it.[104] The Committee refused to consider a later case for that reason.[105]

The third dispute[106] also centered on rival claimants. The Oneida Tribe of Wisconsin and the Oneida Nation of New York both claimed a wampum belt held in Chicago's Field Museum. The Committee recommended further discussions between the two groups to determine an appropriate disposition of the item.

The fourth dispute[107] involved the Hearst Museum and an individual who claimed to be a lineal descendant of Satanta, the original owner of a Kiowa shield. At the conclusion of its only hearing of the claim, the Committee agreed to send a letter to the claimant questioning whether the shield was a sacred object or object of cultural patrimony and whether an individual lineal descendant could base her request on a classification of the object as cultural patrimony. The Committee also agreed to send a letter to the Hearst Museum recommending that it consider transferring the object to the Fort Sill Museum in Oklahoma, in whose territory Satanta had lived. Finally, having noted documentation that seemed to establish the museum's right of possession of the shield, the Committee decided to defer any further discussion of the claim, pending the availability of more information. Subsequently, the claimant withdrew her request.

The fifth and last dispute[108] involved a Native Hawaiian claim for return of a carved wooden support figure in the Museum of Natural History at the Roger Williams Park in Providence, Rhode Island. The salient issues were, first, whether it was a sacred object, an object of cultural patrimony, or an unassociated funerary object; and second, whether the museum had the right of possession of the object. After extensive discussion, the Committee found insufficient evidence to confirm a right of possession and recommended that the city of Providence return the item jointly to a Native Hawaiian organization and the Office of Hawaiian Affairs in Honolulu. This proved to be an unsatisfactory solution. Federal litigation ensued, which in turn led to a settlement of the issues between the parties.[109]

Reflections on the work of the Review Committee

The NAGPRA Review Committee has played a very constructive role not only in helping implement NAGPRA but in serving the broader goals of the legislation. The Committee's modest docket of disputes—only five in six years of meetings—is, however, puzzling. The five disputes involved three Native Hawaiian claims and two Native American claims. Two of the five addressed a dispute between or among rival claimants, one involved a claim that was later withdrawn, and one coincided with a concurrent action in the federal courts. Perhaps the Committee's advisory capacity and lack of sanctions to support its recommendations dampen its appeal to prospective disputants. Perhaps NAGPRA and the agreements it encourages are working well enough to obviate a significant role for the review Committee in resolving disputes except as a penultimate step in the face of prospective litigation. Perhaps it is simply too early to say. Most likely, NAGPRA's encouragement of negotiated agreements between museums and tribes or organizations, together with the Review Committee's monitoring activity, have overcome some of the pressures for formal facilitation of dispute resolution.

Two general conclusions about the work of the Committee are apparent. First, its members have maintained a good working relationship with each other; consensus has been a hallmark.[110] The consensus-based process has served to set a tone of co-operation and mutual understanding for the entire country. Perhaps, though, this consensus has sometimes been achieved at the expense of a diversity of opinion; the minutes of the Committee's meetings reveal somewhat of a snowballing effect once an opinion has been firmly asserted by a member of the Committee. On the other hand, the Committee process has been open to a full range of opinion before a consensus develops.

Second, if reliable conclusions can be drawn from only five disputes, the Committee has not been very effective in facilitating dispute resolution. Only its first recommendation, concerning Native Hawaiian material in the Phoebe Hearst collection, provided a final resolution of a repatriation issue. Rather than facilitating the resolution of disputes, then, the review Committee's paramount role has been as a forum, catalyst, and monitor of NAGPRA implementation. In performing these roles, the Review Committee has been very effective.

Federal court litigation

Only a few NAGPRA-related claims have resulted in published opinions by federal courts. The availability of the federal courts to resolve NAGPRA-related disputes therefore does not explain the limited docket of the review Committee. Neither of the two prescribed methods of dispute resolution has been very heavily utilized. Two of the reported federal decisions addressed only incidental or preliminary issues.[111] Four cases, as follows, are more substantial.

In *Providence v. Babbitt*,[112] the City of Providence brought action against the Secretary of the Interior less than three weeks after the Review Committee had recommended repatriation of a Native Hawaiian support figure from a city museum, as noted earlier. The plaintiff claimed statutory error, violations of procedural due process, and a taking of its property in violation of the Fifth Amendment to the United States Constitution. This claim seemed to be rooted in the plaintiff's presumption that its refusal to comply with the Committee's recommendation—by selling the figure, for example—might subject it to the civil penalties prescribed by NAGPRA. This presumption is doubtful, since only NAGPRA itself, and not the Committee's interpretation of it while attempting to facilitate the resolution of a dispute, would seem to expose a disputant to liability.[113] The city and the claimant Native Hawaiian organization eventually agreed to enter mediation, which resulted in a settlement. Accordingly, the city agreed to donate the disputed figure to the claimant, and the latter agreed to reciprocate with a reported $125,000 donation to the museum.[114]

In *Na Iwi O Na Kupuna O Mokapn v. Dalton*,[115] which also came before the Review Committee, the federal court in Hawaii granted a summary judgment for the defendant on a claim that was concurrently before the Review Committee. In its most important determinations, the court denied standing to the human remains themselves and confirmed several features of the NAGPRA inventory process, including the acceptability of scientific research to determine affiliation and the disclosure by the government of information about the remains.

In *United States v. Corrow*,[116] the Tenth Circuit Court of Appeals affirmed the district court's criminal conviction of the defendant for illegal trafficking in Navajo masks and associated objects that constituted a medicine bundle (or *jish*). Charges had been brought under both NAGPRA and the Migratory Bird Treaty Act.[117] The NAGPRA-related conviction involved the defendant's purchase and offer to sell items of "cultural patrimony." The defendant claimed that the definition of this category of cultural items was constitutionally void for vagueness and that he had purchased the items from their individual owner, the widow of a spiritual chanter, thereby removing the transaction from the scope of NAGPRA. A core issue, however was whether the jish had been individually owned by the widow from whom the defendant had purchased the items, or communally owned and hence part of the Navajo patrimony.[118] The appellate court acknowledged that "the parameters of the designation 'cultural patrimony' might be unclear in some of its applications and at its edges."[119] It decided, however, that a jury could find beyond a reasonable doubt that the ceremonial adornments at issue had "ongoing historical traditional or cultural importance central to the Native American group or culture itself, rather than [being] property owned by an individual Native American."[120]

A particularly troublesome constitutional issue in *Corrow* relates to the prosecutor's examination in court of Navajo spiritual chanters concerning the religious nature of the masks.[121] In allowing such evidence, the court may have encouraged the jury to make its determination of ownership on the basis of its understanding and interpretation of divergent Navajo religious beliefs.[122] Moreover, the masks were never exhibited for the jury to see because of the court's acceptance of the plaintiff's claim that the spiritual nature of the objects did not allow them to be exhibited.[123] The appellate court declined to rule on the appropriateness of the lower court's reliance on religious belief.

The *Corrow* proceedings therefore left unanswered serious issues of doctrinal entanglement[124] by the federal government in violation of the establishment clause, providing for a separation of church and state, of the First Amendment to the U.S. Constitution.[125] In addition, NAGPRA's general protection of Native American but not other sacred material might be seen as an even more sweeping violation of the establishment clause. The apparent preference for Native American religion may be justified, however, as a rectification of past wrongs that resulted in wrongful takings of such items.[126] It is quite another matter, however, for a court to become entangled in, and allow evidence to be based on, divergent interpretations of Navajo religious belief and practice by members of the same tribe and on a religious-based exclusion of otherwise admissible evidence.

Finally *Bonnichsen v. United States Department of the Army*[127] (the "Kennewick Man" case) will be discussed elsewhere in this symposium issued.[128]

Conclusion

During its first decade, NAGPRA has been instrumental in confirming indigenous ownership or control over cultural heritage in the United States. Implementation of NAGPRA's requirements for repatriation of heritage from museums and federal agencies to native groups has led to a profound redefinition of relationships between those groups and collecting institutions. Resolution of disputes arising out of the process of repatriation has not relied heavily on prescribed procedures of the

NAGPRA Review Committee and federal court jurisdiction. Instead, consultations and negotiations have dominated the process.

It is essential to appreciate that implementation of NAGPRA and the resolution of disputes under it are continuing responsibilities. Serious issues remain, ranging from coherent working definitions of "cultural patrimony" and "culturally identifiable human remains" to the critical need for substantial, ongoing funding to facilitate the process of repatriation.

As a hybrid of international and domestic law, rooted in human rights, NAGPRA is a dynamic model in the global system of protecting indigenous heritage. NAGPRA's process of repatriation, in particular, has demonstrated both the significance of cultural heritage issues in human affairs and the broader implications of their resolution for civil society. NAGPRA itself is important heritage.

Notes and references

1. 25 U.S.C. §§ 3001–13 (1994).
2. For a summary of this body of law, *see* Party Gerstenblith, Identity and Cultural Property: The Protection of Cultural Property in the United States, 75 *Boston University Law Review* 559, 579, 586 (1995).
3. "Although protection of our indigenous cultures has become progressively stronger over the course of this century, the legal regime remains inadequate and generally reactive in its formulation." *Id.* at 565. A peculiarity of United States law is that, although regulation of domestic cultural heritage has been limited, the country's cooperation in international efforts to deter and respond to illegal trafficking and other threats to the global heritage has been substantial. *See, e.g.,* James A.R. Nafziger, Seizure and Forfeiture of Cultural Property by the United States, 5 *Villanova Sports and Entertainment Law Journal* 19, 22 (1998) (in a symposium on reclamation of cultural property).
4. 25 U.S.C. § 3002. In this and other respects, NAGPRA is closely related to the Archaeological Resources Protection Act of 1979 (ARPA), 16 U.S.C. 470aa–470mm (1994). ARPA reasserts federal control over archaeological resources on federal and tribal lands and provides stiff penalties for persons who knowingly excavate, remove, or engage in transactions involving those resources without a federal permit.
5. 25 U.S.C § 3002(c). "'Native American' means of, or relating to, a tribe, people or culture that is indigenous to the United States." 25 U.S.C. § 3001(9). The term therefore embraces Indian tribes and Native Hawaiian organizations.
6. 25 U.S.C § 3002(d).
7. 53 U.S.C. § 1170 (1994). Penalties include fines and imprisonment up to five years in the case of a second or subsequent offence, for knowingly engaging in commercial transactions without the right of possession to human remains of a Native American or otherwise in violation of NAGPRA. It is unclear what constitutes a criminal "violation of NAGPRA." Presumably, violations would be limited to commercial transactions in material either taken without permit and against specific federal law from federal or tribal land or obtained from museums or federal agencies after NAGPRA's enactment.
8. *See* Susan B. Bruning, Native American Art and Antiquities, *v IFAR Journal* 17, 18–19 (Autumn 1998).
9. 25 U.S.C. § 3005. NAGPRA does not provide for the repatriation of cultural items from individuals or enterprises that are not museums, as defined, but the law's terms and process of repatriation have helped define claims beyond us scope. *See. e.g.,*

Margaret Loke, Aleut Sacred Objects to be Auctioned at Sotheby's Despite Protests by the Tribe, *New York Times*, November 30, 1908, at B5.

10 The statute requires each institution to undertake a detailed, object-by-object *inventory* of all human remains and associated funerary objects in a collection. 25 U.S.C. § 3003(a). The statute also requires a more general *summary* of unassociated funerary objects, sacred objects, or objects of cultural patrimony. The summary is to describe the collection, its size, and the circumstances of its acquisition. 25 U.S.C. § 3004(a).

11 Although the statutory definition of the term "cultural items" includes all material for which an inventory or summary is required, including human remains, NAGPRA regulations, reflecting objections to the classification of human remains as cultural items, eliminates the generic term "cultural items" and refers only to "human remains" and other specific categories of materials. 43 C.F.R. § 10.1(3) (1998).

12 The statutory definition of "cultural affiliation" refers to "a relationship of shared group identity which can be reasonably traced historically or prehistorically between a present-day Indian tribe or Native Hawaiian organization and an identifiable earlier group." 25 U.S.C. § 3001(2).

13 25 U.S.C. § 3005(a)(1), (2).

14 25 U.S.C. § 3007 allows the Secretary of the Interior to assess a civil penalty against "[a]ny museum that fails to comply with the requirements of this Act." *See* 43 C.F.R. § 10.12 (1998).

15 25 U.S.C. § 3005(a)(1), (2), (4), (5).

16 The statutory definition of "sacred objects" includes "specific ceremonial objects which are *needed* by traditional Native American religious leaders for the practice of traditional Native American religions by the *present day* adherents." 25 U.S.C. § 3001(3)(C) (emphasis added).

17 NAGPRA defines "cultural patrimony" as "an object having ongoing historical, traditional, or cultural importance central to the Native American group or culture itself, rather than property owned by an individual native American, and which therefore, cannot be alienated, appropriated, or conveyed by any individual regardless of whether or not the individual is a member of the Indian tribe or Native Hawaiian organization and such object shall have been considered inalienable by such Native American group at the time the object was separated from such group." 25 U.S.C. § 3001(3)(D). This appears to be "NAGPRA's most difficult definition." Thomas H. Boyd and Jonathan Haas, The Native Museums and Native American Groups, 25 *Arizona State Law Journal* 253, 265 (1992). "[I]dentifying cultural patrimony may require extensive inquiry into both the circumstances surrounding the alienation and the state of traditions and customs as they existed at the time of transfer." *Id.* at 266. Arguably, the result is to create a rebuttable presumption that an object belongs to a claimant tribe's cultural patrimony. Sarah Harding, Justifying Repatriation of Native American Cultural Property, 72 *Indiana Law Journal* 723, 738 (1997). Regardless of this presumption, the interpretive task is demanding.

18 25 U.S.C. § 3005(a)(4).

19 25 U.S.C. § 3005(b).

20 25 U.S.C. § 3005(c). The statutory definition of a "right of possession" is elaborate. Essentially, it requires "possession obtained with the voluntary consent of an individual or group that had authority of alienation." 25 U.S.C. § 3001(13).

21 25 U.S.C. § 3005(c).

22 25 U.S.C. § 3005(e).

23 25 U.S.C. § 3006.

24 25 U.S.C. § 3008.

25 25 U.S.C. § 3011. The review committee is given the responsibility of consulting with the Secretary of the Interior in the development of regulations to carry out the law, 25 U.S.C. § 3006(c)(7). Current regulations appear at 43 C.F.R. § 10 (1998).
26 25 U.S.C. § 3013.
27 *See* Stanley Zamonski. *Buffalo Bill. The Man and the Museum* 32–35 (Renaissance House, Frederick, CO 1987).
28 Jack F. Trope and Walter R. Echo-Hawk, The Native American Graves Protection and Repatriation Act: background and legislative history, 24 *Arizona State Law Journal* 35, 46, 47 (1992).
29 For example, the law failed to take into account such tribal practices as scaffold, canoe, or tree burials. *Id.* at 46. On other statutory and judicially constructed limitations to protection of Indian burials, *see* Gerstenblith, *supra* note 2, at 624–25.
30 Robert M. Peregoy. The legal basis, legislative history, and implementation of Nebraska's Landmark Reburial Legislation, 24 *Arizona State Law Journal* 329, 331 (1992).
31 James Riding In, Without ethics and morality: a historical overview of imperial archeology and American Indians, 24 *Arizona State Law Journal* 11, 25 (1992). *See also* Francis P. McManamon, The reality of repatriation: reaching out to Native Americans, *Federal Archaeology*, Fall–Winter 1995, at 2; Gerstanblith, *supra* note 2, at 583.
32 William L. Merrill, Edmund J. Ladd, and T. J. Ferguson, The return of the *Ahayu:da*: lessons for repatriation from Zuni Pueblo and the Smithsonian Institution, 35 *Current Anthropology* 523 (1993); Fergus M. Bordewich, *Killing the White Man's Indian* 189 (Anchor Books, New York 1996).
33 *See*, e.g. Suzan Shown Harjo, Native people's cultural and human rights: an unfinished agenda, 24 *Arizona State Law Journal* 321, 325 (1992): Rennard Strickland, Implementing the national policy of understanding, preserving, and safeguarding the heritage of Indian Peoples and Native Hawaiians: human rights, sacred objects, and cultural patrimony, *24 Arizona State Law Journal* 175, 190 (1992).
34 The core international agreement, to which the United States is a party, is the UNESCO Convention on the Means of Prohibiting and Preventing the Illicit Import, Export, and Transfer of Ownership of Property, November 14, 1970, 823 U.N.T.S. 231, 10 I.L.M. 289. On the development during the 1970s of general principles for repatriation of cultural property, *see* James A. R. Nafziger, The new international legal framework for the return, restitution, or forfeiture of cultural property, 15 *New York University Journal of International Law and Policy* 789, 799 (1983).
35 *See* James A. R. Nafziger, The underlying constitutionalism of the law governing archaeological and other cultural heritage, 30 *Willamette Law Review* 581, 597 (1994).
36 Conference on security and cooperation in Europe: final act, August 1, 1975, *reprinted in* 14 I.L.M. 1292 (1975). *See* Harjo, *supra* note 33.
37 The Vermillion Accord is summarized in Steve Russell, American Indians seek religious freedom, *Texas Bar Journal*, April 1995, at 368, 370 (emphasizing respect for the wishes of the deceased, the local community, and science, and calling for agreement on disposition of remains). For a stronger Vermillion statement of claims for enforcement of laws, an end to grave robbing and pot hunting, separation of burial material, and reallocation of costs for reburial, *see* Riding In, *supra* note 31, at 29.
38 135 Cong. Rec. S12388 (daily ed. October 3, 1989) (statement of Sen. Inouye).
39 20 U.S.C. §§ 80q–80q-15 (1994).
40 *Reprinted in* 24 *Arizona State Law Journal* 487 (1992) [hereinafter Report on National Dialogue].

41 See, e.g. Trope and Echo-Hawk, *supra* note 28, at 59 ("NAGPRA is, first and foremost, human rights legislation"): Gene A. Marsh, Walking the spirit trial: repatriation and protection of Native American remains and sacred cultural items, 24 *Arizona State Law Journal* 79, 96 (1992) ("NAGPRA is described by leaders in the Native American community as the most important human rights legislation for Native Americans ever passed by Congress").

42 Report on National Dialogue § D(1)(a), *supra note* 40, at 494.

43 G.A. Res. 217A (III), U.N. Doc. A/810, at 71 (1948) [hereinafter UDHR]. Although the UDHR was not intended to be legally binding, it has become a basic component of international customary law, *See, e.g.*, Louis B. Sohn, The new international law: protection of the rights of individuals rather than states, 32 *American University Law Review* 1, 16–17 (1982).

44 G.A. Res. 2200 A (XXI), U.N. Doc. A/6316 (1966), 999 U.N.T.S. 171, 6 I.L.M. 368 (1967) [hereinafter ICCPR]. The United States is not a party to a sister instrument that more directly protects cultural rights, the International Covenant on Economic, Social and Cultural Rights, G.A. Res. 2200A (XXI), U.N. Doc A/6316 (1966), 993 U.N.T.S. 3, 6 I.L.M. 360 (1967).

45 UDHR, *supra* note 43, art. 3; ICCPR, *supra* note 44, art. 9.

46 UDHR, *supra* note 43, art. 6; ICCPR, *supra* note 44, art. 16.

47 ICCPR, *supra* note 44, art. 1. The specific rights to freedom of religion is not easily translated into a right to repatriation of sacred material. The right is defined to "include freedom to have or adopt a religion or belief of [one's] choice, and freedom . . . to manifest his religion or belief in worship, observance, practice and teaching." ICCPR, *supra* note 44, art. 18. The underlying language in the UDHR is similar. UDHR, *supra* note 43, art. 18. The underlying language in the UDHR is similar. UDHR, *supra* note 43, art. 18.

48 25 U.S.C. § 3010.

49 *See* Trope and Echo-Hawk, *supra* note 28, at 60.

50 Diana Drake Wilson has made the point that "[p]articipating in repatriation necessarily brings one into contact with the historical gears of the process of colonization which ultimately give way to less mechanical and more personal strategies of assimilation, denigration, and/or creative transformation between people and nations." *See* Diana Drake Wilson, California Indian participation in repatriation: working toward recognition, 21 *American Indian Culture and Research Journal* 191, 191 (1997).

51 Rebecca Tsosie, Indigenous peoples' claims to cultural property: a legal perspective, 21 *Museum Anthropology* 5, 6 (1997).

52 25 U.S.C. 3001(13) (emphasis added).

53 25 U.S.C. 3001(3)(d).

54 *See* Tsosie, *supra* note 51, at 6.

55 *See, e.g.* Barbara Isaac, An Epimethean view of the future at the Peabody Museum, *Federal Archaeology*, Fall–Winter 1995, at 18, 21 (resulting in a recalculation of the number of human remains from 7,000 to 10,000 and cultural objects tenfold from 800,000 to eight million); Robert Pickering and R. L. Jantz, Look again before repatriating: avoiding a moral and legal morass, *Federal Archaeology*, Fall–Winter 1995, at 36.

56 *See* C. Timothy McKeown, Inside the act: confessions of a bureaucrat, *Federal Archaeology*, Fall–Winter 1995, at 4, 9 ('there has been a dramatic increase in dialogue among tribes, museums, and agencies'); Francis P. McManamon and Larry V. Nordby, Implementing the Native American Graves Protection and Repatriation Act, 24 *Arizona State Law Journal* 217, 244 (1992) (noting NAGPRA's encouragement of

collaborative agreements for access, use, care, and treatment of cultural items); James A. R. Nafziger, The new fiduciary duty of United States museums to repatriate cultural heritage: the Oregon experience. *University of British Columbia Law Review* 37, 40 (Special Issue 1995) ("Encouragement of Creating Partnership Between Institutions and Indigenous Communities"): Dean B. Suagee, Tribal voices in historic preservation: sacred landscapes, cross-cultural bridges, and common ground, 21 *Vermont Law Review* 145, 207 (1996): Martin Sullivan, A museum perspective on repatriation: issues and opportunities, 24 *Arizona State Law Journal* 283, 291 (1992); Rosita Worl, NAGPRA: symbol of a new treaty. *Federal Archaeology*, Fall–Winter 1995, at 28, 29 (emphasizing meaningful consultation as an alternative to conflict between Indians and museums).

57 Gary D. Stumpf, A federal land management perspective on repatriation, 24 *Arizona State Law Journal* 303, 308 (1992).

58 Minutes, Native American Graves Protection and Repatriation Review Committee, www.cast.uark.edu/products/nagpra.dat/rms.001-015.html [hereinafter Minutes], Sixth Meeting, January 23–25, 1994, at 13.

59 At its best, the repatriation process (1) helps to revive cultures: (2) serves to resolve injustices: (3) brings people together: (4) gives museums and universities the opportunity to explain the value of research, collection care, and cultural education; (5) encourages the participation and involvement of Native Americans in our institutions; and (6) encourages the training and employment of members of cultural groups. Michael J. Fox, Repatriation: mutual benefits for everyone, 24 *Arizona State Law Journal* 7, 8–9 (1992).

60 Although Willamette has offered occasional anthropology courses throughout much of its history, it had no in-depth anthropology program until the fall of 1966, when one of the co authors, Rebecca J. Dobkins, and a colleague were hired to establish a comprehensive program. Dobkins coordinated the NAGPRA inventory and summary process after her arrival. She was assisted by Yvonne Lever, former register at Willamette University's Hallie Brown Ford Museum of Art.

61 Nancy Rosoff, in describing the National Museum of the American Indian's process of identifying its much larger inventory of human remains, relates a similar problem of not knowing what the institution possessed until a shelf-by-shelf inventory was completed: "It was initially challenging, however, just to get an exact count of the number of human remains in the museum, a number that kept increasing as staff members continued to encounter human remains in collections storage areas." See Nancy Rosoff, Integrating native views into museum procedures: hope and practice at the National Museum of the American Indian, 22 *Museum Anthropology* 33, 33 (1998).

62 William S. Laughlin, Excavations in the Calapuya mounds of the Willamette Valley, Oregon. 2 *American Antiquity* 147 (1941): William S. Laughlin, Notes on the archaeology of the Yamhill River, Willamette Valley, Oregon, 2 *American Antiquity* 221 (1943).

63 *See, e.g.,* Curtis Hinsley, Digging for identity: reflections on the cultural background of collecting, 20 *American Indian Quarterly* 180 (1996).

64 25 U.S.C. § 3005(4).

65 Devon A. Mihesuah, American Indians, anthropologists, pothunters, and repatriation: ethical, religious, and political differences, 20 *American Indian Quarterly* 229–37 (1996).

66 Elisabeth Tooker, A note on the return of eleven wampum belts to the Six Nations Iroquois Confederacy on Grand River, Canada, 45 *Ethnohistory* 219, 219–20 (1998).

67 *See, e.g.,* Tamara L. Bray and Lauryn Guttenplan Grant. The concept of cultural affiliation and its legal significance in the Larsen Bay Repatriation, *Reckoning with the*

Dead: The Larsen Bay Repatriation and the Smithsonian Institution 153, 153–54 (Tamara L. Bray and Thomas W. Killion eds., Smithsonian Institution Press, Washington 1994).

68 Tamara L. Bray, Repatriation, power relations and the politics of the past, 70 *Antiquity* 440 (1996).
69 *See infra*, text at notes 94–99.
70 *See* Larry J. Zimmerman and Robert N. Clinton, Kennewick Man and Native American Graves Protection and Repatriation Act woes, 8 *International Journal of Cultural Property* 212–28 (1999).
71 At of the time of this printing, the requisite notice of intent to repatriate was awaiting publication in the Federal Register.
72 Roger Anyon et al., Native American oral tradition and archaeology: issues of structure, relevance, and respect, in *Native Americans and Archaeologists: Stepping Stones to Common Ground* 77, 77–78 (Nina Swindler, et al., eds., AltaMira Press, Walnut Creek 1997) [hereinafter *Native Americans and Archaeologists*].
73 Minutes, *supra* note 58. Eleventh Meeting, June 9–11, 1996, at 6.
74 "Repatriation, the quest to recover the remains of the ancestors, has developed into a flexible symbol articulating widely differing points of ideological reference within the Native community. For Native cultures now in the process of forging a collective identity after having survived centuries under the brutal onslaught of colonialist regimes, the past constitutes a crucial contemporary site for this process of retrieval and reinscription, no matter how hybrid, composite or emergent that identity may be." Bray, *supra* note 68, at 445.
75 Carola Goldberg, Acknowledging the repatriation claims of unacknowledged California tribes, 21 *American Indian Culture and Research Journal* 183, 185 (1997).
76 *Id.* at 189–90.
77 Wilson, *supra* note 50, at 197.
78 *Id.*
79 Minutes, *supra* note 58. Fourteenth Meeting, January 29–31, 1998, at 24–25 (discussion of request for repatriation of human remains from a federal agency by the federally unrecognized Chinook Tribe. The Review Committee recommended that the Chinook work with the nearest federally recognized tribe to submit a repatriation request, even though it was explained that the Chinook were not "comfortable with that method"). *Id.* at 25.
80 Steve Russell, The Legacy of Ethnic Cleansing: Implementation of NAGPRA in Texas, 19 *American Indian Culture and Research Journal* 193 (1995).
81 *Id.* at 206.
82 *See* Section IV: A look at Consultation, in *Native Americans and Archaeologists, supra* note 72, for examples of consultation practices related and auxiliary to NAGPRA.
83 In discussing historic preservation efforts in Oklahoma, the state archaeologist Robert L. Brooks has made an observation that could apply to the way some museums seem to have handled consultation under NAGPRA: "One major issue is the conceptual distinction between what consultation means to many in the archaeological/museum community and state and federal agencies as opposed to its meaning to tribes. If we substitute the word 'contact' for 'consult,' it would perhaps be more untrue [as a description of the consultation process]. Tribes are notified of actions or intentions on projects; they are not necessarily consulted." Robert L. Brooks, Compliance, preservation, and Native American rights: resource management as a co-operative venture. in *Native Americans and Archaeologists, supra* note 72, at 217, 218.
84 David G. Rice, The seeds of common ground: experimentation in Indian consultation. In *Native Americans and Archaeologists, supra* note 72, at 217, 218 (referring to both the

type of consultation required under NAGPRA as well as that required by other federal legislation such as the Archaeological Resources Protection Act).

85 *See* Merrill, Ladd and Ferguson, *supra* note 32, at 523.
86 Rosoff, *supra* note 61, at 33.
87 *Id.* at 37.
88 Kathleen S. Fine-Dare, Disciplinary renewal out of national disgrace: Native American Graves Protection and Repatriation Act compliance in the academy, 68 *Radical History Review* 25 (1997).
89 T. J. Ferguson, Roger Anyon, and Edmund J. Ladd, Repatriation at the Pueblo of Zuni: diverse solutions to complex problems, 20 *American Indian Quarterly* 251. 271 (1996).
90 National Park Service, Archeology and Ethnography Program, NAGPRA.
91 *See* Jeffrey Van Pelt, Michael S. Britney, and Tom Bailor, Protecting cultural resources on the Umatilla Indian Reservation. In *Native Americans and Archaeologists*, *supra* note 72 at 167. The authors observe as follows: "As tribes go through the NAGPRA process and see, for the first time, the lists of thousands of ancestral human remains, associated burial items, and sacred objects, our native people are seeing what the 'science' of archaeology has done to our family members and ancestral way of life. To say this is shocking is an understatement!" *Id.* at 169.
92 25 U.S.C. § 3006(c).
93 A copy of the transcript of the Fifteenth Meeting of the Review Committee, June 25–27, 1998, is on file with the authors.
94 *See* Pickering and Jantz, *supra* note 55.
95 Minutes, *supra* note 58, Eleventh Meeting, June 9–11. 1996, at 7.
96 Minutes, *supra* note 58, Thirteenth Meeting, March 25–27, 1997, at 13. Testimony of Carrie Wilson, Quapaw Tribe of Arkansas.
97 Minutes, supra note 58. Fourteenth Meeting, January 29–31, 1998, at 22.
98 *Id.* at 23.
99 *Id.* at 36. A similar process proposed by the state of Iowa was also endorsed.
100 Dispute Resolution Procedures of the Native American Graves Protection and Repatriation Review Committee (c) (1994).
101 Minutes, *supra* note 58, Fourth Meeting, Feb. 26–28, 1993, at 4.
102 *See* Edward Halealoha Ayau, Rooted in native soil, *Federal Archaeology*, Fall–Winter 1995, at 24, 27.
103 Minutes, *supra* note 58, Eighth Meeting, November 17–19, 1994, at 13; Minutes, *supra* note 58, Eleventh Meeting, June 9–11, 1996, at 3.
104 *See* Na Iwi O Na Kupuna O Mokapu v. Dalton, 894 F. Supp. 1397 (D. Hawaii 1995). *See* text, *infra* note 115.
105 Minutes, *supra* note 58, Twelfth Meeting, November 1–3, 1996, at 15 (deciding not to act formally on a request of the Confederated Tribes of the Colville Reservation regarding Kennewick Man).
106 Minutes, *supra* note 58, Tenth Meeting, October 16–18, 1995, at 7; Minutes, *supra* note 58, Twelfth Meeting, November 1–3, 1996, at 8.
107 Minutes, *supra* note 58, Tenth Meeting, October 16–18, 1995 at 9; Minutes, *supra* note 58, Eleventh Meeting. June 9–11, 1996, at 3.
108 Minutes, *supra* note 58, Twelfth Meeting, November 1–3, 1996 at 13; Minutes, *supra* note 58, Twelfth Meeting, March 25–27, 1997 at 16.
109 *See* text, *infra* notes 112–14.

110 *See* McKeown, *supra* note 56; Tessie Naranjo, Thoughts on two worldviews, *Federal Archaeology*, Fall–Winter 1995, at 8 ("[t]he discussions are more like open discussions than formal get-togethers").
111 Pueblo of San Ildefonso v. Ridlon, 103 F.3d 936 (10th Cir. 1996) (establishing that NAGPRA repatriation is not limited by the date when an object was found); Abenaki Nation of Mississquoi v Hughes, 805 F. Supp. 234 (D.Vt. 1992.) (denying NAGPRA's application to construction activity on non-federal land under a permit issued by the federal government).
112 CA 96–668 (D. R.I. Nov. 21, 1996).
113 *See* Minutes, *supra* note 58. Seventh Meeting, May 12–14, 1994 (clarification by departmental consulting archaeologist and discussion among committee members).
114 C.J. Chivas. An intense aloha, *Providence Journal*, August 8, 1998.
115 894 F. Supp. 1397.
116 119 F.3d 796 (10th Cir. 1997), *cert. denied*, 118 S. Ct. 1089 (1998). This case is noted by Dawn Elyse Goldman, 8 *International Journal of Cultural Property* 229–44 (1999).
117 16 US.C.§§701–12 (1994).
118 Because of the allegedly communal nature of ownership of the jish, equitable rather than normal common-law principles shifted the burden of analyzing the original conveyance to the defendant. *See* Ralph W. Johnson and Sharon I. Haensly, Fifth Amendment Takings lmplications of the 1990 Native American Graves Protection and Repatriation Act, 24 Arizona State Law Journal 151, 158–59 (1992).
119 119 F.3d, at 803.
120 15 U.S.C. § 3001(3)(D).
121 United States v Corrow, 941 F. Supp. 1553, 1561 n. 10, 1562 (D.N.M. 1996).
122 Brief of the Antique Tribal Arts Dealers Association as *amicus curiae* in Support of the Petition at 13–16, Corrow v U.S., 118 S. Ct. 1089 (1998).
123 *Id.* at 12.
124 On the constitutional issue of doctrinal entanglement, *see generally* Laurence H. Tribe, *American Constitutional Law* 1231–42 (1988).
125 US. Const. amend. I.
126 *See* Gerstenblith, *supra* note 2, at 659.
127 969 F. Supp. 614 (D. Or. 1997), 969 F. Supp. 628 (D. Or. 1997) (preliminary rulings).
128 *See supra* note 70.

Part II, Section 3

Museums and the care and display of ancient human remains

Chapter 16

Policy and practice in the treatment of archaeological human remains in North American museums and public agency collections

Francis P. McManamon[1]

Claims for control of archaeological resources have increased and now come from a wider range of groups. A century ago, it was common for eccentric antiquarians to be the ones who were most concerned about archaeological sites, with scientists just beginning to become interested in these ancient remains. At present, academic researchers, public agencies responsible for the stewardship of the archaeological record, and descendant communities all assert claims for access or control of the physical record of the ancient and historic past. This is to say nothing of others such as antiquities traffickers, treasure-hunters, and historic shipwreck salvors who also have laid claim to artifacts in archaeological sites. Of special concern for scholars, scientists, public stewards, and descendants are the human remains sometimes found in archaeological contexts. Basic questions regarding these remains include: what is the proper treatment for them, and who should be responsible for determining this?

We can consider the scale of this topic in the United States (national statistics are not available from Canada) by examining some of the quantities of human remains from archaeological contexts that are reported in collections curated by public agencies and museums. When considering only human remains reported as "Native American," the total number is approximately 152,000 set of individual remains. These remains are reported from over 1,000 museums that receive federal funding and public agency offices. Table 16.1 shows summaries of some of the general counts of human remains, as well as examples from several of the large institutions.

In the United States, the largest number of human remains removed from archaeological sites and in agency and museum collections are Native American. Each set of remains counted is believed to represent a single individual. Many of

Source: *Human Remains and Museum Practice*. J. Lohman and K. Goodnow, eds. Paris: UNESCO, 2006. pp. 48–59. Reproduced by permission of Berghahn Books Inc.

these sets of remains, perhaps most of them, are fragments of individual skeletons. Relatively few of them are likely to be even nearly complete. The sets of remains are held by a large number of institutions, over 1,000 reportedly. However, relatively few public museums or agencies have over 500 sets of remains in their individual collections.[2]

Table 16.1 Examples of quantities of human remains from archaeological contexts in United States public agency or museum collections

Number of US public museums reporting Native American (NAm) human remains[a]	689
Number of United States public agency offices reporting NAm human remains[a]	449
Number of sets (minimum number of individuals [MNI]) of 'culturally affiliated' NAm human remains reported by US museums and agencies[a]	29,284
Number of sets (MNI) of 'culturally unidentifiable' NAm human remains reported by US museums and agencies[a]	108,247
Number of sets (MNI) of NAm human remains reported by the Repatriation Office, Department of Anthropology, National Museum of Natural History, Smithsonian Institution collections (3,224+ individual sets have been repatriated)[b]	15,963
Number of sets (MNI) of NAm human remains, National Park Service collections (3,606 of these sets have been determined as culturally affiliated and public notices have described their availability for repatriation to a culturally affiliated tribe)[c]	5,994
Number of sets (MNI) of 'culturally unidentifiable' NAm human remains reported by the Peabody Museum of Archaeology and Ethnology, Harvard University[a]	6,074
Number of sets (MNI) of 'culturally unidentifiable' NAm human remains reported by the Ohio Historical Society[a]	6,700
Number of sets (MNI) of 'culturally unidentifiable' NAm human remains reported by the Tennessee Valley Authority[a]	4,006
Number of sets (MNI) of human remains reported for the African Burial Ground site, New York City[d]	419

Sources:

[a]National Park Service, (2004a), *National NAGPRA Program, Final Mid-Year Report, 31 March FY 2004*, National Park Service, Department of the Interior, Washington DC, www.cr.nps.gov/nagpra/DOCUMENTS/NNReport0410.pdf, information provided by National NAGPRA program leader, 30 August 2005 accessed 24 October 2004.

[b]Flyn, Gillian, (1998), *Annual Report on Repatriation Activities at the National Museum of Natural History, June 1997 to June 1998*, Repatriation Office, Department of Anthropology, National Museum of Natural History, Smithsonian Institution, Washington DC, www.nmnh.si.edu/anthro/repatriation, accessed 28 February 2005.

[c]National Park Service, (2003), Park NAGPRA Updates, 30 June 2003, document on the file, Park NAGPRA Program, Intermountain Regional Office, Denver, Colorado.

[d]Archaeology Magazine, (2003), 'Return to the African burial ground. an interview with physical anthropologist Michael I. Blakey', *Archaeology Online*, www.archaeology.org/online/interviews/Blakey, accessed 28 February 2005; Harrington, Spencer P. M., (1993), 'Bones and bureaucrats: New York's great cemetery imbroglio', *Archaeology* (March/April 1993), 28–38; Lathrop, Stacy, (2003), 'Following the remains of enslaved Africans', *Anthropology News*, November 2003, 15–16.

Other ethnic groups also are represented in some of the collections. At the African Burial Ground site in the center of lower Manhattan, New York City, the remains of over 400 individuals were excavated in 1991–1992 prior to the construction of a public office building. Before the reinterment of these remains in October 2004, they were extensively examined and scientifically analyzed.[3] A smaller nineteenth-century African American burial population (140 individuals) associated with the First African Baptist Church in Philadelphia was excavated in 1983–1984 and analyzed before reinterment in 1987.[4]

So, in the United States there are substantial numbers of sets of human remains from archaeological contexts in the collections of a large number of public museums and agencies. Several national laws and regulations provide guidance on how these remains are to be treated by the organizations that hold them.

National laws and regulations affecting human remains from archaeological contexts

In recent years in the United States, public agencies and museums that are responsible for the care of archaeological human remains have developed general policies and guidance for their treatment. Most specific examples, however, show that a case-by-case approach is usually followed.

The legal regulation of treatment of recently deceased human remains generally is not a matter of national law. Rather, such matters are handled by state or local laws and regulations. In 1997, the Natural Resources Conservation Service surveyed state laws and recorded 38 that specifically addressed "... reburial of human skeletal remains, repatriation of human skeletal remains and grave goods, and/or unmarked grave protection statutes... ."[5]

At national level, the United States has three laws that affect the treatment of human remains from archaeological contexts. In Canada, a national law providing uniform regulation of archaeological resources is being drafted, however, presently, except for archaeological resources within Parks Canada units, provincial laws regulate how such remains are treated. The Parks Canada policy provides its officials with directions for activities regarding human remains, cemeteries, and burial grounds.[6]

In the United States, since 1906, archaeological sites on public lands have been protected. Their investigation, the collection or excavation of artifacts or other remains, including human remains, and curation and public interpretation have been regulated by the Antiquities Act and subsequent laws (Table 16.2). Although this act and its regulations do not make any specific reference to human remains, such remains have clearly been considered as part of the archaeological record and appropriate for archaeological investigation under this statute.

Human remains are specifically mentioned in the second major United States law covering archaeological resources, the Archaeological Resources Protection (ARPA), which explicitly includes "human remains" recovered from archaeological contexts and susceptible to historic or scientific study as being covered by the law. The Native American Graves Protection and Repatriation Act (NAGPRA)

Table 16.2 United States archaeological laws and human remains[1]

Antiquities Act of 1906, 16 USC 431–433	No explicit mention of human remains
Archaeological Resources Protection Act of 1979, as amended, 16 USC 470 aa-mm	"Human skeletal remains" listed as one kind of material remains that are of archaeological interest and therefore covered by the law
Native American Graves Protection and Repatriation Act of 1990, 25 USC 3001–13	"Native American" and "Native Hawaiian" human remains are covered by the law • "Human remains": "means the physical remains of the body of a person of Native American ancestry. The term does not include remains or portions of remains that may reasonably be determined to have been freely given or naturally shed by the individual from whose body they were obtained, such as hair made into ropes or nets." (From the regulations for NAGPRA, 36 CFR 10.2[d][1]) • "Native American": "… of, or relating to, a tribe, culture, or people that is indigenous to the United States." • "Native Hawaiian": "… a descendant of the aboriginal people who, prior to 1778, occupied … the area that is now the state of Hawaii."

Note
1 Readers can access more information about United States laws related to archaeological resources, including summaries of the laws and the statute texts in "Archeological laws: a guide for professionals" at www.cr.nps.gov/archeology/tools/laws/index.html, accessed 22 February 2006.

contains the most detailed direction on how "Native American" and "Native Hawaiian" human remains are to be treated by public agencies and museums subject to the law.

There are several important limitations to the application of these national laws. In general they apply only on public lands, that is, land owned or controlled by the national government. This covers approximately third of the landmass of the United States, so it is a substantial area. They do not, however, apply to private land or to the land held by states. An important distinction of NAGPRA, however, is that it does apply to collections held by museums that receive federal funding. The legal interpretation of receiving federal funding is so broad that in the United States this includes virtually every museum that is open to the public. The collections covered by the law are not limited to those that contain objects or human remains from public lands. NAGPRA's collections-related requirements apply to federal agency collections and to collections held by museums that receive federal funding no matter where in the United States the objects and remains come from.

NAGPRA also contains important restrictions on the kinds of objects it covers. Only a limited range of objects from archaeological sites are covered. Specifically, in addition to human remains, these include: "funerary objects," "sacred objects," and "objects of cultural patrimony." Since this chapter focuses on human remains, the other object definitions are not described, but interested readers can check more specific sources[7] for detailed descriptions. Of course, NAGPRA also applies only to human remains that are "Native American" or "Native Hawaiian" (Table 16.2). Human remains of individuals from other ethnic groups need not be treated following the strictures of NAGPRA and its regulations.

Each of these statutes is supplemented by a set of regulations. Based on the language of the law and consistent with any congressional reports that accompany the law, regulations provide more detailed procedures of what must be done, and by whom, to implement a law.

The regulation most pertinent to the care and use of federal archaeological collections is found in Title 36 of the Code of Federal Regulations, Part 79.[8] Entitled *Curation of Federally-Owned and Administered Archaeological Collections,* it describes the activities necessary by federal agencies for the management and preservation, including appropriate use, of archaeological collections made as the result of their actions under the Antiquities Act, ARPA, and several other statutes. Section 79.10 of the regulation covers allowable uses of federal archaeological collections. Since human remains from archaeological sites may be "archaeological resources," these guidelines apply to them as well as to artifacts and other items from archaeological contexts.[9]

Federal officials are required by the regulation to ensure that collections are available for "scientific, educational, and religious uses, subject to such terms and conditions as are necessary to protect and preserve the condition, research potential, religious or sacred importance, and uniqueness of the collection."[10] When a collection is from Indian land, the relevant Indian tribe or landowner may place additional conditions on any request to study the collection.[11] If the collection is from a site that the responsible federal official has determined is of religious or cultural importance to an Indian tribe with historic ties to the site, the federal official may place additional conditions on any study of the collection.[12] The regulations encourage research on federal archaeological collections, including those that include human remains from archaeological sites. When the study of human remains is proposed, extra planning and review is normally required and certain conditions may be placed on studies in some circumstances.

Similarly, NAGPRA and its regulations do not place an outright prohibition on the study of Native American human remains from archaeological sites. However, under most circumstances, Indian tribes that are "culturally affiliated" with Native American human remains control access to these sets of remains and therefore may prohibit, or set conditions for, any studies of the remains. It is important to understand, therefore, what is meant by being "culturally affiliated." For the purposes of determining whether or not an Indian tribe can have a set of Native American remains repatriated to it under NAGPRA, cultural affiliation between the set of remains and the tribe must be determined.

> *Cultural affiliation* means that there is a relationship of shared group identity which can be reasonably traced historically or prehistorically between a present day Indian tribe or Native Hawaiian organization and an identifiable earlier group.[13]

There are three components to determining that a relationship of cultural affiliation exists. First, there must be a modern tribe as the claimant. For purposes of NAGPRA, the tribe must be one that is recognized formally by the Bureau of Indian Affairs and the Department of the Interior. There must also be an earlier group that the individual set of human remains is associated with and the characteristics of the culture of that group should be fairly well known so that they can be compared with the culture of the modern tribe. The third critical component is that a "relationship of shared group identity" must be "reasonably traced" between the modern and the older group. This last component is usually the most difficult one to establish. For situations involving the relatively recent past, for example, showing a reasonably traced relation of shared group identity between a modern Puebloan or Apachean tribe and a set of human remains from a five- or six-hundred-year-old site near the current location of the modern tribe might be easily done. However, as time depth increases and geographic proximity is reduced, relationships of shared group identity become less generally agreed. In a recent prominent situation in Washington State, federal judges overturned a determination of cultural affiliation made by the Secretary of the Interior regarding an 8,000-year-old skeleton. The Secretary of the Interior had reached his determination based primarily on oral history evidence derived from traditional histories of the Indian tribes that had claimed the remains. Federal judges at both the district and circuit court of appeals levels, evaluating all the available evidence, pointed out that the oral history was contradicted by other evidence that the Department of the Interior seem to have ignored. They also pointed out that the oral history evidence could not be considered reliable and its historical roots were unlikely to extend to 8,000 years ago.[14]

While NAGPRA provides only a simple framework for how to make determinations of cultural affiliation, it does provide a list of the kinds of evidence that should be applied in attempting to reach determinations.

> Cultural affiliation is established when the preponderance of evidence – based upon geographical, kinship, biological, archaeological, anthropological, linguistic, folklore, oral tradition, historical, or other relevant information or expert opinion – reasonably leads to such a conclusion.[15]

This section of the guidance also points out that a "preponderance" of evidence, not overwhelming evidence or evidence beyond the shadow of a doubt, is the standard for making cultural affiliation decisions.

The Native American Graves Protection and Repatriation Act also takes account of a possibly more direct affinity between Native American human remains and individuals. This individual relationship is referred to as "lineal descent." A relationship of lineal descent is said to exist when a modern individual can be shown to trace:

> ... his or her ancestry directly and without interruption by means of the traditional kinship system of the appropriate Indian tribe or Native Hawaiian organization or by the common law system of descendance to a known

Native American individual whose remains, funerary objects, or sacred objects are being claimed.[16]

This kind of strong and especially well-documented relationship is relatively rare and not dealt with any further here.

The next two sections review a number of policies and guidelines developed by different public agencies and museums for research on and interpretive display of human remains from archaeological sites in light of the legal framework sketched above.

Policies and guidance regarding research on human remains from archaeological contexts

In the United States, various public agencies and museums have written policies concerning research on human remains in their collections. The creation of these explicit policy statements has much to do with the requirements faced by federal agencies and public museums required to deal with Native American human remains under NAGPRA since 1990. Some of the policies have been written generally enough to take account of the human remains of other ethnic groups as well. While the information summarized here is not from a comprehensive survey of all the institutions that curate these kinds of archaeological remains, a general pattern can be discerned.

National Park Service (NPS) policies allow for study of human remains from archaeological sites with some conditions being placed on such studies. For NPS archaeological collections, managers:

> … may allow access to, and study, publication [as in a report], and destructive analysis of, human remains, but must consult with traditionally associated peoples and consider their opinions and concerns… . Such use of human remains will occur only with an approved research proposal that describes why the information cannot be obtained through other sources or analysis, and why the research is important to the field of study and the general public.[17]

Consultation with "traditionally associated peoples" is required before a study is approved. Traditionally, associated people are communities or other recognized groups, including Indian tribes, that have multigenerational relationships with the park unit or archaeological site from which the collection to be studied derives.[18] The other main requirement is that the proposed research, whether conducted by NPS staff experts or researchers applying to undertake investigation of NPS collections, must be determined to be important based upon review of a detailed research proposal. Park superintendents are responsible for making decisions about whether or not to permit such research, but their decisions are to be informed by technical and policy advice from NPS archaeologists who also review the proposals.[19] Within these general guidelines, curatorial staff at individual parks may develop more detailed agreements for curation of collections that include human remains from archaeological sites, as has been developed between parks in the Flagstaff, Arizona area and the Museum of Northern Arizona.

The United States Army Corps of Engineers (CEO), which constructs and manages substantial water control facilities and projects throughout the country, has a policy requiring that "District Commanders ensure that archaeological collections are available for scientific and educational uses by qualified professionals ... including access for study ... exhibits, teaching, public interpretations, scientific analysis and scholarly research."[20] When the human remains from collections are subject to NAGPRA, the CEO procedures require compliance with these regulations as part of the conditions before conducting any research activities.

Parks Canada's *Management Directive 2.3.1*[21] applies to human remains from within Parks Canada units that are found *in situ* in archaeological sites, as well as human remains from archaeological contexts now in museum collections. The policy requires that when the remains are determined to be those of "an Aboriginal person" the "... nearest Aboriginal organization or other community of Aboriginal people that is willing to act as the next of kin and whose members have sense of relationship ..." with the person represented by the remains will determine whether any study of the remains will be allowed. The management directive allows for "minimal investigation and documentation ... for identification purposes."[22] However, any additional archaeological or scientific study must be "... deemed necessary or wanted by the culturally affiliated group or next-of-kin ..." in order to be allowed.[23]

In the United States, public museums and university departments that curate human remains have developed specific procedures for dealing with requests for investigations of the remains. A number of examples are summarized in this section. The Department of Anthropology at the University of Illinois at Urbana-Champaign curates archaeological collections that include approximately 815 culturally unidentifiable Native American human remains from about 82 archaeological sites. The department's policy calls for these human remains to be made available to qualified researchers for scientific inquiry, including destructive analysis, if justified.[24] The department's policy requires that proposals be reviewed by the Osteology Committee of the department. The policy acknowledges that culturally affiliated remains subject to NAGPRA will be handled in accordance with NAGPRA requirements. Also, the policy prohibits adding to its collections any human remains that would be subject to NAGPRA for which lineal descendants or culturally affiliated tribes have been determined, without the permission of those entities.

The Florida Museum of Natural History, which reported curating 2,609 culturally unaffiliated Native American human remains from 157 archaeological sites, requires that proposals for testing, study, or loan be reviewed by the appropriate museum curator. The museum recognizes additional legal requirement by stating that further restrictions, which are not specified, may apply to collections from the United States that are subject to NAGPRA.[25]

The University of California at its various campuses that have human remains in their collections applies a consistent set of procedures. The main campuses, Berkeley, Davis, Los Angeles, Riverside, Santa Barbara, and Santa Cruz, report over 11,000 sets of culturally unidentifiable Native American remains from about 750 different sites in their collections. Human remains from archaeological sites normally are accessible for research by qualified investigators subject to approval by the appropriate curator. However, when NAGPRA applies, once a repatriation request has been granted, items covered by the request shall not be used for teaching or research without the consent of the tribal authority that has been determined to be culturally affiliated (that is, granted right of repatriation). Similar conditions apply when a tribe has been determined to be culturally affiliated and other aspects of the repatriation requirements have been met, but the tribe has not yet sought repatriation.[26]

The National Museum of Natural History, part of the Smithsonian Institution, curates nearly 16,000 sets of human remains from archaeological sites (see Table 16.1).[27] The museum allows non-destructive research on human remains. However, if the remains are Native American and have been determined to be culturally affiliated with a tribe, that tribe must either be consulted or give consent to the research proposed.[28]

The American Museum of Natural History in New York City reports curating 1,960 culturally unidentifiable Native American human remains from 395 different sites. The museum evaluates requests for study of these collections on a case-by-case basis.[29] The field Museum of Natural History and Science in Chicago reports curating 1,256 sets of culturally unaffiliated Native American human remains from 122 sites. At the Field, the curator in charge of the collection reviews all study requests. Requests related to Native American human remains require consultation with culturally affiliated Indian tribes and the results of this consultation are taken into account by the curator while reviewing any study request.[30]

In summary, the main issue regarding research of human remains from archaeological sites in Canada and the United states involves whether or not the remains are Native American. For Native American remains, whether or not, not what, kind of research will be permitted is controlled largely by culturally affiliated Indian tribes. For remains for which a cultural affiliation has not been determined, the curatorial facility or museum decides what research is allowed. Readers also should recognize that the term "culturally affiliated" differs between the Parks Canada definition from its management directive and the definition under NAGPRA in the United States.

Regarding the human remains of other ethnic groups, specific laws or procedures have not been established. However, the National Park Service policies and the Parks Canada directive are written generally enough to take account of all human remains, not only those related to modern Indian tribes. The policies, while in effect only within the boundaries of National Park Service and Parks Canada unites, may serve as examples for situations outside of these specific jurisdictions.

Policies and guidance regarding museum display of human remains from archaeological contexts

In the United States and Canada, there are no national laws that deal with issues related to the museum display or exhibition of human remains. This topic has been addressed by some individual public agencies and museums in their own policies because of concerns expressed by representatives of descendant groups. These expressions have come mainly from Native Americans and certainly are consistent with the range of concerns that have received more attention due to the legal requirements established in the United States by NAGPRA. As with the research policies summarized in the last section, policies about display are often written generally enough to cover human remains of other ethnic groups in addition to Native Americans.

In the United States, the National Park Service has written policies on the display of human remains in exhibits at park units. The policy that covers both Native American and other human remains states that:

> Native American human remains and photographs of such remains will not be exhibited. Drawings, render or casts of such remains may be exhibited with the consent of culturally affiliated Indian tribes.... The exhibit of non Native American human remains, or photographs, drawings, renderings, or cast of such remains, is allowed in consultation with traditionally associated people.[31]

This policy was developed taking into account strong and consistent statements by representatives of Indian tribes and other Native Americans with whom NPS officials have consulted. The policy permits the use of illustrations of Native American human remains, such as drawings, casts, or other renderings in displays and exhibits with the consent of culturally affiliated Indian tribes or lineal descendants. The display of photos of non-Native American human remains showing skeletons, as well as other kinds of illustrations is allowed, however consultation with traditionally associated groups must occur before any decision is made on such display.

Among other public agencies in North America whose policies were reviewed for this article, the Parks Canada directive addresses the display of remains only generally because its focus is on the investigation and repatriation of human remains.[32] One of the general principles of the directive provides guidance on the matter of display, noting that:

> Parks Canada will not display human remains to the public. However, reproductions or images may be displayed if consent is given by the culturally affiliated group or next of kin.[33]

In the United States, in addition to the NPS policy summarized above, the Corps of Engineers'[34] policy for cultural resource stewardship prohibits the display of human remains: "human skeletal remains shall not be placed on display or exhibited for public viewing in any fashion." This prohibition is not qualified in any manner and covers human remains from any ethnic group. The policy does not address the use of photos or other kinds of illustrations.

The Department of Anthropology, University of Illinois at Urbana-Champaign has a policy that human remains in its collections may be used for educational and teaching purposes with the approval of the head of department. There is no reference to uses for public display or interpretive displays in the policy. Readers also should recall that the overall policy of the department states that North American human remains for which cultural affiliation or lineal descent has been determined may not be added to the collection without permission of the affiliated tribe or lineal descendants.[35] The Florida Museum of Natural History states in its policies that no specimens, casts, or images of osteological specimens shall be used for public display. In addition, that "images of human skeletal material shall be for research purposes only and such images are not considered appropriate for public exhibition."[36]

At several major public museums in the United States, the Natural History Museum at the Smithsonian, the American Museum of Natural History in New York, and the Field Museum in Chicago, no formal written policies exist regarding the display of human remains in museum exhibits. Decisions are typically addressed on a case-by-case basis. For example, in the *Vikings in America* exhibit which originated at the Natural History Museum, Smithsonian Institution in 2000 and travelled to the American Museum of Natural History and other museums nationally and internationally, human remains from Greenland were included in the displays of the opening section of the exhibition. In the international exhibition *Crossroads of the Continents*, also developed at the Smithsonian and followed by a multination tour, photos of human burials were used along with artifacts recovered from the burial, but no actual bones.

There is a strong pattern in the existing policies, formal or informal, not to display Native American human remains. These policies result from the consistent and frequent statements by Native American representatives that such pubic display, no matter what positive educational results it might involve, is offensive and hurtful to Indian people. By and large, museum and public agency officials acknowledge these statements and have taken account of them in planning and developing new exhibitions and educational materials. Human remains of individuals from other ethnic groups sometimes are included in displays, but only after careful consideration, possibly including consultation with representatives of the ethnic group concerned, and the determination by curators and educators designing the exhibit that inclusion is required for the planned display to be effective. Overall, it seems that use of human remains in museum exhibits in North America is much less common that it may have been in the past.

Patterns of practice in the study or display of human remains from archaeological contexts

Whether evaluating requests by potential researchers to study museum human remains or considering the possible use of human remains in a new display, many public agency and museum policies in North America include consultation with closely related Indian tribes or other descendant groups. When the human remains involved have been determined to be "culturally affiliated" with the tribe being consulted, the consent of the tribe often is required. Reliance on this "cultural affiliation" to determine who will have authority over how the human remains are treated means that the way in which the term is defined and the steps that are used in reaching such determinations are important. The concept has sometimes been extended to establish associations between skeletons of other ethnic groups and modern descendant communities or traditionally associated groups that claim them. The Parks Canada (2000) directive uses a different definition for the term from that used in United States law, basing the relationship on either religious affiliation, if it can be determined, or geographical proximity in the case of aboriginal burials.

Table 16.3 is an attempt to outline who is recognized as the "decision maker" in current practice when living individuals or the remains of deceased humans from different contexts and chronological placement are involved. The list begins with modern individuals who have legal rights to decide whether or not to submit themselves to medical procedures or scientific investigations. The doctrine requiring that "informed consent" be obtained from individuals serving as subjects in medical or scientific studies is well established. Similar requirements of informed consent are applied in other kinds of human subject scientific research.[37]

Unless individuals have left explicit written instructions about how they wish to be treated in case they are incapacitated or die unexpectedly, it is generally accepted that the next-of-kin will make decisions about providing or withholding treatment and whether post-mortem investigations are undertaken. For some individuals from historical archaeological contexts, the concept of "lineal descendant," as defined in United States law by the NAGPRA regulations, might serve as a substitute for next-of-kin in deciding about post-excavation treatment. This hypothetical circumstance is illustrated as category 3 in Table 16.3.

For individual sets of human remains lacking the historical connections to establish next-of-kin or lineal descendant relationships, "cultural affiliation," based upon the concept used in NAGPRA, but more generalized, might be useful for determining who should make decisions regarding treatment.

Table 16.3 Treatment decisions based upon degree of affinity and age of remains

Individual/remains of concern	Authority/decision maker
1. Modern individual	Self, based on informed consent
2. Modern individual, incapacitated	Next of kin; designated individual, informed consent
3. Remains of a historically known individual from archaeological context	Lineal descendant: a modern individual tracing his or her ancestry directly and without interruption by means of a traditional kinship system or common-law system of descendance to the historically known individual
4. Remains of an individual from an ancient archaeological context for whom cultural affiliation can be determined	Culturally affiliated modern group
5. Remains of an individual from an ancient archaeological context for whom cultural affiliation cannot be determined	Public agency or museum officials

Another frequently considered topic regarding research on human remains in the collections of pubic agencies or museums is whether or not proposed research involves any destructive techniques such as removing bone for radiocarbon dating, ancient DNA analysis, or other chemical studies, or thin-sectioning human bone. Such techniques require the consumption of a portion of the human remains being studied. Proposals to conduct research that includes destructive techniques typically require an additional level of review before they are approved. In the United States, when the request involves Native American human remains for which a positive determination of cultural affiliation has been made, consent by the affiliated tribe would be required. In fact, some public agencies and museums would require tribal consent even for non-destructive research on culturally affiliated Native American human remains, as the Parks Canada policy directive.

The simple outline illustrated by Table 16.3 may provide a series of useful categories into which human remains from archaeological contexts can be grouped and for which consistent and standard methods for deciding who should make decisions about their treatment and what kinds of treatments should be allowed can be developed. This simple organizational framework does not delve into questions of how concepts like "cultural affiliation" will be determined in specific instances, what types of evidence are suitable for making such determinations, or how the evidence is evaluated in terms of reliability, independence, consistency, and credibility. Developing agreed concepts and method is essential. Yet there is much ground to be covered in this area. Readers will recall, for example, that even the term "cultural affiliation" is used differently in the United States law and Parks Canada policy described in this article.

Agreed concepts and methods are essential for any generalized system and are among the most complex matters in need of resolution. The difficulty of determining group ownership and of evaluating assertions of group ownership of ancient and historical objects or human remains is recognized by experts who have reviewed this topic.

> Ethical issues are … raised when ownership of historical objects is claimed by a group that defines itself by religious affiliation, tribe, or family line. Group consent is extremely complicated because of the elusive nature of cultural property and its ownership. Existing codes provide little guidance regarding the identification of a relevant group and the duties owed.[38]

In situations for which no individual or affiliated group can claim legitimate authority to determine the treatment of human remains from archaeological contexts, the public authority responsible for the remains, whether a government agency, public museum, or educational organization, might be authorized to do so, as illustrated in category 5 of Table 16.3.

The laws, regulations, policies, guidelines, and procedures developed in North America regarding research on and display of human remains from archaeological contexts provide frameworks for decision-making rather than simple formulas leading to a single "correct" treatment for sets of remains.

The treatment of human remains often is an emotionally charged topic. Recognition that many of the different goals being put forward are worthwhile may help to reduce the antagonism that can arise in confrontations, and even in discussions. Some of the goals may even be compatible, or at least not conflicting.

One important and worthwhile goal, also part of national public policy in Canada and the United States, is respectful treatment for present-day cultural sensitivities and ancestral human remains. Certainly, public concern about how human remains are treated has grown in the last generation. Personal contemporary concerns have been heightened with increased interest in family histories, personal privacy, individual genetic characteristics, and personal records of all sorts.

Another important and worthy public goal is advancing knowledge and providing fuller interpretations and better understanding of the ancient and historical past by analyzing skeletal remains. For over a century, national laws in the United States have been enacted in recognition of this value of archaeological remains. Established national policies and procedures support the scientific and historical study of archaeological sites and their contents, including human skeletal remains. It is important that such studies have as one of their outcomes the provision of broader public access and information about the results of the investigations. Public appreciation of a fuller and improved understanding of the past derived from these studies is necessary at some level for public support for such studies to continue.[39]

In North America, there is an additional challenge for public outreach on this topic. Many North Americans do not recognize the ancient American past and archaeological resources associated with it as a part of their own heritage. If someone does not hold a stake in something, he or she is less likely to be concerned with how it is treated and what happens to it. Yet, if all of us are Americans now, the remains from America's ancient past are ours to care of and make decisions about.[40]

The web of concerns about how to treat human remains from archaeological contexts, whether one regards them as ancestors, informants, or scientific specimens, must be woven into a fabric that can reconcile all these perspectives. The diversity of culture, knowledge, and talent gives the nations in North America one of their great strengths. The ability to work together, appreciating national commonalities, is a skill that North Americans value and strive to achieve. Overcoming difficulties and reaching mutually satisfactory resolutions in the situations dealt with in this article try the strength and skills of those involved.

Notes and references

1. This article has been prepared as work of private scholarship. It is not an official statement of the National Park Service or the Department of the Interior.
2. National Park Service, (2004a) *National NAGPRA Program, Final Mid-Year Report, FY 31 March 2004*, National Park Service, Department of the Interior, Washington DC. www.cr.nps-gov/nagpra (accessed 24 October 2004).
3. Harrington, Spencer P M, (1993). "Bones and bureaucrats: New York's great cemetery imbroglio," in *Archaeology*, March/April 1993, pp. 28–8.
4. Crist, Thomas A J, (2002), "The relevance of mortuary archaeology," in *Public Benefits of Archaeology,* edited by Barbara J Little, University of Florida, pp. 101–17.

5   Natural Resources Conservation Service, (1997), *Compilation of State Repatriation Reburial, and Grave Protection Laws* (2nd edition), Natural Resources Conservation Service, Department of Agriculture, Washington DC.
6   Parks Canada, (2000), *Management Directive 2.3.1 Human Remains, Cemeteries and Burial Grounds (File C-8412)*. Archaeological services Branch, National Historic Sites Directorate, Parks Canada, Ottawa.
7   For example: McManamon, Francis P, (1992), "Managing repatriation: implementing the Native American Graves Protection and Repatriation Act," CRM 15(5), www.cr.nps.gov/archeology/sites/fpm_crm.htm; (2000), "The Native American Graves Protection and Repatriation Act," in *Archaeological Method and Theory: An Encyclopedia*, edited by Linda Ellis, Garland Publishing Inc, New York and London, pp. 387–9, (2003), "An Introduction to the Native American Graves Protection and Repatriation Act,".
8   The shorthand for this regulation is 36 CFR 79.
9   A much fuller discussion of the care and curation of public archaeological collections, including more information about research on archaeological collections, can be found in Childs, S Terry, (2005), *Managing Archeological Collections: An Online Course*, Archeology Program, National Center for Cultural Resources, National Park Service, Washington DC.
10 *Op cit* 36 CFR 79, 10(a).
11 *Op cit* 36 CFR 79, 10(d)(3).
12 *Op cit* 36 CFR 79, 10(d)(4).
13 "Cultural affiliation" is defined in the statute, 25 USC 3001, Section 2(1). It is further described in the regulations 43 CFR 10.1(e). These regulations provide additional directions for implementation of the law.
14 Ninth Circuit United States Court of Appeals, (2004), *Bonnichsen v United States*, 367 F3d 864 (9th Cir 2004), www.friendsofpast.org/kennewick-man/court/opinions/040204opinion.html (accessed 28 February 2005).
15 Title 43 of the Code of Federal Regulations, Part 10, *op cit* 1(e).
16 *Ibid* 2(b)(I).
17 National Park Service, (2001), *Management policies (2001)*, "Stewardship of human remains and burials – research," section 5.3.4, Department of the Interior, Washington DC, www.nps.gov/refdesk/policies.html, accessed 24 October 2004.
18 *Ibid* section 5.3.5.3, p57.
19 National Park Service, (2004b), *Director's Order #28A*, National Park Service, Department of the Interior, Washington DC.
20 Corps of Engineers, (1996), "Chapter 6 – Cultural Resources Stewardship," ER 1130-2-540, 15 November 1996, pp. 6–1 to 6–5, Corps of Engineers, Department of the Army, Washington DC.
21 Parks Canada, (2000), *Management Directive 2.3.1, Human Remains, Cemeteries and Burial Grounds (File: C-8412)*, Archaeological Services Branch, National Historic Sites Directorate, Parks Canada, Ottawa.
22 *Ibid* p10.
23 *Ibid* p14.
24 University of Illinois at Urbana-Champaign, (2001), *Policy for the Acquisition, Treatment, and Disposition of Human Remains and Funerary Objects of United States Origin by the Department of Anthropology*. University of Illinois at Urbana-Champaign.
25 Florida Museum of Natural History, (2004), *Policies for Use of FLMNH Human Osteological Collections*, Museum of Natural History, University of Florida, Gainesville.

26 University of California, (2001), "Policy and procedures of curation and repatriation of human remains and cultural items," Office of the President, University of California, Oakland, accessed 25 October 2004
27 Flynn, Gillian, (1998), *Annual Report on Repatriation Activities at the National Museum of Natural History, June 1997 to June 1998,* Repatriation Office, Department of Anthropology, National Museum of Natural History, Smithsonian Institution. Washington, DC.
28 *Ibid* Smithsonian Directive 600, (1999), *Collections Management,* Smithsonian Institution, Washington, DC.
29 Personal communication, F P McManamon and David Hurst Thomas, Curator, American Museum of Natural History, 24 October 2004.
30 Personal communication, F P McManamon and Jonathan Haas, MacAuthur Curator of the Americas, Field Museum, 24 Oct 2004.
31 National Park Service (2001), *Management Policies 2001*, Section 5.3.4, "Stewardship of human remains and burials – display," National Park Service, Washington, DC.
32 Parks Canada, (2000), *Management Directive 2.3.1, Human Remains, Cemeteries, and Burial Grounds (File: C-8412),* Archaeological Services Branch, National Historic Sites Directorate, Parks Canada, Ottawa *Supra* Note 10.
33 *Ibid* p7.
34 *Op cit* Corps of Engineers, (1996).
35 *Op cit* University of Illinois at Urbana Champaign, (2001).
36 *Op cit* Florida Museum of Natural History, (2004).
37 For example, the United States government requires certain procedures for human subject medical and scientific research, as described in "Protection of Human Subjects." Title 45 of the Code of Federal Regulations, Part 46, Department of Health and Human Services.
38 Andrews, Lori B, *et al,* (2004), "Constructing ethical guidelines for biohistory," in *Science* 304:215–16.
39 McManamon, Francis P, (1999), "The Native American Graves Protection and Repatriation Act and First Americans research," in *Who Were the First Americans: Proceedings of the 58th Annual Biology colloquium, Oregon State University,* edited by Robson Bonnichsen, Center for the Study of the First Americans, Corvallis, Oregon, pp. 141–52.
40 McManamon, Francis P, (2003), "Archaeology, nationalism, and ancient America," in *The Politics of Archaeology and Identity in a Global Context,* edited by Susan Kane, Archaeological Institute of America, Boston, Massachusetts, pp. 115–38.

Chapter 17

Covering up the mummies

Tiffany Jenkins

A confluence of influences has contributed to problematizing the holding of human remains in collections. In particular, these are the crisis of cultural authority contributing to professional activism and weak resistance to it, and the rise of the body as a site of identity and political struggle. So far I have examined this development in relation to remains from overseas indigenous groups, and the formation and impact of a particular Pagan group. This chapter analyses the activity around uncontested human remains, focusing primarily on their display, and further examining the influences and limits to the construction of this problem by looking in greater detail at the interaction between professionals and particular bodies. The impact of concerns about human remains on those uncontested is eclectic and inconsistent, but there is an identifiable impact. I first discuss the exhibition of the bog body Lindow Man, then the covering of Egyptian Mummies at Manchester Museum. Following which I present further analysis of the respect discourse and the policies of particular museums. Finally, I turn to the exhibition *Skeletons: London's Buried Bones*, where I suggest professionals are attempting to reauthorize scientific research and the display of bodies by adopting the discourse of identity work.

Exhibiting Lindow Man

Bog bodies – preserved ancient human bodies found in sphagnum bogs – are an archaeological phenomenon that has attracted extensive scholarly and public attention since the bodies were first discovered, in the eighteenth century, in Northern Europe, Britain, and Ireland. Thanks to the conditions of the bog, many have preserved skin and internal organs, hair and body parts, which means that they resemble the human person more closely than ancient skeletons. As well as extensive academic research, bog bodies have been the inspiration for popular writing, artwork and poetry, such as that of Seamus Heaney (1975).

Archaeologist Nina Nordström (2007) describes how certain bodies from the past become the subjects of great public and academic interest. There are various contributing factors to this, she suggests, deriving from the particular bodies as well

Source: *Contesting Human Remains in Museum Collections: The Crisis of Cultural Authority*. T. Jenkins. New York & Abingdon: Routledge, 2011. pp. 121–139 © Taylor & Francis.

as the cultural climate in which they are discussed. Despite the influence of the present on how we view these bodies, Nordström makes the point that our consistent ambition is to find out 'the truth' about them: who they were and how they lived. This is an observation that should be borne in mind as we discuss the process and outcome of the Lindow Man exhibition.

Lindow Man is the name given to the naturally preserved bog body of a man from the late Iron Age, discovered in the mid-1980s in a peat bog at Lindow Moss, North England. He is Britain's best-known and most studied bog body. Archaeologists Stead, Bourke, and Brothwell (1986) edited the first comprehensive book on Lindow Man, which compiles all the initial different strands of research that had been carried out on the body. This was followed by a number of works (see for instance, Turner and Scaife 1995). Questions considered pertain to discovering who Lindow Man was, how he lived, what he ate, what he wore and hunted with, what religion he might have been, what ritualistic practices he might have partaken in, when he lived, and how he died. He is of particular interest due to speculation that he was the victim of a sacrificial killing.

Hallam, Hockey, and Howarth (1999) explain that with specific cultural and specific institutional contexts, such as the passage of time and the establishment of the coroner's court, the body parts of the dead shift from the category of 'dead body' to that of 'anatomical objects'. As an example of this re-contextualization, they describe the status of Tollund Man, a bog body from the fourth century BC, found in Denmark in 1950. Hallam, Hockey, and Howarth argue that this bog body is no longer considered a 'dead body' because he falls outside of social relationships. Instead, they posit, he has become an anatomical object due to the context in which is displayed: '[H]e became a clinical object, a focus for scientific interrogation, an objectified ornament of antiquity. The Tollund Man, as he is now known, lies in a glass case in the Museum of Silkeborg' (Hallam, Hockey, and Howarth 1999: 92). Given that bog bodies fall outside social relationships, and are not tied to a contemporary claims-making group or associated with a particular past – unlike the human remains of Aboriginal peoples – how is Lindow Man considered in the period of the controversy over human remains?

Lindow Man is usually held in the British Museum, but was loaned for a temporary period to Manchester University Museum (MUM). Earlier exhibitions at MUM in 1987 and 1991 examined Lindow Man's life and times and presented the results of the latest forensic work. The exhibition of 1987 was one of the most popular in the history of the museum (Alberti et al. 2009). The 2008–2009 exhibition *Lindow Man: A Bog Body Mystery* drew upon research carried out over the past 25 years and aimed to explore the different meanings that Lindow Man's body holds for different people. The explicit intention was to reflect changes in society and in academic thinking that had taken place since then. As Bryan Sitch, curator and Head of Humanities at MUM, explained:

> When it accepted the offer of the British Museum to lend the body of Lindow Man for a year, the Manchester Museum was anxious to take account not only of changing academic interpretations of the discovery but

also of increasing sensitivity towards human remains within society more generally.

(Sitch 2009: 52)

Sitch continues: '[H]uman remains had become more contentious, partly because of the Alder Hey scandal, in which it emerged that organs had been removed by hospitals from hundreds of deceased children without the families' permission', and also 'because of the repatriation of human remains to indigenous communities in Australia, New Zealand and the Americas'. In addition, he notes 'the voices of marginalized groups such as pagans, whose relationship with the dead is based on spirituality and a respect for the ancestors', thereby associating these three issues together.

The museum ran a consultation on the exhibition, to which a number of Pagans, archaeologists, curators, and local figures were invited and I attended. Two meetings were held, at the museum, one in February 2007 and the other a year later in February 2008. Piotr Bienkowski, the deputy director of Manchester University Museum, opened the first meeting, stating:

> At Manchester Museum we are increasingly consulting as a museum with all stakeholders. We no longer stand as a single authoritative voice – those days are gone. There is an exciting wide range of voices here: museum staff, university staff, archaeologists, councillor Paul Murphy, the community advisory panel, Pagans, and Honouring the Ancient Dead: I hope I haven't missed anyone out. The plan is to produce a unique exhibition. We don't want to produce just one view, we want to bring out different ways of presenting different views of Lindow Man. We want your views, not just those of the traditional establishment voices.

This represents a clear attempt to portray the new inclusive museum as different to the past, and moving away from the 'traditional establishment voices'.

At the first meeting for the consultation, participants were asked by Bryan Sitch and Piotr Bienkowski, who coordinated the event, how they felt about exhibiting Lindow Man; specifically whether he should be buried and what would constitute respectful treatment. Despite anticipation that there would be disquiet about his display, what was notable about the consultation was that no one argued for the burial of Lindow Man. Nor did participants have firm ideas about how to organize the exhibition. Instead, those consulted raised a variety of different concerns, all of which had very little to do with this particular bog body. In short, Lindow Man became a vehicle for their individual preoccupations.

The Labour Councillor, Paul Murphy, wanted to raise the issue of multiculturalism through the exhibition, and was worried about how to entice local visitors into the museum. He speculated that the museum could show that his constituency was genetically related to Lindow Man, through DNA research, which would make the show relevant to them. He posed the question of how the museum could involve the Afro-Caribbean community members of his ward, which revealed this councillor's underlying concerns about connecting to the electorate. A couple of archaeologists ventured that the exhibition could foster an interest in the past, in order to address contemporary confusion about identity. One Druid suggested that the display of Lindow Man could promote a sense of community. A number of Pagans and archaeologists thought the exhibition could stimulate discussions about death, and confront what they described as the 'death taboo' of the present period. Three archaeologists argued that the display of Lindow Man could draw attention to the problem of the environment, by flagging up the nature of the peat bog in which he was found and how it is threatened by building on the site. As the following exchange demonstrates, the promotion of multiculturalism and identity was an accepted concern of this meeting:

> *Councillor:* It's good to hear about Paganism. It should be central in the exhibition. It shows that multiculturalism is possible through this exhibition.
> *Sitch:* Yes it's important to discuss diversity. Pupils should show an understanding of different views. If they can understand Lindow Man maybe they can understand what it is to be a Muslim.

The particular concerns about diversity are projected on to Lindow Man (and Paganism) as potential themes of the exhibition, although there is no obvious reason why the exhibition of a bog body from the Iron Age would address Muslim identity, or multiculturalism more broadly. Bryan Sitch subsequently suggested that Lindow Man could be an 'ambassador for diversity' – for if the audience could understand Lindow Man, they might be able to 'appreciate that other people are different too'. In the report on the consultation, Sitch wrote:

> Lindow man could be a company ambassador. If schools, children and students can be taught to appreciate his way of life, some sense of his spiritual values in so far as they can be reconstructed from 2000 years ago, how much easier might it be for the same children to understand a present day religion or culture?
> (Sitch 2007a: 8)

In a similar vein, Sitch suggested that the show might help promotion constructive discussion about the environment and terrorism:

> There is also the question of his relationship with the landscape and the importance of green issues in present day society. Potentially there are wider issues involving ethnic diversity, regional identity, and even terrorism.
> (Sitch 2007a: 9)

Overall, nobody argued that having Lindow Man on display was a problem, and very few were interested in the particular body or its history. The majority of attendees at this consultation used Lindow Man to discuss their specific preoccupations. Despite the rhetoric of concern about how human remains should be treated in museums, and the specific consultation on Lindow Man being held ostensibly in response to this concern, the bog body itself was not an object of concern. Rather, Lindow Man was a focus for participants' interests, which were influenced by present day preoccupations that included identity, multiculturalism, and environmentalism.

The main conclusion reached after consultation was that the diversity of opinion and interpretation about Lindow Man, from within academia and the public, should be centrally promoted in the exhibition. This approach was counterpoised to previous ways of exhibiting the bog body, which, it was suggested, falsely implied a degree of certainty about the theories of how Lindow Man lived. Previous exhibitions, it was suggested, exaggerated the knowledge of what is merely speculation about his life, and did not reflect different interpretations. The MUM show would tackle this:

> The exhibition should explore alternative points of view, including archaeological interpretation and more spiritual perspectives. It should be a questioning exhibit, particularly if there are few hard and fast facts or if the facts are disputed. It should not tell people but admit that there are some things we do not know. It could question the sensationalist glamorous interpretation of Lindow Man. There should be stories and contradictory stories.
>
> (Sitch 2007a: 3)

This approach, which questions the possibility of knowing about the life and death of Lindow Man, was made explicit in the show, by promoting a diversity of opinion and taking a pluralist approach. As the feedback to the second consultation notes, the exhibition enacted 'the principle of multivocality or "talking with more than one voice"' (Sitch 2007b: 1). In February 2008, Sitch told me that the exhibition was an 'exemplar in the museum' and that this was an example of the 'museum not speaking with a single authoritative voice'. The deliberate aim was to 'reflect uncertainty'. The show was organized around seven different interpretations of Lindow Man, through recorded personal testimony from the following people: a forensic scientist, a landscape archaeologist, two museum curators, a former peat worker, someone from the Lindow community, and Emma Restall Orr of the Pagan group Honouring the Ancient Dead. Such an approach displaces curatorial authority by presenting these interpretations as equal.

The other central theme promoted throughout the exhibition was that human remains should be treated differently to the way they were before. It was argued that previously archaeologists have treated Lindow Man as an object and that this museum would instead treat him like a person. One of the curators explained in an interview in February 2008, that the old, archaeological way of looking at Lindow Man was problematic:

> I think maybe ten years ago I would have looked at Lindow Man as an example of a wonderfully preserved bit of archaeology […] I think I now see him in a very different way, in a more emotive way and for that reason the approach that we've adopted to display Lindow Man, i.e. displaying him with sensitivity and respect, is one that I personally have a lot of sympathy for.

Archaeology, in the curator's view, was less emotional and sensitive than his own. He was not sure if the public would agree, however, reminding us that concerns about human remains are not driven by public demand.

> I think that our approach; the respectful, sensitive approach, while I find that praiseworthy, my impression is it might be in advance of what the public sensitivity actually demands. I … but I think museums can have a very important role in guiding public attitudes and on this very sensitive and emotive subject … I think it's no bad thing that we actually try and guide … not indoctrinate, but guide our public into perhaps viewing human remains in a different way than they've seen them in the past.

Activists at this museum presented archaeology and museum professionals as unemotional, controlling individuals who need to open up more and consider the different views of dead bodies, to treat them less like objects and more like people. Paradoxically, there was considerably less reflection on this particular body as a person who lived thousands of years ago. There was little discussion, compared to writing and previous exhibitions on Lindow Man, about who this person might have been and how he may have lived. Despite the rhetoric about the need to treat Lindow Man as a person, and with respect, this approach has the consequence of relegating research about his life to a lower priority.

Covering the mummies

At the time of the launch of the Lindow Man exhibition, a controversy broke out when the Manchester University Museum took the decision to cover up the three unwrapped, or partially unwrapped, Egyptian mummies. In May 2008, the unwrapped mummy of Asru, the partially unwrapped mummy of Khary, and the loaned child mummy from Stonyhurst College, usually on display, were covered with white sheets. The stated aim behind this action was to raise questions through public consultation about the treatment of human remains. The museum explained in an official statement, that the covering was due to the recognized issue of the problems with the display of human remains: 'It is now generally recognized that the display of mummies, and indeed of any human remains, is a sensitive matter.' And that 'alongside positive comments', 'a significant number of comments are regularly received from visitors who are concerned or disturbed about their display, questioning the public and educational benefit of displaying unwrapped mummies, particularly a dead child'. It explained that: 'The Manchester Museum is not against the display of human remains; rather it wishes to develop sensitive and respectful methods of displaying them.' (MUM 2008a: 1)

Museum director Nick Merriman told *BBC News:* 'We're asking the public what is the most respectful and appropriate way to display them. It's good practice rather than political correctness.' He continued, asking, 'Is it appropriate to display them this way, given that they were originally wrapped, but then unwrapped in the nineteenth century to satisfy scientific and public curiosity? It's all part of the debate.'[1]

However, Egyptian Mummies are very popular with audiences and a major draw on museum visits (Day 2006). Postcards of mummies at the British Museum are said to sell as well as those of the Rosetta Stone (Beard 1992, cited in Walker 2000: 15). They fall a long way outside of any social relationships. Consequently, there was a strong negative public and professional reaction against the covering of the mummies in this case, which was widely covered in the press. The *Daily Mail* reported Bob Partridge, chairman of the Manchester Ancient Egypt Society, as saying that the cover-up was 'absolutely incomprehensible' (Narain 2008). Partridge continued: 'The mummies have always been sensitively displayed and have been educational and informative to generations of visitors. We are shocked this has been done in advance of any results from the public.' Josh Lennon, a museum visitor, was also reported in the same article as saying: 'This is preposterous. Surely people realize that if they go to see Egyptian remains some of them may not be dressed in their best bib and tucker', and that, 'The museum response to complaints is pure Monty Python – they have now covered them from head to foot rendering the exhibition a non-exhibition. It is hilarious.'

Shortly after this reaction, in July 2008, the museum changed the display and uncovered some of the mummies. In a press release with the title 'Egyptian Mummies: we're listening to your views', it was explained that this was due to the negative public response against the action:

> Director of The Manchester Museum, Nick Merriman, commented, 'We started the consultation process with a total covering of three of the Museum's unwrapped mummies. As public feedback showed that this is not the most appropriate long-term solution, we are trying out a range of different approaches to gauge public opinion. Some of these will include techniques which are used in museums in Egypt.'
>
> (MUM 2008b)

Even so, the organization didn't retract all the attempts to further problematize human remains, in this instance, Egyptian mummies. The museum's press release stated that 'For the next phase of the consultation period, one of the mummies will be left partially unwrapped in its original display state, while another will be partially covered leaving the head, hands and feet exposed.' And that it would continue to debate this issue and undertake research into attitudes regarding display, suggesting that the issue remains potentially problematic, and that the term consultation may be used to promote a particular agenda, while presenting it as open to influence from the public:

> The Manchester Museum utilizes consultation to inform its activities, and is commissioning research into visitor responses to displaying (Egyptian) human remains on the galleries as part of the ongoing consultation process on displaying the dead. The issue of choice as to whether visitors view the mummies on display or not has been addressed by installing panels at either

end of the Egyptian galleries that indicate the presence of human remains, and offering an alternative route bypassing the galleries.

(MUM 2008b)

Future practice planned at the museum involves trying to change public attitudes. In an interview that took place in February 2008, a curator at the museum explained in relation to the Egyptian galleries:

> [W]e prepare the children before we go into the gallery and ask them how they think we should behave when we go into a gallery which is full of in effect dead people really ... and so we programmed in a prayer for the dead at the end of the session so that's very different to the way that mummies used to be the sort of um peep show, freak show, whatever ... and there's still a sense of that that comes through in visitor feedback ... that, you know, 'oh, we want to see mummies because they're scary and repulsive and what have you' ... but I think, I think as people we have the right to take a stand, and say we feel as people that we should treat human remains in a different way.

This curator advocates that the mummies should be treated as dead people, saying a prayer to them after the children have seen them. Contemporary Egyptian curators or communities are not making claims about Egyptian mummies or requesting the treatment, and it is unlikely that the original Egyptians would. The prayer seems therefore to be primarily for the professionals at this museum.

This attempt to extend the problem to uncontested human remains is an example of how certain professionals in the museum sector continue to try and target human remains as an issue. However, there were important limits to their success in doing this. In this instance the lack of claims-making group to support their actions, and strong professional and firm and publicized negative public reaction to the act of covering up the mummies, halted their attempts to problematize these particular human remains.

Analysing the discourse of respect

Piotr Bienkowski and Emma Restall Orr are not the only individuals who have made use of a discourse of respect around the issue of human remains. By early 2000, archaeologists and museum professionals build on this discourse of respect that is used to advocate action and concern in relation to all human remains (Curtis 2003; Lohman, 2006; Brooks and Rumsey 2007). The use of the term in this instance changes over time and can be broken down into three arguments. Firstly, it is argued that respect must be shown is to other cultural values and feelings about human remains. This is either respect for the original community or their present-day descendants. For example, items two and three of the Vermillion Accord, the first code of conduct on human remains, adopted in 1989 at World Archaeological Congress, advocate 'respect' for the wishes of the dead and the local community

(WAC 1990: unpaginated). In a similar vein, the Museum Ethnographers Group guidelines on human remains argues for restricted access to human remains 'where unrestricted access may cause offence or distress to actual or cultural descendants'. (MEG 1991: s.2.2) The guidance also states: 'All requests for the return of human remains should be accorded respect and treated sensitively.' (§ 4.1) Similarly concerned with the feelings of affiliated people today, the International Council of Museums (ICOM) Code requires that public display should be carried out 'with great tact and with respect for the feelings of human dignity held by all peoples' (ICOM 2002: 19), as does the Code of Ethics for Museums, published by the Museums Association, which states that museums should 'respect the interests of originating communities' (MA 2002: 17).

The second part of the case put forward for respect advocates parity of treatment. It is suggested that if some human remains are treated with special care then all should be. Edmund Southworth, curator at National Museums and Galleries on Merseyside and editor for the Society of Museum Archaeologists, points out in an article in the *Museums Journal,* titled 'A special concern', that there is a contradiction between displaying Egyptian mummies and Iron Age men, and hiding Maori heads (Southworth 1994: 23–4). Ratan Vaswani of the Museums Association also comments in the *Museums Journal*, 'The important questions we need to consider are those of consistency. By what standards do we consider it "acceptable" to exhibit Egyptian mummies but decide to withdraw Maori heads from display?' (Vaswani 2001: 35. See also Brooks and Rumsey 2007: 266). In a similar vein, Hugh Kilmister, a curator at the Petrie museum in London, suggests the removal of Egyptian remains, in order to avoid a 'double standard':

> [T]he public is generally positive about the display of ancient Egyptian remains, but we perhaps need to look to the future redisplay of these remains. This has been made more timely by the fact that contentious remains in many museums have been removed from display, but those remains that are unlikely to be repatriated have been left on exhibit, thus creating a double standard.
>
> (Kilmister 2003: 65)

Here, there is a developing sense that if one set of remains is removed from display, others left on exhibit are thus treated without similar consideration.

Thirdly, there is the thinking amongst some professionals that all remains need special treatment and protection because of their unique status. This includes the idea that remains should be taken off display or buried. Commenting on the ICOM Code, Per Kåks of the International Council of Museums Ethics Committee argued that respect is 'not just a question of showing the objects in a solemn setting, but perhaps of not showing them at all, or not allowing them to be handled except by very few and relevant persons' (Kåks 1998: 10). The International Council of Museums Code of Ethics states: 'Collections of human remains and material of sacred significance should be acquired only if they can be housed securely and cared for respectfully' (ICOM 2006: § 2.5). The law academic Charlotte Woodhead argues that proper 'respect' for the dead means that they should be 'undisturbed'. In one of her articles, she makes it explicit that this also means European remains, while referencing the symbolic case of Truganini.[2]

> It is now appreciated that acts such as the exhumation and subsequent display of Truganni's remains, against her last wishes, showed grave disrespect to the dead. While we understand the importance of leaving our loved ones undisturbed, perhaps we should also extend this respect to our own ancestors. One might take heed of the advice: 'You cannot fulfil your dreams if you insult your ancestors'. This should apply not only to indigenous peoples but equally to Europeans.
> (Woodhead 2002: 339)

Woodhead concludes that 'human remains warrant special attention' (p. 346) and that they are different to objects. She argues that all human remains should be treated respectfully because they were once individuals, regardless of public feelings on the matter. They 'deserve special consideration' due to 'the fact they were once individuals'. For this reason, although she recognizes 'there is no widespread movement in Britain for the removal of remains from collections' (Woodhead 2002: 337), she suggests that they should nonetheless be treated differently and suggests that they are left undisturbed and not in museums: 'We in Britain now have an opportunity to ensure this happens and should instigate a clear policy with regard to human remains outside the political arena with the primary intention of affording respect to those remains.' (p. 347) The Human Remains Working Group Report (HRWGR) similarly makes the case that all human remains should be treated as unique and proffers suggestions on the principles for the Human Remains Advisory Service, the second of which pertains to respecting human remains.

> Respect and reverence. Human remains must always be treated with respect. Responsibility for them should be regarded as a privilege. Museums owe the highest standards of care to bodies and parts of bodies within their collections, regardless of their age, origin, or the circumstances of their arrival in the collection.
> (DCMS 2003: 171)

In this principle, the bodies and body parts (note that they are not described as human remains or skeletons) require respect and reverence. This does not apply because of the feeling of the communities or the circumstances of historical acquisition, but because all bodies and body parts require respect.

Even so, what this means in practice appears difficult to articulate. But at its most coherent, as we have seen in relation to the discourse of respect in Chapter 4, the actions advocated concentrate less on the human remains than on the actions of the researcher and the context which the human remains are analysed. In *Human Remains: Guide for Museums and Academic Institutions* (Cassman, Odegaard, and Powell 2007), a publication for the sector on handling and caring for human remains, the discourse of respect and the idea that human remains require special protection is ventured. The book is dedicated: 'To institutionalized human remains wherever they are found' (p. v). The use of 'institutionalized' implies that their holding by an organization is difficult. The foreword outlines that previously 'the treatment of skeletal remains' was 'one of archaeology's dirty little secrets' (Fagan 2007: xviii), a phrase that suggests that there is something sordid about the way archeologists used to treat human remains. Describing human remains as 'the dead' in many instances, this works to humanize human remains, as does the subject of the book's dedication, which would usually be to a named and often, living, person. The introduction makes the point that even the terminology needs to be reconsidered by researchers:

> The use of different vocabularies tends to reveal or impose a level of regard by those that work with the dead. Words that imply the greatest distancing include *artifact, object, specimen, decedent,* and *corpse* [...] Words that convey a sense of connection include *individual, person,* and *human remains*. The latter are used throughout this book to reflect greater respect in order to promote improve care and management.
>
> (Cassman and Odegaard 2007: 1)

With this approach, 'respect' means thinking of and describing human remains as connected to us and as holding human characteristics. 'Disrespect', by implication, is to distance oneself from the remains and consider them as specimens. Similarly in the Human Remains Working Group Report, not treating human remains as people is identified as a problem:

> All these human remains were once parts of living individuals. Museums have tended to objectify them, as this makes them easier to deal with, but many museum staff would now contend that society believes that human remains need special treatment.
>
> (DCMS 2003: 352)

As we have discussed, here the critique is of the museum professionals: their disciplinary background, approach, and how they describe the human remains. This point is explicit in a chapter written by the archaeologist Vicki Cassman and Nancy Odegaard, conservator at Arizona State Museum:

> At a minimum human remains should be accorded gentle handling, and handlers must have an awareness of the potency of the remains, the privilege given to handlers, and their responsibility. Human remains are not specimens; they were people—they are individuals. To begin with, handling should be undertaken only with a specific purpose. One should not browse as if in a library, picking up bones and articulated joints without purpose. Simply put, a mental state of propriety is required of handlers.
>
> (Cassman and Odegaard 2007: 49)

In this extract professionals are instructed that they require a special 'mental state of propriety' when holding human remains. The point is made again that to consider the remains as specimens is to treat them with disrespect. The discourse of respect, or the idea that human remains require special treatment, in this context, appears to apply more to the professional rather than relating to something intrinsic about human remains.

Policies on human remains

Seventeen museums have drafted specific policy on human remains.[3] Many are very similar to the government guidance (DCMS 2005). Most advocate that signs are erected to warn audiences in advance about the display of human remains, even though there is no obvious public demand for this. The Royal Cornwall Museum in Truro, for example, states that it will take care not to show human remains without warning. As the policy outlines:

> Display methods will aim to prepare visitors for viewing human remains respectfully, will warn those who may not wish to see them at all and will display them in such a way as to prevent people coming across them unexpectedly.
>
> (RCM 2006: 6)

The policy continues that it will not be permitted to show images of human remains online or in any publicity material: 'No images of human remains other than wrapped mummies will be available online or will be used for marketing purposes.' (RCM 2006: 6)

Eight policies in particular indicate a significant concern about the display of human remains. These state that human remains should be separated from objects in their stores and collections, or that handling by the public should no longer take place, and that researchers should wear gloves when holding them (B&H 2006; LCMS 2006; NMGW 2006; MoL 2006, RCM 2006; MUM 2007; UCL 2007; HEM 2009). The policy for Leicester City Museums and Galleries explains this in relation to the potential sensitivities of the audience, as well as respect for the remains:

> There is a high probability of the risk of offending religious and other sensitivities far outweighs the benefits of using human remains in handling sessions. A case could be made against this, but it must be carefully considered. At the present time, Leicester Museums and Galleries is not comfortable for human remains to be used as handling material to maintain respect for their past lives.
>
> (LCMS 2006: s.9.1)

There is an unease in using human remains in handling sessions, and this is rationalized in terms of respect for the 'past lives' of the skeletal parts. It should be noted that Leicester City Museum and Galleries contains remains that are uncontested, unclaimed, and ancient. Interestingly, previous to this policy, the organization had not considered human remains as a general overall collection, but rather viewed them as part of different collections organized by disciplines:

> Leicester Museums and Galleries holds human remains in several of its collections. They come in many forms including skeletal, cremated and mummified remains. The human remains in the collections have not previously been assessed as an overall collection and are not always stored appropriately.
> (LCMS 2006 s1.3.1)

Whereas in the past, human remains were not considered 'a collection' but parts of different ways of organizing the whole collection and thus part of different disciplines, this policy begins to consider human remains as a category in and of themselves.

The policy for Brighton and Hove museum also states that contact with human remains should be avoided:

> It will be the aim to place material in individual, marked boxes that also act as auxiliary supports to facilitate handling without direct physical contact. Physical contact will be kept to a minimum although, when absolutely necessary, direct contact with skin will be avoided through the use of conservation standard gloves.

Human remains will be stored so that access to them is allowed only to authorized staff and supervised visitors with specific permission. Where human remains comprise a small proportion of a larger collection, curators will identify a designated area where human remains will be stored, to create conditions supportive of respectful treatment (B&H 2006: § 7.18–7.19).

With these policies, human remains take on a privileged status in the collection and are seen to require extra care that was previously not afforded to them. It should be noted that, in some instances, gloves are already used in institutions, although inconsistently, to protect the material from erosion. This practice now continues, but in the name of 'respect'. As with Leicester Museums and Galleries, the policy for Brighton and Hove museum pertains to human remains that are uncontested and unclaimed. It concerns the archaeological holdings of human skeletal material from the Neolithic through to the Anglo Saxon periods.

The Museum of London policy states that it takes into account (and takes a public stance on) the provenance of the remains; the use of consent; handling; access; specific display methods; privacy; institutional responsiveness to visitors; loans; and internal reviews in relation to human remains. It notes that display requires 'careful thought' (Mol. 2006: § 6.1). Indeed, in 2004, the remains of a boy with rickets were taken off display. The director, Jack Lohman, announced that he had set targets for the Christian burial of other human skeletons from archaeological excavations in London in the museum's collection. This decision was reported in the *Times* newspaper, where Lohman explained these actions as motivated by 'ethical reasons' (Alberge 2004). The policy explicitly includes traditionally marginalized communities, such as Pagans, in its consultation network.

While policies that advocate the different treatment of human remains are present in only eight institutions, none of which are major national organizations, their existence is worthy of note, because it demonstrates a moderate influence of the idea that human remains are a special object that should be treated differently to other objects in the collection.

The idea that human remains require special treatment in not being handled, or that they should be separated from objects, may meet difficulties in practice. This is partly because this is not driven by a rationale or an idea of how human remains *should* be treated and why, and partly because it has to work with other policies that may present contradictions. For example, the access agenda in museums, where policies outline that the public have access to the collection, may be contradicted by policies that advise that human remains are not on display or easily seen. It is worth noting, however, that the policies on human remains are not contested. They may have been adopted by only be a few organizations to date, but as one scientist indicated, professionals are unlikely to challenge their adoption elsewhere, telling me: 'I take a pragmatic approach to these guidelines … if it means I get to do my research, then I'll do it.'

I asked the director of one university collection why it was now policy to separate objects from human remains (in late 2007). She replied, referring also to the rule that handlers would have to wear gloves and that the human remains would have to be hidden or not easily visible to the visitor:

> *Interviewee:* We haven't really started implementing it yet except that in the [museum name] human remains are all now in one part of the store and clearly it's not possible to go into it by accident. I'll suppose we'll have to do something about implementing the handling thing too. There is this thing about university collections being slightly different to other collections, and in the [museum name] everything will either be on display or in visible storage. There won't be anything hidden away … um and I mean … even the … there's some pathology collections here and we are talking about finding ways of putting them in cases so they can be used or examined or when they need to be … but so all the rooms can be used when they need to be, so we have a whole load of neurology specimens, currently in a room that is currently used by the German department [laughs].
>
> *TJ:* How will you reconcile the issue of access and visibility while also putting up warnings about display?
>
> *Interviewee:* Um … ideally one would have a system where they could be in tinted glass, where you wouldn't be forced to confront them if they … if they didn't wish to, but at the same time some wanted to have a handling session or a session with medical students you could do that in the same

room ... So I think what we are exploring is sort of visible storage or visible stroke invisible storage.

This interviewee is a director of a university museum with a broad range of material, including a medical collection. She was medically trained and did not think human remains 'have a special case'. Her museum had not begun to fully implement fully this new policy, which would separate objects from human remains in storage, and would be careful about their display, and it did seem to be a major concern. She acknowledged that there could be difficulties in implementing this practice due to their policy on access, which means that all objects must be available and on display. Another reason is because medical students at the university use and require access to human material as part of their training. To reconcile the problem of removing and storing human remains at an institution that is also meant to have everything on show, this professional suggests a solution of tinted glass. In this instance, while the practice of granting human remains special new treatment contradicts the agenda of other policies in the museum, and the feelings of some of the professionals, this contradiction had not yet become a major problem. There is an attempt to reconcile these different practices without questioning them.

I interviewed the author of one of the policies which states that human remains should not be handled, that warnings should be posted, and that they should be stored separately from objects, to explore further their feelings about the treatment of human remains and the rationale for these rules. The institution held no human remains that were or could be claimed by overseas indigenous groups. I asked her: 'What is it to respect human remains?' The interviewee replied:

> Respect is very complicated, it's about thinking about it really, you think about everything you do with them, and then I think it then it becomes more clear ... We've a case of Roman remains I want to change. They are disarticulated pathological specimens and are just awful ... It's not respectful the way they are ... They've got letters and numbers on them to categorize them in relation to files, but that's a person ... you know ... They are treated as objects or just documents, you need to treat them as people. The scientific outlook that needs to be more social, or personal. You certainly don't separate the parts of the skeleton ... you know, skulls in one case or femurs in another.

For this interviewee, treating Roman remains as objects or documents was a problem. Thinking of them as a person was essential. This means showing respect for the integrity of the body and storing remains separately from objects. The scientific outlook is a clearly identified problem, as is the traditional way these remains were handled and presented, because it does not treat skeletons as people:

> Skeletons are not the same as objects. They have an elevated position – or they should do [...] You know I want to know who they are, not their number. I am not religious at all, but if you've exhumed them, studied

them and put them on display, at least leave a note about what you know about them as people [laughs]. The numbers are bad, some of them are written on the bones, that's awful ... science is too cold really.

Here, the curator identifies as a problem the numbers commonly written on skeleton bone to categorize them. She proceeded to show me a collection of Roman skeleton bones that had numbers written on them in pen and explained that people should not write on them, in pen or in pencil, out of respect. In this interview, it is possible to identify the view that a scientific outlook dehumanizes human remains, because it is 'too cold'.

Skeletons: London's buried bones

The 2008 exhibition *Skeletons: London's Buried Bones* was on display at the Wellcome Collection in London, organized in collaboration with the Museum of London. A sign at the two entrances of this stand-alone show warned, in line with new exhibitions of human remains: 'This exhibition contains human remains, including those of young children.' There were 26 skeletons on show, taken from the Museum of London's collection of 17,000 skeletons. Each skeleton was laid out in its own display case, resting on a bed of black granules. The work of the osteoarchaeologists in determining the age, sex, and pathology of each of the bodies was given on an accompanying label. Photographs illustrated what the burial sites look like today.

Ken Arnold, head of public programmes at the Wellcome Collection, introduced the catalogue for the show with a short discussion of the debate over displaying human remains:

> In the sometimes heated discussions about these issues, scientific approaches to this material frequently seem to be pitted against more empathetic and 'humane' ones. A striking feature of this exhibition is the manner in which it confounds that simplistic dichotomy. For here, the methodical work of osteologists helps to reunite these bones with fascinating, but otherwise hidden, elements of their life stories.
>
> (Arnold 2008: 6)

In this excerpt, we can identify an attempt to justify the exhibition, and the research on and display of human remains, by saying that it brings part of the skeletons' life stories out in the open. Arnold continues by stressing the empathetic character of science in this exhibition: 'This show is about how the scientific study of bones can add to rather than detract from our emotional encounters with this material.' (Arnold 2008: 6)

I interviewed one of the curators in March 2007, when the exhibition was being prepared. He explained:

> The idea for exhibition is ... and this is where the skill and artistry comes in ... would be to, you know, to bring them back to life, i.e. with the skill

of the osteoarchaeologists and medical professionals to say, you know, we can tell this person died somewhere between 1650–1680, they were obviously they were found in Chelsea, they were probably middle class ... we can tell from their teeth they had this in their diet, so you can kind of almost, see this ghostly apparition rising out of a skeleton.

Here, the curator described the display of human remains, and the skill of the medical professionals, as actions that would 'bring them back to life'. He continued by saying: 'the more that the medics tell us about this, the more humanity and the more the human values of these, these gone people come back together'. This would appear to be an attempt to justify the work of curators and medical professionals working on human remains as research objects, at a time when this is questioned, through the presentation of a humanized approach.

Here, we can see that some of those researchers making the case for the research and display of human remains are beginning to incorporate the criticism of their traditional approach. Accused of being insensitive and cold, the researchers repose their potential contribution as humanizing. The dead bodies remain on display, but they are discussed slightly differently, with a deliberate emphasis on the emotional aspect of science, with more reflection on the identity of the skeletons, by scientists attempting to re-legitimize their work.

Skeletons: London's Buried Bones was reviewed in the magazine *Museum Practice*, the sister journal of the *Museums Journal*, by Helen Rees Leahy (2008), who is director of the centre for museology at the University of Manchester. She found the exhibition 'unusually rehumanizing' (p. 38), and compared it to the exhibition, and ethics, of Gunther von Hagens, whom she accuses of anonymizing the corpses on display. The rehumanization that Leahy refers to relates to the Wellcome Collection's contextualization of where and when the remains were found, giving them more of a personal identity. Rees Leahy writes that von Hagens' *Body Worlds* exhibition:

> [I]mplicity promotes the myth of a universal human being, from whom distinguishing marks of colour, age and sometimes sex have been erased. The Wellcome Collection took a very different approach, enabling visitors imaginatively to construct the lives and conditions of the people they encountered through the fragments of their skeletons.
>
> (Leahy 2008: 38)

This is counterpoised to the more imaginative and positive approach taken by the Wellcome Collection, using the following example:

> A young woman with ulcerated lesions on her skull caused by syphilis also had bowing of the bones in her legs, a sign of rickets. She was buried in the Cross Bones cemetery for paupers and prostitutes.
>
> (Leahy 2008: 38)

The approach to displaying human remains that explains the social background of the skeletons, and the diseases that affected or killed them, is considered by Rees Leahy to be humanizing. The skeletons are accompanied by information about their different biographies, in particular their health and the disease from which they suffered, which is well illustrated in some cases by the damage to the bone. This reflects the medical orientation of the Wellcome Trust and this particular exhibition. It also in part reflects contemporary interest in the health-orientated body, as discussed in the previous chapter. In this respect, the exhibition can be seen as an attempt to reauthorize scientific research on the display of bodies in emotional terms and by reference to its contribution to broader issues of identity work. In claiming that the exhibition contributed to an understanding of the self and, in particular, health and the body, it received a moderately favourable reception within museology.

Notes

1 See http://news.bbc.co.uk/1/hi/england/manchester/7413654.stm. Accessed 25 March 2010.
2 Also spelt Truganni in some accounts: for example, Woodhead 2002.
3 These are: SM, 2001; NMGW, 2006; B8H, 2006, BM, 2006; LCMS, 2006; MUM, 2007; MoL, 2006; NHM, 2006; NML, 2006; OUM, 2006; PRM, 2006; SM, 2006; RCM, 2006; Bolton, 2007; UCL, 2007; WT, 2007; HEM, 2006.

References

Alberge, D. (2004) Museum bones 'should have a Christian burial'. *The Times*, London, 6 January.
Alberti, A., Bienkowski, R., Chapman, M., and Drew, R. (2009) Should we display the dead? *Museum and Society*, 7(3): 133–49.
Arnold, K. (2008) *Skeletons: London's Buried Bones*. London: Wellcome Trust.
B&H (2006) Policy for the care and treatment of human remains. Brighton: Brighton and Hove Museums.
BM (2006) British Museum policy on human remains. London: British Museum.
Bolton (2007) Human remains policy. Bolton: Bolton Museum and Archive Service.
Brooks, M. and Rumsey, C. (2007) Who knows the fate of his bones? Rethinking the body on display: object, art or human remains? In: S.J. Knell, MacLeod, S., and Watson, S. (eds.), *Museum Revolutions: How Museums Change and Are Changed*. London and New York: Routledge, pp. 343–54.
Cassman, V. and Odegaard, N. (2007) Examination and analysis. In: V. Cassman, N. Odegaard, and J. Powell (eds.), *Human Remains: Guide for Museums and Academic Institutions*. Lanham, Maryland, New York, Toronto, Oxford: Rowman and Littlefield Publishers, Inc., pp. 49–76.
Cassman, V. Odegaard, N., and Powell, J. (eds.) (2007) *Human Remains: Guide for Museums and Academic Institutions*. Lanham, Maryland, New York, Toronto, Oxford: Rowman and Littlefield Publishers, Inc.
Curtis, N. (2003) Human remains: the sacred, museums and archaeology. *Public Archaeology*, 3(1): 21–32.

Day, J. (2006) *The Mummy's Curse: Mummymania in the English-Speaking World*. London: Routledge.
DCMS (2003) *Report of the Working Group on Human Remains*. London: Department of Culture, Media and Sport.
——(2005) *Guidance for the Care of Human Remains in Museums*. London: Department of Culture, Media and Sport.
Fagan. B. (2007) Foreword. In: Cassmann, V., Odegaard, N., and Powell, J. (eds.), Human remains: guide for museums and academic institutions. Lanham, Maryland, New York, Toronto, Oxford: AltaMira Press.
Hallam, E., Hockey, J., and Howarth, G. (1999) *Beyond the Body: Death and Social Identity*. London and New York: Routledge.
Heaney, S. (1975) *Bog Poems*. London: Rainbow Press.
HEM (2009) Human remains policy. Haselmere: Haselmere Educational Museum.
ICOM (2002) *Code of Ethics for Museums*. Paris: International Council of Museums.
——(2006) *Code of Ethics for Museums*. Paris: International Council of Museums.
Kåks, P. (1998) Human remains and material of ritual significance. *ICOM News* (ICOM '98 Special Issue): 10–11.
Kilmister, H. (2003) Visitor perceptions of ancient Egyptian human remains in three United Kingdom museums. *Papers from the Institute of Archaeology*, 14: 57–69.
LCMS (2006) *The Curation, Care and Use of Human Remains in Leicester City Museums Service*. Leicester: Leicester City Museums Service.
Lohman, J. (2006) Parading the dead, policing the living. In: J. Lohman and K. Goodnow (eds.), *Human Remains and Museum Practice*. Paris and London: UNESCO and the Museum of London, pp. 21–4.
MA (2002) *Code of Ethics for Museums*. London: Museums Association.
MEG (1991) Museum Ethnographers Group guidelines on management of human remains. Museum Ethnographers Group. Available online at: www.museumethnographersgroup.org.uk. Accessed 7 June 2010.
MoL (2006) Human remains policy. London: Museum of London.
MUM (2007) Policy on human remains. Manchester: Manchester University Museum.
——(2008a) Official statement on covering Egyptian mummies. Manchester: Manchester University Museum.
——(2008b) Egyptian mummies: we're listening to your views. Press release. Manchester: Manchester University Museum.
Narain, J. (2008) Fury as museum bosses cover up naked Egyptian mummies to protect 'sensitivities' of visitors. *Daily Mail*, 21 May.
NHM (2006) Policy for the care and treatment of human remains. London: Natural History Museum.
NMGW (2006) Collection management policies: policy on human remains. Cardiff: National Museum and Galleries of Wales.
NML (2006) Policy on human remains. Liverpool: National Museums Liverpool.
Nordström, N. (2007) *De odödliga Förhistoriska individer i vetenskap och media*. Lund: Nordic Academic Press.
OUM (2006) Policy on human remains. Oxford: Oxford University.
PRM (2006) Human remains in the Pitt Rivers Museum. Oxford: Pitt Rivers Museum.
RCM (2006) Policy on human remains. Truro: Royal Cornwall Museum.
Sitch, B. (2007a) Lindow Man consultation report. Manchester: Manchester University Museum.

——(2007b) Feedback to Lindow Man project participants. Manchester: Manchester University Museum.
——(2009) Courting controversy – the Lindow Man exhibition at the Manchester Museum. *University Museums and Collections Journal*, 2: 51–4.
SM (2001) Guidelines on policy for human remains in Surrey museums. Woking: Surrey Museums.
——(2006) Human remains policy. London: Science Museum.
Southworth, E. (1994) A special concern. *Museums Journal*, 7: 23–6.
Stead, I.M., Bourke, J.B., and Brothwell, D. eds. (1986) *Lindow Man: The Body in the Bog*. London: The British Museum.
Turner, R.C. and Scaife, R.S. (1995) *Bog Bodies: New Discoveries and New Perspectives*. London: British Museum Press.
UCL (2007) UCL Policy on human remains. London: University College London.
Vaswani, R. (2001) Remains of the day. *Museums Journal*, 101(2): 34–5.
WAC (1990) Vermillion Accord. Southampton: World Archaeological Congress.
Walker, P. (2000) Bioarchaeological ethics: a historical perspective on the value of human remains. In: M.A. Katzenberg and S.R. Saunders (eds.), *Biological Anthropology in the Human Skeleton*. New York: Wiley, pp. 3–39.
Woodhead, C. (2002) 'A debate which crosses all borders'. The repatriation of human remains: more than just a legal question. *Art, Antiquity and Law*, 7(4): 317–47.
WT (2007) Full Wellcome Trust policy on the care of human remains in museums and galleries. London: Wellcome Trust.

Part III

Interpreting the archaeological past

Introduction to Part III

Robin Skeates

This section explores how the past is interpreted in museums through archaeological remains. This topic sits within the large field of museum communication. An extensive museological literature has been produced over the last two decades offering critical and political perspectives on museum representations of the archaeological past and also of archaeology itself. This has led to changes in museum practice, not all of which have stood the test of time. Indeed, we may be returning to a more pragmatic era, in which curators are simply striving to present archaeological science in an accessible and meaningful manner. Archaeological sites present another opportunity for visitors to engage with the material remains of the past, but the challenges facing archaeological site museums should not be underestimated. New, site-specific, museum architecture can add spectacularly to the fabric of such sites, although architects and gallery designers have been accused of losing sight of the public and their educational needs. Teaching and learning about the past through archaeology is an essential dimension of the museum mission, but requires careful thought. Certainly, public engagement in, and perceptions of, museum archaeology matter, and various initiatives are being undertaken by archaeological museums to make themselves more accessible to the public, whoever and wherever they are. This requires that museum archaeologists understand their audiences.

The first set of readings explores a series of critical and political perspectives on museum representations of the archaeological past and of archaeology. **Chapter 18** is a classic. First published in 1987, it was written by the (then) angry-young-men of British archaeological theory. It critiques the presentation of archaeological work and artefacts in museums, and argues that museums may misrepresent the past to the public, distorting it through selection and classification, and restructuring it through a code of historical representation. English examples considered include the old Museum of Antiquities in Newcastle-upon-Tyne, Greek antiquities in the British Museum, and the Jorvik Viking Centre in York. The chapter concludes with five recommendations for an alternative museum practice: (1) to introduce political content into museum displays, (2) to juxtapose ancient artefacts and contemporary artefacts, (3) to introduce humour, (4) to avoid permanent displays, and (5) to encourage the community use of artefacts outside of the museum. **Chapter 19** examines the ensuing debates that developed surrounding the nature of curatorial authority and of public education in archaeology museums, focusing on texts accompanying exhibitions of prehistoric material in England and Scotland. It also considers the future status and role of text in museums. Continuing the theme of museum representations, **Chapter 20** presents the results of a survey of 55 museums designed to investigate the extent and nature of the scientific content included within UK archaeology displays. Although most respondents recognized the potential for presenting archaeological science in an accessible and meaningful manner, constraints over the increased use of scientific interpretation were also highlighted. **Chapter 21** then examines the variable representation of Saami prehistory in several Nordic museums. Significant differences are identified between majority-community museums and those run by minority Saami communities, reflecting ideologies implicated in building indigenous, nationalist, and pan-national identities as well as in legitimating Saami claims to land and heritage. Following on geographically but broadening out thematically, **Chapter 22** evaluates the prehistory exhibition in the National Historical Museum in Stockholm, Sweden from a gender perspective. Building upon previous feminist critiques of museums which highlighted the absence of women from our constructed past and which called for the engendering of archaeological exhibits in museums, this research paper finds that women have been included in the narratives of the exhibition but that a degree of male gender bias remains.

The second set of readings considers management and interpretation strategies for archaeological site museums. **Chapter 23** tells the story of a single site museum in the UK: the – originally – highly innovative design of the Jorvik Viking Centre in York. Here, the display and interpretation, which were informed by market research, focus on the complete reconstruction of an alley with rows of tenth-century timber buildings and associated Viking figures representing different types of people and activity. **Chapter 24** then explains the thinking behind the new Museum of Altamira. Since its discovery in 1879, the Palaeolithic painted cave of Altamira has attracted large numbers of visitors. In 2001, the new Museum of Altamira was inaugurated, offering to visitors a replica that allows the cave to be experienced with high fidelity while not compromising the preservation of the original cave. Finally, **Chapter 25** introduces the variety of issues facing archaeological site museums in Latin America. These include: ethical considerations, particularly over relationships between site museums and living and descendant communities; the links between site museums and site protection (from looting); the potential of site museums to function as economic motors for their region; and the role played by site museums in identity construction on local and regional levels.

The third set of readings continues with the theme of new, site-specific, archaeology museum architecture. Two case-studies are presented. **Chapter 26** reviews the new Acropolis Museum in Athens, which opened to the public in 2009. It praises the spectacular building, designed by New York's Bernard Tschumi, which establishes a dialogue between the museum and the adjacent Acropolis. But it also criticizes the architecture for dictating the exhibition design, which prioritizes visual display over the archaeological history of the Acropolis. **Chapter 27** then describes the construction of an underground museum exhibition space adjacent to the Yang Emperor Mausoleum of the Han Dynasty at Xi'an in China.

The next reading comes under the heading of designing archaeology displays. A number of our readings touch upon this theme, but **Chapter 28** offers a more focused case study. In particular, it presents an account of a project undertaken to create an interactive virtual reality exhibit about archaeological artefacts found at Port Royal, Jamaica, aimed at school children and other visitors to the Ocean Institute at Dana Point in California.

Following on from this, the next five readings deal with teaching and learning through museum archaeology. **Chapter 29** explores the issues of archaeology education in museum settings – including different educational programme formats – and presents a sample programme for school children visiting a museum. **Chapter 30** offers a critical commentary on the use of hands-on activities in museum archaeology displays. It concludes that a number of museums are successfully using hands-on activities in archaeology displays to stimulate problem-solving learning experiences, but that this experience is predominantly didactic, involving a passive intellectual interaction on the part of the visitor. **Chapter 31** is a case study written by the (then) Regional Education Officer for English Heritage. It details the issues faced by the curatorial team in redisplaying prehistoric Avebury's Alexander Keiller Museum in line with a new National Curriculum. This especially meant focusing on the nature of archaeological evidence and the subjectivity of interpretation based on such evidence. **Chapter 32** offers another example, in this case detailing the Museum of London's initiative to loan mini museums of Roman archaeology to London schools. **Chapter 33** then provides three examples from the Isaac Royall House museum – home to one of the largest slaveholders and traders in Massachusetts during the eighteenth century. Here, visitors are empowered to engage actively in the process of archaeological knowledge production with reference to landscapes, artefacts, and documents. It is argued that this approach cultivates a heightened respect and understanding for what archaeology does, and also makes dialogues of race, ethnicity, class, and culture more accessible and interesting to visitors.

The final set of readings looks in more depth at public engagement in, and perceptions of, museum archaeology. **Chapter 34** explores some of the initiatives being undertaken by archaeological museums in the UK to become more accessible to visitors. These include: digital access, behind-the-scenes access, hands-on learning, provision of loan boxes, outreach work, the targeting of ethnic minorities, and collaborations with artists. **Chapter 35** presents data from a survey about the wide variety of public archaeology activities undertaken at 152 museums in Japan, ranging from displays to practical activities to outreach. A key finding is that activities allowing more public participation are preferred by visitors. The following two chapters focus on museums representations of ancient Egypt. **Chapter 36** is written by the (former) manager of University College London's Petrie Museum of Egyptian Archaeology and by a researcher at the National Children's Bureau. It discusses the results of research commissioned by the museum and carried out in 2000, aimed at understanding the interests and needs of the museum's users, and – more broadly – exploring the nature and limits of the western public's fascination with ancient Egypt. What this research indicates is that, although ancient Egyptian collections in western museums are popular, some visitors bring deep-seated misconceptions and unpleasant prejudices, which the museum would certainly like to question and change. **Chapter 37** describes the theory, practice, and outcomes of the 'Re-imagining Egypt' exhibition that the author curated with the involvement of local school children whilst working as Learning and Visitor Services Officer at Saffron Walden Museum in the UK. This exhibition sought to challenge traditional museum displays of Egypt as the 'Golden Age of the Pharaohs', and to represent Egypt anew as the sum of its many parts, by exhibiting contemporary Egyptian artworks alongside historic objects. **Chapter 38** is a short and accessible article that responds to Barbara Little's question: How have practicing archaeologists and museologists helped US and Canadian First Peoples do their own archaeology and museology? It provides some selected examples of innovative, collaborative, museum-based efforts that benefit Indigenous peoples. **Chapter 39** discusses the collaborative development of a 'living museum' around Chunchucmil in Mexico where members of local descendant communities and archaeologists are recreating an ancient Maya household on the archaeological site. Finally, **Chapter 40** reports on a study that employed a Personal Meaning Mapping methodology to measure the impact of the open-ended, dialogic, and pluralistic temporary exhibition of the 2000-year-old body of Lindow Man at the Manchester Museum, UK. The exhibition's unorthodox concept, design, and construction polarized opinion amongst staff and visitors. However, the study shows that challenging convention, though extremely unpopular in traditional quarters, can add new layers of meaning to the museum experience.

Part III, Section 1

Critical and political perspectives on museum representations of the archaeological past and of archaeology

Chapter 18

Presenting the past
Towards a redemptive aesthetic for the museum

Michael Shanks and Christopher Tilley

'The task to be accomplished is not the conservation of the past, but the redemption of the hopes of the past. Today, however, the past is preserved as the destruction of the past.'

(Adorno and Horkheimer 1979: xv)

Introduction

We have argued for a critically reflexive archaeology which of necessity includes an assessment of the relation of the archaeologist and his or her work to contemporary capitalism (Shanks and Tilley 1992: 46–67). We have also argued the necessity of taking archaeology's presentation to an audience into account, that archaeology is a rhetoric (Shanks and Tilley 1992: 7–28). Archaeologists present themselves and their work to a non-archaeological public through the media, publishing media, actual physical confrontation (archaeological sites, education), and the museum. This chapter considers the presentation of archaeological work – the interpreted artefact – in the museum, which is probably the main institutional connection between archaeology as a profession and discipline, and wider society.

This chapter is intended as an ideology critique, a critique of the museum as an ideological institution. The museum may directly misrepresent the past, distorting it through selection and classification, creating a particular historical narrative. The museum may also restructure the past through its code of historical representation, the *way* it tells its 'story', the way the artefact is presented (*cf.* Berger et al. 1972; Bann 1978).

There are several effective critiques of the way museums directly distort the past as a means of legitimating present sectional interests (Leone 1981b, 1984; Wallace 1981; see also Horne 1984). We shall concentrate more on the museum's aesthetic. In presenting artefacts to be viewed by a visiting public, museums make a statement about the relation of the viewing visitor to the object world. The artefacts are assembled and presented, ordered to make a particular sense to the viewing visitor. Artefacts are mobilized in an aesthetic system (a system of presentation and viewing) to create meanings. We shall be considering this statement, this aesthetic system.

The main part of the chapter is a presentation of a series of interpretations of particular museums and displays. They are not interpretations of a random sample, but neither were the particular museums chosen to make criticism easier. We simply visited a few museums we knew. The series of interpretations builds up a critique of the presentation of the artefact in various forms of museum display. Drawing on our previous discussion of time (Shanks and Tilley 1992: 7–28) we argue that the artefact is turned into a commodity and in effect removed from history. This confirms the present's relation with the object world. It is the present that is preserved, not the past.

We then move on to consider further aspects of the relation between past and present in the museum, the relationship between professional study of the artefact and its subsequent 'public' presentation. Continuing the argument of an earlier chapter (Shanks and Tilley 1992: 7–28), we argue against the possibility of a neutral presentation of an objective past by professional archaeologist or curator. All presentation of the artefactual past is rhetorical performance, an active project of persuasion, an active mobilization of particular modes of presentation which, in the museums we considered, argue for the world as it immediately appears to us, concealing the underlying reality of past and present.

We end by drawing out ideas for a more fertile relation between past artefact and presentation, one that recognizes and assumes that the study of the past artefact and its presentation are inseparable. We reassert that a non-ideological and critically reflexive archaeology cannot be separated from its presentation to a wider social world of people who are not archaeologists.

PART ONE: THE MUSEUMS

The artefact transformed into an object in commodified time

The Museum of Antiquities of the University and Society of Antiquaries of Newcastle upon Tyne: a small museum with two galleries. The first contains a selection of Roman inscribed and sculptured stones, mainly altars and tombstones, from the North-East. There are also models of a Roman milecastle, fort, turret, vallum, and the wall itself. Some cases are used for temporary displays. The second gallery consists of a sequence of cases presenting artefacts from the North-East in chronological order. The artefacts are sometimes juxtaposed with no implied connection other than chronological, are sometimes placed together according to similar type or site of discovery.

The format of the guidebook, a series of photographed exhibits with accompanying notes and references, clearly expresses the organizing metaphor of the museum: the artefact as chronological object, object of academic study, the artefact as specimen. In a mechanical relation of metonymy the artefacts stand for archaeological system.

In the second gallery the cases locate a collection of local artefacts in their archaeological period – prehistoric to medieval. The logical principle uniting the sequence of cases is abstract time, time as a flow divided into conventional lengths – early, middle, and late Bronze Age, Iron Age, Roman, Anglo-Saxon. The only appreciable narrative behind the sequence of cases is a story of technological change. This is change abstracted from the social; it is a story of the production of variety.

The artefacts are conceptually packaged with labels indicating provenance, type, and museum accession number. Any further packaging is limited to the descriptive background: some text and some small models. The artefacts stand in the cases with their academic price tags. Price indicated by price tag is the abstract exchange-value of goods in a shop window; the abstract exchange-value of the artefacts is their being objects for academic study, their antiquarian interest, their academic objectivity.

The objects stand solitarily. The people who made them are irretrievably out of sight and out of mind. (There are figures of Roman soldiers in cases offset from the main sequence, but significantly their armour is replica armour.) The historical subjectivity, which constituted the objects, is denied in their formal identity proclaimed by the labels uniting the objects according to academic exchange principle. The objects are formally equivalent; like commodities in a supermarket their ultimate meaning lies in their formal identity, commodities to be bought, 'historical' objectivity to be decoded by the initiate, manipulated by detached academic subjectivity. The objects are before the visitor in certainty and presence, subjected to archaeological analysis.

The objects form a spatial figure rather than a temporal process; they are cartographically located according to an ontologically and temporally depthless system of archaeological referents. The past is seen, the visitor is distanced, disinterested, 'observer of the ultimately familiar or autonomous picture in which temporality – its threats and its possibilities – has been annulled' (Spanos 1977: 427).

The objects are familiar: the immediate significance of the exhibited objects lies in their relation to contemporary objects, an unremarkable relation of resemblance and difference usually focusing on recognition of function (they had axes in the bronze age!), and appreciation of technical and artistic skill. But in the absence of their determinate social context the meaning of the artefacts lies in their abstract objectivity. The artefacts are objects. Archaeological history stands before the visitor as fetishized objectivity, a detached objectivity mysterious to the visitor, truly fetishistic. A typical label reads:

BELL – DERIVATIVE BEAKER
BOREWELL FARM, SCREMERSTON, N'D
Clarke 706   Class W/MR –
N/MR Hybrid   1948 7

As a coded set, the objects are raw data, objective substance, ready to be worked up into descriptive archaeological narrative. This narrative is implied but almost totally absent from the exhibition. Only the models attest to its possibility.

As we have said, in the second gallery the objects are located by the cases in time, in their archaeological period. The cases themselves represent empty time, time as a container, formal and devoid of social content, but nevertheless filled with the content of archaeology – objects; objects in cases; objects in time. The cases are the content-less temporal form in which the objects are brought to exist.

But time is not a non-relational container of the reality of the past. The reduction of temporality to measured duration separated from the 'content' of the past is an objectification, a commodification of time. So History becomes rooted in empty measured duration, a rigid continuum of ephemerality, a sequence of empty instants. The past exists only in these moments, only in its present. It is over and done with, complete, an 'autonomous picture'. The past thus appears fleeting and distant from the present.

And commodified time is capitalism's factory time (Thompson 1963, 1967; Giddens 1981; Lowe 1982). As John Berger puts it: 'the factory which works all night is a sign of the victory of a ceaseless, uniform and remorseless time. The factory continues even during the time of dreams' (Berger and Mohr 1982: 107).

Remorseless commodified time is the mythical time of the always the same, empty, homogeneous time (Wolin 1982: 48; Benjamin 1973d, esp. Theses XIII and XIV). The visitor is presented with mythical Fate incessantly piling ruin upon shattered ruin, object upon object in an inescapable and rigid continuum of empty moments. Beakers and axe-heads appear in rows; tombstones and altars stand lined up, worn with time. Commodification brings a vision of mythical compulsion to repeat, a failure of memory, a Great Myth, 'the reproduction of the always-the-same under the semblance of the perpetually new' – commodity production (Wolin 1982: 174). History appears as commodity production; the objects in the cases are ultimately familiar because things have always been the same. Commodified time denies remembrance, memory of difference. In this sense the reification that the objectification of the artefact represents is a forgetting (Adorno and Horkheimer 1979: 230). 'History no longer pays its respects to the dead; the dead are simply what it has passed through' (Berger and Mohr 1982: 107). People are the objects, the debris of such a history, forgotten. This is the injustice of the empty cases of objects.

'The factory continues even during the time of dreams': commodified time marginalizes subjective experience of time – individual memory and other forms of experience which have the capacity to undo, unify, and deny the ceaseless passing of empty moments (see Berger and Mohr 1982: 105–06). In proclaiming chronometric history's monopoly of time the museum bypasses the question of other forms of objective as well as subjective temporality (see Shanks and Tilley 1992: 7–28) and the historical roots of commodified time.

The objects have been 'discovered'. The labels indicate provenance and information is given about circumstances of discovery of hoards and valuable objects, but not as a means of adding a geographical dimension to the understanding of the visitor – no maps are provided which indicate either distribution of exhibits or of artefacts of similar type and date. The reference to provenance communicates the idea of space as a non-relational container, an abstract existent analogous to the representation of time within which the substantive object is located. The inclusion of provenance on the labels communicates mere abstract 'discovery'. Subjectivity stands coolly apart from the objectivity of the artefact, seemingly passive yet with an instrumental relation to History, an empty screen of chronometric time onto which it projects the empirical.

But 'discovery' is fascinating. It is part of the romance of archaeology. 'Discovery' links past and present, reaching out from incessant passing of the momentary present, bridging the chasm between past and present opened up by the conception of time as an empty spatial dimension filled with artefacts locked into their respective presents, their archaeological periods.

But this resolution of the tension between past and present is a spurious harmony. The past is not *merely* discovered. 'Discovery' is not an abstract instant of capturing the past. The shock of the moment of discovery shatters the continuity of abstract, commodified time; it is a shock of discontinuity, which reveals the present's practical relation to the past object.

The aesthetic artifact

The British Museum: Greek antiquities: we refer in this section to the typical form of presentation found in the great international museums – free-standing sculpture, ceramics in cases, presented with minimum supporting information, e.g. the Parthenon sculptures.

> In the Russian ikon neither space nor time exists. It addresses the eye, but the eye which then shuts in prayer so that the image – now in the mind's eye – is isolated and entirely spiritualised. Yet the images are not introspective – that would already make them too personal; nor are they ... mystical; their calm expressions suggest no exceptional experience. They are images of holy figures seen in the light of a heaven in which the people believe so as to make the visible world around them *credible*.
> (Berger 1969: 20–21)

Parallel to the homogeneous spatial figure of the past found in the Museum of Antiquities, Newcastle, is the encapsulation of the past in the self-bounded, sealed-off, inclusive image – the artefact as ikon (Spanos 1977: 427). This aestheticization of the artefact is a romantic reaction to the commodification of the past. The lifeless, inert objectivity of analytical study is replaced (or supplemented) by the aesthetic productivity of *Homo Artifex*.

The artefact is displayed in splendid remoteness from the prosaic, from the exigencies of day-to-day life. The concrete and historically variable *practice* of production and consumption is collapsed into the 'aesthetic', an isolatable and universal human experience. Instead of abstract objectivity, the abstract experience of the aesthetic becomes the exchange-value of the artifact, which is again raised to the status of a solitary fetish, a fetish of immanent 'humanity'. Now the formal identity of artefacts in terms of objectivity becomes a formal identity according to spiritual truth, universal values expressed in the exceptional artefact. History is

Figure 18.1 The aesthetic artefact.

again unified. History freezes in the ideological light of the aesthetic artefact, celebrated and exalted, elevated above everyday life.

Display of the artefact conveys the timeless ability of Man (*sic*) as toolmaker-artist. As such the visitor need only approach the artefact with finely tuned sensibilities; the artefact's universal truth is communicated via direct intuition. But whose sensibilities, whose intuition, whose 'humanity'? As the aesthetic qualities of the artefact are supposedly immediately perceptible, context and critical analysis become relegated to optional supplements.

History is differentiated only according to the unifying principle of the technical and artistic triumph of Man. It is divested of the 'trivia' of oppression, of conflict (other than inwardly spiritual), of everything social. The aesthetic artefact is an escape from the nightmare of history. But all culture shares the guilt of society. The aesthetic artefact 'ekes out its existence only by virtue of injustice already perpetrated in the sphere of production' (Adorno 1967: 26).

A constituting subjectivity is now recognized; Man as *Homo Artifex* is recognized as mastering objectivity, objective substance, investing it with a universal message. But where does he belong, where did he come from? Of course *Homo Artifex* is an abstract conception, detached from history, concealing its origins in the cultural values of particular social groups within history.

Bringing the past alive

The anti-rationalism of aestheticized objectivity is related to the secret worrying antinomies at the heart of bourgeois rationality; the success of the analytics of scientific, instrumental rationality, bringing nature and the past to order under a concealed subjectivity, foregrounds the problem of subjectivity. If science, instrumental analytics (exclusive of subjectivity), is the only firm (objective) basis for archaeological reconstruction, then what about human experience, emotion, imagination?

One answer, as we have shown, is to canonize the 'aesthetic' artefact as Art, as repository of the 'human', detached now from the analytics of archaeology, transcending history.

Another answer to this chasm in conventional approaches to the past is the humanizing narrative – setting the artefacts into their concrete 'human' context. In the museum this is represented by the narrative display which provides contextual information (usually text, diagrams, maps) and the situational display, which sets the artefact in a context of contemporary artefacts and features (e.g. the period room).

From another point of view, it has been widely recognized that every visit to a museum is a hermeneutic venture and if museums are to cater for a clientele wider than an initiated elite, the artefacts cannot stand on their own. The visitor faces a slippery indeterminacy in the museum – what do the objects mean? The two forms of display, which have so far been discussed implicitly, propose their own answers to this question – the meaning of the object lies in its objectivity or in the aesthetic. Narrative and situational types of display approach the semiotic indeterminacy of the artefact more directly through contextual information for the visitor.

Narrative display and the artefact as information

The Museum of London: case displays, free-standing artefacts, room interiors, shop reconstructions, paintings, photographs, and much written material are skilfully and efficiently combined to tell the story of London from prehistoric times to the present.

In the Museum of London artefacts are essentially used to authenticate the social description written around them. 'Written', because the museum is in many ways a book around which the visitor may wander. This makes the ultimate message of the past as descriptive information encoded in objects all the more palatable.

The narrative, which was implied but absent from the sequence of cases in the Museum of Antiquities, is foregrounded in the Museum of London, but again an authentic transcendence of the superficial fact is missed.

The displays convey factual information about the past of London. The Museum of London condenses past social practice and experience into information, information tied to the chronological narrative. Information – the fact – is presented as the dominant form in which social practice is stored – news. But as news belongs to a precise point in time, 'the value of information does not survive the moment it was new. It lives only in that moment; it has to surrender to it completely and explain itself to it without losing any time' (Benjamin 1973b: 90). Information lives only in the moment of its novelty. 'In the form of information, experience no longer has anything to teach us; it has simply become another fungible aspect of modern life, an item of momentary interest which will soon cease to be topical and then be promptly discarded' (Wolin 1982: 222). The visitor passes from display to display presumably absorbing 'information' and nothing more.

Indeed, 'you have to be buried alive in order to survive' (Dorfman and Mattelart 1975: 85). Archaeology is precisely the means to a 'living' past. The past has to be buried alive, experience killed off, stultified, pinned down to the moment of its novelty in order to be meaningful in the present as information, a permanent commodity, property, heritage, all preserved, pickled for the future.

Presence, absence, and the authenticating quote

> ὑπάρχουν, ἡ κίνηση τοῦ προσώπου τὸ σχῆμα τῆς στοργῆς
> ἐκείνων ποὺ λιγόστεψαν τόσο παράξενα μὲς στὴ ζωή μας ...
> ἢ μήπως ὄχι δὲν ἀπομένει τίποτε παρὰ μόνο τὸ βάρος
> ἡ νοσταλγία τοῦ βάρους μιᾶς ὕπαρξης ζωντανῆς

> does there exist the movement of the face, shape of the tenderness
> of those who've shrunk so strangely in our lives ...
> or perhaps no, nothing is left but the weight
> the nostalgia for the weight of a living existence
> (from George Seferis 'The King of Asine',
> translated by Edmund Keeley and Philip Sherrard)

The Museum of London quotes with objects. It draws on a quality of aura found in the artefact of the past, its authenticity, genuineness, authority, its unique phenomenon of romantic distance however close it might be physically, a distance located in its testimony to the past it has witnessed (Benjamin 1973c: 223). The aura of the artefacts, their three-dimensional reality, their facticity, all authenticate the narrative of the Museum of London. This is their purpose.

There is a subtle play of difference at work here:

Presence	Absence
Present	Past
Here now	Distant
Signifier	Signified
Trace	Substance

The objects are immediate and real before us, present to our consciousness and sight. As the concrete past, they confirm the meaning of the presentation. But the objects only represent or indicate the past. The past is the referent signified by the object. The object signifies an absent presence: of course the past is not present here and now, but absent, distant. So the objects are signs in our present. They are not the past immediately present before us but signifiers of the past (the signified), traces of the past (the absent referent). 'When we use signs, the being present of the referent and signified, incarnated in the self-present signifier, appears to us immediately, but it is delusion, misperception, dream. There is neither substance nor presence in the sign, but only the play of differences' – difference between signifier and signified, between signified and referent, between presence and absence (Leitch 1983: 44). The objects embody this play of difference, which is tied down by the rhetorical agency of interpretation – the Museum of London producing a substantial past before us in the present, presenting a past. And it is by means of the reduction of difference that the Museum of London confirms its message.

The notion of presence is at the heart of the 'romance' of archaeology. It forms the basis of much of archaeology's appeal and popularity. The objects on view in the museum bring us face to face with the past. The objects have presence, human presence – the features of the burial mask, the thumbprint on the pot. This presence constitutes the object's authority, its authenticity. The presence of the past – the past endures and reaches out to touch us.

The authenticating, romantic presence of the museum object is a restricted, one-dimensional notion of presence, which reduces the dialectic of presence and absence. It suggests that the time of the artefact can be localized, that the artefact *belongs* to the past, to a moment in time when someone made and used it. This is the romance of the object. Time is thus ultimately abstracted and reduced to a derivative of space; time comes to be composed of ultimately timeless moments on a continuum, its essence lying in the measurable 'distance' between moments. The ambiguity of the artefact – the play of semiotic difference encompassing past and present, its nature as sign in the present to and for a past – is stabilized in the name of a fixed and closed-down History.

George Seferis expresses the disturbing tension between presence and absence, the void behind the burial mask, the presence in the human features; the past is both present and absent. We must grasp the full implications of the opposition presence-absence. The makers of the artefact are absent. It is our rhetorical insistence that requires their presence.

The absent creator of the artefact is longed for – if only it were possible to meet and talk with the people of the past, have *them* present before us. But they are absent and what is left? According to some, the archaeologist is confined to describing the tangible (cf. C. Hawkes 1954), doomed to discover only the trivial (Leach 1973). But for the public there is the inspired popularizer, a Michael Wood (1985), a John Romer (1984), who can invoke absent humanity, bring the past alive, make it live, make the people of the past present. The presence of this past *is* our present.

As Eagleton has pointed out (1983: 120–1), structuralism has exposed this humanist fallacy – for archaeology the notion that the artefactual past is a kind of transcript of the living presence of real people who are disturbingly absent. Such a notion actually dematerializes the artefact, reducing it to a mediating element in the present's spiritual encounter with the humanity of the past. Rather, meaning arises through the chronic reciprocity of presence and absence, being and non-being.

Meaning is not simply present in the artefact but is in a sense also absent. Meaning is not identical with itself; the artefactual past exhibits a surplus over exact meaning. Meaning is produced in the material practice of reasoning in the present, which is, of course, in no way identical with the past.

The exhibited past

A period room in the Castle Museum, York: moorland cottage

> Typical of the North-East of Yorkshire ... home-spun and spartan ... The hearth was the centre of family life, providing not only warmth and comfort, but a place for the old cooking pot to simmer above the glowing peat. Bread was baked here: the dough was mixed in the wooden trough beneath the window. In front of the fire is a home-made rag or 'clip' rug ... The country made furniture reflects a tradition of unsophisticated craftsmanship, which was about to pass away. Already, on the mantelpiece, there are factory-made trinkets and ornaments – the pair of Staffordshire pottery dogs, the fancy glass rolling pin and walking sticks, and a cheap but cheerful German clock. In the window hangs a 'witch-ball'. Its glass surface was popularly supposed to reflect from the room the stare of any witch or evil eye.
>
> (Official Guidebook)

In situational display artefacts are brought together in an association that will supposedly enable the visitor to decode a meaning through experience of context. Such associations commonly take the form of period rooms. Figures may inhabit the rooms; they may be the intended focus of attention (e.g. costume). Situational display involves lesser or greater degrees of reconstruction to provide a window to the past.

In traditional case display the artefact demands concentrated attention according to the ritual analytics of archaeology. What matters is not so much the artefact being on view as the significance of its existence, its authenticity. Its exhibition to the public is a concession (the Museum of Antiquities, Newcastle, is a university museum); hence the need for the visitor to be sufficiently initiated to be able to decode the objects.

The aesthetic artefact of the British Museum requires contemplation. Labelling is hardly needed. When exhibited, the aesthetic artefact is to communicate the ritual values of the cull of *Homo Artifex*. Hallowed and venerable achievement, it is the cult-image of *Homo Artifex*, ultimately unapproachable. 'The closeness which one may gain from its subject matter does not impair the distance which it retains in its appearance' (Benjamin 1973d: 245). It is, after all, the product of Man.

The period room focuses on the communicative-value, the exhibition-value of the artefact as opposed to cult-value (Benjamin 1973c: 226–7). Situational display attempts to overcome the distance of the past. Artefacts are reassembled into 'realistic' association and no longer stand on their own. The distance between past and present is suspended in an arrested synchronism. Time is suspended and the objects are viewed through the spatial relations of the display, through their present codification (almost always in terms of function).

The visitor is drawn into the space created by the artefacts to discover their 'meaning'. The visitor herself fills the absence within the period room, the absence of a living constituting agent. The visitor merges with the other because of her absence, but this absence means that the absent living agent of the past artefact is all the more like the visitor. The visitor becomes the figure in a mirror of her present (see Williamson 1978: 77ff.). But it is not so much the past individual who is absent as the present author.

In the period room cult-value is replaced by exhibition-value – the artefact *requires* display; it necessarily includes a communicative function. The artefacts in the period room do not of necessity require concentrated attention or contemplation. The visitor may examine the past, but absent-mindedly.

The semiotic character of artefacts is recognized. They are used as vehicles to a story of the past, as signs in the present carrying information to the visitor. They are given an explicit communicative function. They are a translucent window onto the past 'as it was', immediate, unmediated vehicles to a 'realistic' picture of the past, a photograph of the past (cf. McLuhan et al. 1969, on the pictorial visual form of museum display).

The model of reality behind this notion of the 'realistic' is that of the photograph. The period room is set before the gaze of the omnipresent camera, the clock for making images, for capturing and fixing instants. The period room is 'reality' ready to be photographed, a still life, tableau. But the period room is not so much a 'realist' as a 'naturalist' re-presentation of the past (Berger 1969: 50ff.; cf. Lukács 1963, 1980). The naturalistic display aims to present the immediacy of the past with maximum credibility. It aims at preserving an exact copy of 'the way things were', a replica. There is no other basis for the selection of artefacts to be included in the period room. In this sense naturalism is unselective. The period room shows what there was; it presents an inventory to the visitor and the more complete the inventory the better (Sontag 1979: 22). Nor is inventory a simple listing: 'inventory is never a neutral idea; to catalogue is not merely to ascertain but also to appropriate' (Barthes 1982: 222). Inventory fragments, lists the items the present owns. Naturalist display diverts attention away from the meaning of its inventory, from its constructed nature, from the practical *use* of artefacts as a medium to a past, a historical medium, by emphasizing immediate appearance, by appearing immediately understandable. Indeed, attention is diverted from the artefacts to the empty space between them.

Knowledge of the past is presented as being informational, bureaucratic. In such a conception selection is feared. Recovery and preservation must be as complete and unselective as is inhumanly possible. The past becomes a target for surveillance. Artefacts are preserved and exhibited for scrutiny. The visitor is given the privilege of being in on the act of surveillance. The empirical detail of the past is fed into an interminable dossier (Sontag 1979: 156). The past is atomized, pinned down, defined, controlled.

The visitor is drawn into the period room to fill the human absence and in this aesthetic awareness of and proximity to the artefacts the visitor discovers the familiar. So the past seems closer, understandable, manageable. But this is a tautology. Through the period room's transparent window we recognize the familiar – the fire to relax around, old cooking pot simmering away, china dogs on the mantelpiece. In seeking such a past we must have already discovered it, hence the recognition of the familiar. The past is not explained but acknowledged.

At the same time the period room is attractively mysterious (the 'witch ball' in the window). It invites speculation about its narrative; it begs the question of the link between the artefacts other than their juxtaposition. The more complete the inventory of the period room, the more the period room tells the visitors, the less they know. The period room is a static instant, a disconnected moment. This disconnected temporality and discontinuity with the present creates the mystery. The transparency of the period room is an illusion. Atomistic, manageable, manipulated 'reality' is opaque.

In this world of commodities there is no space for experience, no space for the social constitutive function of subjectivity. There is no space for subjective experience. This also creates a problem of meaning – where is the human narrative? It must be supplied by contemporary experience of the commodity. The visitor lends the objects an experiential context. In the museum department store, the only form of subjective experience allowed is the consumer dream of acquisition and consumption, of alternative lifestyles. The visitor sees, is attracted, desires. The visitor becomes a customer of the past, a tourist of the 'reality' of the past. The past is displayed. Exhibition-value has replaced cult-value.

The arrested temporality of the period room proposes that meaning is instantaneous, located in the disconnected moment, that visible facts convey the truth. The certainty of the existence, the facticity, the 'reality' of the artefacts, the 'look' of the period room confirm this proposal. But it is precisely 'certainty' that is instantaneous. Understanding is temporal and must involve the possibility of denying immediate appearance. (See Berger and Mohr 1982: 89; Sontag 1979: 23.) This is denied in the period room. The significance of the period room is its naturalism, its pretension to immediacy. The period room is not a replica but a *simulacrum,* an exact copy of an original that never existed. The past is transformed into its own image (Jameson 1984: 66).

The erotics of the museum

The relation with the past based on the look of objects is an amorous one (Sontag 1979: 23–4). It is a voyeuristic appreciation and celebration and a simultaneous violation of the body of the past. It is a pornography. Artefacts are promoted to virginal purity (the aesthetic artefact) or prostituted as objects for possession and consumption (the past is subject to immediate consumption in voyeuristic detail).

So the past is revealed to the visitor, exposed and uncovered to be appreciated. In this sense discovery, revelation, includes 'an idea of appropriative enjoyment' (see earlier). Aktaion discovers Artemis, surprises her at her bath and as voyeur enjoys her nudity, her purity and virginity, just as the visitor views the aesthetic artefact. But the sight of Artemis is her violation. What is seen is possessed; to view is to rape (Sartre 1958: 578–79). So the period room invites violation. It invokes subjective emotional detachment and consumption. The visitor stands back detached (no matter how close and familiar the past may seem) and views – there is no space or time, past or present, for drawing close, for subjective experience, for finding out what lies beneath the surface. There is only the pleasure of immediate voyeuristic consumption. 'Knowledge' becomes located in appearance, in instantaneous appropriation, instantaneous consumption, rape.

Artefacts are defined as objects for scrutiny, for display, for exhibition. The past is displayed. Like the pornographic photograph, detail and clarity of reproduction bring fascination, a sense of being in on the act. The desire for certainty of being in on the act rather than understanding leads to the emphasis on explicitness, on empirical mechanical immediacy. The certainty of the 'medium', photography or artefact, confirms the 'reality' of the displayed sexual act, of the displayed past. The pornographic model is displayed, 'available', asking to be taken, to be consumed, a sexual commodity, emotionally detached.

Just as in pornography women are all equivalent as sexual commodities – reduced to sameness in relation to their display and possession in stylized, sterile sex, endlessly repeatable – so too the period room is endlessly repeatable. History is ultimately all the same, abstract temporal sequence, object of display and possession. It is a homogeneous history.

The partner of the eternal virgin Artemis is the whore of the period room brothel, instantly available, open, easily penetrated. But 'the openness of homogeneous history is both seductive invitation and frustrating refusal, since in entering its gaping void you are entering precisely nothing' (Eagleton 1981: 45–6). The ease of penetration is here a sign of the sterility of the relationship.

Sex in pornography is stylized as a system of fetishistic objects – clothing, parts of body, physical acts. Sexuality is bound and immobilized, spectacular. So too with the commodified past. The visitor looks upon 'the past' in the period room. History is appreciated. For this to happen history is stylized, 'history must be complete and fully accomplished. As a process which is fully accomplished, history, with all its promise of future change and development is closed down and confined entirely to what can be exhibited as "the historical past"' (Bommes and Wright 1982: 291).

The George Joicey Museum, Newcastle upon Tyne: Converted seventeenth-century almshouses. The top floor of eleven inmates' cells form a sequence of period rooms in chronological order, from sixteenth to twentieth centuries.

> Is it true, do you think, that if they move us from here they will not let us keep our own furniture? I do hope they will because ... because, well, it's home, you know.
>
> (Inmate quoted just before the almshouses were closed in 1935: Brown 1934: 122)

The bourgeoisie have taken possession of an apartment which they pre-leased from the moment humanity appeared on earth.

(Dorfman and Mattelart 1975: 86)

In the Joicey Museum narrative is tied to situational display. Ideological distortion accompanies the formal elimination of history. The narrative is one of change in furniture. It is a chronology of antiques, the archetypal bourgeois collector's item, uniting the aesthetic and the commodity.

Temporality is again absent. It is the social practice, which is utterly excluded from the sequence of rooms. This is disguised by the linear row of cells, units of homogeneous time. The cells are antique showrooms. The informational text reads like a showroom catalogue:

> In the Regency Period British prosperity grew in combination with naval supremacy and expansion of the Empire, and this is reflected in the style of furniture and the use of new woods. The mahogany table with tip-up top is flanked by a pair of dining chairs, with bowed top and reeded sabre legs. Similar in style is the armchair. The satinwood cabinet in the Sheraton tradition has a bowed central section with a panel painted in the manner of Angelica Kaufmann …

Time is utterly consumable. Pop round the corner after the visit and buy a piece of history – if you can afford it.

The furniture is presented in the form of period rooms, theatres without actors again. Presenting the past; the stage is set, but where are the actors? They are the audience. The actors supplied by the visitor again belong to the present. The rooms represent the nuclear family through the centuries in its living room. The past is a sequence of interior design, redecoration occurring every century or so. Change is the consumerist change of contemporary capitalism; everything changes and stays the same. This is the ideological distortion. What of the constituting reality of social practice – structures of family life, gender, patriarchy? What of the social reality of the almshouses? The past has been evicted together with all her furniture.

Shop-front commodification

The Castle Museum, York: two converted eighteenth-century prisons house a series of 'folk' collections, 'everyday' objects – agricultural implements to toys to truncheons – dating from the eighteenth century onwards. Many were collected by a local country doctor, John Kirk, at the turn of the century. There are two reconstructed streets containing shops, pub, garage, fire station; a watermill, many period rooms; prison cells partly converted into traditional workshops; conventional case displays.

The overwhelming metaphor of the Castle Museum is the shop front, the shop display presenting the consumable variety of capitalist society. 'Kirkgate', the older reconstructed street of the museum, consists predominantly of shop fronts displaying commodities, simply that. The objects simply evoke recognition of empirical similarity and difference to the present, and it isn't all that different (cf. Museum of Antiquities). The artefacts are quite literally commodified. The museum case has literally become the shop front. The museum visit has become a confrontation with empirical commodity change. (Commodification again!)

The shop front has become museum case; the shops and galleries bear the imprint of the 'collector'. Shop fronts display *collections* of gold, silver, Sheffield plate, dinner services. The guidebook proclaims: 'to many people the Castle Museum is "the museum with the street". Kirkgate is a spectacular re-creation that has caught the atmosphere of the nineteenth-century ... It is in constant demand as a "set". But Kirkgate is not, of course, a stage-setting. It is a collection of real buildings and shop-fronts.' Kirkgate is a series of collections, not a street. The 'vivid picture of the everyday life of the past', which a plaque records as the founder of the museum's aim, is a collection of everyday objects.

The Chapel Gallery, which presents the miscellany of the museum, includes cases of horse brasses, weights and measures, model steam engines, lace, knitting, embroidery, drinking vessels, police truncheons; farm implements lie on the floor. Clock pointers, watch keys and clock faces: Kirk's collections of what he termed 'bygones' are the individual units of commodified time. They represent the hysterical compulsion to repeat, the failing of memory, reproduction of the always the same under the appearance of the new, the hysterical compulsion to collect and consume.

But this commodification is the reality of developing capitalism. The rhythm of the 'variety' of the objects reveals their abstract identity. The objects lose their empirical distinctions. The meaning of case after case, shop after shop of everyday objects slides into one of repetition. Meaning is no longer present in the object. This is disguised by the frequent adoption of 'realistic' situational displays; the lack of labelling and supportive material implies that the objects explain themselves.

Yet the 'realistic' display is repeatedly undermined by deconstructing details. Kirkgate's fire station contains cases of objects; the carriage in the street is surrounded by a fence; the street is in perfect order and repair, spotlessly clean; informational text appears on walls. In the costume galleries empty suits of armour stand in a cased mock-up 'realistic' landscape. Further on, in a dark gallery with shored-up 'trench' walls, clean freshly pressed uniforms on shop mannikins fight again in reconstructed Flanders mud. Haute couture dresses revolve in pastel pastoral landscape setting, richly furnished shop window sets.

The prisons play deconstructing counterpoint to the exhibits and displays. Peer through a slit in a door in Kirkgate (locked again) and inside is a padded cell: the hysterical historical? Just as the hysterical, delirious maniac incorporates what he or she sees and hears into his or her self-absorbed fantasizing, so too the museum seizes on manifestations of the past in order to possess them and unfeelingly incorporate them into its myth. We are in the prison of capitalist commodification. Remains of the prisons are frequently encountered: barred windows, iron-grill doors. The cells of one prison, interiors and corridors whitewashed, house workshop collections of blackened tools of Victorian pipe maker, wheelwright, blacksmith, printer. The rooms are obviously cells, some even retain grill doors; they are hardly neutral setting for 'period workshops'. The juxtaposition of blackened tools and whitewashed cells draws further attention to the stark contrast between present artificial setting and display, original carceral use of the settings and the craftsmen's tools. The Castle Museum dismantles its own pretensions to pictorial re-presentation.

Heritage: visiting a mythical past

The North of England Open Air Museum, Beamish, County Durham: 200 acres of countryside are the setting for reconstructed and refurbished buildings, some *in situ*, most transferred from around the North-East, which are meant to represent late-Victorian north-east England. There is a railway layout, colliery, pit cottages, a farm, and a town area with terraced houses, pub, and co-op. A large hall houses collections and archives. Sounds of traditional fairground and brass band, the rattle of trams, the smell of engine oil and steam add considerably to the nostalgic atmosphere; the museum is animated with brass band concerts, engines in steam, passenger trams, summer fairs, whippet racing, pitmen's wives baking bread and scones, and a co-op grocer weighing sugar bags filled with sand.

> We left Gateshead to get away from houses like this.
>
> (Visitor's comment)

'Geordie's Heyday': the declared aim of Beamish, the 'Great Northern Experience', is to preserve the North-East's heritage, the northern way of life 'about a century ago ... when the North-East was in the forefront of British Industrial development' (Official Guidebook). Local heritage is the focus of the visit to Beamish, a visit into a mythical past. Beamish is a commemoration of a mythical past; objects never intended to commemorate anything are transformed into monuments of mythical meaning.

Although the museum houses a reference library and photographic and sound archives, the heritage Beamish outwardly presents is property and artefacts, the property of a utopian community with all classes harmoniously in their place in Hall or terraced house, collecting mounts from stable block or working the colliery steam winder. All the dehistoricized elements of an anaesthetized past have been miraculously transported from Consett, Gateshead, Alnwick to a picturesque rural setting. It is hard to believe that this valley bottom is only a few miles from Newcastle; at Beamish history is isolated from the present.

History, objectified in property, industrial capital, and the object, is the existent (as long as it is carefully preserved) and at Beamish it is eminently visitable and consumable in leisure time. Objects and buildings from the past are extracted from their present context and displayed at Beamish. History is staged as 'historical' sights, images, and events. In this way 'history is abstracted from the historical and becomes an object of generalised social attention' (Bommes and Wright 1982: 290). History is extracted from the present.

We have noted the working of the exchange principle in relation to objects. It applies also to historical sites and to museums themselves. Beamish is eminently visitable, a place for the family to visit on August Bank Holiday. As such it is equivalent to other such places of 'historical' interest: castles, stately homes, cathedrals. The places have meaning overwhelming in relation to one another. History again becomes an 'abstract system of equivalences'. Its relation to everyday life is one of consumption in leisure time. Where should we go this weekend?

But to locate history in sites, monuments, museums, uninhabited places isolatable from the present 'suppresses at one stroke the reality of the land and that of its people, it accounts for nothing of the present, that is nothing historical, and as a consequence the monuments themselves become undecipherable, therefore senseless. What is to be seen is thus constantly in the process of vanishing' (Barthes 1973: 76). Beamish does not provide a window on the past. Beamish is an agent of blindness. The past is transformed into its image, a spectacle.

The past can be visited at Beamish, but this past is another world, a fantasy, a myth, a nostalgia. It is another time; 'as in other aggressive fantasies and the dream of primal bliss, it exists in allegory rather than actual time. It is a reverse image of the weaknesses of the present, a measure of our fall' (Samuel 1983: ii). As theatrical spectacle replaces life so nostalgia replaces history.

Beamish nourishes a 'soft focus nostalgia' (ibid.) for times more congenial when pitmen, 'prodigious gardeners, breeders of animals, and often gamblers' (guidebook) grew leeks (the gardens are set) and raced whippets (there has been whippet racing at Beamish) and yes, took baths in front of the open fire. It must have been this way *really*, mustn't it, because people lived in the terraced cottages until 1976 and provided 'information about how *their* cottages were furnished' (guidebook, our emphasis). Jo, from number 26, died after being rehoused when his cottage was given to Beamish by the National Coal Board, but with the help of his family his cottage has been recreated. He lives on doesn't he?

Beamish capitalizes (*sic*) on the indeterminacy, the ambiguity of artefacts and through selection and relocation at Beamish presents a sentimental experience of an imprecise time and place, a utopian gratification, a euchronia. This movement from the concrete naturalism of the exhibits to imaginary make-believe 'Geordieland' is a neo-tribal gesture, an assertion of 'roots' in the face of the anonymity of everyday life in contemporary capitalism. The transformation from real artefacts to imaginary past occurs through and for the initiate, the Geordie of today. The past is pre-recognized before arrival at Beamish. Beamish confirms recognition of the myth of the past. Older people recognize objects similar to those they lived with but now anaesthetized in the terms imposed by Beamish. Younger visitors listen to their mams and dads, grandmas and grandads.

This recognition and remembrance is not wholly conditioned: 'we left Gateshead to get away from houses like this'. Positive energies of past hopes and dissatisfactions, senses of tradition and freedom are aroused. However, these energies emerge in an isolated realm of leisure, that 'removed and anodyne realm in which gratification is offered for dissatisfaction in relation to work' (Bommes and Wright 1982: 296). As an 'experience' encountered in leisure time, the past is over, finished, relevant only in terms of a visit on Saturday or Sunday or a holiday, a day out with the kids. So why not just remember the good times – the steam engines and trams, leek shows and …? Let's have a good day out at Beamish. We hope to show that such concepts of diversion and amusement – here applied to the presentation of Beamish's nostalgic mythology – are as appropriate in ideology critique as more conventional analysis, which would assign Beamish's displayed past to particular sectional interests, criticizing a story mistold (see Adorno 1967: 30).

History is timeless through the logic of abstract equivalence. The objects and buildings also have a timeless quality because they have endured. They have defeated history's process of decay. Historical time is experienced as degeneration. We nostalgically look back from the edge of an abyss to a time of community and human dignity. This backwards look, and prospect of only further decay, is hindering: we must stop, rescue, and preserve. 'Under the entropic view of history, supported as it is by High Cultural paradigms, "the past" is revalued and reconstructed as an irreplaceable heritage – a trust which is bestowed upon the present and must be serviced and passed on to posterity' (Bommes and Wright 1982: 291). We must preserve the past; it needs servicing, mending, fixing. But fixing is immobilizing.

The rusting items of industrial machinery scattered around Beamish are testaments to history as decay. They proclaim the need to service the past, preserve it, rescue it. They also proclaim its endurance. Together with the work in progress reconstructing buildings, these objects declare Beamish is incomplete.

However, this is not a declaration that history is forever incomplete, or that history is open to human agency. It means *Beamish* is incomplete, a marketing ploy that Beamish will always be open for the visitor to return again and again to view the most recently fixed bit of the past. It means the past is still hanging on, it has endured, it is enduring, just like Jo in his cottage. It means our freedom, our agency, is restricted to being mechanics for a broken-down Gateshead tram.

The past endures, clinging to the present, weighing down the present. A sticky, slimy past sucks the present into its mire. An unfinished past of domination, unfreedom, and suffering seeps into the present and drags us into a mire of compulsive repetition, unresolved conflicts, because the past is forgotten (Schapiro 1977: 147). The past endures with the help of the present but in being preserved in this way the past is forgotten. The truth of the past is suffocated beneath a pile of preserved objects, which only proclaim a self-evident but deadened 'truth'.

Labour and discovery: the archaeologist as hero

Jorvik Viking Centre, York: an underground 'interpretation centre' beneath a shopping centre. Visitors make a 'journey in time' on talking 'time cars' to a street and alleyway in Viking Jorvik, complete with sounds, smells, and models of people. A guide to archaeological excavation is followed by conventional case displays and a museum shop.

'A revolutionary concept in museum design': so claims 'Jorvik Times', an official 'newspaper' produced by the York Archaeological Trust. It is apparently so revolutionary that the label 'museum' cannot be applied to the Jorvik Viking Centre. The centre is a project of the York Archaeological Trust and aims to 'remind people of a forgotten but important and exciting piece of English history, and at the same time explain how archaeologists go about their task' (official guidebook). A visit to the centre is again an experience, the 'Jorvik Experience', a 'journey in time' to Viking Age York, Jorvik brought back to life (Jorvik Times). The experience is of discovery of the past and the labour involved in revivification.

The experience begins with a 'trip back in time', an impressionistic audio-visual presentation, after which 'time stops, history is frozen, this is Jorvik' (time car commentary). The visitor proceeds to view the reconstructed street and alleyway. The past has been discovered and reconstructed through immense archaeological labour, the scientific processing of '15,000 (or is it 30,000) objects! A quarter of a million pots! Four-and-a-half tons of bones!' (commentary). In the supporting literature and commentary, stress is repeatedly placed on the detail and accuracy of the reconstructed street, its basis in enormous amounts of factual evidence. Indeed the reconstruction is said to be so accurate, so real, that 'if the Vikings themselves were to return they would feel completely at home' (Jorvik Times). Yet the objects are made to carry meanings that would have mystified their makers: empirical detail, representational accuracy, inanimate display for educational purposes. Stress is placed on authenticity achieved through science and technology and the sophistication of the audio-visual presentation (see Wishart 1984). The stress is on the identification of empirical accuracy and 'life', the life of Jorvik. But life doesn't live.

After the street comes a jump forward to 1980 and the discovery of what lay buried. The archaeological site is preserved half excavated, a work site, labour in process, finds in a tray, wheelbarrows full. 'Archaeologists from the York Archaeological Trust are revealing the remains of the loos and wells, warehouses, workshops and homes we have just visited … they peel off layer after layer of soil, labelling, measuring, photographing and planning everything as they go' (guidebook).

More labour is revealed: the evidence, having been discovered, is processed. The visitor arrives at the real detective work; 'digging is only the start of the archaeologist's detective work' (commentary). The visitor passes by a desk with work obviously in process and then is presented with a reconstructed conservation laboratory complete with white-coated expert looking down a microscope. Another white-coated figure (a member of an environmental archaeology unit, we are told) sieves biological finds. On the opposite wall life-sized photographs attest to scientific industry. The commentary enlightens the visitor: this is biological detective work, which together with detective work on other material evidence, shows the archaeologist what life was like in the past, what conditions were like, when the enormous three-dimensional jigsaw puzzle is pieced together.

The labour of discovery and reconstructing the past: so great is the stress on authenticity that 'scientific' technique must be shown to the visitor. And science excludes the visitor – the white-coated dummy looks down the microscope, but not the visitor. We are to understand that scientific discovery guarantees the authenticity of the trip, a tourist trip into history. 'You are HERE, and you are THERE, both at the same time' (Magnus Magnusson in guidebook). Time has after all been arrested. The past is present. We are present in the past. This is the actual site of the street. These are the actual timbers. The detective work draws the

Figure 18.2 The past brought back to life. Reproduced with permission of Cultural Resource Management Ltd.

visitor closer to the past. Accordingly it is appropriate that the visitor should be allowed to actually touch the past; panels of potsherds and other objects are attached to a wall.

Between the two white-coated experts is a reminder of the conceptual associate of 'labour' – 'discovery'. A marble slab in the floor records the discovery by two construction workers of the 'Coppergate Helmet' (Anglo-Saxon in date).

'Now come and see the objects'. The penultimate element in the Jorvik Experience is a conventional gallery of 500 case-displayed objects. With the supporting text they form a descriptive account of subsistence and crafts. Finally comes the museum shop where you can 'take your pick from a host of beautifully crafted mementoes of the city the Vikings called Jorvik' (Magnus Magnusson in guidebook).

Jorvik is described as an experience and like any experience it just happens, as does the thrill of discovery, discovery of treasure, of the aesthetic artefact, of the artefact laden with information. The visitor passively experiences, locked for half of the visit in a moving 'time car'. We are guided by the anonymous cultural policeman (but isn't it that kindly Magnus Magnusson?) whose precise rehearsed sentences are truly sentences – *sententiae* – acts of penal speech (Barthes 1977a: 191), telling us what we see, tying down the meaning of the artefacts, tying the artefact to the 'realistic'. The 'journey in time' and visit to reconstructed Jorvik is a sentence against polysemy. There is no turning back; the visitor cannot leave the 'time car'. Museum shop follows object gallery follows object laboratory follows what is presented as the life-world of the artefact. The fixed sequence culminates in the revelation of the meaning of the Jorvik Experience. Object gallery and museum shop are the commodified object of archaeological labour and the reality of commodity purchase, reified object on display followed by an opportunity to buy a memento of the purchased experience, to buy the past (1,000-year-old pieces of timber @ £1 a square inch).

> facilis descensus Averno ...
> sed revocare gradum superasque evadere ad auras
> hic opus, hic labor est.
> (The descent to Avernus is easy ... but to retrace your steps and escape back to upper airs – this is the labour, this is the toil)
> (Virgil *Aeneid* VI: 126–9)

> The present ... is the bull whose blood must fill the pit if the shades of the departed are to appear at its edge.
> (Benjamin 1955: 314)

Aeneas, Trojan hero, visited Cumae where the Sibyl prophesied his destiny and guided him into Avernus, the underworld, where he encountered Rome's destiny. Beamish is a visit to a mythical past. Jorvik is a mythical journey in the steps of the archaeologist as hero.

Like Aeneas, the archaeologist (and later the privileged visitor) is guided on a ritual journey to 'knowledge'. For Aeneas it is a fixed and irresistible destiny and future. For the archaeologist it is 'the past', finally isolated in realistic photographic detail, fixed and certain.

For Aeneas, the irresistibility, the veracity of his destiny and Rome's future is confirmed respectively by his guide, the prophetess Sibyl and her inspiration from the god Apollo, and by the supreme effort and labour required of the hero to gain access to the underworld and there discover knowledge. For the visitor the 'truth' of Jorvik is confirmed by the guides – Magnus Magnusson and other commentators – stressing the 'divine' origins of the reconstruction in scientific endeavour, and also by the supreme effort and labour required of the archaeologist-hero to discover and reconstruct the past.

But there is a striking absence. The *Aeneid* is Virgil's epic. Virgil, the author, is absent from Aeneas's journey. The Sibyl's and Aeneas's prophetic visions of things to come are Virgil's present, his offering to his patron Augustus. So too with Jorvik: the reconstructed street, the result of the labour of the archaeologist hero, and the guiding commentary are self-fulfilled prophecies. They too are irresistible and unavoidable because of the absent author. This is why Jorvik is described as an experience. Like any true experience, it happens, is irresistible, author-less. The Sibyl's certainty and the certainty of Aeneas's experiences belong to Virgil because

Virgil is projecting his present into a mythical past. The truth of the Jorvik reconstruction belongs not in the objects, in the 'past', but in the present, in present archaeological practice, uncovering, unconcealing the fragments of Viking Jorvik.

We may take the classical analogy further. Walter Benjamin also writes: 'The soothsayers who found out from time what it had in store did not experience time as either homogeneous or empty. Anyone who keeps this in mind will perhaps get an idea of how past times were experienced in remembrance – namely in just the same way' (1973d, Thesis XVIIIB: 266). The ancient prophet interpreted phenomena as signs (e.g. flights of birds, hysterical ramblings of a priestess). Uncertainty and doubt existed over the status of phenomena as prophetic signs, over the meaning of the signs and the reality to which they might refer. To perform an interpretation was to arrest the present in grasping the momentary connection of the signs with the future and reduce the doubt over meaning in a prophetic reading. Reservation was repressed, meaning assigned and then asserted – interpretation was open to criticism and debate within the community. So the prophet's experience of time is not empty duration χρόνος but καιρός – the critical moment, conjunction of present and future (Kermode 1967: 46ff.; cf. Leitch 1983: 3–6). To interpret the past is also to play the prophet. Jorvik, or rather its creators, read the fragments of the past and tie them to a particular unmediated meaning, descriptive, empty, its connection with the present forgotten but not absent.

PART TWO: PAST AND PRESENT IN THE MUSEUM

The museum's aesthetic eliminates the concrete author of history; it suppresses the concrete authorship of the past in the present. And this is in spite of the museum's frequent use of a linear 'book' format – using artefacts to carry or support a story line. In presenting the archaeological and/or historical process of acquiring knowledge as one of passive discovery and subsequent description of the past, history is presented as being written by the white-coated expert, a faceless author, a universal author, god, or science. The present's implication in the past is one of objective contingency.

On another level, the present is accepted as being implicated in the museum as an institution. First, the museum is an active intervention in the past as it conserves and preserves artefacts which originated in the past. Secondly, it presents these to the public – the objects are exhibited. Authorship refers to the creativity of interpreting the past for the public – the exhibition is designed. The present's implication in the past is here one of subjective contingency.

At both levels the link between past and present is contingent. The past is fixed and complete; the present turns to the past according to its own subjective decision. The decision is made to turn to the past because it is conceived as valuable to the present, as value-laden. But this is an abstract monetary value: it doesn't really matter what the past was like in its details. The decision is to turn to a past preconceived as fixed, complete, in-itself.

This contingent relation between past and present determines the themes open to discussion concerning the museum as an institution.

1   Does the museum materially preserve the past with efficiency? The management and conservation of collections. Research and collections.
2   The museum and the commodity. Services *for* the community – information services, object identification. The relation of museums to other institutions and bodies (such as local government, planning departments, English Heritage, government departments, local societies, adult education). The museum's contribution to tourism.
3   Education and the museum – museums and educational institutions (schools, universities), loan services. The museum and its message – educational theory and museum applications; traditional knowledge areas (art, history, natural history) and the museum.
4   Is the museum effectively getting across its message? Communicative effectiveness and 'interpretation' in the museum. ('Interpretation': 'an educational activity which aims to reveal meanings and relationships through the use of original objects, by first hand experience and by illustrative media rather than simply to communicate factual information' (Tilden 1957, p. 8).) Exhibition design and layout – use of supportive 'interpretive' material (labels, models, text, diagrams, maps); static and interactive display; object-based and concept-based display. Formal and technical matters.

The majority of work and discussion on museums is confined to these themes (see the comprehensive bibliographies produced by the Department of Museum Studies, University of Leicester).

As a means of critique, we will now consider two particular debates concerning archaeology's relation with the present.

Entertaining the public: 'real' and 'popular' archaeology

The display which aims at the uninitiated visitor and sets out to stimulate, entertain, divert, but ultimately to educate, is the shadow of a 'real' archaeology which is isolated from its determinate context, an autonomous archaeology which searches desperately among the debris of the past for the immediacy and meaning it has overlooked in the present. The popular exhibition is the social bad conscience of 'real', serious archaeology (Adorno and Horkheimer 1979: 135). Archaeologists dig up the past, lodge their finds in the museum, and *may* speculate according to their theoretical models as to the meaning and significance of what they have found. Presenting any of this to a public – those who do not belong to the community of archaeologists – is entirely contingent, a separate matter from 'real' archaeology. Popular presentation is split from the real work of archaeology. The link between archaeology/artefact and public becomes 'interpretation' of archaeology/artefact/history. Interpretation is the function of the museum. The museum becomes a service manned by professionals.

So the museum presents *for* the public, the uninitiated ('knowledge', 'concepts', 'ideas', artefacts – it doesn't matter in this purely technical relation). Experts supply cultural goods, cultural capital for the visitor, manufacturer for customer. The supermarket-museum is simply the physical locus for this transaction.

Archaeology 'is in the end reduced to mere communication. Its alienation from human affairs terminates in its absolute docility before a humanity which has been enchanted and transformed into clientele by the suppliers' (Adorno 1967: 25–6). Reduction to communication, reduction to broadcast: the only form of creativity and agency within this technical relation is the 'creativity' of the curator-entrepreneur, supplying his inventiveness to the marketing of the past, the design of displays. All that can be said to the visitor concerning her agency is 'you too could be an expert'.

Those museums and commentators who draw on progressive educational theory and advocate interactive displays – displays which involve the visitor in some active way, which centre themselves on the visitor – do not alter this relation. They merely comment on the presumed efficiency of the communication, that an interactive display will convey more of its 'message' to the visitor. They are equally manipulative of the visitor (cf. critiques of progressive educative techniques, e.g. Elshtain 1976, Entwistle 1979).

To entertain, inform, educate the present, the past must be presented in an accessible way. Hawkes (1968) has voiced the conscience of humanist as opposed to scientific archaeology. Decrying the inhuman works of scientific archaeologists shored up 'behind ramparts of jargon and other specialist defences' (p. 260), Hawkes wants an accessible humanist archaeology, 'historical (i.e. descriptive-narrative) writing of the quality and humanity of the work of the young Gordon Childe, Mortimer Wheeler, Christopher Hawkes, Stuart Piggott, or even, in his more austere way, Grahame Clark' (p. 256). Hawkes wants historical synthesis, extraction of 'historical' meaning from disparate facts.

For Hawkes, a return to, or re-emphasis of humanist writing would overcome the split she perceived between inaccessible scientific archaeology and traditional archaeology. The link between the archaeological artefact and popular accessible writings is the imaginative *personality* trained in the humanities (p. 261). There is still a split between real archaeology concerned with the past and popular archaeology for the present. The link is the imaginative personality instilling human values into dusty dry artefacts, writing historical synthesis. Clarke also acknowledges the split between real and popular archaeology. For Clarke, vulgarizing archaeology is the last refuge of the humanities-trained archaeologist unable to deal with real analytical archaeology and seeking material gain (1968: 22).

Both of these positions rely on a conception of an autonomous archaeology. For Hawkes, archaeology's autonomy from contemporary society is its basis in eternal human values; archaeology is a pursuit of the cultured (Childe read Pindar after dinner? Hawkes 1968: 261). For Clarke, archaeology is archaeology is archaeology. Analytical archaeology is autonomous in that it is a scientific discipline in quest of knowledge coming to its maturity. Archaeology as culture, archaeology as analytical discipline: both oppose the notion of archaeology fundamentally being for-something-else. Primarily archaeology exists in-itself.

In these conceptions archaeology has no *necessary* link with the public, with a clientele, with its social context. The links that are established between archaeological artefact and the public are due to the social responsibility and sense of social duty of the archaeologist or curator, the personality of the archaeologist or curator.

All the discussion of the reasons behind the archaeologist's quest for the artefact and its eventual residence in the museum is a vacuous rhetoric, a marketing ploy to justify the ideological work done in the name of culture, science, or whatever other reified and alienated realm. Why dig up and preserve the past? Because of natural curiosity, the human will to knowledge and understanding; as an aesthetic quest to secure beauty and variety; to establish symbolic links with the past, a sense of national or human identity; because humans need a past, a communal memory, a sense of the past; because of a sense of social duty – the past is being destroyed; for personal satisfaction; to entertain and divert; for nostalgic reasons – a search for more congenial times; to learn from the past and educate the present; to find a model for inspiration; to reconcile East and West and solve the world's problems (see also the discussion in Shanks and Tilley 1992: 25–7).

The answer lies in the split between real archaeology and its presentation and/or justification to a public. The error is in posing the question after the act of separating real and popular archaeology. Discussing and considering the presentation of archaeology, or its relevance to the present, or justifying archaeology to the present with entertaining or diverting popular works and exhibitions presupposes the gap which such rhetoric is to bridge. The relation between archaeology and the present remains arbitrary because archaeology is absolutized as though grounded in the inner nature of knowledge; it is justified in an ahistorical way by reference to eternal human qualities or values. Archaeology is reified, separated from the present (Horkheimer 1976: 212).

Archaeology is reified, rooted in the antinomies of a fragmented capitalist society. This brings a secret source of comfort in the split between real and popular archaeology. That the fatal fragmentation might some day end is a fatal destiny, nemesis – retribution for archaeology's pretension to autonomy, its hubris (see Adorno 1967: 24). Reification, involving those eternal values of humanity and objectivity must not end. Archaeology must not be contaminated by society's materialism, the mob armed now with metal detectors, wrecking the past in search of material gain. Archaeology must counter this growing barbarism with educative measures, popular works and exhibits accessible to the mob, to justify its civilized alternative, to appease the mob.

Archaeologists as creatures of their times

> Was fällt, das sollt Ihr stossen
> (If it's falling down, give it a shove)
>
> (Nietzsche)

The autonomy of archaeology is potentially violated by the archaeologist and curator who address the public with justifying and entertaining works. The archaeologist and curator are, of course, members of society, but what is the significance of this? Is the autonomy of archaeology compromised?

Fowler writes: 'as a factor in our use of archaeological evidence, the meaning we give to it, the fashion of the times remains potent ... The archaeologist is a creature of his own time ... There is no ultimate, finite truth to be revealed by archaeological evidence ... all interpretation of it is relative' (1977: 136). Fowler separates the artefact, the evidence, from its interpretation by the fallible archaeologist, a creature of his (*sic*) times.

Clarke's controlling models locate the archaeologist in society determining his or her confrontation with, his or her interpretation of the past (1972: 5–10).

Daniel expresses scepticism regarding 'new' archaeologists – they will realize that the past is something to be recorded, described, and appreciated. Their deviations from this empiricist truth are due to their (defective?) personalities, their subjective experience and disposition (1981: 192).

So from these points of view archaeology's autonomy lies in its object. Archaeology is further abstracted from its determination in the present in the assertion that its practitioners belong to the present. Archaeology is judged according to its practitioners who are subsumed, assimilated in an administrative manner into the prevailing constellations of power, *which the intellect ought to expose* (Adorno 1967: 30). The 'artefact' retains its purity and integrity in spite of the potential violation. The present though is absolved from guilt in this absolutization of an immediate relativity.

But the present is not absolved from its duty to the past. Archaeology's autonomy, its truth, lies in the artefact, patiently enduring time and subjective interpretation. The past is objectified as property. The obvious conclusion is that the object past must be preserved, protected. Property is sacred. In the devaluation of the practical confrontation of archaeologist and the past to a universal relativism, the artefactual past is the historical constant, our Heritage to be preserved for interpretation in the future. Every present needs a past to be interpreted. We must preserve the sacred past for the future (Fowler 1977: 192). Museums preserve the future's sacred heritage, its private property. Objectivity is sacred fetishized property. Whose property? The property of Man?

'Disputing the decay of works in history serves a reactionary purpose; the ideology of culture as class privilege will not tolerate the fact that its lofty goods might ever decay, those goods whose eternity is supposed to guarantee the eternity of the classes' own existence' (Adorno 1964: 62, translation by Susan Buck-Morss). We remain hidden in the labyrinth of a commodified past, a labyrinth of deadened and preserved objects. Destruction is necessary to create openings to get out, for the sake of liberation. A way out must be uncovered. In this sense truth is the Greek ἀλήθεια, a practice of unconcealing. The way out has been forgotten (reification is a forgetting), it is hidden behind a heap of decaying objects (see the discussion in Shanks and Tilley 1992: 7–28).

What is the nature of the relation between curator and his or her society? In an analysis of the National Air and Space Museum, Washington D.C., Meltzer makes use of a concept of 'ideology', which he claims to derive from Althusser, 'to view our society's manner of reinforcing and reproducing its economic structure' in the museum. 'The Museum is about air and space, but only on a superficial level; it is more properly about us' (1981: 125). Meltzer utterly neutralizes the concept of ideology in what he recognizes as an apolitical analysis (ibid.: 125). For Meltzer, the museum as ideological institution means that it tells 'us' about 'our' economic structure. 'Our' use of artefacts of the past tells 'us' about 'ourselves'. 'We', presumably, are citizens of the democratic USA, good American capitalists.

Mediating past and present

It is necessary to mediate these two related poles, to mediate a metaphysics of history where history is identified as the past, and a relativization of history where history is a reflex of present social and material reality, present social conditions.

Leone suggests one form of mediation. Drawing on Bloch's proposal (1977a, 1977b) that discussions of the past among most peoples have little or nothing to do with the facts or processes described but are entirely about the present, being models of how society ought to work, Leone claims that the scientist's social structure is replicated when his or her work is presented to the public, in the ritual of public performance. The archaeologist is concerned in his or her professional work with giving the objects accurate meaning (1981a: 12). This search for objective accuracy produces boredom when presented to the public because it ignores the link between past and present. The way out is to 'allow the past to be the image of the present it must be by its very nature in a ritual setting' (p. 13). The professional and private work of archaeology is separate from its ritual and public performance. A bored reception indicates lack of meaning in the original work, an unrealized connection with the present. The solution is to credit the public performances with their private-professional authors. Let the public settings based on interpretations change, 'show them changing and teach how they are changed and what they change in response to' (p. 13; cf. Schlereth 1978).

Leone locates the determinate link between archaeology and the present in its public presentation. The professional-private work of the archaeologist must respect the present's creation of the past if the ritual of presentation, of performance is to be meaningful.

However we would argue that there is no homogeneous present creating the past – the present is fragmented and contradictory. Secondly, professional archaeology and its public presentation are both forms of performance.

Presentation as performance

There can be no 'realistic' objective representation of the past. We have argued that actual past history is not identical to its representation in archaeological reason. There is no genuine past to be brought into harmony with archaeological thought and neutrally re-presented to the public. Archaeology does not provide a mirror to the past nor does it provide an abstract system that expresses the 'reality' of the past. This is to identify reason with the past and does not do justice to the material practice and suffering of human subjects in the past. Such an identification justifies the tyranny of thought over individual human existence, 'it is the triumphant tyranny of the concept, the relentless sublation of discrete particulars to a system radically closed in its very dreary infinity' (Eagleton 1981: 120). The qualitative meaning of the past is lost in the universal authors' quest for the objective past.

Reified, commodified objectivity, empty quantified detail, communicating universal 'truths' of history as progress, decay, or simple objectivity yielding to present reason, destroys the historical meaning of the artefact, its temporality.

The past is not a three-dimensional jigsaw puzzle buried beneath the archaeologist, or a palimpsest. All such conceptions reduce the past to a monolithic structure, a synchronic structure of spatial relationships. Artefacts are not neutral elements with a frozen meaning ready for defrosting, but fields of contention and contradiction with constantly shifting significance and connotation, shifting according to their inscription in past and present social *practice*.

The past is not a tangle of factual details to be decoded, presented to and appreciated by those with an educated 'sense of the past' (Fowler 1981), 'but consists rather of the numbered group of threads that represent the weft of the past as it feeds into the warp of the present … The subject matter of history, once released from pure facticity, needs no *appreciation*. For it offers not vague analogies to the present, but constitutes the precise dialectical problem that the present is called upon to resolve' (Benjamin 1979: 362).

So the museum exhibition is not so much representational or referential as figural and rhetorical. It is the rhetorical performance of the museum, its *act* of interpretation and persuasive intention, which opens up meaning.

There are several implications of the notion of presentation as rhetorical performance. Archaeology and its presentation in the museum cannot begin with an abstractly defined objectivity or a priori method but must begin *in medias res* with the artefact in its present historical circumstance, riddled with error, contradiction, doxa (Benjamin 1973a: 103). The primary question is not ontological or methodological but strategic, political. Not what is the past and how should we approach it, but what do we want to do with the past and why? (cf. Eagleton 1983: 210–11).

Archaeology does not receive its meaning from the artefact. The artefact surrenders and receives meaning in the practice of archaeology and presentation in text or in the museum. This does not sacrifice truth in a relativism whereby it is impossible to decide between rival explanations and presentations if each springs rationally from a particular way of life, from particular social conditions in the present. Such a relativism is only a problem if the concern is with the relation of an *abstract* consciousness or subjectivity in general, formulating explanations and creating presentations, and an abstract object of study. The abstract subject's explanation and presentation of the abstract object is relative to present social context. This problem 'disappears in the concrete process in which subject and object mutually determine and alter each other' (Adorno, quoted by Buck-Morss 1977: 51). Objectivity itself is heterogeneous, not abstract. The artefact cannot be completely defined in terms of abstract, ahistorical, objective qualities such as form, dimension and all related categories of type. It is the insistence and agency of the act of interpretation, explanation, presentation that restricts the ambiguity of the artefact to meaning and understanding. Artefacts have endured and are authentic materially, but they are vulnerable. Their truth is precarious and in constant need of re-articulation. Truth is time-bound, temporal, historical.

The material reality of the artefact is not mythically permanent. The artefactual past is not eternal abstracted objectivity to be appropriated by archaeological reason. The artefact is time-bound, transitory. Non-chronometric time enters into the meaning of the artefact. Material reality is in a permanent state of historical becoming. The past is irreversible, discontinuous, particular, and thoroughly mediated objectivity. The past is not a systematic array of objects and their relationships, a fixed reality of commodified objectivity towards which archaeologists are groping and which may be represented in museum display. Such a conception is a denial of temporality; the past is here presented as an eternal image or myth. The past instead must be realized as the 'subject of a construction whose locus is not empty time but the particular epoch, the particular work' (Benjamin 1979: 352). The artefacts must be broken from historical continuity.

We must renounce all abstract closedness and totality in definitions and re-presentations of artefacts. There is no unified identity behind all artefacts. As such there can be no universal method, no formal principles of interpretation and display.

The contradictory present

Why go to a museum? To see the past because it exists, to be educated? The answers to the question offered by the museum exhibition are inadequate in their masking of aporias, contradictory relations lodged in contemporary social experience. We have tried to show how these contradictory relations lie within the museum's aesthetic, its presentation of the artefact:

spatial	temporal
closed, completed past	open, unfinished history
eternity	history
reified	relational
repetition	particularity
identity	difference
presence	absence
homogeneous	heterogeneous
coercive	explorative
passive	active
monologic	dialogic
forgetting	remembrance
conservation	redemption

The museum manipulates these relations, suppressing contradiction, fixing the past as a reflection of the appearance of the present. The present recognizes itself and is justified. The museum as ideological institution suppresses difference and heterogeneity in advertisements for the world through its duplication in the artefactual past. The museum suppresses temporality and agency. In the museum the past becomes the death mask of the present.

Conclusion: towards a redemptive aesthetic

Some implications can be drawn from our argument:

1. We must retain heterogeneity and difference, the fragmentary and discontinuous reality of the past as a means of overcoming the ideological effects of a reified object world, past and present. The presented artefact is a reified object in the museums we studied. Social relations that provide meaning to the artefact are transformed into an appearance of relationships between objects. The exhibited object's pretence of transparent naturalism is a rendering of society as opaque, of history as homogeneous, always -the -same. Opaque homogeneity, running in a continuous flow through history, conceals the antagonistic and contradictory class-structured present and imposes an image of the present on the past. We must resist the power of reification, shatter the homogeneous past, reveal the social relationship of past and present in a true realism, a social physiognomy that embodies objective social contradiction, which embraces contradiction, discontinuity, and conflict in a dynamic totality (Adorno 1967; Jameson 1977).

2. We must oppose professional preservative History with its archaeologist-curator speaking for a monolithic and murdered past. We should democratize and personalize authorship in an attempt at avoiding the absorption of author-archaeologist and visitor into the product (display, book) (see CCCS Popular Memory Group 1982: 215). This involves an active reconciliation of production and reception of the past, a renunciation of the conventional relationship of professional producing the past *for* a consuming public, of experts presenting an elitist high culture.

3. We must recognize the full implications of authorship and fully embrace reflexivity. So all presentations are to be understood as being precisely that – intimately tied to the present. Their truth is to be found in the present's specific encounter with particular aspects of the past. We must present a specific and unique engagement with the past, an engagement original to every new present (Benjamin 1979: 352). We must present specific acts of construction, work in progress, varied forms of relationship with the artefactual past instead of a fixed relation of representation of a completed past. The museum can allow the visitor to construct a past along with the archaeologist-curator: participation not as a means to a pre-given, pre-discovered end but as an open process of constructing different pasts.

4. The artefact must not be reduced to uniform abstract objectivity. The artefact is not reducible to a one-dimensional representational sign of the past. The past is not fixed, to be represented, but changes according to its specific engagement with the present. So we must detach the artefact from its 'self-evident' meaning as object of scientific study, reveal the artefact as non-identical with its apparent meaning, strip the object of its pretension to being-in-itself, strip the object of its immediacy in order that it might be released from the sterile continuum of the homogeneous history of the always-the-same (Wolin 1982: 125). This may involve enabling the artefact to gesture to its own material inscription in social

practice, its own material existence, at the same time as it conveys a meaning in the context of a museum display. It certainly requires considering recent work on the symbolic meaning and use of artefacts – the style of function (see Shanks and Tilley 1992: 137–171).

Techniques for achieving these ends:

1   Introduce political content into conventional displays – show how the past may be manipulated and misrepresented for present purposes.
2   Break artefacts from fixed chronological narrative and from their original contexts and reassemble them with contemporary artefacts similarly decontextualized: juxtaposition, montage (a) as a means of drawing attention to and engaging with official cultural meanings of the artefact and effecting an ideological critique of commodification, and (b) as a means of illustrating alternative (non-commodified) meanings.
3   Supplement 'objective third person narrative' with exaggeration, irony, humour, absurdity, as a means of stripping the self-evident meaning of the artefact of its power.
4   Avoid permanent displays, emphasize authorship and changing perceptions of the artefactual past.
5   Encourage the use of artefacts of the past outside the institutional space of the museum. Allow community use of museum artefacts, people constructing and presenting their own pasts in the museum.

References

Adorno, T.W. (1964) Nachtmusik. In: T. Adorno, *Moments Musicaux: Neugedruckte Aufsatze 1928 bis 1962*. Frankfurt: Suhrkamp.
——(1967) Cultural criticism and society. In: T. Adorno, *Prisms*. London: Neville Spearman, pp. 17–34.
Adorno, T.W. and Horkheimer, M. (1979) *Dialectic of Enlightenment*. London: Verso.
Bann, S. (1978) Historical text and historical object: the poetics of the Musée de Cluny. *History and Theory*, 17: 251–66.
Barthes, R. (1973) The Blue-Guide. In: R. Barthes, *Mythologies*. St. Albans: Granada.
——(1977a) Writers, intellectuals, teachers. In: R. Barthes, *Image-Music-Text*. Translated and edited by S. Heath. New York: Hill and Wang.
——(1982) The plates of the encyclopedia. In: S. Sontag (ed.), *Selected Writings*. London: Fontana.
Benjamin, W. (1955) *Schriften*. Ed. T. Adorno (2 vols.). Frankfurt: Suhrkamp.
——(1973a) *Charles Baudelaire: A Lyric Poet in the Era of High Capitalism*. London: Verso.
——(1973b) The storyteller: reflections on the work of Nikolai Leskov. In: W. Benjamin, *Illuminations*. London: Fontana.
——(1973c) The work of art in the age of mechanical reproduction. In: W. Benjamin, *Illuminations*. London: Fontana.

——(1973d) Theses on the philosophy of history. In: W. Benjamin, *Illuminations*. London: Fontana.
——(1979) Eduard Fuchs, collector and historian. In: W. Benjamin, *One Way Street*. London: New Left Books.
Berger, J. (1969) *Art and Revolution: Ernst Niezvestny and the Role of the Artist in the USSR*. London: Weidenfeld and Nicolson.
——(1972) *Ways of Seeing*. Harmondsworth: Penguin.
Berger, J. and Mohr, J. (1982) *Another Way of Telling*. London: Writers and Readers.
Bloch, M. (1977a) The past and the present in the past. *Man*, n.s. 12: 278–92.
——(1977b) The disconnection between power and rank as a process: an outline of the development of kingdoms in Central Madagascar. *European Journal of Sociology*, 18(1): 107–48.
Bommes, M. and Wright, P. (1982) Charms of residence: the public and the past. In: Centre for Contemporary Cultural Studies, *Making Histories: Studies in History Writing and Politics*. London: Hutchinson.
Brown, P. (1934) *The Friday Book of North Country Sketches*. Newcastle upon Tyne: Beales.
Buck-Morss, S. (1977) *The Origin of Negative Dialectics*. Hassocks: Harvester Press.
CCCS (Centre for Contemporary Cultural Studies) Popular Memory Group (1982) Popular memory: theory, politics, method. In: Centre for Contemporary Cultural Studies, *Making Histories: Studies in History Writing and Politics*. London: Hutchinson.
Clarke, D. (1968) *Analytical Archaeology*. London: Methuen.
——(1972) Models and paradigms in contemporary archaeology. In: D. Clarke (ed.), *Models in Archaeology*. London: Methuen.
Daniel, G. (1981) *A Short History of Archaeology*. London: Thames and Hudson.
Dorfman, A. and Mattelart, A. (1975) *How to Read Donald Duck: Imperialist Ideology in the Disney Comic*. New York: International General.
Eagleton, T. (1981) *Walter Benjamin: Or Towards a Revolutionary Criticism*. London: Verso.
——(1983) *Literary Theory: An Introduction*. Oxford: Blackwell.
Elshtain, J. (1976) The social relations of the classroom: a moral and political perspective. *Telos*, 27: 97–110.
Entwistle, H. (1979) *Antonio Gramsci: Conservative Schooling for Radical Politics*. London: Routledge and Kegan Paul.
Fowler, P. (1977) *Approaches to Archaeology*. London: Adam and Charles Black.
——(1981) Archaeology, the public and the sense of the past. In: D. Lowenthal and M. Binney (eds.), *Our Past Before Us: Why Do We Save It?* London: Temple Smith.
Giddens, A. (1981) *A Contemporary Critique of Historical Materialism*. London: Macmillan.
Hawkes, C. (1954) Archaeological theory and method: some suggestions from the Old World. *American Anthropologist*, 56: 155–68.
——(1968) The proper study of mankind. *Antiquity*, 42: 255–62.
Horkheimer, M. (1976) Traditional and critical theory. In: P. Connerton (ed.), *Critical Sociology*. Harmondsworth: Penguin.
Horne, D. (1984) *The Great Museum: The Re-Presentation of History*. London: Pluto Press.
Jameson, F. (1977) Reflections in conclusion. In: E. Bloch, G. Lukács, B. Brecht, W. Benjamin, and T. Adorno, *Aesthetics and Politics*. London: New Left Books.

——(1984) Postmodernism, or the cultural logic of late capitalism. *New Left Review*, 146: 53–92.
Kermode, F. (1967) *The Sense of an Ending: Studies in the Theory of Fiction*. Oxford: Oxford University Press.
Leach, E. (1973) Concluding address. In: C. Renfrew (ed.), *The Explanation of Culture Change*. London: Duckworth.
Leitch, V. (1983) *Deconstructive Criticism: An Advanced Introduction*. London: Hutchinson.
Leone, M. (1981a) Archaeology's relationship to the present and the past. In: R. Gould and M. Schiffer (eds.), *Modern Material Culture: The Archaeology of Us*. New York: Academic Press.
——(1981b) The relationship between artefacts and the public in outdoor history museums. *Annals of the New York Academy of Sciences*, 376: 301–14.
——(1984) Interpreting ideology in historical archaeology: the William Paca garden in Annapolis, Maryland. In: D. Miller and C. Tilley (eds.), *Ideology, Power and Prehistory*. Cambridge: Cambridge University Press.
Lowe, D. (1982) *History of Bourgeois Perception*. Chicago: University of Chicago Press.
Lukács, G. (1963) *The Meaning of Contemporary Realism*. London: Merlin Books.
——(1980) *Essays on Realism*. London: Lawrence and Wishart.
McLuhan, M., Parker, H., and Harzun, J. (1969) *Exploration of the Ways, Means and Values of Museum Communication with the Viewing Public: A Seminar*. New York: Museum of the City of New York.
Meltzer, D. (1981) Ideology and material culture. In: R. Gould and M. Schiffer (eds.), *Modern Material Culture: The Archaeology of Us*. New York: Academic Press.
Romer, J. (1984) *Ancient Lives: The Story of the Pharoah's Tombmakers*. London: Weidenfeld and Nicolson.
Samuel, R. (1983) Soft focus nostalgia. *New Statesman*, 27 May 1983 (Victorian Values Supplement ii–iv).
Sartre, J.-P. (1958) *Being and Nothingness: An Essay on Phenomenological Ontology*. London: Methuen.
Schapiro, J. (1977) The slime of history: embeddedness in nature and critical theory. In: J. O'Neill (ed.), *On Critical Theory*. London: Heinemann.
Schlereth, T. (1978) It wasn't that simple. *Museum News*, 56(3): 36–44.
Shanks, M. and Tilley, C. (1992) Ideology, symbolic power and ritual communication: a reinterpretation of Neolithic mortuary practices. In: I. Hodder (ed.), *Symbolic and Structural Archaeology*. Cambridge: Cambridge University Press.
Sontag, S. (1979) *On Photography*. London: Penguin.
Spanos, W. (1977) Breaking the circle: hermeneutics as disclosure. *Boundary*, 2(5): 421–57.
Thompson, E. P. (1963) *The Making of the English Working Class*. Harmondsworth: Penguin.
——(1967) Time, work-discipline, and industrial capitalism. *Past and Present*, 38: 56–97.
Tilden, F. (1957) *Interpreting Our Heritage*. Chapel Hill. University of North Carolina Press.
Wallace, M. (1981) Visiting the past: history museums in the United States. *Radical History Review*, 25: 63–96.
Williamson, J. (1978) *Decoding Advertisements: Ideology and Meaning in Advertising*. London: Marion Boyars.

Wishart, T. (1984) Sights and sounds of 10th century Coppergate. *Popular Archaeology*, 5: 11–14.

Wolin, R. (1982) *Walter Benjamin: An Aesthetic of Redemption.* New York: Colombia University Press.

Wood, M. (1985) *In Search of the Trojan War.* London: BBC.

Speaking for the past in the present
Text, authority, and learning in archaeology museums

Robin Skeates

Introduction

Archaeology museum curators act as persons authorized to mediate between the material remains of past societies and contemporary audiences. They do so in particular through their display of selected classes of silent antiquities, together with texts and images that seek to explain those objects and their original owners. Such texts, which include information panels and object labels, vary greatly both within and between museums, in terms of where they are placed and what they refer to. But often such texts give the reader an impression of detached scientific objectivity, despite the fact that they convey opinions that say as much about the reproduction of the past in the present as about any past reality. Because of this inherent contradiction in the role of archaeology museum texts, they have become closely associated with important debates concerning the nature of curatorial authority and public education in museums. This paper examines the development of these debates, with particular reference to texts forming part of five of the most recent and innovative museum displays of prehistoric archaeology in England and Scotland.

Traditional texts

For over a century, professional museum curators have carefully researched and designed text labels, and displayed them together with collections of objects, as part of educative exhibitions intended to be experienced by a general public. The purpose of such labels has primarily been to enhance the public legibility of the exhibited objects, so that their scientific meaning might be understood immediately and without assistance (Hooper Greenhill 1992a: 205–10; Bennett 1998). Leading on from this perspective, and under the influence of a post-war semiotic approach, it has been possible for some museologists to conceive of text labels as part of a museum communication system, in which the content of an exhibition is transmitted by the exhibitor and received by the visitor (e.g. Pearce 1990: 144–9, 162).

Archaeology museum curators have used text labels extensively in this way, as aids to education and communication. In particular, labels have been used to describe and classify artefacts, with reference to categories such as their display number, archaeological type, form, manufacturing technique, function, raw material, relative age, archaeological culture, provenance, collector, donor, date of discovery or acquisition, and museum accession number. In some cases, labels in archaeology museums also carry statements about the historical significance of the artefacts, and (especially in university or antiquarian society museums) references to authoritative publications providing further information.

Here is a fairly random selection of typical examples of labels from traditional displays in four different types of archaeology museum (national, civic, private society, and university) that I encountered in 2000:

1. from the Early Bronze Age Cyclades section of the Pre-classical Greece galleries, The Louvre, Paris
   3 & 4
   Violin-shaped figurines
   Early Cycladic I
   (32000–2700 BC)
   Pelos Group
   Marble
   This schematic type that has an outline recalling that of
   a violin is the first stylised attempt at the human figure,
   elaborated in the Cyclades.
   Legs Kann, 1949
   Don Koutoulakis, 1949
   3 – Ma 3505
   4 – Ma 3508

2. from Room 1: Paris from its Origins through the Middle Ages, Musée Carnavalet, Paris
   BURIN
   Silex
   Moustérien
   Villejuif (1934–1935)
   Coll. E. Giraud, don. Ch. Sacchia
   PR 1418

3. from Archaeology section, Whitby Literary and
   Philosophical Society Museum
   Fungus, Formes Formentaria
   Starr Carr 1951
   REFS. P.P.S. 1949-1950
   WHIT M. ARC/000

4   from Museum of Antiquities, University of Newcastle-upon-Tyne
    Bell-derivative Beaker
    Lilburn Hill, Wooler, N'D
    Clarke 687. Class S4
    1888.22.1

These examples clearly vary from curator to curator, and between museums, but all arguably aspire to the traditional museological model of education and communication – albeit with reference to different general audiences (such as 'the public' and scholars).

The critique of traditional texts

Despite the presumably well-meant intentions of their authors, traditional museum texts such as these have been subject to much serious criticism since the mid-1980s. At least five general points of criticism have been raised.

Although texts that form part of permanent displays of museum collections often become 'imbued with an aura of unquestioned truth' (Coxall 1991: 93), they are not neutral lists of objective facts; they are, instead, fundamentally interpretative narratives (cf. Shanks and Tilley 1987: 68–9, 90–7; Serrell 1996: 9, 28–31).

Although museum texts may appear to be anonymous, they are in fact social constructs, which can subtly and unintentionally express the value judgements and prejudices of their author-curators, including those relating to education, class, ethnicity, and gender (Coxall 1990, 1991: 92–3).

More specifically, museum texts can be used as political educational tools, although precisely in what way and how effectively is open to question. According to the perspective that regards museums as ideological institutions, museum texts may serve to express and maintain unequal relations of power between experts and their audiences, by constructing particular historical narratives that privilege dominant meanings and silence alternative discourses (cf. Shanks and Tilley 1987: 68, 90; Hooper Greenhill 1999b: 14–23). From an alternative perspective, museum texts produced by reformist museum staff may serve to transform the existing social order, by providing a script for a new social order (Bennett 1998).

Research on museum visitors suggests that traditional texts contribute to people finding museum exhibitions difficult to concentrate on and understand. One cause of this is the museum environment, in which visitors generally have to read museum texts in poor light, whilst standing up, in a distracting space in which other material and visitors compete for their attention (Ekarv 1986–1987: 1; Sabine and Gilmore 1997: 72). But another key reason is that curators have often succeeded in asserting their intellectual authority but have equally failed to consider their visitors, including their differing degrees of prior knowledge, visual ability, interest, and available time (Pearce 1990: 195; Hooper Greenhill 1992a: 210; Serrell 1996: 233–4). They have consequently written texts that contain too much raw information and too many general concepts and inaccessible (specialist) terms. Indeed, many traditional museum displays have been described as illustrated 'textbooks', written in a linear format. Perhaps unfairly, the authors and designers of traditional archaeology museum texts have therefore been accused of being self-indulgent (Schadla-Hall and Davidson 1982: 174–5).

Museum labels can devalue the objects that they accompany, by fixing the objects as authentications and illustrations of curatorial statements about the past, and distancing them further from their former 'social lives' (cf. Appadurai 1986; Shanks and Tilley 1987: 74–6; Hooper Greenhill 1992a: 205; Pearce 1999: 19–20).

The text accompanying the display in the old Prehistory Gallery of the Museum of London (opened to the public in 1976) is an example of a widely criticized traditional archaeology museum text (e.g. Shanks and Tilley 1987: 74–6; Cotton and Wood 1996, 54; Merriman 1996: 60–2). One of the fundamental problems was that 'the work was carried out with little real information on visitors' needs and priorities' (Cotton and Wood 1996: 54). As a consequence, visitors encountered numerous difficulties. The text was over-long and tiring, comprising 10,000 words and large quantities of information. The lack of an introduction or signs was confusing. There was little highlighting or summarizing of key points. The white-on-black captions were unpopular. The text was written in a distanced and authoritative academic style, which offered a single definitive history of London accompanied by relatively high-level factual information, but little consideration of, for instance, the role of women and cultural diversity in the city's long history.

New texts

In response to these criticisms, museum theorists and practitioners have begun to develop a new 'cultural approach' to museum texts. Theorists, drawing upon cultural studies, call for the democratization and personalization of museum authorship, and talk of different members of interpretative communities (with different skills, knowledge and agendas) collaborating to produce and transform negotiated and relevant, reflexive and multiple, interpretative narratives, as well as interactive and rewarding learning experiences, of museum collections (cf. Fish 1980; and e.g. Shanks and Tilley 1987: 98; Hooper Greenhill 1999b: 4, 15–23). Practitioners, drawing upon visitor surveys, talk more about critical awareness and their responsibilities to the public, and the need for accessible visitor-based interpretative experiences informed by audience research (e.g. Coxall 1990, 1991; Pearce 1990: 195, 202). Both have contributed to the development of a new style of museum text.

In fact, a whole body of good practice has been established with reference to the production, display, and evaluation of museum text (e.g. Serrell 1983, 1996; Ferguson et al. 1995). Ekarv, for example, has researched and championed the use of an 'easy-to-read' style of text, which tends to increase visitor reading and comprehension (e.g. Ekarv 1986–1987; Sabine and Gilmore 1997). Characteristic features include:

- the use of simple spoken language, the active form of verbs, and relatively short lines and paragraphs;
- the inclusion of visually referenced information and images;

- the maintenance of close co-operation between the writers, curators, and designers of an exhibition.

To complement this approach, various methods have been devised to assess the effectiveness of museum texts. Relatively simple examples are the Fry and Cloze readability tests, which provide measures of how easy a text is to read and comprehend (Carter 1993); and an elaborate example is the 'scriptovisual evaluation grid', used in Québec to assess systematically the content, layout, and positioning of museum texts (Blais 1995).

This new cultural approach to museum texts has been put into practice in a number of archaeology displays in England and Scotland over the last decade. Here are just a few key examples.

A pioneering example was provided by the archaeology exhibition in Dorset County Museum in the late 1980s, where the scene was set by the first textual statement, 'There is so much we do not know' (Pearce 1999: 26).

The Alexander Keiller Museum in Avebury then took this theme of curatorial honesty and uncertainty further in its redisplay of 1991 (Stone 1994). In planning the new exhibition for non-specialist visitors, the curatorial team (from English Heritage) consulted with a variety of people, including archaeology specialists, school pupils, teachers, and official education advisors. The constraints and challenges offered by the new UK National Curriculum for schools were also carefully taken into account. As a consequence, the curatorial team decided to focus on illustrating the limitations of archaeological evidence and the subjectivity of interpretations based upon such material. Text played an important part in this. For example, the caption in Figure 19.1 accompanies a 'schizophrenic' life-size model of a man, one half presented as a wild and ragged individual, the other half presented as a more sophisticated individual with well-made clothes and body decoration. It also ends by rejecting a stereotypical caveman cartoon image. A series of 'clipboards' was also used to provide additional descriptions of different archaeological sites, as well as raising questions about their locations and functions.

A similar approach was adopted in the archaeology section of the Tullie House Museum in Carlisle, also in 1991. The desire to ensure public accessibility appears to have been a guiding principle in the creation of the display. For example, a simple label accompanying a prehistoric stone artefact manages to provide some interesting and distinctive information in an accessible and succinct way:

KNIFE
This is the finest knife blade and the only one of its type yet found in Cumbria. The edge is extremely sharp. From Bampton.

Curatorial honesty, uncertainty, and questions also formed part of the textual agenda. For example, a text panel on the interpretation of prehistoric stone circles states:

No one is quite sure why they were built: were they for worship? Did human sacrifices take place in them? Perhaps they acted as astronomical observatories? Some people think that they were used as landing stations for spaceships! The pottery, human bones and evidence of fires found in some stone circles would suggest that they were used for religious purposes. Perhaps gods were worshipped to ensure good harvests, good health and the return of the sun in the spring.

These new displays led to perhaps the ultimate example of the application of the new cultural approach to archaeology museum texts, in the 'People before London' prehistory gallery in the Museum of London, which was opened to the public in 1994 (and prematurely closed in 2000). The project was initiated by Nick Merriman, the head of the museum's Department of Early London History and Collections, and the curators were Johnathan Cotton and Barbara Wood (Cotton and Wood 1996; Merriman 1996; Wood 1996; Cotton 1997).

Visitor research played a major part in the redisplay of this 'permanent' gallery. A general survey of visitors to the Museum of London showed that 40 per cent of the annual visitors were children, under 16 years of age, and that at certain times of the year up to 65 per cent of visitors were from overseas. Hence, the curators realized that they could not assume much prior knowledge of London's history and topography, and that they would have to focus on communicating at least basic

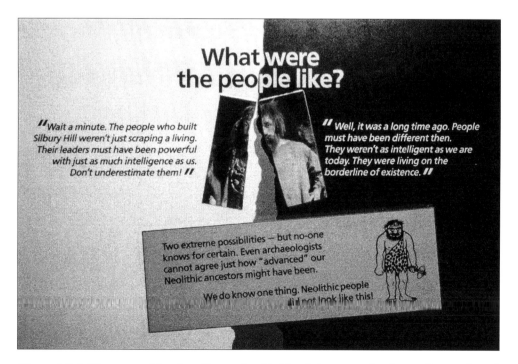

Figure 19.1 Text panel in the Alexander Keiller Museum, Avebury. Reproduced with the kind permission of English Heritage.

concepts in a simple and clear way, accompanied by foreign language summaries and guidebooks. A specific survey then asked visitors to describe what the term 'prehistoric' meant to them as they left the museum. The most common answer was 'dinosaurs', which persuaded the curators to challenge this and other popular stereotypes of prehistory. Thirty-four visitors were also interviewed in detail to assess the accessibility and design of a mock-up text panel. Most were attracted to large dramatic images rather than slabs of undifferentiated text. The curators consequently decided to write clear and straightforward sentences, accompanied by explanations of any technical terms.

Shanks and Tilley's politicized deconstruction of traditional museological representations of the past and radical proposals for future archaeology displays (1987) were also explicitly taken into account by the curators (e.g. Cotton and Wood 1996: 55), who introduced a degree of political content into the display, juxtaposed certain artefacts with contemporary objects, emphasized authorship and the historical contingency of archaeological interpretations, and encouraged people to construct their own pasts in the museum (cf. Shanks and Tilley 1987: 98). As Nick Merriman stated: 'Rather than presenting a single authoritative view of London's history, we will be attempting to show that the process of interpretation is a much more complex and subtle one than often appears in museums, and that other versions of London's history are possible' (Merriman 1996: 62).

The use of text in the new gallery clearly reflected these aims. In order to cater for different visitor requirements, the text was divided according to a four-tier hierarchy of information, consisting of:

- large narrative 'gateway' panels introducing the main chronological phases in a conversational tone;
- smaller panels on specific sites and themes characterized by open-ended discussions that left visitors to draw their own conclusions;
- captions accompanying objects or illustrations;
- loose-leaf ring binders, entitled 'Find out more ...', containing bibliographies and updated news of current projects.

In order to humanize the exhibition and provide basic information at a glance, the text panels were structured with evocative headlines and bullet points. For example, the earliest period of prehistory (known to archaeologists as the Lower Palaeolithic) carried the headline:

> Living on the edge (500,000–28,000 BC): Early humans in competition with each other and the environment

Also, in order to face up to the problems of curatorial authority and voice, the start of the gallery was marked by a signed text panel intended to establish a dialogue between the curators and visitors:

CAN YOU BELIEVE WHAT WE SAY?
The Prehistoric gallery deals with the time 'before history'. By definition, there are no written records . . .

FILLING THE GAP
Archaeology supplies our evidence, although the difficulties of recording the fragile traces of London's earliest part are enormous. Usually it is only possible to salvage shreds of information.

THE PRESENT IS THE PAST
These shreds can be interpreted in many ways, however objectively they are recorded. As each succeeding generation projects its own present onto the past, any number of prehistories are possible.

POLITICALLY PRESENT ... AND CORRECT?
This gallery is a reflection of our present. We have tried to humanize the past by focusing on specific sites and the needs of individual people, and by giving greater prominence to green and gender issues.

How will this standpoint be judged in the future? What do you think?
Johnathan Cotton and Barbara Wood, Curators, November 1994

The final panel in the gallery then asked: 'Now what does prehistory mean to you?'

New reviews

The curatorial team working on the 'People before London' project clearly put a substantial effort into avoiding the problems of traditional displays and into learning the lessons of the new cultural approach to text. But did they succeed in striking the right balance, particularly in terms of text, learning, and authority? Not surprisingly, the answer depends on your perspective.

The three key members of the curatorial team have published generally positive reports on their achievements (see references above). They also refer to summative evaluation, anecdotal evidence and personal observation indicating that most visitors seem to have appreciated their approach. Museologists have also been generally impressed. For example, Simon James states: 'The Museum of London's new prehistory gallery is a fine example of best current practice in planning and executing archaeology projects in museums. . . . Their attitude is miles away from the authoritative statements of truth presented in some museums' (James 1995: 20). Janet Owen wrote: 'the People Before London Gallery at the Museum of London really grasps the post-modernist "nettle" and attempts to expose the contemporary face of archaeology' (Owen 1996: 213). And Susan Pearce commended: 'Honesty in exhibition . . . giving us the kind of sincerity written into the panel texts at the beginning of the Museum of London's new prehistoric gallery' (Pearce 1999: 26).

But there have been some dissenters, particularly over the self-reflective nature of the exhibition and its text. The editors of the popular UK magazine *Current Archaeology,* Andrew and Wendy Selkirk, and a visitor who complained to one of the curators, accused the curators of excessive 'political correctness' (Selkirk and Selkirk 1994–1995: 342; Cotton 1997: 8). Alan Saville, Archaeology Curator at the National Museums of Scotland, was equally outspoken (Saville 1999). Emphasizing the point that the 'People before London' gallery was intended as a permanent exhibition, with an expected life of 20 years, he criticized the curators for their loss of confidence, particularly in rejecting 'tried-and-tested', 'common sense', methods of presenting object-based displays in favour of a short-term 'fad' of academic relativism, characterized by 'distasteful' over-personalization, 'in order to win post-modernist "street cred"'. He also accused them of succumbing to pressures 'to mix it with the heritage centres' in adopting 'tabloid newspaper headlines'.

To a certain extent, these opposing museological perspectives simply reflect basic contemporary political tensions in Britain, in which 'right-wing' Conservatives accuse the governing 'socialist' New Labour Party of 'political correctness' and the 'dumbing-down' of culture. The debate also resembles Pierre Bourdieu's 'classification struggle', in which 'old aged conservatives' and 'irresponsible youths' compete for control over the classificatory system of museums and galleries (Bourdieu 1984). But it should also be noted that this debate is long overdue in British museum archaeology, having previously been considered and resolved in favour of more user-friendly texts, first in the early 1980s in museums of all kinds in America and since 1985 in science museums in the UK, following the publication of the Royal Society report on the *Public Understanding of Science* (Royal Society 1985; anonymous referee pers. comm. 2001).

For my own part, I have mixed feelings about the 'People before London' gallery, particularly in relation to the issues of text, learning, and authority. Like other museum archaeologists, I too remember being both impressed and stimulated when I first visited the gallery. I noted favourably, for example, some clear and concise text on a panel trying to cope with introducing half a million years of prehistory:

> Prehistory of London – 500,000 BC – AD 43
> The first humans arrived during the Ice Age, half a million years ago. Over time they evolved from hunters into farmers and metalworkers. They settled into tribal communities within the area of the Thames. Though trade contacts were strengthened with Rome when Julius Caesar landed in South East Britain in 55 and 54 BC, it was not until 90 years later that the Romans took charge of government.

The gallery also conformed to many of the ideals that I have since promoted in my own writing on the archaeological heritage (Skeates 2000: 118–24). This vision for the future of archaeology sees professionals genuinely engaging in dialogue with their heterogeneous public, providing them with greater physical and mental access to archaeological work and to the material remains of the past, and providing them with questions and food for thought, at the same time offering them new stories about the past. It also highlights the difficult task facing archaeologists in searching for the elusive point of balance between playing the expert and being human. Overall, I think that the Museum of London's curatorial team struck a pretty good balance between self-reflection and getting on with the job of presenting the past for their public. However, that is not to say that they succeeded in overcoming the problem of curatorial authority. Unequal relations of power were still inherent in their display, and especially in their text, which ultimately still spoke for the past and manipulated the visitor. In a sense, all they did was establish a new form of curatorial authority: one that was more subtly masked by written admissions of bias and offers of democratic learning.

Latest texts

Two new displays of prehistoric material in Scottish museums have recently offered fresh opportunities to revisit some of these issues.

The first is the Kilmartin House Museum of Ancient Culture in Argyll, which was co-founded by David Clough and Rachel Butter in 1998, and which has won many awards, including Scottish Museum of the Year and the Gulbenkian Prize for Museums and Galleries (Butter 1999; Ascherson 2000; Heywood 2000). The displays here, which are similar in style to those of the Alexander Keiller Museum and the 'People before London' gallery, clearly conform to the new cultural approach to text. For example, an introductory text panel begins by encouraging visitors to interpret the past for themselves, and then ends with an admission of the limits to scientific and curatorial authority:

> Constructing the Past
> We all play historian, whether by looking at photos, reminiscing, or constructing family trees. Reconstructing the past is an important part of our everyday lives.
> ...
> Our knowledge is always imperfect and ever-changing; for some, understanding may be more spiritual than scientific.

Different versions of the latter statement are reiterated throughout the display, on text panels that admit to gaps in the historical narrative where there is insufficient evidence, but which also have a stab at well-reasoned interpretation. For example, the panel on the Bronze Age landscape states:

> ... No techniques – scientific or archaeological – can yet tell us exactly how the valley was used, but on the evidence of rich artefacts and the disciplined organisation of space, we have envisaged a stratified society with a few important individuals controlling access to and within the valley. ...

Throughout the display, the text-based interpretations remain tentative, and in the case of interpretations of Bronze Age 'carved rocks' visitors are even provided with a list of alternative interpretations and asked what they think, in an attempt to encourage them to reach their own understandings. In terms of my own experience, I must admit that sometimes this curatorial strategy began to frustrate me, but compensation was richly provided in other places by the use of some captivatingly simple and evocative language. For example, the panel on later prehistoric bogs and metalwork begins:

> In about 700 BC someone thrust three swords into a bog on an island 7 miles from Kilmartin ...

This, like much of the display's narrative, in the words of one visitor, 'Caught the imagination and made us want to know more' (museum visitors book 2001).

The second new display, which also opened to the public in 1998, is that of the 'Early Peoples' gallery in the Museum of Scotland. The result here is particularly interesting, in that the curatorial team from the Department of Archaeology, which included David Clarke as Head of Exhibitions and Jenni Calder as script coordinator, have established a quite distinctive, and controversial, position towards museum display and text (Clarke 1996, 1998, 2000; Malone and Stoddart 1999; McKean 2000; Wade 2001).

In order to question and avoid any nationalist bias, they have rejected a culture-historical approach in favour of a primarily thematic display (Clarke 1996). And, in order to 'make the objects do the work' (D. Clarke pers. comm. 2001), and to 'present the stories objects can tell' (J. Calder, quoted in Ascherson 2000: 83), the exhibition is dominated by artefacts from the museum's rich archaeological collections (as opposed to extended text-based discussions of those objects or hands-on activities).

As for the text panels, they are equally, if not more, authoritative than those of the Museum of London. For example, the first half of an introductory panel accompanying a selection of artefacts displayed within a group of Paolozzi sculptures in Room 1 admits to the limitations of archaeological interpretation, but maintains the right to represent a consensus viewpoint that is 'as factual as can be' (D. Clarke pers. comm. 2001), and which asserts a curatorial authority to tell visitors how to experience the exhibition:

> Moving around in their world
> No one knows what early people looked like – with a few exceptions, they didn't make images of themselves. The objects adorning these groups of figures are interpreted as jewellery or dress accessories. These are reasonable and generally accepted interpretations, but nothing is absolutely certain. Moving through this exhibition calls for you to use your imagination to build wider contexts from the objects and related information in order to understand the lives of early people.

Further on, introductory text panels then assume an even greater curatorial authority to speak for the people of the past, by quite literally putting words into their mouths (however based these may be on 'reasonable and generally accepted interpretations'). Here are the opening lines from an example in Room 2:

> A generous land
> Fat of the land
> We ate well and gave thanks, our food plentiful and healthy. At first we lived off what we gathered from the land, the beasts we hunted and the fish we caught. Later, we farmed as well, growing crops and raising animals.

Rachel Butter has appropriately criticized this approach, in arguing that while the literary use of 'we' may help to narrow the gap between the silent material remains of the past and present-day museum visitors, ambiguities surround the unspecified identity of 'we', to the extent that 'one can't help distrusting such a narrator' (R. Butter, quoted in Ascherson 2000: 83). David Clarke has since clarified that 'we' are 'the powerless majority': 'the extensive majority at any period that do not feel a sense of significance, status or power' (D. Clarke pers. comm. 2001, 2000: 221). Butter also pointed out that the displays are, 'highly authorial but do not admit the presence of the *auteur*' (ibid). In response, David Clarke, who certainly has no desire to portray the curator as an expert, claims that 'nothing is gained by adding the name of the *auteur*', and asks, 'would his name add to the visitors' sense of his existence?' (D. Clarke pers. comm., 2001, 2000: 221). However, seen in the context of earlier archaeology museum displays, the text of the 'Early Peoples' gallery still appears to represent a reassertion of an anonymous curatorial authority to communicate and educate. Furthermore, the fact that the exhibition requires some background knowledge and a reading age of 13 (Malone and Stoddart 1999: 486), combined with Clarke's comment that 'It's meant to be tough – you're meant to come back' (pers. comm. 2001), suggests that the display and its text carry unrealistically high expectations of visitors, both to spend time contemplating their messages, and to spend money on repeat visits.

The future of the text

Whether either of these latest examples will come to be used as models for future archaeology museum text writers remains to be seen. But all of the examples of innovative texts accompanying museum displays of prehistoric material that have been discussed above demonstrate both the potential and the limitations of the new 'cultural approach' to museum texts, particularly in terms of their intended role as effective mediators between museum collections and visitors. On the positive side, they have generally served to present archaeological evidence and interpretations in an honest and accessible way, and they have encouraged visitors to reach their own interpretations of the past. But on the negative side they appear to have alienated some regular museum visitors (such as the one who complained to the curators of the 'People before London' gallery, mentioned above), raising new doubts in their minds, not only about the past but also about the role of public museums and their curators, who seem prone to displaying overtly personalized and politicized messages.

At the same time, broader questions still remain over the future status and role of text in museums. Do we still need museum texts? And if so, what do we want from them? Contemporary material culture studies provide a useful starting point in answering these questions, in that they point out that objects do not speak for themselves and that they demand interpretation (e.g. Miller 1994). Archaeology museum texts, as we have seen, are a problematic medium through which to deal with such interpretation, but we should not underestimate the manipulative power and authority vested in alternative media, such as official audiovisuals and live guides.

Texts, then, are perhaps as 'good' or as 'bad' as any other medium of museum interpretation. Anyway, texts must surely remain key elements in our experiences of museum collections for as long as they are missed when they are not there. In the British Museum, for example, Room 63 (covering 'Daily Life in Ancient Egypt') used to lack (as far as I could see) text panels, and I missed them, sensing a lack of clarity about the interpretative themes and information relating to the objects. But that is not to say that texts have to be quite so widespread in archaeology museum displays. A useful warning was provided by focus sessions held in the Museum of London's 'People before London' gallery by the Susie Fisher Group. These revealed that 'Text-based information is ... not popular, and, where used, visitors are looking for it to explain things they can see in front of them (for example, captions) rather than telling a larger story in its own right' (Cotton 1997: 11). Perhaps one way forward, then, is to restrict even further large texts, either to the margins of galleries or to portable guidebooks, where visitors can exert an even greater degree of choice over whether or not to read them. That said, there is surely a limit, which has arguably been overstepped in the case of the new display at Segedunum Roman Fort Museum at Wallsend, where text is mainly relegated to handheld boards, which visitors generally fail to pick up, let alone read (according to my own informal observations). A greater consideration of museum communication in general, and practical guidelines on museum text writing in particular, together with the use of formative and summative evaluation, including readability tests, by museum archaeologists in relation to specific exhibitions and visitors should help to refine this point of balance (McManus 2000). As for the messages that archaeology museum texts contain, perhaps we should not worry unduly about the subtle degrees of curatorial authority that they conceal, or the rate at which they will go out of fashion. Manuals on how to write museum texts are valuable in ensuring that texts are at least comprehensible, but 'there can be no universal method, no formal principles of interpretation and display' (Shanks and Tilley 1987: 96). Likewise, there is no single way of reading a text (Fish 1980: 16). At the end of the day, differences rather than uniformity of curatorial approach and opinion, as expressed through texts, will help to signal a healthy archaeology museum-based learning environment.

References

Appadurai, A. ed. (1986) *The Social Life of Things: Commodities in Cultural Perspective.* Cambridge: Cambridge University Press.

Ascherson, N. (2000) The Museum of Scotland: review. *Public Archaeology*, 1: 82–4.

Bennett, T. (1998) Speaking to the eyes: museums, legibility and the social order. In: S. Macdonald (ed.), *The Politics of Display: Museums, Science, Culture.* London: Routledge, pp. 25–35.

Blais, A. (1995) Scriptovisual evaluation grid. In: A. Blais (ed.), *Text in the Exhibition Medium.* Québec City: Société des Musées Québécois and Musée de la Civilisation, pp. 309–11.

Bourdieu, P. (1984) *Distinction: A Social Critique of the Judgement of Taste.* London: Routledge & Kegan Paul.

Butter, R. (1999) *Kilmartin: An Introduction and Guide.* Kilmartin: Kilmartin House Trust.

Carter, J. (1993) How old is this text? *Environmental Interpretation*, February: 10–11.

Clarke, D.V. (1996) Presenting a national perspective of prehistory and early history in the Museum of Scotland. In: J.A. Atkinson, I. Banks, and J. O'Sullivan (eds.), *Nationalism and Archaeology. Scottish Archaeological Forum.* Glasgow: Cruithne Press, pp. 67–76.

——(1998) New things set in many landscapes: aspects of the Museum of Scotland. *Proceedings of the Society of Antiquaries of Scotland*, 128: 1–12.

——(2000) Creating the Museum of Scotland: a reply to Neal Ascherson. *Public Archaeology*, 1: 220–21.

Cotton, J. (1997) Illuminating the twilight zone? The new prehistoric gallery at the Museum of London. In: G.T. Denford (ed.), *Representing Archaeology in Museums.* Winchester: Society of Museum Archaeologists, pp. 6–12.

Cotton, J. and Wood, B. (1996) Retrieving prehistories at the Museum of London: a gallery case-study. In: P.M. McManus (ed.), *Archaeological Displays and the Public: Museology and Interpretation.* London: Institute of Archaeology, University College London, pp. 53–71.

Coxall, H. (1990) Museum text as mediated message. *Women, Heritage and Museums*, 14: 15–21.

——(1991) How language means: an alternative view of museums text. In: G. Kavanagh (ed.), *Museum Languages: Objects and Texts.* Leicester: Leicester University Press, pp. 85–99.

Ekarv, M. (1986–1987) Combating redundancy: writing texts for exhibitions. *Exhibitions in Sweden*, 27(8): 1–7.

Ferguson, L., MacLulich, C., and Ravelli, L. (1995) *Meanings and Messages: Language Guidelines for Museum Exhibitions.* Sydney: Australian Museum.

Fish, S. (1980) *Is There a Text in This Class? The Authority of Interpretive Communities.* Cambridge, MA: Harvard University Press.

Heywood, F. (2000) Against the grain. *Museums Journal*, 100(10): 10–19.

Hooper-Greenhill, E. (1999a) *Museums and the Shaping of Knowledge.* London: Routledge.

——(1999b) Education, communication and interpretation: towards a critical pedagogy in museums. In: E. Hooper-Greenhill (ed.), *The Educational Role of the Museum.* Second edition. London: Routledge, pp. 3–27.

James, S. (1995) Plumbing the depths of history. *Museums Journal*, 95(7): 20–21.
Malone, C. and Stoddart, S. (1999) Editorial. *Antiquity*, 73: 485–92.
McKean, C. (2000) *The Making of the Museum of Scotland*. Edinburgh: National Museums of Scotland Publishing Limited.
McManus, P.M. (2000) Written communications for museums and heritage sites. In: P.M. McManus (ed.), *Archaeological Displays and the Public: Museology and Interpretations*. Second edition. London: Archetype Publications, pp. 97–112.
Merriman, N. (1996) Displaying archaeology in the Museum of London. In: G.T. Denford (ed.), *Museum Archaeology – What's New?* Winchester: Society of Museum Archaeologists, pp. 60–65.
Miller, D. (1994) Artefacts and the meaning of things. In: T. Ingold (ed.), *Companion Encyclopedia of Anthropology*. London: Routledge, pp. 396–419.
Owen, J. (1996) Making histories from archaeology. In: G. Kavanagh (ed.), *Making Histories in Museums*. London: Leicester University Press, pp. 200–15.
Pearce, S.M. (1990) *Archaeological Curatorship*. London: Leicester University Press.
——(1999) Presenting archaeology. In: N. Merriman (ed.), *Making Early Histories in Museums*. London: Leicester University Press, pp. 12–27.
Royal Society (1985) *Public Understanding of Science*. London: Royal Society.
Sabine, J. and Gilmore, E. (1997) Writing readable texts: evaluation of the Ekarv method. *Museum Practice*, 5(2.2): 72–5.
Saville, A. (1999) Thinking *things* over: aspects of contemporary attitudes towards archaeology, museums and material culture. In: N. Merriman (ed.), *Making Early Histories in Museums*. London: Leicester University Press, pp. 190–209.
Schadla-Hall, T. and Davidson, J. (1982) It's very grand but who's it for? Designing archaeology galleries. *Museums Journal*, March: 171–5.
Selkirk, A. and Selkirk, W. (1994–1995) PC museum. *Current Archaeology*, 12(9): 342.
Serrell, B. (1983) *Making Exhibit Labels: a Step-by-Step Guide*. Nashville, TN: American Association for State and Local History Press.
Serrell, B. (1996) *Exhibit Labels: An Interpretive Approach*. Walnut Creek, CA: AltaMira Press.
Shanks, M. and Tilley, C. (1987) *Re-Constructing Archaeology: Theory and Practice*. Cambridge: Cambridge University Press.
Skeates, R. (2000) *Debating the Archaeological Heritage*. London: Duckworth.
Stone, P. (1994) The re-display of the Alexander Keiller Museum, Avebury, and the National Curriculum in England. In: P.G. Stone and B.L. Molyneaux (eds.), *The Presented Past: Heritage, Museums and Education*. London: Routledge, pp. 190–205.
Wade, M. (2001) Treasure house of the people. *The Scotsman*, 21 February: 15.
Wood, B. (1996) Wot! No dinosaurs? Interpretation of prehistory and a new gallery at the Museum of London. In: A. Devonshire and B. Wood (eds.), *Women in Industry and Technology, from Prehistory to the Present Day: Current Research and the Museum Experience. Proceedings from the 1994 WHAM Conference*. London: Museum of London, pp. 53–63.

Towards presenting scientific research in archaeology museums

Mark S. Copley

Introduction

There is growing interest in the promotion of science education. In the United Kingdom (UK), a government-funded partnership called the Real World Science Project recognizes the importance of science to the British economy. As part of its strategy, the project aims to connect museums with schools (Renaissance South East 2009) through programmes such as Science Links in Museum Education (Bristow 2008). A significant component of this programme supports scientific enquiry, as well as the accumulation of scientific knowledge, mirroring the subtle shift in emphasis witnessed in some quarters from the public understanding of science (PUS) to the public understanding of research (PUR) (Yaneva et al. 2009: 79). The PUS movement attempted to address what they perceived as a worrying lack of scientific knowledge amongst the non-scientific public (Durant et al. 1989: 11–14), whereas PUR encompasses the processes involved in research (Lewenstein and Bonney 2004: 63–73). In museums (predominantly natural history and science museums), much of this is related to hands-on experiences and other activities – but what of the 'traditional' interpretation panels within archaeology museums, the focus of this study?

Aims

The primary hypothesis being tested is that curatorial staff do not possess scientific backgrounds and that this might impinge on their willingness to include science within their archaeology exhibits. To this end, a postal survey of museums maintaining archaeology collections was conducted, which:

1. investigated the educational backgrounds of the curatorial staff;
2. surveyed the curatorial staff's beliefs concerning displaying science in museums;

3   sought to determine the current extent and nature of the inclusion of science within archaeology exhibits; and
4   elucidated topics which curatorial staff wished to display more of in the future.

Background and literature review

The public perception of science

Dunbar (1995) provides an interesting account of what some regard as the origins of antipathy towards science and its misunderstanding among laymen in the USA. He suggests that it starts at school, where students are being turned off by the subject either because it is too difficult, too boring, insufficiently resourced in terms of high-quality science teachers, or due to religious reasons (Dunbar 1995: 3–8). Similarly, in the UK, the perception that science is too hard, too theoretical, or irrelevant to non-academic careers has been cited for the lack of interest in science subjects held by some students (Cleaves 2005: 471–86).

From the late nineteenth century onwards, science became more institutionalized and specialized (Butler 1992: 109) to such an extent that nowadays, science seems to be regarded by the public as a distinctive type of knowledge and expertise (Macdonald 1995: 14). The prevailing view of scientists held by much of the non-scientific public is that they wear white coats, talk a different (mystical) language and work in laboratories that are hermetically sealed from everyday life (Sudbury 1992: 59; cf. van Eijck and Roth 2008: 1074).

Museums and the public understanding of research (PUR)

Education is a core function of the museum, both in terms of lifelong learning and so-called life-wide learning, where all life experiences are affected (Black 2005: 125; MLA 2009a). Our understanding of the nature of learning in museums has changed over the years. The earliest museums were geared towards producing a narrative that was both accepted and expected to be accepted. That is, knowledge existed independent of humans and was there to be learnt by them (the positivism/realism of Plato; Hein 1998, 17). These days, we recognize that knowledge and understanding may be subject to scrutiny and change (Hooper-Greenhill 1999: 71) and, as such, there are fewer immutable 'facts' to be presented within museum environments (Hein 1996: 30; 2001: 1).

This is mirrored in the PUS and PUR movements. The PUS movement identified what they deemed a worrying lack of scientific knowledge amongst the public, the so-called deficit model (Durant et al. 1989: 11–14). Hence, a variety of formal and informal techniques were used to reduce the gap between the 'provider' and 'recipient' of scientific knowledge (seen as the 'expert' and the 'uniformed public'). The deficit model of scientific understanding often used top down prescriptions to increase the understanding of science, and assumed a trust in scientific institutions, which might not be present in all instances (Lewenstein and Bonney 2004: 67; Yearley 2000: 107). More recently, this viewpoint has gradually been replaced by more relational models of interaction through which professionals learn from laypeople and vice versa (e.g., Cohen 2000).

Also emerging from the somewhat unsatisfactory standard models of the PUS is the PUR, where the focus shifts away from trying to ensure that the layperson solely learns 'facts' towards engaging in a greater understanding of the research *process* (Lewenstein and Bonney 2004: 63–4). With respect to scientific research, the research process includes its underlying procedures, data collection methods, model-making, hypothesis testing, and theorizing (Durant 2004: 52), followed by peer review of their work. The public may be particularly unaware of the collaborative nature of modern research (which is actively supported by the main funding bodies in the UK); albeit this collaboration occurs within a competitive field, with research groups vying to be the first to a discovery.

Furthermore, scientists aim to be objective in their work, yet may nevertheless rely on subjective judgements. Their work is usually only provisional in nature, requiring further work to give credence to/falsify their initial findings – this is performed in a completely open manner, with scientists often revisiting and building upon their own research (Paola 2004: 151). Indeed, some PUR proponents go further than simply focusing on the generalized process of research. Rather, they stress the need to concentrate on the understanding of *current* research (Field and Powell 2001: 421–6); current research is characterized by being an incomplete picture, subject to future change and possibly even disagreement amongst peers (Durant 2004: 55).

But why should this be important? It has been suggested that people select to learn scientific information that they feel will be of use in their lives. People may even employ a strategy of not knowing about specific scientific facts as a mechanism to cope with uncertainty in the world (Lewenstein and Bonney 2004: 67). PUR can go some way to address these – an understanding of how scientists do science is transferable between studies/research fields, and does not necessarily require detailed, specialist knowledge. Such an understanding could be utilized to critically assess issues that affect the public at large; for example, the rollout of a vaccination programme, or the background to issues such as climate change. PUR is characterized by the wide range of media that it utilizes to engage with the public, ranging from newspapers to television, and more recently science museums (Farmelo 2004: 1–26).

Individual scientists may not be the best people to translate their work into accessible, everyday language. Conversely, museums actually might not be best suited for learning complex scientific facts and details, yet it can be argued that they do have a role for 'furthering understanding through more general images and messages about the nature of science, its possibilities, its relevance *and* its limitations' (Macdonald 1992: 408; emphasis in original). In museums, a focus on investigation allows for visitors to engage more fully with those involved in the research. Museum visitors may possess different cognitive strengths, such as interpersonal intelligences (Davis and Carter 1999: 100; Gardner 1983), and by focusing on the social nature of research, this may reach out more effectively to audiences who do not exhibit strong bodily kinaesthetic or logical–mathematical intelligences.

Due to it being relatively new, relatively few PUR exhibitions have been provided in museums and science centres, although notable examples may be seen across the world: e.g. The Wellcome Wing at London's Science Museum, Paris' La Cite des Sciences et de l'Industrie and the Current Science and Technology Center at Boston's Museum of Science (Farmelo 2004: 1–26). PUR examples at archaeology museums, the focus of this study, are less easily found. One example is a recent exhibition on the excavations conducted at the Turkish site of Çatalhöyük, which was provided at the Science Museum of Minnesota (Pohlman 2004: 265–75). In this exhibition, social interactions between the specialists were highlighted to illustrate how the process of archaeology operated. Thus, people's interest was garnered by calling on their interpersonal and other intelligences (Gardner 1983). Visitors were not provided with discrete research seen in isolation, but were exposed to a broader framework where methodology, interpretation, and dissemination of ideas and results operated organically through collaborations between specialists. Such an approach at once removes the sterile nature of an academic science article and engages the museum visitor with research practices and processes.

Presenting science in archaeology museums

If visitors have not studied science at school, they might experience a strongly emotional and anxious response when being presented with science within a museum setting (cf. McCombs 1991: 117–27; Wynne 1999: 11), especially in an archaeology museum where they might not be expecting overly scientific content. Curators who do not have scientific backgrounds may have similar responses when deciding whether or not to include scientific elements. Yet, by embedding the science within archaeological exhibits, and presenting it carefully within a specific context, this might be a method of making the science more accessible for visitors. This needs to be completed with care. As Borun et al. (1993: 203) have noted, making a complex concept accessible through the creation of overly simple analogues may not in itself aid the 'novice visitor', with only 'expert viewers' being able to decode and understand the presented information.

As experienced in some science museums, tension may exist between wanting to display science in terms of its products or its processes (Arnold 1996: 58). However, this tension need not be replicated within archaeology exhibits displaying material culture, where the archaeology rather than the science is the primary focus of the exhibition. The study of archaeology is a science, with knowledge being systematically acquired and verified through observation and experimentation (the science of archaeology), although not necessarily to form universal theories. It also employs scientific studies, for example, to determine the provenance of an artefact (archaeological science). Here, these two aspects of study are collectively termed 'archaeology-based science'. Discrete archaeological science research, often conducted within 'traditional' scientific research groups, may operate within narrower hypotheses using different modes of reasoning when compared to the science of archaeology (e.g., Coudart 2006: 138; Wylie 2000).

Therefore, the archaeological process is centred on hypothesis-driven research, with directors of excavations forming hypotheses that inform the way in which excavations proceed. The process of excavation is conducted using the scientific methods of stratigraphy and the finds may be subjected to scientific analyses and treatments. The opportunities for presenting this within museum contexts are enormous.

Methodology

Background

Questionnaires are ideal mechanisms to gain information in order to help understand a specific phenomenon (Moser and Kalton 1971: 2). Postal questionnaires allow a geographically disparate population to be surveyed (Moser and Kalton 1971: 257–58). Non-response may be an issue (e.g., Feitelson 1991: 196–7) although this can be countered by highlighting the importance of the study and the respondent's key role (Heberlein and Baumgartner 1978: 458–60). In this survey, short, anonymous questionnaires (MLA 2009b) were created, using tick-box surveys and rating scales (Oppenheim 1966: 81–92; Taylor and Stevenson 1999: 20) to gauge attitudes to, and the extent of, the presentation of science in archaeology museums.

Design of the questionnaire

The questionnaire was designed to be inviting, quick to complete (five to ten minutes) and had space for additional comments. A large font size was used, with comprehensible language, using clearly divided sections; routing questions were kept to a minimum and were unambiguous when used (Brace 2004: 118, 142, 155–6). In total, eight questions were posed. The first four (Q1–Q4) sought to determine the respondent's background and attitudes to science in museum settings. Two questions (Q5 and Q6) were concerned with the current coverage of archaeological science in their museum, a further question (Q7) asked about future coverage and the final question (Q8) provided space for further comments. Respondents were also offered the chance to receive a summary of the results by email.

Sampling strategy

The Museums Association's *Museums and Galleries Yearbook* (Lucas 2008) provided the required list of accredited and listed UK-based museums. Museum names were extracted from the yearbook, and classified into two groups: the first ($n=101$) was predominantly archaeology-orientated, employed an archaeology curator, or were operated by archaeological societies. The second group ($n=165$) included the remaining museums responsible for archaeological collections and tended to maintain relatively small archaeology exhibits that form a minor component of their overall museum content. A sample of 100 museums was selected using random number tables from a stratified sample based on visitor numbers; i.e. 89

from Group 1 and 11 from Group 2. The questionnaires were sent to those responsible for the exhibits, usually this was a curator of archaeology or curator of a specific gallery. For the smaller museums, these were curators or professionals of other ranks.

Results and discussion

General

The questionnaires were posted on the 2 July 2009. When designing the survey, it was apparent that there were few relevant publications that report response rates and willingness of respondents to provide further comments; hence, these are briefly presented here. Sixty-two per cent of the questionnaires were returned within 90 postal delivery days. This relatively high response perhaps reflects the short period of time required to complete the questionnaire and/or the interest in the subject. Forty-seven per cent asked for a brief summary of the results. A slight majority of the respondents were female (55 per cent), and most had completed archaeology undergraduate degrees (63 per cent). The final question provided the space for respondents to add any further comments; 77 per cent of the respondents decided to add comments, varying from 7 to 151 words in length (mean 54 words). These thoughts proved to be extremely valuable to this study and are provided below.

The respondents' backgrounds

It was hypothesized that the majority of curators of archaeology exhibits do not possess scientific backgrounds. Indeed, most of the respondents' science backgrounds terminated at around aged 16, with more males studying science subjects to aged 18 and beyond (Figure 20.1). Five people claimed to have a postgraduate degree in a science subject. Science teaching at school, perhaps more than any other subject, can shape an individual's perception of the subject throughout life (cf. Davis 2003: 439–68; Dunbar 1995: 3–8). Hence, curators whose scientific education terminated relatively early may be less willing to include more science in their exhibitions. Yet, the survey does not bear this out: 64 per cent of respondents disagreed or strongly disagreed with the statement 'I think "science" and "scientific enquiry" are hard to understand'. Graphs illustrating the responses to all of the statements may be found in Figure 20.2.

In many ways, this question is at the core of presenting science in archaeology museums. The manner in which respondents answered this question will depend upon what they believe to be science (perhaps formed from their educational achievements in science). For example, is it *really* easy to understand the formulae used in the different resistance survey arrays used to provide readings for the location of buried archaeological remains (in geophysical surveys), or to understand the myriad environmental effects that feed into stable isotopic variation of organic

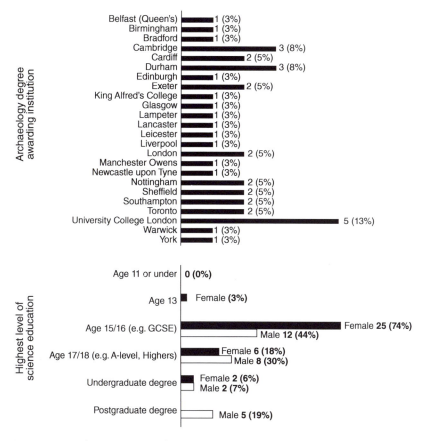

Figure 20.1 Top: the source of respondents' archaeology degree (*n*=39; Q2). Bottom: the respondents' highest level of science training (answered by 61/62 respondents; Q3).

matter (as in biomolecular archaeology)? Face-to-face interviews would help to determine exactly how they defined 'science' and 'scientific enquiry'.

The respondents' views on presenting science in archaeology museums

Museums can offer the space in which visitors' attitudes to subjects can be changed (e.g. Knell 2007; Sandell 2007). Almost all of the respondents (96 per cent) agreed that 'If done sensitively, museums can be an effective place for displaying science'. Despite this generally favourable disposition, fewer respondents (87 per cent) disagreed or strongly disagreed that 'Displays including scientific analyses are not relevant to my museum'.

If proper attention is not afforded to visitors' needs, and concepts are presented in a poor manner, presenting science concepts has the potential to alienate visitors. Yet, 76 per cent of the respondents either disagreed or strongly disagreed that 'Including scientific concepts in our displays may alienate our visitors'. Indeed, most respondents agreed that 'Using everyday language will help to make the

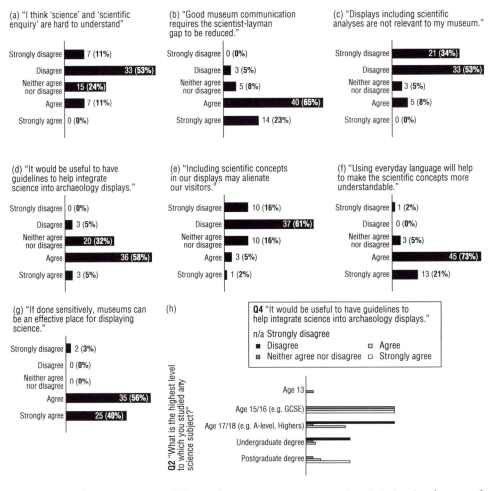

Figure 20.2 Responses (*n*=62) to the seven statements in Q4 (*a–g*); the graphs are presented in the order in which the questions were asked. Normalized responses to the fourth statement according to respondent's backgrounds (*h*).

scientific concepts more understandable'. In the 'additional comments' section, several respondents (17 per cent) specifically highlighted the need to pitch the text at the right level. One telling response was provided by Respondent 3:

> Interestingly, visitors are not content with just the facts, they want to know how these results/answers were achieved. However, it is of critical importance that these scientific facts are conveyed in a short accessible way not to put off visitors. Studying museum text guidelines is important. I have worked with various University Archaeology departments who without exception are generally horrified by these guidelines. However, when left to their own devices these departments have written very inaccessible text.

Hence, the translation of the science into accessible, everyday language is extremely important. The possibility for presenting scientific methodology is an interesting one. Visitors (particularly frequent museum visitors) may be used to being provided with historical debate, but are they able to fully grasp scientific debate (which requires a different knowledge base and set of tools)? As with many of the others, Respondent 41, concurs with these points: 'Getting the balance right is difficult – too much information and the visitor will lose interest'. Perhaps unsurprisingly, most respondents (88 per cent) agreed or strongly agreed with the statement that 'Good museum communication requires the scientist-layman gap to be reduced'. One respondent tellingly crossed out the word 'layman' in this latter question and wrote 'nonspecialist'. Hence, despite their non-scientific backgrounds, respondents were largely favourable to the inclusion of science in their archaeology exhibits, so long as the presentations were provided in an accessible manner for their audiences.

The current extent and nature of the presentation of science in archaeology exhibits

Respondents were provided with a list of scientific topics and were asked which were currently presented in their museum (Table 20.1). No distinction was made as to whether they were within permanent or temporary exhibitions, but the word 'current' was emphasized in order to gain a nationwide snapshot. Only 8 per cent of respondents stated that they did not refer to any of the topics at all.

'Conservation' and 'stratigraphy and the excavation process' (stratigraphy is the study of archaeological layers used during the excavation process) are the most likely subjects currently included in archaeology museum exhibits, with the latter afforded the greatest space for detailed explanation. Conversely, 'biomolecular archaeology' (a relatively new discipline that examines DNA and other molecules), 'general hypothesis building and testing' and 'geophysics and remote sensing' (non-intrusive survey techniques that use differences in the physical properties of the ground to locate archaeological sites and features) are the three least likely subjects to be granted museum space. The lack of geophysics-based displays is perhaps unexpected, since geophysical surveys feature prominently in popular UK television programmes and form an important element of pre-excavation analysis.

In addition to the incorporation of the specific topics outlined earlier, respondents were asked to describe how, if at all, specific themes were covered in depth within their exhibits (Table 20.2). When presented, 'environmental reconstructions' are most likely to be granted the space within a dedicated panel. Furthermore, 'artefact studies' were more likely to be used to illustrate provenance or a specific technology rather than mode of use.

Table 20.1 Responses for Q5: 'For each topic, which best describes how it is incorporated in your museum display?' and Q7 responses: 'Which of the following scientific topics would you like to include more of in your museum?'

The sixteen topics[a]	Q5[b]				Q7
	Not mentioned	Short reference made to it	Explained in depth	Don't know	Want more
Archaeobotany (the study of plants)	29 (47%)	30 (48%)	0 (0%)	1 (2%)	27 (44%)
Biomolecular archaeology (the study of DNA, fats, and proteins)	**55 (89%)**	5 (8%)	0 (0%)	2 (3%)	24 (39%)
Ceramic science (excluding conservation)	38 (61%)	20 (32%)	1 (2%)	1 (2%)	20 (32%)
Conservation	**18 (29%)**	36 (58%)	7 (10%)	0 (0%)	31 (50%)
Dating techniques (excluding radiocarbon dating)	29 (47%)	29 (47%)	2 (3%)	1 (2%)	**40 (65%)**
Evolution (human)	40 (65%)	18 (29%)	3 (5%)	0 (0%)	16 (26%)
Geophysics and remote sensing (the study of non-intrusive survey)	50 (80%)	9 (15%)	0 (0%)	1 (2%)	26 (42%)
General hypothesis building and testing	50 (80%)	9 (15%)	1 (2%)	2 (3%)	**13 (21%)**
History and development of archaeological science	35 (56%)	22 (35%)	4 (6%)	1 (2%)	23 (37%)
Lithic analysis (the study of stone)	33 (53%)	21 (34%)	5 (8%)	2 (3%)	25 (40%)
Materials science (excluding metals, ceramics, and stone)	39 (63%)	20 (32%)	0 (0%)	2 (3%)	19 (31%)
Metallurgy (excluding conservation)	31 (50%)	22 (35%)	5 (8%)	2 (3%)	24 (39%)
Human osteology and palaeopathology (the study of bones and diseases)	29 (47%)	30 (48%)	2 (3%)	1 (2%)	34 (55%)
Radiocarbon dating	27 (44%)	33 (53%)	2 (3%)	0 (0%)	33 (53%)
Stratigraphy and the excavation process	**18 (29%)**	37 (60%)	**7 (11%)**	0 (0%)	34 (55%)
Zooarchaeology (the study of animals)	36 (58%)	22 (35%)	2 (3%)	1 (2%)	25 (40%)

[a] Figures in bold are the highest and lowest in each category.
[b] Any remaining responses unaccounted for in this table were returned unanswered.

Table 20.2 Responses for Q6: 'How are the following themes currently included in your museum?'

Topic[a]	Dedicated panel(s)	Dedicated display(s)	Dedicated exhibition(s)	Not covered	Not answered
Artefact studies using science to determine provenance	12 (19%)	1 (2%)	2 (3%)	41 (66%)	6 (10%)
Artefact studies using science to illustrate technology	10 (16%)	5 (8%)	2 (3%)	39 (63%)	6 (10%)
Artefact studies using science to determine mode of use	5 (8%)	5 (8%)	2 (3%)	45 (73%)	5 (8%)
Conservation methods	14 (23%)	2 (3%)	2 (3%)	41 (66%)	3 (5%)
Environmental reconstruction	**15 (24%)**	5 (8%)	**0 (0%)**	38 (61%)	4 (6%)
Geophysics and remote sensing methods	**2 (3%)**	**0 (0%)**	2 (3%)	**53 (85%)**	5 (8%)

[a] Figures in bold are the highest and lowest in each category.

Additionally, 13 per cent of respondents took the opportunity to write something more about how science is currently incorporated in their museum. For example, Respondent 26:

> We do make reference to scientific topics, but not with 'dedicated' methods as per Question 6, more as an integrated approach: for example, we have a copy of the reconstructed head of a Neolithic period woman, and we explain in the accompanying text about her origins being identified by study of analysis of her teeth. The display is about various aspects of the woman's life and death, not sufficiently dedicated to the science. (Question 6 asks about the current themes covered in their museum)

This demonstrates that the incorporation of science needs not, and perhaps should not, be about the ins and outs of the techniques. One could argue that learning that biomolecules extracted from this Neolithic woman's teeth allowed us to determine her geographical origins is a significant accomplishment in itself.

Fifteen per cent of the respondents discussed the fact that the exploration of scientific elements is best suited to a temporary exhibition, as typified by Respondent 14:

> My museum's temporary exhibition space contains an exhibition entitled 'Reconstructing the past: from the land to the lab' which focuses on the science behind modern archaeology. Many museum staff had concerns that this exhibition topic would alienate visitors but I felt that, with proper explanations, visitors would be able to grasp some of archaeology's complex scientific interpretation methods. In putting together the exhibition panels

> I separated information into stages (i.e. simple sentence of the very basic info, short paragraph slightly more in depth but with no 'complicated' words, then full paragraph with complete explanation). The feedback for this exhibition has been fantastic with no negative comments about concepts being too complex.

The initial disparaging remarks from this respondent's colleagues illustrate the difficulties some museum professionals might encounter, especially if they need to secure the finances to create the exhibition. Yet, the positive feedback provides evidence that integrating science into archaeology displays can be undertaken successfully, if museum text guidelines are followed.

Respondent 59 suggested that scientific topics are not best suited to permanent exhibitions:

> I think your survey questions illustrate a lack of understanding about museum exhibitions. The subject matters you refer to would make very useful topics for temporary exhibitions. Limited space and money would negate their coverage in a permanent display. It depends on which story you are trying to tell.

However, the questionnaire did not differentiate between temporary and permanent exhibitions in the manner this latter respondent supposed. Indeed, Respondent 13 provided examples of what was included:

> Temporary exhibitions since 2002 have included the development of archaeological science, materials science, archaeobotany, osteology, palaeopathology, metallurgy and general hypothesis building/testing and geophysics. This is one of the most useful questionnaires I have seen.

Some reasons for not wanting to include archaeological science within their exhibits

Curators provided several reasons for not wishing, or not being able, to add scientific interpretations to their displays. Museums may use their archaeological collections to tell a dramatic story, which may not lend itself to the inclusion of science within the displays. Seven per cent of respondents volunteered that their exhibition would become too confusing if scientific content was added. For example, Respondent 17 reported:

> Our museum ... was built in 1970 – the main theme concentrating on giving visitors an understanding of the story of the [site] ... illustrated with artefacts.
>
> Incorporating archaeological science into this display would likely confuse visitors/over complicate the narrative. Instead, a separate display on scientific themes would add extra dimension to the visitor experience

and emphasize that the archaeological story is dynamic. This is currently done through guided tours and displays that refer to ongoing research projects. However, this information is limited and ephemeral.

Respondent 6 agrees with this, yet believes science can be integrated:

> We try to tell a fairly dramatic story, but are keen to show the many different ways in which science has enabled that story to be told.

Thirty-two per cent of respondents cited the lack of space for not including more science. Respondent 1 wrote:

> Scientific topics are just one area competing for space in our very small gallery. Such topics are included where particularly important to a particular piece.

Echoed by Respondent 19:

> We do not currently have enough display space to cover all of our collections, let alone cover scientific matters in any depth.

Although Respondent 21 offers one exciting solution:

> ... we are struggling for space to include science (and other thought processes) and have supporting web-based material so people who were interested could explore the subject to whichever level they choose.

Only 15 per cent mentioned funding as an obstacle to having science in their displays. As an example, Respondent 21 mentioned that:

> We have used scientific information in temporary displays made in-house, and will do so again, but we lack the resources to update our permanent galleries at the moment ...

The topics identified by respondents for future inclusion in their exhibits

The survey provided the opportunity for curators to identify which topics, if any, they would like to include more of in future exhibitions (Table 20.1). The top three topics identified for more coverage were: 'dating techniques (other than radiocarbon dating)', 'stratigraphy and the excavation process', and 'osteology and palaeopathology' (the study of human bones and diseases). 'General hypothesis building and testing', 'human evolution', and 'materials science' were the least likely to be chosen. Additionally, some 9 per cent commented further, suggesting that there is a realization that different interpretations of the collections can be made in the future. For example, Respondent 13: 'The archaeology displays were constructed in 1978 and will be completely replaced by 2011 with the emphasis on investigation'.

When asked whether it would be helpful to have guidelines on how science may be successfully integrated in archaeology exhibits, a majority (63 per cent) agreed or strongly agreed. Indeed, Respondent 28 reiterated the perceived usefulness of guidelines in the 'further comments' section. Interestingly, there is not a correlation between those wishing to have guidelines and their scientific education (Figure 20.2h). Most modern archaeology undergraduate degrees in the UK include various scientific topics within their syllabuses. The content and depth of science covered varies between universities and courses offered, yet there is a trend to greater coverage in more recent years as techniques and research has developed. Only 21 per cent of respondents with archaeology degrees were awarded their degrees within the last ten years, and hence there is the potential for their basic understanding of the newer science topics to be more limited. Nevertheless, this does not appear to have hampered their desire to include more science within their displays, with many respondents identifying specific topics that they would like to expand on in future presentations.

In the USA and elsewhere, archaeology is viewed more as a subdiscipline of anthropology, whereas in the UK it is usually viewed as a discipline in its own right. It would be interesting to see whether American curators of archaeology were as keen to have more archaeological science in their museums, and if so which topics.

Other comments made by curators of archaeology exhibits

There are several further points made by respondents that are worthy of note. Respondent 38 highlighted the importance of science education at school and strong community links:

> Hopefully the forthcoming changes to the primary school curriculum will encourage greater cross-discipline interpretation and presentation of local history museum collections. A start would be to present ourselves as a community/heritage resource not just local history.

Indeed, a PUR approach to archaeology-based science could involve local communities with excavations from the pre-excavation phase right through to post-excavation artefact analyses and beyond. This will be more suited to temporary exhibitions and other media with relatively fast processing rates (e.g. the Internet), but could place communities once again at the heart of archaeology and museums at the centre of this dialogue. Respondent 52 stressed the importance of the science to future archaeologists:

> Incorporation of scientific elements should be used more in general as displays are renewed, or started. This would give prospective future archaeologists who visit with their family or school, more of a heads up on what to expect if going on to study in the area.

Although this surely should not be their main target audience! Respondent 42 exclaimed: 'It is of course important to ask your end user how interested they are in these topics!' Despite this latter quote, based on previous answers, this respondent was favourably inclined to the inclusion of science. Naturally, it is important to conduct front-end and formative evaluations (Korn 1999: 5–7; Miles and Clarke 1993: 699).

The whole concept of presenting 'unfinished science' (i.e. science that has yet to be fully verified and accepted by the scientific community) within archaeology museums is intriguing. Durant (2004: 58) recognizes that museums neither know everything, nor can they realistically constantly keep up with the latest developments. Aspects of 'unfinished' archaeological science research can progress at a fast rate, with many articles being published in rapid communications science journals. It cannot be expected that the majority of curators locate, digest, and present this new information. As Respondent 8 ventured: 'It is not easy to find out who is doing what research and how to target them – there almost needs to be a "speed dating" set-up for museums and researchers.'

Although the background science is readily found within archaeological science books, there might be a case for developing a central database specifically for curatorial staff. Such a database could contain the background science, its development, examples of research, summary of cutting-edge developments, contact details for the leading researchers and perhaps some examples of museum text that have been used in the past (both successfully and unsuccessfully). This could go some way in helping the 63 per cent of respondents who specified the need for some guidelines on how science may be successfully integrated in displays.

Conclusions

This preliminary study has investigated the current extent and nature of science displayed within a sample of UK archaeology museums. Curators' attitudes and backgrounds will differ slightly between countries, but the experiences expressed in this study will no doubt resonate elsewhere. Whilst a larger sample size might add slightly more detail, in order to gain a greater understanding of why the respondents answered some of the questions in the manner they did, face-to-face, follow-up interviews are warranted. We now have an idea of what science topics are currently presented in archaeology museums/exhibits, so the logical and necessary next step would be to obtain the views of visitors, non-visitors, and other stakeholders. Different strategies should also be further assessed, such as gallery drama, lecture programmes, hands-on interactive exhibits, and online presentations.

With many governments placing increasing attention on fostering a greater interest in science, archaeology museums possess a unique opportunity using human-focused stories as the hook. Perhaps partly due to historical reasons, natural history museums (and their visitors) view their collections as primarily scientific ones. Archaeology naturally lends itself to more human-centred narratives, from which several of the respondents to this survey acknowledged that they did not want to stray (at least not within their physical exhibitions).

As museums search for innovative ways to interpret their collections, scientific investigation offers a further route that can be negotiated. This survey provides evidence that many museum professionals have included, or would like to include, more references to archaeology-based science within their exhibits. Using approaches advocated by the PUR movement, archaeology museums can illustrate the interconnected nature of archaeological research, whereby numerous specialists communicate in a two-way dialogue that shapes studies, informs data analyses and interpretations, and ensures that the work is disseminated to a wide audience. Arguably, archaeology museum visitors should feature heavily within this audience and museums are well placed to be a central node within this network.

Sixty-three per cent of respondents possess archaeology degrees; the remainder perhaps reflects the varied nature of the museums in which archaeological collections are held (these curators might have social history degrees, for example). To varying extents, modern archaeology degrees usually cover the scientific topics investigated in this study. Hence, the fact that, on average, most respondents terminated their formal scientific education at around age 16 need not necessarily be viewed as a hindrance to increased scientific interpretation in museums. As this study demonstrates, the prospect of reinterpreting the collections, utilizing more scientific perspectives, appears to be extremely enticing to many museum professionals.

References

Arnold, K. (1996) Presenting science as product or as process: museums and the making of science. In: S. Pearce (ed.), *Exploring Science in Museums*. London: Athlone Press, pp. 57–78.

Black, G. (2005) *The Engaging Museum: Developing Museums for Visitor Involvement*. London: Routledge.

Borun, M., Massey, C., and Lutter, T. (1993) Naive knowledge and the design of science museum exhibits. *Curator*, 36(3): 201–19.

Brace, I. (2004) *Questionnaire Design. How to Plan, Structure and Write Survey Material for Effective Market Research*. London: Kogan Page.

Bristow, S. (2008) *Inspiring Science*. Winchester: South East Museum Hub.

Butler, S.V.F. (1992) *Science and Technology Museums*. Leicester: Leicester University Press.

Cleaves, A. (2005) The formation of science choice in secondary school. *International Journal of Science Education*, 27(4): 471–86.

Cohen, L. (2000) Public understanding of science: managing producer/user relations in public sector science institutes. End-of-award report (No. L485274040). Swindon: Economic and Social Research Council.

Coudart, A. (2006) Is archaeology a science, an art or a collection of individual experiments …? *Archaeological Dialogues*, 13(2): 132–8.

Davis, E.A. (2003) Untangling dimensions of middle school student's beliefs about scientific knowledge and science learning. *International Journal of Science Education*, 25(4): 439–68.

Davis, J. and Carter, H. (1999) Open windows, open doors. In: E. Hooper-Greenhill (ed.), *The Educational Role of the Museum*. Second edition. London: Routledge, pp. 99–104.

Dunbar, R. (1995) *The Trouble with Science*. London: Faber and Faber.
Durant, J. (2004) The challenge and the opportunity of presenting 'unfinished science'. In: D. Chittenden, G. Farmelo, and B.V. Lewenstein (eds.), *Creating Connections: Museums and the Public Understanding of Current Research*. Lanham, MD: AltaMira Press, pp. 47–60.
Durant, J.R., Evans, G.A., and Thomas, G.P. (1989) The public understanding of science. *New Scientist*, 340: 11–14.
Farmelo, G. (2004) Only connect: linking the public with current scientific research. In: D. Chittenden, G. Farmelo, and B.V. Lewenstein (eds.), *Creating Connections: Museums and the Public Understanding of Current Research*. Lanham, MD: AltaMira Press, pp. 1–26. Feitelson, E. (1991) The potential of mail surveys in geography: some empirical evidence. *Professional Geographer*, 43(2): 190–205.
Field, H. and Powell, P. (2001) Public understanding of science vs. public understanding of research. *Public Understanding of Science*, 10(4): 421–6.
Gardner, H. (1983) *Frames of Mind: The Theory of Multiple Intelligences*. New York, NY: Basic Books.
Heberlein, T.A. and Baumgartner, R. (1978) Factors affecting response rates to mailed questionnaires: a quantitative analysis of published literature. *American Sociological Review*, 43(4): 447–62.
Hein, G.E. (1996) Constructivist learning theory. In: G. Durbin (ed.), *Developing Museum Exhibitions for Lifelong Learning*. Norwich: The Stationery Office, pp. 30–34.
    (1998) *Learning in the Museum*. London: Routledge.
Hooper-Greenhill, E. (1999) Museum learners as active postmodernists: contextualizing constructivism. In: E. Hooper-Greenhill (ed.), *The Educational Role of the Museum*. Second edition. London: Routledge, pp. 67–72.
Knell, S.J. (2007) Museums, fossils and the cultural revolution of science: mapping change in the politics of knowledge in nineteenth-century Britain. In: S.J. Knell and S. Macleod (eds.), *Museum Revolutions: How Museums Change and Are Changed*. London: Routledge, pp. 28–47.
Korn, R. (1999) Studying your visitors: where to begin. In: M. Borun and R. Korn (eds.), *Introduction to Museum Evaluation*. Washington, D.C.: American Association of Museums, pp. 5–9.
Lewenstein, B.V. and Bonney, R. (2004) Different ways of looking at public understanding of research. In: D. Chittenden, G. Farmelo, and B.V. Lewenstein (eds.), *Creating Connections: Museums and the Public Understanding of Current Research*. Lanham, MD: AltaMira Press, pp. 63–72.
Lucas, C. (2008) *Museums and Galleries Yearbook*. London: Museums Association.
Macdonald, S. (1992) Cultural imaging among museum visitors: a case study. *Museum Management and Curatorship*, 11: 401–09.
Macdonald, S. (1995) Consuming science: public knowledge and the dispersed politics of reception among museum visitors. *Media Culture and Society*, 17(1): 13–29.
McCombs, B.L. (1991) Motivation and lifelong learning. *Educational Psychologist*, 26(2): 117–27.
Miles, R. and Clarke, G. (1993) Setting off on the right foot. *Environment and Behavior*, 25: 698–709.

MLA (2009a) Summary of outcomes and processes. Available at: www.inspiring learningforall.gov.uk/export/sites/inspiringlearning/resources/repository/ Summary of outcomes and PrBlue.pdf (accessed 9 May 2009).

MLA (2009b) Strengths of different research methods in generating statements about learning. Available at: www.inspiringlearningforall.gov.uk/export/sites/inspiring learning/resources/repository/Methods_-_strengths_and_we.pdf (accessed 9 May 2009).

Moser, C.A. and Kalton, G. (1971) *Survey Methods in Social Investigation*. Second edition. London: Heinemann Educational Books.

Oppenheim, A.N. (1966) *Questionnaire Design and Attitude Measurement*. London: Heinemann Educational Books.

Paola, C. (2004) Improving public understanding of scientific research: a view from the research side. In: D. Chittenden, G. Farmelo, and B.V. Lewenstein (eds.), *Creating Connections: Museums and the Public Understanding of Current Research*. Lankam, MD: AltaMira Press, pp. 145–52.

Pohlman, D. (2004) Catching science in the act: mysteries of Çatalhöyük. In: D. Chittenden, G. Farmelo, and B.V. Lewenstein (eds.), *Creating Connections: Museums and the Public Understanding of Current Research*. Lanham, MD: AltaMira Press, pp. 267–75.

Renaissance South East (2009) Science. Available at: www.museumse.org.uk/learning/Science.html (accessed 22 April 2009).

Sandell, R. (2007) *Museums, Prejudices and the Reframing of Difference*. London: Routledge.

Sudbury, P. (1992) Linking scientists to non-science museums. In: J. Durrant (ed.), *Museums and the Public Understanding of Science*. London: The Science Museum/COPAS, pp. 57–64.

Taylor, J. and Stevenson, S. (1999) Investigating subjectivity within collection condition surveys. *Museum Management and Curatorship*, 18(1): 19–42.

van Eijck, M. and Roth, W.-M. (2008) Representations of scientists in Canadian high school and college textbooks. *Journal of Research in Science Teaching*, 45(9): 1059–82.

Wylie, A. (2000) Question of evidence, legitimacy and the (dis)unity of science. *American Anthropology*, 65(2): 227–37.

Wynne, B. (1999) Knowledge in context. In: ed. E. Scanlon, E. Whitelegg, and S. Yates (eds.), *Communicating Science: Contexts and Channels: Reader 2*. London: Routledge, pp. 4–13.

Yaneva, A., Rabesandratana, T.M., and Greiner, B. (2009) Staging scientific controversies: a gallery test on science museum's interacting. *Public Understanding of Science*, 18: 79–90.

Yearley, S. (2000) Making systematic sense of public discontents with expert knowledge: two analytical approaches and a case study. *Public Understanding of Science*, 9(2): 105–22.

Chapter 21

Prehistory, identity, and archaeological representation in Nordic museums

Janet E. Levy

Archaeology and prehistory are contested, both in postcolonial situations in Africa, Australia, and the Americas (e.g., Watkins 2000) and in arenas of nationalist debate as in Europe (e.g., Diaz-Andreu and Champion 1996; Meskell 1998). At the same time, indigenism is contested on a variety of levels (Hodgson 2002; Kuper 2003). These include debates about which individuals are indigenous, which groups are indigenous, and whether indigenousness exists at all. Archaeological and anthropological museums are situated within both of these arenas because they are homes to public representations of the past and culture (Krebs 2003). In Europe, the manipulation, suppression, and even destruction of archaeological evidence by, among others, the Nazis has led to an understandable appeal to depoliticize archaeological heritage. But this appeal can be paradoxical. Although the representation of difference or otherness can be (and, indeed, has been) manipulated for destructive purposes, the denial of otherness can also be destructive. These points can be illustrated with a case study of the Saami, one of the rare populations in Europe that participates in the discourse of indigenism.

It is now widely recognized that archaeology and prehistory are contested arenas, and the past is often used to interpret and legitimate the present. Debate occurs in numerous contexts, including land claims, museum exhibitions, textbooks, repatriation, and the daily practice of archaeology. In North America, these debates are based within complex postcolonial relationships among anthropologists, archaeologists, and Native Americans (Watkins 2000). In contrast, in Europe, debates about the politics of archaeology are infrequently framed within a colonial discourse, and more commonly framed as competition between various national ethnic groups. Within the Nordic countries, as elsewhere in Europe, archaeological dialogue with indigenous people is underdeveloped. Although the Nordic countries are often thought of as ethnically homogeneous, they are not and have not been for centuries. The northernmost regions of Norway, Sweden, and Finland are the home of a minority community of Saami (or Sámi, Sami) people, earlier known as Lapps. The Saami conceive of themselves as the indigenous people of the northern region and refer to the region—known to much of Europe as "Lapland"—as "Sápmi." They lay claim to a cultural and historical distinctiveness in relationship to the majority populations. Yet within the current national borders, Norwegians, Swedes, and Finns might well consider themselves indigenous as well. This ambiguous situation provides a distinctive case study in the politics of archaeological representation.

In this article, I examine some of these issues of identity and archaeological representation as they are exhibited in a variety of museums in Finland, Sweden, and Norway. A few Nordic scholars have commented about museum exhibition (Lundström and Pilvesmaa 1998; Mulk and Bayliss-Smith 1999: 380–1; Olsen 1998). I build on these contributions by looking at a series of museums in a format that resembles James Clifford's (1991) comparison of four Northwest Coast museums, two run by tribes and two run by non-native organizations. I examine the visual qualities of exhibitions about archaeology in far northern Europe to think about some of the intertwining complexities of identity and prehistory and how these are presented to a general public.

This research is situated at an intersection of a growing literature about the cultural politics of representation and the definition of *indigenism* (Dombrowski 2002; Hinton 2002b; Hodgson 2002; Kuper 2003), on the one hand, and discussion and debate within museum studies about display of diverse, minority, and indigenous communities (e.g., Karp and Lavine 1991; Mulk and Bayliss-Smith 1999; Silverman 2002), on the other hand. Although the literature about the ideology of museum exhibition is large, here I turn to Eilean Hooper-Greenhill's (2000) analysis of visual culture in the context of museums.

To summarize my conclusions briefly: The representation of the Saami and their relationship to the past differs significantly between national or regional museums run by majority communities and museums run by Saami communities (for convenience, I call these "majority" and "Saami community" institutions, respectively). These differences reflect a range of ideological and pragmatic factors that ultimately lead to different messages about the history and identity of the Saami. Until recently, Saami prehistory was ignored or marginalized within archaeology exhibitions in majority museums, and it remains marginalized in some museums. Frequently, the Saami have been denied a deep past that is unproblematically granted to the majority population. The identity of the Saami and their links to the past also may be influenced by the expanding ideology of the European Union.

More generally, the Saami museums provide a distinctive example of the politics of heritage in archaeological representation. The past can be used to justify and legitimate present-day claims and power relations or, alternatively, to challenge such claims and relationships. It is understandable that scholars decry the politicization of archaeology. However, the call to depoliticize archaeology inevitably has different implications for majority and minority populations. The representations of the past in museums of archaeology and prehistory communicate statements to the general public about identity, legitimacy, and control of land. In Europe, national and pan-national identities are favoured in public representations: this has the potential to make invisible the identities—and, thus, the rights—of small, non-national groups. There is a variety of ambiguities and paradoxes within this topic, which will be discussed further later.

Ideology of archaeological representation

Kristian Kristiansen, a leading Nordic archaeologist, urges the establishment of "an ethical rule that archaeology and the archaeological heritage cannot and should not be employed for political and ideological claims in the present" (1998: 121). He explains that it is impossible to decide objectively between "good" and "bad" uses of the past; furthermore, there has been so much human movement, cultural mixing, and culture change in Europe that continuity from the past is a fiction. This was written in the context of "ethnic cleansing" and destruction of historical monuments in the former Yugoslavia and elsewhere in eastern Europe. Given the twentieth-century history of manipulation of archaeology by the Nazis (Arnold 1990) and others, this call is a deeply appealing one.

However, in reality, archaeological representation is intrinsically political because it is about who controls interpretation and about connecting people to place. For example, Nadia Abu El-Haj (2001) demonstrates how all aspects of archaeological representation in Israel, from labels of chronological periods to presentations by museum guides, are infused with unspoken assumptions about identity, rights, and power. It is tempting but facile to suggest that the Israeli case is intrinsically different than the peaceful Nordic world. Although the Nordic world thankfully lacks the physical violence of the Middle East, differentials in power nevertheless exist and archaeological representation is implicated in them. Stephanie Moser and Sam Smiles point out that "representation is never innocent" (2004: 1); elsewhere, Moser explains how scientific illustrations are not neutral and unproblematic representations of data but, rather, "powerful rhetorical tool(s)" that inevitably communicate an underlying social agenda (Moser 1998: 15, 18). Where there are minority populations, their agendas and their rhetoric can be very different from those of the majority population. Museums are one way that these rhetorics are communicated to a general public. If this representation denies connection between past populations and present ones, it is not majority populations who will be made invisible. Where the antiquity of minority identity is not discussed, there is a risk that popular discourse will by default establish only majority identity as legitimate.

Among Native Americans, control of representation of the past is one of the most important points of contention with the archaeological community (Watkins 2000: 170). Yet Native Americans have the advantage that their past, although sometimes demeaned or ignored, is recognized as having a reality and antiquity independent of the majority culture. In contrast, in the Nordic area, Saami identity and thus archaeology and history, are fundamentally problematic. A transparent sense of antiquity is granted to "Scandinavianness" but not to "Saaminess." This is communicated implicitly to the public in majority museum exhibitions.

Indigenousness

This article is not about who the Saami "really" are; neither is it about whether there "really" are any indigenous people left in the world. It is about the representation of identity, indigenousness, and the past in public venues: one aspect of the "praxis of indigenism" (Dombrowski 2002: 1062). Anthropologists and others, following

Frederik Barth, think about ethnicity (including indigenousness) as fluid, flexible, and constructed (Hodgson 2002; Jones 1997). Popular understandings, however, identify ethnicity as an intrinsic and clearly bounded category (Hinton 2002a; Kuper 2003), usually with strong links to the past. These understandings have practical implications, in particular for control of land and resources.

There is a core paradox in the claim to indigenousness, and there are calls for minority communities to reject a kind of "false consciousness" of indigenism (Kuper 2003). Certainly, where difference is essentialized and given legitimacy through origin myths, one outcome can be genocide (Hinton 2002b). The strategy of claiming indigenous status can have less virulent but still negative outcomes, including co-optation by outside authorities and factionalism and conflict within communities (Conklin 2002; Dombrowski 2002). But like the call for a non-political archaeology, the call for rejecting "false" indigenism is easy to make from a majority position. The paradox is that an insistence on difference can be destructive, but so can a denial of difference. Where otherness is denied, power differentials do not disappear; instead, they become more hidden, with "unmarked categories of normalcy that privilege, and often legitimate, domination of one type of person over another" (Hinton 2002a: 28). In much the same way, unmarked categories often dominate museum exhibitions about prehistory.

Visual culture of museums

There is a growing literature about the ideological complexities of creating museum exhibitions in a world of diverse, competing human communities. Among others, Christina Krebs (2003) and the chapters in Ivan Karp and Steven Lavine's edited volume (1991) provide an overview. Here, I focus on the visual aspects of exhibitions, following Hooper-Greenhill's (2000) discussion of the visual culture of museums and building on Moser's (1998) analysis of archaeological illustration. Both emphasize the power of visual presentation. Visual arrangements—layout, colors, illustrations, combinations of objects, and so forth—communicate with all-seeing visitors, even those who cannot or do not read texts: children, harried parents, foreign visitors, tourists on a schedule. Visual presentation also communicates in a non-verbal way, making the information presented persuasive but not easily amenable to conscious critical review (Moser 1998: 16). Thus, the visual culture of museum exhibition is a powerful tool of communication.

Hooper-Greenhill (2000) distinguishes between "modernist museums," which originated in the nineteenth century, and "post-museums," which are products of perhaps the last 25 years. The former emphasizes order, categorization, and "progress"; furthermore, they are tied to ideological projects of nationalism and imperialism (Hooper-Greenhill 2000: 16–18, 25; see also Anderson 1991). In contrast, "post-museums" are "reinvented as spaces with more colour, more noise, and which [sic] are more physically complex" (Hooper-Greenhill 2000: 148). These "post-museums" are arenas for performance of intangible heritage, and they often welcome diverse voices into their exhibitions (Hooper-Greenhill 2000: 152; see Krebs 2003, for a comparable perspective using different terminology). The national and regional museums discussed below are examples of modernist museums in Hooper-Greenhill's sense, whereas the Saami community museums fit better into the category of "post-museum."

The visual aspects of museum exhibitions create authoritative canons, "giving authority to certain texts, figures, ideas, problems, discursive strategies, and historical narratives" (Hooper-Greenhill 2000: 19). One of the key canons or master narratives is that of nationalism and national identity (Hooper-Greenhill 2000: 25). The linear layout of many national museums presents this master narrative in physical form. The existence and historical development of the Saami are a problem for the master narrative of nationalism in the Nordic world. It is clear that for many archaeologists, being "Norwegian" or "Swedish" is transparent, whereas being Saami is contested (see discussion below). The question is more complicated in Finland, where questions of scholarly and, in fact, popular interest are "who are the Finns?" or "where do the Finns come from?" From the linguistic connection between Finnish and Saami, one might expect to see intertwined stories, but typically the origin and identity of the Saami are of peripheral interest to the dominant topic of the origin of the Finns (but see Nunez 1987).

If these issues of identity and ethnicity are problematic for archaeologists, they are even more so for the general public, for whom the visual aspect of museum exhibitions have the greatest impact. As noted earlier, bounded ethnic identity is accepted as a given, if a poorly conceptualized given, in popular discourse (and in some scientific discourse, as among geneticists). My interest is the implicit messages of the visual displays, their potential impact on their audiences, and their implications for understanding the political realities of archaeological heritage. The Saami case, based in a kind of internal colonialism, provides a contrast to the more familiar Native American and Native Australian cases.

The Saami

The term *Saami* refers to communities previously called "Lapps," who live in Norway, Sweden, Finland, and northwest Russia (see Beach 1988; Gaski 1997; Hætta 1996; Svensson 1997; Vorren and Manker 1962). Estimates of modern Saami population range from 35,000 to 70,000, with the largest community in Norway, followed by Sweden, Finland, and Russia in descending order.[1] Since the sixteenth century, Saami have been associated, certainly in the minds of outsiders, with herding semi-domesticated reindeer: contemporary media images of the Saami are dominated by reindeer; in Sweden, Saami legal status is tied to reindeer herding. However, there is evidence that both in early modern times and certainly earlier, Saami subsistence depended heavily on a mixture of hunting and fishing, whereas herding is a relatively late and far from universal adaptation. For example, historically, the majority of Saami in Norway relied on fishing. Also important for the Saami during their recorded history was long-distance trade in skins, furs, dried fish, and other goods.

The traditional Saami religion was a variety of circumpolar shamanism, but the Saami have been missionized since about the eleventh century and are now mostly

Lutherans (with Russian Orthodox populations in Finland and Russia). Pietistic and fundamentalist movements from the sixteenth century onward attracted many Saami. This has implications for the issue of repatriation of skeletal remains that, so far, has been of limited interest to most Saami communities. There are about nine Saami dialects within the Finno-Ugrian family of languages. Thus, the Saami language is unrelated to Norwegian and Swedish, but it is related to Finnish, another western Finno-Ugrian language.

The Saami as an ethnic group

The biological position of the Saami has been debated at least since Linnaeus in the eighteenth century. Through the first half of the twentieth century, Saami (then called "Lapps") were conventionally categorized as a separate and inferior race, on the basis of cranial form and measurement (e.g., Coon 1939: 298–306). More recently, there is extensive publication about the chromosomal relationship of the Saami to Finns, to other Europeans, and to non-European populations (e.g., Tambets et al. 2004). The recent genetic literature is oddly similar to the earlier craniology, especially in the emphasis on distinguishing "eastern" and "western" affiliations of the Saami (Coon 1939:299; Tambets et al. 2004), terms that are basically glosses of *primitive* and *modern*. A simplified conclusion of recent research is that there is genetic distance between Saami and other European populations, but that Saami genetic patterns are a restricted subset of broader European patterns (Tambets et al. 2004: 678). In both older and recent literature, the sampling criteria are not discussed; thus, the reader cannot tell how individuals were chosen to be part of the Saami or any other sample. This recent research, although not racialist in character, treats the Saami as an intrinsically identifiable category just as did the earlier craniological research.

My own experience suggests a range of phenotypic variability among self-identified Saami. Today, language use (by the individual or by lineal ancestors) is the major criterion for participation in Saami political institutions; self-identification as Saami is relevant for participating in other community institutions. There is no use of "blood quanta". It is clear that for several hundred years—actually, until very recently—Saami were treated like a colonized people, in that they experienced imposed government, forced taxation, missionization, stigmatization of language, attempted exclusion from traditional subsistence practices, and denigration in racial terms. In recent decades, each Nordic country has allocated more local self-government and cultural autonomy to Saami communities, and Saami-language schools and media are experiencing a renaissance (Gaski 1997). Today, there are Saami parliaments in each of the Nordic countries, charged with advising the national governments and managing certain internal issues including cultural life. However, there is no communal land tenure among the Saami. Although there are some communal Saami usufruct rights, land ownership within the Saami region is by individuals or by the state in the form of national parks and nature reserves. This lack of land tenure has become a striking irritant to Saami political leaders in recent decades (e.g., Finnish National Parliament 1997).

The current generation of Saami politicians and intellectuals has explicitly worked to revive a Saami identity that had declined in the face of discrimination (Eidheim 1997). The Saami, among others (Hodgson 2002: 1038), define themselves as "indigenous people" according to the International Labor Organization's (ILO) Convention 169 on Indigenous and Tribal Peoples, established in 1989:

> peoples in independent countries who are regarded as indigenous on account of their descent from the population which inhabited the country, or a geographical region to which the country belongs, at the time of conquest or colonisation, or the establishment of present state boundaries and who, independent of their legal status, retain some or all of their own social, economic, cultural and political institutions.
>
> (ILO 1989)

Following Barth, many anthropologists argue that ethnicity is not an intrinsic quality of a community or population but, rather, is created in the context of social and economic interaction. However, the Saami themselves, the national governments, and the Nordic public treat Saami identity as a real and bounded category; indeed, they similarly treat Swedish, Finnish, or Norwegian identity. Thus, there is a level at which it is irrelevant who the Saami "really" are: They are understood within the region to be a separate community of some kind, usually defined in cultural and, occasionally, still in racial terms.

Prehistory of Sápmi (a simplified version)

This summary is extracted from recent reviews of Nordic prehistory (Myhre 2003; Siiriänen 2003; see also Forsberg 1995; Zachrisson 1976). Occupation of the far north occurred almost as rapidly as the late Pleistocene ice sheets receded. The earliest archaeological evidence in the region is the Komsa culture, circa 10,000 BP, on the far northern coast of Norway. The evidence suggests that humans moved into the area along the western coast of the Scandinavian peninsula. During the Mesolithic period (ca. 9000–6000 BP), the interior was occupied by people moving inland from the Norwegian coasts as well as by populations coming from east and southeast. Over time, artifact styles suggest affiliations with different outside regions; the literature is variable whether these affiliations are interpreted as immigrations or as influences through diffusion and trade.

For several thousand years, the area was occupied by hunter-fisher-collectors, varying their adaptations between inland and coastal regions and exploiting seals, fish, birds, and mammals, including elk and reindeer. Sites are generally small (although larger along the coasts) and yield pits, hearths, animal bones, occasional wood, or bone carved in the form of animal heads, and a variety of chipped stone tools made of both local and imported stone. Pottery was introduced about 6000 BP. About two thousand years later, asbestos-tempered pottery appears in Finland and eventually spread across the far north; some authors link this with Saami identity (Olsen 1985). Pit systems for trapping elk and reindeer appear about 5000 BP.

A small number of bronzes find their way into the region from southern and eastern cultures in the second millennium BCE. By the beginning of the local Iron Age, circa CE 1, communities using domesticated animals and some farming have expanded northward, especially along the coasts of Norway and of the Gulf of Bothnia, but hunting–fishing–collecting remains dominant in the interior. Sites explicitly identified as Saami appear in the later Iron Age, approximately CE 500–1500; these yield reindeer bones and antlers; decorative bone artifacts carved with geometric motifs; bark-wrapped burials; offering sites of numerous small iron and silver objects; asbestos-tempered pottery; pitfall systems; and distinctive drum beaters (Zachrisson 1976, 1984). There is little written information about the people now called Saami until circa CE 800. Around CE 1600, there is evidence for the beginning of herding semi-domesticated reindeer, as well as both archaeological and ethnohistorical evidence of regional involvement in long-distance trade in northern resources, such as furs.

Archaeology and ethnicity

This simplified summary of archaeological evidence is part of the scholarly background for the museum exhibitions under analysis here. Archaeological publications at least through the 1960s proposed that the Saami (Lapps) are relatively recent migrants to the region, not associated with pre–Iron Age sites. Knut Odner (1983, 1985), using an interactionist perspective on ethnicity based on Barth, suggests that both Saami and Scandinavian identity emerged from the late Iron Age and medieval period economic interactions in the north. Although this approach is situated within the anthropological understanding of ethnicity (and indigenousness) as flexible, contested, and constructed, it is not congruent with popular understandings of ethnicity as an intrinsic and clearly bounded category. For Saami scholars, the key issue is not that ethnicity is misunderstood in popular discourse: It is that only Saami ethnicity is contested in popular discourse. Odd Mathis Hætta writes, "There is *never any problem* in talking about Norwegian ethnicity—or taking it as implied—right from Mesolithic times, whereas Saami ethnicity is often questioned even if one only goes back as far as the Middle Ages" (Hætta 1995: 348). Barbara Scott (1996) and Bjørnar Olsen (1998) provide similar analyses by non-Saami scholars. Thus, the relevant issue is not whether pre–Iron Age sites can or should be identified with an ethnic group. The relevant issue is that in the southern parts of the Nordic world (and, in fact, in many other parts of Europe), pre–Iron Age sites are unproblematically seen as part of a continuum of occupation leading to the modern majority populations. I specifically mean *seen* here, because it is often visual representation that creates this image. In contrast, in the north, a continuum of prehistoric hunter–fisher–collector occupation does not lead unproblematically to the Saami, who are the population documented with a similar adaptation at the time of the first written sources. Museum exhibitions, which communicate to a much wider audience than academics, reflect this asymmetry.

Visiting museums

During academic year 1998–1999 and again in summer, 2002, I had the opportunity to visit a variety of museums in Finland, Sweden, and Norway, all of which had exhibitions, some large and some small, about archaeology and prehistory. These included national and regional museums and those run by Saami communities. I also spoke with a variety of people in the museum and archaeology worlds in the Nordic countries, although these data are limited. Here, I focus on seven museums in particular (the date of my visit is in parentheses):[2]

> National or regional ("majority") museums found in major cities:
> The National Museum of Finland, Helsinki (2002)
> Museum of Northern Ostrobothnia, Oulu, Finland (1998–1999)
> The National Museum of Antiquities, Stockholm (1999)
> The Nordic Museum, Stockholm (1999)
> Museums run by the Saami community:
> Siidá, Inari, Finland (1999)
> Ájtte, Jokkmokk, Sweden (2002)
> Samiid Vuorka-Dávvirat (The Sami Museum), Karasjok, Norway (1999)

Let me start with the exterior of the museums. The national and regional museums not only display "authoritative narratives," following Hooper-Greenhill, they also present themselves in "authoritative" architecture. They are massive stone structures often with architectural details that evoke medieval or Renaissance periods. The museum brochures for the Nordic Museum in Stockholm and the National Museum in Helsinki tell us that the structures were specifically built to evoke heroic periods in the national narrative. However, these styles and this narrative exclude the far north and its more modest indigenous architecture.

If we go inside to the prehistory halls, especially in Stockholm and Helsinki, we see a striking example of what Hooper-Greenhill (2000: 129–30) describes as "carefully spaced and ordered identical display cases, each with its own group of objects systematically placed in their proper places" (Figure 21.1). The two national museums are laid out in long corridors that lead the visitor on a predetermined path. Consciously or not, the national museums are physically laid out to present an authoritative view of prehistory and history, each emphasizing a singular path toward the nation as it is known in the modern world. In a variety of ways, we see the Saami separated from the central narrative.

For example, in both Helsinki and Oulu in northern Finland, the prehistory exhibitions either do not mention Saami (as in Oulu) or mention them in very peripheral ways (as in Helsinki). Exhibitions about Saami culture are found in different galleries and even on different floors than exhibitions about prehistory. Thus, the Saami are excluded from the antiquity of the nation. In Oulu, the archaeology exhibition is explicitly described as stressing the "prehistory of Northern Finland and its special features," yet there is no mention of Saami at all. The path of the prehistory exhibition leads into displays about Finnish peasant life. The Saami exhibition is two floors away.

Figure 21.1 Case in the prehistory exhibition in the National Museum of Finland. Author's photo.

In Helsinki, the prehistory exhibition is housed in a dramatic space resembling a medieval castle. The word Saami appears in one case only, in the Iron Age section where the visitor is told that the Early Saami Iron Age (CE 300–1300) is very poorly known and the Later Saami Iron Age is somewhat better known; no details are given and no artifacts are explicitly affiliated with the Saami. There is a separate case about the widespread pitfall systems used in the north for hunting reindeer, but no statement is made about who was doing the hunting, although this technique was used by the Saami at the time of first written documentation. One long corridor of cases leads toward two dramatically lit cases with life-sized, realistic mannequins dressed in early medieval costume. The visual message is clear: All of this prehistory leads to the people of the Finnish nation. In fact, there are very fine Saami costumes in this museum, but they are exhibited on another floor so they are not integrated into Finnish history. These Saami costumes are represented as barely part of any living community, displayed on faceless metal armatures, not on mannequins. So, the Saami are in the National Museum, but not of the nation. In both Oulu and Helsinki, the Saami galleries emphasize a limited time period, approximately the eighteenth- to early twentieth centuries, they are ethnological rather than historical presentations. The Saami are a classic example of "people without history" (Wolf 1982).

In the Iron Age gallery of the archaeology exhibition in the National Museum of Antiquities in Stockholm, in 1999, a case about the Saami Iron Age was labeled "under development". The text of this case says in Swedish: "The Saami have since time of earliest memory lived in the northern parts of Sweden, Norway, and Finland.

Archaeological finds show connections back in time to the Stone Age" (my translation). Yet the Stone and Bronze Age galleries, which are older installations than the Iron Age gallery, make no acknowledgement of the Saami.[3] Whereas in 1999, this museum continued the story of Sweden from late prehistory on the ground floor into lavish medieval galleries on the second floor, again the Saami were not mentioned; the later historical material about the Saami is found about a mile away in the Nordic Museum, the ethnology and folklore museum. So, although by 1999 concern about exclusion of the Saami had led to some inclusion in the national archaeology exhibition, they were not integrated into the full story of the development of Sweden; their antiquity is ambiguous. The antiquity of Swedes is not explicitly stated; however, it is implicit through the layout of the galleries that the most ancient finds lead eventually to the Swedish nation. The new prehistory exhibition, opening in November, 2005, may provide a different impression.

There are distinctive contrasts with the Saami community museums, of which there is one each in Finland, Sweden, and Norway. The Saami museums are smaller, lower to the ground, rural, and built of wood or stucco. All have outdoor walking trails and reconstructed domestic structures and facilities. Each exhibition contains a prominent map that illustrates a Saami "nation" that cuts across the modern nation-state boundaries.

The exhibitions are less linear than those in the majority museums. At Ájtte on the Arctic Circle in Jokkmokk, Sweden, the layout of the museum is modelled after a reindeer corral: wedge-shaped galleries open in a circle from a central point. In Finland and Norway, the exhibitions are laid out in open rectangles, with displays both along the walls and in the center. The design of the exhibition is most traditional in Norway, which is the oldest of these three museums. Here, individual glass cases with traditional artifact displays line the four walls of the rectangular space; however, the entire space is visible from any point. At Siidá and Ájtte, there are cases dispersed across the open space in a non-linear fashion, and there are more objects outside of cases, sometimes in full-size reconstructions of rooms or structures. In fact, there is nothing particularly cutting edge about these exhibition techniques, but they are strikingly absent from the prehistory exhibitions in Stockholm, Helsinki, and Oulu.

In the Saami community museums, especially the two newer ones in Finland and Sweden, Saami history and culture are closely tied to the natural setting and climate of Lapland. This is done through text and visuals (including life-sized panoramic photographs and reconstructed natural scenes) and even through sounds such as rushing water. Although in the wrong hands, this might be a strategy for "primitivizing" the Saami by connecting them with nature rather than with history, in fact this strategy fits well with Saami contemporary politics. The goal is not to "naturalize" the Saami but to "culturize" the environment; that is, claim it as Saami heritage. Some related processes are occurring among those claiming indigenous status in tropical South America (Conklin 2002). The northern landscape, as it is organized into national parks and preserves, is often discussed in tourist and national literature as empty and pristine, despite millennia of human occupation (Mulk 1997; Mulk and Bayliss-Smith 1999). The Saami museums contest this view by integrating the land, climate, and Saami adaptation into single exhibitions. This strategy is an example of the importance of understanding local motivations in uses of the past, as Helaine Silverman (2002) has suggested. Yet, there is also ambiguity and risk in this strategy of linking culture and nature, as will be discussed below.

Finally, all three Saami museums emphasize the time depth of Saami occupation through visuals, layout, and text. At each, the earliest Mesolithic settlements are claimed unproblematically as ancestral to Saami culture. For example, one enters the main exhibition at Ájtte by walking down a corridor lined with cardboard cutouts of humans doing something typical of the northern regions; the first figure is a Mesolithic fisherperson and the figures then continue in chronological order through medieval periods and in to a modern Saami.

Shared icons

Despite the differences in approach to Saami history and rehistory between majority museums, on the one hand, and Saami community museums, on the other hand, both types of museum actually share key visual icons: repeated striking and familiar images, as described by Moser 1998: 17–19). One visual icon represents Saami in the present: the snowmobile. Two visual icons that represent Saami in the past are the shaman's drum and the *kota* (or *kåta* or *goatte*), the skin tent used during part of the annual cycle of reindeer herding (Figure 21.2).

Figure 21.2 Kota, reindeer herders' tent, the Sami Museum, Karasjok, Norway. Author's photo.

The kota is more visually obvious in exhibits than the drums (besides being bigger, the kota is often displayed in rightly lit galleries, whereas the drums are under much dimmer light, for conservation purposes). All of the Saami community museums and majority of museums in Oulu and Stockholm and a temporary exhibit in Helsinki exhibit kotas. The presence of the kota visually represents a common dilemma of these exhibits. Although the texts may give a somewhat more nuanced view, this visual icon says one key thing: the Saami are migratory reindeer herders. Yet both the use of the kota and the practice of transhumant reindeer herding are only true of a segment of the Saami population and then only true for only limited periods of their history. Both majority and community museums rely on this link between Saami and reindeer herding in their exhibitions, although the background reasoning is probably different. For the majority institutions, the kota fits into the common presentation of Saami as timelessly frozen in about the eighteenth to nineteenth centuries, without an ancient past and, indeed, without a future (this is particularly striking in Helsinki and Oulu).

In contrast, for the Saami community museums, the kota emphasizes Saami distinctiveness and lays claim to the landscape and to certain territorial usufruct rights that are tied to reindeer herding. In the larger political arena, for better or worse, Saami identity and legitimacy are often closely tied to reindeer. This is why Saami political activists raised a kota outside the Norwegian parliament in Oslo during the protests in the 1980s against damming the Alta-Kautokeino River to create hydroelectric power for southern regions. However, this emphasis potentially raises problems for a history of the Saami community because, in fact, the majority of Saami today are not herders and were not for long periods in the past. So, it is understandable why the image of the kota may dominate Saami museum exhibitions, but, like the explicit link to nature, the image is a double-edged sword.

Discussion

There is a temptingly easy critique to be made of these contrasting museums: the national and regional museums diminish or even deny a Saami role in the antiquity of the nation. In contrast, the Saami institutions grant the Saami the same ancientness as the other Nordic populations, the ones that eventually become the national majorities. Yet it is only fair to note that there are pragmatic constraints on the exhibitions. The majority museums, to start with, are confined to buildings with their own heritage significance that has to be respected, to say nothing of structural constraints that have to be worked around. Their funding has been restricted in recent years, so revising older exhibitions is not an easy task and there are demands throughout the collections. New wall texts can be added fairly easily, but major change to the visual appearance of an exhibit is a much more expensive proposition. Indeed, the prehistory exhibit in Helsinki does have a relatively new wall text that explicitly discusses Finnish and Saami origins. However, none of the information is reflected in the displays, and the text itself is ambiguous at best.

In addition, museum exhibitions may be influenced by administrative requirements out of the control of curators. For example, after recent renovations (not including the prehistory exhibition) at the Finnish National Museum, I was told by one curator of the Saami materials that the architect's design requirements—which gave the new Saami display less space than before and demanded that no photos be included—were given priority over the curator's plans for the exhibition.

In contrast, Ájtte in Sweden and Siiclá in Finland are newer facilities. They have the luxury of focusing their exhibitions in a way that the national and regional museums cannot. They are in rural areas, so open-air trails and exhibits are more feasible than in the national museums. They may have better access to EU funding because they are in poorer rural areas to which economic development funds have been directed. Thus, there are a range of factors that impinge on how museums represent the Saami past, and it is overly simplistic to attribute the differences to ideological factors alone.

Nevertheless, the exhibitions ultimately are ideological statements. The lack of information about the prehistory of the Saami at the National Museum in Helsinki is highlighted by the presence of two cases in the prehistory exhibit explicitly about the Iron Age in the Åland Islands, off the southwest coast of Finland. It is almost too easy to see here the difference in contemporary political power reflected in an interpretation of the past: within the Finnish state, the Åland Islands have special political, land tenure, and (Swedish) language rights, whereas the Saami have almost no communal political clout. The distinctive ethnicity of the islanders is made clear in the exhibition while the Saami are ignored.

A key ideological factor derives from the history of archaeology in Europe, in particular the use of archaeology by the Nazis to legitimate their racialist views and imperialistic ambitions (Arnold 1990, 2002). Following the Second World War, many European archaeologists became sensitive to this misuse of archaeological information, in general, and ideas about ethnic identity in the past, in particular (Jones 1997). The response was to turn away from concepts of ethnicity, race, and nation. Thus, out of sensitivity to misuse of archaeology on the subject of ethnicity, the topic largely disappeared from explicit discussion. For majority populations, this is not a problem: For example, in the National Museum of Finland or the National Museum of Antiquities in Stockholm, it will be assumed that the subject is Finns or Swedes, particularly as in both places the prehistory exhibitions physically lead into exhibitions of historic periods. But for minority populations, the issue is more complicated. Sensitivity can mean silence: The result of sensitivity is the virtual disappearance of minority populations from the past, particularly the ancient past.

Identity, power, and the past

Hooper-Greenhill (2000: 19) notes another paradox about museums: They have the power both to present narrow authoritative images of the past and to raise new questions and make visible what had been invisible. The museums examined here reveal a range of ways to approach the complexities of identity and the past in the far north of Europe. At one extreme, there are the National Museum of Finland and the Museum of Northern Ostrobothnia, both of which physically separate the Saami from the story of Finland—the latter museum even excludes Saami from the story of northern Finland—providing them virtually no space within the national discourse. At the National Museum of Antiquities in Stockholm, a similar model apparently once existed. But by 1999, there was concern to include the Saami to some degree in the story of the nation's past, focusing on the later Iron Age and early medieval period, for which scholars can turn to a combination of archaeological and documentary sources to identify ethnic groups in the far north. So, one well-designed case was devoted to the "Saami Iron Age" within the Viking period gallery. In late 2005, redesigned prehistory galleries may integrate the Saami further into the national prehistory.

The Saami have a greater presence in the Nordic Museum, the ethnology museum in Stockholm. The first part of the Saami exhibition is made of miniature dioramas and, again, focuses on Saami and reindeer, placing the Saami in an unchanging ethnographic present rather as is done in Oulu and Helsinki. The dioramas tend to visibly "miniaturize" Saami culture. However, the museum has added new wall text to explain that these display cases represent an old-fashioned view. In addition, there have been added new display cases with life-sized reconstructions of recent Saami houses and activities (including the ubiquitous snowmobile) as well as a photographic exhibition of the modern Saami parliament. The visuals and text of the exhibition are testimony to changing attitudes and to a commitment to bring into view the diversity of modern developments among the Saami, once made invisible by the older exhibition.

The Saami community museums, in contrast, foreground the environmental setting, annual cycle, and modern politics of the Saami. They present the occupations of the north, from the earliest onward, as directly ancestral to the historically documented Saami communities. In recognition of the complexity of ethnicity, there may be textual statements that a specifically recognizable Saami culture appeared in the later Iron Age, but the visual message of the exhibitions is always of continuity back in time to deep antiquity, indeed to the first occupants after the melting of the Pleistocene ice cap. A common phrase in wall text and publications tells the visitor that the Saami have lived in the area "since time immemorial" (e.g. Mulk 1997: 10).

Ultimately, there are pragmatic implications of public understandings of the antiquity of occupation of a region. In Norway, the rights of Saami to claim heritage interest and usufruct right in large areas of land were challenged in the early 1980s by plans to dam the Alta-Kautokeino River, which the Saami protested in alliance with environmental groups (Eidheim 1997; Paine 1994: 153). In 1995, archaeologists testified (on both sides) in a legal case about Saami usufruct rights in north-central Sweden (Beach 2001: 229–33; Svensson 1997). It is notable that during these legal proceedings, there was intensive discussion of how one could identify a Saami archaeological site but no debate about how to identify a Scandinavian one (Gustafsson 1999), demonstrating the reality of Huotta's complaint above. The Saami ultimately lost both cases, but they gained political savvy. In addition, archaeology, for the first time, became part of the public debate about identity, antiquity, and power in the north.

In this context, the paradoxes and ambiguities inherent in the representation of Saami ethnicity are more obvious. The use of symbolic capital from the past is a sensitive operation for anyone, including those who claim indigenous status. The visual focus on the kota and on links to surrounding nature may run the risk of an oppressive, primitivizing essentialism (Kuper 2003); among other things, such essentialism may aggravate internal Saami tensions over the role of reindeer and reindeer herders in self-representation and politics. Alternatively, Saami control and presentation of certain images can be seen as an example of "strategic essentialism" (Hodgson 2002: 1040, 1046, see n.10) that allows the community to "intentionally manipulate, project, and homogenize their public images and identities to accord with 'Western' stereotypes in order to seek recognition and demand rights" (Hodgson 2002: 1040).

Unlike Native American and Native Australians, Saami have few legal claims to land and resources. However, they do have significant control of their own self-representation through Saami educational institutions and media and through museums. Thus, the Saami use the tools of the state—radio, museums, and colleges—to lay claim to autonomy and to resist the state. They do this, in part, by laying claim jointly to the environment and to the past through media and museum images.

Unifying Europe

The dilemma of representation for the Saami has been how to maintain distinctiveness in the face of hegemonic nationalism. Now, continuing Saami control of both representation and heritage is influenced by even larger homogenizing institutional developments: the European Union and related institutions. Despite recognition of national interests in culture and heritage, the cultural apparatus of the European Union is strongly focused on analyzing, defining, and strengthening a non-national "European identity" (Grohn 2004: 144–87; Shore 1995). A well-known archaeological example of this ideological stance is the lavish travelling exhibition, in the late 1990s, on Bronze Age Europe (Council of Europe 1999). The Bronze Age was explicitly chosen as the first truly "European" period. Yet such an approach has potential negative implications for the far north, which only peripherally participated in what are conceived of as truly European cultural developments of prehistory and early history: the Neolithic Revolution, the Bronze Age, the spread of Celtic cultures, and the Roman Empire (Council of Europe 1999: ix; Grohn 2004; Zvelebil 1995). In the new pan-European economy and culture, claims of indigenousness—or, for that matter, any kind of "otherness"—may well be stigmatized as much as, or more than, claims of national interest. The Saami lack the economic and political clout that nation-states can and do use to contest EU directives with which they disagree. Paradoxically, although the Saami past may be conceived of as "non-European" and thus possibly stigmatized, the European Union also provides funding that has benefited a variety of museums in rural areas far from the national capitals (although not in Norway, which is not a member of the European Union).

Summary

Until recently, Saami prehistory has been ignored or marginalized in the Nordic archaeological community. Within the Saami community, although history is considered important, archaeology has only recently and intermittently been a focus of interest. A Finnish Saami student of archaeology told me in 1998 that she felt alienated from the Saami community by her interest in archaeology. A non-Saami archaeology student who worked in far northern Finland found the same indifference. To some Saami intellectuals (e.g., Hætta 1996), much archaeology would be seen as unnecessary if Saami oral tradition were granted the respect it is due. Other Saami scholars (Aikio and Aikio 1989) argue that excavation of Saami sites should be limited until there are Saami archaeologists to control the research agenda. These positions resemble positions held by some Native American activists regarding archaeology. Yet, as Saami continue the struggle for economic and cultural autonomy, I predict that the practice of archaeology will grow in significance within their communities. Among other things, Saami participate in the World Congress of Indigenous People and come into contact there with Native Americans and Native Australians, for some of whom archaeology has become a salient arena of contestation with the majority society.

As noted before, reputable scholars have put forward calls both to take archaeology out of the political arena and to take indigenousness out of the discourse of difference. Ultimately, these recommendations themselves have political implications. For several hundred years, scientific and popular understandings of the Saami (or Lapp) past were the basis for discrimination and forced assimilation. It is bitterly ironic that just as the legitimacy of Saami identity is being acknowledged in the Nordic region, archaeologists put forth arguments, however well intentioned, to stop use of the past for clarifying and strengthening that identity. As tourism, forestry, mining, and power generation expand in the far northern region, rights to land and heritage will become more and more salient and contested. Museums are influential in creating public understandings of past identities, which in turn influence public ideas about who holds legitimate rights to land and resources in the region. One way that the Saami lay claim to identity and rights in the far north is through representations of the deep and recent past in community museums. Over time, there will be increasing pressures on metropolitan museums to acknowledge these identities and rights.

There is a deep desire within archaeology to be safe from politics because we know of the misuse of the past for a range of political causes. But representations of the past are inevitably political because they are fundamentally about connections of people to place. Where claims to land, resources, and identity are contested, where land and resources are being exploited by distant metropolises, and where identity is challenged by globalizing forces, archaeological representation will be political. It is far better to accept this and grapple with the complexities with our eyes open than to propose the goal of a depoliticized archaeological heritage.

Notes

1. I will not discuss the Russian Saami, because I have neither travelled in nor visited museums in Russia.
2. My reading knowledge of Norwegian and Swedish is adequate, but my Finnish is limited. In Finnish museums, I relied on Swedish or English text, one or both of which were always available. Spot checks lead me to believe that the texts were identical in different languages. Conversations with students, scholars, curators, and others were held in English.
3. This plan apparently existed through most of 2003 at which point the prehistory galleries were closed for renovation. As of March 2005, the museum's website, www.historiska.se, says that the main prehistory galleries will reopen following major reconstruction in November 2005.

References

Abu El-Haj, N (2001) *Facts on the Ground: Archaeological Practice and Territorial Self-Fashioning in Israeli Society*. Chicago: University of Chicago Press.

Aikio, M. and Aikio, P. (1989) A chapter in the history of the colonization of Sami lands: the forced migration of Norwegian reindeer Sami in Finland in the 1800s. In: R. Layton (ed.), *Conflict in the Archaeology of Living Traditions*. London: Unwin Hyman, pp. 116–30.

Anderson, B. (1991) *Imagined Communities: Reflections on the Origin and Spread of Nationalism*. Rev. edition. London: Verso Books.

Arnold, B. (1990) The past as propaganda: totalitarian archaeology in Nazi Germany. *Antiquity* 64(244): 464–78.

——(2002) Justifying genocide: archaeology and the construction of difference. In: A.L. Hinton, (ed.), *Annihilating Difference: The Anthropology of Genocide*. Berkeley: University of California Press, pp. 95–116.

Beach, H. (1988) *The Saami of Lapland*. Report 55. London: The Minority Rights Group.

——(2001) *A Year in Lapland: Guest of the Reindeer Herders*. Seattle: University of Washington Press.

Clifford, J. (1991) Four Northwest Coast museums: travel reflections. In: I. Karp and S.D. Lavine (eds.), *Exhibiting Cultures: The Poetics and Politics of Museum Display*. Washington, DC: Smithsonian Institution Press, pp. 212–54.

Conklin, B.A. (2002) Shamans versus pirates in the Amazonian treasure chest. *American Anthropologist*, 104(4): 1050–61.

Coon, C. (1939) *The Races of Europe*. New York: Macmillan.

Council of Europe (1999) *Gods and Heroes of the Bronze Age*. London: Thames and Hudson.

Diaz-Andreu, M. and Champion, T. eds. (1996) *Nationalism and Archaeology in Europe*. Boulder, CO: Westview Press.

Dombrowski, K. (2002) The praxis of indigenism and Alaska Native timber politics. *American Anthropologist*, 104(4): 1062–73.

Eidheim, H. (1997) Ethno-political development among the Sami after World War II: the invention of selfhood. In: H. Gaski, ed. *Sami Culture in a New Era: The Norwegian Sami Experience*. Karasjok: Davvi Girji OS (distributed in North America by University of Washington Press), pp. 29–61.

Finnish National Parliament (1997) Land Rights, Linguistic Rights, and Cultural Autonomy for the Finnish Sami People. *Indigenous Affairs* 33(4).

Forsberg, L. (1995) Saami archaeology in Sweden 1985–1990. *Current Swedish Archaeology*, 3: 97–104.

Gaski, H. ed. (1997) *Sami Culture in a New Era: The Norwegian Sami Experience*. Karasjok: Davvi Girji OS (distributed in North America by University of Washington Press).

Gröhn, A. (2004) *Positioning the Bronze Age in Social Theory and Research Context*. Acta Archaeologica Lundensia Series in 8°, 47. Stockholm: Almqvist and Wiksell.

Gustafson, B. (1998) Arkeologer i rättegång. *Populär Arkeologi*, 1998(4): 29.

Hætta, O.M. (1995) Rock carvings in a Saami perspective: some comments on politics and ethnicity in archaeology. In: K. Helskog and B. Olsen (eds.), *Perceiving Rock Art: Social and Political Perspectives*. Instituttet for Sammenlignende Kulturforskning, Serie B, 92. Oslo: Novus Forlag, pp. 348–56.

——(1996) *The Sami: An Indigenous People of the Arctic*. Ole Petter Gurholt, trans. Karasjok, Norway: Davvi Girji OS.

Hinton, A.L. (2002a) The dark side of modernity: toward an anthropology of genocide. In: A.L. Hinton (ed.), *Annihilating Difference: The Anthropology of Genocide*. Berkeley: University of California Press, pp. 1–41.

——ed. (2002b) *Annihilating Difference: The Anthropology of Genocide*. Berkeley: University of California Press.

Hodgson, D.L. (2002) Introduction: comparative perspectives on the indigenous rights movement in Africa and the Americas. *American Anthropologist*, 104(4): 1037–49.

Hooper-Greenhill, E. (2000) *Museums and the Interpretation of Visual Culture*. London: Routledge.

ILO (International Labor Organization) (1989) Convention 169: Indigenous and Tribal Peoples.

Jones, S. (1997) *The Archaeology of Ethnicity: Constructing Identities in the Past and Present*. London: Routledge.

Karp, I and Lavine, S.D. eds. (1991) *Exhibiting Cultures: The Poetics and Politics of Museum Display*. Washington, DC: Smithsonian Institution Press.

Krebs, C.F. (2003) *Liberating Culture: Cross-Cultural Perspectives on Museum Curation and Heritage Preservation*. London: Routledge.

Kristiansen, K. (1998) Between rationalism and romanticism: archaeological heritage management in the 1990s. *Current Swedish Archaeology*, 6: 115–22.

Kuper, A. (2003) The return of the native. *Current Anthropology*, 44(3): 389–402.

Lundström, I. and Pilvesmaa, M.-L. (1998) Reflections on an unreflected sphere: archaeological exhibitions and nationalism. *Current Swedish Archaeology*, 6: 143–52.

Meskell, L., ed. (1998) *Archaeology under Fire: Nationalism, Politics and Heritage in the Eastern Mediterranean and Middle East*. London: Routledge.

Moser, S. (1998) *Ancestral Images: The Iconography of Human Origins*. Ithaca: Cornell University Press.

Moser, S. and Smiles, S. (2004) Introduction: the Image in question. In: S. Smiles and S. Moser (eds.), *Envisioning the Past: Archaeology and the Image*. Malden, MA: Blackwell Publishing, pp. 1–12.

Mulk, I.-M. (1997) *Sámi Cultural Heritage in the Laponian World Heritage Area*. Jokkmokk: Ájtte, Swedish Mountain and Sámi Museum.

Mulk, I.-M. and Bayliss-Smith, T. (1999) The representation of Sámi cultural identity in the cultural landscapes of northern Sweden: the use and misuse of archaeological knowledge. In: P.J. Ucko and R. Layton (eds.), *The Archaeology and Anthropology of Landscape: Shaping Your Landscape*. London: Routledge, pp. 358–96.

Myhre, B. (2003) The Iron Age. In: K. Helle (ed.), *The Cambridge History of Scandinavia, Vol. 1: Prehistory to 1520*. Cambridge: Cambridge University Press, pp. 60–93.

Nunez, M.G. (1987) A Model for the Early Settlement of Finland. *Fennoscandia Archaeologica*, 4: 3–18.

Odner, K. (1983) *Finner og Terfinner: Etniske Prosesser I det Nordlige Fenno-Skandinavia*. Occasional Papers in Social Anthropology, 9. Oslo: Department of Social Anthropology, University of Oslo.

——(1985) Saamis (Lapps), Finns and Scandinavians in history and prehistory. *Norwegian Archaeological Review*, 18(1–2): 1–12.

Olsen, B. (1985) Comments on "Saamis, Finns, and Scandinavians in history and prehistory." *Norwegian Archaeological Review*, 18(1–2): 13–18.

——(1998) Samerna—Ett folk utan historia? *Populär Arkeologi*, 1998(4): 3–6.

Paine, R. (1994) *Herds of the Tundra: A Portrait of Saami Reindeer Pastoralism*. Washington, DC: Smithsonian Institution Press.

Scott, B.G. (1996) Archaeology and national identity: the Norwegian example. *Scandinavian Studies*, 68: 321–52.

Shore, C. (1995) Imagining the new Europe: identity and heritage in European Community discourse. In: P. Graves-Brown, S. Jones and C. Gamble (eds.), *Cultural Identity and Archaeology: The Construction of European Communities*. London: Routledge, pp. 96–115.

Siiriänen, Ari (2003) The Stone and Bronze Ages. In: K. Helle, (ed.), *The Cambridge History of Scandinavia, Vol. 1: Prehistory to 1520*. Cambridge: Cambridge University Press, pp. 43–59.

Silverman, H. (2002) Touring ancient times: the present and the presented past in contemporary Peru. *American Anthropologist*, 104(3): 881–902.

Svensson, T.G. (1997) *The Sámi and Their Land*. Instituttet for Sammenlignende Kulturforskning, Serie B, 96. Oslo: Novus Forlag.

Tambets, K., Rootsi, S., Kivisild, T., Help, H., Serk, P., Loogvali, E.-L., et al. (2004) The western and eastern roots of the Saami—the story of genetic "outliers" told by mitochondrial DNA and Y chromosomes. *American Journal of Human Genetics*, 74: 661–82.

Vorren, Ø. and Manker, E. (1962) *Lapp Life and Customs: A Survey*. Kathleen McFarlane, trans. London: Oxford University Press.

Watkins, J. (2000) *Indigenous Archaeology*. Walnut Creek, CA: AltaMira Press.

Wolf, E.R. (1982) *Europe and the People without History*. Berkeley: University of California Press.

Zachrisson, I. (1976) *Lapps and Scandinavians: Archaeological Finds from Northern Sweden*. Early Norrland 10. Stockholm: Kungliga Vitterhets Historie och Antikvitets Akademien.

——(1984) *De Samiska Metalldepåerna, Ar 1000–1350*. Archaeology and Environment 3. Umeå, Sweden: University of Umeå, Department of Archaeology.

Zvelebil, M. (1995) Farmers: our ancestors and the identity of Europe. In: P. Graves-Brown, S. Jones and C. Gamble, eds., *Cultural Identity and Archaeology: The Construction of European Communities*. London: Routledge, pp. 145–66.

Chapter 22

Is it enough to make the main characters female?

An intersectional and social semiotic reading of the exhibition Prehistories 1 at the National Historical Museum in Stockholm, Sweden

Annika Bünz

Introduction

Scholars within a range of disciplines have shown that both museum exhibitions and the archaeological discipline to a great extent lean on the grand narratives of evolution, progress, development, and the rise of the West. In these narratives, the white Western man, physically and symbolically, heads the evolution from nature (woman) to culture (man) (Haraway 1989; McClintock 1995; Wiber 1998; Smith 1999; Conkey 2005; Scott 2007; Golding 2009). In this process, the West also develops as opposed to the Rest, the Other (Hall 1992; Pickering 2001; Said 2006). This narrative has also seemed to prevail in many Swedish museums (Bünz and Steen 2008). Nevertheless, due to political decisions and measures from the Swedish government (e.g. the governmental investigation 'Genus på museer' [Gender in museums], Ds 2003), a gender perspective is today more frequently employed in Swedish exhibition designs; a discerning museum visitor can observe a bigger number of women in contemporary museological narratives. But is this casting of women as main characters enough? Is this move sufficient to visibilize and write women into the narratives of prehistory? If so, what about other traditionally marginalized subjects – Others? How does the exhibition represent for example, age, ethnicity, and class?

In this chapter I analyse the exhibition *Prehistories 1* at the National Historical Museum in Stockholm, Sweden. I focus in particular on two parts of the exhibition, which are of specific significance for understanding the relation between *Prehistories 1* and the representation of diversity. I employ intersectionality and social semiotics

Source: *To Tender Gender: The Pasts and Futures of Gender Research in Archaeology.* I.-M. Back Danielsson and S. Thedéen (eds.). Stockholm Studies in Archaeology 58. Stockholm: Department of Archaeology and Classical Studies, Stockholm University, 2012. pp. 97–115. Reprinted with permission of the author.

to understand and discuss these representations and the type of discourses and subjectivities the exhibition produces. My focus is on its displays, visual as well as textual, and I ask a number of questions: what images does this particular exhibition convey of prehistorical subjects? How are people: women, men, children, and elderly presented? What stories are told? How can they be understood?

Theoretical and methodological frame

Museum exhibitions are created to communicate knowledge. This communication occurs by means of, for example, texts, images, reconstructions, and archaeological findings that are brought together and arranged in a space. Communication occurs between creator and receiver, museum curator and museum visitor. The study of communication and representation as the creation of meaning with signs is called semiotics. A semiotician studies how meanings are made and how reality is represented in words, images, sounds, gestures, and objects (Chandler 2002: 2). To investigate something from a social semiotic point of view is to shift focus from signs to sign-making (Kress and Leeuwen 2006: 8; Kress 2010: 9). Sign-making occurs in specific historical and cultural contexts by agents with complex interests and their own specific life histories (Kress and Leeuwen 2006: 7, 12).

When discussing communication and representation with terms from social semiotics the researcher looks at a constantly ongoing process of sign-making wherein individuals have a transformative role as agents in a constant presence of a social context. Conventions shape the resources, and the social structures are inevitably marked by power differences (Kress and Leeuwen 2006: 13). The making of signs involves a procedure where the sign-maker seeks to make representations of objects and entities (Kress and Leeuwen 2006: 7; Kress 2010: 10).

Kress and Leeuwen focus on 'displaying the regularities of visual communication' (2006, p. 14), when they within the frame of social semiotics form a grammar of visual design. According to Kress and Leeuwen (2006: 47–8), there are two kinds of participants involved in the making of signs: the represented participant (people, places, things, 'abstract things') and the interactive participant, that is, the participants involved in communication (who speak, listen, write, or read). Gunther Kress uses the concept of multimodality to discuss sign-making by different kinds of modes and by combining multiple modes. A mode is a resource for making meaning; for example image, writing, layout, music, gesture, speech, moving images, and 3D objects (Kress 2010: 79). 'The signs are made with very many different means, in very many different modes' (Kress 2010: 10). A museum exhibition is composed of many such different modes.

For the most part, the scholars referred to within social semiotics discuss Western culture and only briefly review some aspects of other cultures. The exhibition studied here is designed within a Western and Scandinavian culture. Within the framework of social semiotics I do my analysis as a sign-maker in the role of an interactive participant.

The theoretical framework of social semiotics and sign-making is here used as a method to complement the theoretical perspective of intersectionality. To use intersectionality is to problematize and make visible how relations of power are created within, between, and across categories such as race, class, and gender (de los Reyes and Mulinari 2005: 23). According to postcolonial feminist theorists, white Western middle-class women have been allowed to represent all women while the intersecting oppression that a lot of women live under is forgotten and ignored (Collins 2000; de los Reyes and Mulinari 2005). Chandra Talpade Mohanty argues that Western scholars tend to presuppose that women belong to one single category, a coherent group with 'identical interests and desires, regardless of class, ethnicity, or racial location, or contradictions' (Mohanty 2003: 21). This implies entertaining 'a notion of gender or sexual difference or even patriarchy that can be applied universally and cross-culturally' (Mohanty 2003: 21).

Intersectionality presumes an epistemology where power and subordination constantly is constructed and reconstructed by individuals, ideologies, generally accepted knowledge, discourses, and material conditions (de los Reyes and Mulinari 2005: 24–5). De los Reyes and Mulinari (2005: 23) regard intersectionality as a perspective intended to describe a complex reality and the infinite number of subject positions created in society today. Using intersectionality to analyse a museum exhibition means to look for different subject positions created in the narrative/s and is a way to detect ideologies, generally accepted knowledge and discourses communicated in the process. My study of the exhibition *Prehistories 1* thus entails an examination of how gender, age, social position, and ethnicity produce, and are produced by, such knowledge and discourses.

National museums and the Swedish context

The exhibition *Prehistories 1* is displayed at the National Historical Museum in Stockholm, Sweden. This museum 'administers culture heritage and provides a perspective on our existence in order to strengthen the democratic development of society' (National Historical Museums 2011). The task 'is to preserve and promote Sweden's cultural heritage and provide perspectives on social development and the present' (National Historical Museums 2011).

As stated earlier, this chapter is interested not only in gender, but other sociocultural positions and a distinct Swedish perspective of intersectionality. In this context it should be mentioned that Sweden is a geographically large country and the northern half, called Norrland, is a sparsely populated area with an abundance of natural resources. These have played an important part in the building of the welfare of the entire country, a majority of whose population lives in the southern half of the country. Despite its size and economic significance, and in spite of extensive fieldwork and research having been carried out in the northern parts of the country, the general public still knows very little about the prehistory of Norrland (Bergman 2009: 178). The archaeological records in the north show a variety of cultures during prehistory; peoples in the north and south developed different cultures, and one question raised by the archaeological records of the northern parts, for example, was if an independent kingdom existed in Norrland 1500 years ago (Baudou 1992).

However, what is more commonly known is the history of the indigenous Sámi people who inhabit present-day Norrland as well as the northern parts of Norway, Finland and the Kola Peninsula. In the early twentieth century the Sámi were among those who in the name of science were measured and photographed for eugenic research (Samer 2009). The Sámi people are commonly connected with reindeer herding. In my examination of *Prehistories 1* I look for perspectives on cultural diversity throughout the country including how the Sámi people is presented. What, and who, is included in the grand narrative of prehistoric Sweden? How are human subjects and cultures depicted?

Gender, age, and class in *Prehistories 1*

The exhibition *Prehistories 1* opened in 2005. It presents prehistory through eight different life stories. In the introductory text, the stories are described as 'frozen moments' in time, from ca. 7000 BC to ca. AD 600, and it is declared that: 'The oldest is the woman from Bäckaskog [...] and the youngest the magnate from Vendel [...]'.

Every moment in time comes with a heading that informs the visitor about one or several characters that lived during this period, and period-specific narrative is constructed as lived from the perspective of these characters. The characters are based upon findings of human remains and archaeological materials; women, men, older people and children are represented. The first moment, ca. 7000 BC has the heading 'The Bäckaskog woman', and the second moment, ca. 4800 BC is titled 'The old man and the child from Skateholm'. The third moment is called 'The people of Rössberga', 3500–2700 BC, the fourth 'The Chieftain from Hasslöv and the woman from Stora Köpinge', 1300–1100 BC, the fifth 'The cloak-bearer from Gerum and the child from Bankälla', 200s BC, the sixth 'The man from Öremölla and the woman from Gårdlösa', 200s AD, the seventh 'The men from Kvissleby and Krankmårtenhögen,' AD 200–400 and finally the eighth is entitled 'The lord from Vendel and the aristocratic woman from Köpingsvik', ca. AD 600.

The frozen moments are exhibited in areas that are divided; each period is thus framed in a separate room. The rooms are arranged so as to usher visitors through them in chronological order. All characters are represented in photographic images on textile wall hangings. The representations are, with some exceptions, in natural size. Before entering the display rooms, the visitor is introduced to the exhibition by a film featuring some of the people represented on the wall hangings.

The eight different moments offer stories of twelve different characters, one group of people and some children. Four stories are told by female characters and seven by male. One of the male characters is an old man. Apart from Moment 1, which focuses on the woman from Bäckaskog, and Moment 3, presenting the people of Rössberga, there is always a male character present in the narratives together with a woman, child, or another man. In addition to the main stories, there are side stories in Moment 3 and Moment 4, and in these side stories one male and one female character are mentioned as well. The inference made from the counting is that women are numerically under-represented as main characters in the eight moments in time.

However, when wandering through the exhibition I realized that women are visually well represented. There are several reasons for this. Firstly, they are represented through Moment 1 'The woman from Bäckaskog'. The Bäckaskog woman is the only character presented in two different kinds of environments in a comparatively large area, and she is also represented both by a reconstruction of her head and a photograph on a wall hanging. Secondly, in Moment 3 'The people of Rössberga', there is a side story about a young girl. This girl is represented by an image of a woman, and there is also another image of a middle-aged woman who is not mentioned anywhere in the texts. Both are in natural size (Figure 22.1). The man portrayed in the other side story is represented by a reconstruction of a head, which, without natural colouration, hair, and clothes, appears lifeless. The result is that the two women are given much more space in the visual display than the man.

There are several children mentioned in the texts, but in the images only three children can be counted. One child is together with a man and two children are supposed to represent 'the child' from Bankälla. The Swedish text reads 'children

Figure 22.1 The two top women represent characters in a side story. The women on the bottom row represent characters from the main stories: the woman from Gårdlösa to the left, and the aristocratic woman from Köpingsvik to the right. Author's photo.

from Bankälla' but the English translation only talks of one child. The child depicted with the man could be a girl, five or six years old, and the children representing 'the child' from Bankälla are two boys, approximately five and three years old.

Visually, women and men are represented in a number of situations, as well as in different ages ranging from young to middle-aged. However, they are *not* represented as old. They figure in different social positions, ranging from thrall to aristocrat. 'The old man from Skateholm' is represented by a man in his thirties, even though it says in the text that he was ca. 60 years old. The woman from furthest back in time, the woman from Bäckaskog (Figure 22.2), who has her own narrative and her own moment in time, is represented by a middle-aged woman, a good deal older than the aristocratic woman from Köpingsvik, who lived during the seventh century AD. (Figure 22.1). The woman from Köpingsvik is one of the main characters in the textual narrative, but her visual representation is almost hidden behind a corner. The introductory film at the entrance does not include the woman from Köpingsvik at all. The introductory text excludes the woman from Köpingsvik from the exhibition's grand narrative, and the visual display thus describes her as a side story of no importance to the big picture.

Figure 22.2 The woman from Bäckaskog, ca. 7000 BC. Author's photo.

One of the men living sometime between AD 200 and AD 400, the man from Kvissleby, is depicted as a sitting middle-aged man (Figure 22.3). The man who lived during the seventh century AD, the lord from Vendel, is also represented as sitting. The man from Kvissleby is thin and leans forward, probably sitting on a stool, whereas the Vendel character is a stout middle-aged man leaning back, almost certainly sitting on some kind of throne. From the texts you learn that the lord from Vendel has power over other people and that the man from Kvissleby is called 'a minor king'. One text talks about traces of people living as thralls, and the thralls are represented by three people on a wall hanging, two men and a young woman. In the introductory film, the man from Kvissleby sits with other people, talking and showing an artefact that he holds in his hand while the lord from Vendel is sitting in a throne meeting the onlooker's eye, being served something to drink from the female thrall.

I conclude that the exhibition narrative tells a story where men are young at the beginning of time and middle aged at the end of the story. As the time in the narrative passes, society is described as increasingly hierarchical and complex. The men gradually gain power and are assigned titles such as lords and kings. Women, on the other hand, are older and have authority far back in time but get younger and less important as the narrative moves forward in time. Women are not assigned titles like Lord or Queen; they are only mentioned as 'women'.

Figure 22.3 A representation of the man from Kvissleby, also mentioned as the man by the coast, buried together with a woman in a burial mound in Kvissleby. Author's photo.

Men who have gained power are illustrated sitting down and are being served by others. The lord from Vendel is in the narrative accompanied by the woman from Köpingsvik when the seventh century AD is presented, but in the text that introduces the exhibition, the lord from Vendel is staged as the only representative of the time period.

To summarize the findings about text and images accounted for previously, I reach the conclusion that together the exhibition characters to a certain extent represent a diversified collection of subject positions when it comes to gender, age, and class. But what about cultural diversity and the prehistory of the northern part of the country? What about the women, children, and elderly who also lived there during prehistory? How are they represented in the narrative?

Cultural diversity in *Prehistories 1*

The question about prehistory in the northern part of the country is easily answered. In each exhibited Moment, the graves that are discussed are marked out on a map of Scandinavia. The northernmost marking is actually to be found no farther north than Kvissleby and Krankmårtenhögen in Moment 7. Sweden is thus split into two halves; one entirely without and one with markings, that is, the southern half of the country. This means that nothing is told about the northern half of the country. It seems as if there is nobody – no men, women, children, or elderly – in present-day Norrland during prehistory according to this exhibition. This means that the exhibition offers no perspective on the present when it comes to cultural diversity.

Nevertheless, the Sámi people is mentioned and discussed. This mention occurs in the texts about the man interred in the burial mound Krankmårtenhögen. Next, I examine this moment of the narrative closer. In the following, I do a close reading of this material from the perspective of social semiotics (Hodge and Kress 1988; Leeuwen 2005; Kress and Leeuwen 2006; Kress 2010).

Moment 7: The men from Kvissleby and Krankmårtenhögen

The stories about the men from Kvissleby and Krankmårtenhögen and the period they lived in are told in an exhibition room decorated with two large wall hangings; one frames a photograph of a river running through the woods, the other shows moving pictures of a stream running down a slope. The room is filled with the sound of running water. Two characters from the narrative are depicted on wall hangings, dressed like prehistoric men (see Figures 22.3 and 22.4). In this room you can only see middle-aged men; there are no women, children, or elderly present in the visual representation.

The room seems to be meant to represent the north of Sweden, that is, present-day Norrland. The Krankmårten man in the photograph is walking in the snow dressed in warm clothes trimmed with fur (Figure 22.4). The river runs through the woods, which leads the thoughts to tree trunks transported in rivers, which used to be a common sight in the north. Horns of reindeer and elk can be seen in a showcase. These are elements that together signify Norrland. However, there is something contradictory about the room that can be derived from the lustrous

Figure 22.4 The man from further inland, buried in the Krankmården mound. Author's photo.

yellow tone in some of the showcases and wall hangings. These showcases display artefacts made of gold, silver, and bronze. The colour of the whole room is a blue-grey hue and it is contrasted by highlights of these yellow, golden hues.

Leeuwen (2005: 6–9) discusses how colours are used in *framing*, which is a concept that deals with how elements are connected and disconnected to each other (Leeuwen 2005: 17–19). Colours are important to the understanding of the display in the room where Moment 7 is presented. The representation of the man from Kvissleby is enveloped by a yellow hue (Figure 22.3) and the background colour of the showcases on both sides of the representation is golden yellow. There is also a yellow tone in the image depicting the man. He is here the *represented participant* who signifies the character. The man is connected to the artefacts by what with multimodal terminology is called a colour *rhyme:* the lustrous yellow hue in the images above and the yellow tone in the showcases.

By contrast, the representation of the man in Krakmårtenhögen is bluish with elements of brown and grey, and these colours rhyme with the hue in the illustration and showcase below the representation (Figure 22.4). The representation further rhymes with the blue-grey hue that dominates the room. The represented participant that signifies the man buried in the Krankmården mound is thus connected to the illustration below and the exhibited horns and remains of elk and reindeer. This man is also connected to the room as a whole. According to Kress '*colour*, as a background "wash", frames by establishing the "ground" on which things "are", "belong", "happen", "take place"' (Kress 2010: 151). The character is connected to this room where this moment in time takes place. It belongs to the background wash. And I, as an interactive participant, thereby connect the narrative about the man buried in the Krankmården mound with the north, that is, Norrland. The character 'the man from Kvissleby', on the other hand, is connected to that which by contrast in colour is *disconnected* from Norrland.

To proceed with the analysis, I now perform a closer examination of the two wall hangings representing the two characters (Figures 22.3 and 22.4). The creator of the image, who is also a so-called *interactive participant,* has depicted the man from Kvissleby in a long shot. According to Kress and Leeuwen (2006: 148), a picture from afar indicates an impersonal relationship between the represented participant and the onlooker, the other interactive participant. A medium shot conveys a social relationship and a close shot a personal one. The image shows the whole person, but the legs below the knees are hardly visible in the dark that surrounds the man. The surrounding darkness narrows the shot and puts it somewhere in between a long shot and a medium shot. From this I conclude that the relationship between the represented participant and the interactive participant is of an almost social character. The representation is positioned so that the character meets a full-grown onlooker on an eye-to-eye level. The man is placed in an *equal position* to an adult museum visitor. A child, a short person, or someone sitting in a wheelchair will meet the represented participant's gaze from an inferior position.

Furthermore, the man is facing the viewer almost from a frontal angle, which means that the represented participant, by one interactive participant, has been placed in an *involved position* toward the other interactive participant, the museum visitor. The man also demands something from the viewer, as he looks him/her straight in the eye; the represented participant is a subject interacting with the interactive participant. The long shot indicates an impersonal, almost social, relationship to the museum visitor, but the frontal angle proposes involvement.

The dark colour surrounding the representation conceals whatever is surrounding the man in the image. This darkness surrounding the man is *a locative circumstance*, a specific participant that Kress and Leeuwen (2006: 72) call a *setting*. In this case the setting is darker than the foreground and enhances the yellow glow of the represented participant, making it salient. The lighting in the image can be read as an indoor surrounding.

The wall hanging depicting the man in the burial mound Krankmårtenhögen is placed high above the onlooker (Figure 22.4). This could be interpreted as a power position from which the represented participant looks down on the interactive participant. However, the representation does not gaze at the viewer; it turns its gaze away. This image addresses the viewer indirectly; the interactive participant is not the object, but subject of the look. The man in the Krankmården mound is by the creator placed as an object of a presupposed detached gaze of the museum visitor. The oblique angle showing the man's profile detaches the viewer and the long shot is impersonal. In this picture, the represented participant is dark and the setting is light blue. There are no glowing colours in the image and even though the man's contours are distinct, he is not salient. The setting is as important a participant as the represented character. The facial features are not visible to the viewer; you can only distinguish the contours of his profile. The represented participant signifying the man in the Krankmården mound blends in with the background – it blends with nature.

The way the wall hangings are placed in the room makes the characters turn their backs at each other and the visual display thereby conveys that they do not interact with each other at all. They are actually depicted as each other's opposites. A close-up look at their faces reveals that the man from Kvissleby is depicted with distinct features looking directly at the viewer, while the man in Krankmården mound is depicted with a diffuse profile. The men are thus pictured as almost social vs impersonal, involved vs detached, indoors vs outdoors, sitting vs walking, and relaxed vs striving, in bright saturated colours vs grey unsaturated colours, and as salient vs diffuse being surrounded by artefacts vs remains of animals. One could say that the represented participants, according to the visual design, signify the dichotomies culture vs nature and Us vs Them.

Let me now add something about the texts in this specific room. The time period and the two characters are presented with the subheading: 'Did they ever meet, the minor king from Norrland, and the man from further inland?' This heading connects the man from Kvissleby with Norrland and thereby contradicts the visual design. The text discusses the two men, how they could have lived and how they were buried. A short passage declares that during this period there were jewelleries and plates manufactured from gold and bronze, and they were decorated with animals and humans.

The stories about the two men are elaborated in two other texts. 'The man by the coast' (my translation) is the heading of the text that discusses the man in the burial mound at Kvissleby. The text reads: 'At the mouth of the river Ljungan, in the area of Kvissleby, a couple of burial mounds stand out against the landscape. To be buried in a mound behoved only the very rich and powerful' (my translation). In the next paragraph, the reader is informed that the man from Kvissleby was buried in one of the mounds. But, the text goes on, it was recently discovered that the grave actually contained two people, a man *and* a woman. This is the only mention of a woman in this room. This means that a woman, who was buried together with one of the main characters of this narrative, is neither included in images, nor in the text.

The text about 'The man by the coast' is placed next to the showcase where the artefacts found in the mound are displayed. These artefacts are rather plain with no lustrous colours. The background colour connects the showcase with the representation of the character. It also connects the showcase with the showcases on each side of the image representation. But it is placed in another part of the room, by the picture of the river. The placing in the room does not connect the artefacts with the representation of the character. Rather, it creates a distance between artefacts and character. Had it not been for the colour rhyme, I probably would not have made the connection until I had studied the texts more thoroughly. The showcase with the horns and remains of elk and reindeer on the other hand, is directly connected to the man from further inland, both by the colour rhyme and the placing in the room.

When I look closer at the two showcases on each side of the image representation of the man from Kvissleby, I realize that these artefacts have been found in places all over the country, from Skåne in the south to Hälsingland in the north. They represent the Migration period (ca. AD 400–550) in different parts of the country and are by no means more connected to the finding in Kvissleby, than to Krankmårtenhögen. They comprise a selection of what has been found, and the story about the Migration period is told based on these findings. The showcase to the right of the representation of the man from Kvissleby is placed next to the showcase that displays animal remains, but the background colours disconnect the two showcases. The colours also disconnect the representation of the man in the Krankmårten mound from the lustrous artefacts and thereby also from the Migration period. The two showcases that display the lustrous, elaborate artefacts are both accompanied by texts describing the Migration period. The headings are: 'A time filled with fairytales and myths' and 'Gold, status, and power' (my translation). The latter text informs about the plentiful gold treasures from the Migration period, sometimes called the 'Nordic Gold Age'.

The text about the man in the Krankmårten mound discusses traces of humans who lived in what we today call Norrland and concludes that these traces in some cases differ from traces found in the southern parts of Sweden. The wording 'differ from' the south, suggests that the traces from the north are deviations. These few lines of text are intended to cover the traces of humans in the northern half of the country, although the mentioned finds actually come from the most southern part of Norrland. In the last paragraph you can read that there has been an animated debate about the people in Krankmårten. 'Who were the people buried here? Some think they were Sámi, others insists they were not.' The paragraph ends with the question: 'Does this indicate that there were Sámi people here a thousand years ago?' (my translation).

After reading through the texts in the room I conclude that everything that is told about the Migration period is connected to the man from Kvissleby. Everything that concerns culture and myths, gold and power, is connected to the represented participant that signifies this character. The man from Kvissleby represents this moment in time in the textual narrative. The mentioning in the text of the character as being a minor king from Norrland, whereas the visual disconnects it from the north, indicates a colonial idea of a king living in the south ruling over the north. The man in the Krankmårten mound, possibly of the Sámi people, signifies the Other and his narrative is not part of the grand narrative. Instead, this character is connected to nature and disconnected from culture, gold and power and Us.

Important to note is that the colour rhyme to connect the characters to showcases and artefacts and to disconnect the characters from each other is only used in this room. In the other rooms of the exhibition, all showcases have the same background colour; in one room red, in another green and in yet another yellow, and in these rooms all characters, artefacts, and showcases are framed together in a frozen moment in time by one connecting colour.

To conclude the analysis of the room supposedly signifying Norrland, the diversity of prehistoric subjects including men, women, young and middle-aged, which characterizes the exhibition as a whole, is not reproduced in this room. A woman is mentioned together with the man from Kvissleby, but the man from further inland stands alone as a character representing the Other, perhaps as a representative of the Sámi. If this is the case, it can be concluded that Sámi women, children, and elderly are not included in the narrative at all.

Distance in time and space

The wall hangings depicting the woman from Bäckaskog (Figure 22.2) and the man from further inland (Figure 22.4) are, as opposed to all other representations of characters, placed high above the viewer. This creates a distance between the represented participants and the interactive participant. The woman from Bäckaskog is looking down at the onlooker from a high position, and the man from further inland is depicted on a wall hanging placed high up in the corner of the room, not even looking down at the museum visitor. But if you want to, you can study the woman from Bäckaskog thoroughly in a reconstruction of her head that is exhibited in a showcase nearby, though this represented participant does not meet your eyes. It is placed at eye-to-eye level with a half-grown child. If you were an adult you would be looking down on the reconstruction and even though the woman's eyes look straight forward, the gaze is distant. The character is also represented by a skeleton, the human remains that the character is created from, and thus there are three represented participants that signify the character. You can get close to two of them but only meet the gaze of the third, the one placed high above. The man in the Krankmården mound is not represented in any other way than in the image on the wall hanging. What you can get close to, and scrutinize thoroughly, are the horns and other remains from animals that are exhibited in the showcase beneath the representation. You can also see all the details in the illustration showing how the grave could have looked in the landscape.

Another thing that brings these two representations together is that the characters are depicted in an outdoor setting while the other characters are made salient by a black background and a lighting implying that the characters are indoors. The woman from the distant past is blending with nature in a way that makes it hard to discern her features; she 'is' the woods, and the woods are her (Figure 22.2). The man in the Krankmården mound can clearly be distinguished by the contours, but he is not more salient than the background. The two characters are both depicted as part of nature, they are both hard to get close to, but the woman from Bäckaskog meets your gaze and is a moment of 'our' history while the man from further inland neither meets your gaze nor is represented as a part of the grand narrative of the exhibition.

The blending with nature also occurs in the representation of the child from Bankälla. The two boys are represented in a larger scale than natural children. The setting is a forest. The image of the children and the forest blend in the same way as in the representation of the Bäckaskog woman. But the wall hanging is not placed high above the onlooker; it is placed at eye-level, which signifies equality (Kress and Leeuwen 2006: 148). The children are nature in the same way as the Bäckaskog woman, but they are closer in time and they are not distant in space.

Conclusions

When examining illustrations of human evolution the anthropologist Melanie Wiber concludes that they all share a common plot.

> 'The arduous journey is a common feature of many of them; the harsh struggle for survival is another. [...] Human social and biological evolution has been a great journey, one that has taken us as a species from an animal-like dependence on nature to a human level of independence through culture.'
>
> (Wiber 1998: 49)

Wiber argues that these illustrations take part in a wider field of a larger meta-narrative, and the narrative is an often written and single dominant view of events (Wiber 1998: 49).

Nature, the distant past, as well as distant geographical areas, is often considered to be female (McClintock 1995: 36–8). The journey throughout the history made in *Prehistories 1* starts with a female character represented as blending with nature and ends with a male character sitting on a throne. Stephanie Moser identifies the wild landscape style as a means to illustrate prehistory. Caves, forests, mountains, and large dramatic skies are iconographic means to illustrate the distant past (Moser 1998: 115–16). The Bäckaskog woman character is depicted in the forest and she is also placed in a position in the room that distances her both in time and space. The lord from Vendel represents culture close in space and time. The journey from distant nature (woman) to familiar culture (man) is indeed the plot of the narrative of *Prehistories 1*.

Stephanie Moser concludes that imagery throughout the ages has defined otherness or outsider status. 'The visual language of distant time thus continues an age-old tradition of constructing ancestors, non-western peoples, non-Christians and animals in terms of their opposition to us' (Moser 1998: 172). In *Prehistories 1*, the Sami represent and are depicted as the Other. The dichotomies 'sitting/walking' and 'relaxed/striving' can be read as representing the view that 'We' have finished our arduous journey and harsh struggle for survival and thereby can sit down and relax. The Other still strives and struggles for survival in the distant nature, the wild landscape. The man in Krankemårtenhögen is walking in the (prehistoric) landscape instead of sitting indoors. The character is as distant in time and space as the Bäckaskog woman, even though they are more than 7000 years apart. And the intersecting effect is that the Sámi women, children, and elderly are not only distant, they are excluded – rendered invisible behind a middle-aged man.

Age is something that can promote authority. The lord from Vendel exudes authority, on the one hand by his position on the throne and, on the other, by being middle-aged. The middle-aged Bäckaskog woman also conveys an amount of authority when she gazes down at the visitor, both from being of old age and from her position of power. The female character from the most recent moment in time, the woman from Köpingsvik (as well as most of the other depicted female characters), is depicted as young. She is described as having status, but is visually represented as without authority. The old man from Skateholm is depicted as young and thereby gains no authority by age in the visual representation. Looking at the depiction of authority throughout time, as held by subjects of old age, this is at the beginning described as female, that is furthest back in time, and as male at the end of the journey.

This analysis has only concerned selected parts of the visual design and parts of the texts in the exhibition. There is of course a lot more to analyse in the exhibition *Prehistories 1*. On the one hand there are other identity categories that I have not looked further into, for example, sexual orientation and physical disabilities. On the other hand, the interactive participant, as in the museum visitor, is of varying age, sex, religion, and ethnicity. As Monique Scott puts it, 'diverse individuals bring unique understandings to museum exhibitions' (Scott 2007: 3); that is, understandings that derive from varied cultural histories. Just as the social semiotic approach regards the sign-maker, Scott argues that the museum visitors interpret exhibitions through their prior experiences and through their culturally learned beliefs, values, and perceptual skills (Scott 2007: 3). When I visit this exhibition I can identify with most parts of the narrative as 'my history' because of my background in the same culture as the exhibition narrative seems to be told within. The perspective of intersectionality is a vital reminder that the analysis must not just focus on the represented participants in the museum exhibition; it is equally important to examine the interactive participant's intersecting identities. How would a person with a completely different background interpret the exhibition's messages? How would a person who lives in, and identifies with, the northern parts of the country, perceive what is told? I conclude that further investigations and discussions taking this into consideration are needed to better understand the complexity of representing diversity in historical exhibitions.

References

Baudou, E. (1992) *Norrlands forntid-ett historiskt perspektiv*. Hoganas: Wiken.
Bergman, I. (2009) Norrlands förhistoria i fokus. *Thule: Norrländsk kulturskrift*, 2009: 177–85.
Bünz, A. and Steen, F. (2008) Arkeologi, museiutställningar och intersektionalitet. In: *Arkeologen: Nyhetsbrev från Institutionen för Arkeologi och Antikens kultur, Göteborgs Universitet*, 13(3): 16–26.

Chandler, D. (2007) *Semiotics: The Basics*. London and New York: Routledge.
Collins, P. H. (2000) *Black Feminist Thought. Knowledge, Consciousness, and the Politics of Empowerment*. New York and London: Routledge.
Conkey, M.W. (2005) Dwellings at the margins, action at the intersection? Feminist and indigenous archaeologies. *Archaeologies*, 1(1): 9–59.
de los Reyes, P. and Mulinari, D. (2005) *Intersektionalitet*. Malmö: Liber.
Ds (2003) *Genus på museer*. Stockholm: Fritzes offentliga publikationer.
Golding, V. (2009) *Learning at the Museum Frontiers. Identity, Race and Power*. Farnham and Burlington, VT: Ashgate.
Government Offices of Sweden (n.d.) National Minorities. Available at: www.sweden.gov.se, accessed 15 April 2011.
Hall, S. (1992) The west and the rest: discourse and power. In: S. Hall and B. Gieben (eds.), *Formations of Modernity*. Cambridge: Polity, pp. 275–320.
Haraway, D. (1989) *Primate Visions. Gender, Race and Nature in the World of Modern Science*. New York and London: Routledge.
Hodge, R. and Kress G. (1988) *Social Semiotics*. Cambridge: Polity.
Kress, G. (2010) *Multimodality. A Social Semiotic Approach to Contemporary Communication*. London and New York: Routledge.
Kress, G. and van Leeuwen, T. (2006) *Reading Images. The Grammar of Visual Design*. Second edition. London and New York: Routledge.
Leeuwen, van T. (2005). *Introducing Social Semiotics*. London and New York: Routledge.
McClintock, A. (1995) *Imperial Leather*. New York, London: Routledge.
Mohanty, C.T. (2003) *Feminism without Borders. Decolonizing Theory, Practicing Solidarity*. Durham and London: Duke University Press.
Moser, S. (1998) *Ancestral Images. The Iconography of Human Origins*. Ithaca and New York: Sutton.
National Historical Museums (2011) Available at: www.shmm.se, accessed 8 April 2011.
Pickering, M. (2001) *Stereotyping the Politics of Representation*. New York: Palgrave.
Said, E. (2006) *Orientalism*. Stockholm: Ordfront.
Samer: ett ursprungsfolk i Sverige (2009) Kiruna: Sametinget; Stockholm: Jordbruksdepartementet. Available at: www.sweden.gov.se, accessed 15 April 2011.
Scott, M. (2007) *Rethinking Evolution in the Museum: Envisioning African Origins*. London and New York: Routledge.
Smith, L.T. (1999) *Decolonizing Methodologies: Research and Indigenous Peoples*. London: Zed Books.
Wiber, M.G. (1998) *Erect Men, Undulating Women. The Visual Imagery of Gender. 'Race' and Progress in Reconstructive Illustrations of Human Evolution*. Waterloo, Ontario, Canada: Wilfrid Laurier University Press.

Part III, Section 2

Archaeological site museums

Chapter 23

The Jorvik Viking Centre
An experiment in archaeological site interpretation

Peter Addyman and Anthony Gaynor

The interpretation and display of excavated archaeological sites for the public is rarely attempted in Britain, and even less frequently is it successful. Most attempts hitherto have concerned sites where there are upstanding remains of stone buildings, or reasonably displayable mosaics. The majority of these are monuments in state guardianship, where the well-tried techniques of conservation and minimal interpretation have produced monuments that demand a considerable commitment to learning from the visitor. Early attempts to display the evanescent evidence of excavated timber structures, such as Woodhenge or the Overton circle, have not been followed up. The result is a very considerable imbalance, in the types of archaeological monument available for visits by the public, in favour of the Roman period and of medieval buildings of higher social status, with some periods almost completely unrepresented, and some types of site totally unavailable to the interested layman. Aids to interpretation on the sites that do exist are of the very simplest kind. Even the great spate of excavation which came in the 1970s as the result of the expansion of rescue archaeology in the face of ever more extensive and destructive denudation of the archaeological record by the processes of modern life has produced few new viewable monuments.

It is not that the opportunities were not there, but that the challenge was ducked. Great monuments like the eminently displayable legionary thermae at Exeter, conveniently situated in one of the most heavily visited half acres in the West Country, were reburied rather than exploited as an educational, recreational, and touristic resource, which could already have earned millions for its region, and enormously enriched the experience of visiting Exeter. Three times in the last decade in York, displayable monuments of quite outstanding interest were carefully reinterred, and the sites carefully redeveloped around them, so that a future and more caring – or perhaps more opportunist – generation might at least have the option of displaying them. Sometimes even this luxury could not be afforded. It will certainly be one of the indictments of archaeologists in the 1970s that none of the great series of waterfront structures of Roman and medieval London, nor even the stupendously preserved remains of the original Roman London *Bridge*, have either been kept for re-erection elsewhere, or preserved in *situ*. There mammon won. Always the argument that it was better not to offend developers by holding up development, or redesigning buildings, counted for more than demands that posterity should not be denied its inheritance.

Evidently the public does have feelings on the issue. Where the attempt has been made to show off even a selection of the evidence from an important excavation on the site at which it was found, people have flocked to see it. The Fishbourne Roman palace near Chichester in Sussex is not the easiest place to reach, but hundreds of thousands have made the pilgrimage. The museum display and huge partial cover for the site are both now somewhat dated, and far from the ideal answer to the problem of recreating the ambience of such a site as Fishbourne; but what modest efforts were made were enthusiastically received. The Painted Roman House at Dover, preserved by the archaeologists themselves in a self-help rescue operation, is now sometimes the only place that visitors to Dover pause to see. In York, where excavations have been in progress continuously on a variety of sites over the past decade, visitors have always flocked to see whatever excavation project is open to inspection. Their fascination with what they see probably owes more to the human weakness for watching other people at work than to their understanding of what is being uncovered, for working archaeological sites are often extremely difficult to interpret – even for the archaeologists themselves. However, market research, carried out using returnable visitor comment cards, soon demonstrated that a very large majority of visitors to one of the recent York sites, at Coppergate, had one common reaction. It was a feeling ranging from sadness through despair to outrage that the archaeological remains had to be destroyed by new development.

The Jorvik Viking Centre has been built as one possible answer to the problem of preserving some of the less durable remains of the past in a context where they make some sense. The archaeology of cities is often extremely complex, the excavation sites frequently very deep, and the constraints imposed by the modern built environment usually almost overwhelming. Where, as in York, there are waterlogged conditions, the data survival rate can be extraordinary, making possible the reconstruction of even the most informal details of city life in the past. At the Coppergate site in particular, evidence was recovered which made it possible to postulate with a fair degree of certainty the varying land use in the area from the first century AD almost to the present (Hall 1984). The data were especially full for the Anglo-Scandinavian period (AD 866–1067), when the site had been developed with closely packed timber buildings, alleys, gullies, pits, wells, latrines, and rubbish dumps, which led to drainage impedance, the rapid growth of waterlogged conditions, and preservation of artefacts and natural organisms alike to a quite exceptional degree. The largest and most striking artefacts were the Viking-age timber buildings themselves, sometimes over 8m long, and in some cases still standing almost 2m high. No secular buildings of this period *survive* in England, and it seemed especially important that these buildings should be preserved, to provide for the first time a chance for specialists and the public alike to glimpse the character of vernacular building in the Pre-Conquest period.

There were several options. The usual one would have been to make a full photographic, drawn and written record, and to discard the timbers. Such an answer has proved acceptable to the Irish nation, despite protest marches and a long-running 'Save It' campaign, at the notorious Wood Quay site in Dublin, where somewhat similar remains have been found and excavated in advance of the City Hall development. A second option would have been to remove the buildings, conserve them, then re-erect them in a museum gallery. The option was not practicable in York, for the Yorkshire Museum, built in the 1820s for an already large collection, is now, 150 years later, only very slightly bigger, and quite inadequate for the existing collections; moreover the expense of an extension was beyond the contemplation of either York City Council or North Yorkshire County Council. A further option was to build a special display area away from the site; and a final option was to create an environment on the site itself, below the new shopping development proposed for Coppergate, where the buildings could be set out, more or less where they have been discovered. A scheme was prepared for the last option after professional advice at the highest level of the museum profession stressed the desirability of retaining the buildings at the level, deep below York and in the position, in the city centre, where they had been found. The impact that this would create in the public mind was felt to be a supremely compelling argument in favour of this option. The scheme was rejected by the York City Council, who indicated that an alternative scheme for a ground-level museum, adjacent to the existing Castle Museum, might find more favour. Reluctantly, the York Archaeological Trust turned to this site, and prepared a new scheme, designed by Powell and Moya, fresh from their outstandingly successful Museum of London, to combine a new general archaeological museum with the proposed archaeological exposition of a neighbourhood of Viking-age York. This, too, was rejected by the York City Council, who gave the Trust the option of returning to something very like its first scheme, in the form of an underground archaeological basement below a shopping arcade designed by Chapman Taylor and Partners for Wimpey Property Holdings. This option was taken, and the Jorvik Viking Centre has now been completed.

The York Archaeological Trust is an educational charity, with as its prime charitable objective the education of the public in archaeology, so the Coppergate proposals fall squarely within its remit, although in practice most of its work had hitherto been rescue excavation in and around York. As a charity, however, the Trust had no great funds at its command. It was rapidly apparent that, at least under the Ancient Monuments legislation then in force, the government was not in a position to help finance the display and interpretation of remains resulting from rescue excavation (though under the *National Heritage Act 1983* it is arguable that it could now do so). The local authorities were no more in a position to finance a buried museum than they had been a ground-level one.

In the event the Trust, advised and encouraged by a distinguished and successful Lancashire entrepreneur, C. Ian Skipper, devised a scheme with potential commercial viability which, with the essential prerequisite of a £250,000 grant from the English Tourist Board, proved attractive and sound enough to gain a loan of £1,400,000 from a consortium of seven banks syndicated for the Trust by N.M. Rothschild and Son. The balance of the £2.6m cost for construction and fitting out was loaned by Mr Skipper, or provided through loan facilities from Wimpey Property Holdings plc, the developers. The scheme depended upon visitor figures of 500,000 per year, with an entrance charge at about the level of a cinema ticket, and a profitable shop. Although such a visitor figure would place the Jorvik Viking Centre amongst the most successful 'attractions' in the country, it was nevertheless felt to be achievable with an imaginative display and systematic marketing. The Minster (York's cathedral) and the National Railway Museum have well over a million through the portals annually, and the adjacent Castle Museum has achieved over 800,000. The Jorvik Viking Centre lies physically between these three attractions, and on a direct pedestrian route between two of them. By far the majority of the visitors to York are there because of the city's historic ambience, and are thus already at least potential customers for an archaeological centre designed to present the story of a formative period in the growth of the city.

York Archaeological Trust was invited to design its centre within a basement of some 1500m^2, and in addition it has leased two adjacent shops in the new shopping mall to provide a ground-floor entrance. Administrative offices for the Jorvik Viking Centre are provided at first-floor level. Visitors enter the centre at the end of the shopping mall, through an arcaded brick entrance passage, and are controlled at a computerized ticket desk in the foyer before they make their way down a broad stair or, if they are disabled, descend by lift. Already on the way down there are murals, based on the lines of Viking-age ships excavated in the Roskilde fjord, Denmark, and there is distinctive music synthesized from the notes of a Viking-age boxwood pan pipe excavated on the Coppergate site. From the bottom of the stairs they embark on a carefully programmed sequential experience

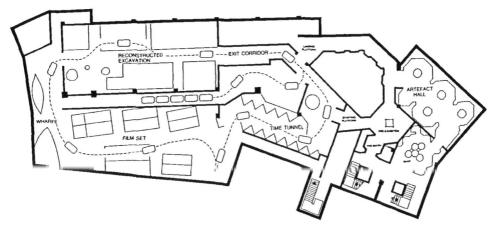

Figure 23.1 Plan of the Jorvik Viking Centre showing the interrelationships between the principal elements in the design.

designed to build up in logical steps an understanding of Viking York, the archaeological process, and the significance both of the Viking contribution to the city's history and the archaeologist's role in elucidating it.

A first element is designed as an orientation area, where the various correct perceptions that average people have about the Viking age are subtly confirmed, while the many appalling misconceptions the Trust encountered in its market research exercises are equally unostentatiously corrected. At this point the visitor steps into a transportation vehicle and enters the second element (the Time Tunnel), which is designed to stress the very long period of time that has elapsed since the Viking age – a simple enough concept, but one which the average person finds extremely difficult to grasp, and which it is difficult to convey meaningfully. The time tunnel gradually leads the visitor away from twentieth-century Coppergate and the sounds of its shopping crowds, to Coppergate with its shopping crowds in the tenth century. A third element presents the visitor with a complete reconstruction of an alley off Coppergate, with rows of tenth-century timber buildings set on long narrow tenements that run back from the street (as indeed the tenements did before the present redevelopment).

This reconstruction is, in fact, a three-dimensional archaeological interpretation of the immensely detailed archaeological evidence. Each building, each activity, and each element of the environment is either directly based on excavated evidence, or deduced indirectly, or, if Coppergate has itself not produced such evidence, based on historical, other archaeological or pictorial sources. The visit to the alley ends at a wharf on the nearby river Foss, after which the visitor enters the fourth element of the centre. Here are laid out the excavated Viking buildings, replaced as near as possible to their original layout, after having been conserved. The area is set out as though the buildings are being revealed in the excavation, just as a visitor to the site in the late 1970s would have seen them. The opportunity is taken to stress how each building in the reconstructed alley is based on the equivalent remains here, and each aspect of that reconstruction is based on archaeological evidence. The archaeological process is also explained. The visitor follows the artefacts and information from the site into a finds shed, where registration processes are in progress, then into laboratories for conservation and environmental study. Finally, visitors move through a photo display of the research and publication processes. The visitor then enters a fifth element, much more like a conventional museum gallery, where the smaller artefacts are displayed in cases and explained in graphics. The sixth and final element is a shop, where reproductions of artefacts in the adjacent gallery, together with souvenirs, guides, and a range of explanatory booklet guides, teachers' aids, and audio-visual products, are sold. Visitors then return to ground level, leaving the building by a separate exit, which ensures that they do not cross the path of those about to enter.

The somewhat rigid layout of the Jorvik Viking Centre is partly determined by the problem inherent in controlling large numbers of people in a constricted underground environment, where fire regulations strictly limit the density of people in any area at one time. It nevertheless also stems from the Trust's conviction that the story it has to tell is immensely complicated, quite new even to most specialist visitors, and best told this way. The sequence has been arranged to build up comprehension cumulatively. There are a limited number of clear take-home messages. Those with limited background knowledge or modest capacity for insight will receive them at one level, while the more experienced will receive a correspondingly more complex story. Those who wish to do so can linger longer in the orientation area, and visitors who wish to examine and ponder the artefact display can do so at their leisure. In the main part of the display, from the Time Tunnel to the laboratory area (elements 2 to 4), the fire restrictions and the nature of the displays have, however, caused the Trust to adopt the device of transporting visitors in four-person battery-driven timecars. Each car has a synchronized low-level commentary, which can just be heard above the general background sound collage, which is provided by a Mackenzie 64-channel sound system in the time tunnel, Coppergate reconstruction and excavation area. There is a choice of three languages for the car commentary.

The creation of so innovatory and complex an exhibition in such an unconventional location has inevitably brought its problems. The Trust has had the benefit of architects Robertson Ward Associates, who have extensive experience of designing for the leisure industry, and whose solutions combine a liveliness and colour boldness not normally associated with the exposition of archaeological data. To create the time tunnel, reconstruction of the Coppergate alley, reconstruction of the excavation and the finds processing area, the Trust has employed the Wakefield-based Yorkshire Communications Group (YCG). YCG has brought together a team with experience in creative design, set construction and dressing, lighting, and communication in various forms. They have decided to make extensive use of figures in the time tunnel, created for them by Derek Freeborn. In the Coppergate alley there are some 20 Viking figures, sculpted in clay and moulded in fibreglass by Graham Ibbeson, the Yorkshire artist well known for his super-humanist figures. There has been constant liaison with York Archaeological Trust archaeologists on details of the dress of these figures, as with everything else, and an archaeological liaison officer has been an essential part of the team. The buildings have been designed under the supervision of Richard Hall, director of the Coppergate excavation, with constant input from the research staff of the Environmental Archaeology Unit of the University of York, and from Dominic Tweddle, finds research director of the Trust. The wharf area has involved consultation with Steve Roskams, formerly of the Department of Urban Archaeology, Museum of London, who has excavated one of the few Anglo-Saxon waterfronts known in England. The Viking Ship Museum at Roskilde, Denmark, has advised on replicating a cargo boat based on their Skuldelev 3 wreck, while the National Maritime Museum donated to the Trust its experimental replica of a faering (four-oared rowing boat) from the Gokstad ship burial, which is also drawn up at the wharf. Veracity of nautical detail has been achieved with the advice of Alan Binns, English doyen of Viking ship reconstruction studies. Carol Morris, specialist in early woodworking techniques, has set up a pole lathe. The various conversations to be heard in the Coppergate alley, all in Old Norse, have been devised by Professor Christine Fell and recorded under her direction by a team of Old Norse speakers. The recordings have been integrated into general sound collages by Trevor Wishart of the Department of Music, University of York. Nothing creates atmosphere in a reconstruction so immediately as smell, and Dale Air Conditioning Ltd of Lytham St Annes have devised a system of balanced olfactory experiences appropriate to various parts of the alley. Lighting for the YCG areas has been designed by Playlight Ltd of Manchester, specialist TV set lighting engineers. The design controller for the areas devised by YCG has been John Sunderland; the set building team has been led by Jonathan Bean, while the YCG team as a whole has been led by Colin Pyrah. The combination of the various disciplines in the academic and communications fields is unique in archaeological interpretation.

The exhibition of Viking-age timbers, long waterlogged, and inherently unstable, has brought its own problems. These started during the excavation itself. Once the decision had been taken to preserve the timbers it became necessary to keep them damp, with constant spraying, throughout the excavation and site recording process. Thereafter, each plank and post was lifted, placed on a pre-constructed wooden former, treated with fungicide, sealed in polythene and then transferred to water storage tanks at a nearby disused aerodrome. Subsequently, each element was transferred, after drawing, to treatment tanks for impregnation, for periods between 6 and 18 months, in polyethylene glycol (PEG), carried out under the supervision of the York Archaeological Trust's Conservation Officer, Jim Spriggs. The timbers, by now relatively stable, were then placed on pre-formed locations in the Viking Centre. Even then, however, particular conditions of humidity were necessary to ensure slow completion of the stabilization process. For this, the hall required special humidification equipment, designed as part of the already sophisticated air handling, heating, and cooling systems for the centre as a whole. During the period in which the stabilization takes place, the timbers are exhibited in polythene tents, and the process of locating timbers will go on long after the exhibition is open to the public, as a kind of living exhibit.

The Conservation Laboratory staff of the York Archaeological Trust have also worked closely with Robertson Ward Associates to ensure excellent environmental conditions in the Artefact Hall. The hall is designed as a series of alcoves, each devoted to a different theme and including a top-lit island case fitted out with a local environment appropriate to the archaeological materials to be exhibited within. Visitors with time to devote to the Artefact Hall can examine at their leisure not only the major finds in the island cases, but also additional supporting material, both artefacts and graphics, in the alcoves behind. Those who are short of time, or whose interest is flagging, can be assured of seeing the most important items simply by walking down the central alleyway between the island cases. The hall as a whole is dimly lit, only the cases being emphasized; though its predominant poppy red and dark-brown colour scheme gives it a richness that helps to promote the importance of the essentially very small artefacts. Here, as everywhere else in the centre, considerable attention has been given to the physical security of the artefacts, and there are a series of surveillance systems, essential not only because of the intrinsic importance of the objects, but also because they belong not to the Trust, but to York City Council. Archaeological curating is by arrangement with the Yorkshire Museum, York.

Figure 23.2 On the street front of Coppergate are market booths, and recreated Viking buildings and their inhabitants are amongst the most striking features of the Jorvik Viking Centre.

The Jorvik Viking Centre shop is an extension of a marketing system developed during and after the Coppergate excavations by Cultural Resource Management Ltd, the commercial arm of the York Archaeological Trust. It was found that visitors to the excavations were anxious to buy a range of interpretative material, together with souvenirs of their visit. After the close of the excavation, a shop opened in York to continue to supply such materials to the general visitor to the city. It does so under the name 'Heritage', and considerable experience has been built up in the marketing of historically or archaeologically associated souvenirs. The 'Heritage' shop has a range largely based on artefacts, which recall past times in York, though replicas from various non-York sources are stocked. The shop in the Jorvik Viking Centre follows the same principles, with emphasis on the site, its artefacts and its story but with supplementary material of Viking association from many parts of Britain and Europe. Special ranges cater for children, and souvenirs vary from the overtly didactic to the frankly light-hearted. The Trust accepts this, and is glad that one of the most popular products is a T-shirt emblazoned 'Erik Bloodaxe rules OK'. It at least causes the purchaser to ask 'Who was Erik Bloodaxe?' – and to convey the news to anyone whom he or she meets. Both the Jorvik Viking Centre products and the 'Heritage' shop range are available by mail order, but purchasers seem to prefer to come to the shops, which are exciting places in themselves, with bright and very cheerful display fittings often commended by the customers.

During the design and construction of the Jorvik Viking Centre a number of specific technical problems presented themselves, the like of which have probably not before been encountered in museum design. Not the least has been the creation of the timecars. The display concept called for a quite different type of vehicle than those encountered in Disneyland and other leisure centres. These gain their impact from speed and excitement. The Jorvik Viking Centre calls for a very slow, silent ride, and the cars themselves have been designed to be as unobtrusive as possible, so that, after the initial surprise of entering a car, the visitor forgets them as anything more than a convenient means of avoiding 'museum leg'. To achieve this, the whole of the main display area has been built on one level, so that minimum propulsion power is required. There is no call for acceleration or braking, and as a result it has been possible to use a very simple technology, with long-life batteries recharged only once per day as the propulsion source. The technology was designed for automated warehouses, but the adaptations, drive systems, and electronic controls have been devised by Peter Millward, an engineer of the highest standing in the field of micro-electronics.

The problems of fire prevention and emergency procedures have been of an order quite different from those encountered in more conventional museum displays, or in buildings sited above ground. While there are fire exits directly into a sunken service yard, many of the restrictions appropriate to an underground building have been applied by the Fire Prevention Officer. The smoke extraction requirements, for instance, necessitated particularly sophisticated and powerful smoke-extraction and air-handling systems, capable of extraction at the rate of 10 cubic metres per second. While every attempt has been made to use authentic material for the dressing of the replicated areas, obviously some of these are highly flammable. The reconstructed buildings should have been of axe-riven oak planks. The materials used in the event were plaster compounds, which achieve the necessary Class 'O' fire rating. The buildings were, it is thought, thatched. Straw was used for one, natural grass from the Askham Bog Nature Reserve on the outskirts of York was used for another, while reed was used for the rest. The thatch was made up on panels, which were then treated with fire retardant. The results passed the most stringent tests the Fire Prevention Officer could devise. Similar methods were adopted for the materials used in construction and dressing of all the underground areas, the whole operation being a story of close and repeated consultation between project manager, designer, architects, heating and ventilation engineers, the local Fire Prevention Officer, and the National Fire Research Station at Borehamwood, Herts.

The Centre has had its critics, not least from the academic world. The main reservations stem from the inability of individual visitors to programme the duration of their visit to each of the display areas. This is particularly true, of course, in those areas through which the timecars travel. However, to cater for the specialist, the JVC has on its staff an Assistant Keeper whose primary task is to deal with inquiries of an academic nature. Full documentation for every artefact on display is available and, in addition, a manual has been prepared which explains the archaeological justification for all aspects of the reconstructions and the evidence upon which they are based.

The overwhelming reaction to the scheme has, however, been very positive and enthusiastic. The initial excavations at Coppergate attracted the most prestigious patronage: HRH The Prince of Wales, Queen Margrethe of Denmark, King Carl Gustaf of Sweden, Crown Prince Harald of Norway, and the President of Iceland. Magnus Magnusson was a most enthusiastic and energetic Chairman of the Stewards – a body composed of influential people in academic, financial, and diplomatic fields. The volume of work required to service this level of patronage, plus the deliberate and planned media coverage that has been generated, has led to the creation of three full-time staff posts. The tourist industry has warmly welcomed (and substantially financed) the Viking Centre, and Mr Michael Montague, Chairman of the English Tourist Board, referred to it as the most exciting tourism project yet seen in this country. Dr Joseph Veach Noble, past president of the American Association of Museums and a trustee of the Archaeological Institute of America, welcomed the design as a brilliant new concept in archaeological interpretation.

The York Archaeological Trust has been ever conscious of the need to maintain the total academic integrity of the display whilst at the same time educating the public in archaeology in an entertaining and enjoyable manner. In this way we feel that we have created a substantial and meaningful archaeological experience for far more people than normally enter the portals of a conventional museum.

Reference

Hall, R.A. (1984) *The Viking Dig: The Excavations in York*. London: The Bodley Head Ltd.

Chapter 24

The new Museum of Altamira
Finding solutions to tourism pressure

José Antonio Lasheras Corruchaga
and Pilar Fatás Monforte

History of the Cave of Altamira

The paintings of Altamira—the first to be cataloged as Paleolithic—were discovered in 1879 by Marcelino Sanz de Sautuola. Since then, Altamira has become a symbol of prehistoric art throughout the world because of its antiquity and, above all, the magnificence of its art. It constitutes a milestone in an art form that proliferated in Europe, from Gibraltar to the Urals, more than twenty thousand years ago.

Throughout time, Altamira suffered many natural and artificial transformations. The difficulty of preserving the cave soon became evident. There were several rock falls from the ceiling. In addition, an interest in allowing public visits began in the early twentieth century. In 1924 the authorities in charge began to make the cave more accessible by providing paths and steps and illuminating it with spotlights. A road was built leading to the cave, and the esplanade next to its entrance was turned into a parking lot.

In 1939 the authorities focused on increasing tourism, and in 1955 Altamira was visited by more than fifty thousand people. This began a critical period for preservation of the cave: experts in charge of its conservation wanted to reduce visitor numbers, but politicians thought large numbers of tourists were an economic boon of vital importance to fostering tourist activity in Cantabria generally.

This disastrous cultural policy led to visitor numbers of more than 177,000 in 1973. At that time the cave was the main tourist attraction in the region and one of the most frequently visited sites in Spain. The situation was so bad that if the number of visitors had increased, the paintings would probably have disappeared as a result of extreme changes in humidity and temperature causing physical, chemical, and microbiological problems.

Source: *On the Past, for the Future: Integrating Archaeology and Conservation.* Proceedings of the Conservation Theme at the 5th World Archaeological Congress, Washington, DC, 22-26 June 2003. N. Agnew and J. Bridgland (eds.). Los Angeles: The Getty Conservation Institute, 2006. pp. 177–183. Reprinted with permission of the J. Paul Getty Trust.

In 1978 the cave was given to the Spanish state, which since then has been responsible for its management. In 1979 the National Museum and Research Center of Altamira was created by the Spanish Ministry of Culture to preserve and manage the cave. That same year the cave was closed to the public, and a team of specialists began to study environmental parameters. On conclusion of the study, a fixed daily number of visitors was determined that would not alter its inner climatic environment, and in 1982 Altamira was reopened for a reduced daily-maximum number of visitors, with an absolute limit of 8,500 people a year. The aim was to maintain its microclimate and to ensure the preservation of the paintings and engravings.

Altamira and tourism: finding solutions

As a general philosophy, the fundamental aim of conserving heritage should be to enable its use. When we talk about using heritage, we have to consider its sustainability, because present exploitation should never exhaust its future use. This is the approach applied in the management of public visits to the cave of Altamira. Visits are not restricted to specialists; the general public may, by prior request, visit the cave, and this will continue as long as conservation conditions permit. The only condition governing their selection is that visitors must be over twelve years old; the order of appointments is based on a waiting list.

The temporary closure of the cave in the 1980s was hotly disputed since it had a profoundly negative effect on tourism. On the one hand, there was the need for proper management of the cave; on the other, a large demand to visit. The cave's fragility left no doubt that the two situations were incompatible. The solution was to offer a high-quality alternative.

The idea of reproducing Altamira became a much-discussed topic. Of course, outside cultural circles, the main motivation was to relieve the crisis suffered by the tourist industry. Many arguments were advanced to support this: economic, political, social, and educational. All were in agreement that a solution must be found that served all parties and interests involved.

Since 1982 the main preservation problems have been addressed. However, some outstanding issues affecting the cave were yet to be resolved: (1) it was necessary to repeat and complete the research work carried out in 1979; (2) there was no permanent recording system that might allow the verification of preservation parameters; and (3) environmental risks, such as sewage and traffic, had not been totally resolved. These concerns, combined with the availability of modern techniques for data recording and the application of new approaches, were reasons to search for a solution from a broader perspective.

In 1992 this solution materialized as a museum project for Altamira that was approved by the museum consortium and begun in 1993. Since then the Ministry of Education and Culture has invested significant funding in scientific equipment and in research agreements with other institutions, as well as in the purchase of the land above the cave. The multifaceted project included measures to improve conservation of the cave art and other heritage held by the museum, planning of a multidisciplinary research project to advance scientific knowledge about Altamira, and various communication strategies to popularize this knowledge. In other words, the project responds to the three main functions of a museum: conservation, research, and communication.

The aims of the project were (1) to satisfy the great demand to visit Altamira; (2) to improve the preservation of the paintings and engravings in the cave; and (3) to create a focal attraction that could contribute to the development of the regional tourist sector. The tools needed were a protection plan; construction of new infrastructure (supply and sewage systems, roads, paths, etc.); and a new building to house the reproduction of the cave, a large permanent exhibition on the Paleolithic period in Cantabrian Spain, new areas for laboratories, research, and administration, and any other public or semi-public facilities that the museum as a whole may require.

The Altamira project encompasses all of these. The cultural offerings of the new Museum of Altamira include not only the reproduction of the cave but also a permanent exhibition dedicated to the "Times of Altamira" and many other activities such as workshops, conferences, and guided visits.

The project has solved the problems of preservation by carrying out a diagnosis of preventive preservation requirements and increasing the amount of land owned around the cave by 80,000 square meters, enabling traffic and supply and sewage systems to be moved more than half a kilometre from the cave. It has answered the demand for knowledge about and visits to Altamira by constructing a replica, creating the exhibition "Times of Altamira," and reshaping the landscape. And, of course, it has helped to regenerate regional tourism.

The neocave of Altamira

The name "Altamira" creates high expectations because it is a landmark in the history of art and has become a legend throughout the world. This implies a responsibility on the part of the museum not to disappoint those expectations.

Using a replica could be a problem because of the tendency to attribute value exclusively to originals and to reject copies and reproductions (sometimes the term "falsification" is even used, confusing quite disparate concepts). The solution was to ensure that the project's conception, design, and execution were of the highest quality and based on scientific research.

Using the results of this research, the replica of Altamira re-creates the original cavern space as it was during Paleolithic habitation rather than as it is today: that is, natural rock falls, supporting walls, paths, and other arrangements made in modern times have been suppressed.

By applying computerized modeling to the cave's topography, more than 40,000 sample points per square meter were measured and shaped; the reproduction has an accuracy of one millimeter. The paintings have been reproduced using the same techniques and natural pigments employed by Palaeolithic artists. Thus, high technology and artisan techniques were combined to achieve the best results.

This high-quality alternative to visiting the original cave does not compromise preservation of the original, yet it allows it to be known with absolute fidelity. It is an "open book" about Altamira based on scientific data and an original museological concept based on quality and singularity. The new museum provides an interesting opportunity for everyone to experience this heritage, and it allows Altamira to be shown without restriction to a larger number of visitors. More than one million people have visited the new Museum of Altamira since 2001; the number of visitors is expected to stabilize at over 200,000 per year, which is more than the number that came to the original cave during the 1970s (Figure 24.1).

The Neocave of Altamira is part of a huge permanent display on the Paleolithic consisting of original pieces from various museums as well as multimedia presentations; it is intellectually accessible to all and motivates intelligent interaction and pleasure in learning through analogy to present-day life. The new museum has become a model of visitation for other heritage sites; many requests for technical information have been received for use by other museums and cultural spaces.

Figure 24.1 The Neocave: ceiling with paintings.

Other tourism-related implications

The tourism industry has recovered in Santillana del Mar and its surroundings. Tourism pressure justified the important investment in this multifaceted project, because it helped to guarantee not only the cultural and economic profitability of the project and the surrounding environment but also a departure from seasonal visitation patterns. That is why the project has been linked to tourism and was attached to a European Union Support Framework, "Valuation of Cultural Resources of Tourist Interest," wherein it responds to the third defined strategy: "aspects relating to the recovery and maintenance of cultural resources of tourist interest." The project revalues Altamira by making tourist use possible.

There is another collateral benefit: the new museum helps to arouse people's interest in the fragility of heritage and the need to restrict visits to the cave. For example, in September 2002 the cave was closed again in order to restudy conservation conditions. This time the public reaction was very different from that in 1979; the reasons for closure were well understood by the general public, and they have access to an extremely interesting alternative, the Neocave.

Another key to appropriate management of the cave is entrusting it to museum technicians, basically curators. While the main task is to preserve the cave, staff are also trained in communication, dissemination, and provision of scientific information to all interested parties.

The Museum of Altamira is a cultural reference point for the tourist destination of Cantabria and "Green Spain" in general. The museum and Paleolithic art are used to portray Cantabria in the current tourist campaign of "Green Spain." The bison of Altamira are among the themes selected by Turespaña in its international campaign, "Spain Marks," which promotes Spain as a cultural and tourist destination. The regional government of Cantabria includes the Museum of Altamira in its promotional efforts. The museum collaborates in this promotion; its communication department personally welcomes tourism and travel journalists sent by the Promotion of Tourism Service of the Cantabrian government and tour operators referred by the Regional Society of Tourism. Through its booking department, the Museum of Altamira pays special, personalized attention to visits organized by travel agencies, booking centers, and hotels.

The Museum of Altamira disseminates information about its cultural offerings and sends a quarterly newsletter published by the Friends of the Museum Association to tourism offices. In summer 2003 the Museum of Altamira made available a new brochure edited especially for tourist establishments: hotels, tourist offices, travel agencies, and so on.

A final consideration is the professional relationship between the museum and tourism, which is difficult because no relationship exists between the Spanish Ministry of Tourism and the Ministry of Culture. In 2002 the "Plan to Promote Cultural Tourism" was presented to the Ministry of Culture. This was developed by the Secretary of State for Tourism to promote the heritage resources of Spain as tourist attractions. The first general aim outlined was the creation of a cultural tourism offering (a cultural offering becomes a cultural tourism offering when the rights to its use and enjoyment are available for acquisition in the tourist market), which involved measures designed to increase information on cultural products and to reinforce the promotion and support of the commercialization of cultural products.

Step by step, the results of the campaign are being seen. At present, museums are listed on the official website of Turespaña, cultural icons have been incorporated in the campaign "Spain Marks," and museum activities have been included in the cultural calendar. Recently, the Museum of Altamira participated in another initiative designed to meet the goals of sensitization to and structuring of the cultural tourism sector. A number of training sessions were held, aimed at cultural and tourism technicians, agents of archaeological venues, civic groups, parks, and cultural landscapes, to analyze Altamira as a cultural tourism resource. However, in most cases, each museum must establish its own relationship with tourism institutions and companies, and this usually depends on the goodwill of the professionals in charge of communication departments, where they exist. Broader collaboration is recommended in the future between the cultural and tourism sectors in order to obtain cultural products of high quality.

Chapter 25

Archaeological site museums in Latin America

Helaine Silverman

Introduction

Over the past twenty years, museums have been receiving critical attention from scholars in various disciplines. Among the many topics considered in the literature are the history of museums, museums and nationalism, museum architecture, the relationship between museums and tourism, and museums as contested spaces of class display, identity formation, public culture, and representation. However, within the burgeoning field of museum studies, scant attention has been directed to archaeological site museums. Most revealing of this situation is the fact that the International Council of Museums (ICOM) has offered only a skeletal definition, dating to 1982, stating that the archaeological site museum is a museum located "at the point where excavations have taken place" (cited in Hudson 1987:144). Other kinds of site museums recognized by ICOM are ethnographical, ecological, and historical. All of these site museums are supposed to protect natural or cultural property, moveable and immovable, on its original site and to "acquire, conserve and communicate material evidence of people and their environment" (Article 2, ICOM Statutes, 1989, 1995, 2001).

The recent interest taken by the United Nations Educational, Scientific and Cultural Organization (UNESCO) in site museums of all kinds—archaeological, historic, urban, natural is therefore most welcome. In his editorial for a thematic issue (called "The Site Museum") of UNESCO's journal, *Museum International*, Gadi Mgomezulu (2004), director of UNESCO's Division of Cultural Heritage, contemplates the complexities of site museums, archaeological and otherwise:

> [They] do not exist in isolation; they take on meaning in a web of interpretative and exhibition systems that are primarily developed within museal institutions. ... [T]he site [i]s a space and the museum [i]s a place which produces knowledge and which is symbolic of the relationship between societies and their heritage at a given moment. ... [T]he museum

Source: *Archaeological Site Museums in Latin America*. Gainesville, FL: University Press of Florida, 2006. pp. 3–17.

simultaneously anchors this relationship and functions as a mediation zone ... a museum is not only an instrument which explains the site in a static relationship that is updated according to the rhythm of new museographic developments. The site and the museum each designate a space of heritage whose limits adapt and transform themselves, occasionally overlapping when a heritage space takes on the characteristics of a museum.

I extrapolate from his remarks that the key issue for archaeological site museums—specifically the concern of the volume *Archaeological Site Museums in Latin America* (Silverman 2006a)—is their imbrication of heritage, cultural mediation, and representation. The case studies of almost all of the authors in this volume illustrate this point.

As commonly understood by archaeologists, an archaeological site museum (henceforth referred to as a site museum) is a building located at an archaeological site in which exemplary excavated materials from the site, and perhaps from related sites, are displayed, accompanied by explanatory texts that interpret the site and its archaeological culture for the public. Barbara Kirshenblatt-Gimblett observes, "The museum is an integral part of the site. The museum does for the site what it cannot do for itself. It is not a substitute for the site but part of it, for the interpretive interface shows what cannot otherwise be seen. It offers virtualities in the absence of actualities" (1998:169). Other features of site museums may include laboratory and storage facilities. They may or may not have an organized educational program. They may or not have housing for a resident archaeologist and/or site protection personnel.

The location of these museums runs the gamut from world-famous monumental sites (such as Teotihuacan, San Lorenzo, Copán) to sites having much less striking—albeit archaeologically important—material evidence (such as the Vegas occupation of the Santa Elena Peninsula in Ecuador). In *Archaeological Site Museums in Latin America* (Silverman 2006a) the contributors amplify the concept of site museum to encompass not just buildings with displays pertaining to a site or group of related sites but also buildings whose exhibits address broad regional prehistories, as well as entire historic districts and even landscapes that are scripted as museums by particular agents.[1]

The site museums discussed in *Archaeological Site Museums in Latin America* include some of the greatest sites of Latin America. These sites are and will grow as tourist destinations because they are part of the ineluctable process of globalization within which the heritage and tourism industry operates. Site museums in Latin America are particularly interesting because of the frequent tension they embody—narrative as well as real—between perceived pre-Hispanic glory, the usually disadvantaged situation of the local and/or descendant communities, and the pressure for development, often in the form of tourism. The contributors to this volume consider a range of site museums and the uneasy as well as successful engagements occurring among diverse local and outside interest groups.

Ethical considerations

The field of archaeology has become increasingly self-critical and self-reflexive as it interrogates its own practices. At the international level this is seen most noticeably in the meetings and publications of the World Archaeological Congress (for example, the One World Archaeology series beginning with the 1986 meeting in Southampton; see, as examples, Bond and Gilliam 1994; Gathercole and Lowenthal 1990; Layton 1989a, 1989b) and the Society for American Archaeology in the United States (for example, the SAA Committee on Ethics, Committee on Native American Relations, Committee on Repatriation, Public Education Committee; see Lynott and Wylie 2000; Zimmerman et al. 2003a; see also, inter alia, Kohl and Fawcett 1995; Shackel and Chambers 2004; Vitelli 1996). Beyond anthropological archaeology per se, a range of ethical issues has been raised by the field of critical museum studies, in which the representation of O/others and relationships with living and descendant communities are among the most salient for archaeologists.

We, as archaeologists, should be informed and enthusiastic about archaeological site museums because, among other reasons, they have the potential to fulfill six of the eight principles of archaeological ethics guiding the Society for American Archaeology (Lynott 1997). Indeed, the museum work or museum critiques of the contributors to *Archaeological Site Museums in Latin America* (Silverman 2006a) specifically engage these principles in the following way:

Principle 1. Site museums can promote local stewardship of the archaeological record.
Principle 2. Site museums should function in consultation with affected groups.
Principle 4. Site museums fulfill the mission of public education and outreach.
Principle 6. Site museums present the knowledge of archaeological investigation to the public in accessible form.
Principle 7. Site museums can function as appropriate depositories of materials and records.
Principle 8. Site museums can sponsor training workshops that teach contemporary standards of professional practice to the local community so that local individuals and organizations are able to appropriately conduct any program of research they initiate or in which they participate.

Each author is well aware that "today's archaeology calls for 'active ethics': the awareness that essentially everything we do as professionals has ethical implications" (Zimmerman et al. 2003b: xvi). Moreover, many of these archaeologists are proactive, not only aware of the ethical implications of their actions but also actively seeking to better the circumstances of the communities in and around which they work.

Site museums and site protection

In compliance with SAA Ethical Principle #1, site museums can promote stewardship of the archaeological record. In so doing, they should function in consultation with affected groups, in compliance with SAA Ethical Principle #2.

But the process may go awry. Here are four true stories from Peru that concern the relationship between site museums and site protection. I offer them as lessons.

Story 1: one site museum, widespread looting

In 1914 Max Uhle, the German father of Peruvian archaeology, lamented, "As soon as I had left the scene [the Ica Valley in 1901 and Nazca region in 1905] of my last explorations, my workingmen, who had become quite experts, under my training, continued alone and in secret to search for this valuable and rare pottery [Nasca, dating to ca. AD 1–750]. Thus a vast amount of this beautiful ware was unearthed and found its way to Lima, where all was greedily acquired by dealers. Many additional cemeteries were located by these huaqueros [tomb robbers] and entirely rifled" (Uhle 1914: 8). Twelve years later, looting was so intense that it prompted Julio C. Tello, the Peruvian father of Peruvian archaeology, to comment in a letter dated 29 October 1926: "In the short space of 25 years [since Uhle's discovery of the Nasca style], the looters have opened about 30,000 tombs. Their vandalized trophies are found dispersed all over the world as mere curiosities. They have lost, perhaps forever, their historical and scientific value" (cited in Tello and Mejía Xesspe 1967: 156). Archaeological excavations have an afterlife that can be either advantageous or deleterious, depending on the decisions made by archaeologists once a project has ended.

The only site museum in the valleys of the Río Grande de Nazca heartland where ancient Nasca society flourished (see Silverman and Proulx 2002 for overview) is the Maria Reiche Museum, dedicated to the life and discoveries of the German investigator of the region's geoglyphs, with an accompanying exhibition of archaeological materials from the major ancient cultures of the area.[2] Neither the Maria Reiche Museum nor the small municipal and private museums in the towns of Nazca and Palpa nor the major regional museum in the city of Ica are thus far having an ameliorative role with regard to the area's unabated looting (notwithstanding looting's diminishing returns, caused by a century of exploitation), despite their admirable public outreach.

Story 2: a site museum, rare looting, but no research

Between 1925 and 1930, one of the most important archaeological sites in Peru was excavated by a team from Peru's national museum. The site is Paracas (actually composed of five distinct loci; see Silverman 1991), dating to circa 200 BC–AD 200 and famous for its exquisite textiles. In 1930 a military revolution overthrew the government and shut down the archaeological project as the political winds of favor shifted. In the absence of an archaeological project, the site was immediately devastated by looters.

In 1964 a site museum was created by the wealthy Swiss archaeologist Frederic Engel, who was working at the site and in the region. No other archaeologist has excavated at Paracas since Engel, and empirical knowledge about the in situ Paracas habitation zones and cemeteries has not advanced, although the material culture has been continuously studied by many scholars. Looting virtually ceased with the construction of the museum.[3]

Story 3: site versus local population versus major museum versus site museum

In February 1987 a small group of looters living in the northern coastal village of Sipán discovered a gold-filled royal tomb in a prehistoric mound alongside their homes. Infighting led to rumors of their discovery leaking to the police, who then informed the director of the regional museum, Dr. Walter Alva. Looted materials from the tomb that had not yet been sold to the illicit antiquities market indicated the extraordinary wealth of what had been plundered. As has been dramatically recounted in the popular press (Alva 1988; Kirkpatrick 1992; Nagin 1990), a real shoot-out determined whether the academic field of archaeology or the shadowy world of the looters would control the site. Within days of the confiscation of the artifacts still in the village, a police presence was established on the mound, and Dr. Alva began a salvage excavation. Scientific excavation proceeded thereafter. Dr. Alva's results are so important that they have revolutionized Mochica (the name of the ancient society to which the remains pertain, circa AD 200–750) archaeology. In addition to the permanent police station, a rustic site museum was created at Sipán to inform visitors and presumably educate the local people. In November 2002, a state-of-the-art museum for the spectacular remains excavated at Sipán was inaugurated in Lambayeque, the provincial capital, located thirty-five kilometres away from the site of origin. It is ironic that the April 2004 issue of *Art News* (cover, page 99; it is a magazine devoted to the sale of art and education of collectors) heralds the Royal Tombs of Sipán Museum as one of "the top ten museums (you never heard of)," while page 8 contains a full-page color ad for an exhibition sale of pre-Columbian pottery at a Chicago art gallery. The recent history of Sipán and its two museums is poignant and illuminating in this context. The local population at Sipán still protests their poor share of the wealth generated by the site in their backyard (see Silverman 2005).

Story 4: a site museum integrates the local community and furthers archaeological research and community development

An example is found at Kuntur Wasi, an important Formative period site in the northern highlands. Prior to the arrival of the Japanese Archaeological Mission of the University of Tokyo in 1988, there had been several interventions in the site (excavation by a Peruvian team in 1946, topographic mapping in 1982–1983, analysis of the 1946 ceramic collections: see discussion in Onuki et al. 1995: 3). As it did elsewhere in Peru in its prior projects, the Japanese Mission made a long-term fieldwork commitment to the site. What makes the Kuntur Wasi archaeological project extraordinary (beyond the always high quality of the Japanese Mission's research) is the social commitment that it simultaneously tendered to the local community, resulting in the creation of a community-based, decision-making, not-for-profit Kuntur Wasi Cultural Association and a superb co-managed site museum (Onuki 2006).[4] Today, the site museum is the pride of the community as well as a source of gradually increasing income and modernization. Despite the repeated discovery of gold-filled tombs at Kuntur Wasi (dating to circa 800 BC) by the Japanese Mission, there has been no looting at the site, nor has the museum suffered any loss despite housing more than two hundred gold artifacts in addition to outstanding pottery; there are also in situ carved stone monoliths.

These four scenarios illustrate four different directions that cultural patrimony preservation can take with and without the presence of site museums. I could provide other examples, but these suffice to show the range from least to most successful outcome for both the ancient people (that is, preservation of the archaeological site) and the living local community. As the remarkable initiatives of various contributors to *Archaeological Site Museums in Latin America* (Silverman 2006a) clearly demonstrate, site museums can play a positive determinant role in the survival of the material record and betterment of the lives of the community around it, making local people true stakeholders. Thus, site preservation matters. Beyond giving archaeologists access to a database with which to reconstruct the past, archaeological sites can be deployed in the present as sources of employment, local and regional development, and proud identity. Site museums are on the front line of these endeavours, since archaeological sites cannot speak for themselves.[5]

Site museums and development

In large and small, thriving and would-be urban centers around the world, museums have been seized upon as a sign of cities' promising futures and facilitator of their economic present. Speaking of heritage in general, Kirshenblatt-Gimblett (1998:155) notes its role as "an instrument of urban redevelopment." The boom in signature architect-designed museum buildings (Henderson 2001) is inextricably linked to municipal plans for development (Solomon 2001). Museums are "premier attractions. Museums are not only destinations on an itinerary: they are also nodes in a network of attractions that form the recreational geography of a region and, increasingly, the globe" (Kirshenblatt-Gimblett 1998: 132).

In a greatly scaled-down form, this is what archaeologists and local communities are quite literally banking on with site museums.[6] Site museums can generate and support sustainable, income-producing activities in an expanding tourism circuit or corridor—and employment diminishes the need for looting. Site museums can function as economic motors for their region. Indeed, starting from the premise that cultural tourism was already unstoppable and would continue to grow exponentially, the 1976 International Seminar on Contemporary Tourism and Humanism (organized by the International Council on Monuments and Sites, or ICOMOS) specifically recognized that archaeological sites can be a source of economic benefit and cultural education in their regions, and ICOMOS argued for better management (also see the 1967 Norms of Quito [ICOMOS 1967]).

The issue is not just the conundrum of indigenous people in a postcolonial small-scale community seizing on the Western-in-origin concept of a museum as a sign of their engagement with modernity and as a facilitator of their construction of identity (see Hastorf's (2006) discussion of Chiripa), it is that museums actually can generate revenue and development through their insertion into the global economy. Indeed, developing countries present their museums to diplomats and visiting foreign entrepreneurs as an assurance of their political stability, cultural worth, and amenable climate for investment. Visiting tourists pay entrance fees, need guides, consume soda and chips sold in kiosks by residents, have their vehicles washed by local teenage boys after the dusty ride, adventurously stay in family-run local lodgings, eat in a local restaurant, and want souvenirs (another form of heritage consumption; for a larger discussion see Lury 1997). Thus, just before the gala inauguration of the Royal Tombs of Sipán Museum in 2002, a proposal for an adjacent open-air Mochica artisans village was approved by the Ministry of Trade and Tourism and is now functioning. Lambayeque artists/artisans sell to tourists their own replicas of ancient Mochica pottery, textiles, and metalwork, along with ethnographic crafts, thereby achieving employment and income.

The ability of site museums to promote development, however, should be constrained by what Kirshenblatt-Gimblett (1998:171) calls a "responsibility to their 'product' that distinguishes them from market-driven amusement, whose primary responsibility is profitability. They are responsible for giving form and space to concerns animating public life in the communities they serve." The site museums discussed in *Archaeological Site Museums in Latin America* (Silverman 2006a) are philosophically and pragmatically in agreement with Kirshenblatt-Gimblett's admonishment.

It is also important to bear in mind that development predicated upon site museums in Latin America is a different process with a radically dissimilar social and historical context than the one problematized by Hewison (1987) in his famous discussion of Britain's heritage industry. Hewison attributes extensive recent museum growth in the United Kingdom to a replacement of "the real industry upon which this country's economy depends. Instead of manufacturing goods, we are manufacturing heritage. ... The reason for the growth of this new force is [that] this country is gripped by the perception that it is in decline" (Hewison 1987: 9). In the case of the towns near the archaeological sites treated by contributors to *Archaeological Site Museums in Latin America* (Silverman 2006a), they have not declined. Rather, they have not been thriving centers for centuries or millennia. In Latin America the issue is not to put heritage on display so as "to give dying economies and dead sites a second life as exhibitions of themselves" (Kirshenblatt-Gimblett 1998:7). Instead, these site museums are intended to assist the development of long-marginalized regions while valorizing and enabling the local population to define its own identity/ies.

Site museums and the construction of identity

Construction of identity is a leitmotif coursing through technical discussions of cultural heritage management (for example, 1996 ICOMOS Declaration of San Antonio; 2001 UNESCO Universal Declaration on Cultural Diversity; see Cleere 1989: 8) in addition to ethnographic studies of appropriations of the past in local communities whose prehistories (antecedent or merely geographically sedimented) are deemed "greater" or more "glorious" than their current socio-economic reality (for example, Silverman 2002). For instance, the ICOMOS Declaration of San Antonio states that heritage sites can carry a deep spiritual message that sustains communal life, linking it to the ancestral past (ICOMOS 1996). The 2001 Universal Declaration on Cultural Diversity recognizes that "culture is at the heart of contemporary debates about identity, social cohesion, and the development of a knowledge-based economy" (International Journal of Cultural Property 2002).[7] Mgomezulu (2004), speaking of site museums in general, argues that by paying "particular attention to preserving or reinterpreting memories and history in relation to issues of the present ... they contribute to developing cultural equilibriums which are necessary for managing and living in peace." He goes on to specifically observe that "[i]n Latin America, more than anywhere else, the integration of local communities and cultural minorities into the life of the museum [is] one of the most important factors in changing the missions of the museum and its reorientation toward socioeconomic objectives." This is well documented in *Archaeological Site Museums in Latin America*.

If we accept the premise that construction of a strong (albeit invented) identity is important for an emotionally fulfilling life (not to mention the economic perquisites discussed above), then site museums are important at the local and regional level because of the role they may play in identity construction. The "new museology" (Vergo 1989) is especially concerned with community development (Mayrand 1984, 1985) and recognizes the need for creation of local museums that "actually involve the community in developing an appreciation of its own places" (Walsh 1992:161).

But identity construction and its related sense of place are not just phenomenological pleasantries, undertaken nostalgically and without cost. They are highly political, spatially assertive, and contestatory social acts (for example, Appadurai 1996). Way (1993: 125), for instance, has observed of regional and indigenous museums that "[t]o the extent that indigenous identity is not subsumed to national citizenship, these museums will reflect a discourse between nationalist representatives in museum administrations and representatives of the varieties of indigenous peoples within the national borders. In any event, such efforts depend on the tolerance of cultural pluralism and internal ethnic political stability." For Latin America I would rephrase Way's statement and apply it to site museums to mean that these museums, by their very location, are provincial and local: they are not in national capitals, and site preservation is such that they are typically in the countryside/non-urban areas where non-elites—often indigenous or descendants therefrom—reside and constitute the majority of the population. This essentially rural location is also the implicit premise of Riviére's (1985) "ecomuseums"[8] although this need not be the case (see, for example, Duitz 1992; González and Tonelli 1992; Jones 1992; Tchen 1992 [all of whom are dealing with urban community museums]; see also Hayden 1999).

Ecomuseums are implicated in the new museology, a museology that espouses "the idea of the 'active' museum—museums which are concerned with involving people in the processes of both representation and interpretation" (Walsh 1992: 162). Riviére (1985) argued that the ecomuseum is the mirror with which the emplaced local population views itself to discover its own historically contingent image/identity (that is, encompassing preceding peoples in the territory), and a mirror held up to visitors so that they will understand and respect this emplaced local population. It is very much a "social construction of space" paradigm in the sense of Lefebvre (1991). As explained by Walsh (1992: 164), "The ecomuseum is . . . concerned with the facilitation of an understanding, or awareness, of how places are a construction of human interaction with environments across time and space."

Marliac (1997) has suggested multifarious relationships between archaeology and development (understood as "in developing countries"). He sees identity as a core problem of development, arguing that any improvement in standard of living (usually the desired outcome of development) will necessarily be effected through sociocultural transformations impacting "people who possess an identity and a history" (Marliac 1997: 325). Because archaeology "rebuilds past societies as neither history nor ethnology can do, its intervention in development is clearly solicited" (Marliac 1997: 325–6). However, as is well known, the archaeological operationalization of the concept of identity is neither procedurally nor theoretically unambiguous (see, for example, Jones 1997; Olsen 2001; Shennan 1989, to name only the most obvious examples), and a host of ethical dilemmas may result from the archaeological identity enterprise (for example, Barkan and Bush 2002; Meskell 1998; Schmidt and Patterson 1995), not to mention outcomes of outright violence (see, for example, Arnold 1992). Although Marliac strays from his title's topic, the issue is important, and Marliac is correct in recognizing the fundamental importance of identity construction as offered by archaeologists and as manipulated by a public.

Site museums can be a rallying point for the generation of local identity, and this is precisely what has happened in some of the case studies presented in *Archaeological Site Museums in Latin America* (Silverman 2006a). For instance, the town of Chepén, near San José de Moro, has erected a life-size statue of the Priestess of San José de Moro excavated by Luis Jaime Castillo and Christopher B. Donnan (Donnan and Castillo 1992; Castillo Butters and Holmquist Pachas 2006). Chepén is claiming a Mochica identity; some townsfolk speak of the priestess as the fiancée of the excavated Lord of Sipán in Lambayeque (Krzysztof Makowski, pers. comm. 2004), thereby generating a neo-Mochica territory and tourism corridor covering the northern range of the archaeological Mochica (see also Elera and Shiada 2006). In other areas, the living local community does not claim to be the descendant community of an archaeological civilization but takes significant pride of place based on the local pre-Columbian remains. Of course, in the cases of Copán (Mortensen 2006), Kuntur Wasi (Onuki 2006), Pukara (Paredes Eyzaguirre et al. 2006), Chiripa (Hastorf 2006), and Cusco (Silverman 2006b), many people living in and around the great archaeological sites are indeed the descendants of those who created the monuments.

Conclusion

Museums began in Europe as the famous cabinets of curiosities and were displays of elite knowledge and power (see, for example, Findlen 1994). Even as they and royal collections developed into modern museums, these museums remained elite private institutions until their democratization through, for instance, the French Revolution's Louvre (McClellan 1994) and the founding of Oxford's Ashmolean Museum (1683) and the British Museum (1759)—although admission to the English museums took some determination and perseverance even 123 years after being opened to the public (Ames 1992: 20); the Victorian disciplinary project resolved this problem, albeit through elaboration of the much-criticized exhibitionary complex (see Bennett 1995: 59–88). Stocking's (1985: 7) historical survey of museum development documents the establishment in Europe of a number of museums of a more anthropological nature during the first half of the nineteenth century, such as in Denmark (1816), Leiden (1837), and Petrograd (1836).

After the US Civil War, there was a burst of art museum construction in the North, as exemplified by New York's Metropolitan Museum of Art (Duncan 1995: 48–71). Despite being virtual palaces built by the country's wealthy and powerful families, these fine art museums were public institutions, contradictions about access notwithstanding. With the interdigitation of the exhibitionary complex and the growth of anthropology, museums began a new phase of their existence in the United States, quickly evolving into such recognizable scientific (natural history, anthropology) institutions as the Field Museum of Natural History in Chicago, originally the Field Columbian Museum, arising out of the 1893 World's Columbian Exposition. But this was not the only influence on their formation. The US Smithsonian National Museum of Natural History was founded in the 1850s explicitly as a research and educational institution (Ames 1992: 26). By contrast, Phineas T. Barnum's American Museum was intended to be a profit-making business venture (Ames 1992: 26). The two kinds of museums—art and natural history/anthropology—still dominate the cultural scene and coexist with moments of crossover and redundancy (as when the Metropolitan Museum of Art acquired the collections of the Museum of Primitive Art). The differences in their scripts are still notable, even outside the United States, as Manzanilla points out in her essay on Teotihuacan's site museums (Manzanilla 2006).

In the English-language literature, very little scholarship has been directed at Latin American museums of any kind (see, for example, Errington 1993,1998; Florescano 1993). In general, independence from Spain led to the rapid establishment of national museums throughout Latin America as anti-colonial statements of autonomy that reached back to the pre-Hispanic era to ground and legitimate the new nation state. Florescano (1993: 87) is clear that in Mexico there was a "compulsive need to create a historical and cultural identity for the new nation" and that out of this arose "the idea of establishing a Mexican museum." The Mexican Revolution at the beginning of the twentieth century again created the need for a new national museum, for the oppressed indigenous peoples of Mexico had come to be seen as historical protagonists, and "pre-Hispanic civilization [was situated] at the very base of the history of Mexico" (Florescano 1993: 97, 98). Archaeological excavations at Teotihuacan were conducted "to bring out the founding nature and original character of the ancient indigenous civilizations" (Florescano 1993: 98). The great new Museo Nacional de Antropología, inaugurated in 1964, was the culmination of the Mexican Revolution ideology that "recognized the pre-Hispanic past in its historical and cultural development and in the traditions of indigenous and popular groups, values and symbols that identified them as the genuine part of the nation's soul" (Florescano 1993: 99).

In Peru, too, "antiquities ... were in the thoughts of the founders of the nation, the sacred symbols of our history and basis of a national idea" (Ravines 1989: 23). Not only was the Inca past (at that time the many pre-Hispanic archaeological cultures were undifferentiated) mobilized for the construction of national identity, but less than one year after independence, a law was passed declaring that Peru's ancient monuments were property of the nation "because they pertain to the glory that is derived from them" (Supreme Decree Number 80, 2 April 1822, cited in Ravines 1989: 23).

Today, site museums in Latin America are being created and valorized as local iterations of these nationalist sentiments, as first lines of defense in the protection of cultural (archaeological) patrimony, and as new promoters of economic development in their immediate regions. Moreover, as the contributors to *Archaeological Site Museums in Latin America* (Silverman 2006a) recognize, archaeologists, local communities, and site museums are tightly enmeshed in cross-cutting webs of intercultural understanding and misunderstanding pertaining to cultural heritage management, economic development, political empowerment, and production of personal and group identity. Our awareness and involvement is a fairly recent development in archaeological professional practice, and one that is so important that Shackel and Chambers (2004) specifically call it "public archaeology as applied anthropology" (also see comments by Castillo and Holmquist 2006 and Pyburn 2006). Archaeologists are increasingly associated with "community-based activities that seek to empower historically subordinated groups" (Shackel 2004: 1)—the kinds of groups that characterize the Latin American populations within which site museums are embedded.

Site museums are another fascinating stage in the centuries-old and varied history of museums around the world, exemplifying the remarkable flexibility of this institution. Negotiating the tensions between tradition and modernity, and locality and globalization in the societies in which they are found, site museums offer a new perspective on some of the most important issues impacting Latin America and the developing countries of the world.

Notes

1 Thomas (2002: 132) says that "an archaeology museum is anything that publicly presents something important from the past. America contains thousands of such museums, from the largest urban natural history museums to major archaeological sites like Cahokia and Chaco Canyon."
2 Nasca written with an *s* refers to the archaeological culture. Nazca written with a *z* refers to the town and geographical area of the Río Grande de Nazca drainage.
3 In late July 2004, several pre-Nasca tombs, known as *cavernas*, were looted within throwing distance of the Paracas Site Museum. This looting, however, was quickly detected and found to be the work of an eccentric schoolteacher from the region,

4   The museum-community relationship at Kuntur Wasi can be positively compared to Riviére's (1985: 182) concept of "ecomuseum" as "an instrument conceived, fashioned, and operated jointly by a public authority and a local population. The public authority's involvement is through the experts, facilities and resources it provides; the local population's involvement depends on its aspirations, knowledge and individual approach."
5   Kirshenblatt-Gimblett (1998: 168) argues that the "inability of sites to tell their own story authorizes the interpretation project itself." A site of extraordinary beauty such as Machu Picchu could be an exception. That site currently does not have a site museum. Indeed, I would argue that for tourists the essence of the visit to Machu Picchu is the emotional-aesthetic experience of it. In my observations, many tourists are not overly concerned with the archaeological details of the site. Indeed, that information may conflict with their own constructions and performances of meaning, particularly among those with New Age beliefs.
6   The Royal Tombs of Sipán Museum falls somewhat outside this parameter of "greatly scaled down" inasmuch as it is a multimillion-dollar state-of-the-art facility designed by a distinguished Peruvian architect, Celso Prado Pastor. The museum is at the heart of plans for a comprehensive north coast tourist circuit or corridor.
7   An excellent framing discussion on heritage and identity is provided by Lowenthal (1994). The relationship between cultural heritage and construction of identity/production of locality is contravened by documents such as the 1972 World Heritage Convention, which argue for the universality of cultural heritage (for discussions about "universality" see Cleere 2001 and Omland 1997, inter alia).
8   This is an infelicitous term because it suggests the meaning "ecological museums." In fact, the term *ecomuseum* refers to museums "concerned with the total ecology and environment, natural and human, of a defined locality" (Boylan 1990: 32). A good site museum would fulfill this mission. Thus, because of the semantic confusion created by the term *ecomuseum*, I will not use it.

References

Alva, W. (1988) Discovering the New World's richest unlooted tomb. *National Geographic*, 174(4): 510–48.

Ames, M.M. (1992) *Cannibal Tours and Glass Boxes: The Anthropology of Museums*. Vancouver: University of British Colombia Press.

Appadurai. A. (1996) Then production of locality. In: A. Appadurai (ed.), *Modernity at Large*. Minneapolis: University of Minnesota Press, pp. 178–99.

Arnold, B. (1992) Germany's Nazi past: how Hitler's archaeologists distorted European prehistory to justify racist and territorial goals. *Archaeology*, July/August: 30–37.

Barkan, E. and Bush, R. eds. (2002) *Claiming the Stones, Naming the Bones: Cultural Property and the Negotiation of National and Ethnic Identity*. Los Angeles: Getty Research Institution.

Bennett, T. (1995) *The Birth of the Museum*. London: Routledge.

Bond, G.C. and Gilliam, A. eds. (1994) *Social Construction of the Past*. London: Routledge.

Boylan, P. (1990) Museums and cultural identity. *Museums Journal*, 90(10): 29–34.

Castillo Butters, L.J. and Holmquist Pachas, U.S. (2006) Modular site museums and sustainable community development at San José de Moro, Peru. In: H. Silverman (ed.), *Archaeological Site Museums in Latin America*. Gainsville: University Press of Florida, pp. 130–55.

Cleere, H.F. (1989) Introduction: the rationale of archaeological heritage management. In: H.F. Cleere (ed.), *Archaeological Heritage Management in the Modern World*. London: Unwin Hyman, pp. 1–19.

——(2001) The uneasy bedfellows: universality and cultural heritage. In: R. Layton, P.G. Stone and J. Thomas (eds.), *Destruction and Conservation of Cultural Property*. London: Routledge, pp. 22–9.

Donnan, C.B. and Castillo, L.J. (1992) Finding the tomb of a Moche priestess. *Archaeology*, 45(6): 38–42.

Duitz, M. (1992) The soul of a museum: commitment to community at the Brooklyn Children's Museum. In: I. Karp, C. Mullen Kreamer, and S.D. Lavine (eds.), *Museums and Communities: The Politics of Public Culture*. Washington, D.C.: Smithsonian Institution Press, pp. 242–61.

Duncan, C. (1995) *Civilizing Rituals: Inside Public Art Museums*. London: Routledge.

Elera, C.G. and Shiada, I. (2006) The Sicán Museum: guardian, promoter, and investigator of the Sicán culure and the Muchik identity. In: H. Silverman (ed.), *Archaeological Site Museums in Latin America*. Gainsville: University Press of Florida, pp. 217–33.

Errington, S. (1993) Progressivist stories and the Pre-Colombian past: notes on Mexico and the United States. In: E. Hill Boone (ed.), *Collecting the Pre-Colombian Past*. Washington, D.C.: Dumbarton Oaks Research Library and Collection, pp. 209–49.

——(1998) Nationalizing the Pre-Colombian past in Mexico and the United States. In: S. Errington (ed.), *The Death of Authentic Primitive Art and Other Tales of Progress*. Berkeley: University of California Press, pp. 161–87.

Findlen, P. (1994) *Possessing Nature: Museums Collecting, and Scientific Culture in Early Modern Italy*. Berkeley: University of California Press.

Florescano, E. (1993) The creation of the Museo Nacional de Antropología of Mexico and its scientific, educational, and political purposes. In: E. Hill Boone (ed.), *Collecting the Pre-Colombian Past*. Washington, D.C.: Dumbarton Oaks Research Library and Collection, pp. 81–103.

Gathercole, P. and Lowenthal, D. eds. (1990) *The Politics of the Past*. London: Unwin Hyman.

González, A.M. and Tonelli, E.A. (1992) Compañeros and partners: the CARA Project. In: I. Karp, C. Mullen Kreamer, and S.D. Lavine (eds.), *Museums and Communities: The Politics of Public Culture*. Washington, D.C.: Smithsonian Institution Press, pp. 262–84.

Hastorf, C.A. (2006) Building the community museum at Chiripa, Bolivia. In: H. Silverman (ed.), *Archaeological Site Museums in Latin America*. Gainsville: University Press of Florida, pp. 85–98.

Hayden, D. (1999) *The Power of Place: Urban Landscapes as Public History*. Cambridge, Mass.: MIT Press.

Henderson, J. (2001) *Museum Architecture*. Gloucester, Mass.: Rockport Publishers.

Hewison, R. (1987) *The Heritage Industry: Britain in a Climate of Decline*. London: Methuen.

Hudson, K. (1987) *Museums of Influence.* Cambridge: Cambridge University Press.
ICOMOS (International Council on Monuments and Sites) (1967) The Norms of Quito. Available at: http://www.icomos.org.
——(1996) The Declaration of San Antonio. Available at: http://www.icomos.org.
Jones, J.P. (1992) The colonial legacy and the community: the Gallery 33 Project. In: I. Karp, C. Mullen Kreamer, and S.D. Lavine (eds.), *Museums and Communities: The Politics of Public Culture.* Washington, D.C.: Smithsonian Institution Press, pp. 221–41.
Jones, S. (1997) *The Archaeology of Ethnicity: Constructing Identities in the Past and Present.* London: Routledge.
Kirkpatrick, S.D. (1992) *Lords of Sipán: A True Story of Pre-Inca Tombs, Archaeology, and Crime.* New York: William Morrow.
Kirshenblatt-Gimblett, B. (1998) *Destination Culture: Tourism, Museums, and Heritage.* Berkeley: University of California Press.
Kohl, P.L. and Fawcett, C. eds. (1995) *Nationalism, Politics, and the Practice of Archaeology.* Cambridge: Cambridge University Press.
Layton, R. ed. (1989a) *Conflict in the Archaeology of Living Traditions.* London: Unwin Hyman.
——(1989b) *Who Needs the Past: Indigenous Values and Archaeology.* London: Unwin Hyman.
Lefebvre, H. (1991) *The Production of Space.* Oxford: Blackwell.
Lowenthal, D. (1994) Identity, heritage, and history. In: J.R. Gillis (eds.), *Commemorations: The Politics of National Identity.* Princeton, N.J.: Princeton University Press, pp. 41–57.
Lury, C. (1997) The objects of travel. In: C. Rojek and J. Urry (eds.), *Touring Cultures: Transformations of Travel and Theory.* London: Routledge, pp. 75–95.
Lynott, M.J. (1997) Ethical principles and archaeological practice: development of an ethics policy. *American Antiquity,* 62(4): 589–99.
Lynott, M.J. and Wylie, A. eds. (2000) *Ethics in American Archaeology: Challenges for the 1990s.* Washington, D.C.: Society for American Archaeology.
Manzanilla, L. (2006) The site museums at Teotihuacan, Mexico: the view of art historians versus the view of archaeologists. In: H. Silverman (ed.), *Archaeological Site Museums in Latin America.* Gainsville: University Press of Florida, pp. 21–9.
Marliac, A. (1997) Archaeology and development: a difficult dialogue. *International Journal of Historical Archaeology,* 1(4): 323–37.
Mayrand, P. (1984) A new concept of museology in Quebec. *Muse,* 2(1): 33, 36–7.
——(1985) The New Museology proclaimed. *Museum International,* 148: 200–01.
McClellan, A. (1994) *Inventing the Louvre: Art, Politics, and the Origins of the Modern Museum in Eighteenth-Century Paris.* Berkeley: University of California Press.
Meskell, L. ed. (1998) *Archaeology Under Fire.* London: Routledge.
Mgomezulu, G. (2004) Editorial: the site museum. *Museum International,* 223: 4–6.
Mortensen, L. (2006) Experiencing Copán: the authenticity of stone. In: H. Silverman (ed.), *Archaeological Site Museums in Latin America.* Gainsville: University Press of Florida, pp. 47–63.
Nagin, C. (1990) The Peruvian gold rush. *Art and Antiques,* May: 98–145.
Olsen, B.J. (2001) The end of history? Archaeology and the politics of identity in a globalized world. In: R. Layton, P.G. Stone, and J. Thomas (eds.), *Destruction and Conservation of Cultural Property.* London: Routledge, pp. 42–54.

Omland, A. (1997) World Heritage and the Relationship between the Global and Local. M.A. thesis.

Onuki, Y. (2006) The Kuntur Wasi Museum in northern Peru. In: H. Silverman (ed.), *Archaeological Site Museums in Latin America*. Gainsville: University Press of Florida, pp. 64–71.

Onuki, Y., Kato, Y. and Inokuchi, K. (1995) Las excavaciones en Kuntur Wasi: la primera temporada, 1988–1990. In: Y. Onuki (ed.), *Kuntur Wasi y Cerro Blanco: Dos Sitios del Formativo en el Norte del Perú*. Tokyo: Hokusensha, pp. 1–126.

Paredes Eyzaguirre, G.R., Fattorini Murillo, G., and Klarich, E. (2006) The Tourist Circuit Project at Pukara, Peru: perspectives from a local site museum, In: H. Silverman (ed.), *Archaeological Site Museums in Latin America*. Gainsville: University Press of Florida, pp. 72–84.

Pyburn, K.A. (2006) Exhibiting archaeology: site museums and cultural resource management in Latin America. In: H. Silverman (ed.), *Archaeological Site Museums in Latin America*. Gainsville: University Press of Florida, pp. 256–66.

Ravines, R. (1989) *Los Museos del Perú: Breve Historia y Guía*. Lima: Instituto Nacional de Cultura.

Riviére, G.H. (1985) The ecomuseum: an evolutive definition. *Museum International*, 148: 182–3.

Schmidt, P.R. and Patterson, T.C. eds. (1995) *Making Alternative Histories: The Practice of Archaeology and History in Non-Western Settings*. Santa Fe, N. Mex.: School of American Research.

Shackel, P.A. (2004) Working with communities: heritage development and applied archaeology. In: P.A. Shackel and E.J. Chambers (eds.), *Places in Mind: Public Archaeology as Applied Anthropology*. New York: Routledge, pp. 1–16.

Shackel, P.A. and Chambers, E.J. eds. (2004) *Places in Mind: Public Archaeology as Applied Anthropology*. New York: Routledge.

Shennan, S. (1989) Introduction: archaeological approaches to cultural identity. In: S. Shennan (ed.), *Archaeological Approaches to Cultural Identity*. London: Unwin Hyman, pp. 1–13.

Silverman, H. (1991) The Paracas problem: archaeological perspectives. In: A. Paul (ed.), *Paracas Art and Architecture: Object and Context in South Coastal Peru*. Iowa City: University of Iowa Press, pp. 347–415.

——(2002) Touring ancient times: the present and presented past in contemporary Peru. *American Anthropologiost*, 104(3): 881–902.

——(2005) Embodied heritage, identity poltics, and tourism. *Anthropology and Humanism*, 30(2): 141–55.

——ed. (2006a) *Archaeological Site Museums in Latin America*. Gainsville: University Press of Florida

——(2006b) The historic district of Cusco as an open-air site museum. In: H. Silverman (ed.), *Archaeological Site Museums in Latin America*. Gainsville: University Press of Florida, pp. 159–83.

Silverman, H. and Proulx, D.A. (2002) *The Nasca*. Malden, Mass.: Blackwell.

Solomon, D. (2001) Forget the art—it's all about the building. *New York Times Magazine*, December 9.

Stocking, G.W. Jr. (1985) Essays on museums and material culture. In: G.W. Stocking Jr. (ed.), *Objects and Others: Essays on Museums and Material Culture*. Madison: University of Wisconsin Press, pp. 3–14.

Tchen, J.K.W. (1992) Creating a dialogic museum: the Chinatown History Museum experiment. In: I. Karp, C. Mullen Kreamer, and S.D. Lavine (eds.), *Museums and Communities: The Politics of Public Culture*. Washington, D.C.: Smithsonian Institution Press, pp. 285–326.

Tello, J.C. and Mejía Xesspe, T. (1967) Historia de los Museos Nacionales del Perú. *Arqueológicas*, 10: 1–268.

Thomas, D.H. (2002) Roadside ruins: does America still need archaeology museums? In: B.J. Little (ed.), *Public Benefits of Archaeology*. Gainesville: University of Florida Press, pp. 130–45.

Uhle, M. (1914) The Nazca pottery of ancient Peru. *Proceedings of the Davenport Academy of Sciences*, 13: 1–16.

Vergo, P. ed. (1989) *The New Museology*. London: Reaktion.

Vitelli, K.D. ed. (1996) *Archaeological Ethics*. Walnut Creek, CA: AltaMira Press.

Walsh, K. (1992) *The Representation of the Past: Museums and Heritage in the Post-Modern World*. London: Routledge.

Way, J.E. (1993) The modern gallery exhibition as a form of Western-Indigenous discourse. In: D.S. Whitten and N.E. Whitten (eds.), *Imagery and Creativity: Ethnoaesthetics and Art Worlds in the Americas*. Tucson: University of Arizona Press, pp. 108–27.

Zimmerman, L.J., Vitelli, K.D., and Hollowell-Zimmer, J. eds. (2003a) *Ethical Issues in Archaeology*. Walnut Creek, CA: AltaMira Press.

Zimmerman, L.J. (2003b) Introduction. In: L.J. Zimmerman, K.D. Vitelli and J. Hollowell-Zimmer (eds.), *Ethical Issues in Archaeology*. Walnut Creek, CA: AltaMira Press, pp. xi–xvi.

Part III, Section 3

New archaeology museum architecture

Chapter 26

The new Acropolis Museum
Where the visual feast trumps education

Katie Rask

The glittering new Acropolis Museum opened on June 20, 2009, amidst a flurry of international attention and press coverage. The need for a new museum was already apparent in the 1970s, but it took the intervening 30 years to become a reality. The new structure, designed by New York's Bernard Tschumi and curated by Dimitrios Pandermalis, replaces a predecessor that first opened its doors in 1874 and welcomed travellers, families, and archaeological superstars for more than a hundred years.

The new incarnation is a far cry from its dark and crowded ancestor. Located to the south of the Acropolis on Dionysiou Areopagitou, it rests on huge pylons above a recently excavated portion of the ancient city. Visitors, after passing through a TSA-worthy security apparatus, move up a wide ramp lined with artifacts from the Acropolis's slopes. The second floor is shaped like a colonnaded temple and contains the Archaic sculpture room, several displays that highlight the Periklean building program, and glowing niches set into the walls for smaller finds. The space is organized both thematically and chronologically, beginning in the Bronze Age and ending with a gleaming display of seventh-century CE gold coins. The escalators, placed within the central "cella," glide up to the top floor, where one can walk among the Parthenon marbles while enjoying a spectacular view. The museum has two gift shops, a well-priced café, and a balcony whose bold lunge toward the Acropolis provides an undisturbed view of both the Parthenon and the meticulously coiffed olive grove included in the museum's grounds.

Most striking about the artifacts on display are their sheer number: about 4,000 – too many to have ever graced the older and much smaller museum. New visitors will be enthralled by the veritable forest of Archaic sculptures. Any questions can be answered by the discreetly hovering docents, employed specifically to wander the museum and engage people in conversation. Those not troubled by vertigo will be thrilled to walk on glass floors above the newly excavated remains of the Late Antique city; walkways are planned that will allow guests to climb down among the ancient streets. Those long familiar with the previous Acropolis Museum will see well-known, old friends—the Kritios Boy, the Bluebeard Pediment, the

Source: *Near Eastern Archaeology*. The American Schools of Oriental Research, 2010. 73(1): 56-59.

Figure 26.1 The Erechtheion's caryatids on display, now visible from all angles. Courtesy of the Acropolis Museum.

Figure 26.2 The Parthenon Gallery interacts with the Athenian Acropolis. Courtesy of Bernard Tschumi Architects.

Rampin Rider—but will also be delighted by the newer additions: the Seated Scribes, the painted votive plaques, the hordes of wedding vessels (*loutrophoroi*). Expect to be pleasantly surprised by details not normally visible in a display of this sort such as the chisel marks on the back of the Parthenon's frieze blocks or the elaborate and lush braids trailing past the shoulders of the Caryatids. Especially charming is the Hellenistic foundation pyre that greets visitors upon entering; in a modern foundation rite, a last pot was interred in the pyre and the deposit symbolically sealed in the glass floor during the televised opening ceremony.

The objects themselves are gorgeously illuminated by the natural light. The purified "low iron" glass used to make up the walls eliminates the hot summer's glare and adds instead a soft, silvery texture to the light. Thanks to the spacious 150,000 square feet, the sculptures and architectural fragments stand away from walls and corners and can be minutely examined from all angles. Other artifacts, such as metal attachments, votive terracottas, and pottery, are displayed in recessed cases in the east and west walls; the handful of free-standing cases are small and serve as accents to display one or two particular artifacts.

As a whole, the building is a spectacular example of a site-specific museum. The dialogue between the museum and the adjacent Acropolis is at once subtle and unmistakable, already evident as one takes in the exterior of the building. Towering above visitors, its size and shape are akin to the huge limestone outcrop that it celebrates. The wide ramp in the interior, lined with artifacts from the slopes, recalls the entrance ramp that once led supplicants upward to the sanctuary; present-day crowds make the pilgrimage much like the ancient Athenians. In the Archaic sculpture room, the white luster of marble contrasts with the slate grey of the concrete piers and walls, recalling the interaction of the white Pentelic marble and grey Eleusinian limestone on the Acropolis, so beloved of architecture aficionados.

The topmost floor, aligned at an off-kilter angle that directly mirrors the neighboring Parthenon, is a breath-taking achievement. A magnificent, panoramic vista greets the visitor upon exiting the central "cella." The concrete buildings of the modern city stretch to the south, while to the north the green hills of Lykabittos, Philopappos, and the Acropolis stand close enough to touch, as if artfully arranged by long-ago geological forces for our viewing pleasure. The sight is so impressive that one has to wrench one's gaze back toward the display, to what many consider the entire ideological underpinning of the museum: the Parthenon Marbles (Elgin Marbles), both the originals that remained in Athens and the casts of those still in the British Museum. The room's form abstractly replicates the sculptured façade of the Parthenon, making it possible to wander along the temple's faux colonnade, looking in toward the famed marble figures. With their original, fifth-century BCE resting place visible beyond the glass walls, the sculptures of the frieze, the metopes and the pediments have been arranged around the central cella and hung at several heights and planes, creating a segmented surface through which the visitor can walk. This spatial partitioning encourages viewers to zigzag in and out of the Parthenon's external layers in a way never before possible. The design has, in fact, created an entirely new way to experience the temple; it adds a distinct, schematic, and original labyrinth that visitors can explore mere minutes after gazing at, photographing, but never entering, the temple on the Acropolis itself.

The casts of the missing pedimental sculptures, the center of so much media attention, stand at either end of the Parthenon Gallery, facing east and west, as they did in antiquity; now, however, the modern viewer stands practically nose to nose with the classical Greek gods of the pediments. One could not imagine a more remarkable and intimate way to see and experience the Parthenon Marbles, a point made abundantly clear in the international media blitz surrounding the museum's opening.

Particularly characteristic of the Parthenon Gallery, and the museum at large, is the extensive use of glass, which floods the interior with natural light. As anyone who visits will notice, there is a particular character to the light that beats down on the Acropolis, something that the museum's architect has exploited to great effect. Glass is everywhere. Not only are the walls composed of it, but so also are sections of the floor and ceiling. With its three levels and a basement housing an excavation, the glass building becomes a symbolic manifestation of an archaeological site, a three-dimensional embodiment of stratigraphy. Looking down is a reminder of the many ancient strata that lie beneath the modern city streets. Looking up, one sees a living palimpsest with the surreal scampering of children on the floor above. Of course, as eye-popping as the effect may be, the designers were clearly not women wearing skirts on a hot Athenian day. Visitors are strongly advised to dress accordingly!

Perhaps because of its modern sensibilities, the museum's design seems to celebrate the nineteenth-century view of ancient Greece, highlighting rationality and simplicity. The lines are clean and the forms basic. Even the muted color palette serves to create a mood reflecting the idealized classical Acropolis—no gaudy ancient color-clashing or Byzantine ochres here. Instead, the shades are cool: the hard grey of limestone, the dusky blue of the afternoon sky, the cream-colored marble of the temples. Yet, for some, the color palette, combined with the museum's concrete, metal, and glass, might have a cold and sterile feel; the architectonic lines, the industrial girders, the metallic lining of the artifact cases—these may more readily bring to mind the skeletal cranes and hardware of the Parthenon's reconstruction project than any classical past.

While the aesthetic experience is stunning, it seems to have dictated and controlled the role of pedagogy in the museum's design. The press pamphlet mentions that "Signage has been developed to be both visible and yet to be as discrete as possible, recognizing that signage and wayfinding must not compete with the artifacts" (*Acropolis Museum Media Kit*, 2009: 4). The signs and labels are easy to miss, because they fade into the background and bear only regular, black text. The lack of photographs, illustrated reconstructions, and other drawings is conspicuous, especially given the rich photographic tradition available from the excavations, as well as the hundreds of drawings and paintings showing the later life of the Acropolis. There are very few maps to aid orientation, although three charming and delicate models of the Acropolis are a pleasure to see; one can only wish that they had been larger, so as to compete with the more massive, beautifully articulated, and gleaming-white models of the fifth-century Periklean buildings. The information provided by the signs is generally too vague and elementary, lacking in detail and with little attention given to chronology or disagreements in interpretation. For example, the function and contents of the Periklean buildings are ignored in favor of their architectural and sculptural details—there is no discussion of the altars beneath the Nike Temple, no mention of the scholarly

Figure 26.3 The Archaic Gallery on the second floor of the Acropolis Museum. Courtesy of the Acropolis Museum.

kerfuffle over whether the Parthenon was a temple, and no exhibit dedicated to the cult statues, not even that most famous product of Phidias, the Athena Parthenos. Fortunately, the objects from the sanctuaries on the slopes highlight daily life and the social function of the slope sanctuaries. These displays are especially strong on ancient marriage customs, gender roles, and the domestic experience. The slim discussion of ancient ritual, however, notably the Panathenaic procession, the sacrifices to Athena, and the various altars and cult statues on the Acropolis, is cause for disappointment. In short, the museum's approach to signage reflects a larger philosophy evident throughout: the artifacts are central, while historical and archaeological contexts pass to the wayside.

Melina Mercouri's campaign to retrieve the Parthenon Marbles, begun in 1983, continues in the Parthenon Gallery, where dull white plaster casts stand in place of the missing sculptures. Yet the sculptures removed by Elgin are not the only glaring omission from the Museum; one likely to receive more attention as time passes is the absence of entire periods of history. The displays officially cover

Figure 26.4 The entrance to the Acropolis Museum includes a view of the recent excavations. Courtesy of Bernard Tschumi Architects.

the Mycenaean through Roman periods, although the emphasis of the collection and its educational literature rests on the Archaic and Classical periods, a fact, one might argue, that was dictated more by the interests of the nineteenth-century excavators than by anything else. Still, even the geological history of the limestone outcrop and its position in the topography of the Mesogeion plain is not explored, so that the Acropolis is presented as having no connection at all to its wider landscape (a trend continued by the failure to connect the Acropolis's history in any way to the Agora or other parts of the ancient city). The Roman period is very poorly represented, both in objects and labelling, so that visitors will have no idea that a temple to Roma and Augustus stood among the Classical structures, or that Herodes Atticus once built a theater there in honor of his murdered wife. A beautifully filmed short video on the top floor is the only concession to the post-Roman Acropolis; computerized reconstructions give a delightful but extremely brief synopsis of the Parthenon's history up until Elgin's departure. Unfortunately, the video is too short to address the later history of the building in any depth, and it does not address the rest of the Acropolis. Most interested visitors will never know that the Parthenon became a sacred site for the Byzantine worship of the Theotokos (Mother of God); that in the medieval period the Acropolis was a fortified site, with a last remaining tower still standing to this day; that a mosque and minaret stood there in the midst of an Ottoman-era town; or that the Acropolis became a symbol of resistance during the Nazi occupation. The entire account of the archaeological excavation is summed up in one sentence. Ultimately, the museum's presentation of the history of the Acropolis effectively terminates with the Roman period, all but ignoring its subsequent life.

The museum's architecture, though it has its detractors, mirrors and reinterprets the limestone rock and its buildings in an enthralling and constantly surprising way. Moving through the building and among its artifacts is an encounter that is to be highly recommended. That experience, however, subsumed the didactic function of the museum. Those interested in exploring the archaeological history of the Acropolis, rather than just its art, will likely be disappointed. In the end, as an aesthetic experience, the new Acropolis Museum is a resounding triumph, but as a place to learn about the long, complex, and fascinating history of Athens's most important cultural landmark, it is a missed opportunity.

Chapter 27

Development and utilization of underground space for the protection of relics in the Yang Emperor Mausoleum of the Han Dynasty

Zhilong Chen, Ping Zhang, and Juxi Li

Connotations of cultural relics protection by means of underground space

Underground space can be characterized as protective, quakeproof, environmentally stable and insulated from the outside, which are favorable for the exhibition and preservation of cultural relics.

Compared with common architecture, underground space, completely enclosed or covered by soil, offers better protection from all kinds of natural disasters. It is part of the geosphere, differing from the above hydrosphere and aerosphere, and characterized by compactness and long-term stability of each component unit, making it much less vulnerable to the destructive effect of earthquakes than aboveground architecture. A large underground space is one or two grades higher in quakeproof capability than aboveground architecture of the same kind. Insulated from the ground, underground structures have excellent fireproof performance and with their few entrances and exits, they are safer than aboveground architecture. The advantages of placing some invaluable cultural relics underground are: most parts are not exposed to aboveground space; the limited entrances and exits make it easy to watch and inspect the relics, and therefore theft-proof; the powerful anti-disaster capability of underground space provides necessary safeguards when disaster occurs (Geng and Zhao 2001).

With underground architecture, functionally contradictory constructions can be set nearby, and the land no longer exploitable or already used can be put to good use. The deeper the underground structures are and the fewer openings, the better the effect of noise and quake insulation. The underground museum takes advantage of the nice insulation effect of the stratum to reduce noise index and promote the utilization of the environment.

Source: *Frontiers of Architecture and Civil Engineering in China*. Gaodeng Jiaoyu Chubanshe, 2007. 1(2): 229–233. Reproduced with permission of Springer Verlag.

Analysis of the utilization model of underground space in the construction of museums at home and abroad

Model 1: In the expansion projects of building relics at historical and cultural sites, the protection of the surrounding historical features makes it impossible to devote more space to display museum artifacts. In this case, the underground space may be the only recourse available.

The Louvre in Paris, one of the world-famous palaces, enjoys lobbies and halls with large capacity, which, however, are only suitable for the display of artwork. In terms of other functions for a large-scale art museum, there is much left to be desired. The need of expansion also arose from the scarcity of the internal management warehouses and research rooms and it was lagging increasingly further behind the standard of a modern museum. However, the fact that there was no more land for development around the Louvre, it was impossible to move to another place, and the regular distribution and perfect profile of the original palace permitted no additional structures on the ground. The eventually successful construction of an underground museum by using the underground space below the Napoleon Square retains the overall pattern of the classical architecture and at the same time meets the demand of the use of such a modern museum (Tong 2005).

In order to highlight the image of the general way-in and way-out, and provide natural lighting for the underground central hall, pyramid-shaped glass skylights that concurrently serve as the main entrance were designed at the crossing of two major axes of the original palace at the center of the Square, and the central hall thus becomes the main entrance and exit. With the glass skylights, the main entrance achieved harmony to a certain degree with the original palace (Chen and Wang 2005).

Model 2: To exhibit the relics of some site museums, because of the immovability of the ground sites, underground space must be developed, which is decided by the burial position of the relics (Gao 2004).

The exhibition of Emperor Qin's Terracotta Warriors and Horses is the world's largest underground military museum, and a site museum built on the original site for laying the terracotta warriors. The total area of Pit 1, 2, 3 is 34,730 m^2. All the terracotta figures are displayed in the 5-metre deep pits in the ground. The halls are arch-domed steel structures, and have over 20 supporting facilities such as the expanded relic warehouses, and the comprehensive exhibition halls of cultural relics. The safety of the relics and artifacts are guaranteed by good ventilation, lighting, fire-resistance, and theft-proof facilities.[1]

The destruction of the relics would mean that the site museum will lose its value of existence. The establishment of relic halls is one of the many protection methods, which applies to special cultural relics that have significant scientific value and are kept in good state. This method has the advantage of both effective protection and rational use, enabling not only those alive but also future generations to appreciate the basic characters of the cultural inheritance as well as to gain enlightenment and education.

Emperor Qin's Terracotta Warriors and Horses make use of an underground exhibition hall to protect the relics. Due to the original location of the burial sites, the pits of the natural relics are only 2–3m deep, so the entire building cannot be placed underground. The entrances and the exits have to be set on the ground, therefore, despite the protection of the relic pits by making use of the characteristics of underground space and various technical means, since the space for visitors and the Terracotta Warriors are not completely isolated, the pits are wholly exposed. Thus, the surface of some relics has been weathered, causing the loss of their original characters. To make it even worse, the ground building distorts the whole outlook of the surrounding environment, bringing into contradiction modern architecture and the protection of historical sites. Yet, the underground exhibition hall has played an important role in the protection of underground relics in terms of the cultural relic protection methods, display requirements, and evaluation criteria.

Development and utilization of underground space in the construction of the Museum of the Yang Emperor Mausoleum, Han Dynasty

The Museum of the Yang Emperor Mausoleum of the Han Dynasty lies next to the emperor mausoleum, in the northern suburb of Xi'an. It is an entirely underground construction, with a total floor area of 6,513m^2, and a quakeproof capacity of 8°. The ground, unchanged and covered with lawn, has soil 0.6m in depth. The ground of the main entrance hall is 6m lower than the ground level. The bottom of the outer-store pit is 7m from the ground. The principal part of the architecture exists in the first underground floor with a height of 6–9.9m. The depth of the underground museum is 13m (Figure 27.1)

The plain view drawing of the Han Yang Tomb is square. It faces east and lies in the west-central of the mausoleum. The main entrance to the exhibition hall is located north of Sima Road and of the same location as the Tomb. However, the best exposure of the underground constructions is southern, southeastern, or southwestern, which allows sunshine and natural light to shine into the depth of the architecture. The site of the museum takes into full consideration the protection of its overall historical pattern, and the interrelationship between the outer-store pit and the emperor's underground palace. The design depth and style of the main entrance not only provide good natural lighting but economize on energy. The main way-in and way-out of the exhibition hall are located at the 45° symmetrical point of the emperor's mausoleum, where the east and north outer-store pits meet. Considering the shared exit of the north and east exhibition halls in the future, such a practice connects the two halls, reducing visitors' time spent in repeatedly going from the ground to the underground via the connection between the underground space.

The primary and secondary entrances also take into account the possibility of future construction and connection with the outer-store pit by referring to and using the present primary and secondary entrances and lobbies. In the northern part of the sunk courtyard, broad openings can be adopted to let in sunshine. The construction form and materials of the museum further promote the penetration of natural light and sunshine. Tourists, after visiting the pits, can first enter the main entrance hall and subsided yards by way of the long ramp in the northwest corner of the lobby to have a rest before arriving at the ground. The exhibition hall has

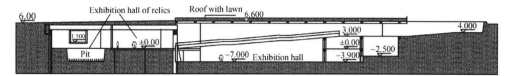

Figure 27.1 The section drawing of the underground museum.

three staircases, connecting both the entrance and exit. Except the partial subsided openings, there are no other protrusions on the ground, thus preserving the historical state of the mausoleum.

Precious historical relics have strict requirements for storing conditions such as temperature and humidity. The optimal environment for preserving relics is shown in Table 27.1. Temperature of underground space is insulated from the outside temperature. The deeper it is, the more stable the temperature is. In winter it is warm and in summer it is cool. With every increase of 10m in depth, temperature stability also rises. The perennial temperature of the shallow annex basement is 8–25°C, its relative humidity 60 per cent to 70 per cent, its summer temperatures 20–22°C, and relative warm winter temperature 12°C. The main body of the museum is underground and semi-underground structures, temperature control (18±2)°C, humidity control (55±5) per cent. The museum runs −13m underground, the maximum structural height of the relic hall is 1.15m, the net height of the lobby for rest is 8.25m. There is no column in the middle of the relics, and the largest span is 31m. This combination of appropriate width, height, and depth of design dimensions, in addition to light and sunlight penetration, and the design and size of the space connecting outdoor environment, decreases claustrophobia caused by underground activities, bringing both material and mental comfort. The Museum has made use of the environmental stability of the underground space: its shallow regionality not only provides a favourable protective environment for the optimal temperature and humidity of relics and pits, but also improves the level of people's activity underground.

The ground of the museum is decorated with carpets of green grass, offering a lawn for visitors to take a rest, maintaining the original natural features and

Table 27.1 Optimal environmental condition for preserving relics[2]

Name of exhibits	Temperature /°C	Difference in temperature	Humidity %	Difference in humidity/%	Illumination/ lux
Painting and calligraphy	18±2	2–5	50–55	5	50–100
Textile	18±2	2–5	50–55	5	50–100
Lacquerwork	18±2	2–5	60–65	5	150–200
Folk-custom	18±2	2–5	50–65	5	100–200
Metalwork	18±2	2–5	45–50	5	200–250

landscape, protecting the ground of the Han Dynasty and the historical environment of the mausoleum. Standing on the ground, people cannot see any architecture, such as houses, but only two tall tombs. The underground museum avoids damaging the overall features and primitive condition, beneficial to the protection of cultural heritage.

The underground protection and exhibition hall completely separates visitors from the relic pits and relics via advanced modern technology. With respect to the display mode, the scientific "Slovenian protective display model" is introduced in which a glass walk is laid on the trenches, and two long soil beams are removed from the side of the graves, providing two upper and lower channels for a close and multifaceted view. Cold lighting and advanced temperature and humidity conditioning equipment are fixed within, well protecting the painted terracotta, paintings, lacquerwork, silk, and other organic relics.

Many large site museums in China have different forms of display or exhibition halls: some are on the ground, some semi-underground, but because of the failure to completely insulate relics and artifacts from visitors, they are exposed to ultraviolet radiation, harmful gases, and dust intrusion. Inappropriate measures to control the temperature and humidity, in addition, cause the surface of the relics to weather, the colored paintings to change color, and organic relics to chap and disintegrate, incurring irreparable damages.

The museum makes use of the natural −7m underground relic pit, and takes into account relic protection characteristics of the underground space. Advanced technology and sophisticated equipment result in the good adaptability of the Museum to the underground space. The existing mode of seeking compatibility with the environment reminds tourists of the original state of the cultural relics newly unearthed and the integrity of the environmental outlook. The underground museum conforms to the earth's morphology or configuration under the natural ground, and its good natural condition being decisive for the use of underground space.

Conclusion

To sum up, from the perspective of the protection of the features of historical relics and sites, attention should be paid to the use of underground space for immovable cultural relics and sites. At such places, it is advisable to conduct pilot investigation and feasibility study, and to make full use of the protection traits of the underground space, based on the geological and natural conditions. Moving the functional space of the museum under construction underground saves ground space, meeting the need to preserve the original historical ground environment. In terms of energy conservation, the good heat insulation effect of rock and soil avoids the various ground factors that cause temperature variations. Placing all the architecture in the underground rock and soil is dramatically less energy-consuming than ground buildings. The energy-saving ratios of underground versus ground architecture are as follows: service architecture, 60 per cent; warehouse, 70 per cent; and semi-earthed underground structures, 69 per cent, hence the low environmental cost of the underground museum. With regard to technology, concerning the exact requirement of the interior environment, advanced technology and sophisticated equipment are necessary even for an outstanding underground environment. In fact, in many ways, sophisticated equipment plays a more satisfactory role when applied to underground relic protection due to the latter's thermal stability, quakeproof and isolating characteristic (Gideon et al. 2005).

In China, the restrictions of the economic and technological standards as well as people's different views on the protection of cultural heritage lead to the slow utilization and development of underground space for relic preservation. The common understanding is to avoid such development, causing the destruction of both surface and underground relics, bringing about high cost and construction intensity. Therefore, if not properly handled, trouble might occur. However, protection and development are interrelated, and development is a positive protection. We should learn from foreign experience, take our own into account, and at the same time fully understand the characteristics of the development and utilization of underground space, so that the underground space can have greater flexibility, adaptability, and freedom.

Notes

1 Emperor Qin's Terracotta Warriors and Horses Museum www.bmy.com.cn (in Chinese).
2 Huang Yalu. On the scientificity and necessity of the classifying storage of museum collections. Chinese Cultural Relic Academic Exchange Network www.chinacov.com (in Chinese).

References

Chen, Z. and Wang, Y. (2005) *The Urban Underground Space Planning*. Nanjing: Southeast University Press.
Gao, D. (2004) Underground space utilization for museum. *Architecture Journal*, 5: 66–8.
Geng, Y. and Zhao X. (2001) *The Urban Underground Space Architecture*. Harbin: Harbin Industrial University Publishing House.
Gideon, S.G. et al. (2005) *The Urban Underground Space Design*. Trans. F. Xu and H. Yu. Beijing: China Building Industry Press.
Tong, L. (2005) *The Underground Space and the Development of Urban Modernization*. Beijing: China Building Industry Press.

Part III, Section 4

Designing archaeology displays

Chapter 28

The Port Royal Project
A case study in the use of VR technology for the recontextualization of archaeological artifacts and building remains in a museum setting

Harry Helling, Charlie Steinmetz, Eric Solomon, and Bernard Frischer

Background

The Port Royal Project resulted from the collaboration of the UCLA Cultural Virtual Reality Laboratory (hereafter: CVRLab; www.cvrlab.org) and the Ocean Institute in Dana Point, California (hereafter: OI; www.oceaninstitute.org/). The work was initially sponsored and conceived by Charlie Steinmetz, a supporter of the lab and one of its project managers. Additional support was received from Spiegel TV. The chief modeller and researcher for the project was Natalie Tirrell. Training and supervising her was CVRLab Associate Director Dean Abernathy. Information about Port Royal was kindly provided by Laurel Breece (Long Beach City College), an archaeologist who has worked at Port Royal; and by Donny Hamilton, the Director of the Texas A&M Port Royal Project.

Port Royal was the principal English colony in Jamaica in the seventeenth century. The original settlement was begun as a naval base for British operations against the Spanish during the wars that continued for many decades in the 1600s in the Caribbean and elsewhere. Almost immediately, a small settlement of traders clustered around the fort, whose name was changed from Cromwell to Charles after news of the Restoration reached Jamaica in 1660. In that year, we also get our first census, which records 690 freemen and 50 slaves. In the next two decades, Port Royal became a crucial British naval base against the Spanish Main. Since the British Admiralty could not afford to send an adequate number of warships to Jamaica, the governors of Port Royal were forced to rely on the assistance of pirates like Henry Morgan in their prosecution of the war against Spain. Such

Source: *On the Road to Reconstructing the Past*. Computer Applications and Quantitative Methods in Archaeology (CAA). Proceedings of the 36th International Conference. Budapest, April 2–6, 2008. E. Jerem, R. Ferenc and V. Szerényi (eds.). Budapest: Archaeolingua, 2011. pp. 229–235.

pirates were called privateers, and with the peace treaty of 1680, the naval forces at Port Royal turned on their erstwhile allies, rid the area of pirates, and secured the Caribbean for commercial trading ships. Not surprisingly, the volume of trade and the size of the town mushroomed. By 1670, the census counted 2,181 inhabitants; 22 years later that number had grown to an estimated 6,500. Much of this growth reflected the increasing number of slaves brought from Africa. The slaves were needed both at Port Royal and on the interior plantations of Jamaica. The port served the interior plantations by exporting their rum and sugar while importing nearly everything else including silver, pewter, luxury clothing from Europe as well as timber from North America, and even silk and ceramics from faraway China. After the earthquake, the site was abandoned and was used only as a naval station. The town of Kingston was founded on the mainland and quickly grew to take Port Royal's place (on the history of Port Royal see Pawson and Buisseret 2000: 7–108).

A great deal of documentation survives that can be brought to bear on a model of the seventeenthcentury town: maps, views, property records, wills, and archaeological finds. In fact, it is possible to reconstruct not only the street grid but even to identify many of the structures by owner, function, chronology, and architectural style (see Pawson and Buisseret 2000, 109–164). Long after 1692, substantial remains of the town could be seen below the water in Kingston Bay. The first sightings are recorded in the nineteenth century, but the first serious survey of the remains was not undertaken until 1959. In the 1960s, further studies were undertaken by Norman Scott and Robert Marx. In the late 1960s, Philip Mayes surveyed the remains on land and worked out a sequence of scaled maps showing the development of the dockyards of Port Royal, which he then excavated in 1970. His work was continued by Anthony Priddy (for the history of archaeological investigations, see Pawson and Buisseret 2000: 203–210). From 1981 to 1990, Donny Hamilton and a team of underwater archaeologists from Texas A&M came to Port Royal to initiate new underwater studies.

Sponsor's goal for the project

As project sponsor and manager Charlie Steinmetz notes, there has been much discussion about using VR in museums but very few concrete projects involving true VR (as opposed to computer animations; on the distinction see, e.g. Vince 1998: 3–6). This lack is doubtless in large part the result of the high cost of VR systems, at least until Desktop VR became a reality in the last few years (cf., e.g., Pimentel and Teixera 1995). But another factor is the very conception of the museum, its mission in educating the public, and its understanding of how this role might best be accomplished (see, most recently Antinucci 2003, where strong arguments in favour of the use of VR are presented).

Steinmetz came to the Port Royal Project through three overlapping interests in the educational work of the OI, in archaeological education, and in the promotion of literacy. Knowing that the Ocean Institute was keenly aware of its responsibility to educate the public, and that its approach to learning could be ultimately traced to the constructivist theories of Jerome Bruner and others (see, e.g., www.instructionaldesign.org/theories/constructivist.html), Steinmetz thought that it would be the most appropriate venue in Southern California for an experiment to see if VR could live up to its promise in a museum setting; his buildings at the intersection of Queen Street and Lime Street just to the north of the area explored by Marx. The excavations brought to light many buildings and articles of everyday life.

As Pawson and Buisseret note, "the history of Port Royal is better documented than that of most English towns of comparable size for that period" (Pawson and Buisseret 2000: xiii). Study of the town's history can thus shed a great deal of light on the everyday life and customs of the first British settlements in the New World. Since Texas A&M generously lent a number of its typical small finds to the Ocean Institute, it was natural that the Institute would take a special interest in this history and in ways of presenting it to its primary audience of schoolchildren from all over the Southern California area.

Hunch was that because of its immersivity, interactivity, and ability to provide a compelling simulation of the lost world, such as seventeenthcentury Port Royal, VR could be a useful tool for arousing students' curiosity about the Port Royal underwater excavations some of whose small finds are on display at the Ocean Institute. He also thought that curiosity arousal might be a stimulus to improved reading skills, on the assumption that once a student was exposed in an effective way to new information about Port Royal, their appetite would be whetted, and they would pursue this new interest in the topic through reading. Steinmetz notes that there is very little research on the relationship between curiosity arousal and literacy (for an analogous project that uses real objects instead of VR models to arouse curiosity and hence reading, see Lewis and Fisher 1999), and so a secondary goal of the Port Royal Project was to see, on the anecdotal level, if such a research program was potentially useful.

The UCLA CVRLab

The UCLA CVRLab (www.cvrlab.org) was founded in 1997 with the mission of creating scientifically authenticated real-time 3D computer models of cultural heritage sites around the world. Such models have been found to have useful applications in education, research, and commerce. Thus far the lab's models have ranged in time from the Iron Age in Europe and the Near East to the colonial period in the New World; and, in terms of space, from Peru to Israel. The Port Royal Project relates to the lab's longstanding interest in the use of visualization to promote learning through curiosity arousal (cf. Frischer 1982: 272–282; and note that CVRLab Associate Director D. Favro supervised Snyder 2003 and Abernathy 2004 on the use of VR technology in architectural education). Given the time and budgetary constraints on the project, the CVRLab could not utilize its normal modelling methodology, which is heavily reliant on the active participation of world-recognized authorities (see Frischer 2004). Instead, the roles of model-maker and expert had to be played by Natalie Tirrell, a student in Art History at UCLA. Some expert information was provided by a number of sources, including staff at the OI, Laurel Breece (an archaeologist with field experience at Port Royal), and Donny Hamilton (Director of the Port Royal Project).

The Ocean Institute

The non-profit Ocean Institute is located in Dana Point, California, USA at the base of the Dana Point Headlands and the entrance to the Dana Point Marine Life Refuge. The OI annually hosts over 90,000 kindergarten through college-age students in innovative learning experiences that increase competencies in science, technology, engineering, and math. The center serves as a field trip destination site and a laboratory for developing, testing, and disseminating new educational programs that help teachers and students meet state and national content standards. Programs range in length from two hours to five days and take place in the Institute's facilities including the 130' tallship Pilgrim, tallship Spirit of Dana Point, 70' research and education vessel R/V Sea Explorer, Ocean in Motion traveling classroom van, Chaparral to Ocean residential science camp and the new 33,000 sq. ft. Ocean Education Center (opened in 2002). With the opening of the new Ocean Education Center, the Ocean Institute has been able host over 50,000 general public visitors per year through a range of weekend exhibits, programs, and informal learning experiences.

Sea floor science: context for the Port Royal exhibit

In 2003, the OI was successful in attaining National Science Foundation support for a three-year project called Sea Floor Science, which develops more effective tools for translating current science to public audiences. The informal science education community consisting of museums, science centers, and nature centers has been challenged with a number of perennial problems: exhibits that hold visitor's attention for only a short time (often less than 1 minute); exhibit and program materials that do not reflect current science; and exhibition spaces that cannot be updated. Sea Floor Science responds to that challenge by developing exhibits that have the capacity to be converted from introductory presentations for general audiences to in-depth teaching stations for an 18-hour, inquiry-based middle-school program. In addition, Sea Floor Science develops and tests new processes to help researchers effectively translate science concepts for informal learning environments. Finally, Sea Floor Science explores new ways to add updatability to museum settings. Sea Floor Science opened with three collaborators: Texas A&M/ Institute of Nautical Archaeology (INA), Jet Propulsion Lab in Pasadena, California, and Scripps Institution of Oceanography in La Jolla, California.

The work with Texas A&M was focused on translating the archaeological research from INA and, in particular, on the sunken city of Port Royal, Jamaica, where Dr Donny Hamilton of INA had conducted underwater excavations. This was a compelling choice because middle school students in California are tested on their understanding of plate tectonics. Port Royal, a wonderfully colourful city whose short history is filled with pirates and merchants, was destroyed in 1692 when a sea floor earthquake liquefied the sand, and a significant portion of the town slid into shallow water. Researchers at INA assisted with the development of convertible exhibit solutions, checked texts for accuracy and authenticity, facilitated the acquisition of artifacts, maps, and resources for exhibit and program designers, and contributed to teacher workshops and staff training. The resultant exhibit focused on a replicated

1-meter quadrant from the underwater excavation that afforded students the opportunity to learn underwater survey, mapping, and recovery techniques. Students take data on underwater dive slates, build and test their own magnetometers and imitate diver protocols employed by INA. A conservation lab was set up where students build electrolysis tanks, make plaster casts, and interpret and label artifacts.

The introduction of the Port Royal model by UCLA's CVRLab

In the Fall of 2003, a new collaboration between UCLA's CVRLab, MIT's DeepArch Lab, Texas A&M/Institute of Nautical Archaeology, and the OI was born to further explore tools and techniques in underwater archaeology in a 4-month public presentation called Explorations! UCLA's CVRLab had the task of developing an exhibit update in the form of an interactive computer model for Port Royal that depicted the town (just before the earthquake) as well as the underwater excavation site. The new computer model met the overall Sea Floor Science goals by having the capability of being converted from a public exhibit to an in-depth teaching station for middle-school students. In addition, the computer model allowed students and visitors access to current research on how complex data sets are assembled and turned into interactive archaeological research tools. What emerged was an elegant solution that housed computer equipment, Port Royal artifacts, texts and monitors in a large 3'× 3' × 7' furniture-quality crate (Figure 28.1). The front section of the crate

Figure 28.1 Port Royal display case at the Ocean Institute (visitor, left; docent, right).

attractively displays Port Royal artifacts and contains electronic equipment and a computer cabinet. Mounted on the top of the crate is a 43" plasma screen monitor that crisply depicts movement within the model to larger audiences.

To be truly convertible, and serve a broad audience, the computer model needed to meet a range of scalable visitor challenges. Public visitors needed the opportunity to virtually walk along the various streets, to examine the architecture, to enter some of the structures, and to find various locations. Middle-school students needed all these experiences and they needed the opportunity to "swim" within the underwater archaeological site in search of the real artifacts that were on display. They were challenged to find the artifacts, discuss their location, and the possible context of their use. Students began to develop spatial relationships that were difficult to grasp with 2-D maps and to use the computer model in the same way as UCLA CVRLab scholars.

Reaction of OI staff and visitors to the Port Royal model

The UCLA CVRLab model made a strong and successful contribution to both the weekend public and middle-school overnight programs. Evaluations showed that the model helped translate current science by allowing visitors to understand how today's archaeologists employ technology to describe and understand sites. The interactivity of the model and the ability for visitors to explore houses and shops helped make the Port Royal story relevant to visitors and, therefore, lengthened stay-times and facilitated inquiry-based investigation and discussion. The Port Royal computer model was also successful in the Overnight Program as evidenced each morning with students able to accurately explain the role of computer models in describing and understanding spatial relationships at archaeological sites.

One of the interesting findings is the strong appeal this particular format has for teenage students. Because the technology is so very suitable for this age group, it is not a surprise that our high-school interns, serving as exhibit facilitators for weekend public exhibits, were interested, motivated, and easy to train. The technology, in fact, serves as an excellent bridge for all of our teen audiences. It is common to find teens teaching teens, teens challenging each other with what they can find, and teens coming up with new ways to use the model. The comfort level with this technology for our young audiences makes this a particularly attractive vehicle for communicating science in informal environments.

Port Royal model installation

The model is run using an SGI Open GL Performer on a Dell Dimension 8300 series computer (Intel Pentium IV, 2.60 GHz, 512MB RAM, 128MB ATI Radeon 9800 graphics card, 80 GB hard drive) and displayed on a 43' Pioneer DPD-433CMX plasma screen. The interface is achieved using a Gyration Ultra GT cordless optical mouse. The Gyration mouse allows the operator to stand at any distance up to 30' from the CPU and navigate the model with simple hand movements, eliminating the need for a tabletop or other surface to operate the mouse. The Ultra GT can also be operated as a standard optical mouse, allowing visitors, students, and those otherwise unfamiliar with the Gyration technology to navigate the model with a more familiar mouse interface. Occasional keystrokes are achieved using a standard wireless keyboard.

As for software, the Port Royal model was created by the CVRLab using MultiGen Creator (www.multigen.com/products/database/creator/index.shtml). The Creator OpenFlight file format is then explored by the user by means of UCLA's vrNav scene navigation program (www.ats.ucla.edu/at/vrNav1/default.htm). Normally, CVRLab models are georeferenced by on-site survey and given a radiosity solution with Autodesk's Lightscape before they are considered complete and ready for release; but, in the case of the Port Royal Project, constraints of time and budget forced us to eliminate these elements of the model-making process.

The physical requirements of a successful public exhibit are often different from those of a successful student-centered teaching station. Meeting the needs of one while not compromising the other presented some of the greatest challenges. Our student programs require the use of reading materials, Internet access, digital media, equipment storage, and reduced or eliminated signage. The public presentation, however, must provide a more "user-friendly" interface that can function effectively with no staff or volunteer mediation. In this mode, visitors will approach and interact with the exhibit entirely on their own. This requires some form of instructional and interpretive signage, an easily understandable interface, and reduced or eliminated access to stored equipment and other program-related functions. The exhibits must also be able to function effectively with varying degrees of staff or volunteer mediation and in this way be a fully scalable experience. The approach of the OI to meeting this challenge was to consider the student-centered teaching station as the highest level of the scalable experience and to create a continuum of degrees of interactivity and instructional mediation that ranged from entirely visitor-operated, through varying degrees of staff or volunteer mediation, and finally to a teaching station capable of serving an 18-hour overnight program. The model's installation reflects this approach.

The system is installed into a 3' x 3' x 7' wooden case modelled after a shipping crate with the face removed. Built into the crate are two primary components: an acrylic artifact display case, and an electronic equipment rack with a darkened acrylic door. The case stands directly over network and Internet access ports, and a false front below the artifact case allows easy access to these ports. Artifact lighting is provided from within the crate, mounted above the acrylic case. A 43' plasma monitor is mounted on top of the crate with an articulated swivel arm to allow for adjustments as necessary.

The equipment rack houses the model's computer, a second computer for program use, a second monitor, and program materials. The darkened acrylic front allows the second monitor to be viewed by the public when desired but effectively hides other equipment and materials. This case is opened for educational programs and remains closed during public visitation. Signage intended for public visitors is mounted on the door and is effectively hidden when the door is opened for educational programs.

The artifacts on display were recovered during an excavation of Port Royal and are on loan from Texas A&M and the Jamaican National Trust. These include an onion bottle, chamber pot, Chinese porcelain bowl, cannon balls, locks, and a few epoxy molds of keys and an iron. These artifacts can be found in the excavation model, allowing students to conduct archaeological investigations based on the context in which the items were found and a study of the artifacts themselves. The context itself is easily scaled in terms of time and space. The CVRLab model permits the artifact to be seen in the immediate surroundings of the site as it appeared during the modern underwater excavations or at the same spot in the reconstructed seventeenth-century city. The historical spot can itself be contextualized within the larger urban fabric of streets, buildings, docks, etc.

Future improvements and follow-up research

Currently, public visitors can navigate the Port Royal model only with assistance from OI staff or volunteers. OI high-school interns show visitors how to operate the mouse to travel through the city, or the interns act as navigators under visitors' direction. The goal of the OI is to provide a public interface that allows visitors to navigate the model with no direct assistance. This will require an intuitive "public-proof" interface and a certain degree of self-correcting behavior within the model so that visitors cannot find themselves inadvertently below ground or lost near the outer edges of the model. The OI is currently testing joystick and other gaming-type interfaces.

At UCLA, D. Favro will be undertaking new research on the effectiveness of the model as a learning tool for visitors to the OI. Given the fact that the model of Port Royal was not created according to the methodology developed by the CVRLab in terms of lighting, georeferencing, and scholarly oversight, we end by expressing the hope that the model is not considered finished but will be continued to be enhanced in the coming years as a 3D database containing information needed to illuminate the history of a site that has sometimes justly been called "the Pompeii of the New World."

References

Abernathy, D. (2004) Computer visualization and simulation as a medium for architectural and urban history pedagogy. Dissertation UCLA.
Antinucci, F. (2003) *Comunicare nel museo*. Rome and Bari: Editori Laterza.
Frischer, B. (1982) *The Sculpted Word*. Berkeley and Los Angeles: University of California Press.
Frischer, B. (2004) Mission and recent projects of the UCLA Cultural Virtual Reality Laboratory. In: R. Vergnieux and C. Delevoie (eds.), *Acts of Virtual Retrospect 2003, Biarritz, France 6–7 November 2003*, pp. 65–76.
Lewis, M. and Fisher, R. (1999). Curiosity kits. *Literacy Today*, 20 (September).
Pawson, M. and Buisseret, D. (2000) *Port Royal, Jamaica*. Second edition. Barbados, Jamaica, Trinidad, and Tobago: The University of the West Indies Press.
Pimentel, K. and Teixeira, K. (1995) *Virtual Reality through the New Looking Glass*. Second edition. New York: McGraw Hill Inc.

Snyder, L.M. (2003) The design and use of experiential instructional technology for the teaching of architectural history in American undergraduate architecture programs. Dissertation UCLA.

Vince, J. (1998) *Essential Virtual Reality Fast*. London: Springer-Verlag.

Part III, Section 5

Teaching and learning through museum archaeology

Chapter 29

Teaching the past in museums

Joanne Lea

Archaeology education can take place in a variety of venues, but the single most common place where the public meets archaeology continues to be the museum. Museums are important for archaeology on a fundamental level because they house and exhibit archaeological artifact collections and because many archaeologists are employed or funded by museums. They are a place (often the only place) where the public comes into contact with the pots and projectiles that have been gathered during archaeological research. For much of the public, museums are archaeology.

The museum-going public has been growing, albeit more slowly recently than its doubling from the 1950s to the 1960s (Roberts 1997: 65). While the usual museum visitor is an educated, middle-class person in his or her twenties (Zyskowski 1983: 124), the future for museums lies in how it attracts and relates to young visitors, especially school groups. What the public will think about archaeology, about museums, and about continued public funding for these will be shaped by museum education programs for children and by community outreach (Duncan 1985: 21).

For these reasons, archaeologists need to consider themselves to be part of the museum education team. They may be either museum educators themselves, or they may work in co-operation with the other education staff at museums. The archaeology educator developing programs for schools ought to have a clear understanding of how museums provide basic archaeology education to the general public, and especially to the literally millions of North American schoolchildren who visit them each year. This chapter explores the issues of archaeology education in museum settings and presents a sample program for schoolchildren visiting a museum.

What are museums?

Museums are institutions for learning. Their focus may be history, science, nature, the arts, or some combination thereof. They may be large and government or business sponsored, or local and volunteer operated. They may been seen as tourism

Source: *The Archaeology Education Handbook: Sharing the Past with Kids*. K. Smardz and S.J. Smith (eds.). Walnut Creek, CA: AltaMira Press, 2000. pp. 315–327.

sites (Boniface and Fowler 1993: 102), as sites of "edutainment" (Soren 1990: iii), as academic guardians of "Great Objects of Great Value that represent Great Traditions" (Roberts 1997: 60), and as "repositories for the collection and study of documents and objects" (Walker 1997: 33).

What they have in common and what defines museums (Martin Lewis, personal communication, 1985) are their functions, outlined by the acronym *ACRE,* namely:

Acquisition	the policies and processes for obtaining a collection
Conservation	the policies and processes for keeping stable, restoring, or protecting collections
Research	the policies and processes for understanding and interpreting the collections
Education	the policies and processes for sharing the museum's collections, expertise, and research

Of the four main museum functions, three relate to the internal museum workings. Only education technically requires consideration of the external world. Each function, however, affects how archaeology is represented. In fact, it is the impact of these functions in combination that have produced the image of archaeology that many people hold for a lifetime.

For instance, acquisition policies both dictate what museums collect and reflect what is considered worthy of being collected. Archaeology has, since its inception, been the main vehicle by which historical museums acquired their collections, so archaeology thereby became the *meaning* of those collections.

Conservation practices defined the public perception of archaeology by dictating the selection and method of exhibiting collections that would be displayed to, or accessed by, the public. To protect collections from breakage, light, humidity, or motion, only the more stable artifacts became part of permanent exhibits. Thus, to most people, archaeology came to be seen as groups of pottery and stone tools, guarded behind glass, removed from everyday life, and protected from everyday people. It was, and is, remote.

Research established the authority of the museum and its reputation by virtue of its collection and conferred on the museum staff the power over interpretation of the artifacts. Archaeologists were authorities to a truth that they controlled. Educators changed the balance of power in the museum world, and with the change came different definitions of archaeology.

What is museum education?

Education in museums is not a new concept. The original 1753 mandate of the British Museum was "not only for the Inspection and Entertainment of the learned and the curious, but for the general Use and Benefit of the Public" (British Museum 1997). In 1973, the American Association of Museums created its standing professional committee on education. What is new about education in museums is illustrated by the statement of Stone and Molyneaux (1994: 17): "Most archaeologists want to teach archaeological skills and ideas; ... whereas educationalists look for the means to stimulate the educational, rather than the archaeological development of children."

What is new about education in museums, then, is a focus on the visitor as participant, as learner rather than as recipient of a particular body of knowledge. Roberts sees this change as an empowerment issue, driven by educators over the objections of many curators because it transferred authority from the curators (including archaeologists) first to the educators, and "later, even to the visitor" (1997: 45, 60, 73).

Once empowered, a museum visitor's own experiences become part of his or her comprehension of the collection. Educators use this understanding of "meaning-making" to develop exhibits or programs that enhance the visitor's involvement with the objects. The educator includes the needs of the visitor along with those of the museum (the "C" and "R" functions) when selecting and interpreting artifacts. The tools used to accomplish the newer approach to museum education include:

1. "market research" or visitor-tracking through exhibits, which lead to more engaging traffic flow patterns, light levels, labels, color and topic selection, graphics, and the use of varied and interactive technologies;
2. exhibits and programs that are seen as "communication systems" (Pearce 1990: 159) based in communication theory studies and in which the visitor is an integral part;
3. entertainment, even to the degree of a call to use some of the techniques of Disney (Lumley 1994: 66);
4. a co-operative approach that involves museum staff (curators, educators, designers) in a team and that seeks to work with other communities that participate in the museum (such as school boards, amateur and a vocational societies, and ethnic societies); and
5. an understanding of education as a formal field of study, in particular as it relates to the developmental stages of learners and the learning processes and the museum's collection.

Collection-based programming

It seems obvious that a museum would develop educational programming based on its own collection, but this has been a debated point (Herbert 1983: 35). Some have questioned whether an educational mandate goes beyond the immediate museum collection to meeting the curriculum needs of the local community (i.e., suggesting that the museum ought to present an Inuit program, whether or not its collections contain any Inuit artifacts, because Inuit Life is taught in Grade 4).

This debate about curriculum versus collection-based programming is underscored with educational program slogans such as that of David Hurst Thomas, cited by Crow Canyon staff, "It's not what you find; it's what you find out" (Ricky Lightfoot, personal communication: 1997). Although this is an obvious truth to archaeologists on the one level, on another—and certainly in museums—it misses the point. Of course it's "what you find." Museums exist because of what was found; they proclaim it in each of their labeled, properly lit glass cases, and they attract the public because of it. Noel-Hume defined archaeology, too, in terms of what was found by calling it "material culture with dirt on it" (1978: 21).

School groups are especially attracted to museums because of its objects. With the high costs of field trips and transportation, most teachers cannot get permission to leave the classroom unless they can obtain experiences for students that they can't provide in the classroom by themselves (i.e., to look at or touch [not talk about] "real" artifacts). To deny that archaeology in a museum setting is about "the object" is to be self-defeating, or at least, lonely.

Object-based learning

The issue, then, is the implications of an object-based focus for educational programming. First, programs should start with the collection, with an assessment of what it contains and its strengths. Next, the education staff should meet with community representatives (for example, teachers), to assess their needs and relate these to the collection. Museum educators then need to collaborate with other museum staff and to work in concert with the acquisition, conservation, and research functions of the institution. These steps could result in the following:

1. modifying acquisitions policies to develop collections that reflect local needs and the cultural diversity of the community;
2. deaccessioning duplicate artifacts from the collection for educational use and handling by the public;
3. creating reproductions of artifacts for public use (see Box 1);
4. researching and designing exhibitions that specifically address curricula;
5. incorporating conservation practices, such as wearing gloves for handling fragile artifacts, into educational programs.

BOX 1

Is It Real Or Is It ... ?

Reproduction artifacts can be perceived as "real" even when not authentic because of the context in which they are presented. Research has shown (Orvell in Roberts 1997:102) that museum visitors are satisfied with the reality of an experience, if it is presented with accuracy and integrity. This holds even when the visitors know that they are not experiencing the seventh century or wearing a genuine Roman toga. The backdrop of integrity provided by a museum's collection of authentic artifacts and the accuracy of museum research gives the aura of reality to the use of reproductions.

---

6. promoting archaeological stewardship, in contrast to the emphasis on obtaining artifacts that is highlighted by museum exhibits; and
7. providing space where educational programs can take place.

This last point implies calculating floor space per anticipated visitor, a designated area for coats, food, and supplies storage, sufficient washrooms to meet health code requirements, and adequately sized activity areas with running water and janitorial supplies. Child-sized furnishings (chairs, tables, coat racks, and toilets) are another consideration.

Museums such as Jorvik Viking Centre, at York, England, present the visitor with a simulated experience of that city's Viking past by combining the authentic and the real. Visitors ride a train back in time, traveling through part of a village peopled by costumed mannequins engaged in day-to-day activities. Facial features are even replicated using computer imaging from actual skulls found by archaeologists in the Viking-period cemetery (Karolyn Smardz, pers. comm. 1997). The trip ends at the archaeological site that uncovered the evidence used to replicate the village, seemingly left just as it was when the archaeologists departed.

Interpretive centers (i.e., museums) at archaeological sites, historic sites, or heritage attractions, such as at Wanuskiwin, L'Anse Aux Meadows, or Old Fort William, in Canada or in Williamsburg, Virginia, and many "living history" centers in the United States, authenticate the reality presented by exhibiting excavated objects as proof. The object, therefore, remains central to the experience.

Museum programs will therefore be object centered. Museums are ideally suited to this approach because well-designed exhibits make connections for the visitor by displaying the objects in historical and often chronological context. This is an advantage museums have over archaeological sites in which the object's context is as an excavated artifact.

Educational program formats

A museum has several format options for educational programs. These may be dictated by practical considerations such as available floor space and staffing; by philosophical considerations about the nature of education, of archaeology, of history, and so forth, or by research about human learning processes and visitor preferences. Among these options are:

The self-guided exhibit tour

Visitors tour the museum with the aid of labels or brochures. This type of program can accommodate a large number of visitors in limited amounts of time for low costs. However, in this type of situation the public deals with the objects superficially. Visitors have been observed to spend only twenty to thirty seconds reading individual labels (Zyskowski 1983: 123; Zorpette 1992: 96). This format also imparts understanding at a superficial level, mostly in the form of facts and terminology. These are, in turn, labeled "knowledge" by educational psychologist Bloom, who defines "knowledge" as the lowest cognitive domain in his taxonomy of learning objectives (Bowd et al. 1982: 301; Geraci 2000: 95).

Visitors feel alienated by museum labeling that is too detailed and academic. Conversely, visitors have been found to be alienated by too-brief labels, made with the intent of not unduly influencing the visitor's own interaction with the object

(Zorpett 1992). When using this option, museums should consider the reading ability and first language of their visitors. Accessibility for younger, older, or challenged visitors may dictate Braille or large-print labels at wheelchair or child height and/or audiotape cassette recordings of exhibit information.

The guided tour or lecture

In this case, visitors' experiences with objects are augmented through the additional expertise of the docent or guide combined with an opportunity to ask questions and the enhanced experiential value of a personal relationship. Language and access issues are more readily addressed. The cognitive focus remains primarily knowledge, but can expand through discussion to include analysis, synthesis, and evaluation. While large numbers of visitors can still be accommodated, this format is less useful for groups of children. This is due to the limitations of their attention span, coupled with the greater impact of an active learning program on young students; research shows that children learn best by doing rather than by seeing or hearing (see Herbert 1983; Ellick 2000).

To conduct a guided tour, a museum guide or archaeology educator should be trained not only in the history and interpretation of the collection, but equally important, in educational theory and interpersonal communication. Knowing a great deal about Blue-Willow–patterned or cord-wrapped ceramics does not necessarily make one a good archaeology educator, museum tour guide, docent, or interpreter.

The discovery program

In this format, visitors may be accompanied by either museum staff or by printed or taped information. Questions are provided to aid exploration by observing specific artifacts or collections. By answering the questions themselves over the course of their museum experience, visitors interact with the objects and learn to analyze the components of objects and exhibits. Sensory experiences enhance the sense of discovery. The interpretive centre at Sainte Marie-Among-The-Hurons in Midland, Ontario, Canada, includes walls covered in locally trapped furs and scents of the spices sought by explorers in its exhibits, while Jorvik Viking Centre, described above, uses essential oils to replicate smells of the barnyard, fish-drying racks, and even the Viking privy (Karolyn Smardz, pers. comm. 1998). Some museums, such as the Royal Ontario Museum (ROM) in Toronto, Ontario, Canada, have 'Discovery Rooms' with deaccessioned collections used for exploration activities.

The hands-on program

This is the most demanding program format for a museum in terms of staffing, material, and preparation. It is therefore the most costly for visiting school groups. Hands-on programs offer the participant a personal understanding of the artifact's meaning through their interaction with it. The interaction may be as simple as holding an artifact or reproduction, or being dressed in a costume while in an exhibition gallery with a guide. More complex versions of this format could include:

1. detailed explorations of artifacts (by drawing them, taking rubbings of them, measuring them, smelling or tasting them);
2. making or using reproductions of artifacts (for example, pottery);
3. participation in structured (tell them what to do) educational activities that guide the visitor's interpretation (for example, give a student a bone awl and a steel needle to sew a leather garment; then, ask students to comment on the effects of European contact on Native American lifeways vis-à-vis technology); and
4. participation in unstructured (don't tell them what to do) educational activities in which the visitor's experience with the object becomes its interpretation (for example, give students typical household items and ask them to improvise a scene from the daily life of that culture; then, discuss how the objects affected and reflected the lifeways of that culture in daily life).

The responsibility of museum education

Whatever program format is used by museum educators, the goal is empowerment. Along with power comes the responsibility that museum educators have to ensure that all visitors are themselves empowered by contact with the object. As noted above, this responsibility can start with providing wheelchair access to exhibits and washrooms and displaying labels that are understandable. The responsibility goes beyond this level. It acknowledges the constructivist perspective that meaning is given by the visitor to an object from their own experience, as much as it is imparted by the museum. This is apparent when one hears a museum visitor exclaim, "My grandmother had one just like that!" followed by a flood of personal recollections.

The matter of responsibility to the visitor has been brought home in the public reaction to museum exhibits that deal with controversial subject matter. Notable in recent years have been the "Into the Heart of Africa" exhibit at the ROM, the "Enola Gay" exhibit at the Smithsonian Institution National Air and Space Museum (NASM), "The Peopling of London" exhibit at the Museum of London, in England, and the "Holocaust" exhibit at Beth Tzedec Temple, Toronto.

Each exhibit focused on objects in the museum's collection respectively: African artifacts brought to Canada by Christian missionaries and personal items of the missionaries; the airplane "Enola Gay," from which the first atomic bomb was dropped on Japan; artifacts illustrating the occupation of London, England; and artifacts from the Nazi concentration camps of the Second World War. Each exhibit was developed with academic rigour, historical accuracy, and current education and programming theory, yet the two former were met with storms of public controversy (Krauthammer 1995: 68), and were closed. The latter two exhibits were considered successful. Why?

A key factor was that the ROM and NASM exhibits represented power over interpretation being maintained by museum staff, whereas the London and Beth

Tzedec exhibits included the museum visitor in the interpretation process. Staff curators wrote the text for the ROM and NASM exhibits (see Canizzo 1989). Merriman's "Peopling of London" exhibit's development process involved hiring liaisons to meet with representatives of nineteen of the culturally diverse groups within the community (Coxall 1997: 99). Beth Tzedec's exhibit reflected the stories and artifacts from the community itself.

Dismissing the need for inclusivity in museum education goes beyond the immediate effect of cancelling exhibits to creating a legacy of distrust toward museums and marginalizing segments of a population. Native North Americans feel robbed by museums of their material culture; denied their voice in telling its story; and denied their cultural values, which placed "artifacts" in a living cultural context, rather than in a glass case (McMaster 1990: 36). The Woodland Indian Cultural Centre on the Six Nations Reserve, in Brantford, Ontario, deliberately avoided naming itself a "museum" because of the discomfort within the community about such institutions (Tom Hill 1986: pers. comm.). Legislation in the United States (i.e., the Native American Graves Protection and Repatriation Act) addresses the issue of inclusion, but the museums themselves will bear the responsibility for restoring a relationship with the Native community. Postcolonial African countries are noted as beginning to consider the potential of museum education to regain identities that were hidden from them by museums that exhibited only the artifacts of the colonizers (Stone and Mackenzie 1990.) To succeed, museums need not only be inclusive in their programming, but responsive. Zorpette (1992: 98) cites publicly funded curators who still question whether they "sometimes have to give the public what it wants." In answer: the Beth Tzedec exhibit contained an artifact that bore such emotional weight for the community that there was a request to remove it from the exhibit. It was removed. The curator at Beth Tzedec replied, by action, to the curators cited by Zorpette with a resounding "Yes."

Components of an education program

After having selected the artifacts for display; having wrestled with the responsibilities to the community; having consulted the contributors to the interpretive process; and having decided on the best program format, the museum educator finally faces the creation of a program. Programs for groups of school children require organization and the following components:

1. A pre-visit information package, sent to the visit coordinator (i.e., teacher), containing:
    - the cost-per-participant and payment options
    - directions to the museum
    - on-site facilities (washrooms, food services, cloakrooms)
    - accommodations for special needs students (such as wheelchair ramps)
    - duration of the program
    - recommended supervision ratio of adults to students
    - appropriate age for program participants

- curriculum related to the program
- an outline of program goals
- an outline of program content
- required materials to be brought (for example, pencils)
- suggested pre-visit activities
- suggested post-visit activities
- the name and contact method (phone, e-mail) for educational staff.

2 Program goals should be age appropriate, relevant to both curriculum and audience, and limited in number. A "three-item rule" is helpful. If, at the end of the program, participants can demonstrate understanding of three concepts to which they have been introduced, the program has been successful. To learn more than three may be too demanding. The content of the "items" may vary with the sophistication of the audience, from "What is a stratum?" to "How did pipe designs demonstrate matrilineal kinship in Iroquoian society?"

3 Museum staff should give an introduction to both the facility and the program. It contains:
- the name of the museum staff working with the group
- the locations of: washrooms, telephones, cloakroom, food services, elevators, stairs, office where payment may be made
- the time constraints of the visit
- security and discipline expectations for the visitor (both students and adults)
- the format and logistics of the program (including a gallery map)
- an activity to focus the group's attention on the program content and help the group feel comfortable in its surroundings.

4 Program content should reflect the stated goals, and therefore also be specific or limited in focus. It should be presented in "bite-sized pieces" such as three fifteen-minute activities or discussions. Each should relate to one goal and be in the format of a mini-lesson, with its own introduction, application, and conclusion. By varying the pace of the activities, interest is better maintained.

   Please note that the use of pencil and paper activity sheets should be undertaken with caution. Some students are too young for this format or may not have sufficient English skills to complete it comfortably. Others will focus their attention on completing a worksheet rather than on learning or on experiencing the collection. Worksheets can become litter, not lessons, especially if subjected to wind or rain during a museum visit.

5 A concluding activity should review the content covered during the program. This provides an opportunity for museum staff to evaluate the effectiveness of the program by gauging the level of understanding gained by visitors. A formal, written evaluation form should also be provided and a response requested of the group's supervisors – preferably before leaving the museum.

A brief program outline follows as an example (see Box 2).

> **BOX 2**
>
> *A Brief Program Outline*
>
> **TITLE:** Native American Technology
>
> **CURRICULUM RELATION:** Grade 7 history unit: Native Peoples
>
> **GOALS:** To complement Native Studies programs in elementary schools by establishing the relevance of the topic to modern life, addressing attitudes about Native cultures and peoples, and engaging visitors at the "Knowledge, Analysis, and Synthesis" levels of cognitive development.
>
> **OUTCOMES:** The participant will:
> - identify three examples of Native American technology
> - explain the technological processes involved in producing artifacts exhibited
> - evaluate cultural relevance in respect to technology
>
> **INTRODUCTION:**
> 1. Museum staff will orient the school group to the museum.
> 2. Museum staff will ask the group for two lists of adjectives to describe Native American technology in the past, and contrast it with present-day technology. Staff will record the lists for the group to see.
> 3. The participants will be divided into three groups and the logistics and activities of the program will be explained to each group.
>
> **PRESENTATION/APPLICATION:** At three activity centers located near exhibits that contain examples of the artifacts to be studied, participants will use provided supplies to either duplicate the exhibited artifacts or to replicate how those items would have been used in the daily lives of the people that produced them, that is:
>
> 1. cordage
> 2. basketry
> 3. stone tools.
>
> Participants should rotate among the three centers at fifteen- to twenty-minute intervals, so all students experience each activity.
>
> **CONCLUSION:** Participants should gather as a group to discuss:
> - Have their perceptions of Native American technology changed?
> - Would they revise the lists of adjectives created earlier? Why?
> - What would they consider the main differences between Native American technologies of the past and present-day technologies?
> - Give examples from each activity center.
>
> **FOLLOW-UP ACTIVITY:** Define 'technology'.

Conclusions

Education is a key function of museums. It is the one that is external to the museum in outlook and that links the public to the artifact. Because it is the collections that define a museum, and many of these are archaeologically obtained, museums ARE the face of archaeology for much of the public, especially school-aged children. How they perceive that face, the understanding they have of it, and the personal relationship they develop with it can affect the future of public or private funding for archaeological research or for museums themselves. It can affect how important the issue of stewardship of archaeological resources is to the public. It can affect how people see themselves in light of the knowledge of the past, and the kind of future they choose to build upon that knowledge. Archaeologists share with museologists the responsibilities and the rewards of bringing the past to the present.

References

Boniface, P. and Fowler, P. (1993) *Heritage Tourism in the Global Village*. New York: Routledge.
Bowd, A., McDougall, D., and Yewchuk, C. (1982) *Educational Psychology*. Toronto: Gate Publishing Limited.
British Museum (1997) Education Service.
Canizzo, J. (1989) *Into the Heart of Africa*. Toronto: Royal Ontario Museum.
Coxall, H. (1997) Speaking other voices. In: E. Hooper-Greenhill (ed.), *Cultural Diversity*. Washington, D.C.: Leicester University Press, pp. 99–115.
Duncan, D. (1985) Keep those visitors coming. In: *Let's Get Organized*. Toronto: Ontario Historical Society, p. 21.
Ellick, C.J. (2000) Against the clock: introducing archaeology in time-limited situations. In: K. Smardz and S.J. Smith (eds.), *The Archaeology Education Handbook: Sharing the Past with Kids*. Walnut Creek, CA: AltaMira Press, pp. 183–91.
Geraci, V.W. (2000) Learning and teaching styles: reaching all students. In: K. Smardz and S.J. Smith (eds.), *The Archaeology Education Handbook: Sharing the Past with Kids*. Walnut Creek, CA: AltaMira Press, pp. 91–100.
Herbert, M. (1983) Museums and schools. *Journal of Education*, 7(4): 34–8.
Krauthammer, C. (1995) History hijacked. *Time*, 13 February: 68.
Lumley, R. (1994) The debate on heritage reviewed. In: R. Miles and L. Zavala (eds.), *Towards the museum of the Future*. New York: Routledge, pp. 57–70.
McMaster, G. (1990) Problems of representation. *Muse*, 8(3): 35–41.
Noel-Hume, I. (1978) Material culture with dirt on it. In: I. Quimby (ed.), *Material Culture and the Study of American Life*. New York: W.W. Norton, pp. 21–40.
Pearce, S. (1990) *Archaeological Curatorship*. New York: Leicester University Press.
Roberts, L.C. (1997) *From Knowledge to Narrative*. Washington, D.C.: Smithsonian Institution Press.
Soren, B. (1990) Curriculum-making and the museum mosaic. Unpublished thesis, Department of Museum Studies, University of Toronto.
Stone, P.G. and Mackenzie, R. eds. (1990) *The Excluded Past: Archaeology and Education*. London: Routledge.

Stone, P.G. and Molyneaux, B.L. eds. (1994) *The Presented Past: Heritage, Museums and Education*. London: Routledge.

Walker, S. (1997) Black cultural museums in Britain: what questions do they answer? In: E. Hooper-Greenhill (ed.), *Cultural Diversity*. Washington, D.C.: Leicester University Press, pp. 32–49.

Zorpette, G. (1992) What do museum visitors want? *Art News*, 91(10): 94–8.

Zyskowski, G. (1983) A review of literature on the evaluation of museum programs. *Curator*, 26(2): 121–8.

Interaction or tokenism?
The role of 'hands-on activities' in museum archaeology displays

Janet Owen

'Hey, Mum, they decorated these pots like we make pies ... the bloke who made it had bigger hands than me though.'
                (Overheard comment of a 10-year-old child at a medieval pottery activity day, City & County Museum, Lincoln, 1993)

Archaeologists have a long tradition of encouraging people to handle archaeological material at museum open days, site events, and other outreach activities. However, it is only really in the last decade that archaeologists have begun experimenting with the use of hands-on activities in archaeology displays as part of a more general trend to involve the visitor in a personal process of discovery. Though it is recognized that there are many practical issues involved in developing this medium, the chapter will focus on the philosophical aspect of using these activities. As a result perhaps of the obvious physical and social interaction that they inspire, hands-on activities are often termed *interactives* and are assumed to be more 'interactive' than any other form of exhibition medium. However, what is the nature of any intellectual interaction that takes place? Do these hands-on activities inspire the visitor to think creatively about the ideas presented in the narrative? How do the authors of a narrative perceive and influence this intellectual interaction between visitor and activity? Are museums using hands-on activities to involve the visitor in a personal process of discovery or are they just a token gesture towards providing greater intellectual and physical access to our collections and the work of the museum?

    This chapter will focus on the last two questions: the museum agenda. A study of the visitor agenda is outside the scope of this work though ultimately both museum and visitor agendas work together to define the nature of any intellectual interaction taking place between visitor and activity. However, the complexity of this interaction will be examined briefly to provide a framework for discussion of the display authors' *intended* learning role for hands-on activities in a selection of

Source: *Making Early Histories in Museums*. N. Merriman (ed.). London: Leicester University Press, 1999. pp. 173–189. Reproduced with permission of Bloomsbury Publishing Plc.

archaeological displays in the UK. This chapter does not attempt a comprehensive survey of current practice, but is rather a commentary on experiments to date using hands-on media.

What do we mean by 'interaction' and 'hands-on activities'?

'Interaction' is defined as 'acting on each other'. Fundamentally, all exhibition media have this property: text is designed to be read, photographs and illustrations to be viewed, objects in cases to be scrutinized, hands-on activities to be handled – all with the intention of having some kind of impact upon the visitor who in turn 'brings [his or her] unique experience, knowledge and perception into play' (Kaplan 1995: 41). Various exhibition media and the visitor therefore *act on each other* in any individual's interpretation of an exhibition; some form of interaction takes place. The nature of this interaction can vary considerably: it can be physical, emotional, social, intellectual, or a combination of any or all of these. It is determined to a great extent by the objectives and design of individual media and the exhibition within which these sit, as well as by the agenda of the individual visitor. A *hands-on activity,* for the purposes of this chapter, is one requiring, or expecting, at the least a *physical* interaction between the person and the activity.

Using this definition, hands-on activities can take many forms; these can be divided into three main categories. Activities can involve people touching the material evidence of the past, the 'genuine article' (handling a real medieval pot, for example); the use of replicas, models or physical displays of the type seen in science centres; and computer interactives where the physical interaction involves pressing a touch screen or moving a joystick.

Inspiring creative thought?

A good deal of evidence exists to suggest that hands-on activities help to create an atmosphere conducive to learning and development by encouraging people to relax in the museum environment, enjoy themselves, and to interact socially with friends and strangers (Coles 1984; Cox 1996; Freeman 1989; Gunther 1994; Peirson Jones 1995). Authors of museum narratives regard this emotive and social interaction as an opportunity that can be built on to inspire visitors to think more closely about the objects and ideas presented. Recent work in the field of learning theory suggests that a large proportion of people learn more from doing things than from reading about them. Through the use of hands-on activities visitors can be encouraged to use their senses of touch, sight, sound, and smell to analyse objects and ideas within the context of the exhibition and within the context of their own experiences and perceptions of the world around them (Hooper-Greenhill 1991). Research by Piaget amongst others suggests that this opportunity is particularly valuable for young children (Jensen 1994), but older children and adults can also benefit from *learning by doing* (Gunther 1994).

The three categories of hands-on activity will each influence the visitor's learning experience in its own unique way. Those activities that emphasize 'the genuine article' will perhaps inspire a stronger emotive and social response than those centred on the use of replicas. Computer interactives will contain an element of fun for some visitors, but might frighten the computer-illiterate museum visitor (Johansson 1996; Tyler 1990). However, the intention of all these varied activities is to use a basic element of physical interaction as a starting point to encourage further intellectual interaction between visitor and museum narrative.

The nature of the intellectual interaction can vary across a broad spectrum from a *closed, passive interaction* at one extreme to an *open, active interaction* at the other. The author of the narrative may choose to predetermine the outcome of the interaction taking place, or may design the hands-on activity in a way that encourages interaction between visitor and narrative but does not fully direct its form. The potential of hands-on activities to encourage visitors to think for themselves and to become actively involved in creating the narrative is perhaps their most exciting aspect. Interpretation in museums is currently focusing on providing greater access to collections and ideas, and is also keen to provide the visitor with enhanced freedom and choice about what they experience during a visit. Now aware that facts are relative, that all narratives are subjective, and that every individual interprets any narrative in their own unique way, museums are increasingly concerned with empowering the visitor; with facilitating learning development rather than dictating any particular direction which that learning experience should take (Freeman 1989; Peirson Jones 1995).

In 1986 Birmingham City Museums and Art Gallery began a project to redisplay its ethnographic collections. The 'Gallery 33' project had two primary objectives: to encourage visitors to address the issue of cultural relativism, and to think about the issue of cultural representation in museums (Peirson Jones 1995). Hands-on activities are used as a means to actively involve the visitor. An interactive video supports a diorama entitled the 'Collector's House', both exhibits focusing on the issue of cultural representation in museums. The video provides the visitor with a number of perspectives on the subject of the return of cultural property, and encourages people to make up their own minds regarding this issue. Formal evaluation carried out for the Museum suggests that a third of visitors found the programme had influenced their views on the repatriation of artefacts to countries of origin.

The people behind the Discovery Gallery at the Royal Ontario Museum in Toronto, Canada (ROM), have analysed the nature of intellectual interaction taking place between the visitor and activities in detail. The gallery is based on Mosston's discovery learning concept (Freeman 1989), which recognized that various types of intellectual interaction could take place within the learning environment, and arbitrarily classified them into three categories (Figure 30.1). Freeman argues that a truly open, individual, learner-designed programme is not possible in the museum environment where inevitably through selecting and designing the activity the museum keeps a certain degree of control over the learning experience. However, experience at the ROM suggests that a mixed approach of problem-solving and guided discovery works best. Those who wish to explore issues in their own way are able to do so, but those who feel less comfortable working to their own agenda still feel able to participate.

Guided discovery	Problem-solving	Designed programme
• instructor-led	• instructor poses problems	• leaner poses problem
• convergent thinking	• divergent thinking	
• discoveries lead to predetermined conclusion	• alternative solutions	• solution pursued independently

Closed, passive interaction ←─────────────→ Open, active interaction

Figure 30.1 Muska Mosston's concept of discovery learning (after Iles 1991: 16), annotated with the 'open–closed interaction' scale proposed in this text.

The ROM's evaluation findings and the resulting approach adopted suggests that some people do find having to think completely for themselves a little daunting, a conclusion echoed by experiments elsewhere (Fisher and Lalvani 1996; Gunther 1994). Therefore, hands-on activities should perhaps be used in ways that provide opportunities for both open and closed intellectual interaction.

The role of hands-on activities in the making of archaeological histories in UK museums: the museum agenda

Archaeologists are currently very keen to develop narratives that are more meaningful to the wider community and more relevant to people's everyday lives (Merriman 1990; Owen 1996). Encouraging an active physical and intellectual interaction with archaeological material is one way of enabling a more personal encounter between the visitor and artefacts or narratives regarding the distant past. Archaeology is an ideal subject for exploiting hands-on media and for encouraging active intellectual interaction. It fascinates and captures the imagination and, as a discipline, places great emphasis on active problem-solving. Archaeologists draw on evidence from a variety of sources to create a narrative, and with the influence of postmodernism on archaeological theory the place and value of alternative narratives is gradually being recognized by those responsible for creating archaeological histories (for example, Bender 1993; Cotton 1997; Merriman 1990; Owen 1996; Shanks and Tilley 1992; Stone 1994).

Do the authors of archaeological histories in museums use hands-on media to provide opportunities for both open and closed intellectual interaction between visitor and narrative? This chapter will look at two sources of evidence to discuss this question: the nature of a sample of exhibits themselves, and the display authors' intended objectives for these exhibits. Information has been gathered from the literature published on the subject, the responses to an informal questionnaire sent to colleagues in nineteen museums known to be working in this area, and various site visits made since 1995 (Figure 30.2).

Museums/organizations sent questionnaires	Museums/organizations visited
Archaeological Resource Centre	Archaeological Resource Centre
British Museum	Colchester Castle Museum
Colchester Castle Museum	Lawn Archaeology Centre, Lincoln
Doncaster Museum and Art Gallery	Leicestershire Museums
Glasgow Museums	Manchester University Museum
Hampshire Museums Service	Museum of London
Jorvik Viking Centre	Reading Museums
Lawn Archaeology Centre, Lincoln	Stoke-on-Trent Museum and Art Gallery
Manx National Heritage	Verulamium Museum
Museum of London	
National Museums and Galleries on Merseyside	
National Museums of Ireland	
National Museum of Scotland	
Plymouth Museums	
Reading Museums	
Royal Cornwall Museum	
Ulster Museum	
Verulamium Museum	
Winchester Museums Service	

Figure 30.2 A list of museums sent informal survey questionnaires and a list of museums visited.

The nature of the exhibits

A number of museums have recently redisplayed their archaeological collections, or are in the process of doing so. The majority of these redisplays will undoubtedly incorporate some element of hands-on interaction. Hands-on activities are an integral aspect of the galleries at the Verulamium Museum in St Albans, the Roman Gallery at Colchester Castle Museum, and the Early Ireland Gallery at the Ulster Museum, for example. Various museum and archaeological organizations have established, or are planning, hands-on activity centres physically separate from narrative displays but intended to complement the latter's communicative role. York Archaeological Trust established the Archaeological Resource Centre (ARC) in 1990; Hampshire Museums Service opened SEARCH, their Hands-on Centre for History and Natural History in 1995; and the British Museum, the National Museums and Galleries on Merseyside (NMGM), and Reading Museums are working on projects still in the planning stages. A number of museums intending to use hands-on activities in permanent gallery redisplays have explored visitor reaction to the medium through a series of evaluated temporary exhibitions. NMGM have held a number of 'Have a Go at Archaeology' exhibitions since 1991, and will use their experiences and evaluation findings to shape exhibits proposed for the new NMGM Discovery Centre (Southworth 1994).

A range of activities has been devised by museums to engage the visitor in the various processes used by archaeologists in their work. An activity that encourages the visitor to sort artefacts by their material type is popular and has been used by the NMGM, the ARC in York, Winchester City Museums, and the Lawn Archaeology Centre in Lincoln. Text- and image-based aids provide the visitor with all the information necessary to sort a mixed tray of stone, pottery, animal bone, and tile fragments and place them in the stone, pottery, bone, and tile trays. This activity requires the visitor to think about the characteristics of the different materials in order to solve the problem. However, there is a correct solution, and the outcome of the activity is to a great extent predetermined. Other similar activities encourage the visitor to identify bones from different parts of an animal's skeleton and identify different pottery types.

Museums experimenting with these activities do employ a number of aids to enhance the interactive problem-solving value. At the ARC and in the NMGM staff are on hand to discuss the task further with the visitor and potentially a more visitor-led exploration of the activity could be facilitated. However, the staff must be tightly briefed to ensure that as far as possible they provide a balance between assisting visitors and giving them space to develop their own ideas. At the ARC, extra reference material is also provided for the staff to access if relevant to their discussions with visitors. In some instances, the text complementing a particular activity will contain questions to encourage visitors to look at artefacts closely and to develop their own ideas about what they observe. In 1994, NMGM introduced this approach into their experimental temporary exhibition programme. The label extract below is taken from an activity that encouraged visitors to think about how archaeologists date pottery.

> Match up the pieces with the pots in the case and put them into trays.
>
> Hint: Is it rough or smooth?
> Is it plain or decorated?
> Was it made by hand, on a potter's wheel or in a mould?
> (From 'How do archaeologists know how old their finds are?' 'Have a Go at Archaeology' display 1994, National Museums & Galleries on Merseyside)

Formal evaluation of the display (Pennington 1994) suggests that its intentions were achieved and that some visitors began to consider further the differences in the pottery shards available,

> some in relation to improvement in manufacturing techniques over the years and others that they look similar but have different textures and qualities.
> (Pennington 1994)

Visitors to the ARC and Hampshire Museums Service's SEARCH Hands-on Centre for History and Natural History are invited to assist the archaeologists in their sorting of soil samples. A microscope is provided and individual visitors are able to search the sample for any interesting faunal remains. Using tweezers they remove the remains from the sample for researchers to analyse at a later date. This type of activity does give visitors the impression that they are contributing to the archaeological process, and does give them space to interpret what they say or do in their own way: 'What material is important and therefore should I be selecting?' Though again the learning experience is stage-managed and predetermined, the activity is more open-ended than the sorting of various types of material.

Both NMGM and Stoke-on-Trent City Museum & Art Gallery have experimented with an activity that encourages the visitor to think about how a complete ceramic can be reconstructed from a heap of shards. At NMGM visitors were provided with moulds of a complete post-medieval vessel to act as a guide. Visitors placed shards of a replica pot (made specifically for this purpose) inside in order to reconstruct it. A complete original of the ceramic was displayed in a case nearby. The problem posed does require the visitor to think hard about the solution and to look closely at the material. However, again the solution is predetermined: the mould firmly guides the visitor as to the relationship between each of the shards on the table and the form of the complete vessel (Longworth 1994).

A number of museums provide opportunities for visitors to handle archaeological material as part of a chronological or themed interpretive narrative, with the intention of adding a personal and interactive dimension. Visitors to the 'Early Ireland' display at the Ulster Museum can touch various prehistoric artefacts on open display, including two Palaeolithic hand-axes, a 'Bann' flake, and a bronze flat axe. The Prehistoric and Roman Galleries at the Museum of London provide opportunities for visitors to touch replica pottery, hand-axes, and Roman tiles. Boxes of pottery are laid out in a 'mock-museum' storage area at Stoke, and visitors are encouraged to open the lids and have a look at the material inside. At Colchester, visitors are invited to touch a replica of a decorated samian bowl to feel the quality of the fabric and the relief of the decoration. A replica of a suit of armour is available and visitors are able to try it on, to feel how heavy it is, and to sympathize with the soldiers who had to wear the originals! In 1993, Glasgow Museums prepared a travelling exhibition, 'In Touch With the Past', which aimed to introduce various aspects of prehistoric technology to visually impaired and sighted people. It incorporated approximately fifty objects from the reserve collections which visitors were able to handle and examine closely, including flint waste, polished axes, and ceramics (Batey 1996).

Whether an opportunity to touch and handle an artefact provides a closed or open intellectual interactive experience depends very much on the design of the activity of which it is a part. The museums visited in preparation for this chapter predominantly used handling material to reinforce issues and concepts discussed in the text. In the 'Technology Before Fire' section of the Prehistoric Gallery at the Museum of London, various raw materials are available for visitors to feel and interpret in the context of what is described on the panels. Any interaction is of a relatively passive nature: visitors are expected to look at the objects with a predetermined conclusion in mind; there is no active encouragement to think further about the objects and what they might mean. This is a point perhaps borne out by the findings of a summative evaluation on the gallery by Susie Fisher (1995), which suggests that hands-on media could be used more effectively. Interestingly, hands-on activities are not used to explore one of the key objectives of the exhibition – to demystify the archaeological and museological process behind the gallery (Museum of London, undated a) – an objective that focuses on the active role of the individual in any narrative. Fisher's survey (1995) suggests that the current focus on using text as the key medium to communicate these philosophical ideas is not working effectively; perhaps hands-on has a role to play.

In the Ancient Egypt Gallery at New Walk Museum in Leicester, visitors are able to open drawers under the display cases containing shabtis to reveal more of the same from the reserve collections of the Museum. This is an activity that has a long history of museum use, and is increasingly exploited in archaeology displays. In the Early Ireland Gallery at the Ulster Museum, drawers below the tool case in the hunter-gatherer section contain additional specimens to those on display and also exhibit their suggested modern equivalents: a Mesolithic borer is displayed alongside a Black & Decker drill, for example.

These drawers do provide greater access to elements of the museum collection, which are too fragile to be made available for handling or touching. They incorporate an element of discovery in the process of opening the drawer and seeing what is inside (Longworth 1991). To many visitors that may be the extent of their fascination; to others it may bring home the fact that museums have material that is not always put on show, and may help them to appreciate the great diversity of material found by archaeologists and housed in museum collections. To a small few, metal detectorists for example, it may be a facility that helps them to identify material of their own. These visitors will interact with the exhibit, but for many, unless they are encouraged to work with the material in the drawers, any intellectual interaction will be of a passive nature.

Museums are experimenting with activities that encourage visitors to have a go at making replica artefacts. At the ARC staff are on hand to help visitors make a Roman shoe and weave using a replica Viking Age 'upright warp-weighted loom'. The visitor is faced with a problem, for example, how to make a shoe from stiffened leather or how to work the loom, and has to come up with a solution. Again there is a definitive finished product, as suggested by the archaeological evidence, but there is scope for visitors to devise their own solution to the task in hand, with or without the assistance of staff.

Hands-on activities are also used to explain broader archaeological concepts, as well as inspiring visitors to think about the objects on display. These activities vary greatly in design and approach, and provide ample opportunity for stimulating open interaction between the visitor and the narrative. However, many identify a problem that needs to be solved and the visitor works towards a predetermined conclusion: in the Ancient Egypt Gallery at New Walk Museum, Leicester, for example, the visitor is asked to consider 'How Egyptian Writing Works'. The text panel explains how the hieroglyphic language uses pictures rather than letters to represent particular sounds, and the interactive encourages visitors to investigate this principle further. The activity is a good example of where 'having a go' helps the visitor to understand quite a complex concept. However, the solutions to the problem are fixed: the visitor needs to match up the correct pictures, which create a given word in order for the activity to be successfully concluded.

Museums are beginning to explore the potential of computer interactives as an element of archaeology displays. These enable the author of a narrative to provide visitors with further information as and when they wish to view it. At the Manchester University Museum, visitors can use a terminal located in the archaeology gallery to interrogate a computerized database containing further information about items on display. Visitors can select the particular artefact to be investigated further, and the type of information to be retrieved. This activity does have the potential to stimulate active interaction, particularly if the visitor has a 'problem' in mind that they wish to explore further. However, if this is not the case, the activity may be less effective because of the lack of any clear problem-solving structure. Visitors may meander through the information concerned to have a go at the technology rather than to review the information.

At Verulamium Museum a touch-screen computer interactive allows the visitor to access further information about Roman food, and the use of rooms in a Romano-British villa. At the ARC visitors can examine a laser disk containing an archive of photographs and other information from the excavations at Coppergate in York. They select the historic period to be viewed and individual photographs of interest. The new 'House of Manannan' exhibition at the Peel Heritage Centre on the Isle of Man incorporates a number of computer interactive facilities, which enable further exploration of aspects of Iron Age life on the island. Visitors are able to choose the type and level of information they wish to access according to their own particular agendas. However, the information content of many of these interactives is still predominantly didactic: visitors may choose the line of enquiry, but the results are still presented as fact.

The majority of the activities outlined above draw on the problem-solving nature of archaeological work and interpreting the past, but do so in a way that emphasizes the closed intellectual end of the interactive spectrum. Visitors undoubtedly develop invaluable observational and problem-solving awareness as a result of these activities (Robertson 1991) and understand more about the work of archaeologists (Davis 1991; Pennington 1994). These activities do perhaps satisfy many of the learning needs of those visitors who do like museums to provide them with a didactic experience. However, because they focus almost completely on closed interaction, these activities ignore the uncertainty, subjectivity, and diverse nature of the archaeological process. Visitors are not set a more open-ended problem and encouraged to work towards alternative solutions, to develop greater confidence in their own ideas.

The display authors' intended objectives

A study of formalized aims and objectives for some of the activities discussed above suggests that most authors had clear learning experiences in mind for visitors who used those activities. In most cases, there is an emphasis on providing an enjoyable learning environment and there is obvious intent to actively engage visitors in the exhibition narrative:

> [The SEARCH Hands-on Centre for History and Natural History] encourages children to investigate with help from specially trained demonstrators or interpreters.
>
> (Hampshire County Council, undated)

> To introduce visitors to the work of archaeologists and the range of skills and techniques employed ... To provoke interest in, and enjoyment of archaeology by breaking down the barriers that surround it and making it approachable to non-specialists.
>
> (Iles 1991: 26)

> The aim of the Centre is to explain the work of Archaeologists in the context of the Roman, Viking and Norman periods of Lincoln. This is done through a series of 'hands on' tasks which require Information Recording, Planning, Drawing and Sorting.
>
> (City of Lincoln Archaeology Unit, undated, pages unnumbered)

Hands-on activities are also regarded as a means of providing greater access to material in collections, and to information about those collections, in a way that enables visitors to choose the level of information they wish to access:

> to ... improve physical and intellectual access to the collections.
>
> (Longworth & Philpott 1993, pages unnumbered)

> to make use of parts of the reserve collection ... to introduce various aspects of prehistoric technology to both visually impaired and sighted people.
>
> (Batey 1996: 19)

Only one of the objectives documents analysed includes any explicit intention of using hands-on activities to explore the subjective nature of archaeology and archaeological interpretation. As a result, the objectives identified for individual activities are primarily didactic in nature:

> The purpose of this section was to explain what archaeologists find out from pottery.
>
> (Longworth 1994)

> 1. To demonstrate the finds recording system operated by the York Archaeological Trust.
> 2. To allow visitors to handle small finds.
>
> (Iles 1991: 78)

The objectives outlined for the Time Machine element of the proposed Rotunda History Centre at the Museum of London were the exception:

[the visitor will be given] the chance to explore both the known parts of an object and the deduced, interpreted aspects of its past use and importance in society ... [and will be encouraged] to appreciate the difference between known fact and essentially subjective, and therefore debatable, interpretation.'

(Museum of London, undated b)

This innovative approach to museum interpretation, whereby visitors would be encouraged to select an object and investigate it at a series of workstations to answer key questions about the object, has unfortunately failed to secure the necessary financial backing required for its development.

The picture evolving from this brief analysis is primarily one of emphasis on developing a closed intellectual interaction between visitor and narrative. A similar picture also emerges at a more informal level: the questionnaire sent to a small sample of museum archaeologists in the UK asked respondents to consider why hands-on activities had been incorporated into archaeology displays in their museums.

The replies placed a great deal of emphasis on the benefits of *doing* as a means to learning; and the feeling that there is value in providing direct access to real collections and artefacts in an entertaining way came through strongly:

> Transfer of knowledge would be better served by displays encouraging activity rather than passivity.
>
> (Isle of Man)

> There is nothing better than being able to touch real objects.
>
> (Glasgow Museums)

> Hands-on activities involve participation, which can be fun. An enjoyable experience is also potentially the best form of communication.
>
> (Plymouth Museums)

A number of respondents mentioned the role of hands-on activities in stimulating an intellectual interaction between visitors and the themes of the exhibition.

> Computer interactives also enable the creation of a hierarchy of information which enables the visitor to choose the level at which he/she wants to investigate a subject.
>
> (Isle of Man)

> The hands-on elements were designed with the [National] Curriculum in mind where children have to discover and work things out for themselves.
>
> (Verulamium Museum)

It is generally proven that they allow an additional way of interpreting the past which due to their interactive nature allows people to discover the past for themselves, and provides a physical link to the past.

(Winchester Museums)

However, in answering the question posed no one explicitly mentioned the potential for using hands-on activities to encourage people to explore the uncertainties of archaeological evidence and to inspire visitors to think in more active and creative ways about their past.

How can we develop hands-on activities that inspire a more active participation by the visitor in the creation of an archaeological narrative?

A brief analysis of the nature of the exhibit and the intentions of the authors using hands-on activities in archaeology displays suggests that museums might benefit from experimenting further with problem-solving activities that encourage visitors to think actively about alternative solutions. What form could such activities take? Anne Fahy's point that all interactive media used in museums are ultimately shaped by curatorial action is taken (Fahy 1995), but it should be possible to 'stage manage' a hands-on activity that encourages people to consider alternative solutions to a problem and to input their own ideas.

The desktop assessment aspect of the archaeological process perhaps has potential: visitors could be supplied with relevant information about a non-confidential, past planning application in the local area, and also with the known archaeology of the proposed development site, and asked if they would recommend archaeological intervention or not as a result of analysing the information available to them. The museum could then identify and explain the archaeologist's decision in this case.

Another form of activity might focus the visitor's mind on what an item could have been used for, an inevitable unknown for a great number of archaeological artefacts. The visitor could be encouraged to look at the object for clues of use – its size, form, material of manufacture, surface treatment, weight, decoration, etc. and from these observations suggest possible uses for the artefact. Their thoughts and ideas about the object could then be compared with an archaeologist's interpretation. This is the type of approach that the Museum of London proposed developing in the 'Time Machine' element of its Rotunda History Centre. The museum commissioned front-end evaluation for the project incorporating focus-group work with both museum visitors and non-visitors (Fisher and Lalvani 1996). The results suggest that the attraction would have been eagerly awaited by participants, and interestingly that:

they [the interviewees] have difficulty grasping the concept of objects as a means of exploring and understanding history. This is because they believe history to be known already – a given, not a mystery. To be related to them, not worked out.

(Fisher and Lalvani 1996)

It is, therefore, much to be regretted that this dynamic and innovative project has not so far attracted the backing of the Heritage Lottery Fund. The findings of Fisher and Lalvani (1996) suggest that the Centre would certainly have challenged people's perceptions of archaeology and the past.

Computer interactive technologies provide museums with the opportunity to encourage visitors to think about alternative interpretations of archaeological material culture by, for example, providing various interpretations of particular material culture evidence. Visitors could select various interpretations to consider, and be encouraged to develop personal opinions about the alternatives proposed. In a paper presented at the Society of Museum Archaeologists Conference at the Museum of London in 1995, Ian Hodder discussed plans to use virtual reality technology to interpret the archaeological site of Çatalhöyük in Turkey in such a way that a visitor could explore alternative reconstructions of the site and alternative interpretations of the material culture evidence discovered.

Conclusion

It has been mentioned from the outset that this chapter is a commentary on, rather than a comprehensive survey of, the issue under debate. However, the evidence to hand suggests that a number of museums are successfully using hands-on activities in archaeology displays to stimulate problem-solving learning experiences. It also suggests that the intended nature of this learning experience is predominantly didactic, involving a passive intellectual interaction on the part of the visitor. Museums now need to explore further the potential of hands-on media to stimulate a more open and active engagement between the visitor and the narrative of a display, and to seek ways of evaluating the learning experiences taking place as a result. Undoubtedly the planned discovery centres springing up around the UK will provide an ideal opportunity (with their emphasis on providing adequate space and resources for hands-on activities) to explore these open interaction possibilities further. However, there is no reason why the hands-on media used to complement archaeology display narratives could not reflect a greater balance between open and closed intellectual interaction. Only then will the interactive role of hands-on activities be developed to its full potential and visitors recognized as contributing authors in the making of early archaeological histories.

References

Batey, C. (1996) In touch with the past at Glasgow museums. In: G.T. Denford (ed.), *Museum Archaeology: What's New?* The Museum Archaeologist 21. Winchester: Society of Museum Archaeologists, pp. 19–23.

Bender, B. (1993) Stonehenge contested landscapes (medieval to present day). In: B. Bender (ed.), *Landscapes: Politics and Perspectives*. Providence, RI: Berg, pp. 245–80.

City of Lincoln Archaeology Unit (undated) Lincoln Archaeology Centre booking form. City of Lincoln Archaeology Unit, unpublished.

Coles, P. (1984) *Please Touch: An Evaluation of the 'Please Touch' Exhibition at the British Museum 31 March to 8 May 1983.* London: Committee of Inquiry into the Arts and Disabled People/Carnegie Trust.

Cotton, J. (1997) Illuminating the twilight zone? The new prehistoric gallery at the Museum of London. In G. Denford (ed.), *Representing Archaeology in Museums.* The Museum Archaeologist 22. Winchester: Society of Museum Archaeologists, pp. 6–12.

Cox, M. (1996) *Just Like Drawing in Your Dinner ...: Start, the First Interactive Art Gallery Experience Designed for Three to Five Year Olds.* Walsall: Walsall Museum and Art Gallery.

Davis, W (1991) The Archaeological Resource Centre: an educational evaluation. Unpublished MA dissertation, Department of Archaeology, University of York.

Fahy, A. (1995) New technologies for museum communication. In: E. Hooper-Greenhill (ed.), *Museum, Media, Message.* London: Routledge, pp. 82–96.

Fisher, S. (1995) How do visitors experience the new prehistoric gallery? Qualitative research. Unpublished report for the Museum of London. London: Susie Fisher Group.

Fisher, S. and Lalvani, S. (1996) A qualitative evaluation of visitor reactions to the London Slice and Time Machine. Unpublished report for the Museum of London. London: Susie Fisher Group.

Freeman, R. (1989) *The Discovery Gallery: Discovery Learning in the Museum.* Toronto: Royal Ontario Museum.

Gunther, C.F. (1994) Museumgoers: life-styles and learning characteristics. In: E. Hooper-Greenhill (ed.), *The Educational Role of Museums.* London: Routledge, pp. 86–97.

Hampshire County Council (undated) What is SEARCH? In: *SEARCH Information Pack,* Hampshire County Council.

Hooper-Greenhill, E. (1991) *Museum and Gallery Education.* Leicester: Leicester University Press.

Iles, R. (1991) Interactive communication and evaluation at the ARC. Unpublished MA dissertation, Department of Museum Studies, University of Leicester.

Jensen, N. (1994) Children, teenagers and adults in museums: a developmental perspective. In: E. Hooper-Greenhill (ed.), *The Educational Role of the Museum.* London: Routledge, pp. 268–74.

Johansson, L. (1996) The electronic family album: a case study. Unpublished MA dissertation, Department of Museum Studies, University of Leicester.

Kaplan, F.E.S. (1995) Exhibitions as communicative media. In: E. Hooper-Greenhill (ed.), *Museum, Media, Message.* London: Routledge, pp. 37–58.

Longworth, C. (1991) My interpretation of the Discovery Centre. National Museums & Galleries on Merseyside internal document, unpublished.

——(1994) Discovery Centre: Evaluation Report 28 May–5 June 1994. Have a Go at Archaeology. National Museums & Galleries on Merseyside internal document, unpublished.

Longworth, C. and Philpott, F. (1993) The Discovery Centre. National Museums & Galleries on Merseyside internal document, unpublished.

Merriman, N. (1990) Dealing with present issues in the long term: 'The Peopling of London Project'. In: E. Southworth (ed.), *Ready for the New Millennium? Futures for*

Museum Archaeology. The Museum Archaeologist 17. Liverpool: Society of Museum Archaeologists, pp. 37–43.

Museum of London (undated a) Museum of London Prehistoric Gallery: Objectives. Museum of London internal document, unpublished.

Museum of London (undated b) The Rotunda History Centre. Museum of London internal document, unpublished.

Owen, J. (1996) Making archaeological histories in museums. In: G. Kavanagh (ed.), *Making Histories in Museums*. Leicester: Leicester University Press, pp. 200–15.

Peirson Jones, J. (1995) Communicating and learning in Gallery 33: evidence from a visitor study. In: E. Hooper-Greenhill (ed.), *Museum, Media, Message*. London: Routledge, pp. 260–75.

Pennington, A. (1994) Report of formative evaluation of two elements of the Have a Go at Archaeology display. National Museums & Galleries on Merseyside internal document, unpublished.

Robertson, J. (1991) A case study of the ARC, focusing on object orientated learning. Unpublished BA dissertation, University of York.

Shanks, M. and Tilley, C. (1992) *Re-Constructing Archaeology: Theory and Practice*. Second edition. London: Routledge.

Southworth, E. (1994) Archaeology and ethnology, 'The Discovery Centre'. A development plan. National Museums & Galleries on Merseyside internal document, unpublished.

Stone, P. (1994) The re-display of the Alexander Keiller Museum, Avebury, and the National Curriculum in England. In: P. Stone and B.L. Molyneaux (eds.), *The Presented Past: Heritage, Museums and Education*. London: Routledge, pp. 190–205.

Tyler, J. (1990) Interactive videos in museums. Unpublished MA dissertation, University of Leicester.

Chapter 31

The redisplay of the Alexander Keiller Museum, Avebury, and the National Curriculum in England

Peter G. Stone

Background

The Avebury sites

The World Heritage Site of Stonehenge and Avebury is made up of two distinctive and separate parts – the first comprising Stonehenge and its surrounding prehistoric landscape, the second, about 25 km to the north, comprising the area around the prehistoric henge monument of Avebury. The latter area includes six prehistoric sites presently under the management of English Heritage, the national organization charged with the statutory protection of the historic environment in England. These sites are: (1) the huge bank and ditch of a neolithic henge monument enclosing the substantially re-erected remains of a number of circles of undressed standing stones and enclosing much of the modern village of Avebury; (2) the remains of the causewayed enclosure of Windmill Hill; (3) the largely re-erected section of part of the West Kennet Avenue of stones that seems to link the henge monument at Avebury to (4) the site of another stone circle known as the Sanctuary; (5) the excavated and rebuilt remains of the Long Barrow funerary monument of West Kennet; and (6) Silbury Hill, the largest artificial structure in northern Europe (see, for example, Coupland 1988). In addition to these monuments, this part of the World Heritage Site also contains the remains of numerous other prehistoric structures. All of the sites lie within an easy two-hour drive of a series of major urban centres including London.

There has been extensive interest in the Avebury area since (at least) the seventeenth century, for example the work of antiquarians John Aubrey and William Stukeley (see Ucko et al. 1991), and more recently a whole plethora of popular books has been produced to satisfy the demands of the interested lay public (for example, Burl 1979; Pitts 1986; Malone 1989). Four of the English Heritage-

Source: *The Presented Past: Heritage, Museums and Education*. P.G. Stone and B.L. Molyneaux (eds.). New York & Abingdon: Routledge, 2004. pp. 190–205 © Taylor & Francis.

managed sites (the main henge, West Kennet Long Barrow, West Kennet Avenue, and the Sanctuary) were extensively restored in the early and middle part of this century after archaeological investigation (Ucko et al. 1991).

The museum in Avebury is named after the millionaire archaeologist Alexander Keiller, who worked in the area in the early part of this century, and is housed in a building itself protected by law for its historic value as the stable block of a largely extant sixteenth-century manor house. The main holding of the museum is the Keiller bequest – collected by Keiller over a number of seasons of excavation in the 1920s and 1930s at Windmill Hill and Avebury and embellished by artefacts he collected and bought from abroad. The museum also holds most of the finds and archive of more recent excavations at West Kennet Long Barrow and Silbury Hill (Piggott 1962; Atkinson 1967, 1968, 1969, 1970) and is the official repository for all archaeological finds from the local area.

School visits to the Avebury region

For the past 20 or more years Avebury has been a popular location for school visits, with over 11,000 schoolchildren visiting the museum annually. It is estimated that at least a further 10,000–15,000 schoolchildren annually visit one or more of the sites without visiting the museum. Until recently, the majority of these children have been in the 7 to 11 age range – the time at school where prehistory is most commonly taught (although see below). Most of these visits were supported by materials produced in school by teachers, although two specific handbooks for teachers on the Avebury sites have been produced (Coupland 1988; Stone 1990a).

However, this situation is in the process of changing. All schoolchildren in England now have to follow a prescribed National Curriculum that leaves little time for teaching about the prehistoric past (DES 1989; Stone 1992; and see Corbishley and Stone 1994). The history curriculum (DES 1991) is made up of a core of compulsory units of work covering topics such as 'Tudor and Stuart Times' and 'Victorian Britain' supplemented by a series of optional courses such as 'Ships and Seafarers' and 'Writing and Printing'. There are no core units that cover any prehistoric period. Because of the huge amount of historical material included in the curriculum, most teachers try to combine core and optional units – for example by teaching about ships and seafarers in Tudor and Stuart England. Teachers, therefore, have very little opportunity to introduce their own ideas or content into this curriculum. Moreover, the new curriculum has been introduced very quickly with, initially, few new resources for a large number of (especially primary) teachers who have never had to teach history before.

Despite this somewhat gloomy picture, opportunities do exist for teaching about prehistory within the new curriculum (Stone 1990b, 1992) and for using museums in particular (NCC 1990; Stone 1993). One of the optional units for 11- to 14-year-olds has to cover 'An episode or turning point in European history before 1914' and in its advice to teachers on the history curriculum the National Curriculum Council (NCC), an advisory body to Government, has suggested studying the 'Neolithic Revolution' for this unit (NCC 1991). Teachers can also use museums and prehistoric sites while working on optional 'local history' units or data from prehistory when working on optional units such as 'Houses and Places of Worship' or 'Food and Farming'.

The redisplay

For a number of years the English Heritage Regional Team (that has collective accountability for the monuments and museum at Avebury) has been aware that the exhibition in the Keiller Museum, originally set up in the 1960s, was in dire need of redisplay. Limited funds for this work were made available for the financial year 1990/1. The team included the Ancient Monuments Archaeological Inspector for the sites, representatives from the English Heritage Museums Group, an in-house Design and Interpretative Manager, and me, the Regional Education Officer. At various times during the year this core group was assisted by architectural, mechanical and engineering, and works staff.

A more extensive project to develop a Visitor Orientation Point in a building in the central car park at Avebury at the same time as the refurbishment of the museum, was put aside until longer-term plans for the presentation of the whole of this part of the World Heritage Site have been finalized. This delay meant (and means) that the new exhibition in the museum was to be (and will be for the foreseeable future) the only point of interpretation (other than brief interpretation panels for individual sites) for the prehistory of the area.

It was my prime concern that the redisplayed museum would relate as closely as possible to the constraints, attitudes, and opportunities imposed and offered by the new National Curriculum. This especially meant focusing on the nature of historical (archaeological) evidence and the subjectivity of interpretation based on such evidence (see below). However, the education policy developed for the museum (see, for example, Hooper-Greenhill 1991) was based on the redisplay being interesting and, we hope, informative, for the general visitor as well as for education groups. Educational requirements were to have a high profile in the work of the project team, but once the redisplay was complete, education groups would have to compete for gallery space with all other visitors and would have no special area or handling collection set aside for them within the museum. (There is, however, a classroom-sized study base available for education groups to book within the village but away from the museum.)

The constraints

As mentioned above, the museum collection is housed in a protected building that cannot be extended or altered. This gave maximum internal dimensions for exhibition space of just under 50 square metres. We also only had one year in which to carry out the project – from initial plans to completed redisplay. If we went over the financial year-end the money would disappear. Finally, the budget was very small – £30,000 to cover the cost not only of actually redisplaying the museum but also of script writer, external designer, new sales counter and facilities, associated building work, and exhibition-related electrical modifications.

Given the timescale for the project, the limitations of space and especially the extremely tight budget, it was clear from the start that we were not going to be able to introduce the latest examples of interactive museum display techniques, nor were we going to be able to replace, for example, all of the old display cabinets. The new exhibition was going to have to rely substantially upon graphics and revised text rather than any major renewal of presentation hardware and this in itself was a major and stimulating challenge.

What to present?

Our first real problem was to decide what type of exhibition we wanted to put on in the museum. What particular message(s) – if any – did we want to give to our visitors? In this we were somewhat constrained by the Keiller bequest that partially directed us as to what should be displayed. However, within these limitations we still had the opportunity to focus on, for example, the entire World Heritage Site, or the six monuments under our management, or the Neolithic of southern England more generally, or a little of all three. We were very conscious that the museum was, and still is, the only place where a display focusing on the prehistory of the area is really possible or appropriate.

Before making any final plans as to the content of the redisplay we discussed our plans with a number of archaeologists who were specialists in the Neolithic, or who had worked on the Avebury sites in particular. Not surprisingly, after consulting six different people we had six very different views! However, through this exercise we gathered a host of relevant and interesting ideas – many of which were finally welded into the overall framework with which we attempted to underpin the exhibition (see below). I also carefully went through all of the National Curriculum subject documents – especially history, science, technology, English, mathematics, and art – to identify where teachers and children might be able to use the material available in the museum collection to develop their work.

We also looked carefully at the visitor profile for the museum. It has been estimated (Cobham Resource Consultants 1990) – that about half a million people visit Avebury every year. Of these, only about 40,000 visit the museum. About 15,000 of these visitors gain free access as members of either English Heritage or the National Trust (a nation-wide charity whose members support the conservation of the historic and natural environment) and a further 11,000+ receive free access as formal educational groups (mainly schools but also including university and college groups and some adult education parties). This leaves only 14,000 or so visitors out of the original half a million who were willing to pay for access to the present museum at the door. Leaving aside the complex issue of charging for heritage attractions and museums, the figures were depressing. Obviously, the museum was not attracting a complete cross section of the population. Visitors in the UK expect to have to pay for access to most sites and most museums and, practical problems apart (visitors have to be particularly persistent to find the museum building, located as it is away from the main tourist route through the site), we had to assume that part of this reluctance to visit was due to the type and content of museum display (museum staff had commented that quite a lot of people peeked in through the door and then left without paying to look around the museum). Because they are usually expected to pay, visitors have become increasingly demanding of the quality of exhibitions and displays. The Keiller Museum was obviously not fulfilling visitor expectations and they were staying away.

As educational groups make up over a quarter of the visitors, I arranged for a number of schools to ask their pupils what they would want a new museum display to tell them about the people who built the Avebury monuments. All of the children involved were from first, primary, or junior schools (with an overall age range of 5–14). We combined the children's responses and drew up a table of the twenty things the children most wanted to know. The results are shown in the Appendix and paint a salutary picture for archaeologists. Nearly all the questions refer to those areas that archaeology cannot reveal with any level of certainty. They wanted to know about social, religious, and practical things that are central to their own world – and would have been central to the world of those people living in the Avebury area in the Neolithic – but which have left little or no evidence in the archaeological record. They had presented us with quite a task! We also discussed the most appropriate types of display for older children with a few secondary-level teachers and Education Authority advisors.[1] Time constraints made it impossible for us to survey undergraduate and other students in higher education as to their thoughts on the most useful type of display for them. We therefore had to assume that many of the points raised by those university-based archaeologists we had already approached would have covered what they wanted their students to get out of the museum.

Earlier general surveys (for example, Hodder et al. n.d.; Stone 1986) had already given some ideas as to the relevant interests of the general public, and further information about this group, including the questions most frequently asked at the museum and comments made about the 1960s display, was forthcoming from the museum staff. From these sources we inferred that many general visitors would be interested in many of the questions raised by the school survey. Museum staff also indicated that visitors had expressed interest in those antiquarians and archaeologists who have studied Avebury and its monuments over the centuries – the story of the re-emergence of Avebury – and that people would be especially interested to be able to see some of the actual tools and instruments used by Keiller and his workforce during the early twentieth-century excavations.

Armed with this background information we decided on our own particular approach. We argued that the great strength of the museum was its unique collection of artefacts from a range of neolithic sites. However, we suggested that only a few (usually archaeologically specialized) visitors would be interested in the artefacts for their own sake. We therefore agreed that the redisplay would concentrate on the strengths of the collection and would be object-led, using artefacts found during excavation of the six sites under our management. However, we were also convinced that there should be a running theme behind the displays that would place the objects in a more general context and which, we hoped, would begin to address many of the questions raised by the children – a theme that would almost certainly provoke more questions than it would ever be capable of answering. This idea was finally formulated in an internal memo:

> The key concept is that of 'prehistoric cosmology'. The monuments in the Avebury landscape were theatres for rites and ceremonies which both reflected and supported prehistoric ideas of world order, the place of people within that order, the relationship of people and gods, and the nature and transmission of authority (whether spiritual, educational or political). Over a period of about a thousand years these separate theatres became linked into one huge theatrical landscape. The monuments are thus the collapsed and grass-cloaked clues to an integrated system of religious, social and political beliefs which may well have been quite as complex as (though different from) our own… . As regards Avebury, unfortunately we do not know what the cosmology was! So we have to use the monuments (and their contents) to try to build a picture of that crucial motivation for their construction and use.

Our theme was to show how archaeologists interpret such fragmentary, 'grass-cloaked' evidence from the past and that, while the data of archaeology may in themselves be regarded as a collection of 'objective' artefacts, any interpretation of these data is necessarily subjective and always open to question and modification. We were, however, conscious that we had to balance this view of our understanding of the interpretation of the past with the desire on the part of many of our visitors to be told in a more didactic way 'what it was like'.

The new display

One of our fundamental decisions, taken early on in the project, was that we would drastically reduce the number of artefacts on display. We argued that a display of twenty similar arrowheads may be extremely interesting to a specialist but would tend to alienate and bore the majority of our visitors – especially if it nestled between displays of twenty similar flint scrapers and twenty similar pieces of hand axe! The whole collection would, of course, have to be available to those who wanted to study it, but our duty in the redisplay of the museum was to non-specialist visitors. This decision freed some space in display cases to add more illustrative material and generally to lessen the density of display. It also meant that we were able to remove some display cabinets entirely. One set of cases had always been a problem as they were too high for children to see into. Their removal provided a far better visitor circulation pattern, generally created more space in the museum, and gave us space to display some of Keiller's tools and instruments and to introduce a small 'hands-on' section where visitors can feel the weight of a hafted axe and handle (modern) antler picks.

The central feature of the redisplay is a chronological tour of the six sites. Each display is object-led but also has a newly commissioned artist's illustration, in colour, of the site in the Neolithic. Objects in the display are, wherever possible, seen in context in the illustration. Each case also boasts a new air photograph of the site as it is today. Throughout, we attempted to address our theme of the subjectivity of archaeological interpretation by continually thinking back to the children's questions. Our lack of ability to answer them satisfactorily kept us constantly aware that what we were trying to interpret were the intangibles of the past rather than any concept of a past well understood and definitive in nature.

We decided to dot around the new display a series of 'clipboards' that could be used to raise questions in visitors' minds about the various sites and their particular functions and locations. They also describe what can be seen from the various sites. The text on the clipboards is easily changed so if new questions come up – a site that might be affected by nearby development, for example – they can be updated relatively easily. We also hope the clipboards will encourage visitors to the museum to go out into the landscape and visit the other sites. The last clipboard, which is much larger than the others and is, in fact, the last major display in the museum, raises the contemporary issues of conservation and preservation and gives the visitor a brief idea of the work of English Heritage and its role as regards these issues.

The practicalities

Our first major problem was a disagreement within the project team as to whether or not the new display should include a full-size 'neolithic figure'. The debate concentrated on the contradiction between the desirability of having a figure to draw in visitors and to give them a strong message about the people in the Neolithic and the well-rehearsed arguments about lack of detailed (any?) knowledge about people's appearance. If we were to have a figure, what clothes would he (or she?) wear? Trousers? Kilts? Cloaks? Jackets? What would they be made from? Would they be dyed with rich colours or plain? What footwear should we give the figure? Would the figure be tattooed? What about body painting? Jewellery? If male, would the figure be clean-shaven or bearded; long-haired or crew cut? The questions were endless and answers were in short supply. The only thing we could agree on was that no figure should be produced which could possibly support the 'dinosaur-hunting grunter-groaner' image of prehistory (Richardson 1987: 76).

We eventually agreed to use our own disagreement to re-emphasize our major theme – illustrating the limitations of archaeological evidence and the subjectivity of display. Our figure was to be schizophrenic, full size but presented in two halves: one side showing a fully dressed yet ragged individual, coping with existence – but only just; the other side illustrating an individual from a society more interested in its presentation and, perhaps, rather more 'sophisticated' – painted, tattooed, with well-made clothes and bedecked with jewellery (Figure 31.1). Neither side has any attributes that were not potentially available to anyone living in southern England in the Neolithic. Below our character a caption suggests to visitors that, because of the nature of archaeological evidence, 'the experts' are unsure about what people really looked like in the Neolithic and that the two options shown in the figure are two extreme views and – importantly – what do they, the visitors, think? Next to the caption sits a cartoon firmly dispelling the image of the 'grunter-groaner'.

We also guessed (steered by the results of the general surveys mentioned above) that most visitors would, perhaps subconsciously, be more at home with the less sophisticated view of the model. We therefore agreed to angle the figure so that this was the image visitors would see on their arrival at the museum – the more sophisticated side would only be revealed as visitors moved around the display. This angling has quite a dramatic effect as visitors are suddenly confronted by the figure's 'sophisticated' side. We hoped that this would cause them to pause for a moment to question their own preconceived views of what people in the Neolithic may have been like, and initial comments from museum staff indicate that many visitors really do confront the issue and discuss the relative values of the two sides of our figure as they learn more about neolithic technology and life from the rest of the museum display.

We decided to continue this 'schizophrenic' theme in some of the newly commissioned artwork for the redisplay. In one instance the same scene is presented in two illustrations with individuals sitting and standing in the same places but dressed differently in the two illustrations – in much the same way as the two sides of our figure. We also have the figures doing slightly different things in the two illustrations in an attempt to get visitors to think about what they are looking at and about what life would have been like in the Neolithic.

Figure 31.1 The symbolic presentation of 'fact' versus 'imagination' through the use of a divided image. Photo: English Heritage.

As a team, we were very aware of the complex debate now in progress with regard to the use of human remains in archaeological exhibitions (for an overview of issues and history of the debate see Hubert 1988, 1991). Interestingly, museum staff had informed us that a child skeleton was the most popular exhibit of the old display with young and old visitors alike. Despite this, we agreed that we were content for human remains to be on display only given that (a) no group claims that the remains are those of their group's ancestors and prefers the remains not to be on display and (b) there is a valid reason for the display of the remains. We were not content for human remains to be exhibited for sensationalism or just for the sake of it.

To our knowledge no group has, to date, attempted to lay claim to any prehistoric human remains from England. However, our second concern was equally important. In the end, it was decided to keep the child skeleton as a justified and relevant part of the redisplay as it provided a further example of the subjectivity of interpretation and acted as an emotional handle to help bridge the gap of 5,000 years between the builders of the monuments and the modern museum visitor.

The panel above the skeleton now reads:

Charlie/Charlotte?

This may be the closest we shall ever get to someone from the neolithic world. Known to custodians and visitors as 'Charlie', this skeleton of a child has been in the museum for nearly fifty years. Yet we are not even sure whether it was a boy or a girl.

The bones are lying just as they were found in the 1920s in the outer ditch at Windmill Hill. The child was buried about 5,000 years ago, with the head facing the rising sun. The curled-up position resembles sleep: perhaps the child was expected to 'wake' again after death.

Charlie was about three or four years old. The shape of the head is odd, and some experts have suggested the child died of hydrocephalus ('water on the brain'). However, the deformity may have been caused after death by weight of soil in the grave.

Who was 'Charlie'? And what would Charlie think of us, if we could meet?

The display of human remains is an extremely complex issue. However, it seems that the display of Charlie has been justified by the positive response it has provoked. To our knowledge there have been no complaints over the display of the child's remains and teachers frequently comment on the beneficial impact the remains have had on their children – turning the past from something studied in textbooks to something that really happened. The remains have also been used by teachers as a stimulus to introduce the topics of what museums should display and who controls the presentation of the past.

All new exhibitions need a period of assessment and review where the visitors put designers' ideas to the test. This review is central to any redisplay and we are in the process of such a review at present. What we have tried to do in the new exhibition is to create an atmosphere where questions are raised not only about the Neolithic but also about our own understanding and presentation of the period, its objects and people. The review and clipboards should give us the opportunity to react with relative ease to the constantly changing questions that are raised by new interpretations of the Neolithic period in general and of the Avebury sites in particular.

The redisplay and the National Curriculum

In National Curriculum history the content of the history study units taught to children is tested against three 'Attainment Targets' that are regarded as being the fundamental attributes of a good historian. Each Attainment Target has ten levels of attainment with only the brightest child being expected to reach Level 10 at the end of their school career. These Attainment Targets are:

1 *Knowledge and understanding of history*
  The development of the ability to describe and explain historical change, and analyse different features of historical situations.
2 *Interpretations of history*
  The development of the ability to understand interpretations of history.
3 *The use of historical sources*
  The development of pupils' ability to acquire evidence from historical sources, and form judgements about their reliability and value.

(DES 1991)

With the emphasis in the redisplay as described above on the subjectivity of archaeological interpretation, the new museum is especially suited to the development of an understanding of the last two Attainment Targets. Specially prepared notes for teachers on how to use the museum display as a tool to develop these skills have been produced and are sent out to teachers on request. These, together with other articles in the educational literature (for example, Stone 1992) and some general DES guidelines that, for example, stress that all children 'should have opportunities to learn about the past from a range of historical sources' that include 'artifacts and buildings and sites' (DES 1991: 13), begin to question the wide-ranging misunderstanding that there is no place for the teaching of the prehistoric past within the National Curriculum.

Given this support material, and the NCC guidelines mentioned above, it can be seen that the National Curriculum does offer a limited but potentially secure position for the teaching of at least one period of prehistory. However, the point to emphasize is that many teachers who now have the opportunity to teach about prehistory do not know enough about the subject. They need help. Museum archaeologists are in a unique position to give that help. The NCC has already published a guide to the National Curriculum for museum and site staff (NCC 1990). It cannot be emphasized too strongly that museum and site staff need to get to know the National Curriculum well and quickly. If we, as museum educators, can show teachers how they can approach a range of subject areas through visiting our museums, then they will build visits into their timetables. If we do not make these contacts, a golden opportunity will have been lost and timetables will have been filled with other work.

Conclusion

We have attempted to redisplay the Alexander Keiller Museum in a way that is interesting, educational, and fun. We have tried to explain some of the techniques of modern archaeology and of those antiquarians and archaeologists who have studied the monuments before us: techniques and a history that underline our contemporary understanding of the Neolithic and of these monuments in particular. We have tried to explain what we know – and to point out what we do not know – about the Avebury sites and the Neolithic. We hope we have achieved an environment that is more welcoming to visitors – be they specialist academics, general visitors, or educational groups. The museum is intended, especially for the latter, to serve as an example of how the evidence of prehistory can be accommodated within the constraints of the prescribed National Curriculum. Time alone will tell whether we have been successful.

Note

1 We tried to get older pupils to answer the questionnaire, but unfortunately curriculum constraints (most older children tend to visit the museum later in the year) and our own timescale did not allow this to happen.

References

Atkinson, R. (1967) Interim report on excavations at Silbury Hill. *Antiquity*, 41: 256–62.
——(1968) Note on excavations at Silbury Hill. *Antiquity*, 42: 299.
——(1969) Note on excavations at Silbury Hill. *Antiquity*, 43: 216.
——(1970) Note on excavations at Silbury Hill. *Antiquity*, 44: 313–14.
Burl, A. (1979) *Prehistoric Avebury*. New Haven: Yale University Press.
Cobham Resource Consultants (1990) Interim report on Avebury visitor survey. Unpublished.
Corbishley, M. and Stone, P.G. (1994) The teaching of the past in formal school curricula in England. In: P.G. Stone and B.L. Molyneaux (eds.), *The Presented Past: Heritage, Museums and Education*. London: Routledge, pp. 383–97.
Coupland, L. (1988) *The Avebury Monuments: A Study Pack for Teachers*. London: English Heritage.
DES (1989) *National Curriculum: From Policy to Practice*. London: Department of Education and Science.

——(1991) *History in the National Curriculum*. London: Department of Education and Science.
Hodder, I., Parker Pearson, M., Peck, N., and Stone, P.G. (n.d.) Archaeology knowledge and society. Unpublished survey material.
Hooper-Greenhill, E. (1991) *Writing a Museum Education Policy*. Leicester: Department of Museum Studies, University of Leicester.
Hubert, J. (1988) The disposition of the dead. *World Archaeological Bulletin*, 2: 12–39.
——(1991) After the Vermilion Accord: developments in the 'reburial issue'. *World Archaeological Bulletin*, 5: 113–18.
Malone, C. (1989) *The English Heritage Book for Avebury*. London: English Heritage.
NCC (1990) *Guide for Staff of Museums, Galleries, Historic Houses and Sites*. York: National Curriculum Council.
——(1991) *History Non-Statutory Guidance*. York: National Curriculum Council.
Piggott, S. (1962) *The West Kennet Long Barrow*. London: HMSO.
Pitts, M. (1986) *Footprints through Avebury*. Avebury: Avebury Press.
Richardson, W. (1987) Isn't it all about dinosaurs? An experiment in a junior school. In: S. Joyce et al. (eds.), *Degree, Digging, Dole: Our Future*. Southampton: Department of Archaeology, University of Southampton, pp. 66–77.
Stone, P.G. 1986. Are the public really interested? In: C. Dobinson and R. Gilchrist (eds.), *Archaeology, Politics and the Public*. York: Department of Archaeology, University of York, pp. 14–21.
——(1990a) *The First Farmers*. Southampton: Department of Archaeology, University of Southampton.
——(1990b) Teaching the past, with special reference to prehistory, in English primary education. Unpublished PhD thesis, University of Southampton.
——(1992) The magnificent seven: reasons for teaching about prehistory. *Teaching History*, 69: 13–19.
——(1993) Life beyond the gallery: education, archaeology and the new millennium. In: E. Southworth (ed.), *'Ready for the new millennium?' Futures for Museums Archaeology*. The Museum Archaeologist 17. Winchester: Society for Museum Archaeologists, pp. 53–6.
Ucko, P.J., Hunter, M. Clark, A., and David, A. (1991) *Avebury Reconsidered from the 1660s to the 1990s*. London: Unwin Hyman.

Appendix: The twenty most common questions asked about prehistory

(In no particular order but ★ = probably the most common questions asked)

1★ Where did they go to the toilet? – How did they get rid of it?
2★ What clothes did they wear? – What were they made of? – How did they make them? – Were they really tatty? – What did they wear on their feet? – Did they have jewellery?
3★ How did they die? – How old were they when they died? – Where did they go when they died (means both how were they buried and did they go to 'heaven')?
4★ What were their houses like? – Did they have an upstairs? – What were houses made from? – Where did they sleep? – Separate rooms or all together?
5 What did they use for light?
6★ What did they wash with? – Did they wash? – Did they have brushes and combs? – Did they have make-up? – Did they cut their hair? – Did they shave?
7 What language did they speak?
8 Did they have wives? – How many?
9 What did they eat? – What animals did they hunt?
10★ Did children have to go to school?
11 How did they get around? – Did they have any kind of transport – especially when they were old and could not walk?
12 Were there any old people? – Were they looked after well?
13★ Did they have Christmas/birthdays? – Did they have parties?
14 Did they draw/do art? – What did they draw?
15 Did they have shops? – Did they have any nice things?
16★ What toys/games did they have?
17 What did they think about the world?
18★ What were their weapons like? – What were they made of?
19★ What animals did they have? – What animals didn't they have that we have now?
20 Were there any physical differences between them and us?

Roman boxes for London's schools
An outreach service by the Museum of London

Jenny Hall and Hedley Swain

Introduction

The Museum of London has developed a project intended for London's schools to improve the access to its nationally important Roman archaeological collections. It would like to provide a 'mini-museum' of Roman material, suitably packed and presented, to every state and special school in greater London – a total of over 2,000 schools. If the museum achieves its aim, it will be the largest ever deposition of museum artefacts to British schools and it is hoped that it will form a model for other institutions seeking to increase educational access to museum collections.

The Museum of London Archaeological Archive

The London Archaeological Archive holds the secrets to the lives of past Londoners. The museum views London as one big archaeological site and each individual excavation contributes a snapshot to the bigger picture. In all, the Museum of London holds the archives for over 3,000 individual excavations. A recent survey (Swain 1998) has shown that the London Archaeological Archive (the accumulated remains from all London excavations) is over three times larger than any other in Britain. At present, it includes 120,000 boxes of artefacts, 4,000 environmental samples, and 265 timber pallets of medieval stonework. These figures continue to increase annually (Swain 1999).

In 1998 the archive moved from its rented store into the Museum of London's own resource centre. However, it is currently stored there in cramped conditions with only minimal access and no room for expansion. The museum is now planning a completely new approach to caring for the archive. It is faced with two main challenges: first, the effective storage of the archive to ensure its long-term preservation; secondly, and perhaps more importantly, the maximizing of access to and the use of the archive. It is widely accepted that archaeology and the study of

Source: *Archaeological Displays and the Public: Museology and Interpretation.* 2nd edition. P. McManus (ed.). London: Archetype Publications, 2000. pp. 87–95. Reproduced with the permission of the authors.

our past is important. However, it is very difficult to translate this into giving wide public access to some very complicated records and to box after box of flints and pottery sherds. Obviously much of the task of providing access falls to museum curators who study the material and explain it to the public through gallery displays, temporary exhibitions, and books. However, it is the Museum of London's goal to provide a far more exciting level of access to this material. The school boxes scheme will be one element of this access initiative.

The museum's plans for the archive to involve the creation of the London Archaeological Archive and Resource Centre (LAARC). This facility will be based in the museum's resource centre in Hackney, which currently holds the extensive social history collections not on display. The building will be enlarged to take current archaeological material and allow room for expansion as new sites are excavated. Public areas are also to be included and the museum is working closely with local archaeological societies, universities, and other educational groups to design a programme of access and events in order to make LAARC the prime centre for archaeology in London. The project has received funding from both a public appeal and from the Heritage Lottery Fund.

The Museum of London's provision for schools

One of the museum's strategic aims is 'to make 100% of the Museum's core collections physically available and interpreted in an accessible and enlivening way' (Museum of London 1999). The museum's current services for schools studying the Romans focus on the Roman London Gallery – the most popular gallery for school visits at the museum. The gallery visits are always fully booked and it is not possible to accommodate all the schools wishing to use the gallery. As many as 5,000 pupils are denied access each year. The museum's educational sessions on Roman themes and artefact handling sessions are also the most oversubscribed in its extensive educational programme.

Museum research has shown that, despite offering free admission for schools during term-time, trips out of school are too expensive for the poorest schools. The cost of travel prevents many from reaching the museum and as a consequence they cannot benefit from access to the collections. In addition, schools in London have only limited access to other sources of Roman material. The British Museum does not offer sessions for artefact handling and only a few of London's local museums have their own archaeological collections that are used for teaching purposes. Currently, the Museum of London's Roman sessions, mainly involving visits to the museum, are used by about 200 London LEA schools, barely 10 per cent of the total of London's state primary schools.

A unique educational resource

It is widely accepted that there is nothing to compare with being able to touch real artefacts. If managed correctly, the first-hand experience of historic objects will greatly enhance a learning experience (see, for example, Durbin et al. 1990). To try to assist schools in studying the Romans, the museum has drawn on its expertise in working with children over the years and has assembled a series of artefact boxes for its teaching sessions. It is hoped that, by using actual objects in the classroom, London's schoolchildren will be better equipped to learn about the Romans. Classes study the Romans as part of the National Curriculum Key Stage 2 – Study Unit 1: Romans, Anglo-Saxons, and Vikings in Britain. This is the stage in the National Curriculum when pupils are required to learn about the Roman conquest, its impact on Britain, everyday life, and the legacy of Roman rule.

The development of the boxes project

The school boxes project therefore developed out of what proved to be several complementary factors:

- The museum wishes to provide greater and better access to its collections, and specifically access to its Roman collections to schoolchildren.
- The museum cannot satisfy the demand for access to its Roman London Gallery by schools.
- The museum holds the London Archaeological Archive, which includes in its great bulk some material that is of limited academic value.
- The museum, through the ordering and management of the archive, will be able to identify archaeological material that does not warrant full curation within the museum, is of limited academic value, and which is suitable for use in school boxes.

The idea was born to use material of no academic value from the archive to create boxes of material that could go out to London schools.

The design of the box

Detailed consideration was given to the appearance of the box. It was important that the box should both look good and be practical in its use as a mini-museum. During research for the type of box, project staff visited museums that run loan-box services to find out how they organized the services and the suitability of materials. They also talked to teachers. The following criteria were drawn up to assist in the final choice of the box:

- It needed to be bright and colourful.
- It needed to be made of durable material to survive the test of time.
- It needed to be strong and secure enough to protect the archaeological contents.
- It needed to be more than just a storage box so that it could double as a classroom display.

A metal box was chosen because it was thought to be the most durable for classroom use. To get such a box made to order would have been prohibitively expensive and project staff then looked to see whether there was anything readily available. They found that metal boxes, made for craftsmen to keep their tools safe, were already on the market. These boxes had metal trays of varying depths and configurations with a top-opening lid. Approaches were made to the manufacturers (Talco plc) to see whether they would sponsor the project by supplying the boxes either free or at cost. The firm thought that the project was very suitable for sponsorship and were happy to supply the boxes at cost but with additions made to the drawer configurations to suit the project's needs. They also added a set of wheels to make the box more manoeuvrable and produced them in the chosen colour at no extra charge.

It had been decided that the objects to be stored inside the box needed to be securely packed. In museums, it is standard practice to store objects packed in inert foam or polystyrene boxes. To help teachers and pupils distinguish between real and replica artefact, the smaller real objects were to be packed into polystyrene boxes held in place in the drawers by foam (Plastazote). Instead of tissue, the artefacts were to rest on crumpled clear film (Cryovac) inside each plastic box. The replicas were to be set into shaped recesses cut in the foam. Again the team approached manufacturers of storage materials (The Stewart Company [crystal boxes for the finds], SJ Gaskets Ltd [foam packing]) and again manufacturers were very happy to help. Some were prepared to supply the materials at cost and others generously supplied materials free of charge as a form of sponsorship. As all the replicas were standard to each box, it was possible to approach a firm to get the shapes machine-cut, saving much time and effort on the part of the project team.

The inclusion of archaeological archive material from the museum's collections

Some still find the idea of using museum collections in this way difficult to accept. However, the very particular nature of archaeological archives, particularly those from very old excavations, does mean that there is almost always material that does not contribute to a museum's aims.

All the material for the boxes will come from the museum's archaeological archive held within the LAARC. The objects that are selected:

- will not come from accessioned collections
- will be clearly identified as owned by the museum
- will be fully recorded, before being selected
- will come from 'unstratified' archaeological contexts, which make no significant contribution to the understanding of a site's history or from material for which no associated records survive
- will be of a mundane and repetitive type, which has no intrinsic academic value.

Much material of this kind exists, and is indeed common to all archaeological assemblages. This programme fits securely with the current professional museum and archaeological debate about gaining maximum value from material while not retaining it simply through precedent (see, for example, Merriman and Swain 1999). The process of deposition will include a clear record of the material, to be kept at the museum.

Figure 32.1 One of the Roman School Boxes. The bottom shelf contains the actual Roman artefacts. Photo: Museum of London.

Legal ownership of the box

It had been intended to donate the box to a school but the issue of ownership of the archaeological material was raised as a problem. It was felt that the museum should retain ownership of these pieces, not so much because it might want them back at a later date but to impress upon the school that the pieces were, in their own way, a valuable part of the archaeological record and should, therefore, be kept safe and secure. The project team did not want see the material appearing on the antiquities market, and the schools were also asked to confirm that they would not discard, hand on, or sell any material that is deposited with them. Each piece of archaeological material has been numbered and a brief record made of what each box contains. Consequently, the schools were required to sign a deposit agreement in which it was stated that, if the school at any time no longer required the box, it should be returned to the museum.

The content of the boxes

Each box is designed as a Roman mini-museum with a graphic panel about the Romans, the Museum of London, and archaeology displayed in the lid. It contains a mixture of real material taken from the Archaeological Archive and replicas of Roman objects. There are teachers' notes, classroom worksheets, and a training and demonstration video to accompany the objects, all of which are designed to support the use of the artefacts.

The artefacts

The artefacts are the most important part of the box. They are high quality and reasonably large, chosen to be easily appreciated and understood when used for non-specialist teaching. Nearly all the items are ceramic, selected for their durability. Each box that has been distributed as part of the pilot scheme contains a carefully chosen selection of Roman pottery. All pottery sherds are clearly recognizable as being from pots, normally rim or base fragments so that the shape of the original can be appreciated. At least one large piece of pottery, of a more awkward shape, has been included and there is a deep drawer in the box to house it.

It would not have been possible to select identical sherds for every box but, in general terms, every box has two sherds of the red glossy tableware, samian, at least one of which had some form of moulded decoration, and an effort was made to select either sherds with either animal or figural decoration to enable children to describe the scene. To provide a balance, a fragment of plain locally made cooking or storage pot was chosen. It has also been possible to include a large fragment of mortarium, the Roman mixing bowl with a gritted interior, which was widely used in Roman kitchens. By including fragments of the abrasive surface, children can appreciate the technological reason behind its original design. Some boxes have a portion of amphora – the large containers that were used for transporting foodstuffs throughout the Roman Empire. Sometimes it may be one of the vessel handles, part of the rim from the top, or the spike from the bottom of the container that acted as a shock absorber.

In addition to vessels, fragments of ceramic building materials have been included. There is one piece of building tile and samples of flooring. The tile might be identifiable as a roof tile because of an upturned edge or might have an animal footprint impressed on the surface. The Romans are renowned for their decorative mosaic floors, but there are many other different types of flooring found from Roman London. Two or three small cubes (tesserae) of clay from plain red tessellated floors are included. The only artefact included, which is not ceramic, is an oyster shell to introduce the dietary theme. The selection of this real material therefore enables many of the themes in the National Curriculum Study Unit to be covered.

The replicas

It was decided that it was important to also include replicas in the school box. This was for two main reasons: replicas could enhance the learning potential of the partial remains of the original artefacts because they could assist the pupil in visualizing the whole object; replicas could also illustrate themes in the Study Unit not covered by the real artefacts and could be made in materials that do not survive in sufficient numbers in the archaeological record to be included in the boxes. The replicas were chosen with care to ensure that they were as close copies as possible to original artefacts and that they were quality products. Some were actual copies of material found from Roman London and all (except for the coin packs which were already in general production) were commissioned especially for the boxes.

Two pottery replicas, a mortarium and a samian cup, help the pupils to understand the size and shape of the complete object, for which they have incomplete examples in the box. Also included is a replica clay Roman lamp, directly based on an example from the Museum of London collections, in the shape of a human foot wearing a shoe.

A replica bronze manicure set with tweezers, nail-cleaner and an ear-scoop, and a replica glass bottle to hold perfumed oil for a trip to the public baths is included. A replica set of wooden writing tablets with a layer of wax set in the recess are hinged together by cord, which makes it possible for children to see how such documents could be sealed and sent. The implement used for writing on the wax is a stylus, a tool with a point at one end for writing and a flattened rectangular end at the other in order to smooth the wax for use as an eraser. A bronze example is included. A pack of two replica coins, one bronze and one silver, shows that coins were a means of communicating important events throughout the empire. Finally, it was decided to include a resin copy of a jet head of Medusa, the mythological creature who could turn people to stone.

The teacher's notes

Three booklets have been especially produced for the box. One provides background information on Roman London, covering such topics as Roman London's first settlers, the port and trade, people in Roman London, everyday life, religious life, homes and houses. A second booklet is solely about the Roman Box and its contents. It advises teachers on how to care for the box, gives information about the suppliers and replicas, and then gives details and illustrations about all the objects, both real and replica, that are contained in the box. The third booklet, entitled *Using Objects – A Teacher's Resource*, is concerned with guidelines for teaching with objects. It provides a sample worksheet for children to help them learn to research objects and suggests activities, including cross-curricular activities, that teachers could use in combination with the Literacy Hour, mathematics, design and technology, and art and design activities. Also included are copies of a booklet on Roman food, reproduced from the Roman London gallery, a sheet giving the chronology of events in Roman London and Roman Britain, and a photocard pack, which had already been produced for teachers for classroom work prior to a school visit. The pack contains ten laminated colour photographs of Roman objects on display in the gallery.

The video

A video, produced to accompany the box, can also be stored in a box drawer. The video is divided into three parts. One section explains to the teacher how to use the objects in the box. The second section consists of a performance by an actress playing the part of a maidservant living in one of the Roman London's houses. It is a performance that, with prior booking, is presented to those schools visiting the reconstructed rooms in the Roman London gallery. She tells the children about her life and brings into the performance some of the replicas that are included in the box. The final section shows pupils how it is possible to find out about the Romans by the process of archaeology and looks at what materials may survive long-term burial.

The trial project

During the autumn of 1999, the boxes, storage materials, and replicas were assembled in the museum's store in Hackney. It was then necessary to retrieve suitable material from the London Archaeological Archive, which was to prove a very time-consuming process. As it had been decided that the pieces had to be informative, there were many sherds that were deemed to be unsuitable. The material was also dirty, needing to be wiped clean and then marked with an identification number.

Two hundred boxes in the pilot scheme were delivered to schools in greater London early in 2000. Half of the schools were chosen because they regularly used the museum's education services and were invited to participate. The museum then approached local education authorities for suggestions of those schools less likely to volunteer to participate. The team wanted to be able to compare the differing uses that such schools might make of the scheme. This will be monitored during the evaluation process.

Before the boxes were distributed, a teacher from each of the schools was required to attend a training session. Two sessions were held at the museum's store in Hackney and attending teachers were allowed to choose and pack the contents of their own boxes. The project team decided that other sessions should be held at appropriate centres throughout Greater London to save teachers from travelling distances. These sessions, held in museums in Croydon, Fulham, Enfield, Newham, and at the main Museum of London building, consisted of a curator talking about the objects and replicas, a conservator who demonstrated how to look after the box, and a museum educator who advised on how to use the objects for teaching purposes. The initial reaction of the teachers to the boxes was pleasing as they saw their teaching potential. Following the training sessions, all the boxes were delivered to the schools.

The boxes are now under trial and the evaluation process is underway. The boxes and their contents were expensive, but it is hoped that they will withstand the test of time. The scheme has also proved costly in staff time and would not have been possible without the generous sponsorship of the manufacturers. The Department of Education and Employment acknowledged it to be a prime example of increasing public access for schools and supported the pilot scheme with a grant of £41,000. The results of the evaluation will determine whether the museum seeks to raise the necessary sponsorship in order to proceed with its intention of furnishing every state primary and special school in greater London with its own mini-museum of Roman artefacts.

References

Durbin, G., Morris, S., and Wilkinson, S. (1990) *A Teacher's Guide to Learning From Objects*. London: English Heritage

Merriman, N. and Swain, H. (1999) Archaeological archives: serving the public interest? *European Journal of Archaeology*, 2(2): 249–67.

Museum of London (1999) *Museum of London Annual Report 1998–9*. London: Museum of London.

Swain, H. (1998) *A Survey of Archaeological Archives in England*. London: Museums and Galleries Commission.

——(1999) Taking London archaeology to Londoners. *London Archaeologist*, 9(1): 3–5.

Translating archaeology for the public
Empowering and engaging museum goers with the past

Alexandra A. Chan

Introduction

With an increasing number of house museums seeking to incorporate archaeology into their interpretations for the public, there is a need to devise and discuss effective strategies for translating what one scholar has called an 'explosion' of technical archaeological information for a variety of different publics (Jameson 1997: 11). To this end, the idea of 'translation' is in counterpoint to mere 'display'. To translate is to interpret, to explain in terms that can be easily understood and intellectually accessible. Archaeologists committed to engaging in public education and outreach grapple explicitly with the idea of translating the archaeological record for public understanding and consumption (Gathercole and Lowenthal 1990; Vitelli 1996; Jameson 1997; Stone 1997; Herscher and McManamon 2000; Lynott and Wylie 2000). Translation requires more than documenting the material record and presenting it as it is. Archaeologists ask – and encourage lay audiences to ask – questions of the material record, questions about meaning. What does a landscape, an object, or group of objects mean? What were particular actors in the past trying to 'say' with the acquisition, modification, and/or use of these material things?

Although archaeologists have expertise and distinct skill sets related to recovering and interpreting the past, the relationship to the things that they study is non-proprietary. Instead, archaeologists can position themselves as 'caretakers of and advocates for the archaeological record'; people who hold the past in public trust, perhaps, but who strive to inhabit the role of public servant (Society for American Archaeology 1996). The archaeologist's main interest in public outreach, for example, is the idea of *empowering* the public; 'to understand and appreciate' what archaeology has to offer (Jameson and Ehrenhard 1997: 9) and, even more importantly, to be able to critically evaluate the interpretations presented to them and to become knowledgeable consumers of the past. In short, modern archaeologists strive to equip their publics to engage in interpretation, discussion and debate on their own, using the same tools that archaeologists and historians do (Jameson 1997; Chan 2007: 16–18).

A successful collaboration with a museum board provides ripe opportunity for archaeologists to act as caretakers and advocates. When done well, it is also one example of a situation where everybody wins. The archaeologist gains a venue to promote the archaeological process, and make his or her findings publicly accessible and debatable, and the museum gains the opportunity to reach and appeal to a wider cross section of the public than ever before because of the unique allure of the material that archaeology can provide. This logic underlies the interpretive approach that I and other heritage professionals have brought to the Isaac Royall House, a house museum in Medford, Massachusetts, home to one of the largest slaveholders and traders in New England during the eighteenth century.

The purpose of this article is twofold. First, it lays out what many archaeologists hold to be the true goal of any archaeological interpretation: teaching the public how to think about the past with material things and empowering them to be active consumers rather than passive recipients of heritage. The second half of the article is framed to mirror the experience of walking through the Royall House site itself, and it provides examples of how a visitor (here as well as elsewhere) might be taken through the scholarly journey of interpretation in order to learn these skills.

The advantage to this approach is that, in bringing visitors through the interpretive process with us, heritage professionals are able to expose social categories (for example, notions of 'whiteness' or 'blackness') whose legacies still affect our national life today as arbitrary cultural processes, rather than natural facts (Leone 1999). By encouraging the public to *engage* with the past – to be critical consumers of the past – visitors may gain insights into the present and a way of looking at the world that they will take with them when they leave the site of heritage, hopefully to the betterment of society.

The Royall House

The Royall House, in Medford, Massachusetts, was owned by the merchant Isaac Royall and his family, who were involved in all three of the principal elements of the Triangular Trade, from ca. 1703 (when Isaac Royall, Sr and his uncle Joseph bought the sloop *Mayflower*) to 1775 (when Isaac Royall, Jr was forced to flee New England in the wake of the Battle of Lexington at the start of the Revolutionary War). Thus, for the better part of a century, the Royalls had a sugar plantation and rum distillery in Antigua and one foot in the slave trade. And when they returned to New England in 1737 they continued to be one of the wealthiest merchant families in the colonies and one of the largest slaveholding families in the region. The archaeological investigations at the Royall House, however, were not just about slavery. They were about colonialism and the constant process of give and take between those who ruled and those who served. They were about social *relations* (between master and slave), as well as cultural *process* (such as the emergence of 'whiteness' and 'blackness' in eighteenth-century New England or the formation of distinct class categories). And they were about the roles of material things in these dynamic relations and processes (Chan 2007).

As public interest in history and archaeology grows, archaeologists find themselves with increasing opportunities to work in advisory or collaborative roles with other professionals (curators, exhibit designers, teachers, museum boards, public relations specialists, and the like) to interpret the past and bring it to the public. It is not always apparent to non-archaeologists, however, exactly what historical archaeology's unique contributions to the interpretation of our sites and our records can be. Cochran and Beaudry (2006: 192) write that one 'distinctive contribution' lies in the way that archaeologists use material things from a site to paint 'intimate portraits' of individual lives; on a larger scale, these same artefacts can be used to understand the 'construction of personal and social identities' and to reconstruct a society's values, ideals, and daily taken-for-granteds.

At the Royall House, archaeology challenged the museum to grapple with its use of 'things' (which, with a few notable exceptions, consisted mostly of items reflective of a lavish, eighteenth-century domesticity) to convey the much larger ideas of social relations and cultural process that give the Royall House significance on a grander, almost metaphysical scale. The challenge was greater because, as is the case at many small house museums, the Royall House had an established mode of presentation and display whose fixedness was at odds with notions of 'process' and 'evolution' raised by the archaeological work. The real question for a collaboration like this, then, was how successfully to incorporate, or blend, the specialized knowledge and dynamic focus of archaeology with the pre-existing (static) narratives of the site.

The key to a successful collaboration lay in two things: first, the Royall House Association (RHA) was ready for something entirely new in the way it chose to manage and present the site. This choice facilitated the collaboration immeasurably. In other words, the archaeology here was not an outside intervention but a collaboration in the truest sense. The other key lay in communicating first to the members of the museum board and, through them, to the public the dynamic ways that archaeologists look at documents, artefacts, and landscapes. Fortunately, the archaeological process of interpretation or knowledge production can be explained in accessible terms, as demonstrated later in this article. At the Royall House, the heritage process as I implement it is explained through a new archaeology exhibit, signage, newly scripted interactive guided tours, workshops, teacher seminars, after-school programmes, and family events. I find that the interpretive technique of translation has the advantage of naturally rendering the 'inanimate objects' on display, as well as the landscape through which the visitors wander, quite lively and dynamically meaningful. This transformation is something that stays with the museum and with the people who visit it even after the active presence of archaeologists on-site has gone.

A short history of narrative at the Royall House

In 1996, the RHA, under the new directorship of Peter Gittleman, approached one of its members, Dr Ricardo Elia, Professor of Archaeology at Boston University, to embark on an archaeological investigation of the Royall House that would allow the association to create, in the words of another author in this issue, a more 'useable past' for the site (Christensen 2011). Prior to this changing of the guard, the Royall House had inhabited the role of most historical house museum of the twentieth century: as a colonial revivalist shrine dedicated to 'the romantic glorification of the benevolent patriarch and the self-made man' (Chan 2007: 20). Period-appropriate rooms attempted to recreate the house at the height of its glory, as documented in Isaac Royall's 1739 probate inventory. That said, the kitchen chamber, which the inventory indicated had been a sleeping place for a number of enslaved people at that time, had been co-opted by a local Daughters of the American Revolution chapter and set up as a parlour, where they could meet on a regular basis to play cards and drink tea in luxurious surroundings. The kitchen below, which should also rightly have contained several 'Negro beds' among the tables, chairs, buckets, cooking utensils, etc., was neat and orderly with no beds or other signs of human habitation. The garrets on the third floor, where a further number of enslaved people worked and slept, were roped off and left altogether uninterpreted. The outkitchen/slave quarters building, where the majority of the Royalls' enslaved people were kept and which may be the only standing slave quarters in the northern United States, stood empty except for a tinny, upright piano and a number of folding metal chairs to accommodate various local meetings and functions.

The local library is replete with vintage photographs of pageants and plays put on at the Royall House dating back to 1905, which show exactly what the Royall House's established mode of presentation had been prior to 1999 (Chan 2007: 20–2). These pageants were usually preoccupied with period finery; re-enacting the English tea ceremony and important visits from illustrious personages such as Generals Stark, Lee, and Washington; or eschewing historical re-enactment altogether, with young girls draped in veils and ribbons portraying the spirits of Hearth and Home chasing away the spirits of Snow, Wind, and Rain. In these portrayals, the Royalls were shown simply as wealthy merchants, peaceful farmers or benevolent aristocrats – wholly isolated from the uneasy and often violent social context of New England slaveholding and -trading. Prior to the archaeological work done at this site, dialogues relating to the ideas of race, class, gender, or power were non-existent. It was also a point of contention between the RHA, in its traditional incarnation, and the local black community of Medford who, for the most part, shunned the museum altogether.

The invitation to do archaeology on the site, and the reasons for soliciting the work, signalled a monumental change in outlook and attitude on the part of the RHA, one which continues to influence the museum's operation. Excavations began under Elia's direction in 1999, while I took over the directorship in 2000 and 2001. The material culture yield was immense, producing numerous previously unknown features, some 65,000 artefacts, 4,000 animal bones, and hundreds of plant materials indicative of an eighteenth-century way of life for both master and enslaved. The results of these excavations gave wings to the RHA's rather vague intent – to bring a more contemporary interpretation of the site to the public. The archaeological finds formed the entire basis for the new approach, from the kind and the way the exhibits would be constructed and presented, to the structure of the guided tours, to the nature of the public events, to the reasons for which the museum would seek and receive funding.

For example, the first public event after the archaeology had begun was called 'The Forgotten Royalls' and was aimed at interpreting a day in the life of enslaved people on the estate. Tours were oriented around the movements and responsibilities of enslaved people (back doors and servant stairs, the kitchen and grounds etc.). Tours were oriented around the movements and responsibilities of enslaved people. Visitors' experiences were focused on the outkitchen/slave quarters and activities in the work yards. Tours of the 'big house' began at the side door and were restricted to servants' stairs and working and sleeping areas, allowing visitors only to glimpse the more public spaces of the house and to experience a sense of these areas as being off limits or out of reach. African-American re-enactors from the Colored Ladies' Theater Group put on a pageant portraying the old African-American folk tradition that it had been the promise of red cloth that first lured Africans onto European slave ships. Historical crafts and games were centred on archaeological finds relating to leisure time activities and personal adornments of the enslaved. There were bead, marble, and clay-pipe making stations, and games of checkers and mankala using discarded potsherds, stone, and other adaptively reused objects.

The event was a tremendous success and drew hundreds from the Medford community, black and white. Since then, I have led several archaeological workshops at the Royall House, and guest speakers address a range of topics that better represent the multiple realities of eighteenth-century life in the home. Most recently, the museum has also begun applying for funding to renovate the kitchen and kitchen chamber (the former Daughters of the American Revolution tea room) into the ascetic work and storage spaces, as well as sleeping quarters, for enslaved people that they once were.

Over the course of nearly a decade, the collaboration at the Royall House among archaeologists, educators, and other cultural resource and public relations professionals has been an experiment in finding effective strategies for a more holistic approach to the study and interpretation of the past, as well as for making these interpretations accessible to public audiences physically and intellectually. Ultimately, the collaboration has also widened the cross section of public audiences who are drawn to the site manifold. The Royall House does not keep formal records of visitation, but the observational evidence is strong. Tom Lincoln (pers. comm. October 2010), the executive director of the RHA, has reported that the museum has gone from nearly languishing before its change in mission to having robust visitation from a variety of groups. Top among them now are school groups from all over Massachusetts, who come to the Royall House as a regular part of their school history curriculum every year. In frequency, school groups are followed by half- and full-day teacher seminars; college class seminars; interest groups (historical societies, African-American groups, seniors etc.); after-school programmes for children from Boston, Cambridge, and Somerville; and individuals. Lincoln estimates that approximately 10 per cent of visitors today are African American, which is roughly a 10 per cent increase over what it was prior to the archaeological work.

It is important for heritage professionals to be active and hands-on in this kind of collaboration, especially when dealing with historically, culturally, racially, or politically sensitive material (and work at the Royall House is all of these things). In such cases, it becomes an archaeologist's responsibility to be proactive in presenting the results of his or her research in an ethical and sensitive manner – and to anticipate how such results might be interpreted or even misinterpreted by various potential audiences (Potter 1991). One thing that archaeologists at the Royall House were especially keen to avoid, for example, was inadvertently to give the impression that, because slavery at the Royall House and in the North in general may have been different in important ways from the South or the Caribbean, it was somehow easier or more tolerable for its victims. This area was one where a more critical engagement by the public with the displays was indispensable.

Archaeology and public outreach

There was a time when archaeology was thought to exist primarily to stock museum shelves and display cases (Potter and Chabot 1997: 37). As a discipline or profession, archaeology generally faded into the background as an invisible source of 'goodies', which were often shown as isolated objects or perhaps grouped with others sharing certain formal or stylistic traits. Generally ripped from the cultural fabric or context of their actual use, however, such objects were almost entirely divorced from their original cultural meaning. 'Context' in archaeology refers to the layers of soil the object was found in, other objects it was found with and their collective spatial relationship to each other, features, and buildings in the landscape. Without context, an artefact is, metaphorically, mute. What had once been a dynamic component of past cultures was rendered instantly static and silent.

The approach, according to Potter and Chabot (1997: 46), suggested that 'truth' could somehow be 'located at the bottom of a pit' and then displayed for all to see. It belied the interpretive *process* of archaeology and ignored the fact that all 'knowledge' is, in fact, an 'inherently social enterprise' (Chan 2007: 23). This claim is not defeatist, and it is very far from an 'anything goes' approach to interpretation. It is simply a statement of fact, and, if communicated effectively, it can be the first step toward encouraging the public to become more critical in their engagement with heritage sites.

Today, archaeology is an independent profession, and archaeologists are much more active in defining and influencing the ways in which our interpretations are reaching public audiences than in generations past. Much of this shift has been internally motivated. The last 15 to 20 years have seen an increasing desire among archaeologists to extend our teaching about archaeology to a wider audience than our own students and other members of the academy (Franklin and McKee 1994; McKee 1994; Potter 1991, 1997; Stone 1997; Stahl et al. 2004; Chan 2007: 14, 17). In most professional circles today, you will find the past conceptualized as a 'public heritage' and archaeologists as 'stewards' of that heritage, holding it in public trust (Stone 1997: 23). In fact, the Society for American Archaeology (1996) adopted a Code of Ethics that *begins* with a statement about the 'Archaeologist's Responsibility to the Public'. Certainly, these responsibilities are central to any system of archaeological ethics

(Fagan 1996). They include, in part, striving to avoid the single, authoritative narrative voice that has characterized scientific scholarship and writing in decades and centuries past. There is an emerging ideal, borrowed from the neighbouring disciplines of anthropology and ethnography, of working to bring the mechanics of knowledge production to the fore, where they can be examined and, yes, questioned, probed, or argued (see Clifford and Marcus 1986; Stahl et al. 2004; Joyce 2006).

Exhibits constructed in this spirit provide visitors with the 'opportunity' and the 'tools' to learn about what it is that archaeology really does (Jameson and Ehrenhard 1997: 9). Such exhibits are simultaneously able to make the past accessible, tangible, and relevant to a wide range of lay audiences. This achievement is the real allure of incorporating archaeology into public interpretation of the past and probably why an ever-growing number of house museums seek to harness its power. Simply to display the 'goodies', however, is not to harness the power of material culture or its active interpretation.

The heart of public outreach, education, and empowerment must involve an examination of the whole archaeological and heritage process – teaching visitors how insights are actually generated. Modern archaeological exhibits are as much about the archaeological endeavour itself – the process of discovery and interpretation – as they are about what has been found. This insight is no less true at the Royall House, where visitors are invited not only to see the results of the archaeological excavations, but also to learn how archaeologists came to the conclusions that they did based on the artefacts in the glass cases. By going through the interpretive process themselves, museumgoers come away with a much deeper understanding of what was, and is, happening at the Royall House, as well as numerous subtle ways to think about the parallel realities of master and slave on the site and in the country at large.

An archaeologist's toolbox

One of the first things to communicate in teaching public audiences about how archaeological insights are generated is that artefacts are not just inanimate objects. They are metaphorical expressions of culture itself (Prown 1993: 11). Traditional methods of public presentation and display tend to obscure that fact. And yet, this concept – that artefacts do not reflect culture, they actually constitute it – lies at the base of my process as a historical archaeologist. The folklorist Henry Glassie (1995: 425) once said, 'the whole blue world sings with meaning'. This insight resonates with historical archaeologists, who tend to see objects, architecture and landscapes as physical embodiments of the assumptions, attitudes, and values of the people who built, shaped, and used them (Tilley 2002; Cochran and Beaudry 2006).

It is a notion we all implicitly understand: the way that material things can be manipulated to make *statements* about things – who we think we are, how we think the world should be. In fact, I perceive the material world as a kind of 'conversation without words' taking place between 'actors' or 'agents' in the past. The comparison between material culture and text or language is, admittedly, an imperfect one. For one thing, material culture has a physical presence in the world – functional, practical, and technological – which influences (and may even constrain) an object's range of symbolic meaning, whereas words are ephemeral and arbitrary (Hodder 1986: 125). Tilley (2002: 23) concurs: 'A design is not a word and a house is not a text: words and things, discourse and material practices are fundamentally different'. 'Different', he states, but not unrelated. On the one hand, material culture is simpler and less precise than language, its meaning more ambiguous and potentially multivalent. On the other hand, argues Tilley (2002: 24), human beings are metaphorical creatures hardwired to 'see similarity in difference' (e.g. social meaning in physical objects) This disposition is true to such an extent, says Tilley (2002: 24), that artefacts may be seen as the 'material counterpoint to verbal metaphor' or, more succinctly put, 'objectified thought'.

Hodder (1986: 126) claims that the 'notion that material culture is a text to be read has long been tacitly assumed in archaeology'. He points, as illustration, to the fact that archaeologists refer to our data as a 'record'. The textual/discursive metaphor is deeply embedded in our professional psyche, and, if not taken too academically (as lay audiences are unlikely to do), it is a useful one. Thinking of the material record in metaphorical terms such as these allows artefacts to open a window into the mindset of people who no longer exist. At the Royall House, we can, in effect, 'eavesdrop' on these so-called conversations 250 years after they took place because part of those conversations was conducted in the realm of material things.

The majority of inhabitants at the Royall House in the eighteenth century were black and enslaved – at least 64 black men, women, and children, with evidence of many more – and yet we know next to nothing about them through traditional techniques of historical research. Let it not be assumed, however, that these were people 'without history' (for example, Wolf 1982). As I have written previously, 'their histories were simply inscribed in often-overlooked places: in mended vessels from the Great House, in the smooth surface of a stone bead, in the seed remains of berry-picking, or in the butchered remains of animals' (Chan 2007: 4). Artefacts lend tangibility and texture to historical narratives; that has long been the allure of using artefacts in displays and exhibits. But what is frequently less recognized is that artefacts also document the past as much as any deed, letter, or newspaper. For the non-archaeologist, I think it helps to understand how archaeologists think by beginning to see artefacts as 'documents' that can be 'read' (Hodder and Hutson 2004).

What follows are three examples from the Royall House, where public visitors are invited to submit the material world to these metaphorical analyses of 'text' and 'conversation'. These techniques are part and parcel of my standard archaeological toolbox, but, happily, they are also metaphors easily and effectively communicated to the public and used by them experimentally on their own. These exercises are offered to the public at the Royall House through posters and signage that accompany the archaeological displays and facilitate their interpretation, as well as through optional interactive tours and occasional student and teacher workshops.

'Reading' a landscape: material culture and power

The important thing to recognize about landscapes is that they are artefacts too, and, like all artefacts, the metaphors of text and discourse can be applied in the interpretation of meaning. Landscapes can be 'read' as maps of social relations in the past even when the cultural systems that produced them no longer exist. One significant portion of the Royall House archaeology exhibit is dedicated to land use and spatial analysis of the estate.

The Royall House sits at the heart of a meticulously constructed landscape. Obviously, it is a landscape once designed and ordered by Isaac Royall, but it is not enough to merely reconstruct that historic landscape for the public without also trying to address what the landscape might have meant to the various people who inhabited it. In other words, what was Isaac Royall trying to say with his landscape? And to whom? What other meanings could it have acquired for people who experienced the landscape differently (for example, for the people who built it or the people we imagine were forced to maintain it)? In the workshops that I run, I break the audience into groups of two to four people and have them wander the grounds with some background information and a list of questions about potential different meanings, which the group then reconvenes to discuss as a whole after 15 to 20 minutes. When there are no workshops, the same exercise is simulated through signage (to slightly less effect; interactive experience is always preferable to reading about the topic).

Who designed a landscape, who built and maintained it, who displayed it, who visited it and under what circumstances are questions that all cultural resource professionals can and should ask of their publics to get them involved in the interpretation of a landscape's potential social meanings. Public audiences at the Royall House are brought naturally through such exercises (through the use of signage, guided tours, and special workshops) to the realization that there are multiple ways of knowing about the past and multiple 'truths' to describe it.

One truth at the Royall House is that the estate was imposing. There could be no question that it was a seat of power. Rich and elaborate gardens greeted visitors and passers-by alike. We know from the pioneering work on formal gardens in Annapolis, Maryland, that these were neither private landscapes nor passive collections of flowers and trees, but rather material statements of rank and power in colonial society (Leone 1984, 1999, 2003). The Great House itself is of a neoclassical architectural design – avant-garde in the 1720s – with quoined corners, pedimented windows and doors, and faux columns that seem to recall the villas of ancient Rome, giving an apparent temporal depth to the family's influence that was not real (see for example Epperson 1990; St. George 1998 for discussions of the phenomenon of such cultural 'implication'). Indeed, the Royalls were, in today's common parlance, nouveau riche.

The exercise on landscape is, however, less about telling visitors what the Royalls' 'real' standing in Massachusetts society was than it is about getting visitors to see landscapes as multivalent spaces. To this end, the Royal House exhibits and tours examine the same landscape from the perspective of both master and slave. Visitors to the Royall House today are asked to notice the sturdy, two-storey slave quarters, built of brick and clapboards like the Great House itself, and how it forms an L-shaped enclosure with the main house creating a common courtyard (Figure 33.1). They are then asked to consider what the possible meanings are behind the

Figure 33.1 View south of the Great House and Slave Quarters in close proximity and in complementary architectural style. Photograph by the author.

fact that the slave quarters are in such close proximity to the Great House and seem to have been designed to complement it architecturally. My personal experience is that visitors often suggest some version of our own, archaeological, conclusions on the matter, even before discussions have been concluded.

The first thing archaeologists notice about this landscape is that it visually incorporates the quarters into the formal landscape of the estate and hence, one could argue, into the ideology of domination and control upon which it rested (Epperson 1990: 31). It is no accident that Isaac Royall, Sr referred to the people he held as slaves as 'my people' (Royall Correspondence, 15 August 1736). This landscape can be interpreted on one level, then, as a metaphor for the Royalls' views on master–slave relations at this estate. After hearing this perspective, visitors are asked to consider alternative, less benevolent meanings such a landscape could have. The proximity of the house and quarters was a constant reminder of the tight control to which many enslaved people in the North were subjected, for example.

Perhaps most insidiously, the Royall House landscape also gave slavery a refined face – one less frightening, alien or brutal and thus, perhaps, less objectionable – than in other parts of the colonies. This hidden message underscored the Royalls' self-styled image as 'benevolent aristocrats', and it also demonstrates the way that the messages contained in the landscape of the estate could be manifold as well as latently sinister. This exercise opens discussion between docents and visitors about important spatial and social points of contrast between northern and southern systems of slavery.

The purpose of this landscape exercise is to demonstrate, first, that landscapes have and always have had meaning and, second, the exact meanings are and have always been diverse and most likely variable, depending on time and/or circumstance. The common denominator, however, was always this: the built environment at the Royall House was a statement of power. The meanings the Royalls and their peers imbued in this Medford country seat were fluid, not fixed. They represented one side of an ongoing conversation: a statement made by the Royalls about who they thought they were and understood by their peers to be evidence of their mutual group belonging (Cook et al. 1996; Hall 1992; Shackel 1992). The landscapes of inequality in various American slave regimes all betray the hope that white spatial and visual dominance in architecture and the landscape would translate into an internalized acceptance of social and political dominance by peers, dependants, and inferiors alike.

Archaeological excavations around the house and grounds have revealed good evidence of the various construction and refurbishment activities that were undertaken when the Royalls first bought the property. For example, the discovery of an intact and datable cobbled surface in the courtyard between the mansion house and slave quarters marks a functional transition of the space from a work yard in the seventeenth and early eighteenth centuries to a formal receiving area when the Royalls arrived in the 1730s (Chan 2007: 37). A lack of historical topsoil in most of the slave quarters' south (back) yard has also led us to speculate that the Royalls might have borrowed soil from this area for use in the many formal landscaping activities evidenced around the property, leaving the area behind the quarters stripped bare.

Archaeology has revealed not only an aesthetic division in the use of space around the estate, but also a functional one, whereby trash disposal activities were relegated predominantly to the side and backyards of the slave quarters – significantly, in the areas least visible from the Royalls' central post. While no sheet refuse or trash pits were recovered from the courtyard after the laying of the cobbles, fully 79 per cent of the total eighteenth-century artefact assemblage of nearly 65,000 came from the west and south yards of the slave quarters, which evidence suggests were work yards that would have been dirty, smelly, and chaotic (see Chan 2007: 214–17 for an in-depth discussion) (Figure 33.2).

Public exhibitions should (and at the Royall House, do) describe such finds to give visitors a physical sense of 'place'. 'Space' is a physical entity, but 'place' is relational (Thomas 2001: 173). The evidence for drastically different uses of space on the estate pushes visitors to see a patchwork of interrelated and overlapping places. These discoveries betray a cognitive separation in the use of space that was built into the very landscape of the estate. They are significant because the Royalls' social construction of space presents one of our first clues about how the process of constructing/defining the categories of 'white' and 'black' at the Royall House actually might have begun. What is more, we begin to see how *ideas* about social differences could be made tangible and thus, perhaps, more apparently 'real' (see Leone 1984; 2003 for discussions of material culture as ideology; also De Cunzo and Ernstein 2006). The Royalls' own notions of the difference between work and leisure, clean and unclean, master and slave and, ultimately, white and black were structurally embedded into the environment itself, entering people's psyches on a subconscious, sensory level.

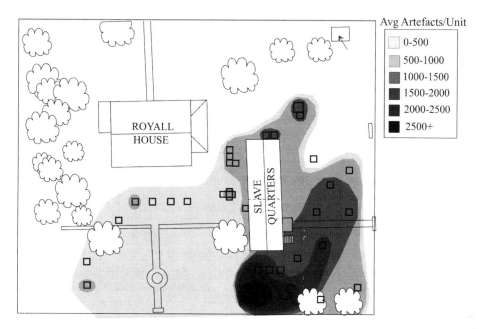

Figure 33.2 Graphic representation of the artefact frequency distribution on the site. These results suggest that social meanings of the use of space on the estate might have contradicted those suggested by the above-ground architecture.

Of course, these yards were also a space belonging to (or at least left to) enslaved people as a place of their own, perhaps a welcome retreat from constant surveillance. We know this to be true because these are the areas where all of the artefacts to do with the work, leisure, childhood and craftsmanship of slaves were recovered. As such, the meanings given to the Royall House landscape in the past were variable and contingent and represented a crack in the façade of total domination that slaveholders sought to project through the manipulation of landscape (see Delle 1999; Epperson 1999).

This message was completely lost in previous modes of public presentation at the Royall House, but visitors now gain an opportunity to understand it on a deep, sensory level because they have gone through the interpretive process on their own. What is more, they leave with a more nuanced and sophisticated way of looking at and perceiving the physical world around them: as a bearer of messages, deliberate or otherwise. Gracelaw Simmons (pers. comm. October 2010), a RHA board member and sometime docent, has said that she has had several visitors comment positively to her about the level of scholarship in the exhibit, noting that they had come to see artefacts but had little idea that they would learn something thought-provoking about landscape and the origins of racial categories. To Simmons, this perspective means that visitors are not overwhelmed by the new approach but rather challenged and invigorated by it.

'Reading' an artefact

The title of this segment is somewhat misleading because one does not really read 'an' artefact in the absence of its physical and social context. I do not want to give the impression that archaeologists are only interested in 'goodies' or that the focus of the archaeological enterprise is on the object. This clarification must be introduced to public audiences when they are presented with archaeological materials, and, in fact, I will say it outright here: archaeologists do not dig for artefacts. They dig for information. An artefact that has been separated from the context of where it was found and with what it was found has forever lost its original meaning and the information we can glean from that meaning.

A good public presentation of archaeological material, therefore, will involve a discussion of why it is good for members of the public to try to 'read' artefacts that have been properly excavated but not so good for them to run out and try to do archaeology on their own by digging up backyards or going out with a metal detector on a sunny afternoon. I always include a brief discussion of this fact whenever I am involved in any kind of public outreach involving non-archaeologists, and I encourage some treatment of the subject wherever archaeology is presented. The ultimate paradox of archaeology is that in digging up a site, one is destroying it forever, and the only way we can justify doing it is by being meticulous in recording what we have done and standardized in the way that we do it. In short, there are rules of engagement. We also justify the archaeological process with strong professional ethics which demand that the results be written up, published, or otherwise brought to a larger audience, because the past belongs to everybody. Archaeologists do not even really talk about artefacts; they talk about 'archaeological resources'. Perhaps this matter is one of semantics, but words are important. They influence the way we think about things.

Asking the public to think about the connotation of the word 'resource' as opposed to 'artefact' will generally cause them to consider what other kinds of things count as a nation's resources. Most likely to come to mind is the idea of natural resources: oil, gas, minerals, timber, etc. The central concern or understanding that we have of natural resources is, of course, that they are finite and non-renewable. Therefore, to call the archaeological record a resource is to recognize that it, too, is finite and non-renewable. The need for managing these resources responsibly, wisely, and with an eye toward future generations becomes apparent. The other implication, of course, is that while 'artefacts' are just objects, 'resources' have shared value.

No documents survive directly to attest the Royalls' personal views on slavery or their rightful relationship with their slaves, but Isaac Royall, Sr does refer to his slaves at one point as 'my people' (Royall Correspondence, 15 August 1736), which indicates the relationship he felt he had with his slaves and the image he strove to project to the outside world. He was also commemorated on his tombstone as a 'kind master'. Calling one's slaves 'my people' was a paternalistic way of naturalizing the master-slave relationship, and it sought to cast the master's authority over the enslaved as a natural extension of the patriarch's obligations to his own family (Epperson 1990).

But what do the artefacts tell us about how the Royalls' 'people' perceived those same relations? Visitors at the Royall House are presented with two stone artefacts that demonstrate the sovereign importance of maintaining an artefact's archaeological context in the interpretation of meaning. The first artefact, in particular, was long something of a mystery at the site, found in the deposits filling an outbuilding foundation in the slave quarters' west yard. It consisted of a stone flake, crudely shaped into the semblance of an arrowhead. I say semblance because it is clear to anyone familiar with stone toolmaking that the material is unsuitable for knapping – rough-grained and cleaving along jagged planes, not easily streamlined and difficult to sharpen.

In flint-knapping terms it was a reworked, or utilized, flake. Except for the two side notches chipped at the base, it is only unifacially worked, with no attempt to create a cutting edge. What this all means in plain English is that, whatever it resembled, this was no arrowhead. A small groove etched between the side notches may have been made to better secure the object from a piece of yarn or leather thong, thus to be hung around the neck or some other part of the body.

Two years after excavating this artefact, I was doing research on the naming practices of the estate slaves. Several of the Royalls' slaves had Akan day names, and it was in an ethnography of the Akan-speaking peoples of the Gold Coast that I first found reference to a belief system in which prehistoric stone projectile points were not made by man at all, but by God, and were thought to have protective powers (Ward 1958). More importantly, it is a belief demonstrably carried over to parts of the Americas (Puckett 1926). The fact that the object at the Royall House was not a 'real' arrowhead was not problematic because, given the right incantations or libations invoking the ancestors over it, any object could be turned into a charm (Chireau 1997: 228). In fact, one can find 'arrowheads' such as this one, nothing more than reworked flakes, sold as good luck charms in New Orleans to this day (Wilkie 1995: 143).

An unusual object was always thought of as something special or lucky, however, and a second discovery from the Royall House may illustrate the point. A stone pestle, pecked and abraded into a rough cylinder, was recovered from the same secondary cellar fill as the amulet, located in the slave quarters' west yard. What was startling about the object was not only that it appeared to be of Native American origin, but also that it dated to sometime between 2,000 and 8,000 years ago, known in North American prehistoric archaeology as the Archaic Period. The pestle was originally made for grinding and mashing, and in one sense it is in fact a prehistoric Native American artefact. The context of its discovery, however – a firmly dated eighteenth-century deposit on a slaveholding estate – makes this artefact likely to have been much more. Within the historically and archaeologically established phenomenon of African curation of Native American lithics (stone tools) for religious or ritual purposes, it seems feasible, if not likely, that this pestle is not just a Native American artefact, but equally an African-American one – even an example of the use of magic and conjuration in the slave population of the estate. As an unusual object with a potentially powerful indwelling spirit, such a pestle might have been used to grind and mash the ingredients of magic, ritual, or medicinal concoctions and considered to lend its own potency to the end product.

Presented with this evidence, and having learned the importance of 'reading' artefacts from their whole physical and historical contexts, visitors at the Royall House are invited to ponder the question of *meaning* once again. What use was magic on this estate and what can it possibly reveal about master-slave relations at this site?

Enslaved people, who generally lacked 'overt and natural means' of obtaining justice, often turned as a result to supernatural forces to aid in the affairs of daily life, loss, or punishment (Puckett 1926: 167). The finds at the Royall House force visitors to consider what the meaning behind evidence of magical practices on the estate of a 'kind' master or in a system of slavery thought to have been 'gentler' than in plantation settings, really is. That is, if northern slavery is popularly considered to be 'not so bad' compared with southern slavery, then what need could there have been to continue to call on supernatural forces in these small, private acts of ritual?

Because physical and spiritual dangers were also perceived to come from fellow bondsmen, the finds might be examined in yet another light, asking visitors to stop thinking of the enslaved as an undifferentiated, internally cooperative, group. For example, the Royalls not only occasionally bestowed their favoured slaves with gifts and extra clothing, but also gave them special consideration in both work and family matters (keeping some together, dispersing others), which suggests a division in the slave hierarchy on the estate that might have been the source of conflict, jealousy, or hostility among these people (Chan 2007: 162–7). Visitors can look at Royall's account book entries to see some of the disparities themselves and consider the emotional effects they had on the enslaved.

Thus, the arrowhead amulet and the stone pestle, as potential artefacts of conjuration, can be interpreted to reflect some of enslaved people's active attempts to gain control over the rigours and dangers of a life under slavery, even in the north and even under masters that liked to think of themselves as kind. They are strong evidence that the Royalls' perception of their paternalistic and protective relationship to their slaves was one-sided. This message represents a profound narrative shift in public presentation at the Royall House, a direct result of the questions raised by archaeological finds. By involving visitors in the same interpretive process, we are able implicitly to avoid the pitfall of having visitors leave the site thinking that slavery here was somehow better than in the south or the Caribbean. It invites them to ponder the mental and emotional abuses of slavery and to think about and appreciate myriad ways that enslaved people survived, coped with, adapted to, and fought against slavery and asserted their humanity within the confines of a brutal system. My observation is that these two artefacts – in their proper context – are profound for many visitors.

'Reading' a document

Visitors to the Royall House are also asked to try their hand at 'reading' a document. The task might seem straightforward, but archaeologists have their own particular ways of reading a document, which, in part, include treating it as an artefact. And here we have come full circle – at the Royall House, visitors begin by trying to 'read' an artefact like a document and end up with trying to treat a document as an artefact. I think most archaeologists pass easily between these two ideas, some understanding of which is something that visitors to the Royall House hopefully take away from their experience there. Our third exercise looks at Isaac Royall's 1739 probate inventory in relation to the tableware and teaware assemblages we recovered archaeologically (Middlesex County Probate Court 1739).

In the archaeological assemblage, porcelain vessels outnumber those of any other material, representing over a third of the non-utilitarian vessel count. The inventory shows that, in life, 71 per cent of the Royalls' tablewares were made of porcelain. Porcelain was expensive – not surprising, the Royalls were rich – but in the interpretation of meaning, we want to do more than just note the presence of fancy tablewares.

Visitors to the Royall House are invited to have a look at Isaac Royall's probate inventory for themselves and to consider a number of things. For example, how many different vessel types can they find listed? The inventory lists tea sets, custard cups, punch bowls, plates, platters, bowls, mugs, and a salt cellar. Archaeological remains include coffee or chocolate cups, decanters, wine glasses, port glasses, tumblers and bottle for wine, port, gin and beer. The variety of vessel forms shows a familiarity with the foreign and novel. It demonstrates that the Royalls had not only the wealth to set a fine table, but also the knowledge of how to use the many different vessel forms and, as one scholar aptly put it, 'the leisure to indulge' (Goodwin 1999: 123).

Docents ask visitors what the significance was of having over a third of one's wares consist of vessels for the consumption of exotic beverages and, further, why have so many vessel types in sets of 6, 8, 12? For most visitors, the answer is clear: in order to entertain. Certainly these numbers show a concern with display, as well as with elegant hospitality. The abundance of vessels for exotic beverage consumption (as well as porcelain and glass trays for their presentation) establishes not only the adoption of the full-blown English tea ceremony at a relatively early date at this site, but also the Royalls' home as a centre of hospitality by the early years of their residence in Medford.

It was not just *what* one did, however, but *where* one did it that also signified. Remember the importance of environment and landscape, which operates not just on the grand scale of vistas, estates, and gardens, but on the very small scale of an ordinary room. Isaac Royall's probate inventory contains spatial information about how these vessels were dispersed around the house and where they were set up as props for life, something that is beyond an archaeologist's ability to reconstruct from the archaeological record alone but is vital to the interpretation of meaning. Looking at the probate inventory once again, visitors consider in what rooms the Royalls kept their fancy teawares and tablewares and ask themselves what the wares' placement suggests about their meaning.

Isaac Royall, Sr's probate inventory shows that all of the porcelain could be found in the best room, front room, and the dining room. Such placement should not be taken for granted. The probate inventory of Andrew Hall – a Medford man of wealth surpassing even the Royalls' – showed all of his most expensive wares being kept in the kitchen, away from public view (Middlesex County Probate 1750). Taken together, we surmise that the Royalls were self-conscious consumers of the fine goods they accumulated. They bought them to show them off.

Thus artefacts found in the ground confirm the Royalls to have been rich, but set against the context of the probate inventory and other documents they take on additional meaning as an important part of the symbolism with which the Royalls cloaked themselves. We also begin to see how a carpenter's son was able to make a perfect ascent to power, in part by his adept manipulation of his physical environment.

Summary and conclusions

The collaboration at the Royall House between archaeologists and other cultural resource professionals has been, and continues to be, a success. Visitation is dramatically up – in overall numbers and in the variety of people and groups that come through the doors. The interactive style of the tours and the thought-provoking archaeological exhibits encourage many visitors to seek out and engage museum staff about their experience in positive ways. The approach at the Royall House can be applied most anywhere and represents a relatively painless way of blending specialized archaeological knowledge, which is generally dynamic, with more traditional modes of presentation, which tend toward the static. Museum managers may find that their displays do not even have to be moved or changed to any great degree. Simply by asking visitors to think about the objects in the display differently, the whole message of the museum can be altered. Equipping visitors with the tools to be active and critical consumers of the knowledge presented to them has the added benefit of making a museum visit seem current, relevant, and interesting to a far larger group of people than ever before, and visitation will rise accordingly. An archaeological collaboration is one obvious way to effect this change.

At the Royall House, we use the metaphors of text and discourse to understand the material world of the Royalls and the many people they held as slaves. Using material symbols, such as personal effects, architecture, and landscape, the Royalls were able to make powerful statements about who they were and how they expected to be seen. It is also arguable that these statements in the material became an organic part of perceived differences between 'black' and 'white' as they were then emerging in New England (Chan 2007). There is also evidence at the Royall House, again in the material, that the Royalls' side of the discourse did not go uncontested by the people they held as slaves. This fact is one of the great strengths and distinctive contributions of historical archaeology at this site.

By inviting one's public(s) to engage with the past in this way, we cultivate a heightened respect and understanding and appreciation for what it is archaeology does. It also enables us to make dialogues of race, ethnicity, class, or culture accessible and interesting to more people than ever before – no longer are these debates the unique purview of 'experts', because, by rendering the process of knowledge production less opaque, we give our publics the tools to engage in these debates on their own. That in itself is a healthy development and a strong justification for thinking about ways to bring archaeology to the public in accessible and interesting ways. An archaeological view of the world almost inherently invites people to perceive and think about physical, social, racial, or economic realities of the modern age in new and astonishing and socially positive ways.

References

Chan, A.A. (2007) *Slavery in the Age of Reason: Archaeology at a New England Farm*. Knoxville: University of Tennessee Press.
Chireau, Y. (1997) Conjure and Christianity in the nineteenth century: religious elements of African American magic. *Religion and American Culture*, 7(2): 225–46.
Christensen, K. (2011) Ideas versus things: the balancing act of interpreting historic house museums. *International Journal of Heritage Studies*, 17(2): 153–68.
Clifford, J. and Marcus, G.E. (1986) *Writing Culture: The Poetics and Politics of Ethnography*. Berkeley: University of California Press.
Cochran, M.D. and Beaudry, M.C. (2006) Material culture studies and historical archaeology. In: D. Hicks and M.C. Beaudry (eds.), *The Cambridge Companion to Historical Archaeology*. Cambridge: Cambridge University Press, pp. 191–204.
Cook, L.J., Yamin, R., and McCarthy, J.P. (1996) Shopping as meaningful action: toward a redefinition of consumption in historical archaeology. *Historical Archaeology*, 95(3): 551–73.
De Cunzo, L.A. and Ernstein, J.H. (2006) Landscapes, ideology, and experience in historical archaeology. In: D. Hicks and M.C. Beaudry (eds.) *The Cambridge Companion to Historical Archaeology*. Cambridge: Cambridge University Press, pp. 255–70.
Delle, J. (1999) The landscapes of class negotiation on coffee plantations in the Blue Mountains of Jamaica, 1790–1850. *Historical Archaeology*, 33(1): 136–58.
Epperson, T.W. (1990) Race and the disciplines of the plantations. *Historical Archaeology*, 24(4): 29–36.
Epperson, T.W. (1999) Constructing difference: the social and spatial order of the Chesapeake Plantation. In: T.A. Singleton (ed.), *I, Too, Am America: Archaeological Studies of African-American Life*. Charlottesville: University Press of Virginia, pp. 159–72.
Fagan, B. (1996) Archaeology's dirty secret. In: K.D. Vitelli (ed.), *Archaeological Ethics*. Walnut Creek, CA: AltaMira Press, pp. 247–52.
Franklin, M., and McKee, L. (2004). African diaspora archaeologies: present insights and expanding discourses. *Historical Archaeology*, 38 (1), 1–9.
Gathercole, P.W. and Lowenthal, D. eds. (1990) *The Politics of the Past*. One World Archaeology Series 12. New York: Routledge.
Glassie, H. (1995) *Passing the Time in Balleymenone: Culture and History of an Ulster Community*. Reprint ed. Philadelphia: University of Pennsylvania Press.
Goodwin, L.B.R. (1999) *An Archaeology of Manners: The Polite World of the Merchant Elite of Colonial Massachusetts*. New York: Kluwer Academic/Plenum Publishers.
Hall, M. (1992) Small things and the mobile: conflictual fusion of power, fear, and desire. In: A.E. Yentsch and M.C. Beaudry (eds.), *The Art and Mystery of Historical Archaeology*. Boca Raton, FL: CRC Press, pp. 373–99.

Herscher, E. and McManamon, F.P. (2000) Public education and outreach: the obligation to educate. In: M.J. Lynott and A. Wylie (eds.) *Ethics in American Archaeology*. Washington, DC: SAA, pp. 49–51.

Hodder, I. (1986) *Reading the Past: Current Approaches to Interpretation in Archaeology*. Second edition. Cambridge: Cambridge University Press.

Hodder, I. and Hutson, S. (2004). *Reading the Past: Current Approaches to Interpretation in Archaeology*. Third edition. Cambridge: Cambridge University Press.

Jameson, J.H. (1997) Introduction: what this book is about. In: J.H. Jameson (ed.), *Presenting Archaeology to the Public: Digging for Truths*. Walnut Creek, CA: AltaMira Press, pp. 11–20.

Jameson, J.H. and Ehrenhard, J.E. (1997) Foreword. In: J.H. Jameson (ed.), *Presenting Archaeology to the Public: Digging for Truths*. Walnut Creek, CA: AltaMira Press: p. 9.

Joyce, R.A. (2006) Writing historical archaeology. In: D. Hicks and M.C. Beaudry (eds.), *The Cambridge Companion to Historical Archaeology*. Cambridge: Cambridge University Press, pp. 48–65.

Leone, M.P. (1984) Interpreting ideology in historical archaeology: the William Paca Garden in Annapolis, Maryland. In: D. Miller and C. Tilley (eds.) *Ideology, Power, and Prehistory*. London: Cambridge University Press, pp. 25–35.

Leone, M.P. (1999) Setting some terms for historical archaeologies of capitalism. In: M.P. Leone and P.B. Potter (eds.), *Historical Archaeologies of Capitalism*. New York: Klewer Academic/Plenum Publishers, pp. 3–20.

——(2003) The Georgian Order as the order of merchant capitalism in Annapolis, Maryland. In: M.P. Leone and P.B. Potter (eds.), *The Recovery of Meaning*. New York: Percheron Press, pp. 235–61.

Lynott, M.J. and Wylie, A. (2000) Stewardship: the central principle of archaeological ethics. In: M.J. Lynott and A. Wylie (eds.), *Ethics in American Archaeology*. Washington, DC: SAA, pp. 35–9.

McKee, L. (1994) Is it futile to try and be useful? Historical archaeology and the African-American experience. *Northeast Historical Archaeology*, 23: 1–7.

Middlesex County Probate Court (1739) Will, probate inventories, accounts of administration of Isaac Royall, Sr. of Charlestown. File papers first series 1648–1871, case #19545. Unpublished material, held at the Middlesex County Probate Court archive.

Middlesex County Probate Court (1750) Probate inventory of Andrew Hall, Esqr. of Medford. File papers first series 1648–1871, case #10098. Unpublished material, held at the Middlesex County Probate Court archive.

Potter, P.B. (1991) What is the use of plantation archaeology? *Historical Archaeology*, 25(3): 94–107.

——(1997) The archaeological site as an interpretive environment. In: J.H. Jameson (ed.), *Presenting Archaeology to the Public: Digging for Truths*. Walnut Creek, CA: AltaMira Press, pp. 35–44.

Potter, P.B. and Chabot, N.J. (1997) Locating truths on archaeological sites. In: J.H. Jameson (ed.), *Presenting Archaeology to the Public: Digging for Truths*. Walnut Creek, CA: AltaMira Press, pp. 45–53.

Prown, J.D. (1993) The truth of material culture: history or fiction? In: S. Lubar and W.D. Kingery (eds.), *History from Things*. Washington, D.C.: Smithsonian Institution Press, pp. 1–19.

Puckett, N.N. (1926) *Folk Beliefs of the Southern Negro.* New York: Negro Universities Press.

Royall, I. (1736) 15 August 1736, Isaac Royall, Sr. to Edmund Quincy about family life, life as merchant, Medford estate. Typed transcript of Royall correspondence. Unpublished material, held in the Royall House Association archive.

Shackel, P.A. (1992) Probate inventories in historical archaeology: a review and alternatives. In: B.J. Little (ed.), *Text-Aided Archaeology.* Boca Raton, FL: CRC Press, pp. 205–15.

Society for American Archaeology (1996) Principles of Archaeological Ethics. Available at: www.saa.org/AbouttheSociety/PrinciplesofArchaeologicalEthics/tabid/203/Default.aspx (accessed 8 November 2010).

Stahl, A., Mann, R., and Loren, D.D. (2004) Writing for many: interdisciplinary communication, constructionism, and the practices of writing. *Historical Archaeology,* 38(2): 83–102.

St. George, R.B. (1998) *Conversing by Signs: Poetics of Implication in New England Culture.* Chapel Hill: University of North Carolina Press.

Stone, P.G. (1997) Presenting the past: a framework for discussion. In: J.H. Jameson (ed.), *Presenting Archaeology to the Public: Digging for Truths.* Walnut Creek, CA: AltaMira Press, pp. 23–34.

Thomas, J. (2001) Archaeologies of place and landscape. In: I. Hodder (ed.), *Archaeological Theory Today.* Cambridge: Polity Press, pp. 165–86.

Tilley, C. (2002) The metaphorical transformations of Wala canoes. In: V. Buchli (ed.), *The Material Culture Reader.* New York: Berg, pp. 27–55.

Vitelli, K.D. ed. (1996) *Archaeological Ethics.* Walnut Creek, CA: AltaMira Press.

Ward, W.E.F. (1958) *A History of Ghana.* London: George Allen and Unwin.

Wilkie, L.A. (1995) Magic and empowerment on the plantation: an archaeological consideration of African-American worldview. *Southeastern Archaeology,* 14(2): 136–48.

Wolf, E. (1982) *Europe and the People without History.* Berkeley: University of California Press.

Part III, Section 6

Public engagement in, and perceptions of, museum archaeology

Chapter 34

Involving the public in museum archaeology

Nick Merriman

Introduction

Museums are a significant and powerful vehicle for the public construction of the past and for public involvement in archaeology. For much of their history, archaeological museums have been relatively inward-looking and have tended to serve the needs of the academic discipline of archaeology over and above the needs of the wider public. In recent years, however, museums in general in the UK have begun to open themselves up to enjoyment and participation by a wider range of people and have begun to play a stronger role in contemporary society. Archaeological museums are taking part in this shift towards a focus on the visitor, with the keynotes being on access, active participation, and even on tackling social exclusion.[1] In this paper, I shall explore some of the initiatives that are being undertaken in the UK, and argue that some of them represent a new way forward for a more publicly oriented concept of archaeology as a discipline which balances the former overemphasis on the needs of the academic community and 'posterity'.

The power of museums

Museums can be described as mass media of the long term. They do not have the day-to-day audiences of television or film, but cumulatively, they are visited by large numbers of people over a long period of time. Thus, a gallery in a museum with 100,000 visits a year, will over the course of a generation (say, 25 years) be visited by around two and a half million people. In the UK, visiting museums and galleries as a whole is more popular as an activity than watching football matches or any other live sporting event (MORI/Resource 2001: 7). A recent survey by the Society of American Archaeology confirmed that a large proportion of the population is exposed to archaeology in museums. The survey, derived from a statistically representative sample of 1,016 American adults, found that 88 per cent of the US population had visited a museum exhibiting archaeological material at some time in their lives (Ramos and Duganne 2000: 21).[2]

Source: *Public Archaeology*. New York & Abingdon: Routledge, 2004. pp. 85–108 © Taylor & Francis.

Museums are powerful media of representation because they deal with the very material on which claims to identity and truth rest. Their concreteness, their possession of 'the evidence', their official status and their association with scholarship, give museums greater authority and claims to truth than many other media of representation. It is this that has made museums important symbols in the struggle to assert national or regional identity claims or to suppress the claims of others (Kaplan 1994). Thus, in many parts of the world, museums were often founded directly out of a desire to promote new identities in emergent states (Lewis 1992) and more generally to produce an ordered, self-regulating civil society which turned away from the temptations of the gin house and learned to be satisfied with its place in the social order (Bennett 1995; Duncan 1995).

A key element in nineteenth century nation-building was the use of archaeology to project backwards in time the idea of a shared ownership of identity within modern national boundaries (Trigger 1995, Skeates 2000: 90–5). Museums played their role in this by amassing material from the past that was found within their modern geographical boundaries and by using this to legitimate the existence of the modern state by situating it in the context of the deeper past (Broshi 1994). In the same way, in the twentieth century, the Nazi regime used the presence of ancient 'Germanic' finds to justify its claims to an expanded Greater Germany, and then used museum presentations of this material culture to justify its invasions and its treatment of certain peoples as inferior or subhuman (Arnold 1990; McCann 1990).

To the public in general, to competing interest groups, to politicians, to economists, to journalists, and to academics, museums – including archaeological museums or those with archaeological collections – continue to matter a great deal. They continue to be powerful cultural and civic symbols; they are used to spearhead economic regeneration and resurgent regional identities, as seen in the construction of the new Museum of Scotland (Ascherson 2000); and they continue to be fundamental targets in conflict, where they are looted and destroyed to erase identity claims, as has been seen recently in Kuwait, Bosnia, and Afghanistan (Layton et al. 2001).

And yet, despite these apparently large visitor figures, and despite the avowed importance of museums as attested by the amount of press coverage and controversy they generate, how effective are they at actually communicating about the past? I have argued elsewhere (Merriman 1991), that the intention of museum founders to disseminate a consensual view of identity amongst the populace has been subverted by the many different readings that museum visitors make of museums, and because many groups in society simply do not visit museums. As a result, the effect of museums for much of their history has been to bind together the educated and advantaged groups in society with a common culture, and to exclude others. The importance of archaeological museums, then, has to a large extent until recently derived from their symbolic role as the repositories of the raw material on which cultural identity is founded, rather than necessarily through the success of any wider educational functions which they may have performed.

Archaeological museums as servants of archaeology

Housing of archaeological evidence, and demonstration of a legitimating presence in the landscape that links past with present have then been the principal social roles demanded of the archaeological museum. This emphasis on 'authentic evidence' has meant that for much of their history archaeological museums have focused on the preservation and documentation of their collections, and on the academic needs of the discipline of archaeology.[3] Even relatively recently, for example, the concluding paper in a publication arising from a conference about museum archaeology in Europe restricted the role of museum archaeologists to undertaking fieldwork, and storing the results of survey and excavation (Biddle 1994).

In common with most other museums, for much of their history, archaeological museums have been 'top-down' institutions where the curators dispensed displays to a passive audience. The training of archaeological curators has been in archaeology, not in communication, and museum archaeologists have tended to look to their peers in other areas of the archaeological community for their validation and approval, rather than to the non-specialist public as a whole.

The difficulty of capturing the headline-grabbing excitement of discovery in the field, the apparent need to serve the rest of the archaeological discipline by coping with the storage of large amounts of material, and the consequent inward focus on matters of curation rather than on audiences, has led to a marginalization of museum archaeology, whereby it is seen to be remote from the interests of most people today (Merriman 1991: 96–103). Indeed, a recent survey of the use of archaeological archives and collections in England (Merriman and Swain 1999) showed that despite the huge resources expended in generating them, they are barely being used even by archaeologists, let alone the public as a whole. A similar 'curation crisis' has been noted in the USA (Childs 1995) and Japan (Barnes and Okita 1999).

The consequences of this lack of focus on the needs of the public can be far-reaching. In Croydon, to the south of London, when local people were asked what sort of things they would like to see in a new community museum that was being planned, the majority said that they wanted nothing before the time which their grandparents could remember back to (MacDonald 1998). As a result, none of the local archaeological material from the prehistoric to late medieval periods found a place in the museum. When consulted, today's ethnically diverse community did not think it of interest or relevant.

The turn towards the public

However, it is the community museum movement that holds the key to understanding the changes that are being experienced by some archaeological museums today. From the 1960s, archaeological museums, like many others, began to experience considerable advances in the *technology* of presentation through the use of models, dioramas, 'reconstructions', and audiovisuals in new initiatives such as the Fishbourne Roman Palace (opened 1968) and the Museum of London (opened 1976). These served to make museums more attractive to visitors, and a combination of greater leisure time and disposable income, effective marketing and presentation, coupled with a genuine desire to hold on to past certainties at a time of rapid change, led to a 'heritage boom' in the 1970s and 1980s. 'Experiences' such as the Jorvik Viking Centre (opened 1984) seemed to show a new way in which archaeology could be presented to popular acclaim. The success of 're-enactments' and first- and third-person interpretation in the United States (Anderson 1984) led to its adoption in open-air sites, such as Ironbridge, and for occasional special events at archaeological sites and museums (Sansom 1996).

While their growth at this time demonstrated the popularity of museums and other heritage attractions, developments were strongly criticized by some academics for producing interpretations of the past which were comfortable and nostalgic and biased in favour of the dominant classes. Specifically for archaeology, Shanks and Tilley (1987: 87) argued that museums such as the Museum of London legitimate contemporary social relations by 'suppressing contradiction, fixing the past as a reflection of the appearance of the present'. The solution for such failings was, it was argued, for museums to become much more self-reflexive, more 'owned' by their communities, to work in partnership with different interest groups, and to represent different voices in their presentations (ibid.: 98–9).

In many ways, the community museum movement already showed the ways in which this might be accomplished. From the 1960s, the changing political climate, which questioned traditional values and promoted civil rights, led to a gradual rethinking of the museum and its role. The movement seems to have started with the Anacostia Neighbourhood Museum in Washington, DC, where the Smithsonian Institution established a branch in a black neighbourhood in 1967 (Hudson 1981: 179–81). The ecomuseum movement began at around the same time under the influence of the thinking of Rivière and de Varine (Davis 1999). In these new kinds of museums, the keynote was on the participation and involvement of the local community in developing museums that met their own needs. In theory at least, the museum was to be run by, and orientated towards, the local people who lived in the area (ibid.: 75).

The access and inclusion agenda

More recently, partly inspired by the success of community museums, and building on the desire to ensure that public services are accountable to taxpayers and serve the needs of the entire community, a much more explicit social agenda has been given to museums in the UK by the government. Elected in 1997 on a manifesto that included improvements in education, tackling social exclusion, and providing access for all to public services, the Labour government has required all of its ministries to identify means of contributing to this overall agenda. The department which covers both archaeology and museums, the Department for Culture, Media and Sport, has as a result placed a high priority, through a series of policy documents, on encouraging educational, accessible and socially inclusive programmes in the bodies it funds (DCMS 1998, 2000, 2001; Dodd and Sandell 1998). This agenda coincides with approaches already favoured by local government, and has influenced other funding agencies, such as the Heritage Lottery Fund, which also place a high priority on the promotion of access to cultural heritage, and the development of educational services. As a result, probably for the first time in the UK there is a situation in which publicly funded museums share an outward-looking agenda, which places the public before collections management. This has itself been reflected in a changed definition of the museum by the UK's Museums Association, from one which focused primarily on processes and collections ('an institution which collects, documents, preserves, exhibits, and interprets material evidence and associated information for the public benefit') to one which stresses outcomes and audiences: 'Museums enable people to explore collections for inspiration, learning and enjoyment. They are institutions that collect, safeguard and make accessible artefacts and specimens, which they hold in trust for society' (Museums Association 1998).

As a result, archaeological museums find themselves in a climate in which their funding bodies, and the public at large, are looking to them to develop programmes which engage contemporary audiences, and which are relevant not only to traditional visitors but which also reach out and connect with people who normally do not visit museums or have any particular interest in archaeology. Whilst the political impetus to use museums to implement government policy must be regarded extremely critically by those working in museums (cf. Moore 1997: 21–2), so far the move towards making museums more socially engaged has had the benefit of giving many of them a much-needed push to address their actual and potential audiences more closely.

As a result, widening 'access', defined simply as physical and intellectual, or further refined into physical and sensory, intellectual, cultural, attitudinal, and financial (Lang 2000), has become the single most important driving force in museum development in the UK in recent years. I shall now turn to examine some of the ways in which this turn to the public has manifested itself in the work of museum archaeologists.

Digital access

One of the principal ways in which access to archaeological collections is being promoted is through the placing of collections information and images on the Internet, which allows them to be accessed in ways that break free of the constraints of the four walls of the museum.

For long seen as something dull but necessary for accountability purposes (Davies 1998), museum documentation has been transformed through digital technology into an element of museum access and communication (Keene 1998). Some museums, such as Hampshire Museum Service, have simply posted their collections information on the Web fairly undigested, but searchable by anyone with sufficient interest. The Petrie Museum of Egyptian Archaeology at University College London has developed a full online illustrated catalogue of all 78,000 objects in its collection, and plans to create a virtual museum linking all of the other Egyptian material excavated by Petrie scattered around the world, starting with a specific link-up with the Manchester Museum for the finds from the site of Lahun, which are held in both museums (MacDonald 2000). At the Hunterian Museum in Glasgow, it is possible to see 'object movies' of prehistoric carved stone artefacts – by clicking on the object it can be made to rotate so that all sides and angles can be seen.

Many museums have moved beyond the object to use the Internet to create a virtual information resource. At the Museum of Antiquities of the University of Newcastle, it is possible to see a 'virtual exhibition' about Late Stone Age hunter-gatherers, enter the Hadrian's Wall education website, and explore the museum's recreated temple to Mithras three-dimensionally by moving around the room and clicking on elements of interest (Museum of Antiquities Website 2001).

Beyond the UK, the Alexandria Archaeology Museum in Virginia, USA, is one of the fullest archaeological explorations in a museum context of the possibilities of online access and information. As well as providing information on how to find the museum (including online maps) and its current programmes, the website provides details of its current and past exhibitions, of the 'Archaeology Adventure Lessons' held in the museum, and other activities such as the summer camp, public dig days, and archaeological site tours. There are 'Kids Pages' which provide online or downloadable activities, and details of how to join the Friends' programme, become a volunteer, or apply for an internship. There are also short online catalogues relating to publications and merchandising, with downloadable order forms, and, as an incentive to visit, 'eSavings coupons', which can be used by actual visitors to the museum to obtain discounts. In addition, there is 'behind the scenes' information on how collections are cared for and conserved, extracts from the collections policy, details on how the new storage facility was created, explanations about the laws on archaeological preservation and metal detecting, and downloadable forms for archaeologists such as a 'Request for Preliminary Archaeological Assessment'. Finally, there is extensive information on local sites currently or previously excavated, themes from Alexandria's past, and a bibliography of publications relating to the archaeology of the town (Alexandria Archaeology Museum Website 2001).

Most Internet access involves remote visitors accessing a pre-prepared site. However, some museums are beginning to exploit the Web's potential for interactivity and broadcast. The National Museum of Wales' excavation of a Viking Age settlement at Llanbedrgoch became the focus of a project called 'Digging for Vikings. Archaeology as it Happens' in 2000. Perhaps borrowing from a format established by the television series *Time Team*, web pages were set up giving the background to the excavation, details of the site team and their jobs, site reports, site plan, educational information, and daily updates. Enquirers were invited to send emails with their questions to the excavation team, which the team would reply to on a daily basis (National Museum of Wales Website 2001). Taking this a step further, a British Museum team excavating the Palaeolithic site at Elveden in Suffolk is experimenting with webcam broadcasts (British Museum 2000), in a manner similar to that already undertaken in the National Museums and Galleries on Merseyside for scientific expeditions as part of the JASON project (Phillips 1998).

Digital media clearly provide a new dimension to the accessibility of museum archaeological resources. However, they are not the panacea that they are sometimes seen to be, because access to the Web is generally limited to those with the resources to afford it (Sarraf 1999: 233). The further provision of Internet access through the People's Network, which will hook all libraries to the Internet, and Culture Online, which is a new government agency devoted to providing digital content, may transform this situation, but at present there is a fairly close match between Internet users and those who tend to visit museums (ibid.). Non-visitors tend also to be non-users of the Internet, except perhaps in the case of young people, who are more likely to be Internet users but less likely to visit museums.

Paradoxically too, the use of digital media to provide 'access' to museum archaeological collections, can actually take people away from the real objects themselves by focusing their attention on digital reproductions of them. While digital information may alert users to the existence of certain collections and stimulate more enquiries to see the objects themselves, it is not clear whether digital media really provide any more 'access' to collections than photographs in books.

Behind the scenes

Another strand of the access agenda does however bring users into closer contact with the museum's collections themselves, for example, through the opening-up of storage and other 'back of house' facilities such as conservation, through the handling of collections in discovery centres and loan boxes, and through programmes of outreach beyond the museum building itself.

In the archaeological context, the opening-up of collections formerly held in store away from public gaze can mean the provision of pull-out storage drawers in the body of display cases, a reinvented Victorian tradition seen, for example, at the Verulamium Museum, St Albans, or it can mean the availability of the whole stored collection in a publicly accessible resource centre. The Museum of London's London Archaeological Archive and Research Centre, for example, makes the entire archive of some 3,000 excavations available to students, researchers, archaeological societies, and interested members of the general public (Hall and Swain 2000: 87). Other museums that do not have the resources to develop facilities such as these will often have open days with guided tours behind the scenes, where visitors have the opportunity to see material in store and ask questions of the curators (CBA Website 2001).

The opening-up of the museum has also resulted in the exposure of previously hidden processes to public scrutiny. For archaeology, this seems to have begun with the Archaeological Resource Centre in York which, from its opening in 1990 (Jones 1995), not only allowed visitors to gain an insight into finds processing and analysis (see below), but also had offices with glass walls so that archaeologists could be seen at work.

Archaeological conservation has been brought out of the laboratory and into public view by the National Museum of Wales through its 'Celtic warrior' programme, which presents an in-gallery performance designed to show how materials survive or deteriorate. The 'warrior' (played by a member of museum staff), and his clothes and weapons are described to the audience who then help 'bury' him under a mound. The warrior is removed via a trapdoor and replaced by his grave as if it has just been excavated by archaeologists. Conservators then discuss with the audience how different aspects of the body, clothes, and grave goods have changed in the course of burial. Using X-rays, photomicrographs, and tools, they then show what excavation and conservation can discover about what may originally have been deposited. At the end, the Celtic warrior returns so that the visitors can again compare what was placed in the grave with the work of the conservators (National Museum of Wales Website 2001).

The most ambitious attempt to develop public access to conservation has been at the Conservation Centre in Liverpool, which is part of the National Museums and Galleries on Merseyside. The Centre provides accommodation for all of the museum service's conservation needs, including archaeology, and was designed from the outset to promote public access and understanding. It has a visitor centre, is open seven days a week, which explains the processes of conservation in an interactive display, and at scheduled times visitors can sit in a small lecture theatre that has a live video link to the laboratories. They can use this link to engage in an active question-and-answer session with conservators working in the labs. Tours of the labs themselves are also available at scheduled times (Forrester 1998).

It is notable that one of the characteristics of these initiatives to bring out formerly hidden museum functions into public view is that it seems to be only the technical processes themselves which are exposed. It is taken for granted that museums must undertake storage and conservation, for example, and debates about the ethics of collecting, disposal, and conservation do not form part of the presentation. Visitors are, it seems, invited to admire the extent of the collections, and the expertise and scientific prowess of the museum staff, but not question the fundamentals of what they do or why they do it.

Hands-on the past

A major way in which visitors have been given further access to archaeological collections is by breaking a long-held taboo and being allowed to touch and handle some of them. To a large extent this has been influenced by the development of hands-on discovery centres, particularly those relating to scientific principles, of which the first was the Exploratorium in San Francisco in 1969 (Caulton 1998: 3). Owen (1999) has summarized recent approaches to hands-on learning in archaeological museums showing that the principles of discovery learning are well-suited to archaeological collections (but see her reservations, below).

For archaeology, the pioneering 'discovery centre' has been the ARC in York (Jones 1995), which concentrates primarily on providing hands-on experiences for booked school groups and family visitors. Visitors handle archaeological finds from sites, sort them into categories (pottery, bone, etc.), and are encouraged, through this, to understand something of the archaeological process. Staff are on hand to guide visitors through the process and answer questions.

The ARC is unusual in being a stand-alone facility entirely devoted to archaeology. Rather commoner is the generalized discovery gallery in which archaeology plays a part alongside other disciplines, such as the Discovery Centre at the National Museum of Scotland. Here, from amongst six activity areas, visitors can unpack a Roman soldier's kitbag, write on a wax tablet, handle artefacts from a Viking grave, or make a seal's tooth pendant. As well as being available for the general public, the Centre is aimed specifically to meet the demands of the curriculum for 5 to 14-year-olds. It has times reserved for school visits and is supplemented by teachers' packs and teachers' in-service courses. In a similar vein, Hampshire Museum Service's hands-on centre, SEARCH, is aimed principally at primary school groups studying National Curriculum topics in science and history. One of the areas is 'Archaeology in Action', which has workstations equipped with microscopes and hand lenses for examining material. Following a slide show about evidence found during an excavation, children are encouraged to handle and sort real and replica Roman and Anglo-Saxon material, look for clues about their use, and build up ideas about the life of the inhabitants.

The Museum of London has taken the notion of 'discovery' through participation in archaeological activities a stage further in its temporary exhibition, 'The Dig', which was held in 2001. Here, visitors were able to participate in a mock excavation over twenty-four 'trenches', using trowels and brushes to uncover real and replica objects (Martin 2002).

Hampshire's 'SEARCH' is subtitled 'Hands on education centre for learning by discovery', and it is clear from all of the above initiatives that a consensus has developed that it is educationally beneficial for visitors to handle and closely examine authentic archaeological material. However, as Owen (1999) has observed, there is next to no work that actually demonstrates quite what the educational benefits of hands-on or discovery learning are for visitors. Despite this, they seem to be popular, and may well justify themselves from the enjoyment they provide through the experience of handling ancient objects alone, rather than through any enhanced learning, which they may, or may not, stimulate. It is also uncertain how far such hands-on initiatives actually broaden the audience for archaeology rather than provide a richer experience for the existing profile of visitors, as currently visitor studies on this topic do not exist.

Loan boxes

One of the ways in which museums have been attempting to widen hands-on access to archaeological collections, and broaden the profile of their audience, is through the use of loan boxes, which are one of the oldest forms of museum outreach. Despite being quite well developed in the period before the Second World War (Markham 1938), many museum loan services were curtailed in the post-war period because of local authority funding cuts. However, with the rise of the access and education agenda, loan boxes have been reborn in many museum services as a vital component of educational outreach. The loan service run by Reading Museum, one of the few to survive intact for nearly a century, now consists of some 2,000 foam-padded boxes containing 20,000 objects, including a significant archaeological component comprising prehistoric, Roman, Anglo-

Saxon, medieval, Ancient Greek and Ancient Egyptian material. The boxes are delivered to schools in the local area each term to support their curriculum needs and each year around 4,000 loans are made, which are used by 33,000 schoolchildren (Swift 1997).

Moreover, as part of the general move of museums to bring behind-the-scenes processes out into the open, Reading Museum has developed a 'box room' right by its entrance, which consists of a hands-on area where visitors can examine some of the loan boxes not currently out on loan and handle some of the objects, and an area where staff work in the open, preparing boxes for loan, receiving returned loans, and administering the scheme as a whole.

In a further development of the idea, the Museum of London has reinvented the loan box as a permanent transfer to local schools. Enquiries showed that the museum's schools' sessions on the Roman Gallery were not able to accommodate all of the school parties wishing to use it, and as many as 5,000 children a year may have been turned down (Hall and Swain 2000). In addition, it was found that the poorest schools were not able to afford to travel to visit the museum. As a result, the museum developed a scheme whereby boxes of Roman material were given to 200 schools in the London area. The boxes contain selected unstratified Roman material together with replica material such as a lamp and writing tablet, teachers' notes, and a video. Each school now has a permanent mini-museum available to it, and the Museum has been able to use material that was archaeologically relatively unimportant because of its lack of context.

Outreach and inclusion

As the work with loan boxes implies, the socially engaged museum is now no longer to be conceived of as a building to which visitors are enticed, but as a service, which tailors its work to different target audiences. As a result, outreach work has become an important means of service delivery, both as an end in itself, and as a way in which the museum can publicize itself. Outreach in this context involves moving beyond the traditional provision of travelling exhibitions, which are lent to other museum venues, to the provision of services to non-traditional venues and audiences. In some instances this can mean mounting archaeological displays in places such as the office buildings erected on the sites of excavations, or in pubs, airports or shopping centres, as has been done by the Museum of London, and in other cases it can mean taking mobile museums directly out to the community. Long-established in large countries with relatively few museums, such as India (Jain 1994), mobile museums have had a sporadic history in the UK, but like loan boxes, are becoming revived as outreach and public involvement become more important.

The National Museum of Scotland's 'Discovery on the Move', for example, is a travelling version of its discovery centre that can be booked by museums, libraries, schools, community halls, and other public venues. It focuses on five topics, two of which include the use of archaeology. The first element, on 'How we use evidence to learn about the past', invites visitors to see what material from today would look like in 100 years' time, and piece together a three-dimensional jigsaw in the form of a broken pot. Another element displays objects and evidence specifically from the local area of each venue, and changes with each destination. A computer information point provides further information about objects and places in Scotland.

However, such forms of outreach do not necessarily mean that new audiences who would not normally consider visiting museums (particularly 'the socially excluded') are reached. The issue of broadening audiences, particularly of reaching audiences who are socially marginalized, represents a major challenge to museum archaeologists. How can archaeological collections be made to resonate with people's lives today, especially those who feel excluded from museums?

One response to this has been to target specific groups. For example, the county museum services of Shropshire, Herefordshire, and Worcestershire have come together to develop a 'Museum on the Move', which is specifically aimed at providing a community museum service to isolated rural communities, many of them suffering from considerable poverty. A purpose-built 7.5-tonne vehicle housing an exhibition is made available to visit schools, training centres, day centres for the elderly, sheltered housing schemes, village centres, hospitals, youth centres, and shopping centres. As with most of the outreach projects already noted, disciplinary boundaries are dissolved and archaeological material takes its place in thematic displays alongside material from other traditional disciplines. The first exhibition, 'Munch!: A short history of food through the ages', included archaeological material, and featured handleable real and replica objects, 'feely boxes' and 'smelly boxes', tapes, video, and an on-board interpreter who could answer questions.

Glasgow Museums Service, a pioneer of community involvement and outreach in the UK, has developed its 'Open Museum' service, which consists of a series of twenty exhibitions or displays that can be borrowed by community groups, and four handling kits for schools, playschemes, and local events (Edwards 1996). One of the handling kits is called 'The Archaeology Game', designed to be used by visually impaired children as well as sighted ones. It has accompanying Braille notes, as well as teachers' notes. All of the exhibitions and kits are available free of charge.

The exhibitions are distinguished by the fact that they have all been developed in partnership with local people, so the process of exhibition development is as important a part of the project as the final product. Some of the displays include an archaeological component, including one on 'Digging up Govan', which features Viking and other material from Govan Old Parish Church. They tend to be loaned not to other local museums but to church halls, libraries, and community centres.

Archaeology and cultural diversity

Very few museum archaeological initiatives have targeted current ethnic minorities in their programmes, who, surveys show, tend to feel excluded from participation in museum culture (Trevelyan 1991; Khan 2000). This has also recently been emphasized in the UK government's review of the historic environment (English Heritage 2000). Informing it was a large-scale survey of attitudes of the public, and in particular members of ethnic minorities, to the history and heritage of the UK.

The survey showed that black people in particular felt alienated from mainstream white culture and its heritage, and did not feel that the historic environment is 'for them' (MORI 2000).

The issue of how archaeology and archaeological museums in the UK might include people from ethnic minorities in their audiences is a question that has generally not troubled archaeologists, and only a couple of examples are available of projects that might point the way forward. The 'Peopling of London' project at the Museum of London in 1993–1994 combined archaeological and social historical evidence to demonstrate that London's cultural diversity was part of the essence of the city's history from its earliest times (Merriman 1997). The exhibition began with a survey of London in the post-war period, which established what most visitors perceived to be true: that immigration from the Commonwealth had been a significant part of London's story in this period. Visitors then went back to prehistoric times, to the last glacial maximum, when Britain was an uninhibited peninsula of northern Europe. The story then wound from the incursion of hunter-gatherers into lowland Britain following the retreat of the ice sheets, through the establishment of the Roman settlement of London, inhabited by people from all over the empire, the Anglo-Saxon and Norman settlements, the settlement of craft-workers and merchants from overseas in medieval times, England's expansion as a maritime and trading power in the Tudor period, the development of the slave trade and the first Black settlers in London, and through on into the eighteenth and nineteenth century settlements of Irish, Jewish, Chinese, Asian, Italian, German, and African-Caribbean people, back to the present. In doing so, the project involved members of ethnic minorities who previously felt unrepresented and unwelcome in the museum, and told a story that linked their lives with those of Londoners of hundreds or thousands of years ago. In addition to the exhibition itself, there was an extensive programme of events for schools and families, a teachers' pack, a book, a travelling exhibition, and an artist in residence. Nearly 100,000 people visited the exhibition during its six-month run, and survey and other evaluation techniques demonstrated that the exhibition successfully attracted a new audience to the Museum, with 20 per cent of people visiting the museum while the exhibition was on describing themselves as belonging to an ethnic minority, compared with 4 per cent before the exhibition (Merriman 1997).

The Cuming Museum in Southwark, London, is based on an antiquarian collection of Egyptian and British antiquities, which until just over a decade or so ago catered principally for a dwindling audience of mainly elderly people committed to archaeology and local antiquities. The museum's local area is today ethnically highly diverse. Rather than turning their backs on this local audience, in recent years the museum staff have attempted to make connections between the collections and the local people by transforming part of the galleries into a child-oriented hands-on local archaeology and history display with text written in an accessible, personal way and a hands-on excavation pit in the centre. Through the local council's education and outreach department, the museum reaches out to schools and community centres. Through handling sessions in the museum itself, connections are made between archaeological material and the visitor's experience, such as between Roman lamps and similar lamps used by Hindus at home today. Through targeting its very diverse local community, and in particular local schools, the museum now finds that some 60 per cent of its visitors are from ethnic minorities (J. Bird, pers. comm.). Here, perhaps, is an indication that by concentrating on the notion of 'place', archaeological collections can make connections with audiences who do not necessarily subscribe to the notions of a shared identity rooted in a deep common past that until recently archaeological displays promulgated.

'The Art of Archaeology'

One particular method of developing new approaches to the use of archaeological (and other) collections has been through emphasizing the creative and imaginative ways in which archaeological collections can be used. In most museum contexts, this has involved engaging the services of creative artists who have tended to use the collections as a source of inspiration and produce their own interventions in the museum space (Pearce 1999: 21–5). Whilst such interventions may play with ideas of the relationship between the historical display and the artistic installation, and may 'subvert the museum's dialectic by illuminating it with the beams of parody, irony and deliberate fiction' (ibid.: 24), it is not clear how far such questioning and subversion extend beyond the highly culturally literate core museum audience.[4] One exception to this is the work of Mark Dion, an American artist whose work challenges the boundaries between fact and fiction and between science and art, by collecting material in fieldwork 'expeditions' and assembling cabinets of curiosities from his discoveries, which are exhibited in art galleries rather than museums of history or science. His 'Tate Thames Dig' of 1999 was the fourth in a series of 'excavations', which collected debris from different parts of the world and arranged them on tables or in cabinets (Coles and Dion 1999). In this project, the process of collecting, cleaning, and classifying material taken from the Thames foreshore by the sites of Tate Britain and Tate Modern were essential parts of the project, and were carried out in public in tents on the lawn of Tate Britain. Crucially, for this project, Dion chose as his 'field workers' representatives of the local community. Their role was to collect, clean, label, and package the material from the river foreshore, answer questions from the public and attend the lectures given by 'experts' on aspects of the river and its history. This was effectively a kind of community archaeology project, in which over half of the community participants were from ethnic minorities, but took place within the context of an art gallery rather than an archaeological museum.

In order to explore new uses and new audiences for underused archaeological collections, the Society of Museum Archaeologists, the UK's professional organization for archaeologists working in museums, developed a project called 'The Art of Archaeology' which encouraged the creative use of archaeological collections. Ten museums took part between May 2000 and March 2001, helped by funding from the Heritage Lottery Access Fund. Some of these are worth describing in a little detail as they provide good examples of the ways in which museum archaeologists are currently trying to encourage wider use of archaeological collections.

Nottingham City Museums and Galleries developed a project called 'Archaeology Revealed'. One element involved young mothers from a particular area of the city in developing a ceramic art installation for the exhibition, and involved pupils at risk from exclusion in a local school in the production of the exhibition banner, using the Egyptian collection as inspiration.

In urban museums such initiatives are not unusual, although they have rarely been carried out using archaeological collections. It is much more unusual, though, for this kind of work to be undertaken in rural areas, despite their oft-neglected problems of poverty and poor services. Archaeological collections can potentially have a significant role to play in outreach projects in rural areas because they are found in almost every local history museum and because the general robustness of much of the material lends itself to active use.

Shropshire Archaeology Service, for example, used material from a Roman villa and a medieval friary to develop a series of events focused particularly on the Craven Arms district, which is a recognized area of rural poverty. Events included an art installation, song and poem workshops, and a workshop in which a stained-glass artist used medieval stained-glass fragments to discuss with participants how they could be used to reconstruct the past. Two of the workshops were also taken into local schools and all of them resulted in a series of exhibitions that toured local museums and libraries.

In another rural area, Herefordshire Museums' projects included one undertaken in partnership with the local Royal National College for the Blind, in which a five-week course on 'A History of Ceramic Technology' was held, based principally on the museums' collection of archaeological pottery. The course was held for students following a vocational qualification on recreational art and design, and the results of their work were displayed at one of the local museums.

North Lanarkshire Museum targeted two areas, Glenboig and Cardowan, as areas of deprivation and social exclusion, for a programme of creative writing focusing on the industrial heritage of the area through the museum's industrial archaeology and social history collections. Workshops involved a range of participants – from primary school pupils, youth group members, and adults – and culminated in a public reading of their work, and a publication. In a similar vein, Worcester City Museum developed creative writing workshops based on its archaeological collections, involving schools, a leisure club, and adult groups, including a group with disabilities.

Evaluation of the projects made it clear that the majority of projects were successful in bringing new uses and new audiences to archaeological collections. All of the museums involved felt that the projects represented new approaches for them, and would wish to undertake more of this work if resources would allow them to do so. It is clear that it is possible to encourage more extensive use of archaeological collections, and their use by a wider audience. However, it is also clear that such work requires a significant commitment in terms of time by museum staff, and it is not yet clear what the effects are or how long-term they may be (Owen 2002).

Observations

This overview has demonstrated that archaeological museums – or museums with archaeological collections – are now beginning to make significant strides in reorienting themselves to the public following their former focus on the needs of their collections and of the discipline of archaeology. What is remarkable about many of the initiatives is that they represent a new way of thinking about archaeology in which the emphasis is not, as has traditionally been the case, on what the public can do for archaeology, but rather on what archaeology can do for the public (Smardz 1997: 103). This is not to say that archaeology can only justify itself if it can be proved to be 'relevant' to contemporary society, but it does mean that archaeology can no longer be solely justified by reference to notions of disinterested scholarship and objectivity: it must also balance this with a commitment to deliver something back to present-day communities.

In terms of archaeological museums, in many ways the work in the UK leads the way, mainly because of the pressures exerted by non-archaeological impulses on the museums profession as a whole. However, the embracing by the whole archaeological profession of the notion of engaging with audiences, providing access and use of archaeological collections and knowledge, and providing services for different parts of the community is an exciting prospect indeed for a more publicly oriented archaeology. There are nevertheless a good number of issues to be confronted (aside from the obvious ones such as funding), which arise from a review of current practice.

The return to the object

One of the most noticeable aspects of many of the access initiatives outlined above, such as visible storage, online databases, hands-on activities, and the art projects, is that they seem to represent a return to the object. In contrast to some recent approaches to social history in museums (Fleming 1998; Jenkinson 1989), which have argued for a retreat away from the object in favour of historical context and interpretation, much recent museum archaeology has focused on the objects themselves, with minimal if any historical contextualization. The intrinsic properties of the objects are emphasized, be it their tactility, age, or unusual nature. The visitor is invited to engage with the objects as objects, with their apparently intrinsic 'aura', rather than engaging with them as evidence forming an element in the construction of a historical understanding of past cultures. Where contextualization is provided, it tends to be used to demonstrate processes of excavation, storage, conservation, or research, but rarely will the possible historical meanings of the objects be explored beyond classification, date and technical function.

A focus on the objects themselves nevertheless highlights aspects of the visitor experience which engage well with current theories of museum education, which emphasize affective, non-linear, self-directed learning in which the visitor constructs knowledge him- or herself (Hein 1998). Plurality is welcomed, and proximity to 'truth' is not the standard against which visitor understanding is measured. Such approaches stress that what museums do best is to stimulate feelings such as wonder, awe, mystery, and 'otherness' (cf. Tilden 1957). A focus on the individual 'aura' of each object stimulates an approach that is creative, poetic and anti-rational. It is also an approach that is accessible to all, in that knowledge of archaeology is not necessary, nor even encouraged. The visitor can admire the richness of the collections, may react to the aesthetic qualities of the object, and may develop a subjective emotional response to the material, without needing to know anything about the historical context and interpretation of the objects themselves. This is an aesthetic approach, which treats the collections essentially as if they are art objects.

The abandonment of interpretation implicit in such approaches may actually be a legitimate response to critiques of museum archaeological representation, which have seen gallery narratives as irredeemably biased and partial. However, in concentrating on providing access, principally physical, to archaeological collections, museum curators are in danger of promoting the idea that the objects 'speak for themselves', or of concentrating on the exposition of archaeological and museum processes at the expense of historical interpretation. This point has been well made by Sharon MacDonald in relation to science interpretation, where she argues that although 'the active visitor' is seen as an ideal manifestation of democratic and accessible interpretation, the actual range of choices with which visitors are presented can in fact restrict possibilities for critical engagement rather than open them up:

> Thus, rather than just reading off 'democracy' or 'empowerment' from 'activity' or 'choice-making', it is important to try . . . to understand just how activities are conceptualised and performed by those involved, what kinds of questions are asked, and, equally crucially, what are not.
> (Sharon MacDonald 2002: 219)

This partiality of approach could mean that the post-modern fear of the past becoming a plaything, devoid of meaning other than as a thing to be consumed by visitors (e.g Walsh 1992: 113–15), could become fulfilled. Greater access may indeed be provided through such initiatives, but access to what? The challenge must now be for museum archaeologists not only to broaden the demographic profile of their audiences, but also to broaden their minds.

Use of 'informed imagination'

One of the ways in which intellectual access to archaeological collections might be broadened without sacrificing the role of museums to encourage knowledge of the past is to introduce historical contextualization alongside the affective, hands-on, and creative approaches outlined earlier. There already exist some models for this kind of approach, which I would term 'informed imagination'. By this I mean an approach to interpretation which is based on the knowledge of the archaeological and historical context of the material provided by the expertise of the curators, but which acknowledges diversity of views, the contingency of archaeological interpretations, and encourages imagination and enjoyment in the visitors' own constructions of the past.

Elements of such an approach could be seen in the former prehistoric gallery of the Museum of London, which used images of modern stereotypes of prehistory, an explicit agenda in its narrative, the ability to handle objects, links between past and present landscape, and a poetic approach to the writing of text, to communicate a sense of change over a period of half a million years (Cotton and Wood 1996). The latter is also a strong feature of the main text panels in the early displays at the Museum of Scotland, as in this section on 'Bloodshed, weapons and heroes':

> ... At first we fought with clubs and with bows and arrows. Later we fought with swords and spears. Our weapons got better, our warriors grew fiercer. The army of the Romans was uncountable. They moved with the purpose of ants. Their weapons were murderous, their war horses terrifying. But we fought them anyway.
>
> (Clarke 2000: 221)

This represents an entirely new kind of approach to archaeological interpretation in the museum. Instead of the dry and distanced writing of the scholar, we have an emotional, experiential narrative, which draws on poetry and fiction and by implication invites visitors to construct their own stories from the evidence and information they see in the galleries.

Galleries such as these tend to be informed by research on the preconceptions and attitudes of actual and potential visitors (Cotton and Wood 1996), which is one of the reasons that successful communication can occur. The recent temporary touring exhibition, 'Ancient Egypt: Digging for Dreams', mounted by the Petrie Museum of Egyptian Archaeology, Croydon Museum and Glasgow Museums, was similarly informed by such research, particularly amongst people who tended not to visit, such as members of ethnic minorities (Sally MacDonald 2002). The initial sections of the exhibition dealt with popular stereotypes about Ancient Egypt, as shown, for example, in films such as *The Mummy*. The excavation and recovery of the collections by Flinders Petrie were discussed in terms of colonialism, and then the political usurpation of archaeology was explored, such as the Nazis' use of the mummy portraits discovered by Petrie to support racial arguments (ibid.: 4).

The main body of the exhibition was devoted to various issues relating to the relationship between Ancient Egypt and societies today. One of these concerns the treatment of human remains: in the exhibition, mummified remains were in a case covered by a shroud, which visitors could lift if they wished to view them. Visitors were invited to fill out postcards giving their views on the display of human remains. Other parts of the exhibition dealt with issues of race and colour, which were identified in visitor research as being of particular interest to Black people, and the way in which Ancient Egypt is drawn upon by New Age beliefs. A final section examined how Ancient Egypt is marketed and consumed. A short video showed the personal meaning of Ancient Egypt to different people, ranging from an academic Egyptologist to Black schoolchildren (Sally MacDonald 2002).

The last three approaches to the interpretation of the archaeological past in museums offer an exciting prospect for the future, in which experimentation and debate can occur about archaeological interpretations, in which visitors and their understanding are placed at the forefront, and in which the best work on opening up collections can be allied with innovative approaches to narrative and contextualization. The public seem to respond well and without surprise to what are often seen as radical departures by archaeologists and museum professionals. It may be, then, that it is we who are holding ourselves back, through fear of the disapproval of our peers. Perhaps it is time to listen more to the views of our potential visitors, and take a few more risks in what we do.

Notes

1   Social exclusion has been defined by the Department for Culture, Media and Sport as: 'A shorthand term for what can happen when people or areas suffer from a combination of linked problems such as unemployment, poor skills, low incomes, poor housing, high crime environments, bad health, poverty and family breakdown' (DCMS 2000: 7).
2   However, this may be slightly misleading as the survey does not make clear whether visitors specifically went for the archaeology, or indeed whether they looked at the archaeology galleries at all in their visit.
3   There has nevertheless been a strong tradition of support for adult education and archaeological societies amongst museum curators since the expansion of museum provision in the nineteenth century in the form of lectures, evening classes, and field excursions. The audiences for such initiatives, however, have tended to be those who were already strongly committed to archaeology.
4   Although there is some evidence that such approaches do serve to bring in a new audience of young people who relate to contemporary art and popular culture, as was witnessed in the 'Time Machine' project at the British Museum, in which contemporary artists installed artworks in the Egyptian Sculpture gallery (S. Quirke, pers. comm. 2001).

References

Alexandria Archaeology Museum Website (2001) Available at: http://ci.alexandria.va.us/oha/archaeology (accessed 12 June 2001).

Anderson, J. (1984) *Time Machines. The World of Living History*. Nashville: American Association for State and Local History.

Arnold, B. (1990) The past as propaganda: totalitarian archaeology in Nazi Germany. *Antiquity*, 64: 464–78.

Ascherson, N. (2000) The Museum of Scotland. *Public Archaeology*, 1(1): 82–4.

Barnes, G. and Okita, M. (1999) Japanese Archaeology in the 1990s. *Journal of Archaeological Research*, 7(4): 349–95.

Bennett, T. (1995) *The Birth of the Museum. History, Theory, Politics*. London: Routledge.

Biddle, M. (1994) Can we expect museums to cope? Curatorship and the archaeological explosion. In: D. Gaimster (ed.), *Museum Archaeology in Europe. Proceedings of a conference held at the British Museum, 15–17 October 1992*. Oxbow Monograph 39. Oxford: Oxbow Books, pp. 167–71

British Museum (2000) *The British Museum Plan 2000/01 to 2004/05*. London: British Museum.

Broshi, M. (1994) Archaeological museums in Israel: reflections on problems of national identity. In: F. Kaplan (ed.), *Museums and the Making of 'Ourselves'. The Role of Objects in National Identity*. Leicester: Leicester University Press, pp. 314–19.

Caulton, T. (1998) *Hands-on Exhibitions*. London: Routledge.

CBA (2001) Council for British Archaeology. Available at: www.britarch.ac.uk/ (accessed 12 July 2001).

Childs, S.T. (1995) The curation crisis. *Federal Archaeology*, Winter/Spring: 11–15.

Clarke, D. (2000) Creating the Museum of Scotland. A reply to Neal Ascherson. *Public Archaeology*, 1(3): 220–21.

Coles, A. and Dion, M. eds. (1999) *Mark Dion: Archaeology*. London: Black Dog Publishing.

Cotton, J.F. and Wood, B. (1996) Retrieving prehistories at the Museum of London: a gallery case-study. In: P. McManus (ed.), *Archaeological Displays and the Public: Museology and Interpretation*. London: Institute of Archaeology, University College, pp. 53–71.

Davies, M. (1998) Too much data. *Museums Journal*, 98(8): 19.

Davis, P. (1999) *Ecomuseums: A Sense of Place*. Leicester: Leicester University Press.

DCMS (Department for Culture, Media and Sport) (1998) *A New Cultural Framework*. London: DCMS.

——(2000) *Centres for Social Change*. London: DCMS.

——(2001) *Libraries, Museums. Galleries and Archives for All. Co-Operating across the Sectors to Tackle Social Exclusion*. London: DCMS.

Dodd, J. and Sandell, R. (1998) *Building Bridges: Guidance for Museums and Galleries on Audience Development*. London: Museums and Galleries Commission.

Duncan, C. (1995) *Civilising Rituals. Inside Public Art Museums*. London: Routledge.

Edwards, N. (1996) The open museum. *Museum Practice*, 1(3): 60–63.

English Heritage (2000) *Power of Place: The Future of the Historic Environment*. London: English Heritage.

Fleming, D. (1998) Brave new world: the future for city history museums. In: G. Kavanagh and E. Frostick (eds.), *Making City Histories in Museums*. London: Leicester University Press, pp. 133–50.

Forrester, J. (1998) Opening up. *Museum Practice*, 3(1): 59–61.

Hall, J. and Swain, H. (2000) Roman boxes for London's schools: an outreach service by the Museum of London. In: P. McManus (ed.), *Archaeological Displays and the Public. Museology and Interpretation*. Second edition. London: Archetype Publications, pp. 87–95.

Hein, G. (1998) *Learning in the Museum*. London: Routledge.

Hudson, K. (1981) *Museums of Influence*. Cambridge: Cambridge University Press.

Jain, S. (1994) Mobile museums in India. In: S. Pearce (ed.), *Museums and the Appropriation of Culture*. New Research in Museum Studies 4. London: Athlone Press, pp. 129–41.

Jenkinson, P. (1989) Material culture, people's history and populism: where do we go from here? In: S. Pearce (ed.), *Museum Studies in Material Culture*. Leicester: Leicester University Press, pp. 139–52.

Jones, A. (1995) The Archaeological Resource Centre. In: E. Hooper-Greenhill (ed.), *Museum, Media, Message*. Leicester: Leicester University Press, pp. 156–64.

Kaplan, F. ed. (1994) *Museums and the Making of 'Ourselves'*. Leicester: Leicester University Press.

Keene, S. (1998) *Digital Collections: Museums and the Information Age.* Oxford: Butterworth-Heinemann.

Khan, N. (2000) *Responding to Cultural Diversity: Guidance for Museums and Galleries.* London: Museums and Galleries Commission.

Lang, C. (2000) *Developing an Access Policy.* London: Museums and Galleries Commission.

Layton, R., Stone, P., and Thomas, J. eds. (2001) *Destruction and Conservation of Cultural Property.* London: Routledge.

Lewis, G. (1992) Museums and their precursors: a brief world survey. In: J.M.A. Thompson (ed.), *The Manual of Curatorship: A Guide to Museum Practice.* London: Butterworth, pp. 5–20.

McCann, W.J. (1990) 'Volk und Germanentum': the presentation of the past in Nazi Germany. In: P. Gathercole and D. Lowenthal (eds.), *The Politics of the Past.* London: Routledge, pp. 74–88.

MacDonald, Sally (1998) Croydon: what history? In: G. Kavanagh and E. Frostick (eds.), *Making City Histories in Museums.* London: Leicester University Press, pp. 58–79.

——(2000) University museums and the public: the case of the Petrie Museum. In: P. McManus (ed.), *Archaeological Displays and the Public: Museology and Interpretation.* Second edition. London: Archetype Publications, pp. 67–86.

——(2002) An experiment in access. *Museologia,* 2: 101–08.

MacDonald, Sharon (2002) *Behind the Scenes at the Science Museum.* Oxford: Berg.

Markham, S.F. (1938) *A Report into the Museums and Art Galleries of the British Isles, other than the National Museums.* Edinburgh: Carnegie United Kingdom Trustees.

Martin, D. (2002) Great excavations. *Museum Practice,* 7(1): 21–3.

Merriman, N. (1991) *Beyond the Glass Case. The Past, the Heritage and the Public in Britain.* Leicester: Leicester University Press.

——(1997) The Peopling of London Project. In: E. Hooper-Greenhill (ed.), *Cultural Diversity. Developing Museum Audiences in Britain.* Leicester: Leicester University Press, pp. 119–48.

Merriman, N. and Swain, H. (1999) Archaeological archives: serving the public interest? *European Journal of Archaeology,* 2(2): 249–62.

Moore, K. (1997) *Museums and Popular Culture.* London: Leicester University Press.

MORI (2000) *Attitudes Towards the Heritage: Research Study Conducted for English Heritage.* London: MORI.

MORI/Resource (2001) *Visitors to Museums and Galleries in the UK.* London: MORI/Resource.

Museum of Antiquities (2001) Museum of Antiquities. Available at: http://museums.ncl.ac.uk (accessed 12 June 2001).

Museums Association (1998) *Museum Definition.* London: Museums Association.

National Museum of Wales (2001) National Museum of Wales. Available at: www.nmgw.ac.uk/archaeology (accessed 12 June 2001).

Owen, J. (1999) Interaction or tokenism? The role of 'hands on activities' in museum archaeology displays. In: N. Merriman (ed.), *Making Early Histories in Museums.* Leicester: Leicester University Press, pp. 173–89.

——(2002) Society of Museum Archaeologists Art of Archaeology Initiative. Summary Report. Available at: www.socmusarch.org.uk/artofarch.pdf (accessed 15 March 2003).

Pearce, S. (1999) Presenting archaeology. In: N. Merriman (ed.), *Making Early Histories in Museums*. Leicester: Leicester University Press, pp. 12–27.

Phillips, P. (1998) Developing digital resources. National museums and galleries on Merseyside. *Museum Practice*, 9: 54–6.

Ramos, M. and Duganne, D. (2000) *Exploring Public Perceptions and Attitudes about Archaeology*. Washington, D.C.: Society for American Archaeology.

Sansom, E. (1996) Peopling the past. Current practice in archaeological site interpretation. In: P. McManus (ed.), *Archaeological Displays and the Public: Museology and Interpretation*. London: Institute of Archaeology, University College London, pp. 118–37.

Sarraf, S. (1999) A survey of museums on the Web: who uses museum websites? *Curator*, 42(3): 231–43.

Shanks, M. and Tilley, C. (1987) *Reconstructing Archaeology*. Cambridge: Cambridge University Press.

Skeates, R. (2000) *Debating the Archaeological Heritage*. London: Duckworth.

Smardz, K. (1997) The past through tomorrow: interpreting Toronto's heritage to a multicultural public. In: J. Jameson (ed.), *Presenting Archaeology to the Public: Digging for Truths*. London: AltaMira Press, pp. 101–13.

Swift, F. (1997). Boxing clever. *Museum Practice*, 2(2): 9.

Tilden, F. (1957) *Interpreting Our Heritage*. Chapel Hill: University of North Carolina Press.

Trevelyan, V. (1991) *Dingy Places with Different Kinds of Bits*. London: London Museums Consultative Committee.

Trigger, B.G. (1995) Romanticism, nationalism and archaeology. In: P. Kohl and C. Fawcett (eds.), *Nationalism, Politics and the Practice of Archaeology*. Cambridge: Cambridge University Press, pp. 263–79.

Walsh, K. (1992) *The Representation of the Past*. London: Routledge.

Chapter 35

Public archaeology and museums in Japan

Devena Haggis

Introduction

Members of the public do go and visit archaeological sites, heritage places, and attend public lectures about various topics related to heritage. Even a disinterested member of the public is exposed to these paradigms through mediums such as television, newspapers, and popular culture. Popular culture such as the movies series *Indiana Jones* or *Lara Croft* portray archaeologists as adventurers' with bush hats and cowhide whips behind the door of their office and offers a romantic view of the profession. So most people have a vague idea of what an archaeologist does even if they sometimes get confused about the difference between archaeology and palaeontology. However, a very important area of first contact between the artefacts recovered, analysed and presented from archaeological sites and the public is the museum. Relying on traditional methods, such as museum visits to educate the public about archaeology, is limiting as the visitor gains a sanitized and selected view of archaeology. Some museologists consider archaeology as a source for material only and their selection of artefacts for display can shape how the public deciphers the past (Jameson 1997). This is why it is important for those within the discipline to become more involved in public archaeology programmes – as a means of describing up-to-date research and explaining the artefacts within the context of the whole site or culture. This paper presents data from a survey about the types of public archaeological activities undertaken at museums in Japan and discusses the nature of interaction between members of the public and the profession. It also suggests future directions that public archaeology activities may take in order to involve the public more in museum activities.

Public archaeology at museums in Japan

A total of 115 museums were surveyed in Japan and the breakdown in categories is given in Table 35.1. The museums were surveyed during October–November 2006 using a combination of telephone, email, the Internet, and personal contact. The survey attempted to gather information about as many categories of museum and public archaeology activities undertaken as possible throughout the different

Source: *The International Journal of the Inclusive Museum.* Common Ground Publishing, 2008. 1(4): 95–102.

prefectures in Japan. Table 35.1 details the type and distribution of the museums surveyed and the different museum categories refer to the organization or authority that administers the museum. Table 35.2 indicates the type of museum activities surveyed with a brief explanation of these being given below.

Public archaeology programme refers to a programme whereby members of the public are able to participate in an archaeological excavation under the direction of museum staff. *Display* indicates the type of museum display available: *static* – refers to a Permanent display; *audiovisual* and *interactive* refer to museums and displays that have these facilities. *Practical activities* refer to the opportunity for members of the public to have a 'hands-on experience'. *Outreach* indicates efforts by the museum to educate members of the public through use of public lectures, newspapers, or

Table 35.1 Museum categories

Japanese museums	
National	5
Prefectural	41
Municipal	49
University	20
Total	115

Table 35.2 Museum activities

Type	
Public archaeology programme	
Display	Static
	Audiovisual
	Interactive
Practical activities	Children's
	Experimental archaeology
Outreach	Public lecture
	Newspaper
	School visit
Tours	
Library	
Publication	
Volunteers	
Other	

visits. *Tours* refers to the existence of guided tours of the museums. *Library* indicates the availability of a library for research purposes, which allows for public access. *Publication* refers to material published by the museum. *Volunteers* refer to the existence of volunteer groups within the museum, which assist museum staff in any way.

Activities

A variety of activities were undertaken with differences being noted in the 'other' category, which will be discussed later. Table 35.3 gives the breakdown in percentages of the type of public archaeology activities undertaken throughout the range of museums. Generally, the national museums have a fairly good coverage over all the categories. Surprisingly, the categories of 'newspaper' and 'experimental' have lower percentages possibly due to the higher ratio in other areas and allocation of resources towards more traditional activities. University and site park museums have the lowest rate of public archaeology programmes. For universities the limitation in this and other categories is probably due to teaching and practice experience taking priority and staff commitment. Although children's activities rate high in the university category (60 per cent) this is possibly due to staff efforts to integrate the university into the community. The nature of site parks means that excavations may have already been completed with no ongoing excavation after the creation of the site park.

When the museum categories are combined (Figure 35.1) the results reinforce that the more traditional museum displays (static, audiovisual, and interactive) and public talks dominate the dissemination of information about archaeology to the public with the more practical activities such as public archaeology programmes,

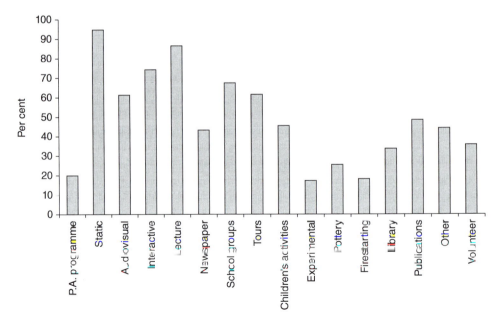

Figure 35.1 Public archaeology in Japanese museums (combined).

Table 35.3 Percentages and activities by museum type

Type	Prog	Static	AV	Inter	Lect	News	School	Tour	Child	Ex	Lib	Pub	Other	Vol
National	100	100	80	100	100	40	80	60	60	20	60	80	60	100
Prefectural	56.6	100	73.2	90.2	95.1	58.8	78	65.9	56.1	51.2	36.6	82.9	48.8	41.5
Municipal	22.4	95.9	73.5	73.5	91.8	61.2	65.3	61.2	51	40.8	26.5	53.1	65.3	34.7
Site park	2.7	100	51.4	73	75	13.5	51.4	51.4	27	37.8	43.2	10.8	24.3	29.7
University	5	100	80	40	70	40	80	60	60	20	60	80	60	20

experimental activities, pottery making and firestarting less prevalent. This indicates that the public archaeology activities in the museums generally still represent a more passive way of learning about the past.

Museums – other activities

However, there are a variety of practical activities offered to the public within the survey museums that facilitate learning about the past and which focus on replicating, in a simple way, ancient technology and processes. Table 35.4 details the type of other activities undertaken in Japanese museums with reference to learning about archaeology. Within the education category Japanese museums organize trips to other excavations and some museums have a full-scale excavation model in the museum as an exhibit. The experimental activities focus on reproducing goods utilizing ancient technology and knowledge. The children's activities place more emphasis on fun although there are specific archaeology classes and weekend sessions for children.

Of particular note is the festival category where museum festivals are held based on a particular period. For example, the Mikata Jomon festival in Fukui prefecture is a yearly festival that incorporates a local festival with museum activities and a celebration of local 'Jomon history' (the fisher-gatherer-hunter period of Japanese prehistory) as represented by the museum exhibits recovered from Torihama shell

Table 35.4 Other museum activities

Category	Type	Examples
Education	General	Loan of materials
		Discovery centres
		Work experience
		School visits
		Museum worksheet
		Special lectures
		Virtual tour
		Visits to excavations
		Full-size excavation model
Historic and prehistoric	Experimental	Stone toolmaking
		Toolmaking
		Jomon clothes
		Rope making
		Lacquerware
		Salt making
		Glass and sculpting
Children's	Participatory	Playing games
		Making toys
		Archaeology class
		Weekend sessions
Other	Festival	Jomon festivals

mound nearby. The importance of this site, the existence of a small park commemorating and explaining the excavation, the oversized characterized 'Jomon man' and its close proximity to the Mikata Jomon museum all contribute to inserting and keeping Torihama in the public perception as an important Jomon site related to the history of their area. In this way archaeology is used to reinforce a sense of local identity and is a common aspect of public archaeological activities in Japan (Fawcett 1996).

Public archaeology and the 'public'

The use of the past to reinforce local identity is an example of Owen's (1996) suggestion that museum history can reinforce or legitimize dominant social and political norms. In Japan, identity and social memory are implicitly connected, in some cases regarding the archaeology of a place or people as the precursor of modern identity whether or not these linkages exist. In comparison, archaeologists study the material remains of the human past and the artefacts that comprise museum displays and collections are an incomplete reflection of the past and can have no connection to people today who often relate only to the present (Owen 1996). Both these situations exist and these contrasts show that archaeology and by extension 'public archaeology' can be a powerful tool to extend and educate public knowledge of the past. The role of archaeology within a society is a reflection of how that society views its archaeological heritage and the importance it places on preserving and maintaining that heritage in order to understand the past and to preserve it for future generations. Archaeologists everywhere consider the role of prehistory and history within the context of national and international spheres and the value of artefacts to the general and world community and how best to protect and educate members of the public through education programmes. The extent to which members of the public become involved in archaeology is partly influenced by how archaeology as a profession responds to public input and opinion.

Public opinion

Information from the museum survey indicates that public archaeology activities at these museums in Japan focus more on passive learning rather than activities where there is contact and communication between archaeologists and the public. Trying to promote the development of an archaeologically aware public is a step towards redefining the relationships between archaeologists and the public and contributes to the continued and ongoing development of the discipline (Davidson 1995). An appreciation of cultural heritage can be developed, reinforced, or discouraged depending on the experience of the visitor and a constant challenge that museums face is keeping the public interested in what they do. One way to maintain this interest within the community is to facilitate the participation of the public in museum activities.

A small test survey ($n=64$) was undertaken in order to ascertain which museum activities members of the public found interesting or more useful in learning about archaeology and the past. The activities offered at the museums were grouped according to associated learning strategies derived from education theory. These are *individualistic learning* whereby the learning environment of one student is independent and separate from other people in the group (Johnson and Johnson 1991), which suggests an environment where members of the public learn about archaeology independently or separately. Museum examples in this category include newspapers, magazines, library resources, museum displays (static, audio visual and interactive), lectures, school groups, site tours, and media interviews. *Co-operative learning* occurs when students work collaboratively towards a common goal (Panitz 1997) and can be represented by situations where members of the public work together with archaeologists collaborating towards a common goal. These include public archaeology programmes and volunteer activities. *Collaborative learning* occurs when students are in control of their own learning outcomes (Panitz 1997); and similarly, situations where members of the public co-operate with each other and archaeologists but are in control of their own learning process could be considered collaborative. Examples include experimental and replicative archaeology (pottery making, firestarting, making stone tools etc.) and children's activities.

Members of the public were asked to make a series of pair-wise comparisons in regard to which type of learning they found more useful in understanding archaeology at museums. These were then entered into a matrix and weightings were obtained for the three types of learning category (Figure 35.2). The results indicate that collaborative and co-operative learning are the preferred options. Comparing these results with the activities survey indicates that there is a discrepancy between the main public (displays, lectures) offered at museums and those that the public find more useful. The first public preference of the learning categories, co-operative learning (0.426) indicates that the public believe participation and

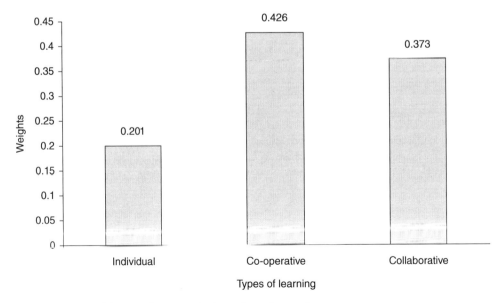

Figure 35.2 Public preferences in learning about the past.

working together with archaeologists in activities, such as excavations, would be more useful in learning about archaeology. The second of the learning categories, collaborative learning, indicates that while children's activities are covered relatively well in museums experimental activities are limited. Public preference for a more practical and 'hands-on' experience at a museum can contribute to the increase in interaction between archaeologists and the community and a broadening of their educational experience, which in turn facilitates an increase in archaeology and heritage consciousness.

Conclusion

A wide range of public archaeology activities are undertaken at museums in Japan and encompass different learning strategies to teach people about archaeology and the past. However, public preferences indicate that activities which allow more public participation are preferred. Therefore, the development of programmes to cater for the public preferences of collaborative and co-operative learning opportunities should be promoted.

References

Davidson, I. (1995) Introduction. In: I. Davidson, C. Lovell-Jones, and R. Bancroft (eds.), *Archaeologists and Aboriginals Working Together*. Armidale: University of New England Press, pp. 3–5.

Fawcett, C. (1996) Archaeology and Japanese identity. In: D. Denoon, M. Hudson, G. McCormack, and T. Morris- Suzuki (eds.), *Multicultural Japan*. Cambridge: Cambridge University Press, pp. 60–77.

Jameson, J.H. Jr. (1997) *Presenting Archaeology to the Public*. Walnut Creek, CA: AltaMira Press.

Johnson, D. and Johnson, R. (1991) *Learning Together and Alone*. Third edition. Sydney: Allyn and Bacon.

Owen, J. (1996) Making histories from archaeology. In: G. Kavanagh (ed.), *Making Histories in Museums*. Leicester: Leicester University Press, pp. 200–16.

Panitz, T. (1997) Collaborative vs cooperative learning: comparing the two definitions help understand the nature of interactive learning. *Cooperative Learning and College Teaching*, 8(2): 5–7.

Uncovering ancient Egypt
The Petrie Museum and its public

Sally MacDonald and Catherine Shaw

Introduction

> Here are invalids in search of health; artists in search of subjects; sportsmen keen upon crocodiles; statesmen out for a holiday; special correspondents alert for gossip; collectors on the scent of papyri and mummies; men of science with only scientific ends in view; and the usual surplus of idlers who travel for the mere love of travel.
>
> (Edwards 1877: 1–2)

Amelia Edwards was a popular writer and journalist with a passion for Egypt. When she died in 1892 she left her collection of Egyptian antiquities, together with some money, to University College London (UCL), to promote 'the teaching of Egyptology with a view to the wide extension of the knowledge of the history, antiquities, literature, philology and art of Ancient Egypt' (Will of Amelia Edwards, dated 8/3/1891, copy in Petrie Museum archive). Edwards clearly hoped that the new academic department she helped establish would have an impact, long term, on the wider public understanding of this ancient culture.

Her bequest funded the UK's first Chair in Egyptology. Flinders Petrie, her protégé and first Edwards professor, added his collections to hers and through his annual excavations and purchases built UCL's museum into one of the most significant collections of early Egyptian material in the world. What came to be called the Petrie Museum remained nevertheless a university rather than a public museum: 'The collection is largely supplementary to the national collection, and consists of objects for study rather than for popular show' (letter from W.M.F. Petrie to Provost, UCL Managing Sub-Committee Minutes 5/11/1907 minute 10).

For Petrie and his immediate successors the collections were primarily there to support the teaching of UCL's Egyptian archaeology students, although the quality and range of the collections inevitably attracted specialist academic researchers from all over the world. It was not until the 1970s that museum staff took steps to broaden its audience and welcome interested amateur Egyptologists. External (non-UCL) visit numbers rose from around 200 per annum in 1970 to around 3,000 by 1997 and nearly 9,000 by 2000. As the museum became more heavily used by an 'outside' audience the inadequacies of its current accommodation grew more apparent and the need to find a safer, more spacious, and more accessible home grew more acute. The search began for a suitable site, and at the same time the museum began a programme of research on its existing and potential audiences and what they might want from new displays on ancient Egypt in the new museum. This paper reports on that research, which examined for the first time, in relation to a museum of Egyptian archaeology, the attitudes of existing users alongside those of non-users such as the modern black and Egyptian communities in London, and the perspectives of amateur enthusiasts and children, alongside those of academics.

Audiences and questions

The process of defining existing and target audiences involved – as it would in any museum – understanding what was known about current visitors (here mainly from observation and old visitors books); looking in detail at the subject matter of the collection; and considering other potential interest groups and the media through which they currently access ancient Egypt. It was a long and rather woolly process involving much discussion and it is not over yet. Many museums – particularly in North America and more recently in the UK – now undertake formative research of the kind described here when planning new displays or programmes. This is part of a general trend away from single-perspective didactic exhibitions and towards more open, reflective presentations that take account of the perceptions, beliefs, and biases that audiences – and, of course, curators – bring with them to any subject (Merriman 1999: 7). Although this kind of research appears inclusive and potentially allows many voices to be heard, it has to be remembered that it is almost always museum staff who set the agenda, decide the questions, choose the respondents, and, in the end, decide whether to use or ignore what they hear.

Amateur and 'alternative' Egypt

On the basis of observation, staff at the Petrie Museum broadly defined their existing adult audience as consisting of professional and amateur Egyptologists. The professionals are those who earn their living, or aspire to earn their living, from the subject; most hold relevant higher education qualifications. The amateurs are those for whom the subject is an interest rather than a job. Many members of the museum's thriving Friends organization would fall into this latter category. In practice the difference between professionals and amateurs is not always clear-cut. Amateurs at the traditional end of the spectrum belong to many of the same societies as professionals, and read some of the same books. Many amateur Egyptologists develop specialized knowledge and some earn money and academic status by giving lectures or writing articles.

Move towards the alternative end of the amateur spectrum and a great divide appears to open up. Roth identifies this alternative sector as a broad grouping of New Age spiritualists, those who believe in reincarnation, or the mystical powers of pyramids and crystals. She points out that the media tend to emphasize disagreements between professional and alternative Egyptologists in favour of a good story (Roth 1998: 221). However, it is tempting to conclude that each side plays down the points of agreement between them. I have often heard academics refer to alternative Egyptologists as 'nutters' or 'pyramidiots', while alternative archaeologists seem to relish the banner of 'forbidden archaeology'. But as a group, alternative Egyptologists are too numerous and too diverse to dismiss. The Questing Conference of 'forbidden archaeology', held in London in 1999, attracted over 800 people to hear papers on labyrinths, pyramids, and the evidence for ancient astrology. Feder, who has catalogued and dissected many examples of what he calls archaeological pseudoscience, acknowledges and analyses their wide appeal and refuses to draw easy distinctions between what he calls 'scholars, charlatans, and kooks' (Feder 1996: 252).

The academic/amateur distinction was not, of course, an issue in the early years of the museum, when the discipline was also in its infancy. Petrie encouraged amateurs, organizing the Egyptology Library for lending as well as reference, to help those who could only study at home, and supporting specialized research. In his inaugural lecture in 1893 he remarked, 'Someone may not be able to touch more than a minute subject, in a few spare hours, now and then; but let him do that fully and completely and every student will thank him' (in Janssen 1992: 102). Montserrat has pointed out that Dr Margaret Murray, Petrie's assistant at UCL and a professional Egyptologist, was at the same time also a practising witch (Montserrat 2000: 21). Today the distinctions seem more clearly demarcated. In fact academic, popular, and alternative Egyptologies seem polarized in a way that might appear very strange to someone coming from another discipline.

Academic Egypt

But while amateur Egyptology appears to be growing in all directions, academic Egyptology is a narrow field; in this country Egyptology is a 'minority' academic subject (as defined by the Higher Education and Funding Council for England). Some see a link between these developments. As Roth has pointed out: 'ironically, the academic field of Egyptology is increasingly being marginalised by the very popularity of its subject matter' (Roth 1998: 222). The experience of the Petrie Museum's curator, that within academic circles Egyptology is considered academically inferior to the study of other, less widely appealing, ancient cultures, supports this view (S. Quirke pers. comm.).

Roth argues that academic Egyptologists should welcome the public interest in their subject and engage with it. Instead she sees many of her colleagues retreating into more specialized studies which earn them peer recognition yet distance them not only from the lay public but also from colleagues in other academic disciplines (Roth 1998: 229). There are additional reasons for these interdisciplinary divisions.

Thomas points to the traditional separation of classics departments from those concerned with the Near East and Egypt as being 'a relic of the secular separation in the late 18th century of classics from the study of the Bible' (Thomas 1998: 15). As a university museum, the Petrie is very much affected by these academic divisions. For most of its history, it was part of UCL's Egyptology Department. It was only in 1993 that the department was officially incorporated within the Institute of Archaeology (the Greek and Latin Department is still separate). Despite incorporation, the old disciplinary divisions are still in evidence. The museum houses extensive collections from Hellenistic and Roman Egypt, but remains little known and almost unused by Institute of Archaeology staff teaching courses other than Egyptian Archaeology (Merriman 2000: 1). It can easily be argued that discipline-bound thinking is a problem throughout academia. But within the academic study of archaeology ancient Egypt seems isolated in a way that, for instance, Bronze Age Greece does not.

The Petrie Museum is a university museum seeking to broaden its audience, both within and outside academia. Museum staff felt it was important to understand the common ground between academic and more general audiences. After all, Feder's surveys of college students found they were just as likely to believe in unorthodox archaeological statements as the general public (Feder 1996: 3–5). What periods and themes were of greatest interest? What meanings did ancient Egypt have for them? What was their attitude to modern Egypt, and more specifically, to archaeology in modern Egypt?

African Egypt

There are numerous recent examples of ethnographical and social history museums engaging with traditionally excluded audiences in an effort to redress the historic biases of their displays (Simpson 1996). Archaeological museums have been criticized for lagging behind, for failing, often, to see the relevance to their institutions and displays of such issues as cultural diversity (Merriman 1999: 3). In a recent UK survey researchers found that three out of four people believed that 'the contribution of black people and Asians to our society is not thoroughly represented in heritage provision' (MORI 2000). The archaeology of Egypt presents interesting questions in this respect.

There is a long history of black scholarship on the subject of Ancient Egypt and its relationship to the rest of Africa (Hilliard 1994). Some of the more extreme aspects of what is often called Afrocentrism have been rightly criticized (for example by Howe 1998) as being themselves racist, and some academics argue that it is both misleading and dangerous to seek to establish, as many black scholars have done, what colour the Ancient Egyptians were (e.g. Brace et al. 1996: 162). To do so is, they argue, to apply modern concepts of race, which did not exist in Ancient Egypt. Most of them would, however, acknowledge that, for almost two centuries, the study of Ancient Egypt in the Western world has been distorted by Eurocentric and racist bias (e.g. Young 1995: 118–41).

UCL has no black Egyptologists on the teaching staff. Of those students undertaking research or taught courses in Egyptian archaeology, less than one in ten is black. Friends of the Petrie Museum defining themselves as black are a tiny minority (less than 1 per cent). The proportion of black visitors to the museum is also, from observation, very low, though some have recently criticized the museum's displays and labelling as racist (T. Golding pers. comm.). This research sought to draw black audiences – both Egyptologists and members of the general public – into discussion about Ancient Egypt, its appeal, significance, and representation in museums. It also took issues that have been important to black historians – Ancient Egypt's relationship with the rest of Africa, the skin colour of the Ancient Egyptians – and raised them in discussion with white audiences.

Egyptian Egypt

Modern Egyptians might be regarded as another group excluded by traditional Egyptology. The slow growth of indigenous Egyptology in the last century has been attributed in part to the prevalence of pan-Arab politics, favouring a study of Islamic rather than earlier periods (Trigger 1984: 359) and in part to the appropriation of Ancient Egypt by Western scholars and archaeologists (Reid 1985: 234). According to one source, less than 5 per cent of visitors to the Cairo Museum are Egyptians (Stone and Molyneaux 1994: 21). Professor Fekri Hassan, an Egyptian archaeologist and currently Petrie Professor of Egyptology at UCL, summarizes the modern Egyptian relationship with the country's ancient past as follows:

> the Pharaonic past is a political card. It can arouse passionate responses among certain intellectuals, but it has not effectively become an integral or a predominant element of the materiality of Egyptian life. Perhaps the only vibrant continuity with Egypt's Pharaonic past is the Nile river. But it no longer floods and is imprisoned within its bounded channel. Lined with high rise Western hotels it belongs to the European and Arab tourists who can afford them.
>
> (Hassan 1998: 212)

Although UCL has an Egyptian Professor of Egyptology, the proportions of students and museum Friends who are Egyptians are again very low (one in twenty students, 1 per cent of Friends). This research sought the views of Egyptians, most of them Egyptologists, on general issues relating to the study and presentation of ancient Egypt. It also asked wider audiences about the issue of chronology, of when, in their view, ancient Egypt began and ended. It has been argued that the term Egyptology has imposed time limits on the subject, denigrating, for instance, a study of Coptic and Islamic Egypt (Reid 1985: 234). The narrowness of the academic field of study may also have restricted the interests of more general audiences. A study of visitors to the British Museum in 1998 indicated that most visitors made no connection between ancient and modern Egypt (Motawi 1998). In the research discussed here this issue was explored further with people who had visited Egypt, as well as those who had not, to establish whether a personal encounter with modern Egypt might be significant in reshaping attitudes to past and present.

Specific areas of interest included tourism and archaeology. Wood has concluded that

> Europeans, even 'Egyptologists' must still have been motivated by a desire to possess 'treasure', if only for the prestige its ownership would entail ... This cavalier attitude ... that Europeans have the right to excavate, study and export Pharaonic remains however they see fit is rooted in an attitude that feels that, in the end, Egypt's past does not really belong to its present day inhabitants.
>
> (Wood 1998: 190)

Given that the museum is part of a department that employs and trains archaeologists, and whose staff and students excavate in Egypt, it seemed appropriate to ask questions about attitudes to archaeology, and to the ownership and treatment of what is excavated.

Children's Egypt

For some years now Ancient Egypt has been an option on the English National Curriculum history programme of study at Key Stage 2 (i.e. for children aged 7–11). It is not possible to establish how widely the subject was taught in English schools prior to that date, nor how many schools now choose the Ancient Egypt option from the seven options currently available to them as a World History Study (the alternatives are: Ancient Sumer, the Assyrian Empire, the Indus Valley, the Maya, Benin, or the Aztecs). Anecdotal evidence from advisory teachers suggests however that it is a popular choice (D. Garman pers. comm.).

The National Curriculum requires the study of the key features of the chosen past society, which must include 'the everyday lives of men, women and children; the society in relation to other contemporary societies; chronology; the reasons for the rise and fall of the civilisation; significant places and individuals; distinctive contribution to history' (QCA 1999: 19). At Key Stage 2, children are also expected to acquire knowledge, understanding, and skills applicable to any historical subject. Amongst other things they are required to be taught how to find out about the past from a range of sources (examples given in the guidance include documents, artefacts, and visits to museums, galleries, and sites). They should also be taught 'about the social, cultural, religious and ethnic diversity of the societies studied' and 'to recognise that the past is represented and interpreted in different ways, and to give reasons for this' (ibid.: 17).

The curriculum thus maps out what can be interpreted as a radical and stimulating agenda for the study of Ancient Egypt at primary level. However, although standard attainment targets (SATS) are set for history, they are not tested as they are for the core subjects of English, Maths, and Science and there is no way of knowing, other than through inspectors' reports on individual schools, whether or not they are being attained. On the particular issue of cultural diversity, for instance, it has been said that 'Ancient Egypt is frequently chosen and taught as if this civilisation were actually white' (Claire 1996: 12). Certainly there are few currently available primary level support materials, in print or video format, that address questions of diversity or differences of interpretation in the study of Ancient Egypt.

There is evident demand from primary teachers for access to museum displays about Ancient Egypt. In the 12 months from November 1999 to November 2000, 1,032 school groups booked into the Egyptian Galleries in the British Museum, and according to the museum's Education Department the Egyptian galleries are more popular with schools than even the Greek displays, despite the fact that the study of Ancient Greece is compulsory, and that of Ancient Egypt an option (information from British Museum Education Department).

Since the Petrie Museum began offering sessions for primary schools in October 1998 these have been considerably oversubscribed. We wanted to understand through this research how we could best meet teachers' needs and which aspects of Ancient Egypt they wished to prioritize. We also wanted to understand what interested children, who access Ancient Egypt, as adults do, outside formal education; through toys and stories – Asterix, Lego, Scooby Doo – referring to the secret passages, codes, and curses common in Western popular fiction. Their interests would be unlikely to accord exactly with the priorities of a curriculum written by adults.

About the research

There are two strands to the findings presented in this paper. The first has to do with examining the similarities and differences between academic and amateur Egyptologists in terms of their particular areas of interest. These findings are important in informing the museum's management about the interests and needs of its current users: those who visit in order to study. The second strand involves taking a broader and more exploratory look at perceptions, attitudes, and beliefs relating to both ancient and modern Egypt. These findings provide a basis for developing the museum for a visitor population with a more general curiosity about Egypt. These two strands are fundamentally related to the overall aims of the research, which was to inform decision-making about access, display, and service issues for the Petrie Museum. It did this by reviewing the particular areas of interest, research needs, and priorities of existing study-users, and potential ones such as Key Stage 2 history teachers and their pupils, by exploring the nature of people's fascination with Ancient Egypt, and by examining attitudes to modern Egypt and its links with the past, including attitudes to archaeology.

In order to address these objectives effectively it was necessary not only to target a range of different respondents, but to employ a number of research methods.

Surveys of existing specialist user groups

The purpose of these surveys was to build an accurate description of what these 'core' groups of existing users wanted from the museum, and how much common ground there was between them in terms of themes and periods of particular interest.

In August 1999 a questionnaire was sent to all 650 Friends of the Petrie. A total of 252 completed questionnaires were received, representing a response rate of 38 per cent. A survey of students took place nine months later. Questionnaires were sent to all undergraduate and post-graduate Egyptology students at UCL (including those just taking a module as part of another degree) using the university's internal mail system. Thirty-nine responses were received, a response rate of 43 per cent, one-third of whom were studying for higher degrees.

Survey of known potential users – primary school history coordinators

As already described, Ancient Egypt is an optional area of study at Key Stage 2 (KS2) of the National Curriculum. This opens up the potential for thousands of school-age visitors to the Museum each year. What would the interests and particular needs of this age group be, and to what extent would they overlap with those of older or more advanced students? Equivalent questions about themes and periods of interest to those asked of Friends and students were therefore included in the survey of KS2 history coordinators.

We decided to take primary schools within reasonable travelling distance from central London as our target population. As a high response rate was not anticipated, the questionnaire was mailed to a large number of schools, in order to ensure a return large enough to yield meaningful findings. A sampling fraction of 50 per cent was selected, and questionnaires were sent to the KS2 history coordinators of the 1,167 state and independent schools in Greater London thus randomly selected; 165 replies were received.

In-depth interviews

While the surveys were able to provide a quantitative description of the range and prevalence of particular themes and periods of interest within the existing user groups, they were unable to provide any insight as to why and how the individual respondents had developed their particular specialized areas of interest, nor their attitudes to various aspects of the subject. To this end, in-depth interviews were conducted with a sample of 24 individuals with a known interest in Egyptology. Interviewees were purposively selected to include both professionals (such as academics and museum workers) and amateurs, including those with alternative or fringe interests in Egyptology. Three of the interviewees were themselves Egyptian, another five were black, but not Egyptian, and the remainder were white.

Amongst other topics, the interviews explored the meaning and significance of Ancient Egypt for interviewees, their impressions of present day Egypt, and their attitudes to excavation. These interviews, which lasted for up to 90 minutes, were tape-recorded and fully transcribed.

Focus groups

The fascination that Ancient Egypt holds for the general population was studied by means of a series of focus groups, commissioned from the Susie Fisher Group (Fisher 2000). The focus group setting allows respondents to explore and develop ideas and perceptions about a subject within a stimulating but non-threatening environment. Five groups were conducted: one of schoolchildren aged 9–10 who had studied Ancient Egypt; people who had visited Egypt (one group of backpackers, and an older group of 'Nile cruisers' who had been on a cruise or organized tour); and two groups of people aged 25 to 45 who had never visited Egypt (one group of white and one group of non-white UK-born respondents). Each group contained six to eight respondents and the session lasted between 60 and 90 minutes.

Research findings

The findings presented below are drawn from the analyses of the questionnaires, interviews, and focus groups. A large amount of varied data covering a wide range of themes was collected during the course of the research, but in a paper of this length it is possible only to summarize responses to some of the key questions.

Most popular themes

The questionnaires presented respondents with lists of pre-coded themes, of which they could tick as many as they wished. These lists were very similar on each questionnaire, although sub-themes were omitted from the teachers' version. Many general enthusiasts (particularly among Friends and undergraduates) took the opportunity to tick virtually every box, whereas academic specialists (including some Friends) indicated just one or two themes. There were nevertheless large areas of common interest to be found between students, Friends, and primary school teachers (on behalf of their pupils). The results are presented in Table 36.1.

Five broad themes proved to be of universal interest, each indicated by over half of each of the user groups:

- daily life
- architecture (including pyramids)
- language and communication
- pharaohs, politics, and government
- religion, gods, and goddesses.

These five areas were particularly strongly indicated by primary-school teachers, the group which proved most homogenous in their interests, for reasons presumably related to the requirements of the National Curriculum. More than two-thirds of teachers expressed an interest in these themes and also in those of death/mummification, agriculture and arts/crafts. Perhaps of greater significance is the blanket *lack* of interest in certain aspects of Ancient Egyptian life. All groups of respondents showed a singular lack of enthusiasm for women, trade, and war.

Table 36.1 Themes of interest to Petrie Museum user groups (%)

	Students (n = 39)	Friends (n = 252)	Teachers (n = 165)
Daily life	69	64	95
Society and social relations	56	55	44
Women/gender	36	35	
Agriculture, food, and farming	21	37	73
Science and technology	36	50	46
Language/script (all or any)	59	64	85
Hieroglyphs	46	50	
Hieratic	23	15	
Demotic	18	11	
Trade, travel, transport	33	48	43
Architecture (all or any)	67	80	90
Temples	33	53	
Tombs	38	56	
Pyramids	33	51	
Palaces	28		
Arts and crafts	46	58	73
Pharaohs, politics, and government	56	61	67
Religion, gods, and goddesses	67	64	94
Death and burial – mummification	64	49	92
War and weapons	28	30	22
Archaeology and archaeologists	51	53	
Other	23		

Shaded boxes indicate themes or sub-themes that were absent from a particular questionnaire.

Most popular periods

The same user groups were also asked about which periods of Egyptian history were of most interest (Table 36.2).

It is perhaps of no surprise to find that Egypt under the Pharaohs is by far the most popular period among all three groups surveyed: 85 per cent of students, 94 per cent of Friends and an overwhelming 97 per cent of primary-school teachers expressed an interest in some or all of the period. Within this broad time frame, interest for both Friends and students – we did not expect teachers to go into such detail – peaks at the Old Kingdom, Middle Kingdom and, in particular, the New Kingdom, after which interest tailed off markedly. Relatively little interest was expressed in the intermediate and late periods.

However, there is even less enthusiasm for more recent periods of Egyptian history, and expressed interest gradually declines. By the time the Islamic age is

Table 36.2 Periods of interest to Petrie Museum user groups (%)

	Students (n = 39)	Friends (n = 252)	Teachers (n = 165)
Pre-dynastic Egypt	51	57	12
Egypt in the period of the unification	44	48	
Egypt under the Pharaohs (all or any)	85	94	97
Early Dynastic Egypt	33	49	
Old Kingdom	39	58	
First Intermediate Period	23	36	
Middle Kingdom	39	58	
Second Intermediate Period	31	41	
New Kingdom (all or any)	59	63	
Amarna Period	36	56	
Ramesside Period	28	52	
Third Intermediate Period	18	32	
Late Period	15	27	
Graeco-Roman Egypt (all or any)	33	43	10
Ptolemaic	26	26	
Roman	26	19	
Byzantine/Coptic (early Christian)	13	16	
Islamic Periods (all or any)	18	14	2
Medieval	10		
Ottoman	5		
Contemporary	8		

Shaded boxes indicate themes or sub-themes that were absent from a particular questionnaire.

reached, we are down to a handful of individuals, some of whom indicated an interest in *every* period listed and therefore cannot be assumed to have any particular specialist interest in Islamic Egypt.

These findings are borne out by those of the focus group research; 'virtually nothing is known about modern Egypt or times since the pharaohs, and there is no desire to know' (Fisher 2000: chart 6). Among more general audiences there was no evidence of an understanding of chronology or sense of historical perspective: 'Ancient Egypt is a sealed bubble in which pharaohs, pyramids, slaves, tombs and Cleopatra float around in a rich soup' (Fisher 2000: chart 7).

Most resonant ideas and images

The focus group research identified a number of 'mythic themes' associated with Ancient Egypt in the minds of general audiences: death; power; wealth; treasure; extinction; slavery; monumental building; command of the heavens; creativity, and religion (Fisher 2000: chart 17). The most resonant images appeared to revolve around the size and splendour of the architecture (pyramids, tombs, sphinx); the exoticism of the landscape (sand, heat, camels); a collection of historical/mythical individuals (Cleopatra, Tuthankhamun, Indiana Jones) and a general sense of awe and mystery:

> I'd like to know how they built, like their pyramids and got everything perfect. The dimensions are so intelligent, it's scary.
>
> (non-white adult)

For non-white respondents ancient Egypt had a greater role, symbolizing 'the theft of cultural capital' by white Europeans (Fisher 2000: chart 13).

The focus group findings suggest that, for general audiences:

> Ancient Egypt is a concept. It is not only a country. It is not purely history. It is not just a tissue of myths and artefacts. It is an amalgam of all of these; a magic terrain where myths may be real. The concept is created by school, media, archaeology, myths and museums, and is completely self-contained and satisfying.
>
> (Fisher 2000: chart 16)

The researchers found that white people seemed untroubled by the mix of fantasy and fact in their vision of ancient Egypt, whereas non-white respondents were more conscious of distortions (Fisher 2000: chart 33):

> I suppose I want to think that Cleopatra looked a bit like Elizabeth Taylor.
>
> (white adult)

> People think it's European history, Richard Burton and Elizabeth Taylor.
>
> (non-white adult)

In the in-depth interviews, it was not uncommon for a preoccupation with Ancient Egypt to develop from a more generalized interest in ancient history. However, for those interviewed, Egypt rapidly took over, exerting a stronger fascination which eclipsed previous interests. One interviewee refers to the study of Greeks and Romans as being a 'poor relation', these periods being 'too accessible, I suppose, and there didn't seem to be quite the mystery to them' (white, amateur). This is an interesting comment in relation to the survey finding that fewer people were interested in the later periods of Egyptian history. Another respondent describes how his interest wanes as more modern times are reached:

> We're then starting to come into the classical world, they were Macedonians from Greece, they themselves were Egyptian and they adopted the Egyptian culture and religion ... but it's not the same ... I have no interest in studying classical Greece or Rome or any other ancient civilisation.
>
> (white, professional)

What colour were the Ancient Egyptians?

The research concluded that the question of colour was an interesting and provocative one for all the adult respondents. White adults found questions about the skin colour of the Ancient Egyptians 'profoundly disturbing and largely unexpected'. There was evidence of a desire to maintain a white Egyptian identity (Fisher 2000: chart 35):

> Hollywood makes out they were white Europeans. Why didn't it dawn on me? I assumed they were all white and the dark ones were Nubian slaves.
> (Nile cruiser)

Non-white respondents felt passionate rather than threatened by the question. They were clear that Ancient Egypt had been appropriated as part of white history (Fisher 2000: chart 37):

> I went to the library, looking in the African section. It came under European history!
> (non-white adult)

> The black Africans were supposed to be ignorant, but we could build the pyramids.
> (non-white adult)

Feelings about modern Egypt and its relationship to Ancient Egypt

The focus group researchers found that most people, particularly white respondents, made no connection between ancient and modern Egypt, which was 'below nowhere on most people's agenda':

> Modern Egypt is simply the country you have to get to so that you can physically experience the myth of ancient Egypt. Many people aren't quite sure where it is, but ... this doesn't matter because spiritually they feel ancient Egypt belongs to them too.
> (Fisher 2000: chart 26)

Those respondents who had visited Egypt seem to have come away with negative and racist views:

> The monuments are too breathtaking for words. It knocks you away and now they can't mend your toaster.
> (Nile cruiser)

The focus group researchers noted the strong contrast between Western European perceptions of the Ancient Egyptians ('aloof, spiritual, powerful, clever') and of the modern Egyptians ('grasping, pushy, poor, backward), looking for their own roots among the first group. Non-white respondents were 'more open, insightful, sympathetic' (Fisher 2000: chart 29).

While the Egyptologists (amateur and professional) interviewed were more knowledgeable about Egypt's geographical location (as most of them had visited the country) they expressed similarly negative attitudes to modern Egypt and Egyptians. Many of their comments were indistinguishable from those of the focus group members. For example:

> I wasn't too sure about modern Egypt, which I thought was very run down, poor and I didn't particularly like it very much. But ancient Egypt, yes, it lived up to everything I hoped it would.
> (white, professional)

Another interviewee, who had never visited, remarked sardonically:

> Well, apart from the heat, the flies, the food and the terrorism, it sounds wonderfully appealing ...
> (white, amateur)

Other interviewees spoke as if there was almost a duty – which was sadly neglected – for Egyptians to make their country more palatable for tourists. One interviewee described her surprise at the 'dirt' and the 'culture shock' she experienced on every visit:

> No matter how much they try, and they do try much harder nowadays because they get so many Western visitors, it is still difficult ... the argument that it's the climate ... doesn't really pass muster, that's not really true, it's a cultural thing. They don't bother ... I've never understood it.
> (white, professional)

> They pester you constantly ... they want to stick to all the Europeans, thinking they can get as much money from them as they can, but they don't understand the European mentality.
> (white, amateur)

Among the interviewees a clear distinction was drawn between rural and urban Egypt. Most of the unpleasant images were derived from the cities or tourist areas whereas the countryside was viewed as very much unchanged from ancient times – 'like a Bible picture coming to life' (white, professional) – with agricultural practices most often being cited in this context.

Modern Egyptians were sometimes criticized by interviewees for showing insufficient interest in their own heritage, or for simply taking it for granted through familiarity. They 'don't give a toss about it' according to one amateur Egyptologist, although, on reflection, she does not judge them too harshly:

> I was angry they didn't treat it any better but also, the poverty of the country in comparison to our wealth here, I could see they had other priorities.
>
> (white, amateur)

It would, however, be unfair to present too one-sided a picture here, and it should be acknowledged that other – more sympathetic – views were also expressed in the interviews, particularly by those who had become more immersed in modern Egyptian life and had made Egyptian friends.

Feelings about archaeology

The focus group respondents, children and adults, were almost wholly positive in their view of archaeology, seeing it as a virtuous search for artefacts with a 'Boys' Own' appeal:

> I would like to find a flight of stairs in the rock. They found the Anubis seal and there were four rooms blocked off.
>
> (child aged 9–10)

> They don't give up that chance they'll find something. It's a hobby and the achievement of finding something becomes an obsession. Your moment of glory.
>
> (Nile cruiser)

The researchers felt that some young men saw it as a kind of game 'as though the Egyptians had buried their artefacts, daring future generations to find them' (Fisher 2000: chart 38). There appear to be strong parallels between people's descriptions of archaeologists and fictional representations such as Indiana Jones or the Tomb Raider video game. This theme was echoed in an interview with a professional archaeologist, who had been inspired by the glamorous heroine of a Hollywood movie:

> So the image that I had was her in a safari suit with leather boots, chiffon scarf and a pith helmet, which is what I always wanted to be.
>
> (white, professional)

Among the focus group members the only person expressing disquiet about archaeology was a child:

> If I found a tomb, I would leave them. I wouldn't want to be dug up when I should be resting.
>
> (child aged 9–10)

Some of the in-depth interviewees shared this concern, in particular those who approached Egyptology from a mystical or religious angle:

> Being a spiritual person by nature, I'm not sure about the merit of digging up people's tombs, when they obviously put so much effort into preserving their own dignity.
>
> (white, amateur)

The interviewees for the most part were more aware than focus group members of the debates around the subject of excavation, and expressed more equivocal views. Arguments in favour of continued digging included the thirst for more knowledge and increased archaeological skills, the benefit to the local Egyptian economy, and the race against time in a climate of deteriorating environmental conditions. On the other hand, there was an awareness that there already exists an enormous quantity of uncatalogued and inadequately conserved finds, a feeling that enough was known already, and that nothing was being left for future generations to discover. Most interviewees were ambivalent in their views.

However, there was a clear consensus among interviewees that finds should remain in Egypt – 'they belong to the country that they're in' (white, amateur) – with just one dissenting voice:

> Ultimately it depends on the arrangement between the Egyptian authorities and the excavators ... who finances the digs and so on. You can't afford to be sentimental about that.
>
> (non-white, professional)

It was assumed by white focus group members that archaeologists would be white Europeans or Americans (Fisher 2000: chart 40):

> We sort of had to do it, as they couldn't be trusted to look after it themselves.
>
> (white adult)

Sadly, this perception was borne out by the personal experience of a number of professional Egyptologists we interviewed. A young British Egyptologist is contemptuous of the attitudes of some of her colleagues:

> I do see a heck of a lot of 'We're the foreigners, we're here, we're going to dig your country, we're going to tell you all about it, and you're going to sit and listen'... . It's astounding, it's, 'We don't speak to them because they're Egyptian'. It's, 'We do our thing, they do their thing.'
>
> (white, professional)

Whereas this Egyptian describes the struggle to be accepted as a trainee on a dig in his own country:

> Still, after all these years, you can see it in foreign expeditions digging in Egypt, it's all foreign, they are happy to take foreign students to train them, they never take Egyptian students to train them... . I had to force myself

onto anybody to take me for training, nobody was interested. They just don't take Egyptians.

(Egyptian, professional)

Some non-white focus group respondents had a conviction that finds and findings should be shared:

I think they should acknowledge and apologize and keep partnerships. A commonwealth, where everything is catalogued.

(non-white adult)

The following interviewee went further, suggesting that knowledge should be shared not only across nations, but between different interest groups in Egyptology, blaming academics for not making their work more accessible to lay or specialist audiences.

There's enough information around for God's sake, the academics are sitting on it, they're not sharing it ... And I find that is very controlling and manipulative ... and they make it into something boring and dry and unapproachable. So if there's any academics listening, get your arses into gear and you'll be more popular.

(white, amateur)

Contemporary relevance of Ancient Egypt

All the interviewees were asked what they felt the legacy of the Ancient Egyptians had been. Most responses referred to social or spiritual concepts. Perhaps surprisingly, only a few mentioned the physical remains such as art and architecture. Two interviewees made a link to the people themselves, one describing the Egyptians as a 'root race' (white, amateur), while the other, an Egyptian, referred to the 'relics of our own ancestors', both material and spiritual. Some of the black interviewees highlighted the connections between ancient Egyptian society and language with aspects of modern and traditional African life. Others pointed to the connections between ancient and modern Egyptian cultures:

There is a gradual harmonious transport of ideas from ancient Egypt to Coptic Egypt to Islamic Egypt, and you just need to scratch the surface to see ancient Egypt.

(Egyptian, professional)

For many, Egyptian society was represented in an almost Utopian way, for example, 'perfect' (white, amateur), 'tolerant' (white, professional), 'non-racist' (non-white, professional). One interviewee suggested it should be revived as a model society:

> Very dedicated, obedient, liked working in groups, teamwork and things like that ... If we go back to those disciplined days ... it would be good for everybody.
>
> (Egyptian, professional)

Many of the amateur Egyptologists interviewed were interested in the spiritual aspects of the subject, and this is reflected in their comments about the legacy of the ancients, which emphasize the mythic archetypes, mysteries, and mysticism associated with Egypt. For some, a deep religious truth endures:

> They knew something about the afterlife ... there's something really important there, they're trying to say ... they've left messages if you like.
>
> (white, amateur)

As one interviewee pointed out, 'legacy can mean different things to different people' (Egyptian, professional), and as the examples above show, the meanings attributed by the interviewees were indeed very personal, underpinning, and supporting their fundamental belief systems.

Children and education

One area that would clearly repay further work is that of children's interest in Ancient Egypt. The focus group report described children's vision of Ancient Egypt as 'bursting with life ... a magnificent adventure playground' (Fisher 2000: chart 8):

> I want to see a tomb, go into a tomb, get the curse of the mummy.
>
> (child age 9–10)

> They had mummies in Egypt. I would have tea with them if they came to life.
>
> (child age 9–10)

The primary-school teachers' survey indicated that 75 per cent of respondents chose the Ancient Egypt option, rather than one of the others, at least partly because 'pupils find it interesting or inspiring'. Leaving aside the National Curriculum requirement 'to study an ancient civilisation', selected by 86 per cent of respondents, children's interest was by far the most significant factor in choosing the option.

Even before the National Curriculum, some schools had taught about Ancient Egypt, sparking the interest of around one-third (32 per cent) of respondents to the students' survey. School was the most commonly chosen source of early interest in Egypt for this group (now mainly in their twenties and thirties). The survey also suggests that formal education is more significant than other media or catalysts (such as films, magazines, exhibitions) in laying the foundations for later interest. Given that, because of the National Curriculum, a higher proportion of children are receiving formal education about Ancient Egypt, it seems possible therefore that the schoolchildren of today are more likely than their counterparts in previous generations to become Egyptology enthusiasts. This raises questions about how that interest might best be fostered in secondary and higher education and in informal settings such as museums.

Conclusions for museums

This research provides museums like the Petrie Museum with a basis for audience development and communication on a number of levels, many of which it has not been possible to examine here in detail. For now the most significant implications, and questions, to consider appear to be these:

- **Broadening audiences.** In theory it should be possible for museums like the Petrie to serve both a general and a specialist audience; they share an immense enthusiasm for the subject matter. The research confirmed the strength and diversity of interest in Ancient Egypt. If museums can harness this appeal together with the considerable academic resources at their disposal they have powerful tools with which to inform and inspire people.
- **Children.** There is a need to understand the role of formal education, and of museum visiting as part of this, in developing children's evidently high level of interest in this subject. In the meantime, the level of enthusiasm for the subject among children implies that a high priority should be placed on this audience.
- **Difficult subjects.** Museums now have to decide how hard they should try to 'burst the bubble' in various areas. How far should they temper their broadly educational mission with an acceptance of the interests, or lack of interest, of their audiences? For example:
    - **Chronology**. It would appear that general audiences have little idea of and little interest in understanding the chronology of Ancient Egypt. Educational audiences are required to be more interested, but curricula have their own demarcations. Some of the periods represented in the Petrie Museum's collections, for example, appear to have significantly less appeal than others, and the museum will have to work harder to 'sell' these. Alternatively, it may be decided that a chronological presentation is not always appropriate.
    - **Unappealing themes**. Both general and specialist audiences may be less receptive to certain themes that museums may feel it is important to cover, such as trade. Again more work and effort may need to be put into presenting these themes in an appealing way, or working them into more attractive subject areas.
    - **Modern Egypt and archaeology**. Although modern Egypt is rarely, if ever, the theme of museums of Egyptian archaeology, it may be important to include Egyptian people and perspectives in the displays in order for visitors to engage. However, it also needs to be borne in mind that attitudes to modern Egypt among some of the target audiences are very negative, and there is apparently little general interest in the ethics of archaeology.

- **Race and colour**. This is not a theme traditionally addressed within academic or popular Egyptology, except by black historians. Many academics fight shy of it as impossibly complex, dangerous, and misleading territory. For white audiences the question will be disturbing. Nevertheless if museums are to address black audiences it is a fundamental issue to tackle.
- **Using science**. There is widespread support for an open approach to the subject, one that is academically honest but allows for alternative readings and leaves some questions unanswered. There is a history of argument and debate around many aspects of the subject and this could be present in displays. There is a general desire to know more about the science of archaeology; science and the techniques of archaeology could be a bridge between the academic and popular audiences.
- **Using romance**. Effective communication with general audiences will require museums to address (and probably use the appeal of) the 'mythic themes' generally associated with Ancient Egypt as a framework for understanding the objects in the collections. In practice, this may be difficult to achieve. Some of the popular myths – that slaves built the pyramids – may be too entrenched for museums to counter, and some of the romance more powerful than the evidence.
- **What makes Egypt special?** For many people, including some professionals, the study of Ancient Egypt has a contemporary relevance of a social or spiritual nature. It will be a challenge to create museum displays that allow for and support these personal readings while at the same time enabling people to reflect on and question them.

Inevitably the next stage, as far as the Petrie Museum itself is concerned, will involve a good deal of trial and error, testing, and evaluating the most effective means of presenting important issues, unimaginable chronologies, unappealing or contentious subjects. However, exploring the effective communication of difficult subjects seems an entirely appropriate area for a university museum. Inspiring a broader audience to research this subject in more depth, to ask informed questions and to reach new interpretations is an aim of which Amelia Edwards, this museum's founder, would probably have approved.

Each must interpret for himself the Secret of the Sphinx.

(Edwards 1877: xvii)

References

Brace, C.L. with Tracer, D.P., Yaroch, L.A., Robb, J., Brandt, K., and Nelson, A.R. (1996) Clines and clusters versus 'race': the case of a Death on the Nile. In: M.K. Lefkowitz, and G.M. Rogers (eds.), *Black Athena Revisited*. Chapel Hill and London: University of North Carolina Press, pp. 103–11.

Claire, H. (1996) *Reclaiming our Pasts: Equality and Diversity in the Primary History Curriculum*. Stoke-on-Trent: Trentham Books.

Edwards, A.B. (1877) *A Thousand Miles up the Nile*. London: Routledge.

Feder, K.L. (1996) *Frauds, Myths and Mysteries: Science and Pseudoscience in Archaeology*. Mountain View: Mayfield.

Fisher, S. (2000) Exploring peoples' relationships with Egypt: qualitative research for the Petrie Museum. Susie Fisher Group (unpublished report).

Hassan, F.A. (1998) Memorabilia: archaeological materiality and national identity in Egypt. In: L. Meskell (ed.), *Archaeology under Fire: Nationalism, Politics and Heritage in the Eastern Mediterranean and the Middle East*. London: Routledge, pp. 200–16.

Hilliard, A.G. (1994) Bringing Maat, destroying Isfet: the African and African diasporan presence in the study of ancient KMT. In: I. Van Sertima (ed.), *Egypt, Child of Africa*. New Brunswick and London: Transaction Publishers, pp. 127–47.

Howe, S. (1998) *Afrocentrism: Imagined Pasts and Imagined Homes*. London: Verso.

Janssen, R.M. (1992) *The First Hundred Years: Egyptology at University College London 1892–1992*. London: University College London.

Merriman, N. ed. (1999) *Making Early Histories in Museums*. Leicester: Leicester University Press.

——(2000) Institute of Archaeology Teaching Collections: Staff Survey (unpublished).

Montserrat, D. (2000) *Ancient Egypt: Digging for Dreams*. Glasgow: Glasgow City Council.

MORI (2000) Attitudes towards the heritage: research study carried out for English Heritage. London: English Heritage. Available at: www.english-heritage.org.uk.

Motawi, S. (1998) Egypt in the British Museum. MA Dissertation. Institute of Archaeology, University College London.

QCA (Qualifications and Curriculum Authority) (1999) *History: the National Curriculum for England*. London: HMSO.

Reid. D. (1985) Indigenous Egyptology: the decolonisation of a profession. *Journal of the American Oriental Society*, 105: 233–46.

Roth, A.M. (1998) Ancient Egypt in America: claiming the riches. In: L. Meskell (ed.), *Archaeology under Fire: Nationalism, Politics and Heritage in the Eastern Mediterranean and the Middle East*. London: Routledge, pp. 217–29.

Simpson, M. (1996) *Making Representations: Museums in the Post-Colonial Era*. London: Routledge.

Stone, P.G. and Molyneaux, B.L. eds. (1994) *The Presented Past: Heritage, Museums and Education*. London: Routledge.

Thomas, R. (1998) Learning from Black Athena. *British Museum Magazine*, Autumn/Winter: 12–15.

Trigger, B.G. (1984) Alternative archaeologies: nationalist, colonialist, imperialist. *Man*, 19: 355–70.

Wood, M. (1998) The use of the pharaonic past in modern Egyptian nationalism. *Journal of the American Research Centre in Egypt*, 35: 179–96.

Young, R.J.C. (1995) *Colonial Desire: Hybridity in Theory, Culture and Race*. London: Routledge.

Chapter 37

Re-imagining Egypt
Artefacts, contemporary art, and community engagement in the museum

Gemma Tully

Introduction

What does Egypt conjure up in your imagination? Powerful pharaohs, towering pyramids, arid deserts, modern revolutions? Egypt has experienced many different cultural influences stretching back over 300,000 years. All eras of Egypt's past have helped shape the country today, yet for most of the world Egypt is only about one [his]story – the 'Golden Age' of the pharaohs. The exhibition 'Re-imagining Egypt', held at Saffron Walden Museum, UK, between 26 November 2013 and 23 February 2014, aimed to challenge this narrow view. Community engagement was central to this process as almost 100 local school-age children were involved in a series of workshops at the museum that explored artefacts spanning the breadth of Egypt's past, from prehistory to present. Encouraging participants to make connections between different eras and themes, the workshops sparked creative ideas, which looked beyond traditional representations of Egypt. The result was multiple artistic creations, which were curated collaboratively alongside the historical objects and new artworks by the contemporary Egyptian artist Khaled Hafez, who was invited for a residency. The combination of art and artefact, ancient and modern, Egyptian and local (North West Essex) perspectives in the exhibition set out to create a fresh vision of Egypt, both personal and historical. This chapter will discuss the theory, practice, and outcomes of this process; analyse 'Re-imagining Egypt' as a model for future community engagement in museums and ask whether the exhibition achieved its goal of representing Egypt as the sum of its many parts.

The legacy of ancient Egypt

The study and presentation of ancient Egypt is coloured by over five hundred years of Western tradition. Excluding accounts from ancient Greece and Rome (Strassler 2007), sources as early as the sixteenth century reveal the Western fascination for collecting ancient Egyptian artefacts. From the ingestion of *mummia* (ground mummy powder) for health (Dodson and Ikram 1998: 64) to pride of place in cabinets of curiosity Impey and MacGregor 1985; MacGregor 1994; Bredekamp 1995) and later in the first museums, ancient Egyptian items offered a source of mysticism and grandeur on a previously unparalleled scale. This was important at a time when Western nations were building the foundations of modern science and struggling to establish their place in the world.

Ancient Egypt provided a source of both intellectual challenge and national competition. However, by claiming the world's 'greatest' ancient civilization for its own, the West divorced living Egyptians from this heritage. Powerful orientalizing discourse (Reid 1985, 2002) divided ancient and modern populations with the coming of Islam. Disenfranchising ancient history from the modern population, this process appeared to justify European excavation, collecting, and control (Wood 1998). Yet inability to translate the hieroglyphs until 1822 meant that for the first three centuries in which ancient Egypt was slowly entering western consciousness audiences and 'experts' could do little more than stare in wonder and speculate about their 'rediscovered' ancestors. As a result, the focus for collecting was on the 'magnificent and the monstrous': monumental sculptures, mummies, sarcophagi, and temple reliefs (Moser 2006). Without access to the true meaning of the ancient texts, concepts of 'divine wisdom' (ACTS 7, 22 [New Revised Standard Version])[1] accompanied by classical, patristic, hermetic, gnostic, and alchemical traditions came to form lasting impressions of ancient Egypt in popular and scholarly doctrines (Assman 2003: 427). The power of these first associations, which established a narrow set of understandings of ancient Egypt, focused on elite individuals, death and religious practices, endures in twenty-first century representations of Egypt's past. While our understanding of Egyptian society and culture has moved on, it is inevitably morbid curiosity that still dominates popular visions of Egypt and continues to drive much Egyptological research.

From historical fiction, to films and archaeology exhibits,[2] Western 'Egyptomania' (Curl 1982, 1994) is still very much alive. The implications today are that historical awe eclipses more accessible daily life narratives and, perhaps more significantly, positions modern Egypt as a nation disconnected from, yet living in the shadow of, its past. As a result, exhibitions about Egypt rarely live up to the aims of contemporary museum practice which acknowledges that while institutions are important in inspiring marvel they also have a social and ethical role to play in contextualizing cultural and temporal differences, challenging stereotypes, and diversifying the voices involved in the interpretation process (Peers and Brown 2003).

Across the world, the majority of 'Egyptian' exhibitions focus primarily on the dynastic era. The Roman, Coptic and Predynastic periods are generally found in annex rooms, or tacked on to the end of exhibits, marginalizing them in relation to the wider 'pharaonic' chronology. The Islamic period, if present, is usually distanced spatially from traditional Egyptian galleries and is predominantly integrated within a general Arab-Islamic history. Similarly, when the prehistoric period is represented, artefacts are normally included in wider evolutionary 'Out of Africa' narratives. In terms of representing modern Egypt in western museums, sixteenth to twenty-first century artefacts make occasional appearances in ethnographic displays but these tend to focus on often nomadic, Nubian, and Bedouin lifestyles. Such exhibits do not reflect the diversity of modern Egyptian life and instead reinforce the apparent chasm of difference between Egypt's ancient and modern populations as established by orientalism (Tully 2010).[3]

Interestingly, some Egyptian museums are beginning to promote a different vision of Egypt's past compared to the orientalist rhetoric of the West. While the first museums within Egypt were initiated by Westerners, predominantly to house Egyptology collections, and thus segregated pharaonic, Coptic, and Muslim culture (see also Mitchell 1991; Reid 1997), many of today's Egyptian curators are beginning to focus on more encompassing accounts of Egyptian history that challenge the western view.[4] By using similar styles of display technique and by integrating various eras of history together through a more thematic focus, a unified history is being created that positions 'indigenous' eras of Egyptian heritage alongside the present. This approach aids the legibility of Egyptian history by superimposing a clear 'material relationship between native cultures over the episodic expression of each individual period' (Doyon 2008: 13–14). Reflecting cultural palimpsest in this way, ancient Egyptian history can be reclaimed for contemporary Egypt while maintaining a positive place within other cultural dialogues, such as the development of western civilization. Providing a narrative of continuous cultural exchange and overlap (see Doyon 2007, 2008), this approach finds parallels with an emergent trend in anthropology which promotes the reconsideration of artefacts from final products – 'objects' (Gell 1998) – to 'things' caught up in a number of processes which gather together the 'threads of life' in diverse ways (see Heidegger [1971] 2001; Miller 2005; Henare et al. 2007). By viewing past items as part of a continuing process of meaning-making which remains relevant to modern life, it helps audiences to consider different ways of seeing the world.

The idea of representing continuity and change, and allowing for multiple interpretations of a country's past to coexist, provided the central concept for 'Re-imagining Egypt'. However, visitor research with audiences at existing European Egyptology displays has revealed how visitors tend to focus on objects which reinforce their existing knowledge, rather than seeking to challenge it, and that specially exhibited 'star objects'[5] win attention from other artefacts and new information (Tully 2010). This is a problem experienced with traditional museum display methods in general because while they offer objects up for contemplation, they single them out from the general flow of life (Gosden 2004: 35). It was clear, therefore, that simply placing objects from all eras of Egypt's history in a single gallery would struggle to challenge the traditional viewing process and our didactic programming, which tends to isolate cultures into distinct hermetic units. Thus, an approach was needed that would challenge expectations of an Egyptian museum display by taking audiences out of their comfort zone and encouraging them to stop and reconsider 'taken for granted' ideas regarding Egypt's past. Working collaboratively to include contemporary Egyptian voices as well as local voices in the interpretation and curation process, rather than simply imposing a singular (albeit non-traditional) curatorial vision, provided part of the solution.

Collaboration in the museum

Over the last two decades, it has become increasingly accepted that archaeologists and museum curators have long been guilty of privileging their 'specialized' forms of knowledge and presentation over other interpretations of cultures and histories (Faulkner 2000; Peers and Brown 2003). This is problematic as academics and institutions are sanctioned 'knowledge-makers' with the power to challenge or enforce commonly held beliefs. Collaborative archaeology and collaborative museology therefore aim to democratize the production of knowledge by working from the premise that 'wherever material is housed, it has a history that is shared among many people who all have a stake in it' (Curtis 2003: 31). While it would be impossible to consider the views of every stakeholder, it is acknowledged that understanding can be enhanced and new questions asked when the voices and methods involved in interpretation move away from singular 'authoritative' perspectives.

Collaborative museology emerged from the movement towards 'critical museology' and notions of the 'post-museum' (Hooper-Greenhill 2000). The sub-discipline engages with the moral, national, historical, and ethical implications of display in order 'to introduce a plurality of practice and develop new genres of exhibitions, which can engage with the panoply of wider cultural practices which have stimulated it' (Shelton 2001: 146–7). 'Re-imagining Egypt' developed from this premise with the aim of creating a multi-perspective, experimental display that would simultaneously inform the present as well as the past. However, if evidence suggests that artefacts would not 'speak for themselves' (Tully 2010), even if put in new collaboratively curated object groupings, it was also unlikely that by simply adding alternative interpretative voices, in the form of text, that this would do justice to the aims or participants of the exhibition process; dramatic visual intervention was needed! Thus, contemporary art provided the second part of the solution.

Contemporary art and archaeological display

Contemporary visual art, alongside collaborative curation, offers a powerful medium through which museums can engage with contemporary debate, incorporate multiple narratives, and become more fluid spaces for cross-cultural and cross-temporal exchange. Colin Renfrew (2003: 7) describes the visual arts of today as an 'uncoordinated yet somehow enormously effective research programme that looks critically at what we are and how we know what we are – at the foundations of knowledge and perception, and of the structures that modern societies have chosen to construct upon these foundations'. Art has agency (Gell 1998) and is therefore a useful facilitator for the generation of deeper understandings by its producers and consumers in terms of engagement with the past.

Since the 1980s, art has been breaking free from the art gallery as artists and indigenous communities have challenged the way their work/culture is categorized and displayed (Stocking 1985). This has led to the development of numerous contemporary art-human past partnerships across various museum contexts: ethnographic, historical, artistic, and archaeological.[6] Art and archaeology, in fact, share much common ground. Both practices reflect an expression of society (Haskell 1993: 4), an attempt by the artist/curator/interpreter to make sense of their personal experiences as they come face-to-face with different aspects of the material world (Renfrew 2003, 21; Laneri 2003: 181). However, where archaeology achieves this through passive, often static, modes of academic engagement, which cannot help but classify and compartmentalize concepts, the visual arts can assimilate many differing but equally complex ideas regarding people, places, objects, and histories more fluidly. This provides for a more emotive and imaginative experience, both for the producer and the audience, as it avoids the imposition of direct curatorial narratives and instead provides artistically 'couched' dialogue that can challenge ideas without appearing explicit (Dutton on Kant 2009: 58–9). As such, artistic interpretation can both sit alongside and challenge Western institutionalized methods of historical/archaeological display and transform exhibition spaces. Anthony Shelton suggests this process could convert museums into 'a hive of creative activity which would open the way for interventions and reinterpretations that would proactively challenge received expectations and stereotypes and encourage an active viewing public, rather than simply reproducing more familiar tomb-like galleries which congeal meaning and demand only a passive voyeuristic gaze from its audiences' (Shelton 1993: 15). It is exactly this form of 'active viewing' that is needed to revive Egyptian display and enable alternate narratives to gain visibility alongside knowledge of 'the Golden Age of the Pharaohs'. Thus, a collaborative approach bringing together multiple visions of Egypt's past by Egyptians, locals and museum staff, through art-artefact unions, could help meet the needs of Egyptian and Western stakeholders who want to see 'Egypt in context' and find personal resonance in museum exhibitions.

The importance for artists of an awareness of the past, and the art of the past, in the creation of meaningful works (Eliot 1920), was also significant to the 'Re-imagining Egypt' exhibition. While heritage is internalized by many contemporary Western artists, explicit visual references are more commonly made by artists from North Africa and the Middle East where the loss and destruction of heritage is more prevalent. Acting as a means of preserving and reclaiming lost or appropriated heritage, it is the integration of wider cultural markers that makes contemporary art from nations such as Egypt particularly suited to the archaeological museum context.[7] Khaled Hafez, for example, the artist who created new works inspired by the Saffron Walden collection, focuses on the assimilation of ancient and contemporary icons to reflect the culture of recycling and how aspects of Egyptian art, from various periods, have influenced today's universal visual culture. The result is the splicing of 'superheroes', e.g. Anubis with Batman, and Catwoman with Bastet, added to the frames of magazine models, and presented alongside Arab Islamic, Mediterranean, and Judeo-Christian motifs. The work reveals the palimpsest of Egyptian and global identities, and uses repetition, irony, and humour to bring into question the dichotomies of East/West, ancient/modern, sacred/profane, good/evil, war/peace. The use of collage within his work and the 'dripping paint effect' reinforce the message that these binaries, like his paintings and all museum exhibitions, are constructed and should therefore be challenged. Held together by a contemporary message that crosses cultures, Hafez's use of pop language, collage, and vibrant colour was something I felt would appeal and be accessible to local school-age participants from Saffron Walden during workshops, as well as to visitors to the final exhibition.

In terms of the artwork produced by local children, only a century ago the idea that children's art could be of any use to the adult world, let alone that we could glean new meanings from it, was inconceivable. However research by developmental psychologists since the 1980s (Gardener 1980) has begun to highlight the importance of both children's perceptions of the world and the accessibility of their thoughts through art.

Creative methods of expression are one of the richest sources within teaching to access a child's needs, thinking, and emotion (Lowenfield 1959: vi). Art production is a useful way for young people to make sense of the world at a time when thoughts may be difficult to vocalize (Gardener 1980, 12). Art also allows for much greater levels of experimentation than traditional forms of learning as there is not the same fear of being 'wrong' (Dailey 1984: 8). It is also suggested that, 'drawing liberates other thoughts and connections' (Boulter et al. 2002: 13). The potential for art, therefore, to reveal numerous shades of understanding is highly appropriate in terms of the collaborative aims of 'Re-imagining Egypt'. The approach would provide a unique insight into young participants' understanding of Egypt, as well as help them clarify and expand upon their existing knowledge and share their ideas with visitors of all ages and backgrounds. However, for both Khaled Hafez and the school-aged participants' artworks to achieve the goal of enhancing audiences' understanding of the museum objects on display and creating a more dynamic viewing experience – from Egyptian prehistory to present – it was essential to ensure that art and artefact were placed in specific contextual dialogues linking to the exhibition's central theme.

Creating contextual dialogues

When dealing with communication across time, culture, and media – art/artefact – maintaining direct contextual links is essential to an exhibition's success. As discussed by Dutton (2009: 53), the combination of art and artefact creates a layering of experience, which 'can be most effective when separable pleasures [archaeological item and contemporary artwork] are coherently related to each other or interact with each other'. It must not be forgotten that while art can enhance understanding, aspects of contemporary art may appear illusive to some viewers. Thus, artefacts' relationships and traditional labels for artworks and objects can provide a sense of security for visitors who may not take naturally to an unexpected viewing context. Selectivity, in terms of art and artefact is therefore essential in creating a balanced exhibition space, which highlights the merits of integrating 'art' and 'science' to provide new insights on the world. Significantly, it is not only the artefacts and audiences who benefit in terms of extended understanding through this form of display partnership. Through hands-on engagement with artefacts and the collaborative curation process, the artists/participants are also able to expand their artistic practice through new experiences and by carrying out their own form of 'fieldwork' within the museum and presenting their own 'data' (Durand 2008: 77). This balance and the resulting mutual benefits are important to overcome curatorial concerns about exhibition rooms being transformed into 'art shows', and artists' anxieties as to whether positioning work within non-art museums reduces them to ethnographic subjects (Elliott 2008: 93). These issues were all addressed in 'Re-imagining Egypt' through a focus on the creation of site-specific artworks/installations developed during Khaled Hafez's residency and workshops with children from the local community. Combined with continuous consultation on how art and artefact should be presented to maintain optimum communication, the approach aimed to highlight the artists' messages and their ramifications for new historical interpretations, while providing gravitas for the artworks through their links with each other and significant items from over 300,000 years of Egyptian history.

The exhibition process

Preparation for 'Re-imagining Egypt' took place over six months prior to the opening of the exhibition. Starting with Saffron Walden's collection, every item from Egypt was catalogued. This involved working between our ethnographic, archaeological, and ceramic collections, and resulted in a huge haul of potential artefacts from stone tools, to ceramics and textiles. Gaps in our collection were then identified, namely classical period and early Islamic items, and kindly filled by object loans from the Fitzwilliam Museum, Cambridge. A basic timeline was then developed, illustrated with artefacts, where possible, from Stone Age to present Egypt, including modern tourist souvenirs, photographs, and images from the recent political turmoil (Table 37.1). The timeline provided the starting point for workshops with five different groups of school-aged children local to Saffron Walden: St Mary's School Year 5/6 (29, 9–11 year olds), Friends' School Year 7 (31, 11–12 year olds), Friends' School Sixth Form A-Level Art students (15, 16–18 year olds), Home School Art Club (15, 7–13 year olds) and Museum regulars (8, 7–10 year olds). Each group looked at Egypt's history chronologically, handling artefacts where appropriate before discussing similarities and differences in design, language, technology, governance, and so on across eras. Hand-on experience of the artefacts was particularly important, especially for the younger children, as the physical experience of a subject is essential in developing understanding (Pearce 1997: 238). With a more contextual awareness of Egypt, its people and diverse cultural influences in place, each group began picking out objects and themes that particularly interested them. The artistic projects and artefact groupings to go on display evolved from there. Each group was able to dedicate different amounts of time to the project, which influenced the scale and scope of their final product and the level of curatorial input; artworks were produced from one single three-hour session up to six two-hour sessions over consecutive weeks.

Table 37.1 Timeline and artefacts for show/handling

Time period	Artefacts
Stone Age circa 300,000–4000 BC	Stone tools
Predynastic 4000–3100 BC	Pottery, make-up palettes, stone blades
Pharaonic/Dynastic 3100–332 BC	Amulets, shabtis, statuettes, inscriptions, alabaster containers, ceramics
Classical (Ptolemaic Egypt 332–30 BC, Roman and Byzantine Egypt 30 BC–AD 641)	Lamps, coins, mummy portraits, statuettes, textiles, glass
Middle Ages (Arab AD 641–969, Fatimid AD 969–1171, Ayyubid AD 1171–1250, Mamluk AD 1250–1517)	Lamps, calligraphy, textiles, stonework, jewellery, coins, tiles, woodwork, glass
Early Modern (Ottoman AD 1517–1867, French AD 1798–1801, under Muhammad Ali AD 1805–1882, Khedivate of Egypt AD 1867–1891)	Lamps, calligraphy, textiles, stonework, jewellery, coins, tiles, woodwork, glass
Modern Egypt (British occupation 1882–1953, Sultanate of Egypt 1914–1922, Kingdom of Egypt 1922–1953, Republic 1953–2011)	Photographs from the era, lamps, calligraphy, textiles, stonework, jewellery, coins, tiles, woodwork, glass, tourist souvenirs
Revolution 25 January 2011 to present	Graffiti, images of protests, landscapes and scenes of contemporary life, modern products e.g. clothes, toys, technology, souvenirs, daily life items

The human figure

St Mary's school chose the human figure as their theme, with a particular focus on two very different types of 'doll' – ancient Egyptian shabtis, created to work for the deceased in the afterlife, and modern-day arusa (Arabic for doll) made by children to sell to tourists. After learning about shabtis in more detail, the children began to design '21st century shabtis' upon which they wrote 'spells' which would make their lives easier today; do my homework and tidy my room featured frequently! Crafted with felt and fabric pens, before being stuffed and stitched, the shabtis were then displayed together in a 'shabti box', as they would have been in a tomb, alongside a real shabti from the museum's collection. The art-artefact installation was explained by a label in the display, which included a translation of the genuine shabti's hieroglyphic text to emphasize the link between the ancient and modern requests.

For the arusa, we thought about what life was like for children in Egypt today. The focus was on those from poor rural families on the West bank of the Nile in Luxor, an area that is particularly well known for the homemade dolls, along with other souvenirs, which are made to sell to tourists. Made from recycled clothes, as in Egypt, the children from St Mary's fashioned their own arusa based on costumes from different eras of Egyptian history. Titled 'It's a small world', the dolls were displayed on the wall in a 'dancing formation' next to two arusa recently purchased in Egypt, an image of a little girl who makes them, and a brief explanatory text.

The shabtis and the arusa were positioned in close proximity to each other and close to the display of statuettes from other eras of Egypt's history. The inclusion of multiple artistic and archaeological representations of 'people' in the gallery was important to help repopulate visitors' visions of Egypt, ancient and modern, compared to traditional images which tend to present the country as a sparsely populated agricultural land or as a barren desert inhabited only by monuments and camels. The vibrant colours used in both works added to their impact. Standing out from the plain gallery walls, they drew the eye and complimented both the colours of the artefacts and those used by Khaled Hafez and the other community groups. Creating a more cohesive unit between art and artefact, this colour symmetry helped reinforce the exhibition's message that Egypt has an interconnected historical narrative. The humour of the shabti spells and the personal nature of each arusa were also important in the creation of a more emotive and relaxed viewing environment where the identities and ideas of multiple artists/authors/curators provoked audiences to laugh, discuss and add their own thoughts to the mix.

Signs and symbols, lines and language

The Home School group selected Egypt's many languages as the focus of their project. Starting with the symbols of Predynastic Egypt known from Naqada pottery, we discussed the idea of written language evolving and changing with new cultural influences and invasions. Where possible we looked at real artefacts containing hieroglyphic, Coptic, Greek, Latin, and Arabic script. The decorative side of written language was also addressed, from hieroglyphs on tomb and temple walls to Arabic calligraphy, before participants began to design their own new language inspired by one or a combination of Egypt's alphabets.

The final designs were drawn on to thin linen with fabric crayons, pens, and paint before being transformed into a giant wall hanging which was positioned near artefacts incorporating numerous Egyptian symbols and languages in the exhibition. The work found resonance with the cross-temporal dialogue of the shabtis' spells – ancient and modern - while enforcing the concept of Egyptian history as palimpsest through the literal layering of Egypt-inspired icons.

Gods and goddesses

Most children (and adults) are fascinated by the ancient Egyptian gods, especially their often hybrid nature – part human, part animal. The children from our Museum Regulars group wanted to create new gods with a modern twist. We began by studying the ancient Egyptian gods and goddess, printed images, statuettes, and reliefs were used. We discussed the kinds of creatures represented, the way they are often drawn with their bodies facing forward and their heads side on, and the colours used in ancient times. Inspired by the surrealist game the exquisite corpse (more commonly known as picture consequences), each child was then given a sheet of paper folded into three parts for the different sections of the body (head and shoulders; arms and body; waist and legs). Each segment of their god or goddess had to be different (e.g. one part human, one part animal, one part sea creature), thus pushing the boundaries set for ancient Egyptian goods.[8] The 'New Gods of the Nile' were then transferred on to good quality art paper and recreated with layers of colour produced by wax crayons and vibrant paints. Each god/goddess was individually framed and hung in the gallery near artefacts depicting various Egyptian religious icons and opposite the work of Khaled Hafez, who also incorporated interpretations of sacred characters and motifs into his new works. Once again the colours helped draw the different areas of the exhibition together and the tongue-in-cheek 'formula' for creating a god offered a playful alternative to traditional Egyptological theories.

Crowning glory/pots and patterns

The shapes and patterns found on artefacts spanning the breadth of Egypt's history formed the basis of artistic inspiration for both groups from the Friends' School. The 11–13 year olds recreated the crowns of ancient Egypt with card and papier mâché and decorated them with the motifs from multiple eras, including contemporary Egyptian culture. The Sixth Form group used the same approach to design and decorate Predynastic-style pots.

The crowns were mounted in a niche in the exhibition space, surrounding a panel that made explicit the legacy of ancient Egypt. This was significant as the crowns of ancient Egypt are only known from artistic depictions. They have never been found in artefact form, and may have been purely symbolic. The label for the new crowns explained this and offered up the modern creations as a representation of Egypt's wider historical glories.

The pots were placed in a museum vitrine alongside other ceramics and containers from Egypt, which dated from 5,000 BC to the twenty-first century. The students' contributions neatly summarized these 7,000 years, and while they looked very much at home among the artefacts they injected an element of surprise and encouraged viewers to look more closely at all the objects and question their provenance.

In vitrines where artworks were not present, the focus remained on a mix of religious and daily life objects, presented cross-temporally, which referenced both Khaled Hafez's and the community's art: e.g. stone tools, amulets, make-up paraphernalia, oil lamps, textiles, and stonework depicting religious scenes.

The writing is on the wall

To add further Egyptian voices to the display, a number of quotes were added to the upper-section of the gallery walls. Reinforcing the messages evident in Khaled Hafez's art, the statements were extracted from interviews carried out in Egypt between 2007 and 2009 as part of my PhD research into Egyptian perceptions of identity and history (Tully 2010). The artistic presentation of the quotes in blue calligraphy, 'floating' above the display, alongside their somewhat poetic nature helped bridge the divide between the more factual text panels and labels and the vibrant colours and personal interpretation of the art and artefacts. At the same time, the excerpts continued to pursue the exhibition's aims of challenging narrow visions of Egypt as a country with a single 'great' past and revealing the multiple layers that form Egyptian identity today:

> Egyptian religion, history, culture, and art are like a ring, a chain of evolution and continuation …
> (Elham Salah Eldien, Curator at the Coptic Museum, Cairo)

> All periods of history played a part in shaping the next and were shaped by what went before. In Egypt all history blends into one.
> (Myrium Gergis Hanna, Student at the American University in Cairo)

> Current society is a culmination of all Egyptian civilizations and this is what is great about Egypt, you can see history everywhere.
> (Haitham Saeed, Engineer, Luxor)

> The objects of the past and the narratives of both history and the present are twins, to separate them is to alienate them.
> (Amir Nasr, Shopkeeper, al-Quseir, Red Sea coast)

> Egyptian identity is complex and multilayered. It interweaves Islamic, Jewish, Christian and Ancient Egyptian influences.
> (Khaled Hafez, Artist, Cairo)

Outcomes and evaluation

From a purely statistical perspective the exhibition was a success. The museum's visitor numbers for the quarter the exhibition was open were the highest since 2009 (a time when the Museum had a larger staff and budget!). In terms of changing perceptions of Egypt, informal interviews with visitors and the monitoring of 'dwell time' within the temporary exhibition space revealed that 'Re-imagining Egypt' held people's attention. It was also clear that the exhibition got people talking within their social/family groups a great deal more than usual as they discussed artworks and objects, what they liked and disliked, explained things to one another and often confessed that they hadn't thought about Egypt in this way before. There was also more frequent laughter, often provoked by the shabti spells or people's comments on the art. However, the most important outcome from my perspective as the project's co-ordinator, as well as the Museum's Learning Officer, was the impact of involvement on the school-aged participants.

Putting the children in control, letting them act as the creators of knowledge, valuing their unique opinions, and exhibiting their work as equal in status to important artefacts and creations by a famous Egyptian artist was clearly transformative. Some participants came back almost every week with a different family member to show them their artwork and to 'talk them through' the exhibition. Young people's attitudes and patterns of behaviour are much less 'fixed' than those of adults, meaning that they are more willing to synthesize new knowledge within their existing frames of reference (Anderson 1997, 36). At the same time, children are an incredibly powerful source in the dissemination of new ideas to adults. Thus, the quality of the exhibition's communication was undeniably enhanced, at least at local level, through recognition of participants' achievements, which prompted them to act as ambassadors of new understandings about Egypt and to challenge and extend others' perceptions of the past.

On a more general note, the concept underlying 'Re-imagining Egypt' is significant as it caters for numerous narratives rather than merely representing a single form of knowledge. The collaborative aspect, crossing generations, cultures, and forms of communication – art and artefact – supports the argument that new methods of display can act as a launch pad for active meaning-making in the museum (Roberts 1997, 3) and cut through century-old stereotypes and traditional 'ways of seeing' (Berger 1972). Engaging with communities, putting cultures into context and making connections with modern life are essential if museums are to survive and maintain relevance in the twenty-first century. 'Re-imagining Egypt' is proof that museums can do more than simply inspire marvel in the case of Egypt, and I am confident that multiple global cultures and histories could be equally successfully 're-imagined'.

Notes

1. A great deal of scholarship developed from the biblical notion of ancient Egyptian divine wisdom. One such example is William Warburton's Hebraist study, *The Divine Legation of Moses* (1738–1741).
2. The influence of modern Egyptomania is evident in historical fiction, such as the *Ramses* series by Christian Jacq (1997, 1998a, 1998b, 1998c, 1999), films such as *The Mummy* (both 1959 and 1999 versions), and exhibitions such as *Tutankhamen and The Golden Age of the Pharaohs* at London's O2 arena (2007–2008).
3. For detailed discussion and analysis of displays of Egyptian history, see Tully 2010.
4. For example, the Nubia Museum, Aswan and plans for the new Grand Egyptian Museum (GEM) in Cairo.
5. For example, the Rosetta Stone at the British Museum or the bust of Nefertiti at the Neues Museum in Berlin.
6. Examples include: art in archaeological displays (see Edmond and Evans 1991; Putnam 2001; Renfrew 2003; Renfrew et al. 2004); ethnographic exhibits (see Shelton 2001; Herle 2003; Gunn 2005; Leach 2005, 2007; Raymond and Salmond 2008); dissecting the museum as an institution and attracting new audiences (see McShine 1999; Jameson Jr. et al. 2003; Tully 2010).
7. For examples see Tully 2010, 302–20.
8. Most of the ancient Egyptian gods are presented as fully human, fully animal, or a combination of one part animal, one part human. The only common exception is Ammut, 'the devourer', a goddess who has the head of a crocodile, the mane and body of a lion, and the rear end and legs of a hippopotamus.

References

Anderson, D.A. (1997) *A Common Wealth Report on Education in Museums*. London: Department of Culture, Media and Sport.

Assman, J. (2003) *The Mind of Egypt: History and Meaning in the Time of the Pharaohs*. New York: Metropolitan Books.

Berger, J. (1972) *Ways of Seeing*. London: BBC and Penguin.

Boulter, C., Tunnicliffe, S., and Reiss, M. (2002) Probing children's understandings of the natural world. Paper presented at the Institute of Education, University of London. October 2002.

Bredekamp, H. (1995) *The Lure of Antiquity and the Cult of the Machine: The Kunstkammer and the Evolution of Nature, Art and Technology*. Translated by A. Brown. Princeton: Princeton University Press.

Conner, P. ed. (1983) *The Inspiration of Egypt. The Influence on British Artists, Travellers and Designers 1700–1900*. Brighton: Brighton Borough Council.

Curl, J.S. (1982) *Egyptomania: The Egyptian Revival. An Introductory Study of a Recurring Theme in the History of Taste*. London: George Allen and Unwin.

——(1994) *Egyptomania: The Egyptian Revival: A Recurring Theme in the History of Taste*. Second Edition. Manchester: Manchester University Press.

Curtis, G.W.N. (2003) Human remains: the sacred, museums and archaeology. *Public Archaeology*, 3(1): 21–32.

Dalley, T. (1984) *Art as Therapy: An Introduction to the use of Art as a Therapeutic Technique*. London: Routledge.

Dodson, A. and Ikram, S. (1998) *The Mummy in Ancient Egypt: Equipping the Dead for Eternity*. London: Thames and Hudson.

Doyon, W. (2007) Representing Egypt's past: archaeology and identity in Egyptian museum practice. Masters of Art, University of Washington.

——(2008) The poetics of Egyptian museum practice. *British Museum Studies in Ancient Egypt and the Sudan*, 10: 1–37.

Durand, C.A. (2008) Fieldwork in a glass case: artistic practice and museum ethnography. In: R. Ramond and A. Salmond (eds.), *Pasifika Styles: Artists inside the Museum*. Cambridge: Cambridge University Museum of Archaeology and Anthropology, pp. 75–80.

Dutton, D. (2009) *The Art Instinct*. Oxford: Oxford University Press.

Edmonds, M.R. and Evans, C. (1991) *The Place of the Past: Art and Archaeology in Britain*. Cambridge: Kettles Yard.

Eliot, T.S. [1920] (1997) *The Sacred Wood: Essays on Poetry and Criticism*. London: Faber and Faber.

Elliott, M. (2008) Some anxious moments: the mechanisms and pragmatisms of a collaborative exhibition. In: R. Ramond and A. Salmond (eds.), *Pasifika Styles: Artists inside the Museum*. Cambridge: Cambridge University Museum of Archaeology and Anthropology, pp. 89–95.

Faulkner, N. (2000) Archaeology from below. *Public Archaeology*, 1. 21–33.

Gardener, H. (1980) *Artful Scribbles. The Significance of Children's Drawings*. New York: Basic Books.

Gell, A. (1998) *Art and Agency: An Anthropological Theory*. Oxford: Oxford University Press.

Gosden, C. (2004) Making and display: our aesthetic appreciation of things and objects. In: C. Renfrew, C. Gosden, and E. DeMarrais (eds.), *Substance, Memory, Display. Archaeology and Art*. Cambridge: McDonald Institute, pp. 35–45.

Gunn, W. ed. (2005) *Creativity and Practice Research Papers*. Dundee: Creativity and Practice Research Group, Visual Research Centre, University Dundee.

Haskell, F. (1993) *History and its Image: Art and the Interpretation of the Past*. New Haven: Yale University Press.

Heidegger, M. [1971] (2001) *Poetry, Language, Thought*. London: Harper.

Henare, A., Holbrand, M., and Wastell, S. (2007) Introduction. In: A. Henare, M. Holbrand, and S. Wastell (eds.), *Thinking through Things: Theorising Artifacts*. New York: Routledge, pp. 1–31.

Herle, A. 2003 Objects, agency and museums. Continuing dialogues between the Torres Strait Islanders and Cambridge. In: L. Peers and A.K. Brown (eds.), *Museums and Source Communities*. London: Routledge, pp. 194–207.

Hooper-Greenhill, E. (2000) *Museums and the Interpretation of Visual Culture*. London: Routledge.

Impey, O.R. and MacGregor, A. eds. (1985) *The Origins of the Museum: The Cabinets of Curiosity in Sixteenth and Seventeenth Century Europe*. Oxford and New York: Clarendon Press.

Jacq, C. (1997) *Ramses: The Son of Light*. London: Warner Books.

——(1998a) *Ramses: The Eternal Temple*. London: Warner Books.

——(1998b) *Ramses: The Battle of Kadesh*. London: Warner Books.

——(1998c) *Ramses: The Lady of Abu Simbel*. London: Warner Books.

——(1999) *Ramses: Under the Western Acacia*. London: Warner Books.

Jameson, Jr. J. H., Ehrenhard, J.E., and Finn, C.A. eds. (2003) *Ancient Muses: Archaeology and the Arts*. Tuscaloosa, Alabama: The University of Alabama Press.

Laneri, N. (2003) Is archaeology fiction? Some thoughts about experimental ways of communicating archaeological processes to the external world. In: J.H. Jameson Jr., J.E. Ehrenhard, and C.A. Finn (eds.), *Ancient Muses: Archaeology and the Arts*. Tuscaloosa, Alabama: The University of Alabama Press, pp. 179–92.

Leach, J. (2005) Disciplinary specialisation and collaborative endeavours: some challenges presented by sci-art projects. In: W. Gunn (ed.), *Creativity and Practice Research Papers*. Dundee: Creativity and Practice Research Group, Visual Research Centre, University Dundee.

——(2007) Differentiation and encompassment: a critique of Alfred Gell's theory of the abduction of creativity. In: A. Henare, M. Holbrand, and S. Wastell (eds.), *Thinking through Things: Theorising Artifacts*. New York: Routledge, pp. 167–88.

MacGregor, A. ed. (1994) *Sir Hans Sloane: Collector, Scientist, Antiquary. Founding Father of the British Museum*. London: The British Museum in association with Alistair McAlpine.

McShine, K., Williams, C., Lowry, G., and Arnold, E. (1999) *The Museum as Muse: Artists Reflect*. New York: Museum of Modern Art.

Miller, D. (2005) *Materiality*. Durham: Duke University Press.

Mitchell, T. (1991) *Colonising Egypt*. Cambridge: Cambridge University Press.

Moser, S. (2006) *Wondrous Curiosities: Ancient Egypt at the British Museum*. Chicago: Chicago University Press.

Peers, L. and Brown, A.K. eds. (2003) *Museums and Source Communities: A Routledge Reader*. London: Routledge.

Putnam, J. (2001) *Art and Artefact. The Museum as Medium.* London: Thames and Hudson.

Reid, D.M. (1985) Indigenous Egyptology: the decolonisation of a profession. *Journal of the American Oriental Society*, 105: 233–46.

——(1997) Nationalising the Pharaonic past: Egyptology, imperialism, and Egyptian nationalism 1922–1952. In: I. Gershoni and J. Jankowski (eds.), *Rethinking Nationalism in the Arab Middle East.* New York: Columbia University Press, pp. 127–315.

——(2002) *Whose Pharaohs? Archaeology, Museums and Egyptian National Identity from Napoleon to World War One.* London: University of California Press.

Renfrew, C. (2003) *Figuring it Out: The Parallel Visions of Artists and Archaeologists.* London: Thames and Hudson.

Renfrew, C., Gosden, C., and Demarrais, E. eds. (2004) *Substance, Memory, Display: Archaeology and Art.* Cambridge: McDonald Institute.

Roberts, L.C. (1997) *From Knowledge to Narrative: Educators and the Changing Museum.* Washington, D.C.: Smithsonian Institute Press.

Shelton, A. (1993) Re-presenting non-western art and ethnography at Brighton. *The Royal Pavilion and Museums Review*, 1: 1–14.

——(2001) Unsettling the meaning: critical museology, art, and anthropological discourse. In: M. Bouquet (ed.), *Academic Anthropology and the Museum: Back to the Future.* Oxford and New York: Berghahn Books, pp. 142–61.

Stocking, G.W. (1985) *Objects and Others: Essays on Museums and Material Culture.* Madison: The University of Wisconsin Press.

Strassler, R.B. ed. (2007) *The Landmark Herodotus: The Histories.* Translated by A.L. Purvis. New York: Pantheon Books.

Tully, G. (2010) Answering the calls of the living: collaborative practice in archaeology and ancient Egyptian daily life display in western museums. PhD thesis, University of Southampton.

Warburton, W. (1738–1741) *The Divine Legation of Moses.* London: T. Cox.

Wood, M. (1998) The use of the Pharaonic past in modern Egyptian nationalism. *Journal of the American Research Centre in Egypt*, 35: 179–96.

Working towards greater equity and understanding

Examples of collaborative archaeology and museum initiatives with Indigenous peoples in North America

Sarah Carr-Locke and George Nicholas

Readers of the *Vancouver Sun* were recently treated to a rare view of a Squamish Nation *sxwayxway* mask that is to be shown at the North Vancouver Museum (Griffin 2010). These masks were traditionally owned by high-ranking Squamish families and used in spiritual cleansing rites. This mask was gifted from Xats'alanexw Siyam (Chief August Jack Khatsahlano), a spirit dancer, to Maisie Hurley, a non-Native who was an activist for Native rights in the 1940s and 1950s, demonstrating a high degree of mutual friendship and respect. Hurley's collection of 190 objects was eventually donated to the North Vancouver Museum. Due to their spiritual power, *sxwayxway* masks have not been shown in museums in the last thirty years and the fact that this is occurring now demonstrates a shift in the relationship between museums and First Nations. What made the display of this mask possible, notes journalist Kevin Griffin, is that the North Vancouver Museum "brought aboriginal people into the decision-making process." Through this process it was determined that the mask was safe to display since it had not been danced or used in ceremony. This kind of informed and sustained relationship is at the center of efforts to make archaeology and museums more accessible to, representative of, and beneficial to Indigenous peoples.

The *sxwayxway* exhibit is an example of how Indigenous concerns are successfully being addressed through recognition of and respect for cross-cultural differences regarding heritage concerns, cultural authority, and identity. It thus provides an apt opening to addressing Barbara Little's request to write on 'how have practicing archaeologists and museologists helped US and Canadian First Peoples do their own archaeology and museology.' This is a formidable topic, with so much happening in the last decade alone that even a book-length treatment would be hard pressed to do it justice. We've therefore chosen to focus on select examples of innovative collaborative efforts that contribute to Indigenous peoples in North America achieving their goals and benefitting from new modes of archaeological practice and museum initiatives.[1]

We begin with a brief historical review of archaeological and museum-based projects or initiatives that directly involved Indigenous peoples. Building on this, we then provide examples of archaeological and museum endeavours that benefit Indigenous peoples (as well as others). We reiterate here that this is illustrative, not exhaustive, and also emphasize that our division of these examples is somewhat arbitrary and increasingly difficult to recognize or justify, since collaborations with Indigenous peoples have increasingly underscored the need to look at heritage matters as a whole.

Over the last twenty years there have been significant developments within archaeology as a result of greater integration of, or response to, Indigenous peoples and other descendant communities. To be sure, there was very early involvement of First Nations in archaeology. Arthur C. Parker, himself Seneca, was the first President of the Society for American Archaeology and more famously, the collaboration between George Hunt and Franz Boas, but these were rare instances. Generally, the role of Indigenous people in anthropological endeavors was as informants, guides, and labourers, with little direct benefit flowing to their communities (Hollowell and Nicholas 2009).

However, by the 1970s archaeologists, anthropologists, and museologists began to react and to address Indigenous concerns in a sustained manner in response to the increasing politicalization and cultural revitalization efforts of Native Americans (e.g. Deloria 1969), the passage of various legislative acts (such as the American Indian Religious Freedom Act of 1978), and an emerging awareness within the discipline of the political and intellectual challenges confronting anthropology (e.g. Hymes 1974). Archaeology and museums were increasingly seen as a colonial enterprise at this time. This view fed a 'crisis of representation', precipitated by the critiques and protests of Indigenous peoples who saw museums presenting their cultures without their input and often in conflict with their belief systems (Cooper 2008). For North American museums, the most significant changes came about in the late 1980s and early 1990s when formal policies in the form of the Native American Graves Protection and Repatriation Act (NAGPRA) in the United States and the Assembly of First Nations/Canadian Museum *Association's Task Force Report* in Canada – outlined the rights of Indigenous peoples over decisions made about their heritage and demonstrated a need for consultation. Repatriation of human remains, burial items, and sacred and communal objects to communities, as well as the removal of culturally sensitive material from public view, was also an important part of this movement.

In response to these events, what followed was a series of important developments worldwide that would open a new chapter in the relations between Indigenous peoples and archaeologists. In North America, pioneer initiatives, such as the Zuni Archaeology Program, established in 1975, illustrated what a tribal-based heritage program could achieve. A variety of post-secondary education programs and training opportunities provided interested Indigenous youth and others with the means to obtain training and provide capacity in their communities. And such organizations as the Society for American Archaeology and the Canadian Archaeological Association called for, and supported, greater participation of Indigenous peoples in the discipline.[2]

These efforts have yielded many benefits to Indigenous peoples, including a greater involvement in issues affecting their heritage. This is aided today by an impressive number of those who are practicing or even teaching archaeology and related fields (Nicholas 2010), or whose knowledge of archaeology is assisting them in their administrative duties as council members, for example. Benefits also flow from First Nations developed and operated heritage programs and cultural centers, whose primary mandate is to serve community needs, but also welcome the public (e.g. Ziibiwing Center of Anishinabe Culture and Lifeways in Michigan).[3] In a similar vein, the Mashantucket Pequot Museum and Research Center in Connecticut[4] not only has a substantial public education program but also a very active archaeology program headed by Kevin McBride. Large, public institutions, such as the Canadian Museum of Civilization in Ottawa and the National Museum of the American Indian in Washington DC, have also provided a venue for Indigenous peoples to tell their own stories through collaborative exhibits.

At the same time, non-Indigenous practitioners have benefited substantially from a deeper and more complete understanding of other ways of seeing "the past," and the different ways that tangible and intangible heritage are treated in non-Western settings. What has emerged from both individual and collaborative efforts are new models of archaeological practice (Dowdall and Parish 2003); of museum acquisition, display, and curation, such as virtual exhibits (e.g. Srinivasan et al. 2010); and of knowledge creation and dissemination (e.g., Sleeper-Smith 2009).

As a result of these efforts, archaeological and museological practice today is far more inclusive and accommodating than ever before. Nonetheless, a variety of topics, issues, and challenges are on the agenda for the coming decade that relate to, amongst other things:

- substantial inequalities in heritage management and benefit flow;
- viewing heritage as a living and dynamic, rather than as a static, artifact-oriented representation of the past;
- honoring and acknowledging different ways of interpreting and talking about the past;
- achieving a more holistic study of culture (disrupting the academic silos that separate archaeology, anthropology, history, ethnology, and museum studies; and
- more equitable modes of information sharing and protection that recognize and respect Indigenous cultural values.

The benefits of collaborative archaeology

Moving beyond the generally improved relationship that Indigenous peoples today have with the discipline of archaeology, we offer some examples of innovative studies to demonstrate that new research collaborations stand to enhance, rather than restrict the research process, thus increasing the benefits of archaeology to descendant communities.

Exemplary approaches to archaeological practice that directly benefit communities are found in the efforts of TJ Ferguson and Chip Colwell-Chanthaphonh, both individually and together. One example must suffice. *History is in the Land: Multivocal Tribal Traditions in Arizona's San Pedro Valley* (2006) focuses on a collaboration between the Hopi, San Carlos Apache, Tohono O'odham, and Zuni that shifts the frame of reference of heritage "as things" to heritage "as relationships." In doing so, archaeological materials and information become part of a wider sphere of cultural heritage, along with ethnohistory and other ways of knowing. Heritage values and stewardship strategies are thus revealed and contextualized by Indigenous knowledge and the landscape itself. The result is a history that emphasizes the continued connections of people to the land and to those who came before: As Micah Lomaomvaya states in that volume (p. 249), "Our interpretations are based on experience, not hypotheses. That's why this continuity is so important to us. To us it reaffirms ties to the land—it's one element of our identity, who we are."

Issues of reburial and repatriation have long been contentious, representing a collision of politics, science, and traditional beliefs. While the passage of NAGPRA in the United States marked a watershed moment in North America for archaeology (and museums), it was not the end of the world as many archaeologists feared at the time. In fact, some would argue that it forced a long-overdue dialogue that has benefitted both descendant communities and archaeology itself. What has received far too little attention is that First Nations across North America have been turning to archaeology to provide them with information on ancestral remains prior to reburial, including radiocarbon dating and DNA studies (see Nicholas et al. 2008). In addition to First Nations archaeologists and community members becoming directly involved in the recovery and analysis of ancestral remains, new research projects are underway to negotiate some of the difficult questions associated with recovery and analysis, knowledge production and intellectual property associated with these remains.

An example of this is the "Journey Home Project," which involves the repatriation of ancestral remains from the University of British Columbia's Laboratory of Archaeology (LOA) to the Stó:lō Nation/Tribal Council of southwestern British Columbia, Canada. This collaboration includes Susan Rowley (LOA), David Schaepe, and Sonny McHalsie (Stó:lō Research and Resource Management Centre) working with the Stó:lō House of Respect Caretaking Committee as cultural advisors in this dialogue. For the Stó:lō, knowing about the life histories and antiquity of these ancestors informs the repatriation process. This community-initiated project is addressing questions central to the Stó:lō's relationship with both their ancestors and the LOA, and seeks aims to provide guidelines for generating knowledge within a mutually acceptable framework of authority, control, and use. The initiative is a component of the "Intellectual Property Issues in Cultural Heritage (IPinCH) project."[5]

One final example of the benefits of archaeology concerns initiatives that help to connect elders with youth, while also generating new and useful knowledge about the past. The "Arviat Archaeology and Oral History Project" (Lyons et al. 2010) was a collaborative project between Inuit elders and community historians from Arviat (in Nunavut, northern Canada) and archaeologists. The project was conceived and jointly developed to provide new archaeological information but more important was to integrate this with existing community histories to make it meaningful. What was especially important to the participating Elders was connecting with Inuit youth—a theme highlighted in many community-based archaeology programs in northern Canada. They wanted "to educate their young people to think, learn, and thrive in an Inuit way. They are weaving a thread of Inuit knowledge through past, present, and future generations that makes the land and histories of their forebears comprehensible and useable to their children and grandchildren, who will inherit them" (Lyons et al. 2010: 21).

The benefits of collaborative museology

While archaeological practice involves researcher/excavators and community partners, the public forms a third stakeholder community with respect to museums. The public nature of these spaces accounts for their focus as sites of both resistance and of collaboration. Despite the calls for collaborative methodologies and their mention in ethical guidelines,[6] museum curators and staff have not always been sure about the shape that collaborative museology should take and how Indigenous voices might be included in museum displays (Ames 2004; Shannon 2009). On a wider scale, there is a need to redress museums' role in colonial programs, which imagined Indigenous peoples and their cultural heritage as stuck in the past and irrelevant to contemporary cultural practices.

An innovative example of collaboration and re-contextualizing museum objects is the Reciprocal Research Network (RRN), a project co-developed by the Musqueam Indian Band, the Stó:lō Nation/Tribal Council, the U'mista Cultural Society and the Museum of Anthropology.[7] The RRN is a virtual space where researchers, community members, and museum professionals can collaborate on research and projects concerning the cultural heritage of the Northwest Coast of British Columbia. The website features the collections of sixteen institutions who have uploaded collections' images and information so that they can be accessed from anywhere using the World Wide Web. This enables rural First Nations community members to access information about collections held in museums and cultural centers around the world and to play an important role in enriching understanding about them. The information provided by community members and researchers about objects also feeds back into institutional databases and enriches the information available to visitors to the brick-and-mortar institutions, making the effects of reciprocal research wider than the RRN project. As the website states, "the RRN is groundbreaking in facilitating communication and fostering lasting relationships between originating communities and institutions around the world."[8]

In 2007, the Department of Anthropology of the Denver Museum of Nature and Science launched a program to research their entire collection more fully (Colwell-Chanthaphonh et al. 2010). In order to do this in an ethical way, the

Indigenous Inclusiveness Initiative was launched as a vital part of this program. The intended purpose of this program is to include Native American perspectives and voices in the museum and to cultivate partnerships that create better and more holistic understandings of Native American culture and history in general, and the Denver Museum collection specifically. Several programs that fall under this initiative are aimed at supporting aboriginal people with training and capacity building: a Visiting Indigenous Fellowship Program; Native American Science Scholarships for college students; Native American science internships; and a Native American Science Career Day.[9] The lofty goal of the Denver Museum is to have the "best understood, and most ethically cared for anthropology collection in North America," and they understand that this is realizable only through collaboration and partnership with their stakeholder communities.

The Makah Cultural Center in Washington State is a good example of an Indigenous-run institution that participates in both museology and archaeology. The Makah Indian Tribe created this museum on their reservation after undertaking a collaborative archaeological project at Ozette as a place to store and display material culture recovered in the project. The museum is a collaborative venture with non-Makah researchers, with the Makah retaining control over project approval. While Western knowledge and expertise is employed by the Makah center, tribal worldviews and sensibilities are reflected in the way collections are stored, sorted, and labeled. Rather than sorting objects according to archaeological or traditional museum categories, the community decided to sort the objects by ownership according to household, thus enacting contemporary cultural practices. These sorting methods have enriched understanding of both the objects in the collection and on Makah language and ways of understanding the world (Bowechop and Erikson 2005). This integration of archaeology, language, education, place-name research, and the like within Indigenous-run museums is quite common and reflects the seamless relationship of these aspects of life and culture in Indigenous communities.

Conclusions

In recent decades, archaeologists and museologists have sought to make the work they do, and their use of other peoples' cultural heritage, more meaningful to and respectful of descendant communities. The challenges are substantial because of the historical legacy that has so deeply affected their lives, and has been exacerbated by the difficulties of cross-cultural communication.

What Indigenous peoples want more than anything else is to have the right to be involved in the management and presentation of *their* past and culture. Moving beyond "working together," new collaborations are shifting the focus from research *results* to the research *process*. Indigenous peoples' roles as full and equal partners in collaborations, or as lead developers, ensures that they benefit from research on their heritage. As the examples provided here demonstrate, this can serve to enhance, not constrain, the research process.

It is only fitting to end by noting the theme of the forthcoming World Archaeological Intercongress[10]—"Indigenous Peoples and Museums: Unwrapping

Postscript

A few days after this piece was submitted for publication, the *sxwayxway* mask was removed from the North Vancouver exhibit due to Squamish community feedback. According to Deborah Jacobs, head of education for the Squamish, the coverage in the *Vancouver Sun* was alarming for some members of the community. Although she acknowledged that the article itself was balanced, community members reacted to the front-page photo of the mask, which did not identify it as three-quarter replica that had not been danced. The mask was removed in a ceremony overseen by a Squamish Elder. (Griffin, Kevin, 2011, Squamish remove replica mask from Hurley Exhibit; community reacts after images in *Sun* story cause concern. *Vancouver Sun*, 27 January.)

Error: our original article lists the Griffin coverage in the *Sun* as being Jan 22, 2010, when it should be 2011.

Notes

1. Our approach is informed by our respective experiences and interests in overlapping realms of applied anthropology: Carr-Locke, with community archaeology and involvement in museum projects, and Nicholas, with Indigenous archaeology and collaborative research practices.
2. This has taken various forms, such as the SAA's Native American Scholarships (http://saa.org/AbouttheSociety/Awards/SAANativeAmericanScholarships/tabid/163/Default.aspx), and the CAA's Statement of Principles for Ethical Conduct Pertaining to Aboriginal Peoples (http://canadianarchaeology.com/caa/node/901).
3. www.sagchip.org/ziibiwing/
4. www.pequotmuseum.org/
5. IPinCh is an international consortium of over 50 scholars and 25 partner communities and organizations that is investigating how and why concerns and harms about intellectual property emerge, and how best can they be avoided or resolved (www.sfu.ca/ipinch). One component of this seven-year project is a set of 15 community-based initiatives that investigate local heritage at ground level, which are co-developed with Indigenous communities.
6. Several recent publications provide extensive examples of more ethical and effective research methodologies (e.g. Denzin et al. 2008; Lydon and Rizvi 2010).
7. www.moa.ubc.ca/RRN
8. www.rrnpilot.org
9. The Museum has been able to offer three to five scholarships each year, and has secured funding for three internships each year for the next ten years (Chip Colwell Chanthaphonh, pers. comm.).
10. June 22–25, 2011, in Indianapolis, Indiana. For information: http://wacmuseums.info/

References

Ames, M. (2003) How to decorate a house: the renegotiation of cultural representations at the University of British Columbia Museum of Anthropology. In: L. Peers and A.K. Brown (eds.), *Museums and Source Communities*. London and New York: Routledge, pp. 171–80.

Bowechop, J. and Pierce Erikson, P. (2005) Forging indigenous methodologies on Cape Flattery: the Makah Museum as a centre for collaborative research. *American Indian Quarterly*, 29(1–2): 263–73.

Colwell-Chanthapohonh, C., Nash, S.E., and Holen, S.R. (2010) *Crossroads of Culture: Anthropology Collections at the Denver Museum of Nature and Science*. Boulder: University Press of Colorado.

Cooper, K.C. (2008) *Spirited Encounters: American Indians Protest Museum Policies and Practices*. Lanham, Maryland: AltaMira Press.

Deloria, V. Jr. (1969) *Custer Died for Your Sins: An Indian Manifesto*. Norman: University of Oklahoma Press.

Denzin, N.K., Lincoln, Y.S., and Tuhawi Smith, L. eds. (2008) *Handbook of Critical and Indigenous Methodologies*. Thousand Oaks, CA: Sage.

Dowdall, K. and Parrish, O. (2003) A meaningful disturbance of the earth. *Journal of Social Archaeology*, 3(1): 99–113.

Ferguson, T.J. and Colwell-Chanthaphonh, C. (2006) *History is in the Land: Multivocal Tribal Traditions in Arizona's San Pedro Valley*. Tucson: University of Arizona Press.

Griffin, K. (2010) Rarely seen artworks on display: North Vancouver Museum exhibits spiritually significant works from the Squamish First Nation. *Vancouver Sun*, 22 January.

Hollowell, J. and Nicholas, G.P. (2008) A critical assessment of uses of ethnography in archaeology. In: Q. Castenada and C. Matthews (eds.), *Ethnographic Archaeologies: Reflections on Stakeholders and Archaeological Practices*. Lanham, Maryland: AltaMira Press, pp. 63–94.

Lydon, J. and Rizvi, U. (2010) *Handbook of Postcolonial Archaeology*. Walnut Creek, CA: Left Coast Press.

Lyons, N., Dawson, P. Walls, M., Uluadluak, D., Angalik, L., Kalluak, M., Kigusiutuak, P., Kiniksi, L., Karetak, J., and Suluk, L. (2010) Person, place, memory, thing: how Inuit elders are informing archaeological practice in the Canadian North. *Canadian Journal of Archaeology*, 34(1): 1–31.

Nicholas, G.P. (2008) Native peoples and archaeology. In: D. Pearsall (ed.), *Encyclopedia of Archaeology, Vol. 3*. Oxford: Elsevier, pp. 1660–69.

——ed. (2010) *Being and Becoming Indigenous Archaeologists*. Walnut Creek, CA: Left Coast Press.

Nicholas, G.P., Jules, J., and Dan, C. (2008) Moving beyond Kennewick: alternative Native American perspectives on bioarchaeological data and intellectual property rights. In: H. Burke, C. Smith, D. Lippert, J. Watkins, and L. Zimmerman (eds.), *Kennewick Man: Perspectives on the Ancient One*. Walnut Creek, CA: Left Coast Press, pp. 233–43.

Shannon, J. (2009) The construction of Native voice at the National Museum of the American Indian. In: S. Sleeper Smith (ed.), *Contesting Knowledge: Museums and Indigenous Perspectives*. Lincoln and London: University of Nebraska Press, pp. 218–47.

Sleeper-Smith, S. ed. (2009) *Contesting Knowledge: Museums and Indigenous Perspectives.* Lincoln and London: University of Nebraska Press.

Srinivasan, R., Becvar, K., Boast, R., and Enote, J. (2010) Diverse knowledges and contact zones within the digital museum. *Science, Technology, and Human Values,* 35(5): 735–68.

Conversations about the production of archaeological knowledge and community museums at Chunchucmil and Kochol, Yucatán, México

Traci Ardren

In the mid-1980s, the noted Mexican anthropologist Guillermo Bonfil Batalla wrote that, while every Mexican schoolchild knew something about pre-colonial periods, and was aware of the great archaeological monuments that serve as modern national symbols, the glorious prehistoric past was experienced as something dead, something apart from themselves, something connected by territory but little else (Bonfil Batalla 1996: 3). Bonfil was writing *México Profundo*, a complex analysis of modern Mexican culture, where, in Bonfil's own words, the imaginary dominant Western culture continues to confront and suppress the *profundo*, or large, resources of indigenous Mesoamerican culture, which continue to reside and survive in most Mexicans. Part of this struggle has been the appropriation of the past, where ancient monuments and archaeological sites have been made into the history of Mexicans instead of the history of the indigenous population of México. This is particularly striking to Bonfil in the National Museum of Anthropology in México City, where the spatial design of the museum emphasizes the prehistory of México on the ground floor and all references and exhibits having to do with indigenous culture are segregated to the second floor. Bonfil lays the responsibility in the lap of his "imaginary México," the Western-trained intellectuals more likely to speak French than an indigenous language, as well as the school of *indigenismo* led by Manuel Gamio, a colleague of Franz Boas, who simultaneously exalted the "positive values" of Indian cultures yet acknowledged the necessity of a homogeneous society to forge a new nation (Bonfil Batalla 1996: 116). Gamio advocated Indianizing the dominant culture to a certain degree while Westernizing the Indians. One outgrowth of this philosophy was the education of all children in México in its "national" history, one that merged the accomplishments of native states like the Maya and Olmec with the

Spanish colonial period. Unique Indian cultures were gradually replaced with the "superior" national culture. It is not surprising, then, that schoolchildren who visit the national museum feel disconnected from the accomplishments of their ancestors, even to the point of seeing no connection between the dead past and the living present. Bonfil's prescient observations foreshadow a current debate within the field of archaeology, a debate framed by issues diverse from those with which Bonfil was concerned, but a debate which is illuminated by Bonfil's honest explanation of the uses to which archaeological data were put by those involved in modern nation building in México. One question Bonfil did not ask, but which is relevant here, is: what responsibility do archaeologists have when children, especially indigenous children, feel separated from their past?

This paper chronicles a shift in research priorities as a result of sustained interaction with members of the local communities in which a Maya archaeological site is located. Over the last five years the Pakbeh Regional Economy Program, an archaeological project directed by academic archaeologists Dr Bruce Dahlin of Howard University and myself with a staff of several graduate students from universities in the United States, Europe, and México, has shifted the research focus from a clearly outlined processual program concerning the ethnic nature of an ancient trading enclave, to a collaborative plan of research and development that uses academic archaeological inquiry as a foundation from which to generate tourism within the local communities. Open dialogue with interested community members about the archaeological knowledge generated by academic research, as well as local priorities for development, has been the key component in the evolution of a community-based methodology. Our priorities as directors have shifted, our research has been adjusted accordingly, and we find ourselves engaged in ongoing discussions with community members and other academics about how archaeology is to be done in the twenty-first century (Stone and MacKenzie 1990; Patterson 1995; Ferguson 1996; Swidler et al. 1997; Kehoe 1998; Watkins et al. 2000; Gosden 2001).

Initial research goals at Chunchucmil

The original research strategy at Chunchucmil addressed a current concern with evidence for ethnicity in the archaeological record (e.g. Dahlin and Ardren 2002; Bawden 1993; Blanton and Feinman 1984; Spence 1996). Chunchucmil is a major, Classic Maya urban center near the Gulf of Mexico coast in north-western Yucatán (Ardren 1999). Although demographically large, with 16 square kilometers of settlement, Chunchucmil is located in one of the poorest regions in Mesoamerica for agriculture (Vlcek et al. 1978). The north-western peninsula has an unpredictable seasonal rain cycle with an annual deficit. Soil is another limiting factor, with up to 80 per cent of the landscape having thin to no soil—50 per cent of the landscape is bare bedrock—and, where soils do exist today, they have largely developed over the last 1,000 years since urban abandonment (Farrell et al. 1996). Palaeo-ecological analyses demonstrate that conditions were no better in the past, and research has proceeded from the hypothesis that an urban population of 20–30,000 must have been fed with imported maize (Beach 1998).

The built environment of Chunchucmil exhibits a number of unique features that set it apart from most other Classic Maya centers of its size: streets, stone fences, a central barricade, a relative lack of sculptural monuments and, most fundamentally, a decentralized monumental core (Magnoni 1995; Dahlin 2000; Hutson et al. in press). Chunchucmil's uniqueness is also reflected in its strategic location with respect to maritime trade routes and salt flats, regional subsistence patterns, and artifacts (Dahlin et al. 1998). The original research program was designed to test the hypothesis that the deviations Chunchucmil demonstrated were due to its economic organization as an ancient trade center. Excavations and testing were designed to establish the degree to which economic factors organized Chunchucmil's economic, political, social, and religious life.

Following Michael Spence and others, we have identified a list of traits by which to identify ethnic enclaves, realizing that how ethnic groups choose to display ethnic traits can appear arbitrary until large-scale patterns are distinguished (Spence 1996). Spence suggests that ethnic markers will appear in certain central institutions, such as the arrangement of ritual space, artifacts—especially the style of serving or domestic vessels, as well as their source of origin, and skeletal traits and/or mortuary practices that can be distinctive. We agree with Garth Bawden and others that ethnic markers are primarily communication mechanisms, used by a community of members to manifest an identity to others (Bawden 1993: 43). As such, the material record can carry the physical expression of certain structural components of a society.

There is some architectural evidence for ethnic enclaves at Chunchucmil. A cluster of modest platforms east of the central area has the only known Puuc style masonry represented at the site, and may be an architectural signature of ethnic identity. Approximately 12 kilometers to the north and 20 kilometers to the east, the Puuc established large cities dominated by their distinctive architectural style. One working hypothesis is that this cluster at Chunchucmil represents an attempt by the Puuc to establish a presence and perhaps a central role in the trade economy of Late Classic Chunchucmil during a time when hostile forces were in control of the northern and eastern coasts of Yucatán.

Another indication of non-local influence on the architectural record emerged in recent excavations. In a residential group within the central urban zone, a 3-meter high platform was built in a typically central Mexican architectural style known as the talud-tablero. The presence of this architectural form in the Maya area has usually been interpreted as an indication of extensive influence, especially economic and military, emanating from the early urban capital of Teotihuacan upon all of Mesoamerica during the Early Classic period (Marquina 1964; Heyden and Gendrop 1980; Giddens 1995; Blackmore and Ardren 2002). Other examples of talud-tablero-style architecture are found at Chunchucmil's nearest urban neighbour, the ancient capital of Oxkintok, where the style has been interpreted as an indication that the political and economic life of this city was directly tied to non-local, central Mexican, power (Ricardo Velasquez personal communication 2000).

Midden testing at modest platform groups has already demonstrated a relatively high level of material wealth at all levels of Chunchucmil society (Hutson 2000). Consistent with excavations at the port site of Punta Canbalam on the coast, Chunchucmil middens have yielded a high percentage of foreign ceramics from the central Gulf coast region, jade and obsidian from the highlands, chert from the coast of Belize, and significant amounts of marine shell ornaments (Stanton et al. 2000).

The stone walls that surround the majority of house lots at Chunchucmil suggest either a need to enforce local cultural norms regarding the use of public versus private space or a heightened concern for the use value of land. Though Maya house lots are not the same as enclosed fields, soil testing has determined that kitchen gardens were certainly grown in the enclosed households at the site (Beach 1998). Given the poor nature of the soils for subsistence plants such as corn, the house lots may have been dedicated to market-oriented crops such as cotton or achiote, a native dye and condiment (Watanabe 2000). Artifactual patterning from excavations in non-mounded areas of the house lots indicates an intensive use of house-lot areas for processing raw materials such as shell and obsidian. Over a thousand obsidian fragments were recovered from less than 2 square meters of fill off a small platform in a residential area (Hutson 2000). A heightened commercialism of the residential realm would be consistent with certain trade-center models.

Given an environment that is severely limited in agricultural potential, the modern inhabitants of the land around the ruins have diversified their economic strategies just as the ancients did. Although the current population of the area is much smaller than what has been projected for ancient times, the ruins of Chunchucmil are split between five separate *ejidos*, or modern land grant communities, that date from the dissolution of large hacienda landholdings after the Mexican revolution (Figure 39.1). Each of these communities is quite distinct; their economic bases are very different and thus the lifestyles and values of their citizens are different. The modern village of Chunchucmil is largely supported by wage labour in the nearby state capital of Mérida. The village of Kochol is primarily agricultural, with farmers shifting from traditional crops, such as maize, to cash crops like *habanero* peppers and papayas. Coahuila and San Mateo are small agricultural communities with less active use of their *ejido* lands within the site boundaries, while Halacho is a county seat some distance from the ruins, which uses land for pasturage of range cattle. In each *ejido*, the majority of the population is ethnically Yucatec, but there are long-standing historical and cultural conflicts between the communities, which often lead to mutual mistrust. The Pakbeh Project has dealt primarily with the members of Chunchucmil and Kochol, as these two communities control the land on which the majority of archaeological research has taken place.

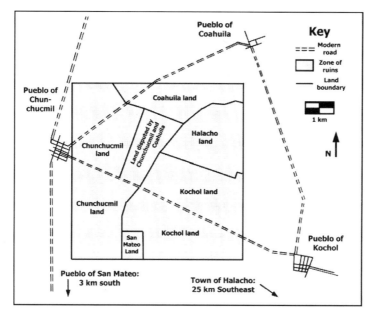

Figure 39.1 Division of archaeological ruins into five modern community boundaries. Illustration by Scott Hutson.

Tourism and archaeology in the Maya world

The overarching power and influence of tourism in México is evident to anyone conducting archaeological research in Yucatán. Over the last twenty years, Pakbeh staff members, Mexican archaeologists, and Yucatec Maya communities have all witnessed the dramatic expansion of tourism on the peninsula. Many studies have documented the growing role of tourism in the Mexican economy: it is currently the third largest national industry, the main arena of overseas investment and the second largest employer after agriculture (Austin 1994; Clancy 1999). Because México has assumed a "statist" approach to its tourism economy, where the federal government has a direct hand in planning, funding, and promoting tourism as a means to fund regional development, tremendous changes have occurred in Yucatán as a result of the boom in tourism since the 1960s when FONATUR, the state tourism ministry, was created (Van Den Berghe 1994; Clancy 1999). The Mexican government has relied so heavily upon foreign tourism that they have demonstrated a willingness to pursue tourism plans despite opposition from local groups, or at the very least with minimal local involvement (Long 1991). Members of small Yucatec communities have experienced tourism as something imposed by the state, not something initiated on a local level. Paradoxically this is an industry based in large part on Maya cultural heritage, albeit in a heavily commercialized form (Brown 1999). Despite its intrusion into people's lives, tourism on the peninsula is generally desired because it is seen as one of the primary ways in which to receive infrastructural support from the government. Roads are paved when tour buses demand it, new electrical lines are run when ecotourism resorts are built in rural areas.

Despite the improvements in infrastructure, the economic benefits of this $6.4 billion/year industry are small for most Maya communities. Hotel industry ownership and control is confined to large-scale Mexican chains and foreign investors (Clancy 1999), while electrical and telecommunications service is consistently targeted to places where large numbers of tourists are expected, like the Maya Riviera/Cancún-Tulum corridor (Brown 1999). Objective evaluation of the tourism industry in México leaves no doubt that it benefits primarily multinational corporations (Clancy 1999). A small but growing nature or sustainable tourism industry holds the promise of greater local control (Savage 1993).

An awareness of the economic potential of tourism existed in Chunchucmil and Kochol prior to the commencement of archaeological research at the site. These villages are literally in the shadow of Uxmal, the third most commonly visited site on the peninsula, and, although most villagers have not been to Uxmal, it holds a place of meaning or significance in their lives as a major tourism center. Tourism is so pervasive in Yucatán, that few communities would deny the attraction of an archaeological project because the potential economic benefits are so obvious to *campesinos* trying to support themselves in a changing world where cash is needed for children who want Nikes, but also for fertilizers to make a semi-agricultural lifestyle viable (Re Cruz 1996). Señora Gomez, a staff member at one of the few locally operated archaeological museums in nearby Hecelchakan, emphatically stated that as archaeologists we should start a local museum in Chunchucmil, "para avanzar con turismo el pueblo [so the village could move forward through tourism]."

The evolution of a dialogue about archaeological research

The initial receptivity on the part of Chunchucmil and Kochol village leaders to a foreign-run archaeological project at their ruins was due in large part to the wages we would pay to excavation assistants. A small number of local leaders, especially the schoolteachers from both villages, Gualberto Tzuc Mena and Fernando Rodriguez, believed in the potential for excavations to draw tourists to the site. At the outset of archaeological research, there was little interest expressed in excavation as a way to reveal the ancient history of the villagers or their ancestors. Unlike certain areas of the Yucatán peninsula, here there are no remaining traditional *h'men* (shaman) in any of the villages near the ruins of Chunchucmil. These specialized keepers of traditional knowledge are key individuals within Yucatec villages for the dissemination of stories about the ruins as powerful places where spirits must be appeased and ancestors honored (Ardren 1991; Brown 1999; Freidel et al. 1993). Thus, as a generalization, it might be fair to say that members of the local communities near the ancient site of Chunchucmil saw the ruins as agricultural land, where contested boundaries have caused conflict between the communities, much more than they saw the area as a historical or cultural resource. Cultural anthropologist Lisa Breglia is currently conducting research on the changing attitudes of locals toward the archaeological ruins.

The enthusiasm expressed by Pakbeh staff members about the site as the remains of an ancient trading city with royalty and historical-political interconnections to other ancient Maya cities was soon communicated to locals employed by the project to work on excavations at the site. The archaeological messages of cultural inheritance and empowerment at first stood in stark contrast to the messages from local workmen of fear and anxiety that we would take away the site or facilitate the Mexican government taking away the site. At a formal meeting between the project and the men of Kochol in 1999, the second year of excavations, many local individuals challenged project members with the accusation, "Ustedes son los gringos que siempre ganan de la tierra de nosotros [you are the outsiders who always profit from our land]." While certain immediate fears were ameliorated by providing specific information about our inability to take away the land, indeed our dependence upon them for permission to work, as well as our requirement as foreigners to abide by Mexican federal and state laws which mandate removing archaeological materials to state facilities, it also became clear that facilitating access to the processes of archaeological research, and especially to the results, would be essential to building a relationship of trust and mutual collaboration.

Through dialogues with village elders and regular evening meetings of project members and interested community members, we have continued this dialogue about what happens on an archaeological project and who ultimately benefits. In these conversations a crucial element is the willingness of some community members to speak up about the value they see in archaeological research; thus the conversations abandon the traditional power dynamic of academic authority in favour of a more balanced dialogue in which everyone present is entitled to express an opinion. Speaking to other villagers in a video about the archaeological project, Gualberto Tzuc Mena, the Chunchucmil village schoolteacher and an historian of local history, said:

> Para mi, este proyecto que está realizado por mis compañeros que vinieron de los Estados Unidos, ha sido de muy suma importancia para.... Kochol y Chunchucmil ya que ha beneficiado a los campesinos dandoles remedios para tener un poco de recursos económicos para sustentar sus familias ... y realmente conocer la historía de Chunchucmil, de los antiguos mayas, para mi, es de suma importancia. [To me, this project organized by my co-workers from the United States is very important. It has already given the people of the villages a chance to earn some extra wages to help support their families, and to really know the history of the archaeological site of Chunchucmil and the ancient Maya. To me, this is really important.]

The project, including Gualberto in his capacity as laboratory manager, encourages locals to handle and explore certain archaeological materials, such as whole ceramic vessels, before they are removed to the state museum of archaeology. While artifacts are compelling, the sharing of archaeological knowledge produced by excavation is more fundamental to this exchange, and, when artifacts are mutually examined by staff members and community members, a profound sense of mutual trust and respect is fostered. Many members of the Pakbeh Project have given presentations to the communities on their research and encouraged questions, reactions, or alternative interpretations from the audience. Permanent poster exhibits with photographs, maps, and text have regularly been produced and donated to local community centers to encourage access to the information for those who are unable to attend our presentations.

In 1999, the project produced a short video expressly for the local communities in which basic concepts of excavation were explained and demonstrated by local leaders who work with the project. Narrated in Spanish and Yucatec Maya, the video was very popular and prompted new questions about archaeological research from individuals who had not had any significant previous associations with the project such as teenagers and women. After Gualberto Tzuc Mena showed the video to his elementary students, he suggested we provide tours of the excavations for kids from both villages. Each season, first to fifth graders are given a morning to crawl up the pyramids and ask questions about ceramics, obsidian, and the other materials recovered that day. These are fine opportunities for the local community members who work with the project as excavation assistants to explain to children from Kochol and Chunchucmil, often using their first language, Yucatec Maya, what they have found in excavations as well as why kids should be interested in archaeology. After one visit, the Secretariat of the *ejido* of Kochol, Marcelino Cahuich, told me:

> La arqueología es bonita y más gente debe aprender sobre la arqueología ... hay mucha gente en Kochol, y no todos tienen interés en este trabajo, pero algunos sí. Este programa de visitas de alumnos esta buena porqué los alumnos van a sus casas y hablan con sus familias sobre las cosas que han visto, hablan mucho, y ahora más gente están preguntando sobre la arqueología y las que cosas estamos buscando. [Archaeology is a good thing and more people from the village should know about it ... there are many people in Kochol and not all of them are interested in archaeology, but many are. This program of visits by schoolchildren is good, because the kids go home and talk about what they have seen, they talk a lot, and now more people are interested in archaeology and what we are finding.]

In addition to the maintenance of exchanges about what happens on site and what it means to all interested parties, our research and excavation strategies have been shaped by ongoing dialogue between village elders and members of the archaeological project about what would attract paying visitors to the site. With many monumental centers already open to the public in the immediate region, and a relative lack of carved monuments or visible monumental architecture at Chunchucmil, we have agreed that excavation and consolidation of household groups might pose the best chance of attracting the interested public. To date there are no Maya tourist sites that demonstrate the experience of the majority of ancient Maya, those who lived in modest residential platform groups in and around the monumental pyramids, palaces, and ball courts of the royalty. Members of Kochol first commented on the similarity they saw between the ancient house mounds dug up on site and the dimensions and orientations of their own homes. They joked about moving into the newly reconstructed platform groups, where it would be quieter and cooler than in their own homes.

A suggestion from the Pakbeh staff to form a community museum around the conception of a living museum, where members of Kochol would, on a rotational basis, spend time "living" in one or more of the reconstructed residential groups has been met with preliminary endorsement from Marcelino Cahuich, the Secretariat of the *ejido* of Kochol, and other community members interested in developing tourism at the site. When I suggested a garden of native plants could be nurtured, Galdino Canul, the Mayor of the *ejido* of Kochol, suggested papaya trees, since they are the economic backbone of modern Kochol. Everyone was in agreement that pre-contact turkeys, chillies, and corn could easily be raised and various types of leather worked; however, Marcelino and other leaders were less sure that anyone in the area still had the skills to spin and weave native cotton or knap obsidian. Marcelino suggested nearby potters who still mine clay and create coil-based pots be brought to teach interested members of Kochol. Other excavation assistants from Kochol have offered to demonstrate native beekeeping, roof thatching, and medicinal plant tending. A woman's group, "Promotores de Salud" (Health Advocates), led by Señora Irma, the nurse from Kochol, was very enthusiastic about the proposed living museum, and offered their skills as experts in household maintenance. Clearly the concept will evolve given the interests of Kochol citizens to enliven the archaeological knowledge that provides a base, but only the barest of backbones, for a thoroughly modern exploration of an ancient Maya household. The Kochol community museum will become another ongoing and evolving experience through which members of the local community and staff archaeologists can share in the production of archaeological knowledge.

One of the most common themes to emerge in the conversations between Pakbeh archaeologists and locals is the explanation and translation of the concept of tourism. While most members of Kochol and Chunchucmil are aware of the broadest outlines of the tourism economy, and its importance in bringing cash into small communities, they have a limited concept of who tourists are or what they might pay money to see. Some conversations leave little doubt that workers on the site see tourists as a group of people who are always travelling, for whom travelling is a way of life. Descriptions of tourists by locals often utilize an ethnic metaphor: there are Yucatecans, Mexicans, Cubans, gringos, and *turistas*. Thus, while the Pakbeh staff has provided information about the modern process of tourism, as we understand and experience it, we have also learned a great deal about the distance that exists between modern Yucatec Maya and even the best-intentioned tourists who pass through the area. Conversations about the living museum have thus included comments by all parties that this attraction would be different from many others, because tourists and locals would interact, learn about each other; perhaps even get to know one another a bit. The scale of the living museum appeals to all parties as a departure from the highly compartmentalized and formalized interactions that take place in most tourist locales on the peninsula.

During the next field seasons, Pakbeh project staff and community leaders will finish consolidation of the archaeological remains at the first platform group, as well as reconstructing perishable structures and creating access to the group from the road. Additional collaboration will focus upon the elaboration of textual material to guide visitors, although the goal is to allow much of this instruction to happen face-to-face, between members of Kochol and tourists. Interested volunteers from Kochol will be identified by community leaders and begin training in the basic mechanics of maintaining the living museum and interacting with the public. Proposals to the highest levels of México's administration of archaeological sites have received enthusiastic support, in part because the innovative concept of a living museum has a strong educational component and does not violate any federal laws about how actual archaeological structures or artifacts must be curated. We are optimistic that the living museum will move forward the goals, shared by the Pakbeh Project and both local communities, of increased revenue generated for local families, increased access to and production of knowledge about the ancient Maya past for members of the local communities, and innovative tourist opportunities for the public that foster a real interaction between tourist and local.

Future directions for community archaeology in Yucatán

There is a growing awareness in the field of archaeology that one of its greatest challenges is to be both responsive and relevant to what have been called "descendant communities" (Stone and MacKenzie 1990; Patterson 1995; Ferguson 1996; Swidler et al. 1997; Kehoe 1998; Gosden 2001). A recent iteration of this theme utilizes the framework of postcolonialist studies in order to argue for an archaeological practice that responds to the calls of indigenous people that academic archaeology is the ultimate usurpation of their past, by reformulating the relationships between native peoples and archaeologists especially in regard to construction of "the past" (Gosden 2001). What follow are some programmatic thoughts about how a postcolonial archaeology, in which Native people are full partners in key decisions about how cultural materials are managed, should be conducted in the Maya area. These observations are most relevant for south-eastern México, because great variation exists in native perceptions of archaeological research within the Maya area alone.

In Latin America, the direction of archaeological research toward the interests and goals of local communities does not yet seem to be self-evident to many researchers, but this may be due in part to the multiple descendant communities that exist and contest each other's claims to the archaeological past. México presents a complex situation, for, though archaeologists are not required by law to consult with local native populations about archaeological research, they are required to abide by the demands of the nation state and of the tourist economy. In Yucatán, multiple descendant communities can be identified, and each has distinct demands. Local Yucatec Maya communities, who share control of the ruins, are a clearly distinguished group, although, as seen at Chunchucmil, the members of Maya communities are diverse in their perceptions of the ancient ruins. Descendants of the hacienda owners or historic landowners, today often wealthy Ladino businessmen, are also a distinct and powerful group. Archaeologists and anthropologists who work for the state of Yucatán and the nation of México claim the ruins as their national patrimony and use images, artifacts, maps, and archaeological knowledge for a variety of purposes, including economic development and ethnic identification. Even the interested public, who visit México in very large numbers to visit the ruins and whose dollars drive the state economy, have specific considerations and needs. Each of these populations can claim the ruins where archaeological research is conducted as part of their heritage, as a space in which they find meaning and experience cultural perpetuation. Archaeologists are only doorkeepers of the past, we open the door and anyone can step through.

This is not to say there are no differences in the relative levels of privilege and connection these multiple descendant groups may claim. Historic and modern power imbalances in México and the broader Maya zone have shown that Maya communities are largely excluded from the process of interpreting archaeological data (Warren 1998; Montejo 1999). Descendant groups that are comprised of people with culturally continuous or territorially historic claims to an archaeological resource must be given priority of control over the management of cultural materials. But archaeologists must also become more aware of, and responsive to, the other members of descendant communities with which we work. Clearly, as public funding of archaeology increases, and public interest increases, only by acknowledging our responsibility to the interested public as a unique descendant community will we ensure the continuation of the discipline. Chris Gosden suggests archaeologists develop the notion of layered knowledge, an idea he borrows from Aboriginal Australian culture where both public and secret interpretations of art and ritual exist simultaneously (Gosden 2001: 258). Each distinct descendant group in Yucatán is both interested in, and looking for, a different contextualized meaning from archaeological data. Archaeologists must begin to negotiate these intersecting layers of knowledge as we move between descendant groups.

There are other aspects of the social context of archaeological research in Yucatán that demand attention and dovetail with the needs of descendant communities. Briefly, these include the modern economic setting, the historical landscape, and the local patterns of consumption of archaeological knowledge. As outlined above, one economic setting of the Pakbeh archaeological research is the tourist economy of Yucatán. Further considerations relevant to local community members include the role a project plays in employing local people, and specifically the rate of pay relative to other employment options and the distribution of work opportunities. Mayanists are all too often unaware of how profound an impact their "scientific" project may have on the local economy and community. Archaeological field schools, in particular, where large numbers of transient students bring highly disposable cash into a rural or isolated setting, can have a profound effect on the values of a local community and upon how archaeology is perceived by the host community. In comments to participants in a session on the social context of Maya archaeology, anthropologist Richard Wilk likened an archaeological field school in Honduras to setting loose untrained, largely unsupervised anthropologists to conduct research on an unwilling population. An archaeological project that will employ local people must have an understanding of the local wage system and rates, what alternative employment opportunities locals may or may not have, and consider the impact the appearance as well as the disappearance of their wages will have on the local economy.

Consideration of the historical landscape must encompass much more than the traditional survey of environmental change that may have occurred at a site. A real consideration of landscape must include people, and the actors who experienced the site over time, especially those who have cultural or experiential claims to the land. If an archaeologist is going to be responsible to the needs of descendant communities, it is imperative to know the nature of relationships between the land and various communities. Has the site been continuously utilized or have the archaeological ruins been co-opted from traditional use by another interest? What constitutes traditional use in a given region? Within the Maya area some prehistoric sites have been abandoned for hundreds of years, some are under cultivation, some have been held in private hands, some are the site of continuous religious experience and some provide political refuge. For any given archaeological zone, tracing the history of how the site came to be available to excavate will inform the relationship of various communities to the land, and thus improve the interpretative power of the archaeologist. In Yucatán, it is significant to many Yucatec Maya that numerous ruins were returned to them for agricultural purposes after the Mexican revolution and land reforms of the 1930s. This moment stands as a benchmark in their ongoing experience of these landscapes and their past. It is also extremely significant to them that these sites can be taken away at any time when the nation state determines they are of archaeological importance to the national patrimony. An understanding of this particular local history helps us understand the protective but fragile connection Yucatec Maya have with their archaeological heritage.

A final aspect of the historical landscape that can be crucial but is often ignored by archaeologists is documentation of who has experiential knowledge of the site. Communities that are spatially close to ruins may travel over them on a regular basis, or they may not. Groups that claim religious significance in the ruins may have greater experiential knowledge of the ruins, and can thus contribute to the interpretations offered by an archaeologist. A real commitment to understanding the entire landscape of a site includes a willingness to engage in dialogue with groups that may have very different motivations for accessing archaeological space. As Quetzil Castañeda has shown for the ancient Maya capital of Chichén Itzá, where 40,000 tourists appear on the vernal equinox each year, the demands and interests of these pilgrims have had as profound an effect as any archaeological project on the reinvention of Chichén Itzá (Castaneda 1996).

Finally, one of the most deliberately overlooked aspects of modern archaeological research, and one of profound impact on relations between archaeologists and local communities, is the specific local pattern of consumption of archaeological knowledge. Certainly, archaeologists are taught early on that they have an obligation to publish their findings and make these available to the field. But, after this obligation, many archaeologists withdraw from any engagement with the information they have written, and move on to the next research opportunity. These technical reports, journal articles, and monographs are then consumed by a variety of interests for a variety of purposes, which vary according to the region, and which have been the study of recent scholars who examine ethnicity and nationalism (Kohl and Fawcett 1995). Michael Dietler has shown how Iron Age archaeological evidence from France has been manipulated in the name of Celtic identity since the time of Napoleon the First and continues to be used by pan-national movements like the European Union (Dietler 1994). A cautionary tale is told by native ethnographer Victor Montejo, who claims the depiction by archaeologists of the ancient Maya as obsessed with blood sacrifice was absorbed by the military dictatorship of Guatemala and used as a justification for the widespread massacres of modern Maya, whom the military identified as subhuman pagans (Montejo 1993: 15). Certainly, the Guatemalan military had motivations for massacre that went far beyond any historical or archaeological justification, but Montejo's statement does illustrate the power of archaeological knowledge to be manipulated for political means, as well as the high level of mistrust between the archaeological community and native ethnographers. Such observations should not act to silence our production of knowledge, but as a call for anthropological archaeologists to share in the responsibility for the images we create about the world. A postcolonial archaeology that acknowledges the verifiable uses to which archaeological data can be put, such as land claims or language revitalization, can contribute productively to the field of postcolonial theory by adopting substantive political engagement with indigenous peoples (Sturm 1996; Begay 1997; Nicholas and Andrews 1997; Warren 1998; Lilley 2000; Gosden 2001).

Collaboration between Native Americans and archaeologists in North America has shown that conflicts over the uses to which archaeological data will be put are often mitigated when indigenous communities are put in control of research issues or are at least fundamentally consulted in the development of research proposals (Ferguson 1996; Begay 1997; Cypress 1997; Ravesloot 1997). What kinds of research might native descendant communities suggest? As noted by Bruce Trigger and others, the emphasis on environmental determinism or empirical quantification that characterizes much of processual archaeology is of little interest to most native groups in North America (Trigger 1997). Kay Warren describes the interest of female Kaqchikel Maya linguists in a native chronicle written down in the sixteenth century that preserves oral histories from much earlier times. *The Annals of the Kaqchikels* contains a passage about women warriors, which was compelling to Kaqchikel Maya scholars because "it demonstrates that women were held in respect and occupied positions of prestige in the original cultural system" (Warren 1998: 154). To these female scholars, the textual passage that described women joining with men in the uprisings at the ancient capital of Iximché, supported their own positions as women joining a mostly male movement of cultural revivalism. In addition, Warren notes that the message of ancient women and men working together was meaningful because the female scholars felt increasingly under pressure from non-local development groups to see themselves as exploited by men within their culture. In this instance the native interpretation was not one of female independence but rather co-operation across gender lines. Warren's observations would suggest that research on ancient gender roles, and especially the negotiation of resistance to imposed European gendered expectations, could be of very real interest to modern communities of Maya women and men.

Native ethnographer Victor Montejo has articulated the frustration of Maya intellectuals and activists that they are "continually placed in the position of being listeners" (Montejo 1999: 14). Montejo addresses the power imbalance present in Western academic control of intellectual knowledge about Maya culture, and argues for a "decolonization" of the process by allowing "insider" voices to be heard and respected (Montejo 1999: 13). Montejo's own version of ancient Maya history, briefly summarized as a backdrop to his ethnography of the modern political exile experience, compares the accomplishments of the ancient Maya to coeval accomplishments in Europe with statements such as, "When democracy was flowering in the Attic world, our ancestors were forming city-states such as Tikal, Uaxactun, and Quirigua" (Montejo 1999: 26) but ultimately emphasizes the independence of Maya communities prior to Spanish arrival. Montejo's writings suggest that a productive avenue of research would be for Western and Maya scholars to collaborate on interpretation of new archaeological materials, and underscore the crucial importance of increased funding targeted for Maya scholars to facilitate educational and occupational training in archaeology.

Demetrio Cojti Cuxil, an influential Guatemalan Maya scholar, has argued forcefully that "the appropriate role for North American anthropologists should be one of helping to identify continuities in Maya culture, the timeless characteristics that make Mayas Maya" (Warren 1998: 74). While a significant challenge to academics attempting to move far beyond the essentializing history of anthropology and archaeology, Warren and I see Cojti Cuxil's ideas as a call for scholarship on the rejection of Spanish or Western definitions of Maya culture, such as investigation of the material remains of Maya resistance during the Colonial period.

A productive dialogue about research priorities arose from an accidental discovery found on another archaeological project on which I worked in Yucatán. In the course of architectural testing at the Classic period Maya site of Yaxuna, a human burial dating to the historic period was recovered from one of the rooms of standing architecture within the site. A juvenile skeleton complete with porcelain button and musket ball was found just beneath the floor surface inside the Classic period building (Suhler and Freidel 1993: 45–6). This individual appears to have sought out shelter in the ruins of the archaeological site, died from a musket ball wound and was buried in the remains of an ancient palace (Bennett 1993: 155–6). Within the local Yaxuna community, this individual stimulated much more interest than any previous burial, and it was immediately interpreted by locals as the remains of a refugee from the Caste Wars, a series of Maya independence movements during the nineteenth century, and a significant event in the history of the local village. Stories from the Caste War are told in this village, and it is a very real and present part of the historical landscape, much more immediate than the ancient Maya history that attracts so much more research attention. Even some of the older women from the village made the walk over to the research laboratory to see "los restos del pobrecito [the remains of the poor little guy]." Lacking a specialist in historic archaeology, and given the strong interpretative certitude of the villagers, burial 10 has remained a Caste War victim in everyone's minds. The experience of intense interest in possible Caste War remains, as well as the ensuing dialogue about the lack of archaeological research on this period of history, illustrates that recent historical events are a good candidate for further community archaeology in Yucatán and echoes the calls for more study of Maya resistance that come from Guatemalan Maya scholars.

Concluding thoughts

The Pakbeh Regional Economy Program has taken some small but significant steps toward the goal of practising an archaeology that is both more responsive and more relevant to our host community. In addition to respecting and implementing the goal of bringing tourism to the villages, we have a commitment to education that encompasses many levels of participation. Working in conjunction with the primary school teacher of Chunchucmil, we have given tours to area teachers and encouraged them to bring students on site. High school students are working in the laboratory in the hope that they may continue in the field of archaeology once funding is secured for scholarships to the University of Yucatán. Most fundamentally, we are involved in an ongoing dialogue with all interested members of the villages of Chunchucmil and Kochol about what the artifacts and structures mean, to us, to them and to the interested public. Much of our work still lies ahead, but the satisfaction of positive relations with the Yucatec communities on both sides of the site is evidence to us that we are on the right track.

From my viewpoint, there can be no greater failure for archaeology than to accept that children will feel no connection to their archaeological heritage or that native peoples will reject the entire archaeological discipline as exploitative. There are signs of hope that archaeology is moving into a theoretical maturity that accepts some of the critiques of postcolonial analysis. A growing number of native people entering the field, the incorporation of archaeological ethics into graduate and undergraduate curriculums, and a greater accountability to descendant communities, however they are constructed and defined, are all signs that we have indeed left behind the days of archaeology as an isolated laboratory endeavour and are moving toward a greater sense of cultural responsibility.

References

Ardren, T. (1991) Modern Maya perceptions of the Ancient Maya: the creation of a history. *Yale Graduate Journal of Anthropology*, 3: 46–51.

—— (1999) Chunchucmil: a preliminary chronology and summary of research. Paper presented at the Annual Meeting of the American Anthropological Association, Chicago.

Austin, A. (1994) Fonatur leads efforts to mold México's resorts. *Hotel and Motel Management*, 209(9): 4–6.

Bawden, G. (1993) An archaeological study of social structure and ethnic replacement in residential architecture of the Tumilaca Valley. In: M. Aldenderfer (ed.), *Domestic Architecture, Ethnicity, and Complementarity in the South-Central Andes*. Iowa City: University of Iowa Press, pp. 42–54.

Beach, T. (1998) Soil constraints on Northwest Yucatán: Pedo archaeology and subsistence at Chunchucmil. *Geoarchaeology*, 13: 759–91.

Begay, R.M. (1997) The role of archaeology on Indian lands: the Navajo Nation. In: N. Swidler et al. (eds.), *Native Americans and Archaeologists*. Walnut Creek, CA: AltaMira Press, pp. 161–6.

Bennett, S. (1993) 1992 burials from Yaxuna, Yucatán. In: C. Suhler and D. Freidel (eds.), *The Selz Foundation Yaxuna Project: Final Report of the 1992 Field Season*. Dallas: Department of Anthropology, Southern Methodist University, pp. 144–54.

Blackmore, C. and Ardren, T. (2002) Social landscape in a market economy: archaeological investigations of the Pich and Lool groups at Chunchucmil, Yucatan. Paper presented at the 67th Annual Meeting of the Society for American Archaeology, Denver.

Blanton, R. and Feinman, G. (1984) The Mesoamerican world system. *American Anthropologist*, 86: 673–82.

Bonfil Batalla, G. (1996) *México Profundo: Reclaiming a Civilization*. Trans. P.A. Dennis. Austin: University of Texas Press.

Brown, D.F. (1999) Mayas and tourists in the Maya world. *Human Organization*, 58(3): 295–304.

Castañeda, Q. (1996) *In the Museum of Maya Culture*. Minneapolis: University of Minnesota Press.

Clancy, M. (1999) Tourism and development: evidence from México. *Annals of Tourism Research*, 26(1): 1–20.

Cypress, B.L. (1997) The role of archaeology in the Seminole tribe of Florida. In: N. Swidler et al. (eds.), *Native Americans and Archaeologists*. Walnut Creek, CA: AltaMira Press, pp. 156–60.

Dahlin, B. (2000) The barricade and abandonment of Chunchucmil: implications for Northern Maya warfare. *Latin American Antiquity*, 11(3): 283–98.

Dahlin, B. and Ardren, T. (2002) Modes of exchange and their effects on regional and urban patterns at Chunchucmil, Yucatán, México. In: M. Masson and D. Freidel (eds.), *Ancient Maya Political Economies*. Walnut Creek, CA: AltaMira Press, pp. 249–84.

Dahlin, B., Andrews, A.P., Beach, T., and Benzanilla, C. (1998) Punta Canbalam in context: a report on a peripatetic coastal site in Northwest Campeche, México. *Ancient Mesoamerica*, 9: 1–15.

Dietler, M. (1994) "Our ancestors the Gauls": archaeology, ethnic nationalism, and the manipulation of Celtic identity in modern Europe. *American Anthropologist*, 96(3): 584–605.

Farrell, P., Beach, T., and Dahlin, B. (1996) Under the roots of the Chukum tree: a preliminary soil analysis of the Chunchucmil region, Yucatán/Campeche, México. *Yearbook, Conference of Latin American Geographers*, 22: 41–50.

Ferguson, T.J. (1996) Native Americans and the practice of archaeology. *Annual Review of Anthropology*, 25: 63–79.

Freidel, D., Schele, L., and Parker, J. (1993) *Maya Cosmos: Three Thousand Years on the Shaman's Path*. New York: William Morrow.

Giddens, W.L. (1995) Talud-tablero architecture as a symbol of Mesoamerican affiliation and power. MA thesis, University of California–Los Angeles.

Gosden, C. (2001) Postcolonial archaeology: issues of culture, identity, and knowledge. In: I. Hodder (ed.), *Archaeological Theory Today*. Cambridge: Polity Press, pp. 241–61.

Heyden, D. and Gendrop, P. (1980) *Pre-Columbian Architecture of Mesoamerica*. New York: Electa/Rizzoli.

Hutson, S. (2000) Excavations at residential groups A'ak and Chiwo'ol. In: T. Ardren (ed.), *Chunchucmil Regional Economy Program Report of the 1999 Field Season*. Tallahassee: Department of Anthropology, Florida State University, pp. 24–30.

Hutson, S., Magnoni, A., and Stanton, T. (in press). Corporate groups at Chunchucmil. In: J. Lohse and J. Neely (eds.), *Corporate Groups in Mesoamerica*. Scottsdale: University of Arizona Press.

Kehoe, A.B. (1998) *The Land of Prehistory: A Critical History of American Archaeology*. London: Routledge.

Kohl, P.L. and Fawcett, C. (1995) *Nationalism, Politics, and the Practice of Archaeology*. Cambridge: Cambridge University Press.

Lilley, I. (1999) *Native Title and the Transformation of Archaeology in the Postcolonial World*. Sydney: University of Sydney Press.

Long, V. (1991) Government–industry–community interaction in tourism development in México. In: M.T. Sinclair and M.J. Stabler (eds.), *The Tourism Industry: An International Analysis*. Oxford: CAB International, pp. 205–22.

Magnoni, A. (1995) Albarradas at Chunchucmil and in the Northern Maya Area. BA thesis, Institute of Archaeology, University College, London.

Marquina, I. (1964) *Arquitectura Prehispánica*. Second edition. México, DF: Instituto Nacional de Antropología e Historia.

Montejo, V. (1993) In the name of the pot, the sun, the broken spear, the rock, the stick, the idol, ad infinitum and ad nauseum: an exposé of Anglo anthropologists' obsessions with and inventions of Mayan gods. *Red Pencil Review: A Journal of Native American Studies*, 9(1): 12–16.

——(1999) *Voices from Exile: Violence and Survival in Modern Maya History*. Norman: University of Oklahoma Press.

Nicholas, G.P. and Andrews, T.D. (1997) *At a Crossroads: Archaeology and First Peoples in Canada*. Burnaby: Department of Archaeology, Simon Fraser University.

Patterson, T. (1995) Archaeology, history, *indigenismo*, and the state in Peru and México. In: P.R. Schmidt and T.C. Patterson (eds.), *Making Alternative Histories: The Practice of Archaeology and History in Non-Western Settings*. Santa Fe: School of American Research Press, pp. 69–86.

Ravesloot, J.C. (1997) Changing Native American perceptions of archaeology and archaeologists. In: N, Swidler et al. (eds.), *Native Americans and Archaeologists*. Walnut Creek, CA: AltaMira Press, pp. 172–8.

Re Cruz, A. (1996) Thousand and one faces of Cancun. *Urban Anthropology*, 25(3): 283–311.

Savage, M. (1993) Ecological disturbance and nature tourism. *The Geographical Review*, 83(3): 290–301.

Spence, M.W. (1996) A comparative analysis of ethnic enclaves. In: A.G. Mastache, J.R. Parsons, R.S. Santley, and M.C. Serra-Puche (eds.), *Arqueología Mesoamericana: Homenaje a William T. Sanders*. México, DF: Instituto Nacional de Antropología e Historia, pp. 333–53.

Stanton, T., Ardren, T., and Bond Freeman, T. (2000). Chunchucmil as a specialized trade center in Western Yucatán. Paper presented at the Annual Meeting of the Society for American Archaeology, Philadelphia.

Stone, P. and MacKenzie, R. eds. (1990) *The Excluded Past: Archaeology in Education*. London: Unwin Hyman.

Sturm, C. (1996) Old writing and new messages: the role of hieroglyphic literacy in Maya cultural activism. In: E.F. Fischer and R.M. Brown (eds.), *Maya Cultural Activism in Guatemala*. Austin: University of Texas Press, pp. 114–30.

Suhler, C. and Freidel, D. (1993) *The Selz Foundation Yaxuna Project: Final Report of the 1992 Field Season*. Dallas: Department of Anthropology, Southern Methodist University.

Swidler, N., Dongoske, K.E., Anyon, R., and Downer, A. (1997) *Native Americans and Archeologists: Stepping Stones to Common Ground*. Walnut Creek, CA: AltaMira Press.

Trigger, B. (1997) Foreword. In: G.P. Nicholas and T.D. Andrews (eds.), *At a Crossroads: Archaeology and First Peoples in Canada*. Burnaby: Archaeology Press, Department of Archaeology, Simon Fraser University, pp. vii–xiii.

Van den Berghe, P. (1994) Marketing Mayas: ethnic tourism promotion in México. *Annals of Tourism Research*, 22(3): 568–88.

Vlcek, D., Garza de Gonzalez, S., and Kurjack, E. (1978) Contemporary farming and ancient Maya settlements: some disconcerting evidence. In: P. Harrison and B.L. Turner (eds.), *Pre-Hispanic Maya Agriculture*. Albuquerque: University of New Mexico Press, pp. 211–23.

Warren, K.B. (1998) *Indigenous Movements and their Critics: Pan-Maya Activism in Guatemala*. Princeton, NJ: Princeton University Press.

Watanabe, T. (2000) Form and function of metates in Chunchucmil, Yucatán, México. MA thesis, Department of Anthropology, Florida State University, Tallahassee.

Watkins, J., Pyburn, K.A., and Cressey, P. (2000) Community relations: what the practicing archaeologist needs to know to work effectively with local and/or descendant communities. In: S. Bender and G. Smith (eds.), *Teaching Archaeology in the 21st Century*. Washington, D.C.: Society for American Archaeology, pp. 73–82.

Chapter 40

Us and them
Who benefits from experimental exhibition making?

Pete Brown

Introduction

As a university museum, the Manchester Museum (United Kingdom) has a track record for developing collaborative and audience-focused projects and programmes, whilst simultaneously challenging staff to be experimental and innovative – to take risks rather than play safe. Examples include 'Alchemy', an Arts Council–funded project inviting artists (through research fellowships) to present new ways of interpreting the collection;[1] 'Collective Conversations', an opportunity for a diverse range of people to respond to the collection and have the resulting dialogues filmed for others to view;[2] and 'Myths About Race', a temporary exhibition focused on issues arising from the 2007 UK national 'Revealing Histories' project commemorating the abolition of the British slave trade in 1807.[3]

This paper offers a glimpse into the effect of the museum exhibition as 'museological laboratory' on visitors' learning and enjoyment. It demonstrates that, as long as it is backed by sound ethical principles, taking an unconventional and potentially controversial approach, though unpopular in some quarters, can provide an enlightening and rewarding experience for visitors and the institution. The context is a research project focused on a yearlong temporary exhibition (April 2008–April 2009) based on the loan of Lindow Man's body from the British Museum. Lindow Man – a 2000-year-old 'bog body' uncovered during peat excavation near Manchester – had been on display at the Manchester Museum twice before, in 1987, just three years after his discovery, and again in 1991. The coroner's decision to release the body to the British Museum on the grounds that the discovery was of national significance triggered a passionate, though unsuccessful, community campaign to bring Lindow Man 'home' to Manchester.

The research project set out to examine the role of the university museum in challenging people's habits, beliefs, and perceptions. It aimed to test whether 'provoking a debate', which is a key element of the Manchester Museum's mission

Source: *Museum Management and Curation*. New York & Abingdon: Routledge, 2011. 26.2: 129-148
© Taylor & Francis.

statement, and part of its twin purpose of 'promoting understanding between cultures' and 'developing a sustainable world', is just an academic, postmodern indulgence that bewilders and alienates visitors, or whether it has real value for audiences. The research explored the tension within museums and the sector as a whole, between a cultural institution's role as educator, activist or philosopher, and its function as a visitor attraction. The Lindow Man exhibition became a case study to assess the impact of the Museum's unorthodox approach on visitors' learning and enjoyment. 'A Bog Body Mystery' offered an opportunity, over a sustained period, to learn how the Museum's visitors make sense of this kind of presentation, whether the lack of definite 'facts' frustrated people seeking the authority of the museum voice, or liberated them to define and explore their own interpretations.

There were a number of hazards inherent in the Museum's 2008 treatment of Lindow Man: the first lay in the decision to raise issues around the ethics of collecting and displaying human remains, rather than simply taking an authoritative line; secondly, the exhibition team chose to depart from orthodox museum display techniques and materials, risking the wrath of the traditionalists; thirdly, the museum decided to share expertise and authority, acknowledging the lack of absolute facts and incorporating multiple perspectives and, finally, the approach was empathic rather than forensic – creating an emotional encounter unlike the 'objective' tone which many visitors are used to.

'Lindow Man: A Bog Body Mystery' looked and felt quite unlike the previous two presentations of the archaeology, which were more conventional and authoritative displays. This exhibition was poly-vocal and involved an open, constructivist type of experience (Hein 2000) offering evidence, contextual information, and hypotheses, as well as inviting visitors to make sense of it in their own way and in accordance with their individual experience, knowledge, and beliefs. It used as its core structure interviews with seven people who have personal experience of Lindow Man, including the peat diggers who discovered the body, a local woman who was a child when Lindow Man was found and took part in the 'repatriation' campaign, a forensic scientist who examined the body, a Druid priest, a landscape archaeologist, and two curators – one from the Manchester Museum and the other from the British Museum. Each person was invited to contribute to a 'scrapbook' of personal effects, ephemera, artefacts, and specimens that contextualized and illustrated their connection with Lindow Man. Additional information was made available in ring binders labelled 'Find out More' and placed alongside relevant books on shelving (Figure 40.1).

At the entrance (and the exit) there was a 'welcome board'[4] holding an introductory panel and a short gallery guide that visitors could take with them into the exhibition. Just inside the gallery, visitors encountered a graphic panel introducing the seven interviewees and their stories. Two temporary Visitor Service Assistants were hired specifically to engage with visitors in the exhibition. With such a departure from conventional archaeological presentation, the marketing campaign had to 'sell' the different approach so that people knew what to expect. The Museum decided to use a multi-pronged strategy, extracting four themes from the exhibition content: historical/archaeological, scientific, spiritual, and nostalgic.

Figure 40.1 Discovering the body: section showing construction with object cases, applied interview quotes, and 'Find out More' shelf with seating.

These themes would appeal in different ways to different visitors, so four posters were produced, each with an image illustrating that aspect of the exhibition.

The materials (mainly medium-density fibreboard and chipboard) and colours selected for the exhibition construction were chosen to evoke the landscape of Lindow Moss, where the body was found, and to reflect the impermanent, unfinished, and incomplete nature of the story. The construction was deliberately left rough and unfinished, recalling the shuttering used to line archaeological trenches. The horizontal, modular units were also reminiscent of library stacks.[5]

The key goal of the exhibition was to contextualize Lindow Man in a way that encouraged respectful reflection, inviting visitors to question the interpretation of archaeological evidence and the practice of displaying human remains in museums. The 'postmodern' concept sought to expose the process of development and construction, and to present various interpretations of what little evidence exists. 'A Bog Body Mystery' also attempted to deconstruct the idea of 'exhibition', laying bare some of the machinations behind the 'glossy museum show'. For example, British Museum objects were displayed conventionally in a case as a single object – a traditional mini museum within the exhibition – that contrasted with the interviewees' 'scrapbooks'.

The interpretation strategy was guided by a public consultation exercise with the terms of engagement clearly explained on the day – that no promise could be made to include all the consultees' suggestions. The workshop was attended by a wide range of participants, including professionals and enthusiasts in archaeology, anthropology and local history, and people with pagan beliefs. Following a presentation by the Museum's Curator of Archaeology, the attendees were divided into small groups and asked to share and discuss their priorities and suggestions for an exhibition centred on Lindow Man's body. The process was surprisingly consensual, as you might expect pagans and forensic anthropologists to be at each others' throats – but there was very little disagreement.

What emerged was a set of principles and suggestions for approach and content that the exhibition team used as the foundation for the development process. The key points were as follows: Lindow Man should be presented as a person rather than as a museum object; he should be given a context that helps people to understand his world and ours; the exhibition should be a reflective, contemplative experience with opportunities to share ideas and feelings; the lack of factual information about him should be acknowledged and different perspectives explored and, if possible, Lindow Man should be situated away from any interpretation to allow visitors to choose whether to view his body or not. It quickly became clear that not all the suggestions could be included – in fact, some of them were contradictory – but the team strove to keep to the spirit of the consultation day, referring back frequently to the report and checking whether the ideas could be incorporated. The Museum reported back to consultees by email, by post, and through a second, all-day workshop.

The fact that so little is known about Lindow Man – where he came from, his family background, his social status, his trade or profession, even his name reinforced the exhibition team's decision to present the evidence, together with a number of hypotheses about his life and death, and to invite visitors to consider (alongside experts such as archaeologists and museum curators) the relative merits of the different interpretations. Ironically, the 2008 approach, leaving the mystery of Lindow Man open, rather than proposing a definitive interpretation, presented him as less of a complete person than he seemed in previous exhibitions, which included imaginative recreations of his world and a facial 'likeness' constructed from scans of his skull. For some visitors (and staff), this was a serious omission and an abdication of the Museum's responsibility to educate the public through expert testimony. For others, it felt more inclusive, validating their own thoughts and theories as part of the shared experience of 'public history'.

Some Manchester staff firmly believe that the exhibition approach was perverse, flying in the face of what *we know visitors want*. For them, leaving the interpretation open is taking the lazy way out – it is a museum's job, as 'expert', to filter information and present the authorized version.[6] Gurian (2006: 12) would disagree, noting:

> Fairness demands that we present our audiences with the broadest range of conflicting facts and opinions within the exhibition – or alternatively, having taken a single viewpoint, reveal ourselves (the authors) by name, bias, class, education and opinion. To do otherwise suggests that audiences are children unable to think for themselves.

Is provocation just a publicity stunt? Against a background of fundamental disagreement on human remains and public disputes about the value and role of museums, the Manchester Museum's mission to 'provoke a debate'[7] might seem superfluous – it was likely to happen anyway with this subject matter – but there is a difference between creating the conditions for constructive argument and simply standing by while controversy rages around you. The Museum framed the exhibition within a year-long programme of events and activities, many designed to facilitate debate. Visitors were invited to share their views and opinions on comment cards in the exhibition and via the Museum's website. Staff and volunteers were briefed and trained to engage visitors in discussion about the issues arising from the retention and display of human remains, and the interpretation of archaeological evidence.

Since Lindow Man was first exhibited at the Manchester Museum, the widely accepted attitudes and procedures regarding the research, display, and interpretation of human remains have been hotly contested both by academics and professionals, and in the public arena. The intervening 17 years saw a fierce debate erupting over questions of retention, repatriation, and reburial, with diehard forensic archaeologists facing militant 'source communities' and other claimants, each side entrenched with no-man's-land between. The language of the protagonists is often bellicose, expressing a deep conviction in all camps that there will be dire and lasting consequences if the battle is lost. During the same period, following notorious cases such as Alder Hey in Liverpool where children's remains were retained by the pathology department for research without parents' consent, public awareness of human remains issues, along with sensitivity and scepticism, had grown (Alberti et al. 2009).

The second significant shift in context was within the museum sector. Many institutions had been following a gradual postmodern trajectory, moving away from their traditional authoritative position and acknowledging alternative interpretations and world views. In the two earlier exhibitions, Lindow Man was presented as an 'archaeological treasure', a 'find' and a piece of evidence, and this is how he is still described by traditionalists. In contrast, one of the aims of the 2008 exhibition, suggested through consultation with a broad range of interested parties, was to emphasize his humanity – casting him more as 'one of us' rather than a historical artefact. In 'A Bog Body Mystery', Lindow Man was consciously and consistently described as 'he' rather than 'it', and the case that contained the body was deliberately not given an 'object label'. For some people, these measures accorded the man due respect. For others – Emma Restall Orr for example, one of the seven interviewees[8] – they were no more than window dressing: the very act of displaying the body turned him into a museum specimen.

As the exhibition was taking shape, the subject of museums and human remains was developing a high profile in the Museum and beyond. Manchester staff members were playing a leading role in a national debate about the ethical treatment of human remains (Bienkowski 2009), while a panel of staff with consultees from outside the institution developed a human remains policy for the Museum. The policy states that human remains should be displayed only 'in a culturally appropriate, sensitive and informative manner and always accompanied by explanatory and contextual interpretation'.[9]

In order to ensure consistency of practice, and in response to feedback from visitors who felt that displaying unwrapped bodies was disrespectful, Manchester's human remains panel decided to gauge visitor reaction by conducting a test 'cover up' of the mummies in the Ancient Egypt galleries. The resulting outrage took the Museum by surprise and was reported by news media across the world.[10] The Museum eventually contained the furore by producing a series of panels through the gallery, explaining what was happening, and directing them to an evaluation board inviting visitor feedback through comments cards. At the end of the consultation period, permanent panels were installed near the Museum entrance, alerting visitors to the presence of human remains in the galleries and describing routes avoiding those displays. During the same period, the Museum of Science & Industry in Manchester hosted Gunther von Hagens' *BODY WORLDS 4: The Original Exhibition of Real Human Bodies*. Comparisons between the Manchester Museum's personal approach and the anatomical engineering of *BODY WORLDS* added to the 'human remains debate' in the city and further afield (Alberti et al. 2009).

Context of the exhibition

'Experimental' and provocative exhibition-making practice in museums is viewed by some as self-indulgent navel gazing, a sop to political correctness, of no benefit to visitors and a waste of public money. It puts the museum's hard-earned authority at risk and devalues curatorial expertise.[11] For some time now, museum ethicists have questioned the power balance between museums and their audiences, weighing attributes such as transparency, accountability and social responsibility alongside academic authority and expertise. Yakel frames the debate in terms of power and possession (Yakel 2000: 278): 'Who has the authority to interpret history to the public – indeed, who "owns" history?' To Walker Laird and Braden, the answer seems clear: no one and everyone. Braden believes that there could be serious consequences if museums do not deal with the question of ownership (Braden 1998: 489–98) – 'No one has a proprietary claim to history, yet if we do not participate in the process of examination, or worse yet, are forced into non-participation, we all lose.' Walker Laird reminds us of how much is at stake (Walker Laird 1998: 474–82): '... public history engages public money, public treasures and public beliefs.'

Many people still trust museums more than other institutions, but audiences have been losing patience with the didactic approach. More than a decade ago, Boyd (1999, 185), wrote 'Museums are no longer perceived as infallible; they can no longer presume the privilege of issuing unquestionable pronouncements.' Neil Harris (1995: 1104) said, 'Our very notion of museum truth is now questioned.' Hood agreed, but put it more poetically (Hood 1994: 1011–19), '... the curatorial key is no longer the only one to fit the lock.' Museums have never been apolitical or 'objective', however much they may have tried to maintain the 'fallacy of authoritative neutrality' (Janes 2009: 59). Gurian (2006: 69) asserts, 'It is clear that no museum has ever been "value neutral" and 'There is no longer a belief that the object will tell its own story or that there are neutral or objective truths' (Gurian 2006: 77).

Collections, by the nature of the way they were acquired and have been interpreted, are provocative in many ways to different people. Today, audience consultation, involvement, and engagement are as much a part of museum theory and practice as documentation and conservation. Collections in publicly funded museums belong to everyone, and each of us is an expert with regard to our own experience, opinions and, reactions, whatever the origin of that understanding. Authorship ensures transparency and invites critical thinking, just as anonymity conceals and inhibits. As Janes (2009: 80) puts it, 'The implication in maintaining this anonymity is that there is one perspective or interpretation, and the museum owns it.' Acknowledging and validating diverse responses and encouraging a dialogue make collections more useful and relevant to a wider range of people. It shifts the balance from the institution to the individual and helps empower disadvantaged citizens.

If museums shy away from controversy or allow funders and stakeholders to prevent them from engaging in contemporary debates, they may lose an opportunity to reinvigorate their purpose. Janes (2009: 17) is convinced that rising to that challenge is the only way forward for museums. He maps out in stark terms the downward spiral in store for those institutions that fail to engage, from 'privileged societal position of trust and respect' to 'incremental irrelevance at a time of increasing urgency' (Janes 2009: 173–4). Janes acknowledges that it will not be easy and uses a term coined by Canadian essayist John Ralston Saul to discuss the uncomfortable consequences of reaching out (Janes 2009: 94). Saul describes the 'psychic discomfort which inevitably accompanies active engagement in the public sphere'. It may be, however, as Lynch and Alberti suggest, that 'discensus' is a more powerful creative force than consensus (Lynch and Alberti 2010: 13–35).

I argue that a more inclusive and equitable relationship enriches the museum experience rather than diluting it. The broadening or democratization of interpretation may appear to be an attack on curatorship, as though pluralism necessarily leads to a decline in standards, but it need not be so. Sharing authority does involve a change of status, but does not have to mean redundancy, as diverse interpretations should enhance rather than replace the curator's perspective. Gurian, in describing this tendency to frame the debate in terms of 'either or', reminds us of 'the importance of "and"' when considering 'excellence and equity' (Gurian 2006). When these concepts are embodied in exhibition design and construction, 'traditional' museum visitors can feel disoriented, out of place, and insecure. The exhibition space no longer feels like home, the structure is unfamiliar, the rules are unclear, and their interests appear to be marginalized. If we are aware of this effect, is it ethical to disadvantage one group for the benefit of another, even if the former has had privileged access in the past?

Methodology

In order to assess how effective the Museum was in balancing the needs of visitors, with its desire to innovate and its mission to provoke, the research project aimed to compare feedback from visitors with the perceptions of staff and volunteers, and to set this in the context of media coverage and correspondence from interested parties outside the institution. As the Lindow Man exhibition was developed in consultation with external contributors, their views would also be considered.

Visitor responses were captured using the Personal Meaning Mapping (PMM) method developed by Falk, Mousourri, and Coulson (1998) and contextualized through a brief questionnaire which people were asked to complete after they had finished the PMM exercise. The questionnaire was designed to assess – as far as possible within the parameters of the study – the participants' prior experience, knowledge, and understanding of museums in general and of Lindow Man specifically, as well as their motivation for visiting. Bearing in mind that people might make comparisons between this exhibition and others that they had attended, particularly the previous Lindow Man exhibitions, it would also be useful to find out what expectations they had, if any, about what they were going to see. A question about educational background and a request for the participant's postcode was added to provide the option to test whether there was a link between socio-economic status and the response to the exhibition approach. The questionnaire also requested that the visitors rate individual elements of the exhibition on a five-point Likert scale, according to how useful they felt these elements were in terms of 'learning and enjoyment'.

The PMM method involves a very open-ended 'mind mapping' exercise where participants are given a sheet of paper with a stimulus word or phrase in the centre (in this case 'Lindow Man'), and then invited to share any knowledge, thoughts, ideas, or feelings that they may have on the subject. They write their contributions using one colour pen before the visit and then add any new thoughts afterwards using a different colour pen (Figure 40.2).

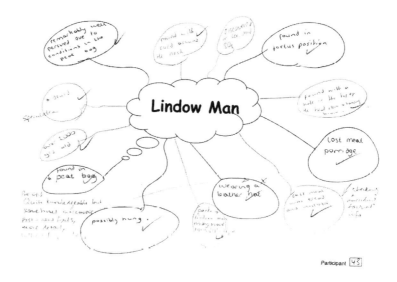

Figure 40.2 Personal Meaning Map 43. Two colours show darker and lighter: text outside bubbles is the author's.

Analysis of the charts followed the process designed by Falk and Dierking (1998). The written responses were categorized and analysed according to four progressively more complex 'dimensions' that aim to identify the depth and breadth of an individual's understanding. The purpose of the 'random' sample of adult visitors was to include a range, from first timers to regulars. This could provide insight into whether there is a difference in expectations between new visitors and those who have some experience of the particular Manchester Museum offer – in a sense, whether the Museum is 'training' visitors to expect, and hopefully welcome, a certain kind of interpretive approach. It was important to get an idea of what the subjects of the study anticipated before they entered the exhibition space, so people were approached before they entered the gallery and the experience was followed through with them when they came back out. The aim was also to use this front-end evaluation to explore some of the prevailing 'myths' around what visitors want. It is worth noting that there is a discrepancy between the number of PMM charts and questionnaires completed: 98 people filled in the questionnaire, but only 97 of them finished the PMM chart.

Results and discussion

Questionnaire data

In summary, the vast majority of the participants (80 per cent) were visiting with family or friends. Most of them visit museums between one and five times a year (64 per cent) and are highly educated (43 per cent completed their education after the age of 18).[12] Considering the strong perception within the Museum that visitors had been shocked by the unorthodox approach, the answers concerning whether the exhibition was what they expected was surprising: 52 per cent said it was what they expected; 48 per cent said it was not. Forty-two per cent reported a special interest in Lindow Man, which is quite high, as most visitors usually report just a general interest in the Museum's themes and content.[13]

In order to address the visitor aspect of the research question 'Who benefits?' it was important to understand what value these visitors placed on the experience and what motivated them to visit. The visitors were asked to rate different motivating factors on a rising scale of 0–10. Their conscious motivation for the visit was overwhelmingly education and entertainment, which is what one would expect, although the sociocultural aspect of the experience should not be underestimated. Indeed, it is a key element of the constructivist model of museum learning, along with physical and psychological factors (Falk and Dierking 2000), and its influence was evident in some of the responses to the PMM exercise. People were aware of, and often interested in, the way others interacted with the exhibition. There was also a very positive response to the interventions of the handling station volunteers and certain Visitor Services staff – when the right people are in place, 'live interpretation' of whatever form can significantly enhance learning and enjoyment.

Judging by the questionnaire responses, the drive for education and entertainment for most visitors was largely satisfied by all aspects of the exhibition.

However, there were individual exceptions, including people who strongly objected to the design and construction and, interestingly, the handling station.[14] It would clearly be necessary to probe more deeply in order to assess the accuracy of this initial impression.

PMM exercise

The survey took place over ten days during November and December 2008. In an effort to randomize sampling, each third person or fifth person entering the exhibition was approached, depending on how busy the Museum was. In some ways, it would have been easier and perhaps more productive in terms of the PMM methodology to work with a more 'captive' audience, such as organized groups or some of the Museum's community partners who might have been willing to devote more time to the activity. For this study, however, the aim was to gather the experiences of visitors in as natural and unrehearsed a way as possible.

Because people were unprepared, rather than being recruited as part of a longer and more formal activity, this project was able to capture only a snapshot of each participant's meaning-making experience. It would require a more intensive longitudinal study, combining PMM with contact over a longer period (as Falk, Dierking, and Foutz suggest in their family learning research), in order to assess the way that visitors' understanding of the exhibition experience changes over time (Falk et al. 2007). However, the spontaneous nature of this 'brief encounter' research may have the advantage of minimizing the tendency that participants have to 'overthink' the exercise and attempt to provide what they think the researcher wants. Despite the introduction stressing that the activity was not a test of recall – that there were no right or wrong answers – some participants were definitely striving to remember facts from the exhibition as if playing a memory game.

The number of completed samples totalled 97 out of 113 people approached (seven people declined to take part[15] and nine either dropped out part way through the process or were found not to have completed the activity). Most of the participants were with other people who often asked if they could take part as well. The only criterion for refusal was if they had already visited the exhibition. After introductions, the project was described to the selected participants and the PMM process was explained. Bearing in mind that the process would eat into people's scarce leisure time and that I was catching them unawares, the exercise was designed to last just a few minutes before and after the visit.

I used my University of Leicester graduate student identity, rather than revealing my position at the Museum, which I felt might inhibit people's ability to speak or write openly about their experience. It was made clear that they could opt out at any time, though fortunately almost all completed the exercise. All of the participants were happy to take part – in fact, many thanked me at the end for involving them in the research. All in all, I think the technique provided a more open approach to gathering feedback that stimulated a fuller, richer, and more personal response than a conventional questionnaire format on its own would have done.

PMM analysis

Firstly, in order to judge the general educational and emotional impact of the experience, the quantity of relevant vocabulary was logged. The next step was designed to chart the respondents' range of understanding and the responses were sorted into different concepts or subject areas. Twenty separate categories emerged, all of which corresponded to the themes or aims of the exhibition: discovery, aesthetics of the body, preservation, forensics, speculation as to how Lindow Man died, different perspectives, other bodies, local links, repatriation, peat extraction, wetlands, archaeology, the Iron Age, recent history, pagans, ethics (human remains), design, construction and so on, personal connections, emotional response and curiosity. The third stage was to move more deeply into the language, assessing the profundity of each individual's grasp of the concepts and subject areas. The PMM process ends with the fourth dimension, which brings together the previous three stages, rating each participant's response in terms of its sophistication and expertise. A scale similar to that suggested by Alison James[16] was employed to determine each participant's mastery of the subject matter, ranging from 'novice' to 'expert'.

In addition to the PMM process, with the visitors' prime motivation in mind (education and entertainment), the personal meaning maps were analysed using the Inspiring Learning for All Generic Learning Outcomes (GLOs) that were developed by the Museums, Libraries and Archives Council (MLA) in the United Kingdom to measure the learning impact of visitors' experiences.[17]

Clearly, there is a high level of subjectivity in this analysis, as it is the researcher who chooses the concept groupings and gauges the participants' command of a subject. Had it been practical, it would have been prudent, as James did, to have different researchers cross check the results. However, the fact that three people in that case found a 'high level of agreement' suggests that this linguistic system can provide a robust measure of learning if thoughtfully applied.

PMM dimension 1: quantity of relevant vocabulary

The numerical analysis was entered into a Microsoft Excel database to enable comparative graphs to be created. The total number of words generated by the 97 PMM charts tripled after the visit (from 2,167 before to 6,614 after), which suggests that people were stimulated by the exhibition and prompted to share their new ideas and impressions through the research exercise. The most striking finding was that more than a third of these 6,614 words related to one category: 'design, construction and atmosphere of the exhibition', which reveals what a strong impression the presentation method and materials had on visitors. The total number of individual comments classified under the 20 concept or subject categories increased from 299 before to 436 after visiting, but the change was even greater in the average length of discrete thoughts and ideas expressed. This more than doubled, from 7.3 words before the visit to 15.2 after. This increase in the length of responses correlated with comment card reports,[18] which concluded that the exhibition triggered longer and more considered feedback than usual.

Most participants referred to more than one category on their personal meaning maps, but the most 'popular' categories were not always predictable. Comparing the number of references per category before and after the visit is quite revealing: some of the increases are related to themes that visitors might not be expected to comment on before experiencing the exhibition, such as 'different perspectives' and 'pagans', while others are less obvious. Some themes highlighted in the exhibition, such as 'forensics' and the 'repatriation campaign', seem to have struck a chord, whereas 'wetlands' and 'archaeology' left people cold. There were fewer post-visit comments about other bodies or discoveries of this kind compared with pre-visit, but this is to be expected as the only references to other bodies were in the 'Find out More' folders. What is surprising is that the discovery of Lindow Man's body and its preservation in the peat also provoked a lower response after the visit. Perhaps this was because people's curiosity had been satisfied or maybe these aspects of the exhibition were not stimulating enough. One thing that is clear from the density of language on the personal meaning maps is that the exhibition approach prompted visitors to speculate about Lindow Man's life and death; to consider different perspectives; to engage emotionally with the themes, and to explore the ethics of displaying human remains. This may explain why so few of the comments relate to objects – most are to do with issues, ideas, and concepts.

PMM dimension 2: range of understanding

As noted above, the categories that include the longest and most considered responses were those most closely identified with the exhibition's unorthodox qualities: 'different perspectives', 'ethics of displaying the dead' and 'design, construction and atmosphere'. Of these, 'design, construction and atmosphere' prompted by far the strongest response: 73 per cent of the visitors included comments about it on their personal meaning maps. In addition, the comments in this category were much longer on average (33.4 words as opposed to 20.9 for its nearest rival: 'ethics of displaying the dead').

When the personal meaning maps were analysed for the range of different subjects or concepts, there was a clear difference between pre-visit and post-visit responses. The personal meaning maps contained references that related to between 0 and 10 different categories.[19] The results showed a definite shift towards a broader range of understanding following the exhibition experience. Over a quarter of the participants more than doubled the range of categories covered by their personal meaning maps, and a number increased the range of categories by much more than that. This indicates that the exhibition experience had prompted visitors to think about concepts or issues that did not occur to them before entering the gallery. However, that general picture does not tell the whole story. A few of the personal meaning map results showed the opposite. Three of the respondents (24, 33, and 41) had a significantly *reduced* range of categories after the visit. All of them were very knowledgeable about the subject and experienced museumgoers. Two of them critiqued the exhibition with an 'expert' eye, one from a negative standpoint and the other positive about the approach. The third was a local person with very strong opinions about Lindow Man and the environment where he was found.

EXPERIMENTAL EXHIBITION MAKING   647

In order to ascertain why the post-visit responses of these three individuals were significantly less broad-ranging than before, it is worth looking at each personal meaning map in more detail and, following the Falk and Dierking model, consider the 'personal, sociocultural and physical' aspects of their experience.

Respondent 24's personal meaning map referred to eight different categories before the visit, but only one (design, construction and atmosphere) afterwards (Figure 40.3). She visited with her spouse (respondent 23). She identified herself on the questionnaire as a 'historian' and 'PG Library Dip'. Both respondent 24 and her spouse were experienced visitors with very traditional expectations that appeared to be thwarted by the unorthodox approach of the exhibition. My impression on talking to respondent 24 after she had completed the exercise was that her experience of the exhibition had been so dominated by her extreme disappointment that this emotional reaction had unfortunately blocked any chance of learning or enjoyment. This 'cognitive dissonance', as N. James (2008, 770–7) calls it, may explain why respondent 24's post-visit response took the form of an extended diatribe focused on the design and construction of the exhibition.

With respondent 33 the difference was not quite so marked, as she referred to five categories before the visit and two afterwards. She revealed, through the personal meaning map and questionnaire, a very strong personal link to Lindow Man. Before the visit, respondent 33 used Lindow Man's nickname (Pete Marsh), identified herself as a repatriation supporter and described Lindow Moss as 'nice place'. She speculated about Lindow Man's death being a sacrifice, calling him 'poor fella' and wishing he could be 'laid to rest once and for all'. Respondent 33 chose to add nothing to the personal meaning map after the visit, although she did reiterate her personal connection on the questionnaire, declaring 'he be … semi-local to moi!' She seemed generally satisfied with the exhibition but did not share

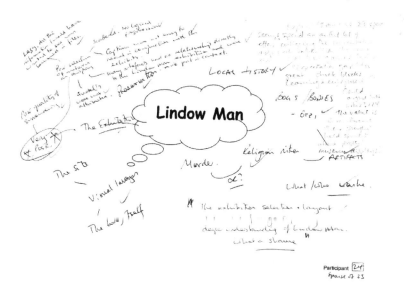

Figure 40.3 Personal Meaning Map 24.

any new thoughts or insights. Perhaps the experience of communing with her 'neighbour' was too private to divulge on the personal meaning map.

The range of categories on respondent 41's personal meaning map went down from 10 before the visit to 6 after the visit. Respondent 41 identified himself as having a 'forensic archaeology background' and felt disappointed that he could not recall many 'facts' before the visit. Several of his pre-visit thoughts were questions about Lindow Man's death, the ethics of displaying him, the local connection, links to the Museum collections and about how other visitors might react to the body. These thoughts seemed to come together post-visit, addressing many of the questions and, although focused on fewer categories, the comments were profoundly reflective. In this case, the narrower range of subjects or concepts did not mean that respondent 41 was repelled like respondent 24. It was quite the reverse, as the language used suggests that the exhibition provoked some profound emotional and philosophical thought processes. And unlike respondent 33, respondent 41 felt able to share those thoughts on the personal meaning map.

PMM dimension 3: grasp of concepts and subject areas

Linguistic analysis of the personal meaning maps revealed the depth of visitors' engagement with the exhibition and subject matter. The questionnaire results identified education and entertainment as the prime motivators for the visitors (therefore an effective measure of the value of the experience to them), so the GLOs were employed to identify evidence of learning impact. Applying the GLOs revealed that 91 out of 97 participants' personal meaning maps showed clear evidence of learning and many of these demonstrated learning in more than one category (see Figure 40.4).

A total of 225 comments could be directly linked to four out of the five GLOs. Of the six personal meaning maps where evidence of learning was questionable, all of the relevant comments related to 'attitudes and values'. Only two, respondent 22 and respondent 32, both 'experts' (forensic anthropology and archaeology student, respectively), appeared to find nothing of value in the exhibition. They were looking for 'the facts' about Lindow Man's period in history and were clearly not engaged by the multi-vocal, open-ended approach. They were unwilling or unable to use the unconventional facilities to uncover information that might have been of interest.

Three others (respondents 23, 24, and 50 – all very knowledgeable and articulate) were so incensed by the exhibition approach that the potential for learning appeared to be severely restricted. While conducting the GLO analysis, a question mark was placed against 'attitudes and values' for these three people because there may be a benefit in the provocative approach, serving to reinforce their strongly held beliefs about the subject and museums in general – especially as it provided opportunities to 'sound off'. The two most disturbing personal meaning maps (respondent 64 and respondent 73) revealed a very emotional encounter with Lindow Man that seemed to traumatize rather than enlighten the participants. On the evidence of their painful testimony ('disgusting, ugly, freaky, weird' and 'awful death, terrible') (Figure 40.5), it is difficult to imagine what benefit they might have gained from the experience.

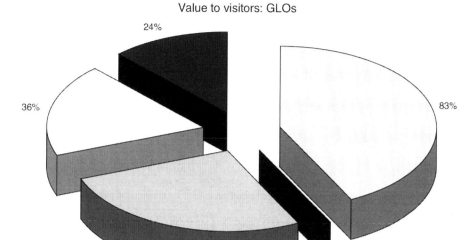

Figure 40.4 Value to visitors – Generic Learning Outcomes (GLOs).

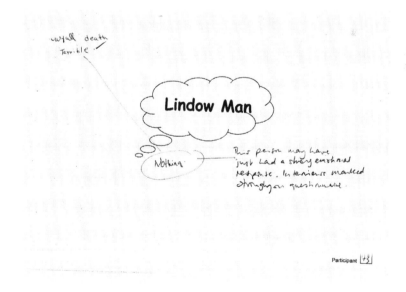

Figure 40.5 Personal Meaning Map 73.

From Figure 40.4, it is immediately evident that the 'skills' GLO does not appear in the analysis and this requires explanation. The exhibition did set out to encourage skills development in assessing and interpreting evidence, so the learning that was recorded as 'knowledge and understanding', or 'attitudes and values', could also have been placed under an 'interpretive skills' category. However, based on the available evidence, it is not possible to determine whether the participants already had those skills or had developed them through the exhibition.

The balance between 'knowledge and understanding' and 'attitudes and values' is interesting. Through an exhibition that, to some, seemed light on facts and dominated by opinion, the vast majority of participants reported picking up new knowledge and understanding. At the same time, more than half felt prompted to question and explore their own and others' perspectives on issues such as the retention and display of human remains in museums. For most of the participants, it seems the exhibition approach enabled the traditional factual transmission of information whilst also facilitating a more philosophical kind of learning experience.

It is also significant that more than half of the participants felt creatively engaged, inspired or encouraged to want to find out more about Lindow Man and the issues that surround his story. Many of these people felt moved to ask themselves quite profound questions while in the exhibition, and to explore them further through the PMM exercise. Some intended to carry out their own research and, in one case, to visit Lindow Moss where Lindow Man was found, and 'drink in the history of it all'.

PMM dimension 4: mastery of subject matter

The scale used to determine the participants' level of understanding or engagement ranged from 'novice' to 'expert'. To begin with, four categories were used – (N) novice, (Q) quite knowledgeable, (V) very knowledgeable, and (E) expert – but it soon became clear that intermediate categories would be needed to record the nuances that were appearing in the personal meaning maps. Participants' language identified their level of understanding or engagement, and based on this evidence there appeared to be a progression from one phase of the exercise to the other. However, without further information from the participants, it was not possible to judge whether the experience had facilitated a shift along the spectrum or whether the person simply felt more able or willing to express his or her expertise after visiting the exhibition. The latter seems much more plausible, as brief engagement with a museum exhibition can increase knowledge and understanding but is unlikely to transform 'novice' to 'expert'. Some of those who were clearly 'expert' wrote very little before entering the exhibition and much more afterwards.

The research findings demonstrate that the exhibition, depending on an individual's perspective, was seen as groundbreaking, experimental and challenging, or shoddy, lazy, and unprofessional. The opinions that have been articulated in various ways about Lindow Man suggest that one person's 'innovative' is another's 'rubbish' and, by implication one person's 'traditional and reassuring' is another's 'boring and irrelevant'. Furthermore, because every exhibition visit is a highly personal experience, getting it right for a particular individual may be more a matter of luck rather than judgement.

Conclusions

The Manchester Museum's unconventional approach to the third Lindow Man exhibition prompted strong reactions from visitors, staff, the museum profession and the media at large. 'A Bog Body Mystery' gave rise to a huge increase in comment card feedback; divided opinion sharply within the Museum; prompted three measured critiques in academic and professional journals (Rees Leahy 2008; Burch 2008; James 2008), and triggered a blast of invective from media blog Manchester Confidential.[20] Loathed by some, the exhibition was feted by others: it was listed by *The Times* as a top-five attraction;[21] was named in December 2008 by the *Museums Journal* as one of two outstanding exhibitions of the year outside London, and won the temporary exhibition category of the national *Design Week* awards 2009.

Although, as Oscar Wilde remarked through the character of Dorian Gray, it may be better to be talked about than not,[22] the museum's purpose in staging Lindow Man in the way it did was not to court publicity. The aim, through a creative and multidisciplinary approach, was to engage a wider range of people with Lindow Man's story, and to encourage a debate about the appropriateness of the display and interpretation of human remains. In the context of this research project, the question is whether, on balance, this 'experiment' was of value to visitors or whether it benefited the museum at the expense of the learning and enjoyment of its audience.

Was the approach self-indulgent? The museology behind the inclusion of exhibition features such as the 'mini museum' case passed most visitors by, so it could be argued that it was, and that the Museum was taking advantage of its benevolent university host to play academic games with visitors' expectations. However, that argument would ignore the serious audience development work that has underpinned the Museum's philosophy and its commitment to greater accessibility and inclusivity.

Feedback, both positive and negative, is now an essential part of the relationship between any public organization and its users. However, feedback is not always what it seems. Harris (1995), recalling people's responses to publicly funded contemporary art in the 1930s and 1940s in the USA, notes, 'These angry reactions, remember, were not simply about art, they were about attitudes toward social reality, toward national character, official values, progress, and standards of life.' Some visitors' vehement criticism of what they called the 'poor' and 'lazy' design and structure of the Lindow Man exhibition may mask a broader plea to preserve the traditional place of the museum in their lives.

Museums, like the British Broadcasting Corporation (BBC) and other publicly funded organizations, have to come to terms with the result of inviting users to 'interact'. Following the BBC Radio 2 'Ross and Brand affair' in 2008 (when presenter Jonathan Ross and comedian Russell Brand scandalized 'Middle Britain' by phoning and insulting the granddaughter of actor Andrew Sachs live on air), Emily Bell in *The Guardian* described a radical shift in the relationship with audiences. Thousands of people had contacted the BBC to demand punishment for the perpetrators, despite the fact that many of them had not heard the offending programme. The story itself prompted people to 'press the red button'. Bell wrote:

> Interactivism is changing the terms of engagement for media organisations, politicians, companies and individuals ... Complaint becomes a participation sport in a digital world, where totals are electronically tallied and regularly updated. Most importantly, by participating, the public expects to influence the outcome of events.[23]

This was certainly the case with 'A Bog Body Mystery' – there were even calls for the people responsible to be sacked.

Did the exhibition 'bewilder and alienate' people? There is evidence that the exhibition upset and angered some visitors (and staff), particularly those who are wedded to the tradition of museum as authority and expert. It did not seem to cross the minds of people incensed by what they saw as the 'tackiness' of the construction – that the choice of constituents and construction methods was intentional. The rough, everyday materials and finishes were particularly problematic for people who equate slick and polished with quality and professionalism. They saw no rationale behind it; for them it was merely a result of incompetence and idleness. There were many others, however, who appreciated the pared down presentation and dilution of the commanding museum voice.

With hindsight, I think the Museum could have made the thinking behind its approach more overt, describing the complex challenge that faces archaeology when there is so little contextual evidence and explaining more clearly why there are so few 'hard facts'. In addition, the lack of certainty or 'closure' about the death of a fellow human being may have been too emotionally or intellectually disturbing for some visitors. The Museum's decision to present impartially several theories as to how Lindow Man died, reflecting the ongoing debate in academic and archaeological circles, was viewed as an abdication of responsibility by some people. This was the 'politics of expertise' in action (Janes 2009: 159). Towards the end of a seminar that I led for the University of Manchester's Art Gallery & Museum Studies Masters course, one of the students vented her frustration with the approach by saying 'Somebody must know!' It seems we have some way to go if we are, as Janes suggests, to 'cultivate a respect for uncertainty' in museums (Janes 2009: 13). It is also possible that combining an open-ended, poly-vocal approach with the 'incomplete' raw-edged design was just too much and too soon for some people. I wonder whether either technique on its own would have triggered such a violent response from the quarters it did.

One of the benefits to the Museum of the 'provocative' approach was the opportunity for the staff to practise their skills in facilitating debate through exhibitions and programmes, including the potential to learn from this by reflecting on their own responses to hostile feedback from some visitors and stakeholders. It is clear from the research that while staff may have understood and accepted the rationale behind the mission to provoke and the potential benefits for audiences and the institution, there are significant reservations about how prepared the Museum was for the consequences of challenging convention. Unless there are mechanisms clearly in place to facilitate a dialogue between the museum, its staff, and visitors who find their ideas and values challenged (including policies and systems to support staff), criticism can leave people personally and professionally exposed. The ability to anticipate, absorb, and learn from feedback, good and bad, will be a key skill for museums and their staff in the years to come.

The team that created 'A Bog Body Mystery' took the opportunity to flirt with conventions and explore creative ways of interpreting the themes and issues triggered by the discovery, study, and display of Lindow Man. This definitely did not work for everyone, but it seems clear from the research that almost all the participating visitors learned something, were moved by the experience and felt able to contribute to the debate surrounding the 'bog body mystery'. In his review of the Lindow Man exhibition, James (2008) both posed and answered the question, 'Other than students, should a museum challenge its visitors?' He responded, 'Public life in Britain badly needs the imaginative quality of critique offered by *Lindow Man*.' He concluded his review by throwing down his own challenge to the sector: 'Despite decades of sociological research we still know little about how learning can grow from leisure. It is vital, for any museum, that challenges such as *Lindow Man*'s should be understood.'

Notes

1. www.alchemy.manchester.museum/ (accessed 19 January 2011).
2. www.museum.manchester.ac.uk/community/collectiveconversations/
3. www.museum.manchester.ac.uk/whatson/exhibitions/pastexhibitions/revealing historiesmythsaboutrace/
4. This was redesigned following the post-opening evaluation meeting to assist with visitor orientation and understanding.
5. Some visitors instinctively seemed to recognize this and happily rooted through the books and folders.
6. Staff were invited through questionnaires to share their views on the exhibition. One senior person wrote: 'Public consultation is good, debate is good, but in the end the museum has a role and a duty to present the *facts* as researched and integrated by specialists. This is a *university* museum, with an academic research, study and teaching role.'
7. The Manchester Museum Strategic Plan 2007–2011.
8. Private correspondence, April 2008.
9. www.museum.manchester.ac.uk/aboutus/reportspolicies/fileuploadmaxl0mb, 120796,en.pdf
10. For the Manchester Museum's official statement: www.museum.manchester.ac.uk/ aboutus/pressreleases/pressreleasesarchive/fileuploadmaxl0mb,136438,en.doc
11. A letter from a visitor reads: 'Was this the idea of a work experience kid? Or is there a professional (being paid a lot more money than I earn) coming up with inane ideas like this? It's just awful. Shameful... . When I was there everyone was walking around just

looking at each other saying "this is absolute shit". And it is; it's just absolute shit.' In addition, a member of staff wrote on a questionnaire for this study: 'The museum needs to learn from the overwhelmingly negative comments that the public made. It cannot afford to put on poorly thought-out exhibits and disguise them as "experimental"'.

12 Seventeen per cent left education at age 16 or under, which might suggest a broadening of the Museum's visitor base, and 32 per cent were still in full-time education, perhaps reflecting the Museum's university status.
13 Morris Hargreaves McIntyre (April 2008) *Knowing your Visitors: Visitor Segments at North West Hub Venues,* www.mla.gov.uk/what/programmes/renaissance/regions/north_west/news/~/media/North_West/Files/2008/Newsletter_Oct 08.ashx
14 Feedback suggests that certain people excluded themselves from this feature because they felt it was for children.
15 To some degree the sample is self-selecting and therefore may not be representative of all visitors' experiences. In this kind of research work, with people being approached and asked for their opinions by someone who looks 'official', those visitors who find such interactions intimidating will often opt out.
16 Alison James, *Visitors' meaning maps at the Pitt Rivers Museum,* www.alison-james.co.uk
17 www.inspiringlearningforall.gov.uk
18 Part of the Museum's standard evaluation process.
19 Zero was scored when the individual either reported that he or she knew nothing before the visit or had nothing to add afterwards.
20 www.manchesterconfidential.com/index.asp?Sessionx = IpqiNwImNwIjIDY6IHcij NwB6IA
21 22–28 November 2008, timesonline.co.uk/theknowledge
22 Oscar Wilde, *The Picture of Dorian Gray*: 'There is only one thing in the world worse than being talked about, and that is not being talked about.'
23 *The Guardian,* Saturday 1 November 2008.

References

Alberti, S.J.M.M., Bienkowski, P., Chapman, M., and Drew, R. (2009) Should we display the dead? *Museum and Society*, 7(3). Available at: www.le.ac.uk/ms/museum society.html (accessed 3 October 2016).

Bienkowski, P. (2009) Museum, authority, knowledge, and conflict. *Museum Identity*, 3. Available at: www.museum-id.com/magazine-detail.asp?newsID=71 (accessed 3 October 2016).

Boyd, W.L. (1999) Museums as centers of controversy. *Daedalus*, 128: 3.

Braden, D.R. (1998) Whose history is it? Planning Henry Ford Museum's 'Clockwork' exhibit. *Technology and Culture*, 39(3): 489–98.

Burch, S. (2008) Lindow Man: a bog body mystery, Manchester Museum. *Museums Journal*, 7: 50–51.

Falk, J.H., and L.D. Dierking. 1995. *Public Institutions for Personal Learning: Establishing a Research Agenda*. Washington, DC: American Association of Museums.

Falk, J.H. and Dierking, L.D. (2000) *Learning from Museums: Visitor Experiences and the Making of Meaning*. Lanham, MD: AltaMira Press.

Falk, J.H., Dierking, L.D., and Foutz, S. eds. (2007) *In Principle, in Practice: Museums as Learning Institutions*. Lanham, MD: AltaMira Press, pp. 21–22.

Falk, J.H., Mousourri, T., and Coulson, D. (1998) The effect of visitors' agendas on museum learning. *Curator*, 41(2): 107–20.

Gurian, E.H. (2006) *Civilizing the Museum*. London: Routledge.
Harris, N. (1995) Museums and controversy: some introductory reflections. *The Journal of American History*, 82(3): 1102–10.
Hein, G.E. (2000) *Learning in the Museum*. London: Routledge.
Hood, A.D. (1994) The practice of [American] history: a Canadian curator's perspective. *The Journal of American History*, 81(3): 1011–19.
James, N. (2008) Repatriation, display and interpretation. *Antiquity*, 82: 770–77.
Janes, R.R. (2009) *Museums in a Troubled World*. London: Routledge.
Lynch, B.T., and Alberti, S.J.M.M. (2010) Legacies of prejudice: racism, co-production and radical trust in the museum. *Museum Management and Curatorship*, 25(1): 13–35.
Rees Leahy, H. (2008) Under the skin. *Museum Practice*, 43: 36–40.
Walker Laird, P. (1998) The public's historians. *Technology and Culture*, 39(3): 474–82.
Yakel, E. (2000) Museums, management, media, and memory: lessons from the Enola Gay exhibition. *Libraries & Culture*, 35(2): 278–301.

Index

acquisition 2, 8–11, 43, 47–9, 57–8, 61, 73, 104, 144, 183, 189, 194, 201–12, 216–18, 245, 294, 323, 347, 431, 466, 474–6, 522, 610; donation 2, 8, 48, 57–8, 67–8, 82, 189, 201–3, 208, 211–13, 217, 249, 258, 347
aesthetics 1, 14, 19, 110, 121–4, 193, 208, 312–13, 316–18, 321–5, 331–3, 336, 340–1, 452, 455, 532, 558, 645; modernism 19, 382–3
anthropologists 9, 240, 251, 379, 381, 385, 412, 609, 617, 622, 627, 630, 638
antiquarians 1, 161, 269, 314, 347, 500, 504, 510, 554
antiquities dealers 8, 168, 187–96, 199, 203–7, 220, 243, 435
archaeological fieldwork 3–4, 43–4, 49, 52, 55, 64–6, 75–80, 83–4, 88–90, 94, 101–3, 112, 147, 190, 401, 436, 456, 545, 555, 599, 626–7
archaeological heritage 3, 17–18, 189, 198, 354, 379, 381–3, 395, 569, 628, 631
archaeological site museums 16–18, 27, 307–8, 415, 432–42, 457, 460
architectural design 19, 65, 68, 117, 308, 392, 417–18, 437, 443, 449, 451–2, 457–9, 530–1, 617
archives xvii, 2–4, 12, 24, 43–4, 47–61, 64–8, 71–3, 77–96, 99–102, 105–6, 158, 192, 197, 207, 238, 249, 318, 327, 474, 493, 501, 513–17, 520, 544–5, 549
art 1, 8–12, 15, 18–20, 23, 25, 68, 91, 114, 123, 130–2, 143–4, 184, 188–9, 193, 201–17, 248–9, 253, 285, 309–10, 317–18, 421, 426–30, 436, 441, 455–7, 503–7, 512, 519, 555–8, 572, 588, 593, 596–604, 627, 635, 651
audiences *see* visitors
audio 24–5, 53, 56, 330, 358, 420, 478, 545, 565–6, 570
Australia xvii, 9–10, 12, 183–4, 234–41, 379, 383, 394–5, 627
authenticity 4, 17, 43, 98, 188, 193–4, 198, 214–15, 251, 318–21, 330, 339, 349, 424, 465–6, 476–7, 545, 551

bias 1, 14–16, 23–5, 189, 307–8, 312, 342, 350–2, 355–6, 394, 546, 558–9, 573–5, 594, 597, 604, 638

Canada 26, 215, 249, 269, 271, 276–8, 280–2, 477–9, 487, 609, 611–12
care of collections *see* conservation
children xv, 4–6, 13, 16, 20–23, 95, 143, 152, 161, 287–92, 300, 309–10, 335, 351, 382, 400–8, 411–13, 419, 423, 452, 465, 473–80, 483–6, 494–5, 501–12, 515, 518–19, 526, 529, 533, 545, 551–4, 559, 565–73, 577–80, 586, 589–90, 593, 598–604, 612, 617–18, 622–4, 631, 636–9
China xvii, 5, 24, 28, 221, 224, 309, 456–61, 464
civilization 1, 142–4, 187, 190, 207, 440–1, 577–8, 583, 589, 594–5, 603, 610

classification 14, 157, 243, 257, 307, 312, 354, 557; typology 20, 102–4
cleaning xv, 5, 52–4, 72, 109–16, 121–4, 129, 169–70, 174, 326, 520, 555
collaboration 6–7, 10–11, 20, 25–6, 53, 63, 68, 90, 95, 102–3, 134, 192, 214, 238–43, 247–55, 300, 309–10, 324, 349, 361–4, 418, 430–1, 463, 466–7, 476, 523–8, 546, 553, 556, 570–1, 588, 593–8, 604, 608–13, 618, 623, 626, 629–30, 635, 644
collections management 2–3, 10, 43, 47, 69, 95, 547; disposal 2–3, 44, 55–8, 67, 71, 75, 86–8, 235, 550; exchange 2, 58, 67, 103, 142, 207–9; export 8, 183, 195–7, 199, 202–12, 219, 242–4, 464, 577; loan 2–5, 8, 24, 49–52, 58–60, 104, 202, 206–11, 217, 222n, 229n, 276, 286, 290, 297, 309, 334, 419, 469, 515, 549–53, 568, 599, 635; reburial 9–10, 114–16, 183, 233–7, 240, 244–5, 255–6, 271, 416, 611, 639; repatriation 9–12, 26–7, 55–8, 64, 74, 114, 183–4, 212, 216–17, 233–60, 271–4, 277–8, 287, 293, 379, 384, 434, 480, 487, 609–11, 636, 639, 645–7; retention 3, 44, 71, 77, 121, 124, 162, 209, 639, 650; sale 2, 74, 101, 187–91, 192–7, 206, 209, 215, 436; selection 3, 14, 21, 44, 71, 100, 112, 307, 312–13, 322, 328, 356, 410, 417, 474, 485, 518, 564
colonialism 1, 9, 18, 26, 73, 234–6, 246, 383, 410, 441, 465, 523–5, 530, 559, 609, 612, 617–18, 630
commodification 186, 313–16, 324–6, 332, 337–42
community museums 16–18, 292, 308, 383, 389–95, 439, 545–6, 553, 617–31
conservation xv, 2–6, 10–12, 18–20, 27, 43–4, 48–57, 61, 63–6, 69, 72–3, 79, 82–5, 94–6, 99–102, 106, 108–34, 142–5, 159, 169, 183, 186, 192, 198, 200, 210, 219, 238, 247, 253–5, 268, 271–3, 282, 293–7, 312, 330, 334, 340, 369–71, 391, 416, 420–2, 426–30, 460, 467, 474–6, 503, 506, 520, 548–50, 557, 613, 641
consolidation 5, 112, 125–7, 132, 159, 624–6
constructivist theory 20–1, 464–5, 479, 636, 643

consultation 10–13, 18, 26, 48, 52, 55, 58–9, 69, 75, 81–2, 102–4, 114, 142–6, 184, 196, 237–8, 243, 246–56, 260, 275–9, 287–91, 298, 350, 421, 424, 434, 480, 503, 545, 599, 609, 626, 629, 637–42
contextualization i, 19, 21, 286, 301, 342, 463, 470, 557–8, 560, 594, 611–12, 627, 636–7, 642
copyright xviii, xix, 7, 60
crowd-sourcing 7
cultural diversity 253, 282, 288, 349, 402, 406, 438–9, 476, 553–4, 575, 578
cultural heritage 23–6, 51, 57, 65, 73, 93, 96, 99–101, 187, 234–9, 242–6, 249, 259–60, 282, 308, 319, 327–9, 337, 374, 380–2, 389–94, 401, 418, 423, 429–33, 437–9, 442, 460–1, 465, 477, 489, 493, 503, 523–4, 527–8, 546–7, 553–6, 564, 571, 575, 585, 594–7, 608–13, 621, 627
cultural resource management (CRM) i, xvii, 2, 58, 63, 65, 77, 252
curation crisis 2, 43–6, 63, 69–70, 75–8, 81, 545

decay *see* deterioration
democracy 14–15, 338, 341, 349, 355, 401, 441, 558, 596, 630, 641
Denmark 17–19, 33, 150–1, 286, 419, 421, 425, 441
designers 20–1, 27, 224, 307, 349–50, 424, 475, 502, 509, 524
deterioration 5, 17, 19, 52–8, 109–22, 126–8, 133, 144–6, 177–8, 194, 210, 329, 337, 339, 549, 587
digital technologies xv, 2–3, 7, 17, 24–6, 43, 49, 60, 77, 84, 87–90, 133, 169–70, 241, 309, 469, 547–9, 652
dioramas 15, 393, 487, 545
discovery of the past 20–1, 24, 89, 99, 149–51, 156, 161, 211–12, 286, 308, 313–16, 323, 329–33, 347, 363, 435–7, 478, 485–9, 492, 497, 528, 532, 535, 545, 549–52, 568, 630, 635, 645–6, 653
documentation xv, 2–4, 8–10, 17, 26, 43–4, 48–61, 64–6, 81, 98–103, 106, 117, 128–9, 176, 190–3, 204–14, 217–18, 229, 246–51, 257, 275–6, 299, 309, 388, 424, 522, 545–7, 628, 641; accessioning 2–3, 43–4, 47–51, 56–61,

64, 72–6, 314, 347, 516; cataloguing 2–4, 7, 26, 43, 50, 60, 100–1, 105, 124, 187–8, 300, 322, 325, 547–8, 574, 587–8, 599; deaccessioning 2–3, 43–4, 47, 57–8, 63, 66–9, 72–6, 209, 216–18, 253, 476–8; identification 4, 43, 50, 98–102, 162, 171, 230n, 243, 248, 251–6, 276, 334; indexes 4, 50, 66, 90, 94, 102–6; inventory 2–4, 10, 43–4, 47–9, 53–61, 64–5, 72, 75, 99–106, 195–7, 243, 246–8, 251, 254, 258, 322–3, 420, 525, 537–8; records 2–3, 7, 49–66, 77–81, 84, 87–9, 93–6, 99, 106, 158–60, 248, 282, 353, 401, 434, 514–16, 524; registration *see* inventory; thesauri 4, 101–5

ecomuseums 18, 439–40, 443, 546
economics 3, 17–18, 161, 246, 263, 308, 337–8, 385–6, 392–5, 401, 426–7, 430, 437–9, 442, 461, 539, 544, 619–23, 625–7, 642
Ecuador 18, 433
Egypt 4–6, 13, 18–21, 25, 45, 129, 142–7, 184, 187–8, 196, 214, 285, 290–3, 309–10, 358, 492, 547, 552–6, 559–60, 572–91, 593–604, 640
empowerment 18, 21, 24, 249, 256, 309, 442, 475, 479, 487, 522–3, 528, 558, 623, 641
English Heritage 22, 79–85, 89–90, 309, 350–1, 500–7, 554
environmental conditions 2, 5–6, 45, 53–5, 68, 79, 109–11, 115–20, 127, 142–6, 160, 169, 173–9, 422, 427, 430, 456–61, 587
ethics 1, 3, 5–11, 17–18, 45, 48, 56–8, 69, 72–4, 117–19, 183–5, 191–4, 197–8, 201–18, 234, 243, 281, 293, 298, 301, 308, 381, 434, 440, 527, 534, 550, 590, 594–6, 612–13, 631, 635–6, 639–41, 645–8
ethnicity 12, 20, 246, 256, 271–80, 288, 309, 348, 379–86, 392–3, 399–401, 413, 439, 475, 538, 545, 553–5, 559, 577, 618–20, 625–9
evaluation 13–15, 20–1, 27, 349–50, 353, 358, 375, 458, 468, 478, 481, 487–91, 496–7, 520–2, 554–6, 591, 603, 622, 640, 643

exhibition design 6, 13, 20–5, 54, 143–6, 279, 308–10, 325, 329, 333–5, 346, 352, 389, 393, 399–400, 409, 413, 418–24, 428, 431, 462, 466, 476–7, 486–8, 491–2, 495, 514–19, 529, 549–50, 553, 556, 599–602, 619, 639, 641–7, 651–3
exhibition messages 14–16, 20–7, 187–9, 198, 308, 312–14, 317–20, 323–5, 334–5, 342, 348–9, 352, 355–8, 362–3, 372, 375, 380, 383, 387–8, 393, 399–413, 421, 433, 439, 485–97, 503, 506, 524, 528–9, 531–3, 536–8, 558–60, 589, 594–604, 623, 629

fakes 4, 8, 44, 104, 187, 193–4, 204, 214–17
Finland 16, 379–80, 383–95, 402
forgeries *see* fakes
funding xv, 2–7, 11–12, 15–17, 57–9, 63, 67–9, 73, 77–82, 86–90, 94–5, 106, 212, 237–9, 245–7, 254, 260, 269, 272, 361–3, 373, 391–4, 418, 427, 473, 480, 483, 497, 502, 514, 526, 546–7, 551, 555–7, 572–4, 621, 627, 630–1, 635, 641, 651

gender 15–16, 20, 197, 308, 325, 348, 353, 399, 401–2, 406, 453, 525, 581, 630
Germany 151, 196, 239, 298, 321, 435, 544, 554
Greece 5, 8, 11, 16, 107, 132, 187, 201–2, 206–7, 220–1n, 307, 316, 337, 347, 452, 552, 575, 578, 583, 593, 601
green issues 15, 288, 353
group identity 16–18, 27, 249–51, 254–5, 265, 273–4, 285, 288–9, 301–2, 308, 314, 336, 340, 357, 379–86, 391–5, 413, 432, 437–42, 544, 555, 569, 584, 602–3, 608, 611, 619, 629, 644
guardianship *see* stewardship
guided tours 4, 17, 21–4, 59, 373, 524–6, 529–30, 538, 548–50, 565–6, 570, 624, 631

handling 2, 5, 22, 47, 51, 55, 59–60, 102, 110, 114–16, 125–7, 143, 177, 294–9, 461, 476, 485–6, 491–4, 502, 505, 514, 549–554, 559, 599–600, 623, 643–4
hands-on *see* interactivity

INDEX 659

heritage professionals 23, 43, 183, 198, 523, 527
human remains xv, 2, 6–13, 26–7, 55, 58–9, 94–5, 114, 142–55, 159–62, 183–4, 188, 219, 234–51, 254–60, 268–82, 285–302, 384, 402, 411, 432, 452, 490, 508, 559, 609, 619, 630, 636–40, 645–6, 650–1; Egyptian mummies 13, 21, 142–4, 147, 184, 188, 206, 285–301, 559, 572, 580–1, 589, 593–4, 640; Lindow Man 13, 26, 285–90, 310, 335–9, 642–53
human rights 10, 244–6, 260

ideology 16, 194, 308, 312–13, 317, 325, 329, 336–42, 348, 380–2, 392, 394, 401, 441, 451, 531–2
illicit trade in antiquities 7–10, 27, 48, 183, 198, 201–3, 207, 218–19, 242–4, 258, 269
imagination 17, 22, 318, 356, 488, 507, 558, 593
Indigenous Peoples 10–12, 16–18, 26, 114, 183, 234–47, 252–4, 259–60, 272, 285–7, 294, 299, 308, 310, 379–82, 385–9, 394–5, 402, 437–9, 441–2, 576, 595–6, 608–13, 616–18, 626, 629; Australian Aboriginal 9–10, 26, 234–8, 627; Canadian First Peoples 26, 310, 608–12; Native American 10–12, 26, 55, 58–9, 64, 73–4, 142, 183–4, 237, 242–59, 269–81, 379–83, 394–5, 434, 479–82, 535, 609–10, 613, 617–18, 629; Native Hawaiian 12, 26, 242–3, 246, 251, 256–8, 272–4; Saami 16, 308, 379–95
information panels 14–15, 20–3, 291, 331, 346, 350–8, 361, 369–71, 491–2, 502, 508, 517, 559, 602, 636, 640
interactivity 20–25, 309, 334–5, 349, 361, 375, 400, 408–13, 465–9, 475, 478, 485–97, 503–5, 524, 527–30, 538, 548–54, 557–8, 565–6, 570–1, 598, 652
international conventions 8–9, 11–13, 183, 195–6, 198–9, 203–5, 208–9, 211, 385, 443

Jamaica 20, 309, 463–6, 469
Japan xvii, 25, 127, 309, 436–7, 479, 545, 564–71

labels 2, 6, 14, 22, 26, 43, 51–5, 58, 72, 106, 143, 156–8, 300, 314–16, 321, 326, 329–30, 334–7, 349–50, 381, 388, 452–4, 467, 475–9, 490, 555, 576, 598–602, 613, 636, 639
law xv, 1–2, 7–11, 13–15, 19, 47–8, 56–8, 67–9, 73, 81, 73, 100–1, 181–5, 190–7, 201–12, 215–18, 234, 237–8, 240, 242–7, 251, 254–8, 260, 271–6, 277–8, 280–2, 293, 383–5, 393–4, 418, 442, 480, 501, 517, 548, 609, 623, 626
legislation see law
Lewis Chessmen 7, 11, 45, 167–79
looting 8–9, 183, 190–8, 202–6, 210, 213–18, 244, 308, 435–7, 544, 629

marketing 17, 82, 186–9, 296, 329, 335–6, 419, 423, 546, 636
metal detecting 9, 194, 336, 492, 534, 548
Mexico xvii, 18, 26, 202, 310, 441, 617–31
museology 13–15, 301–2, 310, 439, 596, 608, 612–13, 651
museum communication xv, xviii, 14–18, 21, 43, 47, 120, 134, 195–7, 216, 236, 246–7, 253, 307, 316–17, 321–2, 334–5, 339, 347–8, 351, 357–8, 368–9, 376, 380–2, 386, 400–1, 421–2, 428–32, 468, 475, 478, 489, 492, 495, 519, 524, 527–9, 544–7, 559, 569, 580, 590–1, 598–9, 604, 612–13, 619, 623
museum representation 13–16, 124, 307–12, 315, 330, 338–41, 352, 379–95, 399–413, 432–4, 439, 487, 544, 558, 576, 586, 593–4, 601–2, 609–10
museum websites 24, 47, 66, 188, 211, 217, 431, 548, 612, 639

NAGPRA 10–12, 26, 55–9, 64, 67, 74, 183–4, 242–60, 271–80, 609–11
narratives see exhibition messages
national museums 7–11, 15, 45, 65, 142, 167–8, 191, 235–8, 245, 249, 253–4, 264, 270, 277, 293, 354, 383, 387–8, 392–3, 401, 427, 435, 441, 489–90, 548–52, 566, 610, 617–18
nationalism 1, 204, 207, 216, 221, 308, 356, 379, 382–3, 394, 432, 439, 442, 629
Norway 9, 16, 122, 379–80, 383–94, 402, 425

objectivity 13, 89, 106, 198, 313–18, 333, 336–42, 346–8, 353, 363, 381, 505, 557, 622, 636, 640
outreach 3, 18, 23, 282, 309, 434–5, 473, 485, 513, 522, 527–8, 534, 549–56, 565
ownership 2, 5, 9–12, 26, 47–9, 56–8, 61, 74, 80, 100, 149, 183, 194–9, 203–5, 208–15, 235–43, 256–9, 273, 281, 346, 384, 464, 517, 544, 577, 613, 622, 626–7, 640

Parthenon Marbles 11, 449–53
partnership *see* collaboration
photographs 3, 7, 12, 21, 25, 52–6, 60, 66, 77, 90, 124, 187, 205, 249, 278, 300, 313, 318, 322–4, 327, 330–2, 389, 393, 402–6, 418, 451–2, 486, 493, 506, 519, 525, 531, 549, 599–600, 624
pollution 5, 53–4, 115, 159
postcolonialism 25, 379, 401, 437, 480, 626, 629, 631
private collecting 8–9, 48, 60, 67–8, 72, 169, 192–3, 211, 214–18, 237, 247–8, 435, 440, 628
professional guidelines 3–5, 8–10, 48, 50, 63, 67, 74, 83, 88, 134, 183, 202–3, 208–13, 216–17, 255–6, 273–5, 281, 293, 298, 358, 368, 372–5, 509, 519, 611–12
professional museums associations 9–11, 26, 60, 67–9, 100, 202, 212, 238, 293, 365, 425, 430, 474, 524, 547
provenance 2–10, 43, 50–5, 58, 64, 143, 147, 151, 162, 183, 190–5, 198, 202, 208–17, 239, 248, 297, 314–16, 347, 364, 369–71, 602
public archaeology i, xvii, 77, 89, 309, 442, 564–72
public understanding of science 15, 354, 361–2
publications 3, 58–60, 78–80, 100, 161, 183, 208, 211, 215–17, 275, 347, 386, 393, 420, 548, 556, 565–6

race 23, 26, 309, 384–5, 392, 401, 525–7, 533, 538–9, 559, 575–6, 584, 588, 591, 635
reconstruction 17, 21–2, 25, 77, 94, 110–12, 120, 125–8, 132–4, 202, 215, 288, 308, 318, 321, 325–33, 355, 369, 371, 389, 393, 400–3, 411, 417, 420–4, 437, 452–4, 464, 470, 491, 497, 519, 524, 530, 537, 545
reflexivity xvii, 14, 312, 341, 349, 434, 546
religion 11–12, 65, 131, 143, 209, 215, 245, 253, 259, 273, 280–1, 286–8, 296, 299, 351, 362, 383, 413, 504–5, 519, 535, 539, 577, 580–3, 586, 589, 594, 602–3, 609, 619, 628; sacred objects 10, 55, 58–9, 114, 238–40, 243–8, 257–9, 272–5, 293, 609
repair 5, 109–11, 116, 119–21, 125–7, 131, 214, 326
replicas 7, 17–23, 104, 115, 133–4, 308, 314, 322–3, 421–4, 428, 438, 451, 466, 477–8, 482, 486–7, 491–2, 516–20, 551–3, 568–70, 614
repositories *see* archives
research 2–3, 6–19, 24–7, 43–5, 50–60, 64–8, 73–6, 81, 86–90, 93–6, 99–105, 142, 145, 148, 162, 169, 190, 198, 206–14, 217, 240, 256–8, 269, 273–81, 285–7, 290–1, 294–6, 298–302, 334–6, 361–76, 420–1, 427–8, 434–6, 441, 457, 474–6, 483, 519, 549, 557, 564–6, 572–4, 610–13, 618–31, 635, 639
respect 6, 13, 26, 51, 55, 58, 131, 144–7, 184, 213, 247, 253, 282, 285–302, 309, 315, 391, 395, 440, 538, 608–13, 624, 629–31, 637–41
restoration 5, 19, 44, 58, 102, 108–13, 119–22, 128–34

security xv, 2, 20, 53–6, 60, 68, 79, 82, 422, 449, 481, 598
senses 17, 21–2, 478, 486, 532–3, 547
signage 24, 296, 322, 349, 452–3, 469, 524, 529–30
social class 23, 161, 301, 309, 327, 337, 341, 348, 399, 401–2, 406, 432, 473, 524–5, 538, 546, 638
Spain 426–31, 441, 463, 618, 624, 630
stereotype *see* bias
stewardship 8–9, 18, 186, 198, 202, 206, 218, 269, 278, 416, 425, 434, 474, 476, 483, 527, 611
storage xv, 2–6, 13, 26, 43–56, 59–69, 72–94, 99–102, 105, 111–20, 128, 143–9, 191–2, 217, 235, 239, 247–9,

296–9, 433, 477, 491, 513–20, 526, 545, 548–50, 557, 613, 641
sustainability 1, 18, 84, 94, 239, 427, 437, 622, 636
Sweden 16, 308, 379–80, 383–9, 392–3, 399–410, 425
Switzerland 4, 8, 44, 99–101, 195–6, 205–7, 435
Syria 9, 189

Terracotta Warriors 5, 12, 457–8
three-dimensionality 7, 21, 117, 128, 155, 319, 330, 339, 400, 420, 452, 465, 470, 548, 552
tourism 11, 17–19, 25–7, 234, 323, 330, 334, 382, 389, 395, 416, 419, 425–33, 437–40, 458, 460, 473, 503, 576–7, 585, 599–600, 618, 621–8, 631
trafficking *see* illicit trade in antiquities
training xv, 2, 18, 47, 69, 75, 236, 299, 367, 431, 434–5, 463, 466, 517, 520, 545, 553, 588, 609, 613, 626, 630, 643
Turkey 15, 19, 364, 497

United Kingdom xvii, 3–15, 22, 25–6, 44–5, 81–3, 113–14, 117, 131, 183–99, 310, 350, 354, 361–5, 369, 374–5, 438, 486–8, 495–7, 503, 543, 546–8, 552–7, 572–5, 580, 593, 635, 645; England 3–4, 11, 14, 20, 23, 44, 78–9, 82–6, 93, 151, 159, 286, 307–8, 327–9, 346, 350, 417–21, 425, 441, 465, 477–81, 545, 574, 577; Scotland 7, 11, 14–15, 45, 151, 167–8, 308, 346, 350, 354–6, 489, 544, 551–3, 559; Wales 78, 151, 157, 548–50
USA xvii, 2, 8–12, 15, 50, 66, 72–4, 191, 196, 201–5, 208, 211, 214, 217, 237–9, 242–9, 254, 258–60, 269–72, 275–82, 338, 362, 374, 434, 441, 466, 477, 480, 525, 545–6, 548, 609, 611, 618, 623, 651

video 21, 24–5, 56, 454, 487, 517–19, 550–3, 559, 578, 586, 623–4
virtual reality 20, 24, 309, 463–70, 497
visitors 5, 12–27, 43, 54, 82, 89–90, 94, 124, 145, 187, 287–8, 290–2, 296–8, 301, 307–35, 341, 347–58, 363–76, 383, 386–8, 393, 399–402, 408–13, 416–29, 436, 440, 449–54, 458–60, 465–82, 485–97, 502–10, 522–38, 543–60, 564, 569, 573–85, 588–91, 594–8, 601–3, 612, 624–6, 635–53; visitor studies 14, 349, 551
volunteers i, xvii, 4, 7, 20, 72, 469–70, 473, 520, 548, 565–6, 570, 626, 639, 641–3

women 16, 234, 308, 324, 349, 399–406, 411, 413, 452, 529, 577, 580–1, 624, 629–30
World Heritage Sites 17, 22, 500, 502–3

Taylor & Francis eBooks

Helping you to choose the right eBooks for your Library

Add Routledge titles to your library's digital collection today. Taylor and Francis ebooks contains over 50,000 titles in the Humanities, Social Sciences, Behavioural Sciences, Built Environment and Law.

Choose from a range of subject packages or create your own!

Benefits for you
- Free MARC records
- COUNTER-compliant usage statistics
- Flexible purchase and pricing options
- All titles DRM-free.

Benefits for your user
- Off-site, anytime access via Athens or referring URL
- Print or copy pages or chapters
- Full content search
- Bookmark, highlight and annotate text
- Access to thousands of pages of quality research at the click of a button.

REQUEST YOUR FREE INSTITUTIONAL TRIAL TODAY | **Free Trials Available** We offer free trials to qualifying academic, corporate and government customers.

eCollections – Choose from over 30 subject eCollections, including:

Archaeology	Language Learning
Architecture	Law
Asian Studies	Literature
Business & Management	Media & Communication
Classical Studies	Middle East Studies
Construction	Music
Creative & Media Arts	Philosophy
Criminology & Criminal Justice	Planning
Economics	Politics
Education	Psychology & Mental Health
Energy	Religion
Engineering	Security
English Language & Linguistics	Social Work
Environment & Sustainability	Sociology
Geography	Sport
Health Studies	Theatre & Performance
History	Tourism, Hospitality & Events

For more information, pricing enquiries or to order a free trial, please contact your local sales team:
www.tandfebooks.com/page/sales

 | The home of Routledge books

www.tandfebooks.com